Transforming Organizations

Transforming Organizations

Editors

THOMAS A. KOCHAN

MICHAEL USEEM

New York Oxford   OXFORD UNIVERSITY PRESS   1992

Oxford University Press

Oxford   New York   Toronto
Delhi   Bombay   Calcutta   Madras   Karachi
Petaling Jaya   Singapore   Hong Kong   Tokyo
Nairobi   Dar es Salaam   Cape Town
Melbourne   Auckland

and associated companies in
Berlin   Ibadan

Copyright © 1992 by Oxford University Press, Inc.

Published by Oxford University Press, Inc.,
200 Madison Avenue, New York, New York 10016

Oxford is a registered trademark of Oxford University Press

Library of Congress Cataloging-in-Publication Data
Transforming organizations / Thomas Kochan and Michael Useem, editors.
p.   cm.   Based on a conference held in June 1990.
Includes bibliographical references and index.
ISBN 0-19-506504-2
1. Organizational change—Congresses.
I. Kochan, Thomas A.   II. Useem, Michael.
HD58.8.T72   1992   658.4'06—dc20
91-16837

Selected passages of Chapter 4 have been reprinted from "Business Restructuring, Management Control, and Corporate Organization," by Michael Useem which appeared in *Theory and Society*, Vol. 19, Dec. 1990, pp. 681–707.

An earlier version of Chapter 14 by Marcie J. Tyre appeared in *Research Policy*, Vol. 20, 1991, pp. 57–76.

Selected passages of Chapter 16 have been excerpted from *The Corporation of the 1990s: Information Technology and Organizational Transformation*, edited by Michael S. Scott Morton. © 1991 by Sloan School of Management. Reprinted by permission of Oxford University Press, Inc.

Selected passages of Chapter 19 have been reprinted from "Informal Technology Transfer Between Firms: Cooperation Through Information Trading," by Stephan Schrader which appeared in *Research Policy*, Vol. 20, No. 2, April 1991, pp. 153–170.

An earlier version of Chapter 21 by Peter M. Senge and John D. Sterman appeared in a special 1992 issue of the *European Journal of Operational Research*.

9 8 7 6 5 4 3 2 1

Printed in the United States of America
on acid-free paper

Foreword

Organizational change is one of the most important and difficult tasks facing managers today. For this reason this issue is prominent in the research program and curriculum of the Sloan School and every other school of management in the world. But when the challenges facing managers are changing rapidly, as they are now, it is useful to take a fresh look at this subject.

By drawing on the work of Sloan faculty and a select group of industry executives *Transforming Organizations* takes an important step in shaping a new agenda for the study and practice of organizational and social change. The goal was to attempt to define the dimensions of the challenges contemporary organizations face in managing change and to explore the relationships among these dimensions. Given the early stages of our effort, we sought to involve partners from industry in a creative fashion. The result is a book that should provide us and others who share concern for these issues with a rich inventory of ideas to consider in shaping our future agendas for managerial action, research, and teaching.

In addressing the issue of change the contributors to this book build on a rich MIT tradition dating back at least as far as the work of Douglas McGregor in the 1950s and 1960s and extending to the recent work of the MIT Commission that produced the book *Made in America*. But by adopting the working hypothesis that it is *systemic change* that is particularly needed and especially hard to achieve, this book breaks new ground and should serve as a useful opening salvo in what ought to be a major debate in the boardrooms, laboratories, classrooms, and policy forums of the 1990s. In fact, achieving and managing change may be the one sustainable source of competitive advantage that remains open to firms in today's global economy.

Traditionally four factors have contributed to making individuals rich, companies successful, and nations prosperous: natural resources, capital, technology, and skills, where skills included the management skills necessary to coordinate these factors of production. But the competitive game has changed. Natural resources have receded in importance as resource-based industries have declined to the point that they employ only a small fraction of the labor force. In the United States, for example, less than 3 percent of the labor force is employed in resource industries. The advantages of capital in turn are being neutralized as modern information technology speeds the development of and access to world capital markets. Technology continues to be important, however, as the chapters in this book argue, and gaining strategic advantage from technology requires a managerial, technical, and production work force skilled in both developing and utilizing scientific knowledge, inventions, and processes.

This leaves managerial and work force skills as the critical strategic variable in the competitive equation. The argument of this book, and one that many of us at MIT and elsewhere have come to embrace, is that the process of encouraging, adapting to, and managing change is the most critical of these skills.

The authors of this book take the argument a step further by arguing that it is achieving *systemic* organizational change that is critical to success in today's organizations. Managerial skills therefore will increasingly be measured by success in simultaneously adapting corporate strategies, technologies, organizational structures, and human resources. This is a challenge to all of us, given our traditions of specialization and compartmentalization. Indeed, it is a set of skills that we can best learn from each other, and this puts a premium on our ability to work together.

But we must be careful not to define the managerial task or skill set too narrowly. This book develops an important theme in noting that the task of managing change in the future will involve diverse individuals, organizations, and institutions. Organizations live in a macro economy and a society capable of imposing new aspirations and expectations on firms and their managers. No individual firm can respond in isolation and no individual firm alone can produce lasting social change. Thus an important task for future research and discussion is how to go beyond organizational change to achieve the necessary changes in economic and social institutions that lie beyond the traditional boundaries of any single firm. To address this issue will require a similar collaborative effort between the research community and representatives of these diverse institutions.

The quality of this collaborative effort depends on direct involvement of faculty researchers in the key organizational and social policy debates of the day. Our preference is to participate through well-grounded analytical research and active communication with leading practitioners and policymakers. By doing so we hope both to contribute to constructive change and to learn from our customers and constituents. This book follows in this tradition and in doing so helps initiate and structure a debate that is destined to be front and center in management research, teaching, and practice well into the twenty-first century.

Lester C. Thurow
Dean
MIT Sloan School of Management

Preface

Organizations are often slow to change, and the change is often too limited in scope when it does occur. Yet without continuous and systemic organizational change, this book argues, the competitiveness or even survival of many organizations may be at risk.

Continuous change implies that the organization has a capacity to learn from its environment, its various stakeholders, and itself. Systemic change implies that its major components—strategies, technologies, human resources, and internal structures—require simultaneous transformation. Implemented together these forms of change should generate what we term a "learning organization." In this metaphor is a vision of individuals, groups, and networks within an organization committed to continuous learning across the organization through informatior exchange, experimentation, and consensus building.

Our arguments on continuous systemic change and the learning organization emerge from a number of ongoing organizational studies by a set of MIT researchers. Each study concentrated on specific elements of change, ranging from new information technologies to innovations in human resource management and manufacturing methods. Taken together the studies point toward a more comprehensive model of organizational transformation. As a first test of its validity, the research studies were reviewed with a number of industry representatives. The studies and the industry responses are assembled here as an initial step toward generating a new, broader paradigm for the study and practice of organizational change.

Transforming Organizations is thus an endeavor in collective learning. Transcending traditional boundaries in academe and industry, the enterprise includes more than fifty individuals of diverse disciplinary backgrounds and business responsibilities. MIT researchers working in the areas of strategy and policy, management of technology, organizational behavior, and human resources initially prepared reports on their investigations. Industry representatives associated with manufacturing corporations, financial companies, consulting firms, and trade unions joined with the researchers for two and one-half days in June 1990. The conference discussion and debate ranged widely but recurrently came back to the need for systemic organizational change.

The joint endeavor was richly rewarded by the active involvement in many phases of the undertaking by the academic researchers and industry representatives. The generous sharing of their time, experience, and insights provided the essential ingredients for preparation of this book. A number of other individuals contributed invaluably to its completion. Roger Samuel facilitated conference planning and organization; Donald Ephlin, Arnoldo Hax, Robert McKersie, Maurice Segall, and Glen Urban moderated conference discussion; Lisa Quackenbush and Peter Cebon assisted with the conference and the preparation of the book; and Michelle Fiorenza, Pamela Spencer, and Joyce Yearwood contributed related services. Michelle Kamin served as conference and book coordinator, orchestrating an array of tasks to ensure the completion of both.

Preparation of the book and support for the conference were made possible by resources from the Sloan School of Management, the Industrial Liaison Program, and the Leaders for Manufacturing Program of MIT, and from Oxford University Press. The dean of the Sloan School of Management, Lester Thurow, and the vice president and executive editor of Oxford University Press, Herbert Addison, provided backing and guidance throughout the endeavor.

Cambridge, Mass.   T. A. K.
May 1991   M. U.

Contents

INTRODUCTION

1

Achieving Systemic Organizational Change

THOMAS A. KOCHAN AND MICHAEL USEEM

This book is an attempt to meet a challenge first posed over thirty years ago. A former MIT colleague, Douglas M. McGregor, in his classic *The Human Side of the Enterprise* challenged managers to rethink their assumptions about their roles, their organizations, and the values, motivations, and talents of their employees. McGregor's work was motivated by an intense belief that the key to organizational success in the future would be determined, in part, by the progress made in the theory and practice of organizational change and management. In his words:

> It has become trite to say that the most significant developments of the next quarter century will take place not in the physical but in the social sciences, that industry—the economic organ of society—has the fundamental know-how to utilize physical science and technology for the material benefit of mankind, and that we must now learn how to utilize the social sciences to make our human organizations truly effective. (McGregor, 1957, p. 1)

McGregor then went on to challenge theorists and practitioners to develop creative and useful models of organizational change that could turn this "pious hope" into organizational reality.

Have scholars and organizational practitioners lived up to McGregor's challenge? Few would answer yes, judging from contemporary concerns over the ability of firms to adapt to and compete effectively in today's global economy. This concern is voiced most clearly in the United States through reports of various productivity or competitiveness commissions that have been issued in recent years. Groups as wide ranging as the Council on Competitiveness to the National Academy of Sciences Commission on Technology and Employment, to MIT's Productivity Commission report *Made in America,* to the Collective Bargaining Forum and National Planning Association, groups of leaders of major corporations and unions—all seem to agree that changes are needed in the way U.S. firms compete and utilize their human, financial, and technical resources.

Moreover, these concerns are not limited to U.S.-based organizations. Similar debates are occurring across Europe and Asia as firms, nations, and regions search for new organizational strategies and institutional arrangements to take advantage of new opportunities posed by such things as the remarkable political events unfolding in

Europe and the advancing Asian economies. Thus we need to take a broad, international perspective to these issues.

A common theme emerging out of these debates, discussion groups, and reports is the view that systemic and continuous changes in organizational practices will be needed if firms are to compete successfully in today's and tomorrow's global economy. Moreover, a view is emerging that changes in any single organization are not enough. For a national economy and society in general to benefit, these changes need to be diffused broadly across organizations.

By calling for change, these groups have opened a debate over the organizational practices that can best serve advanced industrialized economies and societies of the future. But the debates to date leave a number of very basic questions unanswered: What is the new model of organizations that underlies the changes being advocated? Do these changes fit together in a coherent, internally consistent fashion? What evidence is there to suggest this new model or these new practices are superior to the traditional approach? What groups, forces, and policies must be mobilized to achieve systemic organizational change? Finally, how are systemic changes or transformations in organizational practices to be achieved?

COMPETING VIEWS OF ORGANIZATIONS

The current debates about organizational change reflect a deeper, but as yet unjoined debate over two competing views of organizations and their roles in society. These competing conceptions are outlined briefly in this section. We urge the reader to keep this broader debate in mind while examining the more specific issues and evidence presented in the individual chapters included in this book.

The Traditional Conception

In the traditional conception, the central purpose of the corporation is to maximize shareholder wealth. The primary legal and fiduciary responsibility of management and the board of directors is to promote shareholder interests. An effective organization is defined as one that maximizes shareholder returns.

Organizations form when markets are inefficient or incapable of coping with opportunistic (self-interested) behavior. Relations among different organizational participants and relations across organizations are dominated by self-interested behaviors. Controlling self-interest or opportunistic behavior is a critical function of organizational schema and contractual relations. For these reasons, organizations are designed with hierarchical structures, clear boundaries, and sharp divisions of labor, authority, and functional expertise and responsibility.

Organizations have deterministic technologies that are chosen on technical and rational economic criteria, independent of their organizational settings or human context. Technology not only is separate from labor but is a substitute for labor in the production function.

Individual employee voice or participation is to be focused around organizational goals or task-related problem solving. Independent organization or collective articulation of employee interests is to be avoided if at all possible or, if necessary, limited to highly stylized and tightly circumscribed forms of negotiations.

The Transformed View

In the transformed conception, by contrast, organizations are composed of and therefore responsible to multiple stakeholders. Effective change and mobilization of the energies of these stakeholders requires responding to their varied interests and needs. An effective organization is defined as one that meets the expectations of multiple stakeholders, including shareholders, employees, customers, and the societies in which they are located. The effective organization also commands the loyalty and commitment of these stakeholders to the long-term survival of the organization and social network in which it is embedded.

The boundaries across traditional functional units, roles, and organizations are blurring or becoming more permeable. Achieving effective cooperation and coordination across traditional boundaries is critical to organizational effectiveness. This requires building institutions and practices that sustain trust and instilling values of community and concern for mutual welfare into these cross-boundary relationships.

Technology cannot be separated from its human inputs and organizational contexts. A new form of sociotechnical design and conceptualization is critical to effective development and utilization of advances in scientific and technical knowledge.

Employees and other stakeholders are the best judges of their own interests and institutions. Individual and collective voices are critical to change and effectiveness in modern organizations.

Critics of the traditional conception of organizations do not challenge its descriptive validity as much as they challenge its functionality, that is, its ability to meet the varied demands facing contemporary organizations. Yet there is also a concern that transforming organizational practices from one conception to the other is neither an easy nor a natural phenomenon that will occur solely in response to market signals or technological change. Moreover, because of the interrelationships among the components of the alternative models, piecemeal change in one set of organizational practices is unlikely to be sustained or successful in the absence of supporting changes in other dimensions. This, in short, is what is meant by the phrase "transforming organizations." These are the issues and questions we asked our faculty and industry colleagues to consider in preparing and discussing the chapters included in this book.

The chapters that follow are organized into four broad interrelated areas shown in Figure 1.1. As this figure suggests, we see the challenge of achieving systemic changes in organizational practices as involving four highly interdependent activities: (1) strategic restructuring, (2) using technology for strategic advantage, (3) using human resources for strategic advantage, and (4) redesigning organizational structures and boundaries. We next introduce the broad arguments found in contemporary debates over each of these issues and then provide a brief preview of how they are treated in the chapters and discussion to follow.

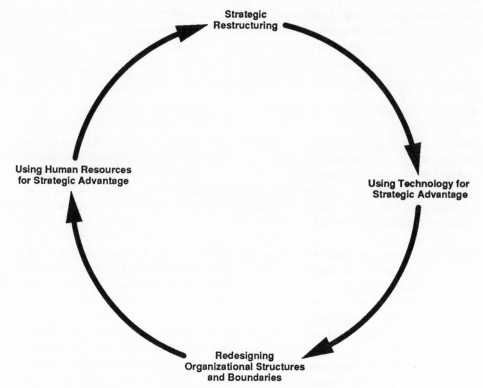

Figure 1.1   Multiple domains for achieving systemic change.

STRATEGIC RESTRUCTURING

The Argument

The central argument in the area of strategic restructuring is that many large firms prospered in the decades following the Great Depression because they adopted strategies that were successful in capturing large and expanding domestic markets. Now the challenge lies in adapting to global markets in a world economy where firms in other nations have caught up to or surpassed the capabilities of many American firms. The question, therefore, is what strategies and processes of adaptation are likely to be most effective?

Given large mass markets, firms adopted strategies that emphasized large volumes, long production runs, mass production of undifferentiated goods, economies of scale, and cost minimization. But today's global markets seem to be calling for more differentiated and higher quality goods and services. And shorter product life cycles put a premium on innovation and time to market. The challenge is for firms to adapt in ways that combine a focus on quality, cost reduction, changing customer needs, and the capacity to innovate.

Yet American firms have been highly criticized for being too focused on short-term cost minimization and profit maximization strategies and for being slow to learn and adapt innovations from other companies and other countries. Some of the reasons American firms tend to adopt these strategies may reflect the incentive structures produced by our financial markets and institutions. In particular, the 1980s witnessed extensive restructuring of American corporations as a result of an emerging market for corporate control. The chapters included in Part I review these developments in the United States and, through the lens of comparisons with Japan and Europe, ask how this approach to restructuring compares with the alternative approaches in other countries.

The Evidence

Ronald Dore starts the debate by describing the process of strategic restructuring adopted by Japanese firms. He points out that we cannot understand how Japanese managers restructure unless we first understand the fundamental assumptions Japanese society makes toward organizations. Organizations are communities, subject to communitarian values and expectations. Employees are highly important stakeholders. Moreover, Japanese financial institutions allow managers to take the long-term perspective expected of them as they adjust to changing markets. Dore's work further suggests that this approach allows Japanese firms both to achieve flexibility and to preserve the trust relationships required to maintain their capacity to innovate. He concludes that this approach to restructuring contributed to success enjoyed by the Japanese economy and its structural adjustments in the past two decades.

Richard Locke argues that patterns of strategic restructuring are not constrained by national models but instead are increasingly shaped by local socioeconomic and historical factors. In recent years, changing conditions of world competition and technological innovation have spurred increasing numbers of individual firms as well as entire industries to restructure. Contrary to traditional political economy analyses, which seek to understand these patterns by focusing on national institutional patterns, Locke argues that the current wave of restructuring is testing and sometimes transcending the boundaries of national regulatory regimes.

Whereas national institutions and arrangements have proven unwilling or perhaps unable to adjust to or even accommodate these changes, individual firms have continued to experiment with a variety of solutions that have transformed their structures and strategies. This combination of micro level effervescence and macro institutional stagnation has provoked the reemergence or renewed salience of local patterns of industrial politics. In other words, to fill this vacuum in the center, more localistic patterns of strategic restructuring, embedded within more regional or local socioeconomic contexts and histories, have emerged. Locke illustrates this more general trend by analyzing the reorganization of two Italian automobile firms. Locke's analysis develops an alternative way of understanding both how organizations like firms change and how the micro and macro levels of national political economies are linked.

Michael Useem then documents two of the dominant restructuring strategies adopted by U.S. firms in the 1980s, employment downsizing and changes in ownership. Useem introduces a new variable for organizational analysis by showing that many of the organizational changes occurring in recent years have been stimulated by pressures from external financial markets. This is not an area traditionally linked to study and practice of organizational change.

Useem notes that restructuring sets off a chain reaction of somewhat predictable internal organizational changes. If the current wave of restructuring follows previous patterns, we are likely to see organizations that are more centralized, less diversified, and perhaps less outward looking.

In the case of leveraged buyouts or hostile takeovers, the dominant hypothesis is that the greater responsiveness to shareholders is likely to reduce responsiveness to the interests of other organizational stakeholders such as employees and the community. Stated more broadly, the argument is that highly leveraged new owners (or executives in firms threatened by the prospect of a hostile takeover) will have shorter time horizons, will invest less in research and development, be less innovative in human resource development and policy-making, and, finally, be less successful.

These arguments, however, must still be viewed as hypotheses in need of more rigorous and extensive testing and examination. Indeed, the very basic question of the effects of different forms of corporate restructuring on corporate financial performance is still subject to intense debate. Paul Healy summarizes the empirical evidence available on these issues. He reports that the evidence on mergers and acquisitions is more positive than critics might suggest, but the long-term performance of leveraged buyouts and hostile takeovers is still uncertain.

Although these chapters stress the impact of external forces as stimuli to organizational change, none of the authors suggest that the course of these changes cannot be shaped by the organization. That is, organizational decision makers are far from passive parties in the change process. Edgar Schein picks up on this point in his chapter by documenting various strategies he has observed chief executive officers (CEOs) following as they manage and shape the change process. His data are drawn from studies of how CEOs use information technology. The CEO is the person in an organization most able to set the direction for change and most influential in the internal change process; thus an understanding of the CEO's role is critical to the overall task of understanding organizational change.

John Henderson and N. Venkatraman use information technology–induced change to show the importance of integrating and aligning an organization's competitive strategies with its policies for managing technology, human resources, and related internal processes and procedures. While this point is especially pertinent to information technology given the evidence of its limited economic return to date, the theme of integration and alignment is apparent in many of the other chapters collected here as well.

Rebecca Henderson's chapter identifies technological change as another external stimulus to organizational change. Moreover, she points out that some forms of technological change are highly problematic for existing organizations because they reposition the relationships among different knowledge bases, expertise, and organizational interactions. She uses the metaphor of architectural change to describe this phenomenon. As she suggests, and as the conference participants wholeheartedly agreed, this metaphor is helpful in conceptualizing the changes in thinking and action required in other organizational domains as well. Indeed, it became the dominant metaphor in our discussion and we draw on it in our final chapter in summarizing the central lessons for the future study and practice of organizational change.

USING HUMAN RESOURCES FOR STRATEGIC ADVANTAGE

The Argument

Advanced industrial economies can be competitive at the standards of living their citizens expect only by excelling in the development and full utilization of their human resources. This will require a public and private partnership to develop a highly educated, motivated, and adaptable work force and organizational practices that utilize these attributes. American society now finds itself behind many other nations in attending to its human resource infrastructure. The challenge therefore lies in:

1. Upgrading the quantity and quality of education and training in the work force.
2. Learning to value the differences and diversity found in the work force of today and tomorrow's global firm.
3. Sustaining a high level of participation and cooperation among employees and managers within organizations.
4. Supporting the transformation of industrial relations and human resource policies, practices, and traditions to diffuse and institutionalize commitment by business, labor, and government to these principles.

The Evidence

If these propositions are correct, the United States and perhaps other nations as well face considerable challenges. As the chapters in Part II suggest, the challenge goes beyond the ability of any single organization and will require a concerted and coordinated response by all of the institutions that affect employment relationships—employers, the government, labor unions, professional societies, and household and family units.

In the first chapter in this section, Lisa Lynch describes the changing demographic and educational profile of the labor force of the future. In doing so, she provides a starting point for the discussion that follows since a necessary precondition for realizing strategic advantages from human resources is that present and future employees be highly educated, skilled, mobile, healthy, and available for work. Only when this labor force is secured can one go on to examine the equally important requirement of designing policies and practices that fully utilize and reward the attributes of the work force. Lynch outlines the various approaches to training and skill acquisition that are currently used by companies and individuals. She challenges organizations to do more to link their training and development policies to other aspects of the organization's long-run strategies.

The key word that describes the work force of the future is *diversity*. The days are gone where the dominant model of a worker was a white male employed in a large firm for an extended period of time with a wife at home taking care of household and family affairs. Although there was always considerable variation around this stereotype of the average worker, in an era where future labor force growth will come largely from women, minorities, immigrants, and/or dual-income families, this stereotype is rendered meaningless. Thus a necessary condition for organizations to gain value from their work forces will be that they become skilled in *learning* from diversity.

Deborah Gladstein Ancona and David E. Caldwell probe the conventional wisdom about the importance of teams by showing that there is wide variation in team performance. They also show that the diversity inherent in cross-functional team composition is sometimes a mixed blessing. On the one hand it provides the diverse technical expertise that is needed to produce creative and efficient solutions. But on the other hand it can reduce team cohesion and thereby hamper internal team processes. Thus again the theme comes through that one type of change, in this case structural change (i.e., cross-functional integration), is not a sufficient strategy for improving organizational performance. What then does make teams work? Ancona's research suggests that at least one key characteristic lies in the ability of teams to both manage internal diversity and coordinate relationships with external stakeholders and clients. This implication leads into a central theme developed in a later section of the book, namely, the importance of cross-boundary coordination and cooperation.

Thomas Kochan and Robert McKersie review the innovations in human resource and labor–management practices that occurred in many leading union and nonunion firms in the 1980s. Kochan and McKersie outline the considerable challenges that must be addressed if labor, management, and government officials are to diffuse and institutionalize these innovations in the 1990s. They see this as becoming a major public policy issue for this decade. Thus we come full circle—strategic choice of individuals, their firms, and their representatives together will shape the larger environment and society in which we all live and work. But through the leverage provided by well-informed public policy, society can also influence the choices made at these micro levels and speed the diffusion of their effects.

Lotte Bailyn then argues that employers and policymakers will have to redefine the relationship between work and family in ways that reflect the growing diversity of the labor force and the need to create a more acceptable balance between the demands of the job and the home. In doing so, she alerts us to a paradox. The participative mode inherent in high-commitment organizations by itself is likely to exacerbate the work–family conflicts of dual-earner or single-parent families. Thus a "whole life" approach will be required—from government and corporations—to deal simultaneously with increasing competitiveness and with the interests of the nation's future workers and consumers.

USING TECHNOLOGY FOR STRATEGIC ADVANTAGE

The Argument

Given the high cost of labor and the standards of living expected by citizens in advanced industrialized countries, firms in these settings will need to adopt strategies that gain competitive advantage from advanced technologies and new product development rather than strategies that emphasize cost minimization. Historically the United States has been a leader in scientific and technological discovery, but mounting evidence suggests that U.S. firms have difficulty in transferring science and technology through the design and manufacturing processes to the marketplace. To improve the transfer process, most management and engineering experts are now stressing the importance of greater teamwork and cross-functional integration in both new product and new process development activities. Thus significant changes in organizational structures and practices will be needed if firms are to gain competitive advantage from advanced technology.

The Evidence

These issues are taken up in several of the chapters of Part III. Taken together they build on a modern variant of the longstanding "sociotechnical" model of organizational and technical systems. As we will see, however, these chapters go considerably beyond traditional sociotechnical models. They extend the hypothesis that it is the integration of a host of organizational, social, and human resource factors with technical considerations that will determine the extent to which new technologies are fully utilized and result in tangible benefits to different organizational stakeholders.

An important theoretical statement and empirical test of this argument is presented in the chapter by John Paul MacDuffie and John Krafcik. They develop the differences between an integrative approach and a traditional engineering approach to the design of technology and production policies, work organization systems, and human resource practices. The integrative approach that is most commonly found in Japanese manufacturing firms requires flexible work practices and a work force that is highly skilled, trained, and motivated. Without these attributes the production system cannot achieve the twin goals of high productivity and high quality. In contrast, the approach to production systems more typical of traditional U.S. engineering practice is to design controls or buffers that ensure against variations in the performance of the human resource system. This chapter provides the beginnings of a new sociotechnical model of technology and production system design and management. Their evidence suggests this new model is not culture bound but, instead, when adapted to reflect cultural differences, it appears to perform well in diverse national settings.

Marcie Tyre's chapter begins by showing that U.S. business units in the firm she studied lagged behind their European counterparts in meeting several standard performance benchmarks for new process development projects and teams. She goes a step further, however, in probing some of the historical and institutional reasons why these differences are observed. She argues that just changing the structure of the organization to introduce greater cross-functional integration and teams will not be sufficient. Instead, one needs to examine the interconnections across different dimensions of what might be called the internal labor market system. Thus Tyre's chapter illustrates the importance of systemic rather than piecemeal organizational change.

Eleanor Westney's chapter demonstrates the additional complexity associated with organizational design and strategy for a global corporation by asking which organizational model—one patterned after the parent corporation or one that incorporates practices that dominate in the host country—firms will adopt in managing organizations in multiple national contexts. She uses the internationalization of research and development activities as her window on these problems, but as she notes, these are generic questions that apply to all functional activities in transnational organizations. Thus she poses what may indeed be the fundamental organizational design question facing today's global firm.

A chapter by Michael Scott Morton summarizes the major conclusions derived from a large-scale study of the effects of information technologies on management and organizational processes. He concludes that the need for integration of technology with its organizational and human contexts is equally critical to achieving the full benefits of information technology as the other chapters have shown it to be for manufacturing technologies. He too reinforces the need for an integrative approach to the study and practice of organizational change and management.

Robert Thomas's chapter extends the discussion beyond the shop floor to the design process by focusing on the early stages of decision making about new technologies. He notes that the choice of a technological system or "solution" to a "problem" is not dictated by technical factors alone. Instead technological choice and the process of implementation are part of a highly contested political process involving a competition over both resources and substantive content. Because the parties recognize the political nature of these decision and implementation processes, the process tends to be highly stylized with defined and limited roles for various technical specialists. Engineering design specialists tend to dominate the early stages of problem definition and the search for alternatives, leaving human resource specialists out of the process until the final stages of implementation. Thomas's case study evidence and theoretical model therefore lead him to suggest that achieving real integration of human resource policies with the design of new processes will require fundamental structural change in organizations.

REDESIGNING ORGANIZATIONAL STRUCTURES AND BOUNDARIES

The Argument

The hierarchical principles upon which today's corporations are structured grew out of the era of mass production and were influenced by the military principles of command and control. In contrast, many voices now argue that organizations need to encourage and support participatory decision making, vertical and horizontal communications, creativity, risk taking, cooperation and teamwork, and coordination across traditional specializations and organizational boundaries. The argument is that innovations in organizational design and structures should occur in several areas:

1. Organizational hierarchies will need to be flatter to encourage the flow of ideas and influence from below.
2. Departmental and disciplinary boundaries will need to be more permeable to promote cross-functional integration, communications, and problem solving.
3. Barriers to cross-firm cooperation and collaboration will need to be overcome.
4. Organizations must be open to continuous learning and improvement.

The Evidence

Opening up organizational structures and boundaries is not only hard to do, but many of the proposed changes are contrary to human and organizational tendencies to specialize and focus on narrowly defined and self-interested behavior. Each of the chapters in this section questions the permeability of internal and cross-organizational boundaries and the stability and effectiveness of the various forms of cross-boundary cooperation and coordination that have been established.

Michael Piore starts this discussion with a broad-ranging analysis and interpretation of the factors that underlie the cross-firm collaborative networks observed in small enterprises in northern Italy. He starts with a theoretical premise that the only way to understand individual and organizational behavior is to see economic action as embedded in a broader social structure and society. From this starting point he emphasizes the importance of building upon community values and an overarching set of shared objectives rooted in local networks. Piore argues that the demonstrated ability of these types of networks to do this flies in the face of traditional economic and organizational theories of human behavior.

Stephan Schrader provides an additional interpretation of factors that affect the amount and stability of cross-organizational information flows. He emphasizes the joint benefits and reciprocal relationships that produce friendships and personal links that feed the flow of information and expertise across traditional boundaries.

Edward Roberts takes up the alternative to change in an existing organization or organizational structure by discussing the alternative design options open to organizational decision makers when confronted with new technological possibilities and markets. He notes that careful strategic choices need to be made in selecting among alternative designs such as joint ventures, outside acquisition, and internal venturing. His concept of the "innovation paradox" captures the dimensions of the challenge to organizations: the more radical the departure from one's current market niche and technological expertise, the greater the risk of failure. The solution to the paradox lies in developing the skills needed to manage cross-boundary organizational designs.

Peter Senge and John Sterman provide an appropriate caveat to the prescription that decentralization and involvement of lower level participants are universally beneficial. They note that unless these structural changes are combined with strategies that ensure local level participants are aware of and take into account the larger system implications of their decisions, considerable suboptimization will occur. This in turn can lead to a counterreaction to recentralize or add a coordination layer of management. They stress the importance of organizational learning and describe how systems thinking and the tools of systems dynamics can foster this type of organizational learning.

THE ROLE OF LEADERSHIP

Changes in organizational practice are not likely to occur in the absence of strong, intelligent, and visionary leadership. For this reason we asked two highly respected and experienced leaders—one from the world of business and the other from the world of labor—to share their views on the types of leaders needed in today's organizations. Their statements were intended to initiate further debate on organizational transformation, and they sparked a lively discussion over the questions of who should be considered a leader, who leaders listen to and learn from, and how leaders from diverse backgrounds and organizations can collectively lead organizations and institutions to change.

CREATING THE LEARNING SITUATION

The interactive nature of our conference was designed to promote mutual learning among the researchers and practitioners present. The discussions and debates that followed the papers generated a range of new ideas and themes that are summarized in our closing chapter. In the chapters that follow, therefore, we have included practitioner commentary on each of the chapters as well as excerpts from the researcher–practitioner dialogue that took place in each section of the conference. This approach is in keeping with our belief that systemic organizational change and transformation can best be accomplished by bringing together individuals and groups with diverse knowledge and experience bases to form a learning community.

If successful, the changes discussed in the book should point toward the creation of learning organizations, the subject of the final chapter of the book. A learning organization, as our authors and industry representatives conceive it, is not a static, transformed mirror image of the traditional organized model outlined earlier in this chapter. Instead, it is a living and evolving entity that engages in continuous learning and adaptation by engaging diverse stakeholders from inside and outside its traditional boundaries in a process of experimentation, analysis, problem solving, and feedback. In short, it is an entity that creates and nurtures a culture that sustains learning and change and that allows change to originate from diverse sources. In this vision leadership and the management process are dispersed activities, along with the power to initiate and the skills to manage change. Organizational transformation does not become an end state but rather a process or mindset that keeps the organization open to opportunities for continuous improvement.

This may sound like an unrealistically visionary view of organizational life, at least as we currently experience it. Yet it is the vision that is generated by the models, data, and experience of those researchers and practitioners who participated in the production of this volume. The extent to which this vision appears to be beyond our current reach may therefore be one measure of how far we, and our organizations, have to travel in the quest to be competitive in tomorrow's world. It also challenges us to examine further the evidence and base of experience that lead such a group to produce this type of vision. Only by delving into the evidence and relating it to our own experiences will we either confirm the validity of this vision or take sufficient exception to it to generate an alternative view. In either case our hope is that this material sparks an intellectual debate that, in turn, stimulates constructive and systemic organizational change. We invite you to now examine the ideas that follow and to thereby join our debate and learning community at this incipient stage.

REFERENCE

McGregor, D. M. 1957. "The Human Side of the Enterprise." Address delivered to the Fifth Anniversary Convocation of the MIT School of Industrial Management, Cambridge, Mass., April 9, 1957. Available from the MIT Sloan School of Management.

I

STRATEGIC RESTRUCTURING

2

Japan's Version of
Managerial Capitalism

RONALD DORE

> The best solution [for overhasty diversification] is for Japanese firms to sell
> unwanted subsidiaries and buy firms which fit with their core business, even if
> this requires a hostile takeover. To make such a reshuffle of assets possible, the
> Japanese will have to ease the regulations governing mergers and acquisitions.
> Last year a Tokyo district court ruled that firms that find themselves the target of
> an unwelcome takeover bid can no longer resort to the age-old practice of
> selling shares at knockdown prices to friendly white knights. This has been the
> favourite way of diluting a hostile investor's stake to below the critical 33
> percent level—above which an investor has the right to call a shareholder's
> meeting and demand changes. The ruling has since been contradicted by another
> court. What is needed now is a government edict to put some administrative
> resolve into the first court's ruling.

The Olympian self-assurance with which *The Economist* (February 10–16, 1990) tells
governments around the world what they should do admits no possibility of coun-
terarguments. Japanese capitalism should grow up. And that means, of course, that it
should grow more and more to resemble Anglo-Saxon capitalism. Never mind that
there are other and materially different—German, Italian, French—models available,
should the Japanese happen to be dissatisfied with their own. If the Japanese are sincere
about "internationalization"—and equal playing fields and all that—then there is no
doubt what "reforms" are needed.

But, of course, there is considerable doubt whether the Japanese *are* dissatisfied
with their own form of capitalism. A quarter of a century ago, when I first started
studying and writing about Japanese firms, there was a general assumption, in Japan as
well as abroad, that in practically every respect, organizationally as well as technologically, Japan was "backward." That assumption is still around, in Japan, too, as
well as in the editorial offices of *The Economist*, as current Japanese discussions of the
takeover rules illustrate. There are today, however, far more Japanese who would say,
rather, we just have a basically different—and better—way of conceiving the nature of
the business firm.

The points which this chapter emphasizes can be put in the framework of recent
arguments that the firm should be seen as the convergent locus of the interests of
multiple stakeholders. They are:

1. In the conception of the firm—or at least of the large corporation—which is overwhelmingly dominant in Japan, among union leaders as well as in the business class, the one stakeholder whose stake is seen to be of paramount importance is the body of employees. The primary definition of the firm is a community of people, rather than a property of the shareholders, and this conception shapes business practice.
2. Certain institutional characteristics of the employment system, reinforcing the sense of community, have the particular effect of blurring the lines of division between two of the key categories of stakeholder analysis, employees and managers.
3. Bits of property cannot be easily anthropomorphized; communities can. Hence Japanese managers readily speak of devoting themselves "to the future of our great company" much as U.S. presidents talk of "the future of our great nation." Contrary to the individualistic utilitarian assumptions of most "multiple stakeholder" writing, "the company" can be seen, not simply as an arena, not simply as an institutional device that allows a variety of stakeholders to pursue their separate interests, but also as a reified entity. As such it can be an object of loyal sentiments and can be seen as itself having interests that transcend the interests of all possible concrete stakeholders.
4. The economic behavior encouraged by these underlying conceptions is more conducive to business efficiency (even if its promotion of X-efficiency, as Leibenstein first dubbed it, is sometimes at the expense of allocative efficiency) than behavior based on the assumptions embodied in American—or for that matter Japanese—corporation law.

THE EMPLOYEE INTEREST

What is the evidence that the employee interest dominates and that the firm is seen primarily as a community of people in Japan? One can, to begin with, start with the rhetoric. A Japanese company chairman addressing his shareholders would be unlikely to make a point of acknowledging the principal–agent relation in which he is engaged by speaking, as his American counterpart well might, of "your company." It would always be "our company" (Sogo, 1981).

There would, to be sure, these days, in our post–Peters and Waterman world, be nothing very unusual in an American CEO emphasizing the community nature of the firm. What *would* be unusual, though, would be for the American employees, especially blue-collar employees, universally to respond to such a statement with a solemn nod of deferential agreement rather than with a sneer or a cynical grin. "Universally" would not apply in a Japanese firm either, but the positive reactions are likely to be overwhelmingly dominant. Natural deference? Partly, perhaps, but also because what counts as normal business behavior in Japan is such as to *reinforce*, rather than undermine, statements about "trust" and "common goals." For example, it is now extremely rare (it was not so rare in the 1950s) for a firm's CEO and any of the executive directors to be "outsiders." The vast majority are men who have spent all, or almost all, their working lives in the firm. They think of themselves, and act like, elders of the enterprise community. As elder senior executives they have high salaries, but not on such a scale as to differentiate their lifestyle radically from that of their fellow employees. A company president's salary is rarely more than ten times the average employee's—compared with three-figure multiples in many American firms.

Moreover, just as within modern nation-states, various symbolic affirmations of common citizenship serve to emphasize the ideal of what de Tocqueville saw in America as a "basic equality of condition," so within the Japanese firm. Often this involves everyone, from the managing director down, wearing a company uniform. Single benefit schemes for retirement and sickness graduated to salary or seniority are normal. Some firms have lunchrooms, weekend resort hostels, and other perks reserved for senior management, but that is not the dominant pattern. Most enterprise facilities are available to all the firm's "members."

The conventions associated with lifetime employment are clearly a key factor. Recruitment is a matter of hiring young people for careers, not particular jobs. Hence great care is taken in personnel selection for full-member employees (who are clearly distinguished from temporary employees, employees of on-site subcontractors, etc.). All the advantages of long-term commitment—the loyalty, the payoff from training, and the accumulation of experience—can be gained only if the commitment really is long term, that is, if the employees can be persuaded to stay with the firm. And that is understood to mean (though the contract is wholly implicit) that the firm for its part must make a strong commitment to keeping them as long as they want to stay (up to the agreed retirement age). In any case, the ability of any community to inspire a sense of attachment in its members is crucially damaged by any form of triage. Hence, first, the concern to avoid the need for redundancy through early diversification to deal with declining markets, and, second, the conventions for dealing with overstaffing problems when they do arise: redeployments, transfers to training schemes, layoffs at 80 percent of pay, freezing and eventually cutting bonuses, cutting recruitment (though not of new graduates), "outposting" surplus workers to subsidiaries or suppliers, the wholesale "loaning" of bodies of workers to other firms for fixed periods, and dismissals as a last resort only after 10–20 percent cuts in managers' pay and a reduction or suspension of dividends.

FACILITATING CONDITIONS FOR THE "COMMUNITY ENTERPRISE"

The Legal Framework

Is it just a difference in values, ideologies, or behavioral habits that explains the differences between these conventional Japanese behaviors and the way American or British managements would behave? Or are the structural constraints different?

Legally there is very little difference between the Japanese commercial code and American corporation law, but there are two relevant differences. Both are matters of statute rather than of judicial interpretation. The first concerns restrictions on "unfair dismissal"; the other concerns the priority given to unpaid wage claims vis-à-vis other creditor claims in a bankruptcy proceedings.

The grounds on which employees have challenged collective dismissals have varied, but judgments have come to turn on one dominant issue: whether managements have done everything in their power to avoid dismissals (Hanami, 1989). Have they, for example, actively sought new markets? Have they eliminated or reduced overtime? Have they actively sought opportunities for the outposting or for the loaning of workers? A subsidiary issue in many cases has been charges of discriminatory selection of the people to be dismissed. Some courts have given priority to the welfare principle: triage should concentrate on those most able to weather the consequences of dismissal—young workers able to find another job. Others have given priority to the efficiency principle: firms are justified in thinking primarily of the health of the firm as a whole by (as they are almost universally inclined to do) cutting off the old and infirm (and expensive). A unified doctrine has yet to be established, though statute has made some intrusion here. Firms can get the benefit of special schemes for declining industries only if their personnel retrenchment plans are part of an overall business plan which they have discussed with their employee unions (Hanami, 1989).

As for the regulations governing bankruptcy, and the restructurings that are its Chapter 11–like near cousins, these *are* a matter of statute rather than judicial interpretation. They not only give priority to full payment of back wages before other claims are settled, but they also give a similar priority to employees' claims on the accumulated Reserves for Employees Retirement Compensation. (These funds reserved for pensions and lump sum retirement payments are at the discretionary disposal of management and an important element in capital employed. They are distinct from, and in volume much larger than, pension trust funds, which also exist in some firms under the control of trustees, not management.) There have been strong tax incentives to increase the size of these reserves, and in 1979 they amounted, for nonfinancial corporations as a whole, to nearly 19 percent of net worth—that is, of the current market value of stockholders' equity (Aoki, 1984)—usually a good deal more than the total possible sum of claims on them.

Financial Markets

A second, extremely important, contextual factor is the financial environment of the enterprise. The main distinctive features of the Japanese situation are as follows:

1. A heavy, though in the last decade rapidly diminishing, reliance on bank loans rather than equity capital.
2. One of the banks is generally considered a firm's lead bank. It may provide only marginally more loan capital than other banks, but it will own more of the firm's equity, it will put more effort into monitoring the company's performance, and it will be the prime mover in any brink-of-bankruptcy reconstructions (Rohlen and Pascale, 1983).
3. A large part of a firm's equity is in the hands of friendly, corporate stockholders: the suppliers, banks, insurers, trading companies, dealers it daily does business with. The holdings are frequently mutual. The distinction between these (rarely traded) equity holdings by "loyal" business partners and the "floating holdings" owned by investors whose sole concern in the stock is to make money out of it is so clear and important that the quarterly company reports regularly list for each firm the percentage of floating stockholdings. For most firms that percentage is relatively small. A 1988 estimate by the American analyst Gideon Franklin puts the figure for the average firm at 23 percent (Emmott, 1989).

4. That immeasurably complicates the task of any would-be takeover bidder.

5. In any case, apart from T. Boone Pickens, who is carrying his missionary torch for true red-blooded capitalism to Japan with an attempt to take over the firm Koito, attempts to mount a hostile takeover are rare. At present, the "enterprise as community" ethic, the rejection of the "enterprise as stockholders' property" ethic, militates against it.

6. Not having much to fear from takeovers, firms do not need to panic if their share quotations fall, even if—after, say, being in the red for two or three years running—their market value falls below the value of their strippable assets. (Japan's spiraling urban land values—not reflected on balance sheets where assets are counted at cost—makes Japan potentially an asset-stripper's paradise.)

7. The lowly position of the shareholder is indicated by actual dividend returns. Most companies pay a standard percentage on the share's face value—which in recent years has hovered below a 1 percent yield on market values. So why does anyone hold equities? *Hitherto* the self-reinforcing spiral of capital gains has provided enough compensation.

8. Note, too, that (in a society with a production ethic rather than a financial wizardry ethic, where enterprises have rather more engineers than lawyers or accountants on their boards) the stock market is generally thought to be a corrupt and sleazy place, rife with insider trading and dominated by four big securities firms capable now and again (when they have particular friends to benefit or claim favors from) of making rather than taking prices. Hence share price movements not only have few practical consequences for managers; they are not, either, taken as indicators of how well "the market" judges managers to be doing their job.

Culture

A third set of facilitating conditions cannot be ignored. Japanese enterprises recruit Japanese. Japanese are brought up in emotionally tightly knit families; they go to schools where there is a great stress on conformity, cooperativeness, belongingness; where the individualistic alienation of anyone from the group is viewed with alarm. They are programmed to be susceptible to the comforts and allurements of community.

Do not forget that the typical statement that "the Japanese are *more* predisposed to seek community" is inevitably *comparative*—a matter of more and less, not all or nothing—and is a statement about population norms, not individuals. Japan has enough awkward-cuss individualists to staff quite a number of American firms in Tokyo, just as America has quite a lot of communitarians who exist happily in Japanese-managed firms.

THE MANAGER–EMPLOYEE DIVIDE

The second proposition was about the assumption in most stakeholder analysis (at least since 1947) that employees and managers are clearly distinguishable categories.[1] The various community membership–affirming devices already described—unified benefit schemes, standard uniforms, and the like—clearly blur category boundaries. So, too, do two other institutional factors.

First, university graduates on managerial career tracks normally start with eight to ten years in subordinate positions. During this time they are members of the enterprise unions that bargain with senior managers over their wages.

Second, in the highly bureaucratized Japanese firm, all remuneration is based on some seniority-constrained incremental scale. The senior managers who bargain with the unions are themselves on the upper reaches of the junior manager scales, which are the subject of union bargaining. Those upper reaches are, to be sure, beyond the purview of the unions, and subject to much greater elements of discretion. But they are not just set by managing directors as the product of one-to-one bargaining. They are set by personnel offices which need to use justifiable rules to protect themselves against charges of favoritism—and tend, consequently, to use much the same rules as for the rank-and-file union member employee. It is likely, therefore, that a senior manager who bargains down the union demands for a wage increase will be lowering his own wage increase. He may earn brownie points which help toward his next promotion, but he will not expect to bargain for a higher salary out of the money he has saved the firm.

THE REIFICATION FACTOR

As suggested earlier, these characteristics of the Japanese firm are not adequately described by saying that employees are preeminent among the stakeholders. They have other implications that can best be elucidated by contrasting the perception of "the firm as arena" with that of "the firm as entity."

Analysis in terms of stakeholders assumes the arena view. It can handle concepts like the firm's reputation and goodwill as collective goods of the stakeholders in much the same way as rational choice political scientists analyzing the functions of the state write about defense, public order, and conservation of the environment as collective goods. But the logic of collective action (with its assumptions that only organizational compulsion can overcome inevitable—and rational—tendencies to be a free rider) seems clearly inadequate as a means of understanding how patriots feel about the reputation of their nation abroad, for instance, how many Americans felt about losing the Vietnam War. It is equally unable to capture what goes on in the mind of employee stakeholders who swell with pride when they tell a stranger which firm they work for, and who attach some real meaning to phrases like "a loyal member of the firm." As a means of understanding that psychology, the entity view makes more sense.

Let us put this in concrete terms. Imagine a production engineer who is asked to work through a weekend to meet the accelerated timetable for getting a new product on the market—a weekend when he had promised to take the kids to the beach. One can see this as in some ways analogous to the situation of a youngster deciding whether to dodge the draft or risk death in Vietnam. The dominant factors will be the pressures of supervisors and peers in the one case, and family and friends in the other; but *behind them* will lie the norms and shared assumptions of the organization/society. Those norms are about not interests but duties, and they are conceived as duties not so much toward the other stakeholders–fellow citizens, but as duties to "the firm" or to "the nation."

One might put the point explicitly in terms of obligations. In a stakeholder arena analysis the sum of the obligations of each stakeholder equals the sum of their rights. In an entity analysis it is greater. In an arena analysis obligations are payments, disutilities; in an entity analysis the satisfaction derived from the performance of obligations can count as utility—though I would agree with Etzioni that the attempt to count it as such and to assume that all human action can be measured in a single unidimensional utility calculus is misguided; the moral dimension deserves separate treatment (Etzioni, 1989).

The point acquires its greatest importance, of course, for analyzing the behavior not of a production engineer deciding on the disposal of nothing of more consequence than his own time, but of managers deploying the resources of the firms—making decisions that are going to affect the interests of all the other stakeholders. Are they just balancing those interests, or are they *also* influenced by a sense of being guardians of "the firm"—of its reputation and of its long-term future?

Note the *also* of that last sentence. It is not suggested that entity allegiance often, or ever, dominates over, much less excludes, arena participation in managers' perceptions of their role. (And that is a fortiori the case with other stakeholders.) The suggestion is, only, that the entity allegiance element is probably too important to be ignored. Scholars and judges may concur that, legally, to consider the corporation as an entity separate from the stockholders is muddleheaded and improper (Freeman and Reed, 1983).[2] But casual empiricism suggests that, even in the United States, a sense of the firm as a entity with a future that may be more or less glorious, depending on their efforts, does enter into the decision-making calculations of many executives—certainly in elite firms.

But if *some* level of entity allegiance is a common feature of all modern industrial societies, capitalist or socialist, that element is especially important in Japanese firms for two particular reasons. The first, elaborated at length earlier, is the extent to which enterprises are regarded as communities of people rather than bits of property. The second is the fact that Japanese managers are more given to planning for the long term.

The relation between the entity view and long-term thinking is two-way. People are not much *motivated* to think long term if they do not think in entity as well as arena terms. And if they *are* thinking long term, there are fewer forecasting problems if they think in terms of the well-being of "the firm" as an entity rather than in terms of the aggregate of the benefits accruing to the separate, not at present clearly identifiable, future stakeholders.

There are other circumstances that predispose Japanese managers to long-term planning and hence to the entity view:

1. They are more likely to have a long-term commitment to the firm.
2. They are fairly secure from the threat of takeover if poor short-term results lower their share price.
3. They are unlikely to be subject to any kind of executive compensation system based on short-run performance criteria.

IMPLICATIONS

My fourth proposition was that these characteristics which distinguish Japanese firms from those of Europe and America, and most sharply from Anglo-Saxon firms—the predominant weight given to the employee interest and the greater predisposition to take the entity view of the firm—give Japanese firms a strong competitive edge in world markets. The advantages they confer—the long-term horizons, the synergies of cooperation—are most obvious when firms face the sort of changes in market conditions that require drastic readjustment. Take the steel industry as an example. The problems which that industry has experienced in all the industrial countries—high energy costs, substitution of new materials, new competing capacity in developing countries—culminated in Japan in the mid-1980s (Dertouzos, Lester, and Solow, 1989). The adjustment of individual companies was made easier by industry-wide agreements to share capacity cuts of a kind that would probably have run into antitrust problems in the United States.

But the objectives of managers in the individual firms were not just to get back into profit by cutting off loss-making sections of the business, becoming leaner and meaner. Nippon Steel, for example, announced its long-term plans for reconstruction in 1987— after two years of substantial losses. It envisaged no reduction, but rather a continuing growth in turnover. The pivotal element was a target for 1995 against which all strategic planning for the intervening years was to be evaluated: 50 percent of sales to be, by 1995, in non-steel business. Plans were developed for moving, not only into obviously related fields, like plant engineering and composite materials, but also further afield into areas such as biotechnology and tourist development. New venture start-ups were sometimes accelerated by recruiting experienced personnel from outside, but for the most part the required technical and marketing expertise was developed internally—by extensive programs, not so much of retraining as of learning, since they relied a great deal on employees' own initiatives. The plan was agreed to by the union; an essential element was agreement on numbers—how far total employment would be reduced, with what phasing, through what sort of early retirement inducements.

The objective was to ensure that, even if no longer describable as a steel firm, the entity, the continuously self-renewing community of people who make up Nippon Steel, should have a flourishing long-term future. As it happened, the arrival of boom conditions helped the company to get back into profit a good deal earlier than might have been expected, but by the turn of the decade the results of the diversification plans were also beginning to appear.

It is a long way from the continuing takeover sagas that preoccupy the top management of USX. The standard recipe for adjustment—in the economic textbooks and by and large in reality in the United States—is adjustment through the market. The steel firm's business, if its markets are contracting, is to cut down until it is back in profit. The financial markets and the labor markets do the job of ensuring that the resources thereby released move under the control of other entrepreneurs with other kinds of expertise in new and expanding industries. In Japan the adjustment mechanism is not so much the market but the managerial decision, redeploying labor and capital *within* the enterprise community—in ways which, because of cross-subsidizing as between divisions, allowing relatively wide margins for risk-taking experimentation.

HOW VIABLE?

Will the system survive, though? After—roughly—forty postwar years of a form of capitalism dominated by the enterprise as community ideal, will Japan revert to the sort of stockholder-dominated form of capitalism that prevailed at the beginning of the century?

There are *some* grounds for answering "yes." Spiraling stock prices cannot offer capital gains forever. Shareholders are likely to become more demanding in their claims on current earnings. Unions, the only organizations likely to mount a real defense of the status quo, are losing, not gaining strength. And perhaps the taboos on hostile takeovers cannot last forever, as Japan becomes culturally and ideologically a less homogeneous society. The arguments of *The Economist* with which this chapter began have many supporters in Japan, and they are supported by the growing influence of foreign investors.

But still the managers of the economy's dominant corporations, who have grown up in and been formed by the system, seem predisposed to preserve it. And there are grounds—most recently moves in some states against takeovers; the sixty-day notice rule for redundancies, and so on—for arguing that, incrementally, the U.S. system is edging toward the Japanese more than vice versa.[3] I would put my money on the probability that those trends will continue.

NOTES

1. R. W. Johnson first added managers to the established quaternity—customer, employee, community, stockholder—according to Preston and Sapienza (1989).
2. *Garner* v. *Wolfinberger,* Delaware High Court.
3. This is a view which is elaborated—though more specifically about Britain than about the United States—in a study published in 1973. I have since reaffirmed that judgment in an "Afterword" to the latest reprinting of *British Factory, Japanese Factory* (1990).

REFERENCES

Aoki, M. 1984. "Aspects of the Japanese Firm." In *The Economic Analysis of the Japanese Firm,* edited by M. Aoki. Amsterdam: Elsevier Science Publishers.

Dertouzos, M. L., R. K. Lester, and R. M. Solow. 1989. *Made in America: Regaining the Competitive Edge.* Cambridge, Mass.: MIT Press.

Dore, R. 1990. *British Factory, Japanese Factory: The Origins of National Diversity in Industrial Relations.* Berkeley: University of California Press.

Emmott, B. 1989. *The Sun Also Sets: The Limits to Japan's Economic Power.* New York: Random House.

Etzioni, A. 1989. *The Moral Dimension.* New York: Free Press.

Freeman, R. E., and D. L. Reed. 1983. "Stockholders and Stakeholders: A New Perspective on Corporate Governance." *California Management Review* 25, no. 3: 88–104.

Hanami, T. 1989. "A Guide to Personnel Management in Japan—Law and Practice. Part IV: Termination of Employment." *Labour Institute Quarterly* (summer), (Tokyo).

Preston, L. E., and H. J. Sapienza. 1989. "Stakeholder Management and Corporate Performance." Paper presented at Conference on Socio-Economics, Harvard Business School, March 1989.

Rohlen, T., and R. Pascale. 1983. "The Mazda Turnaround." *Journal of Japanese Studies* 9, no. 2: 219–263.

Sogo, S. 1981. "Gaining Respect." *Speaking of Japan* (Tokyo) 1, no. 3.

COMMENTARY BY HAROLD E. EDMONDSON

Let me comment in four parts. First, in Japan the company is an entity, a living, breathing entity. In the United States it's usually viewed simply as a collection of "stuff" that is used for the various stakeholders' benefit. While the entity is important in Japan, that feeling is present in many American companies, too. I should preface my comments by saying that I'm speaking mostly about the high-tech industries, which I know better than others. But certainly many other companies in our country also fall into the same category. I am familiar with Johnson & Johnson, and a few other companies represented here, and I think I can say that DEC (Digital Equipment Corporation), HP (Hewlett Packard), and Johnson & Johnson are probably closer to the Japanese model.

That entity idea is important to all of us. When we at HP go home for the night, we all kind of feel like there is this living, breathing thing still present, and when we get back the next day the ghosts of people past will still be there. The entity approach is certainly a good one and one that we should strive for.

The second thing is the relationship of the employees to the managers. Professor Dore characterized the relationship in the United States as being more adversarial and in Japan as more cooperative. I think that's probably accurate in general. But I feel that there is a fair amount of the cooperative or Japanese approach to things in our industry, and I certainly hope there is at HP. By cooperative, I don't mean that the company is going to be managed cooperatively—we're not going to take a vote on things we do— but at least there is a feeling that we're all in this together, both labor and management, and I think we try to run the company that way. The cooperative approach is a better one.

The third issue is the short-term versus long-term mentality, with the United States being on the short-term side and the Japanese being on the long-term side. We are all reasonably familiar with a lot of articles that have told us that. Characterizing American industry once again, I think that there are a fair number of us that do a little of each. Our research and development is oriented to the longer term, while our response to the financial community is short-term oriented. I think the Japanese do much better, which the article pointed out quite well, in making managerial decisions based on the long term.

I would see a kind of combination. There are certain things you do have to concentrate on in the short term and certain things in the long term. It would be good if we did have some research that looked into successful Japanese and American firms and tried to give some sense of what things can be and should be managed on a short-term basis, and what things you need to invest in for the long haul. I do think we suffer at HP from the financial threat. If I didn't think that, I wouldn't call home every night to find out what the stock closed at. But I do.

The last thing is the issue of the stockholder versus the employee as the main group for which the firm is run. The chapter points out that in Japan it's mostly the employees and in the United States it's mostly the stockholders. My view of that is that it's probably pretty nearly true, though in the firms I am familiar with there is a little more employee emphasis.

It seems to me there is another piece that needs to go in there, and that is the need for a triumvirate for which the firm is run: the stockholder, the employee, and the customer. I think the properly run firm will balance all of those things. There is also society in general, and although I don't add that one to the other three, it should be in the equation too.

You see articles all the time about the compromise between two pieces of the triumvirate, but I don't really think there needs to be a compromise. As a matter of fact, if you try to benefit one of the three versus the other two, you will ultimately defeat yourself. As an example, if you try and pay your employees too much money, thinking you are doing them a favor, your firm will not be successful and their employment will go downhill pretty fast. The same thing is true of the other two elements of the triumvirate.

3

The Political Embeddedness of Industrial Change: Corporate Restructuring and Local Politics in Contemporary Italy

RICHARD M. LOCKE

This is an essay about industrial change. Conventional explanations for industrial adjustment emphasize the institutional efficacy (or lack thereof) of certain national institutional arrangements over others. The premise is that there exist different "national models" of regulation, some better than others at adapting to changing political and economic circumstances. Yet the empirical evidence on industrial adjustment in the 1980s suggests the need for a more subtle and differentiated account. Cases of successful adjustment[1] emerged not just in countries with the "correct" mix of institutional arrangements but across several advanced industrial nations with radically different political and economic arrangements. Moreover, in a variety of industrial sectors within the same countries, patterns of industrial renewal appeared to coexist alongside other cases of blocked innovation.

This chapter attempts to account for these divergent patterns of industrial change not only across but also within nations by analyzing how the current wave of industrial reorganization is undermining established national regulatory institutions and norms. It focuses on the recent restructuring of Italian industry since, in many ways, Italy has acted as an advanced laboratory for corporate reorganization during this era of economic turbulence and massive industrial change. Yet the argument holds for other advanced industrial nations as well. In understanding the configuration of the new industrial order in Italy (and elsewhere) two factors are key: (1) changing patterns of international competition and new technologies which have altered markets and challenged traditional business practices; and (2) political struggles, alliances, and compromises among different local industrial actors which shape and reshape the strategic choices of firms and unions. This chapter is part of a larger research project aimed at developing a more robust explanation for the diversity of the adjustment patterns observed within industries and countries in Europe and North America.

THE SETTING: INDUSTRIAL CHANGE IN ITALY

One of Italy's many paradoxes concerns its recent economic revival. In the 1970s, Italy (along with the United Kingdom) was seen as a "sick man" of Europe. It suffered from all the ills of the advanced industrial democracies: unstable governments, terrorism, rigid and militant unions, high rates of inflation, and balance of payment deficits. Three separate but equally critical events—the "hot autumn" of 1969, the collapse of the international monetary system, and the oil crises of 1973 and 1978—contributed to promote Italy's economic crisis.

The consequences of the cycle of worker strikes and militancy commonly known as the hot autumn of 1969 for industrial output, profitability, productivity, and labor costs were substantial. For example, in 1970 alone, average employment compensation rose by 19 percent as opposed to annual increases of 8.5 percent between 1963 and 1969 (Rey, 1982). In the first half of the decade, the number of hours worked per employee decreased by 12 percent and overall productivity growth fell sharply (Rey, 1982). The consequences of the hot autumn on the length of the workweek and labor relations on the factory floor (i.e., reduced scope of employers in dismissing workers, limited internal labor mobility, curtailed use of capital equipment, etc.) were also dramatic.[2]

The domestic situation was exacerbated by international developments. Notwithstanding a series of currency devaluations following the Smithsonian Agreements,[3] Italy experienced a deterioration in competitiveness as expressed by loss of market share of Italian exports abroad and a sharp rise in import penetration (Geri, 1981). With firms caught between increasing labor costs on the one hand and a rise of import penetration on the other, industrial investment, particularly in the private sector, stagnated.[4] Instead of increasing productivity by raising the capital–labor ratio, entrepreneurs sought to decentralize production toward smaller scale establishments or self-employed operators working at home (hence also circumventing trade union restrictions and depressing wage bills; e.g., see Frey, 1975).

As in most other European countries, these years were dominated by inflation (see Salvati, 1985). Firms contributed to this spiral by defending their market power through cartelization, unions by supporting progressively more rigid forms of indexation (i.e., the *scala mobile* agreement of 1975), and the public sector through increasingly indiscriminate use of subsidies. Growth rates and investment continued to decline and currency devaluations were frequent. When the second oil crisis struck, Italy was particularly vulnerable. Given the country's heavy dependence on oil (70 percent of its energy needs), the deterioration of terms of trade was striking.

Restraints on layoffs, overtime, and flexible use of labor imposed by the unions combined with low levels of investment to limit productivity and profitability. Moreover, although employment was defended (Italy almost alone in Europe witnessed an increase in employment in these years), population growth, a return flow of migrants, and increased participation rates by women combined to promote unemployment, especially among the young and in the south.

Economic policy during this period was initially designed to increase government intervention so as to offset some unfavorable consequences of the crisis.[5] Industrial investment by public corporations, especially in the south, rose substantially. Transfer payments to social groups not protected by the unions also increased. These measures, however, met with limited success. In fact, while the effects of increased public expenditures were modest, the public sector deficit swelled.

The structural weakness of the Italian economy—best illustrated by record budget deficits and rates of inflation—continued into the 1980s. Integration into the European

Community and the establishment of the European Monetary System in 1979 fore-closed most protectionist measures and hindered successful devaluations of the lira. Other government attempts at correcting the situation—taxation reform, incomes pol-icy, and various forms of industrial policy—also failed due to the continuing stalemate of Italy's political system.

Various government measures aimed at promoting industrial restructuring, or even facilitating the adjustment processes under way, all appear to have produced limited results at best. For instance, initial attempts by the Italian government to promote industrial adjustment through the use of its huge public sector, Ente Nazionale Id-rocabuki (ENI) and Instituto per la Ricostruzione Industriale (IRI) or to provide finan-cial and organizational support to enterprises in difficulty through GEPI (Gestione e Partecipazione Industriale, a program in which the state would purchase shares of private enterprises in need of restructuring, reorganize them, and then reprivatize them) resulted for the most part in saddling the state with more "lame ducks" and increasing the public deficit (see Posner, 1978; Prodi, 1974).

Likewise, other government programs aimed specifically at industrial restructuring (Law 675 of 1977) and technological innovation (Law 46 of 1982) also suffered from a combination of bureaucratic inefficiency and government incapacity. Several studies found that a combination of political maneuvering by parties and endless bureaucratic infighting blocked the efficient allocation of funds aimed at promoting industrial ad-justment in several sectors. Because of these obstacles, only a small fraction of the allocated funds were ever used before the mandate for the various programs expired.[6] In other cases, government funds were disbursed but without clear purpose and cer-tainly not in any preconceived, rational plan. In short, because of various institutional limitations of the Italian state and due to the ongoing political stalemate of the 1970s,[7] the government was unable to formulate, let alone implement, a coherent policy aimed at promoting industrial restructuring.

Underneath and largely obscured by this national political-economic stalemate, the restructuring of firms and industries at the local level continued apace. This restructur-ing took place in districts of small firms as well as among large enterprises and its results have been quite positive for the Italian economy (see Regini and Sabel, 1989). For example, since the early 1980s, labor productivity in Italy has increased more than in West Germany, the United States, and even Japan. Moreover, while unit labor costs have decreased, profitability, especially in those sectors that have undergone the most extensive restructuring, has improved significantly (see Confindustria, 1988). In fact, if one examines various indicators for structural adjustment in manufacturing (e.g., production, value added, investment), one sees a clear improvement, both in terms of past performance and in comparison with other countries, during these years. How can we account for these recent changes?

To better understand these developments, in the next section I analyze two cases of industrial adjustment in two very different sectors, automobiles and textiles. These two industries were chosen because they possess very different industry structures, technol-ogies, and work forces and thus variables like firm size, capital and labor intensity, type of technology, and skill level of the work force can be controlled. In this way, I can illustrate how local socioeconomic factors shaped firm-level adjustment strategies in both these sectors. This is the focus of the next section.

INDUSTRIAL RESTRUCTURING AND INDUSTRIAL RELATIONS: A TALE OF TWO SECTORS

Chronic Conflictualism: The Case of Fiat Auto

Like most automobile producers in Western Europe and the United States, Fiat Auto experienced very serious organizational and financial problems in the late 1970s. In many ways, Fiat's troubles were related to the more general crisis of the auto industry. A variety of factors, including increased international competition; the rise of fuel costs; changing consumer tastes; more stringent government health, safety, and environmental protection regulations; and increased labor costs all contributed to the crisis of the automobile industry in the West. Yet, because of insufficient capital investments and extremely conflictual and rigid industrial relations practices throughout the 1970s, Fiat's productivity, profitability, and plant utilization rates were all lower than those of its major competitors.[8]

Fiat's crisis became especially visible in 1979, when the automobile division acquired a separate balance sheet for the first time.[9] Suddenly, Italy's largest privately owned firm appeared to be on the verge of bankruptcy. As a result, the firm launched a restructuring process which included the massive introduction of new process and product technologies, a reorganization of its supplier and sales networks, and a radical break with the industrial relations practices of the 1970s. As part of its reorganization plan, Fiat proposed to place 24,000 workers in Cassa Integrazione, a state-financed redundancy fund, during the fall of 1980.

The local union rejected this reorganization plan and broke off negotiations with the firm. Fiat, in turn, declared its intention to fire 15,000 workers, beginning on October 6. Things heated up as the union blockaded the firm and Fiat sent out letters of dismissal. The ensuing strike lasted thirty-five days but rank-and-file participation was low. Finally, on October 14, Fiat foremen and supervisors organized a successful demonstration calling for a return to work. Some 40,000 people marched against the union, among them many blue-collar workers.[10] That very night an agreement was signed which represented a major defeat for the union. The agreement met with resistance from the more militant factions of the local union but was signed and pushed through for approval by the national industry federations. Despite initial attempts by the local labor movement to claim victory in this strike, it marked a major defeat from which they have not yet recovered.

With the union out of the way, Fiat embarked on a major reorganization of its production processes. Its products were rehauled so that many new models with greater differentiation in design but more common components were introduced. The modular design of these new models permitted the automaker to reap greater economies of scale as well. Fiat also invested heavily in new technologies like computer-assisted design and manufacturing and industrial robots. Finally, Fiat rationalized and upgraded its network of components suppliers. This increased collaboration between Fiat and its suppliers both enhanced the quality of its components and stimulated continuous product innovation.

The consequences of this reorganization have been positive for the firm but harsh for its workers and their union. Profits, productivity, production, and investments have all increased dramatically since the restructuring of the firm (Fiat Auto, 1989a, May 31). As a result of these and other improvements, Fiat has increased its market share and now rivals Volkswagen as Europe's number one auto producer. If the results of Fiat's restructuring have been positive for the auto firm, the consequences for the union have not. Immediately following the rupture in relations with the unions in 1980, the firm asserted a hard line with the labor movement. Within the factories this translated into a recreation of traditional hierarchies and control on the shop floor, the expulsion of numerous union activists (see Becchi Collida and Negrelli, 1986), and the reduction of the work force by tens of thousands of workers.

Ongoing antagonism between the local unions and Fiat management foreclosed all possibilities of labor participation in the adjustment processes under way. For the first half of the decade, Fiat management circumvented the unions, negotiating directly with workers over issues concerning retraining, flexible work hours, and modifications of their jobs. These modifications were significant enough to match the changes under way in the organization of production, but they were not sufficiently dramatic to necessitate formal renegotiations of job classification schemes and the like, since this would have legally required union participation. This blurring or bending—but not breaking—of already established contractual rules and boundaries was characteristic of Fiat industrial relations policies over the course of the 1980s.

A recent study of how Fiat workers perceive the technological changes under way in the firm suggests that those workers most vulnerable to being replaced by automation are extremely anxious about their positions and diffident toward the union. Unions are shunned not only because of their failure to protect these workers but also because of fears that union contacts will result in company reprisals in the form of dismissals or Cassa Integrazione (Reiser, 1986). Union membership rates reflect these feelings. At Fiat's various Turinese plants, membership in the local metalworkers union, the FLM, fell from 32,898 in 1980 to 11,589 in 1986.[11]

In sum, the reorganization of Fiat Auto was accomplished in a highly confrontational and unilateral manner in which the firm's "success" was directly proportional to the union's failure and workers' fears. More careful examination of this reorganization reveals potential challenges to the future stability and viability of this model of firm adjustment and raises serious questions about union strategy in today's climate of sweeping economic change. But before this is attempted, let us look at a second, very different case of industrial restructuring. Examination of this second case will not only provide us with a comparative perspective through which to better understand the case of Fiat but also will highlight how local socioeconomic factors shape industrial adjustment.

Negotiated Restructuring: The Case of the Biellese Textile District

The Biellese textile district, the birthplace of Italy's industrial revolution, is a small area located in the mountainous northwest section of the Piedmont. Referred to as the "Manchester of Italy" (Secchia, 1960), this area consists of eighty-three small towns and villages and about 200,000 residents. Yet, despite its isolation and fragmentation, the Biellese area is a leader in the world's textile industry.[12]

With over 90,000 people active in the labor market, the Biellese area has one of the highest rates of labor market participation (45.2 percent) in the country; and with 235 out of every 1,000 residents employed in industry, the Biellese is the most heavily industrialized district in Italy. The Biellese has over 5,000 firms with approximately 44,000 workers. The vast majority of these firms (3,000) and workers (35,000) are employed in the woolen textile industry. In 1986, the textile industry produced 4,400 billion lire in sales, of which one-third was exported (mostly to Germany, Japan, France, and the United States). For an industry that is in crisis almost everywhere in the West, this is a notable achievement (see Toyne, Arpan, Barnett, Ricks, and Shimp, 1984).

Yet Biella was not always this successful. During the 1970s the local textile industry was in crisis. Many firms faced the threat of bankruptcy and a number shut down. Changing conditions of international competition (newly developing countries with lower labor costs are very strong in this sector) combined with increased labor and energy costs to render traditional integrated textile firms uncompetitive. Only through a massive process of industrial restructuring and technological innovation was the industry restored to health.

Major restructuring began in the early 1970s, as a result of a natural disaster (in 1968 a flood devastated the plants of many firms), but continued throughout the decade in response to the previously cited changes in the economy. In essence, traditional integrated firms found themselves consistently outcompeted in an ever more volatile and competitive market. Rigidities in manufacturing and industrial relations practices posed serious problems for firms whose markets demanded frequent product innovations and flexible production processes. Most firms restructured but some did not. However, only those firms that reorganized themselves were able to survive.

Traditional integrated mills restructured themselves by spinning off various phases of their productive cycles, preserving internally only those phases of production in which they were most specialized and/or which most distinguished their products. This process not only changed the industrial geography of the area, eliminating all firms with over 500 workers (Ferla, 1981), but also encouraged the emergence of many new, smaller firms specialized in specific phases of the productive process. Thus while some traditional mills maintained the spinning and weaving phases of production, other newly formed firms performed the dying and finishing phases of the cycle.

Increased specialization promoted innovations in product and process technologies for both the original and newly formed firms. Economies of scale and scope were achieved no longer by producing long series of standardized products but rather through the use of new, more flexible looms, which permitted weaving mills to produce smaller batches of woolens efficiently. While the new dying and finishing operations also invested in new technologies, they were able to reap economies of scale by aggregating orders from several weaving mills into large batches.

A network developed among the different firms engaged in the various processes of production. Cooperation developed not only between traditional weaving firms and their dying or finishing subcontractors but also among the original spinning and weaving firms, which often used the same suppliers. This, in turn, further promoted product and process innovations as firms related their experiences and techniques with new machines, new fibers, and new finishing processes. For instance, several manager-owners of textile plants in the Biellese explained that before buying a new machine or initiating a new process they visit other local plants in the area which already have installed these innovations and conduct tests with their own products. Moreover, a visit to the local Rotary Club, Unione Industriale Biellese (business association), or to certain trattorie (local restaurants) reveals how Biellese textile managers are constantly exchanging information and recounting their experiences with new techniques and technologies.

Cooperation and collective innovation have not only improved product quality but also altered production strategies. Each firm now produces specialized products for specific market niches. Moreover, although Biellese textile firms are still quite competitive with one another and very protective of their individual firm autonomy, they nonetheless unite both to buy raw materials (setting up purchasing cartels) and to sell their finished goods (organizing a biannual fair, IdeaBiella, in which they introduce their latest products).

The unions played a significant role in these developments. Although most (but not all) restructured firms reduced their work forces, the transition from integrated to specialized production was usually negotiated with the union. The union had a say in who was let go or put in Cassa Integrazione and was consulted on plans to innovate and introduce new technologies. It also negotiated a territorial collective bargaining agreement with the local business association in order to extend union strength in certain firms to other weaker sectors of the work force. Not only did this territorial agreement protect workers; it also strengthened the unions by preventing whipsawing, enhancing workers' solidarity, and extending union agreements in large firms to the newly formed smaller firms.[13] As a result, the productive decentralization that took place in this area did not undermine union strength. Workers who remained within the restructured firms were often retrained in the use of new process and product technologies, and many who exited the firms set up their own small businesses, buying old machines from and often working as subcontractors for their original bosses.

Labor relations are not always tranquil in the Biellese area. There were a number of strikes and even a few factory occupations. The local union is militant and factory owners are far from complacent about it. The point, however, is that this process of radical change was negotiated by management and the unions. Both sides recognize their different interests and express very different ideologies (the workers are primarily Communist while most business leaders support the rightist Liberal Party [PLI]), but they nevertheless bargain and reach accords regulating the processes of industrial adjustment. As one local business leader put it, the unions and the managers united in a "pact for development" in order to save the local industry and preserve jobs. The major confrontations between labor and management occurred not in restructured firms but rather in those businesses that did not restructure and thus were forced to close (Neiretti, Moranino, Perona, Dellavalle, et al., 1987).

Cooperation continues between the unions and business leaders. Joint efforts have emerged to promote research and development, technical education and job retraining, and improved infrastructures—all aimed at enhancing the competitiveness of local industry.[14] The results have been positive. Record sales and profit rates for firms have been matched by high rates of employment (people actually commute into the Biellese area to work!) (Unione Industriale Biellese, 1981). Union membership rates are above the national average and the Communist party is the only party able to elect a representative to Parliament from this politically competitive electoral district. For an area only seventy-five kilometers from Turin, the contrast is striking.

Alternative Explanations for Diversity in Corporate Restructuring

Thus we have two cases, one of negotiated restructuring and the other of conflict. How do we account for these different experiences with industrial change? One's first instinct is to attribute these differences to economic or industrial factors. In other words, they can be traced to differences between the automobile and the textile industries. Elsewhere, however, I have compared these two cases of industrial reorganization with matched pairs in the same sectors in order to control for these economic and industrial variables (Locke, 1989). That analysis indicated that the alternative models of industrial politics observed in Biella and Fiat Auto are neither typical of nor attributable to the particular features of the industry or economic sector in which they belong. Within the Italian automobile industry—in fact, even within Fiat (i.e., Alfa Romeo)— more negotiated models of industrial adjustment are found. Likewise, within the Italian textile industry there exist notorious examples (i.e., Lanerossi) of intense labor–management conflict and blocked industrial adjustment.

An alternative way of explaining these diverse models of corporate restructuring employed in this chapter focuses on local socioeconomic factors which shape firm-level behavior. Building on recent work by Arnaldo Bagnasco (1985), Carlo Triglia (1987), and Mark Granovetter (1985) which illustrates how local sociopolitical traditions and institutions influence the strategic choices of economic actors like firms and unions, I argue that three local features—(1) the organizational features of local firms and unions; (2) the ideological outlook or worldview of their leaderships, and (3) the degree of social and political development of the surrounding context—all shape the type of strategies developed by these actors. A reexamination of our two cases illustrates the importance of these factors in shaping contemporary patterns of industrial renewal in Italy.

SHAPING INDUSTRIAL POLITICS: LOCAL PATTERNS OF SOCIOECONOMIC RELATIONS

The development of Fiat along the lines of "Fordism," and the way in which it occurred, had significant effects on both the firm and its work force, as well as on the history of Turin (Castronovo, 1979; Michelsons, 1986). The expansive development of the firm made it not only the biggest but in many ways the only show in town. (Fiat is referred to as "la mamma" by local residents.) The local economy has historically revolved around the firm and the majority of the local labor force is employed either at Fiat or at one of its numerous suppliers.

Due to its hegemonic position, Fiat was able to dominate local government, control local business and cultural associations, and thus more or less determine the development of the city. Fiat management also cultivated an extremely authoritarian, hierarchical vision of its role (Bairati, 1983; Castronovo, 1977).[15] Thus during the early years of the firm, through the long tenure of Vittorio Valletta, and continuing to this day, Fiat management has sought to unilaterally control the firm's development. As a result, management promoted pro-business political forces and company unions. It also sought to tame its work force through a combination of repression and paternalism and undermined all attempts at establishing alternative bases of power (i.e., the post-war workplace councils, the Consigli di Gestione) within its plants.

The local labor movement's development reflects this particular model of development.[16] For instance, peculiar to the local labor movement are its frequent experiences with spontaneous worker uprisings, regularly followed by the politicization of industrial relations (see Golden, 1988). This occurred in 1913, when the rank-and-file supported anarchosyndicalist positions and prevented the local union from negotiating with the firm, and it has been repeated throughout the local union's history. The political development of the local labor movement was such that it developed weak organizations but strong ideologies. Antagonism toward the firm combined with a radical, almost maximalist vision of politics to create a local union which perceived itself (and at times sought to act) as the vanguard of the Italian labor movement (Reiser, 1981).

As a result of the particular way in which industry was developed in Turin and the peculiarities of the local labor movement, stable relations between the firm and its work force never developed. The result was a continuous struggle between these actors in which no long-lasting compromises were possible. Defeat by one meant its almost complete subordination to the other. The wounds of past battles were nourished as the loser prepared for revenge in the next round of struggles. Thus from the factory occupations in 1920 (see Cammet, 1967), continuing through the rise and fall of fascism, the restoration of private capital in the 1950s, the hot autumn struggles in the late 1960s, and the thirty-five-day strike in 1980, labor and management in Turin have been engaged in an all-or-nothing battle.

Moreover, Turin does not possess the sociopolitical resources necessary to mediate the type of conflictual labor relations characteristic of Fiat. Because of the simplicity of Turinese society—composed essentially of two groups, an industrial bourgeoisie and a proletarian working class—organized interest groups and political parties never fully developed in Turin. Membership figures and participation rates in political parties are especially low in Turin (Bagnasco, 1986, Chapter 4). Even membership rates in the union, which has historically been more of a movement than an institution, have been always below the national average. Other interest groups in Turin are dominated by either the firm or the union movement. The only institutions that are independent of these two protagonists are the local churches. But because of their own historical development, even they are quite radical and actually enhance rather than hinder antagonisms between labor and management at Fiat (see Berzano, Cañedo Cervera, Famà, Fornero et al., 1984). In sum, the local union at Fiat and the firm's management developed into highly antagonistic and political actors located in a city lacking potential mediators of industrial conflict. It is no surprise, therefore, that repeated attempts by groups within the local union and the firm to construct a more negotiated and stable form of industrial relations at Fiat failed repeatedly (see Deallessandri and Magnabosco, 1987).

The contrast with Biella is striking. Formative experiences of the local union in the Biellese, which include strong union organizations, a tradition of collective bargaining (the first Italian collective agreement over wages and working conditions was negotiated in Biella), a protagonistic role in political-economic developments (i.e., unionists were leaders in the local resistance), and close integration into a rather complex local community clearly shaped its present politics (see Neiretti et al., 1987; Ramella, 1983). As a result, the local union in the Biellese developed as a strong organization (union membership rates are higher than the national average) with a long tradition of collective bargaining with local firms. Moreover, because it was embedded with a complex social and political network, it was able to negotiate territory-wide agreements which reinforced its position as an organization and facilitated the adjustment of the local industry.

Local firms, in turn, also developed in a way that increased their inclination and ability to negotiate with labor and enter into collaborative projects with customers, subcontractors, and even potential competitors. For example, their shared experiences with natural disaster (the flood of 1968) prompted them to act collectively and develop more collaborative arrangements between individual firms. These practices came in handy in the 1970s as all firms in the Biellese faced similar competitive challenges from low-cost producers. They negotiated a territorial collective bargaining agreement in order to avoid price competition between them and organized buying cartels for raw material and trade fairs of local firms in order to reduce raw material costs and expand their markets. In short, they too developed organizational features and managerial strategies that encouraged patterns of negotiated adjustment at the local level.

Thus local socioeconomic factors shaped the divergent models of industrial change examined here. The firm-centered, authoritarian adjustment pattern at Fiat and the more negotiated model of Biella were both the result of local patterns of industrial development which shaped the strategic choices of unions and firms. At Fiat, this produced a highly politicized but organizationally weak union and a hierarchical and authoritarian management who were unable to negotiate over the firm's restructuring. At Biella, the opposite took place. Strong, territorial-based unions and well-organized business interests formed a "pact for productivity" in order to facilitate industrial adjustment and guarantee employment in the local industry.

Given that these cases are not exceptional but rather indicative of the wide array of diverse patterns of industrial politics manifest at the local level, what does this mean for the future of national systems of industrial regulation and policy?

CONCLUDING CONSIDERATIONS: TOWARD A RECONFIGURATION OF INDUSTRIAL POLITICS?

Conventional accounts of industrial change stress how individual nations with particular institutional histories and varying positions in world markets possess not convergent but rather very diverse industrial, social, and political institutions. As a result, these explanations focus on different macro level institutional arrangements (financial markets, state structures, "neocorporatist" labor arrangements, etc.) to explain divergent patterns of industrial adjustment among nations.[17] "Successful" adjustment (or its failure) depends upon the existence (or lack thereof) of the "correct" mix of particular structures and/or institutionalized patterns of state–society relations (see Katzenstein, 1985; Reich, 1988).

The two cases summarized here challenge these conventional accounts and point to an alternative, more micro and historically grounded model of the adjustment process. This model rests on three distinct but related arguments. The first emphasizes the role of choice open to firms in *how* they respond to external pressures to adjust. In recent years, the new terms of international competition and technological innovation have radically altered markets and the organization of production. The simultaneous globalization and segmentation of national markets has rendered traditional business practices in all advanced industrial nations less effective. Technological innovations have not only shortened product life cycles but also created opportunities for firms to compete along lines that challenge the supremacy of mass production (see Piore and Sabel, 1984; Porter, 1986).

The breakup of national markets has spurred individual firms and regional networks of firms to experiment with a variety of alternative business strategies and structures that test and/or transcend the boundaries of national regimes of regulation (see Dertouzos, Lester, and Solow, 1989; Piore, 1987). Whereas national institutions have proven unwilling, or perhaps unable, to adjust to or even accommodate these changes, individual firms have experimented with a variety of solutions which have transformed their structures, strategies, and relations with labor. This combination of micro level effervescence and macro level paralysis has provoked a series of political struggles between actors of these two levels of the political economy over how best to respond to individual firm needs for flexibility while also maintaining national standards. Given that "success" is not uniquely associated with one set of choices but that a range of alternative strategies is possible, what determines the choice of one solution over another?

The second point is that history matters, that is, local historical traditions shape the strategic choices of individual firms. In other words, given that industrial development occurred in different ways and at different times in the various localities and regions of all national economies, local firms developed divergent organizational resources and attributes which reflect the particular context in which they are embedded. While these differences were latent or perhaps less noticeable during the heyday of national markets, they recently reemerged to fill the vacuum left by anachronistic regulatory practices. This accounts for the increasing divergence in corporate structures, strategies, and labor–management relations manifest not just across but also within industrial sectors, sometimes even between plants within the same firm.

The third point is that local politics matter. The historical legacies that shaped the strategies of firms and unions were at times consolidated, at other times transformed, through political struggles between these actors over their competing choices. These struggles emerged in the 1980s as individual firms and entire industries sought to adjust to changes in the international economy. The outcome of these struggles, whether in the form of complete victory of some actors over others, or the result of compromises and alliances between them, shaped both the subsequent structure of the local industry and the future patterns of relations between labor and management. This is why there is such diversity in industrial adjustment patterns within and not just across industries in Italy.

Moreover, the Italian case illustrates that significant economic change and organizational variety can occur with the same macro institutional regime or mode of regulation. Since such change is continuous and to a certain extent subterranean, it often is overlooked by conventional political-economic analyses, which focus primarily on national institutions and arrangements. Yet because micro level industrial change has been pervasive, the substance (if not the form) of the relationship between local industrial actors and the national institutions regulating them has been transformed over the last decade or so. This institutional transformation can also be detected in recent reforms in labor law and labor market regulations, the structure of collective bargaining, health care and health insurance provisions, vocational education, and economic development programs.

In short, the renewed salience of local patterns of industrial politics shapes not only individual firms and union strategies but also traditional patterns of state–society relations. Increasingly, the division of political or regulatory labor between the national and local levels, or between the public and the private sectors, is being renegotiated in ways that give greater voice to actors at the firm and local levels. While this trend toward localism may be especially pronounced in Italy—given its long historical tradition of regionalism—similar or analogous patterns appear to be emerging in other nations as diverse as Sweden, the United States, and Germany (see Sabel, 1989). How these tendencies are unfolding in these other countries and what they mean for the way we understand organizational and institutional change in today's economy are issues being pursued in the broader research project from which this chapter is drawn.

NOTES

1. A note of clarification. By "industrial adjustment" I mean the reorganization of the structures, strategies, and human resource policies of industrial firms. This entails, for instance, investing in new technologies, changing the organization of production and work, altering relations both internal to the firms (i.e., managerial hierarchies, internal labor markets, labor–management relations) and external (i.e., with suppliers, customers, perhaps even potential competitors).

In this chapter I embrace Peter Katzenstein's definition of "successful adjustment," which includes political as well as economic outcomes (Katzenstein, 1985, p. 29).

2. For more on the hot autumn, see Brandini (1975) and Pizzorno, Reyneri, Regini, and Regalia (1978).

3. The Smithsonian Agreements took place at the end of 1971 and entailed a renegotiation of exchange rates between the United States and its advanced industrial trading partners (Europe and Japan) following the U.S. government-initiated collapse of the gold standard. For more on this episode, see Block (1977).

4. On the low levels of investment during these years, see Enrietti (1981); for the negative impact of this low investment on machine parks, R&D, etc., see Pecchio, Perrucci, and Rollier (1981).

5. For more on economic policy during these years, see Salvati (1980).

6. For more on the failure of these attempts at industrial policy, see Adams (1985), Ferrera (1987), CER-IRS (1986), and Modigliano (1986).

7. For more on the crisis of the Italian political system, see Bartolini (1982) and Pasquino (1983).

8. For more on the crisis and subsequent restructuring of Fiat Auto, see Locke (1989).

9. Fiat Auto is one of fourteen divisions of Fiat S.p.A. In 1988, the automobile division employed about 45 percent of Fiat's total employees, generated over 60 percent of its profits, and consumed about half of its investment. For more details, see Fiat Auto (1989b June 29).

10. For more on this episode, see Baldissera (1984) and Bonazzi (1984).

11. Figures from the Metalworkers Union, FLM, Turin, December 31, 1986.

12. This and the following figures on the Biellese are from Unione Industriale Biellese (1987).

13. Based on interviews with Secretary of the Chamber of Labor, Biella, May 25, 1987. See also Neiretti et al. (1987).

14. Based on interview with head of local business association, Unione Industriale Biellese, May 22, 1987.

15. For a more general discussion of how management worldviews shape organizational features, see Schein (1983).

16. See various essays in Agosti and Bravo (1980) and Gianotti (1979). For an interesting discussion on how formative experiences become institutionalized and continue to shape labor politics, see Brody (1971).

17. For examples of scholarship which seeks to account for differences in state–market relations or even government economic policy by focusing on national political and economic institutions, see Hall (1986) and Zysman (1983).

REFERENCES

Adams, P. 1985. Government–Industry Relations in Italy: The Case of Industrial Policy. Unpublished Ph.D. dissertation. Department of Political Science. Yale University.

Agosti, A., and G. M. Bravo, eds. 1980. *Storia del movimento operiao, del socialismo e delle lotte sociali in Piemonte*. Bari: De Donato.

Bagnasco, A. 1985. "La costruzione sociale del mercato: Strategie di impresa e esperimenti di scala in Italia." *Stato e mercato*, no. 13.

Bagnasco, A. 1986. *Torino: Un profilo sociologico*. Turin: Einaudi.

Bairati, P. 1983. *Valletta*. Turin: UTET.

Baldissera, A. 1984. "Alle origini della politica della disuguaglianza nell'Italia degli anni '80: La marcia dei quarantamila." *Quaderni di sociologia* 31.

Bartolini, S. 1982. "The Politics of Institutional Reform in Italy." *West European Politics* 5 (July).

Becchi Collida, A., and S. Negrelli. 1986. *La Transizione nell'industria e nelle relazioni industriali: L'Auto e il caso Fiat*. Milan: Franco Angeli.

Berzano, L., A. Cañedo Cervera, A. Famà, G. Fornero, G. Girardi, G. Margaria, A. Paini, and T. Panero, 1984. *Vomini Di Frontiera: "Scelta di Classe" & Trasformazioni Della Coscienza Cristiana A Torino Dal Concilio ad Oggi*. Turin: Cooperativa di Cultura Lorenzo Milani.

Block, F. L. 1977. *The Origins of International Economic Disorder*. Berkeley: University of California Press.

Bonazzi, G. 1984. "La lotta dei 35 giorni alla Fiat: Un analisi sociologica." *Politica ed economia* 11.

Brandini, P. M. 1975. "Italy: Creating a New Industrial Relations System from the Bottom." In *Worker Militancy and Its Consequences, 1965–75*, edited by S. Barkin. New York: Praeger.

Brody, D. 1971. "The Expansion of the Labor Movement: Institutional Sources of Stimulus and Restraint." In *The American Labor Movement*. New York: Harper & Row.

Cammet, J. 1967. *Antonio Gramsci and the Revolution That Failed*. Stanford, Calif.: Stanford University Press.

Castronovo, V. 1977. *Giovanni Agnelli*. Turin: Einaudi.

Castronovo, V. 1979. *Imprese ed economia in Piemonte dalla "grande crisi" ad oggi.* Turin: UTET.

CERS-IRS. 1986. *Quale strategia per l'industria?* Bologna: Il Mulino.

Confindustria. 1988. *X Rapporto CSC: Squilibri commerciali e aggiustamento produttivo nei paesi industriali.* Rome: Confindustria.

Deallessandri, T., and M. Magnabosco. 1987. *Contrattare alla Fiat.* Rome: Edizioni Lavoro.

Dertouzos, M. L., R. K. Lester, and R. M. Solow. 1989. *Made in America: Regaining the Productive Edge.* Cambridge, Mass.: MIT Press.

Enrietti. A. 1981. "L'Accumulazione industriale in Italia negli anni settanta." In *L'Industria Italiana: Trasformazioni strutturali e possibilita di governo politico,* edited by L. Pennacchi. Milan: Franco Angeli.

Ferla, P. 1981. "Progresso tecnico e nuove forme organizzative nel comparto laniero Biellese: Analisi empirica di alcuni casi significativi." Tesi di Laurea, Facolta' de Economia e Commercio, Turin.

Ferrera, M. 1987. "Politica, assetti istituzionali e governo dell'industria." In *Stato e regolazione sociale,* edited by P. Lange and M. Regini. Bologna: Il Mulino.

Fiat Auto. 1989a. *Bilancio consolidato al 31 Dicembre 1988.* Turin: Fiat Auto S.p.A.

Fiat Auto. 1989b. *Relazioni e bilancio al 31 Dicembre, 1988.* Turin: Fiat Auto S.p.A.

Frey, L., ed. 1975. *Lavoro a domicilio e decentramento dell'attivita produttiva nei settori tessili e dell'abbigiliamento in Italia.* Milan: Franco Angeli.

Geri, M. 1981. "Il ruolo delle aree nell'equilibrio degli scambi commerciali: Quattro paesi Europei a confronto. In *L'Industria Italiana: Trasformazioni strutturali e possibilita di governo politico,* edited by L. Pennacchi. Milan: Franco Angeli.

Gianotti, R. 1979. *Trent'anni di lotte alla Fiat 1948-1978.* Bari: De Donato.

Golden, M. A. 1988. "Historical Memory and Ideological Orientations in the Italian Workers' Movement." *Politics and Society* 16, no. 1.

Granovetter, M. 1985. "Social Structures and Economic Action: The Problem of Embeddedness." *American Journal of Sociology* 91, no. 3: 481–510.

Hall, P. 1986. *Governing the Economy.* Oxford: Oxford University Press.

Katzenstein, P. 1985. *Small States in World Markets.* Ithaca, N.Y.: Cornell University Press.

Locke, R. M. 1989. Local Politics and Industrial Change: The Political Economy of Italy in the 1980s. Unpublished Ph.D. dissertation. Department of Political Science, MIT.

Michelsons, A. 1986. Turin Between Fordism and Flexible Specialization. Unpublished Ph.D. dissertation. Cambridge University.

Modigliano, F., ed. 1986. *Le Leggi della politica industriale in Italia.* Bologna: Il Mulino.

Neiretti, M., L. Moranino, G. Perona, C. Dellavalle, A. Massazza Gal, and S. Cal di Biella. 1987. *L'Altra Storia: Si-dacato e lotte nel biellese 1901–1986.* Rave: Ediesse.

Pasquino, G. 1983. "Partiti, societa civile, istituzioni e il caso Italiano." *Stato e mercato,* no. 8.

Pecchio, A., A. Perrucci, and M. Rollier. 1981. "Innovazione e progresso tecnico nell'industria Italiana." In *L'Industria Italiana: Trasformazioni strutturali e possibilita di governo politico,* edited by L. Pennacchi. Milan: Franco Angeli.

Piore, M. J. 1987. "Corporate Reform in American Manufacturing and the Challenge to Economic Theory." Department of Economics, MIT, unpublished paper.

Piore, M. J., and C. F. Sabel. 1984. *The Second Industrial Divide.* New York: Basic Books.

Pizzorno, A., E. Reyneri, M. Regini, and I. Regalia. 1978. *Lotte operaie e sindacato: Il ciclo 1968–1972 in Italia.* Bologna: Il Mulino.

Porter, M. 1986. "Changing Patterns of International Competition." *California Management Review* 27, no. 2.

Posner, A. R. 1978. "Italy: Dependence and Political Fragmentation." In *Between Power and Plenty,* edited by P. J. Katzenstein. Madison, Wisc.: University of Wisconsin Press.

Prodi, R. 1974. "Italy." In *Big Business and the State*, edited by Raymond Vernon. Cambridge, Mass.: Harvard University Press.

Ramella, F. 1983. *Terra e telai*. Turin: Einaudi.

Regini, M., and C. Sabel, eds. 1989. *Strattegie di riaggiustamento industriale*. Bologna: Il Mulino.

Reich, R. 1988. "Bailout: A Comparative Study in Law and Industrial Structure." In *International Competitiveness*, edited by A. M. Spence and H. A. Hazard. Cambridge, Mass.: Ballinger.

Reiser, V. 1981. "Come si riproduce un avanguardia." In *Il Mestiere dell'avanguardia*, edited by A. Accornero. Bari: De Donato.

Reiser, V. 1986. "Immagini del progresso technologico e del lavoro." *Ex Macchina*, no. 2.

Rey, G. 1982. "Italy." In *The European Economy: Growth and Crisis*, edited by A. Boltho. New York: Oxford University Press.

Sabel, C. F. 1989. "The Re-emergence of Regional Economies." In *Reversing Industrial Decline*, edited by J. Zeitlin and P. Q. Hirst. London: Berg.

Salvati, M. 1980. "Muddling Through: Economics and Politics in Italy 1969–1979." In *Italy in Transition: Conflict and Consensus*, edited by P. Lange and S. Tarrow. London: Frank Cass.

Salvati, M. 1985. "The Italian Situation." In *The Politics of Inflation and Economic Stagnation*, edited by L. N. Lindberg and C. S. Maier. Washington, D.C.: The Brookings Institution.

Schein, E. H. 1983. "The Role of the Founder in Creating Organizational Culture." *Organizational Dynamics*, pp. 13–28.

Secchia, P. 1960. *Capitalismo e classe operaia nel centro laniero d'Italia*. Rome: Editori Riuniti.

Toyne, B., J. S. Arpani, A. H. Barnett, D. A. Ricks, and T. A. Shimp. 1984. *The Global Textile Industry*. London: George Allen & Unwin.

Trigilia, C. 1987. "La regolazione localistica: Economia e politica nelle aree de piccola impresa." In *La Societa Italiana degli anni ottanta*, edited by U. Ascoli and R. Catanzaro. Bari: Laterza.

Unione Industriale Biellese. 1981. *La Pendolarita' dei lavoratori dipendenti dell'industria Biellese*. Biella: UIB.

Unione Industriale Biellese. 1987. *La Realta' socio-economia Biellese*. Biella: UIB.

Zysman, J. 1983. *Governments, Markets, and Growth*. Ithaca, N.Y.: Cornell University Press.

COMMENTARY BY VEIKKO O. VUORIKARI

Professor Locke's study is interesting from many points of view. First, the history between employers and unions which is touched on dates far back. It represents a time when unions had the government on their side in negotiating the terms and benefits for people. Social benefits like an eight-hour workday and other benefits all came when the unions worked together with governments. This refers to the old Fiat-type conglomerates which are now falling apart in Europe. I think that employment in large companies is decreasing—I saw the figure of 25 percent during the last decade—but I think that in other countries it has decreased even more than in the United States.

The second stage of the development was when the government realized that the country had sufficient money and advanced technology, but no real support for entrepreneurs. It realized it needed to create an entrepreneurial environment, through enforcing requirements for the unions and the employees while also maintaining support of entrepreneurs. That has been the trend in Europe for the last fifteen years. The governments, of late, have been passing legislation and setting up systems to make the entrepreneurs a very highly respected segment of the population, so that the countries' companies can really gear up and compete with other countries. Government has shifted its position from supporting only employees to supporting entrepreneurs as well.

I think Italy is one of the countries that is not controlled by unions and government but in which the government will give support to entrepreneurs in various ways. In my country, Finland, there are liaison officers paid by the government who help entrepreneurs get through the bureaucracy. Today in Europe, the small companies are the key employers of the population, and the word "employer" needs to be changed to the word "entrepreneur."

The other thing is that in the textile business that Locke talked about, he neglected to mention the "gray market" in Italy. The gray market was and is so strong that the government cannot get its value-added and other taxes from that market. The government ordered that if a company had fewer than twenty employees, then they need not pay any value-added tax or other salary-based taxes. I went to visit an Italian manufacturing company that produced shoes, and there were sixteen different companies under one roof. All together, there were about 300 employees. Outside, it looked like one company, but inside it was many, and the division into sixteen companies avoided the VAT and other salary-based-tax cost factors.

All the governments are very concerned about bringing in new technology, management techniques, mechanisms for supporting exports to other countries, and methods of training entrepreneurs. This has resulted in new types of organizations, which are now very local and common in Europe, such as nonprofit organizations, associations, and cooperatives. Other means of supporting small companies are also used, as in the Italian case, to promote local employment.

The role of unions has changed. Government no longer stays on the side of unions but supports economic development through new growth of local entrepreneurship. Unions negotiate with employers over general salary adjustments and nonunionized employers follow these guidelines. The main role for supporting employment, however, is devolved to local municipalities, and they cooperate with entrepreneurs, unions, and larger companies to achieve this goal.

4

Corporate Restructuring and Organizational Behavior

MICHAEL USEEM

Many of the nation's corporations underwent major restructurings during the 1980s. In response to threats of international competition, unfriendly tender offers, declining profit margins, and other pressures, divisions were sold to other companies, plants were closed, and thousands of employees were redeployed. Boards of directors urged top management to enhance earnings, and ownership interests reasserted control through hostile takeovers and leveraged buyouts. American business has always undergone periods of reorganization and adaptation to the environment, but the scope and direction of corporate change during the mid- to late 1980s would appear to have been significantly different from that of earlier decades.

Drawing on a range of research studies and limited preliminary interviewing of my own for a forthcoming study, this chapter examines several interrelated issues in organizational restructuring, ownership control, and company redesign during the 1980s.[1] The chapter argues, first, that restructuring should be viewed as part of a broader transformation in the organization of ownership and managerial control of the corporation. Second, the chapter shows that the scope of restructuring expanded during the mid- to late 1980s and that it affected a large proportion of the nation's major companies. Third, the chapter contends that although much of the restructuring had been undertaken in the name of increasing corporate financial performance, substantial organizational change may be introduced as a by-product of the restructuring. Finally, the chapter argues that top company management has considerable discretionary authority in determining company behavior in nonfinancial areas, and therefore its role is particularly critical in shaping the organizational outcome of the restructuring.

The focus here is on major American firms. This is partly an artifact of methodology, since available studies have generally concentrated on large companies. But it is also premised on an assumption that the wave of restructuring affected large, publicly traded corporations more intensively and in different ways than smaller companies.

RESTRUCTURING AND CONTROL
OF THE LARGE CORPORATION

Much of the recent corporate restructuring can be traced to open contests for control of large business firms. The intensified struggle derives from a weakening of the longstanding dominance of professional managers over the fate of many major corporations.

Professional managers had gradually accumulated control of many large firms as public shareholding expanded and owners became too numerous and dispersed to retain effective control. Although in principle the board of directors was the shareholders' representative, in practice the nomination process came to be controlled by management, ensuring that directors sympathetic to management dominated the board. This "managerial revolution," first identified by Adolph Berle and Gardiner Means in their classic 1932 study, had inverted the organizational chart, with boards and shareholder welfare now subordinated to managerial interests. Powerless to affect policy change or replace management, owners disenchanted with a firm's performance knew that the only realistic course was disinvestment (Berle and Means, 1967).

The managerial revolution, however, did not reach the executive suites of all major corporations. Some remained firmly under the control of family dynasties, others fell under the influence of financial institutions. Still, professional management had acquired de facto control of a majority of the nation's major companies by the 1970s. Of the 200 largest manufacturing firms in 1974, one study estimated that over three-quarters had come under management influence, up from just over one-quarter in 1929 (Herman, 1981). Other studies reported somewhat different proportions, but they generally concurred that inside management controlled the fate of a far larger fraction of major firms than a half-century earlier (Kotz, 1978; Larner, 1970; Mintz and Schwartz, 1985).

Professional managers typically held little direct ownership stake in the firm. Yet many had wrested control on the premise that they would be more effective at serving ownership interests than the owners themselves. The premise had been persuasive. The enormous scale of the new organizational forms and the task of operating them in highly complex environments placed a premium on sophisticated leadership. Decision making came to be viewed as a learned rather than intuitive skill, and a university education and professional management training became the norm for those who would oversee the nation's largest companies (Chandler, 1977; Gordon and Howell, 1959; Pierson, 1959).

The solution of one set of organizational problems, however, ushered in a new set of dilemmas. While professional nonowning managers might come to be the technocratic masters of problem solving, it proved inherently difficult for the owners to ensure that the managers did so in a way that best served shareholder interests. Once professional managements were installed as the owners' agents, the door was opened for personal career and other distinct managerial concerns to intrude into decision making. So too was the decision-making door opened to the concerns of local communities, company employees, nonprofit organizations, and other corporate stakeholders as professional managers were prodded to make their companies more socially responsible. Despite the institution of a host of organizational mechanisms to better align managerial and ownership interests, such as the widespread use of performance-based executive compensation schemes, the door could never be fully closed (Jensen and Ruback, 1983).

This "agency" problem and other possible shortcomings of professional management received little attention during the 1970s. Government regulation was widely viewed, at least by business, as the most important cause of any shortcomings in financial performance (Himmelstein, 1990; Silk and Vogel, 1976; Vogel, 1989). With the rollbacks in federal regulation during the 1980s, however, the cause of poor performance could no longer be credibly laid at the doorstep of the federal government. Instead, the source of the problem was increasingly identified as entrenched managers who had become, by virtue of their de facto control of the firm, unresponsive to shareholder concerns (Jensen, 1989).

While professional managers and their policies came to be viewed by many as the problem, the solutions proposed for increasing "shareholder value" depended on the location of the proponent. Incumbent managements naturally preferred to remain so and to increase company earnings through downsizing of the work force and other means of cost reduction. Corporate "raiders" placed little stock in the ability of incumbent management to reform itself. Institutional shareholders increasingly insisted on exercising a voice in management decisions rather than exiting from them. And still other outsiders moved to install management teams possessing ownership stakes, often through the device of a leveraged buyout, thereby recombining ownership and control of the corporation in the same individuals (Auerbach, 1988; Coffee, Lowenstein, and Rose-Ackerman, 1988).

Incumbent managements, outside raiders, and buyout groups thus vied for the opportunity to restructure the corporation. As the market for corporate control intensified, downsizings, acquisitions, and leveraged buyouts were among the varied strategies for restructuring that emerged during the 1980s. The scale and impact of these initiatives, described in the following sections, suggest that the wave of restructuring during the mid- to late 1980s may come to represent one of those periodic eras in which the organization of American business is significantly altered.

THE BREADTH AND INTENSIFICATION OF RESTRUCTURING

Corporate restructuring is generally considered to include qualitative change in a company's ownership or control, internal organization, employment structure, or market focus. Although we lack comprehensive ways of gauging the scope of restructuring, measures of specific features provide a means for estimating the scope. The focus here is on two elements for which systematic information is available. One element provides a measure of the breadth of restructuring, that is, the proportion of major American firms that had undergone some form of restructuring. For this element we examine the fraction of companies that had undertaken significant reductions of their work forces. The second element furnishes a window on the trend in restructuring during the mid- to late 1980s. For this we utilize changes in company ownership. It is recognized that these measures capture only two of the dimensions of restructuring, and other indicators could reveal other patterns and trends.

The Breadth of Restructuring: Employment Downsizing

One central element of corporate restructuring was substantial reorganization of the work force. Many major companies sharply reduced their employment rolls during the mid- to late 1980s, and such reductions were often accompanied by a range of other changes in employment practices, from the introduction of early retirement schemes to the internal redeployment of thousands of employees (Tomasko, 1990; Useem, 1990). Employment downsizing was a central element of the restructuring trend, and since systematic information is most available upon it, it is used here to provide a gauge of breadth.

The variety of employment restructuring can be briefly illustrated with reference to several major companies whose policies on the employment of managerial and professional personnel were directly observed. One company is a technologically oriented manufacturing and service corporation; the second is an industrial company specializing in office equipment; and the third is a manufacturing firm focusing on information systems. Though facing different competitive pressures, all three initiated extensive reorganizations of their managerial and professional personnel in response to the pressures. The first firm reduced its work force by more than 20 percent during a four-year period in the mid-1980s. Five major manufacturing facilities were closed and a major division was phased out. A number of managerial and professional employees were either encouraged to retire or were dismissed, but some 3,000 others were invited into a retraining program that led to redeployment onto the company's sales staff. The second company reduced facilities and personnel rolls as well. One manufacturing site, for instance, was cut from 11,000 to 6,000 employees, and the company scrapped a longstanding policy that no manager or professional with eight years or more of experience could be terminated without the chairman's approval. It also initiated retraining and lateral movement of its personnel, initially for reassignment into proximate functions but increasingly to more remote areas. The third company managed to avoid layoffs entirely despite a flattening of its revenue growth during the mid-1980s. It instead emphasized the movement of managers and professionals out of headquarters functions back to branch offices. This "rebalancing" of the work force saw some 8,000 employees with main office experience moved into direct contact with the company's customer base.

Surveys of the nation's major firms confirm that a large fraction had undergone significant work force downsizings during the mid- to late 1980s. The research also indicates that the downsizing was uneven, with companies more affected in manufacturing than in the service sector, and larger corporations more vulnerable than midsize firms. Still, substantial proportions of companies in all major sectors and of diverse sizes contracted their employment rolls.

A study of 1,100 companies in mid-1987, for instance, found that 57 percent of the manufacturing firms and 43 percent of the service companies had reduced their employment rolls during an eighteen-month period ending in June 1987. Larger companies (with annual sales of more than $500 million) were more likely than midsize firms (with annual sales from $50 million to $500 million) to have initiated layoffs, though a lower proportion of the work force was affected among the larger companies. More than half of the large corporations, 58 percent, had downsized during the past eighteen months, while 49 percent of the midsize companies had done so. Among both large and midsize firms, the jobs of about one in ten company employees were affected by facility- or company-wide downsizing. Strategies for restructuring varied by company size: significantly greater proportions of the large corporations reported that they would likely use job redeployment, retraining, early retirement, and selective outplacement schemes than would the midsize companies (American Management Association, 1988).

Comparable rates of reductions in company size were reported in a Conference Board survey of 512 large corporations conducted in 1985. This study found that 59 percent had closed a facility or significantly reduced the work force during a three-year period ending in December 1984. Within manufacturing, more than three-quarters (77 percent) had either closed a facility or undergone a substantial reduction in employment rolls. Within financial services, however, less than half (44 percent) had shut a facility or significantly cut employment (Berenbeim, 1986).

These studies also confirm that competitive pressure was a primary force behind the work force resizings. Among the 210 companies in the Conference Board survey which had closed a facility, the leading factor, identified by nearly half of the firms, was change in company markets, including increased domestic or foreign competition and production or process obsolescence (Berenbeim, 1986; also see General Accounting Office, 1987). Among the nation's major firms, then, approximately one in two substantially reduced their work forces during the 1980s partly in response to competitive pressures. The aggregate results were substantial: between 1980 and 1989, total employment among the nation's largest 500 manufacturing firms dropped 3.7 million, a 21 percent decline over the decade (Figure 4.1; Autry and Colodny, 1990).

Some observers suggested that white-collar ranks were particularly subject to reduction. A widely cited estimate, for instance, indicated that as many as half a million middle management and professional positions were eliminated by some 300 companies between 1984 and 1986 (Willis, 1987). One study that explicitly compared rates of job loss among various occupational groups, however, found that managers and professionals were less vulnerable than blue-collar groups (General Accounting Office, 1987).

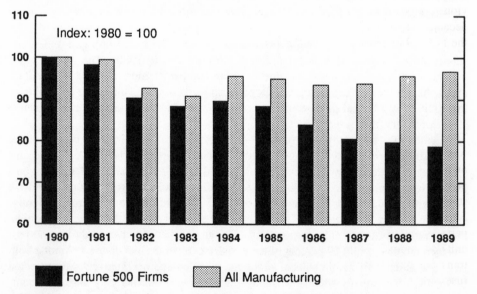

Figure 4.1 Total employment, manufacturing firms, 1980–1989. (From Autry and Colodny, 1990.)

Trends in Restructuring: Changes
in Corporate Ownership

To gauge whether corporate restructuring was intensifying during the mid- to late 1980s, we consider turnover in corporate ownership, a major component of the restructuring process. A data series on mergers and acquisitions compiled from an array of government and business sources provides a useful trend indicator (Grimm, 1990).

Although the number of turnovers in company ownership did not increase during the 1980s, the aggregate value of the turnovers did expand by a factor of more than five, from $44.3 billion in 1980 to $246.9 billion in 1988. Moreover, the proportion of the turnovers involving publicly listed companies substantially increased. Less than one in ten of the transactions in 1980 entailed a publicly traded firm, but by 1988 more than two in ten of the transactions involved such firms: 173 publicly traded companies were merged or acquired in 1980, whereas 462 publicly traded firms came under new ownership in 1988 (Grimm, 1990).

It is evident, then, that restructuring, at least as manifest in work force reductions, was relatively widespread among the nation's major companies during the mid- to late 1980s. And the trend line in the other barometer of restructuring, changes in company ownership, indicated that restructuring expanded through much of the mid- and late 1980s, particularly among larger, publicly traded corporations. The trends, however, were not steadily upward. A strong contraction occurred in 1987, in part because of the sharp drop of the stock market in October of that year. Another contraction began in 1989 and continued into 1990, partially driven by the softening bond market following the bankruptcy of firms that had been at the forefront of acquisitions during the 1980s (e.g., Drexel Burnham Lambert and the Campeau Corporation). The total value of ownership turnover among publicly traded firms in 1989 was down by 22 percent from the year before (dropping to $121.9 billion from $156.1 billion; Grimm, 1990). Previous periods of intensified rates of mergers and acquisitions rarely ran more than a decade (Golbe and White, 1988), and the relatively high rates of restructuring during the later 1980s could be considerably lowered during the early 1990s.

OWNERSHIP AND MANAGEMENT CONTROL
OF THE CORPORATION

The intensifying turnover in ownership among publicly traded firms during the 1980s was accompanied by rising influence of owners over management. The reemergence of ownership control is evident in the transformation of publicly traded corporations into privately held firms. In "going private," a company's shares are purchased from the stockholders, typically with funds borrowed against the assets of the company under acquisition. The buyer may be inside management, an outside organization, or a partnership among several groups. Leveraged purchases sometimes take divisions or units of companies private rather than the entire company. Whether the ownership transformation involves a division or the entire corporation, however, the outcome is to fuse ownership and control. Public shareholding and nonowning professional managers disappear, and corporate resources are placed under the direct decision-making control of owner-managers.

The conversion of publicly owned corporate resources into privately held companies intensified during the 1980s. The total dollar value of buyout transactions involving either company divisions or entire companies rose rapidly during the first half of the decade, with a better than 60 percent annual growth rate in the total dollar volume between 1979 and 1985. Moreover, the merger-and-acquisition field moved increasingly toward the conversion of public to private companies. The proportion of the dollar value of ownership turnovers involving leveraged buyouts between 1981 and 1988 rose almost tenfold, from 4 to 39 percent. While most leveraged buyouts were still of relatively modestly sized firms, the upper end of the transactional distribution reached well into the ranks of the nation's major corporations. The largest buyouts in 1986, 1987, and 1988 were, respectively, of firms valued at $5.4 billion (Beatrice Companies), $3.8 billion (Borg Warner), and $24.9 billion (RJR Nabisco). Again, however, 1989 witnessed a sharp decline in buyout transactions. The total value of such transactions declined to $18.5 billion, only 31 percent of the value of the year before and the lowest total since 1984 (dropping the takeover buyout fraction of publicly traded mergers and acquisition to 15 percent of the total; Grimm, 1990).

The fraction of publicly traded companies going private in any given year remained small, but the aggregating effects became considerable. The total divisional and company resources taken private from 1980 to 1988 stood at nearly $190 billion. The accumulating number of firms that had disappeared from the roster of publicly traded companies also reached a substantial level. One study found that of some 2,500 manufacturing firms that had been publicly listed during the decade ending in 1985, nearly 8 percent, or 199 firms, had been taken private (Hall, 1988).

While the transformation of publicly traded companies into privately held, owner-managed firms remained limited to a relatively small number of companies, the specter of a takeover encouraged many firms to take actions favorable to shareholder interests as a means of fending off hostile suitors. This frequently consisted of lowering administrative costs and raising stockholder dividends. Such actions were also encouraged by the rising power of institutional investors. Their collective stakes in many companies reached a majority during the 1980s. Of the 500 largest publicly traded firms in 1985, for instance, 50 percent of the median firm's common stock was held by insurance companies, investment firms, commercial banks, pension funds, and other institutional holders (Scherer, 1988). For all publicly traded companies, institutions held 45 percent of the value of outstanding shares in 1989, a sharp rise from 29 percent in 1980 (see Figure 4.2). By the late 1980s, some of the largest holders began to seek direct influence on management policy, breaking with a longstanding tradition of selling rather than exercising voice (see, for instance, Bartlett, 1990; Graves and Waddock, 1990; Regan 1990).

The effect of these developments was to make firms more aware of and responsive to shareholder interests. In some cases the potential for hostile shareholder action was sufficient to produce changes in corporate behavior; in others actual changes in ownership control occurred. A complete analysis of the effects of these developments would entail study of those firms taken private or subjected to hostile takeover and those that changed their behavior (but not their ownership or corporate form) in response to the threat of a takeover. Few direct studies are available of such changes in recent years, however, and for guidance we thus turn to analyses of behavioral differences among firms with varying degrees of ownership control.

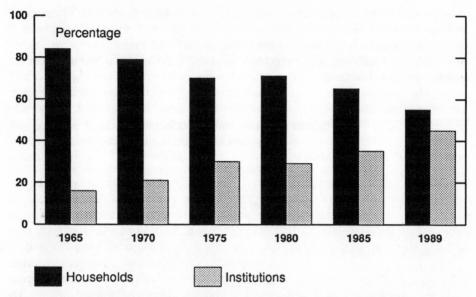

Figure 4.2 Holdings of equities, distribution of stock value, 1965–1989. (From Securities Industry Association, 1990.)

OWNERSHIP CONTROL AND CORPORATE NONFINANCIAL BEHAVIOR

The closing of the gap between managerial and ownership interests may substantially reshape corporate organization and behavior in an array of nonfinancial areas. Previous research would suggest that the restructuring has implications for organizational change in both the company's design of its internal organization and its management of the social and political environment.

It should be cautioned, however, that the results of prior research studies on company ownership may not necessarily apply to current developments. A common strategy in past research has been to compare the behavior or organization of firms with greater or lesser degrees of ownership as distinct from management control. The reemergence of ownership influence during the 1980s, however, may be introducing forms of ownership that are significantly dissimilar from past forms. In prior studies, companies defined as ownership-controlled were often those whose original founders or their descendants had remained in power. By contrast, among publicly traded companies that have been taken private, the new owners have often had little entrepreneurial role in creating the company, and they could thus bring a different outlook to their management of the firm. Many of the new owners, for example, may be less concerned than the old owner-founders with ensuring that control of the firm remains in family hands. Thus inferences from past research should be viewed as only suggestive and will require modification as the strategies of the new owners become more evident.

Internal Organization

Intensification of ownership interests may lead to greater concentration of decision making in the central office and a more unitary form of internal organization. Such changes would be anticipated from a comparative analysis of the internal organization of owner-controlled and management-controlled companies. Firms dominated by their owners are found to be more likely than those dominated by managers to concentrate their plants and facilities near headquarters, rather than dispersing them around the country (Palmer, Friedland, Jennings, and Powers, 1987). Moreover, compared with management-controlled companies, owner-dominated firms more often retain a unitary structure rather than moving to a multidivisional form. Both of these differences remain even after company size, market, and other factors are taken into account. Corroborating evidence comes from another study, which reported that firms whose stock was highly concentrated in the hands of a few major owners were significantly less likely to be engaged in unrelated product lines (Hill and Snell, 1989).

The evidence suggests that ownership restructuring could bring greater centralization of control (though not necessarily reversion to a unitary structure), concentration of resources near headquarters, and consolidation of organizational lines. Centralization of control, however, may focus largely on strategic decisions, and operating decisions may be delegated further down the organizational chart. As new owners seek to consolidate control over their firm, they are likely to require more direct involvement in fundamental decisions on product areas, competitive strategies, and long-term objectives. Yet because of their lean staffs and interest in making operating units as profit centered as possible, the new owners are also likely to devolve operating authority down the line organization. One review of the organizational consequences of large leveraged buyouts from 1979 to 1985 finds such a pattern: under new ownership, company strategy appeared to be more centrally controlled while operating decisions were more decentralized (Easterwood, Seth, and Singer, 1989).

At the same time, available evidence casts some doubt on a related thesis that recent corporate restructuring has pressed companies to sacrifice long-range planning in favor of short-term actions, presumably because the now more powerful owners are more interested in quick returns. Critics of leveraged buyouts and hostile takeovers, for instance, have often charged that the resulting heavy indebtedness creates pressures on short-term earnings that are even stronger than those expressed by institutional investors and other shareholders. Advocates of taking companies private concede that the unrelenting demands of servicing a large debt builds greater pressure on management to achieve steady near-term earnings (compare, for instance, Dertouzos, Lester, and Solow, 1989, pp. 53–66; and Jensen, 1989).

Longer term capital investment, already a problem in some American industries, may thus be even further eroded. One implication of this line of argument is the anticipation of lessened company support for such activities as research and development (R&D) in periods following an acquisition or leveraged buyout. Available evidence, however, does not confirm this expectation. One study of the R&D activity of all publicly traded manufacturing firms between 1976 and 1986 finds that there is little difference in the growth rates of R&D intensity between firms that had undertaken acquisitions and those that had not. Companies involved in mergers displayed little difference in their premerger and postmerger R&D efforts compared with firms not so engaged (Hall, 1988; and Healy, Palepu, and Ruback, 1989, report similar results). Another investigation even revealed that companies with concentrated ownership interests, where ownership power was presumably more effectively expressed, tended to invest *more* in R&D than other comparable companies (Hill and Snell, 1989). These results should be interpreted cautiously, however, since they do not directly assess the effects of unrealized takeover threats on a firm's R&D investments. Still, the intensification of ownership influence or control should not necessarily be assumed to increase short-term performance pressures.

Managing the Political and Social Environment

The corporate restructuring of the mid- and late 1980s could also lead to a greater focus on financial performance and a consequent lessening of concern toward corporate stakeholders other than shareholders. If so, this would reverse a prolonged period of active growth in concern with the social and political environment on the part of company management (Useem, 1984; Vogel, 1989).

Traditionally, the only legitimate corporate stakeholders for publicly traded companies were the shareholders. State statutes required that company officers and directors serve as the responsible agents for the shareholders. During the 1970s and early 1980s, however, many major corporations moved well beyond such limitations, and laws on corporate governance came to reflect the broadened company outlook. A number of states altered their legislation on corporate chartering to incorporate other groups' concerns. Pennsylvania law, for instance, was amended in 1985 so that directors and officers "may, in considering the best interests of the corporation, consider the effects of any actions upon employees, suppliers and customers of the corporation, [and] communities in which offices or other establishments of the corporation exist" (Preston and Sapienza, 1989).

Whereas the 1970s and early 1980s were marked by expanded corporate efforts to manage the social and political environment, the intensification of ownership interests in the governance of many corporations during the mid- to late 1980s may be reversing those efforts. Takeovers and other forms of ownership change were often justified as disciplinary actions to focus management attention on shareholder welfare (see, for instance, Walsh and Ellwood, 1989). Company programs intended to respond to other external stakeholders should be among the first casualties of heightened ownership control.

Patterns of company contributions to nonprofit organizations and corporate giving to candidates for political office indicate that closely held firms tend to be less active. A detailed analysis of company contributions in one major metropolitan area, for instance, found that owner-controlled companies were significantly less generous in supporting nonprofit organizations than were management-controlled firms, even controlling for earnings and other factors (Atkinson and Galaskiewicz, 1988). Similarly, a comparison of the political activities of large privately and publicly held companies revealed that the former were significantly less likely to have formed a political action committee than the latter (Burris, 1987, 1990).

The diminishing of traditional forms of company social and political action may reflect in part a reprogramming of resources to manage what had come to be viewed as a larger threat to firms' autonomy and independence. If the challenges were once from union movements and government regulation, they were now increasingly from institutional investors. As a result, during the 1980s many companies elevated their offices responsible for investor relations. The tactics applied to managing investors were akin to those already perfected in managing other outside pressure groups.

The approach observed in one corporation is illustrative of many. A senior officer with a substantial professional staff maintained regular personal contact with all of the firm's major analysts and investors. The contact ranged from frequent informal telephone conversations to major events for the analysts and investors to meet with the firm's chief executive. A specially prepared newsletter for analysts and investors ensured a steady flow of information that the company deemed appropriate. Changes in the holdings of the major investors were tracked on a daily basis, and investors whose stakes in the company dropped or were substantially below those in other companies in the same industry were lobbied for more. The head of investor relations had also learned the value of the implicit quid pro quo. His staff systematically compared the analysts' forecasts for the company's quarterly and annual earnings with its actual performance. Within hours of the company's announcement of the quarterly and annual results, the first telephone calls were placed to the analysts who had been overly optimistic in their predictions. It was they, the investor manager reasoned, who most needed and therefore would most remember the company's immediate assistance for explaining their errant forecasts.

TOP MANAGEMENT DISCRETION AND ORGANIZATIONAL CHANGE

Corporate restructuring and the rising importance of ownership influence during the mid- to late 1980s could lead to a range of organizational responses. Although the outlines of the changes are often prescribed by market and structural constraints, considerable managerial discretion remains. Senior management's past experience and present perspectives can give a critical shaping to the organizational solutions (see Hambrick and Brandon, 1988; Romanelli and Tushman, 1988). Their choices acquire special significance during a period of restructuring. Exceptionally open opportunities are presented for resizing the work force, redefining relations between managers and owners, and otherwise redesigning the organization.

The importance of managerial leadership in shaping corporate change can be seen in several areas. In the field of organizational design, for example, top management characteristics affect such basic decisions as whether to convert the company from a unitary to a multidivisional structure. Companies led by chief executives with MBAs from top-ranked universities and whose careers had been based in finance or sales (rather than manufacturing) are significantly more likely to adopt a multidivisional structure (Fligstein, 1985; Palmer, Jennings, and Zhou, 1989). In the field of political action, senior management's outside networks shape company decisions on the kinds of public policies, political candidates, and organizations to support. Firms led by senior managers who also serve on the boards of other corporations more often seek collaborative (rather than confrontational) relations with public agencies and more frequently support centrist candidates and organizations (Clawson and Neustadtl, 1989; Galaskiewicz, 1985; Miles, 1987). In the field of human resources, the background experiences of top management often have a fundamental bearing on whether firms adopt innovative programs for involving and supporting employees (Kanter, 1984; Kochan, Katz, and McKersie, 1986).

The discretionary impact of managerial action depends not only on what senior managers bring to the office but also on how they work together. When top management is molded into an integrated team based on shared organizational experience, its capacity to shape the firm's fate is particularly strong (Ancona, 1989; Michel and Hambrick, 1988; Tushman, Virany, and Romanelli, 1987).

The organizational experience of the 1980s is likely to have had an enduring impact on new senior management teams that emerged during the era. Their formative experiences occurred amid heightened career turbulence and organizational flux (Useem, 1990). And while the influence of ownership interests was ascendant, organizational constituencies other than shareholders mobilized to have their voices heard by management as well. Employees sought greater participation in the firm's decision making; environmental groups pressed for stronger protection against disasters; and communities looked for protection against plant closures and takeovers of locally owned firms. Claimants frequently asserted that greater recognition of their stakes in the firm would contribute to, rather than detract from, shareholder value (Freeman and Reed, 1983). With some confirming evidence to bolster the claims (see, for instance, Conte and Svejnar, 1990; Levine and Tyson, 1990), senior management teams have considerable latitude in redesigning their organization to meet the varied constituency concerns while remaining responsive to shareholder interests.

CONCLUSION

After half a century of growing dominance of the large corporation by nonowning managers, the 1980s were marked by a slowing or even reversing of their quiet revolution. Professional managers had come to control the corporation on the premise that they could more efficiently produce shareholder value than the original founder-owners. They turned shareholding into a passive investment on the same premise. As companies faced increasingly competitive pressures during the 1980s, however, the legitimacy of the rule of incumbent management came under challenge. No longer could government interference be blamed for many of the problems facing business; fingers pointed at management itself. As the criticism of corporate leadership gathered momentum, a leading diagnosis focused on one of managerial capitalism's crowning achievements: the autonomous power of professional management.

The critique viewed the managerial autonomy as excessively permissive, the agency system as no longer effective. Professional managers had come to show too much concern for the social welfare of various stakeholder groups and too little concern for the financial welfare of the only stakeholder group that should really count—the shareholders. Many restructuring efforts were thus undertaken in the name of returning companies to the single-minded pursuit of ownership interests. What had stood in the way of such a pursuit was less a matter of government constraint and more a matter of inadequate stockholder vigilance by their appointed agents.

Mindful of the critique, incumbent managements moved during the mid- to late 1980s to improve stockholder returns by paring the work force and cutting other costs. Corporate acquisitions and leveraged buyouts brought new management teams to the fore where others had seemingly fallen short. The resulting restructuring reached a large proportion of the nation's major companies, and the opening of the market for corporate control brought a significant fraction of companies more directly under the immediate oversight of ownership interests.

The reassertion of ownership control over large corporations was usually taken in the name of improving corporate earnings. Would-be takeover groups generally promised more internal discipline and stronger financial performance. Whatever the actual financial impact of the intensification of ownership interests (a sampling of the varied research conclusions can be found in Jensen and Ruback, 1983; Magenheim and Mueller, 1988; Smith, 1989; Weidenbaum and Vogt, 1987; and Healy, Chapter 5, this volume), available research suggests that it has had organizational impact. General company strategies may come to be more centrally guided while specific operating actions devolve further down the organization.

Ownership change and other restructuring steps have also had ramifications on corporate social and political action. That outreach is likely to be less vigorous and more divided. It is also being redirected. During the 1970s and early 1980s, corporate energies focused on reducing government regulation and improving community opinion. Those energies are now increasingly focused on managing their institutional investors and facilitating or resisting restructuring. Companies fought legislation that would limit the process of plant closings and sought legislation to protect themselves against hostile takeovers.

Yet corporate change must not be viewed as isolated managerial responses to changing market conditions. Companies and managements frequently look to one another for guidance in coping with ambiguous circumstances (DiMaggio and Powell, 1983; Granovetter, 1985). Understanding company responses to restructuring pressures therefore requires a focus on intercompany flows of ideas and doctrines as well as purely internally generated responses specific to the company. Reactions to the restructuring pressures that are collectively developed and defined in the broader business community may prove to be as critical as individually fashioned solutions in guiding management approaches to restructuring during the years to come.

NOTE

1. As part of a larger study of restructuring supported by the National Planning Association, extended interviews were conducted with managers in six major companies from mid-1988 through mid-1990. Included in the interviews were a range of senior managers with primary responsibility for strategic planning, finance, human resources, investor relations, and industrial relations, and managers with general company responsibilities, including group vice presidents and presidents of operating units. Five of the companies were manufacturers and one was a commercial bank. The annual turnover of the smallest of the firms exceeded $3 billion. Interviews were also conducted with a range of senior managers involved in acquisitions and buyouts of other companies.

REFERENCES

American Management Association. 1988. *Responsible Reductions in Force*. New York: American Management Association.

Ancona, D. G. 1989. "Top Management Teams: Preparing for the Revolution." In *Social Psychology in Business Organizations*, edited by J. Carroll. Hillsdale, N.J.: Lawrence Erlbaum Associates.

Atkinson, L., and J. Galaskiewicz. 1988. "Stock Ownership and Company Contributions to Charity." *Administrative Science Quarterly* 33: 82–100.

Auerbach, A. J., ed. 1988. *Mergers and Acquisitions*. Chicago: University of Chicago Press.

Autry, R., and M. M. Colodny. 1990. "The Fortune 500: Hanging Tough in a Rough Year." *Fortune* 121 (April 23): 338–345.

Bartlett, S. 1990. "Big Funds Pressing for Voice in Management of Companies." *New York Times*, February 23, p. 1.

Berenbeim, R. E. 1986. *Company Programs to Ease the Impact of Shutdowns*. New York: Conference Board.

Berle, A., Jr., and G. C. Means. 1967. *The Modern Corporation and Private Property*. New York: Harcourt, Brace and World.

Burris, V. 1987. "The Political Partisanship of American Business: A Study of Corporate Political Action Committees." *American Sociological Review* 52: 732–744.

Burris, V. 1990. Special reanalysis of data prepared for this chapter.

Chandler, A. D., Jr. 1977. *The Visible Hand: The Managerial Revolution in American Business*. Cambridge, Mass.: Harvard University Press.

Clawson, D., and A. Neustadtl. 1989. "Interlocks, PACs, and Corporate Conservatism." *American Journal of Sociology* 94: 749–773.

Coffee, J. C., L. Lowenstein, and S. Rose-Ackerman, eds. 1988. *Knights, Raiders, and Targets: The Impact of the Hostile Takeover*. New York: Oxford University Press.

Conte, M. A., and J. Svejnar. 1990. "The Performance Effects of Employee Ownership Plans." In *Paying for Productivity: A Look at the Evidence*, edited by A. S. Blinder. Washington, D.C.: The Brookings Institution.

Dertouzos, M. L., R. K. Lester, and R. M. Solow. 1989. *Made in America: Regaining the Productive Edge*. Cambridge: MIT Press.

DiMaggio, P., and W. W. Powell. 1983. "The Iron Cage Revisited: Institutional Isomorphism and Collective Rationality in Organizational Fields." *American Sociological Review* 48: 147–160.

Easterwood, J. C., A. Seth, and R. F. Singer. 1989. "The Impact of LBOs on Strategic Direction." *California Management Review* 32: 30–43.

Fligstein, N. 1985. "The Spread of the Multidivisional Form." *American Sociological Review* 50: 377–391.

Freeman, R. E., and D. L. Reed. 1983. "Stockholders and Stakeholders: A New Perspective on Corporate Governance." *California Management Review* 25 (Spring): 88–106.

Galaskiewicz, J. 1985. *Social Organization of an Urban Grants Economy: A Study of Business Philanthropy and Nonprofit Organizations*. New York: Academic Press.

General Accounting Office. 1987. *Plant Closings: Limited Advance Notice and Assistance Provided Dislocated Workers*. Washington, D.C.: General Accounting Office.

Golbe, D. L., and L. J. White. 1988. "A Time-Series Analysis of Mergers and Acquisitions in the U.S. Economy." In *Corporate Takeovers: Causes and Consequences*, edited by A. Auerbach. Chicago: University of Chicago Press.

Gordon, R. A., and J. E. Howell. 1959. *Higher Education for Business*. New York: Columbia University Press.

Granovetter, M. 1985. "Economic Action and Social Structure: The Problem of Embeddedness." *American Journal of Sociology* 91: 481–510.

Graves, S. B., and S. A. Waddock. 1990. "Institutional Ownership: Effect on Corporate Strategy." *The Executive* 4 (February): 75–83.

Grimm, W. T., & Co. 1990. *Mergerstat Review 1989*. Chicago: W. T. Grimm & Co.

Hall, B. H. 1988. "The Effect of Takeover Activity on Corporate Research and Development." In *Corporate Takeovers: Causes and Consequences,* edited by A. J. Auerbach. Chicago: University of Chicago Press.

Hambrick, D. C., and G. L. Brandon, 1988. "Executive Values." In *The Executive Effect: Concepts and Methods for Studying Top Managers,* edited by D. C. Hambrick. Greenwich, Conn.: JAI Press.

Healy, P. M., K. G. Palepu, and R. M. Ruback. 1989. "Do Mergers Improve Corporate Performance?" Cambridge, Mass.: Sloan School of Management, Massachusetts Institute of Technology, unpublished.

Herman, E. S. 1981. *Corporate Control, Corporate Power.* New York: Cambridge University Press.

Hill, C. W. L., and S. A. Snell. 1989. "Effects of Ownership Structure and Control on Corporate Productivity." *Academy of Management Journal* 32: 25–46.

Himmelstein, J. L. 1990. *To the Right: The Transformation of American Conservatism.* Berkeley: University of California Press.

Jensen, M. C. 1989. "Eclipse of the Public Corporation." *Harvard Business Review* 89(5): 61–74.

Jensen, M. C., and R. S. Ruback. 1983. "The Market for Corporate Control." *Journal of Financial Economics* 11: 5–50.

Kanter, R. M. 1984. *The Roots of Corporate Progressivism: How and Why Corporations Respond to Changing Society Needs and Expectations.* New York: Russell Sage Foundation.

Kochan, T. A., H. C. Katz, and R. B. McKersie. 1986. *The Transformation of American Industrial Relations.* New York: Basic Books.

Kotz, D. M. 1978. *Bank Control of Large Corporations in the United States.* Berkeley: University of California Press.

Larner, R. J. 1970. *Management Control and the Large Corporation.* New York: Dunellen Publishing Company.

Levine, D. L., and L. D'Andrea Tyson. 1990. "Participation, Productivity, and the Firm's Environment." In *Paying for Productivity: A Look at the Evidence,* edited by A. S. Blinder. Washington, D.C.: The Brookings Institution.

Magenheim, E. B., and D. C. Mueller. 1988. "Are Acquiring-Firm Shareholders Better Off After an Acquisition?" In *Knights, Raiders, and Targets: The Impact of the Hostile Takeover,* edited by J. C. Coffee, Jr., L. Lowenstein, and S. Rose-Ackerman. New York: Oxford University Press.

Michel, J. G., and D. C. Hambrick. 1988. "Diversification Posture and the Characteristics of the Top Management Team." New York: Graduate School of Business, Columbia University, unpublished.

Miles, R. H. 1987. *Managing the Corporate Social Environment.* Englewood Cliffs, N.J.: Prentice-Hall.

Mintz, B., and M. Schwartz. 1985. *The Power Structure of American Business.* Chicago: University of Chicago Press.

Palmer, D., R. Friedland, P. D. Jennings, and M. Powers. 1987. "The Economics and Politics of Structure: The Multidivisional Form and the Large U.S. Corporation." *Administrative Science Quarterly* 32: 25–48.

Palmer, D., D. Jennings, and X. Zhou. 1989. "From Corporate Strategies to Institutional Prescriptions: Adoption of Multidivisional Form, 1962–1968." Paper presented at Annual Meeting of American Sociological Association, San Francisco.

Pierson, F. C. 1959. *The Education of American Businessmen: A Study of University–College Programs in Business Administration.* New York: McGraw-Hill.

Preston, L. E., and H. J. Sapienza. 1989. "Stakeholder Management and Corporate

Performance." Paper presented at Conference on Socio-Economics, Harvard Business School, March 1989.

Regan, E. V. 1990. "Why We 'Interfered' at G.M." *New York Times,* February 11, Business Section, p. 13.

Romanelli, E., and M. Tushman. 1988. "Executive Leadership and Organizational Outcomes: An Evolutionary Perspective." In *The Executive Effect: Concepts and Methods for Studying Top Managers,* edited by Donald C. Hambrick. Greenwich, Conn.: JAI Press.

Scherer, F. M. 1988. "Corporate Ownership and Control." In *The U.S. Business Corporation: An Institution in Transition,* edited by J. R. Meyer and J. M. Gustafson. Cambridge, Mass.: Ballinger.

Securities Industry Association. 1990. Analysis of statistics provided by the Federal Reserve Bank. Washington, D.C.: Securities Industry Association.

Silk, L., and D. Vogel. 1976. *Ethics and Profits: The Crisis of Confidence in American Business.* New York: Simon and Schuster.

Smith, A. 1989. "Corporate Ownership and Performance: The Case of Management Buyouts." Chicago: Graduate School of Business, University of Chicago, unpublished.

Tomasko, R. M. 1990. *Downsizing: Reshaping the Corporation for the Future.* New York: American Management Association.

Tushman, M. L., B. Virany, and E. Romanelli. 1987. "Effects of CEO and Executive Team Succession: A Longitudinal Analysis." New York: Graduate School of Business, Columbia University, unpublished.

Useem, M. 1984. *The Inner Circle: Large Corporations and the Rise of Business Political Activity in the U.S. and U.K.* New York: Oxford University Press.

Useem, M. 1991. "The Restructuring of Managerial and Professional Work in Large Corporations." In *Turbulence in the American Workplace,* by P. B. Doeringer et al. New York: Oxford University Press.

Vogel, D. 1989. *Fluctuating Fortunes: The Political Power of Business in America.* New York: Basic Books.

Walsh, J. P., and J. W. Ellwood. 1989. "Mergers, Acquisitions, and the Pruning of Managerial Deadwood: An Examination of the Market for Corporate Control." Hanover, N.H.: Tuck School of Business Administration, Dartmouth College, unpublished.

Weidenbaum, M., and S. Vogt. 1987. "Takeovers and Stockholders: Winners and Losers." *California Management Review* 29 (Summer): 157–168.

Willis, R. 1987. "What's Happened to America's Middle Managers?" *Management Review* 76 (January): 24–33.

COMMENTARY BY LAURA DIVINE

In response to the chapter, I am going to speak more specifically about some of the experiences of Pacific Bell as part of the telephone company breakup. While we have not experienced any kind of buyout, Pacific Bell was, at the time of the divestiture, financially the lowest rated telephone company in the Bell System. We were considered the "dog" of the Bell companies. In that situation, we were very concerned about a leveraged buyout. We began to look in the mid-1980s at how to increase our performance to our stockholders and community. We went through quite a few actions to improve our performance and we've done very well. We have outperformed all the other Bell operating companies and AT&T from a stock performance perspective.

But what was the price we paid? We have gone through tremendous amounts of restructuring. We are continuing to learn how to be competitive, and we're changing from being more engineering and operations focused to more of a customer focus. We are doing constant restructuring to figure out how to position ourselves to be competitive. Internally it has been a tremendous amount of change, a constant redirection.

While we performed tremendously well, part of our improvement in performance, a large part of it, was through cost cutting by decreasing the work force. We reduced our work force from about 120,000 in 1984 to 63,000 today. About half of this reduction was through transfers to AT&T, and we're slated to reduce 11,000 more in the next five years. What we have learned from that, as we entered the late 1980s and 1990s, is that cutting down employment may have helped us through the first hump of divestiture but we can't continue to go that route. We can't continue to rely on cost cutting as a technique for high performance.

We have begun to learn that we need to be a lot smarter about how we do business. The one thing I would say as we go forward is that we cannot continue to respond only to shareholders. There is really the need to look at the customer, shareholders, employees, and the community, and how we can approach our business and consider all four. We are trying to figure out how to fulfill that objective and still meet the high pressures of the financial community.

5

The Effect of Changes in Corporate Control on Firm Performance

PAUL M. HEALY

There have been dramatic changes in corporate ownership during the past ten years with mergers, acquisitions, and leveraged buyouts reaching record levels. In 1988 merger and acquisition transactions alone totaled $246.9 billion, approximately 57 percent of total business investment expenditures.

The early evidence on the effect of changes in corporate control indicate that target stockholders in mergers and acquisitions earn 30 to 50 percent returns, and acquiring stockholders break even. For leveraged buyouts, the firm's stockholders receive a buyout premium of approximately 40 percent. These stockholder gains have been the subject of considerable controversy. Some argue that stockholder wealth increases because changes in ownership have positive economic effects by reallocating corporate resources to more productive uses (see Jensen, 1986). Others argue that the benefits to stockholders come at the expense of other stakeholders in the firm. For example, stockholder gains can arise from increased monopoly rents or reduced tax payments. Alternatively, the gains may come at the expense of employees, who are laid off or forced to accept wage concessions, lowering morale within the organization (see Shleifer and Summers, 1988).

This chapter summarizes the recent theories and evidence on the effect of changes in ownership arising from mergers and acquisitions and from leveraged buyouts. Several recent studies have attempted to resolve the ambiguities of stock price studies by examining firms' earnings or cash flow performance after changes in corporate control. These studies provide evidence on whether mergers and acquisitions and leveraged buyouts lead to improvements in firm performance. They are also able to provide some evidence on the sources of any improvements in performance. Answers to these questions provide a means of resolving the public policy debate on the desirability of mergers and acquisitions and of buyouts.

The major conclusions of the studies reviewed in this chapter are as follows:

1. Merged firms experience a significant increase in asset productivity relative to their industries in the five years after the merger, leading to higher postmerger cash flow returns on assets. These increases in performance do not appear to come at the expense of long-term growth, because merged firms do not reduce their capital expenditures and R&D rates after the merger.
2. Management buyout firms also experience an increase in operating performance

after the buyout. These effects persist for at least three years. However, there is some question as to whether they will continue in the long term, since the buyout firms examined also reduce capital expenditures, and the only evidence on performance beyond three years after the buyout indicates that performance declines.

The effects of changes in corporate control are discussed next, followed by a review of the evidence on corporate performance in years surrounding mergers and leveraged buyouts.

REASONS FOR CHANGES IN CORPORATE CONTROL

Changes in corporate control provide the new owner(s) with the opportunity to allocate a firm's resources more efficiently. The specific forms of reallocation may differ somewhat between (1) mergers and acquisitions and (2) leveraged buyouts. The specific benefits of each of these forms of change in control are discussed separately.

Mergers and Acquisitions

Mergers and acquisitions potentially provide a wide variety of benefits to acquirers, including economies of scope and scale, increased market share and rents, improved management incentives, opportunities to recontract with employees or other stakeholders, financial slack, and tax benefits. Equity gains from only some of these sources are unambiguously socially beneficial.

Economies of Scope and Scale

Economies of scope and scale can arise if the merger enables the combined firms to improve asset productivity by eliminating facilities that are underutilized if each firm operates independently. Economies of scale or scope typically arise for horizontal mergers, where overlapping production and marketing facilities can be eliminated. They may also be available in vertical integration mergers. For example, Du Pont argued that acquiring Conoco would ensure greater control over the availability of petroleum, its major raw material. Economies of scale have even been used to motivate mergers between firms in unrelated industries, where central office facilities for accounting, personnel, and top management can be eliminated.

Increased Market Share

While horizontal mergers offer the combining firms opportunities to take advantage of economies of scale, they may also lead to increased market share and hence increased monopoly rents. Firms engaged in horizontal mergers are required to obtain approval for the merger from the Federal Trade Commission (FTC) and/or Justice Department. However, these regulatory bodies in recent years have interpreted the antitrust regulations loosely and have permitted a greater number of horizontal mergers. Critics argue that these actions have led to an increase in mergers between firms whose primary motivation is to increase monopoly rents.

Improved Management Incentives

Mergers provide the acquirer with the opportunity to replace inefficient managers within the target or to motivate them to act in shareholders' interests (see Jensen and Ruback, 1983). One form of management inefficiency arises when managers have incentives to reinvest free cash flows in negative net present value projects rather than paying them out to investors as dividends (see Jensen, 1986). Acquirers can then create value by selling unprofitable divisions, changing investment policies, and bonding against future free cash flow problems by increasing financial leverage and/or increasing dividend payouts.

Recontracting Benefits

Mergers may provide the acquirer with an opportunity to renegotiate explicit and implicit contracts between the target firms' stockholders and other stakeholders. For example, the acquirer could abrogate contracts with employees by negotiating wage concessions, changing employment conditions, recapturing overfunded pension assets, and laying off employees (see Shleifer and Summers, 1988). These are likely to result in lower labor costs and a more efficient mix of capital and labor in the merged firms' production functions. However, they can have harmful side effects for the new firm by reducing employee morale.

Financial Slack

Mergers provide an opportunity to eliminate underinvestment problems arising from lack of financial slack. If managers are better informed than investors on a firm's prospects, internal financing of new projects is cheaper than external financing. Financial slack, or unused borrowing capacity, is then valuable, since it increases the likelihood that low-cost funding is available for new projects. This implies that there are gains from a merger of a high-growth–cash-poor firm and a low-growth–cash-rich firm, as explained by Myers and Majluf (1984) and Palepu (1986).

Tax Benefits

Finally, a variety of tax benefits are available from mergers. These include benefits from net operating loss carryforwards that could not be realized by the two firms operating separately, and prior to the 1986 Tax Reform Act, increased depreciation shields from writing up the basis of acquired assets (see Gilson, Scholes, and Wolfson, 1988; and Hayn, 1989). Mergers may also provide increased tax shields to the merged firm through additional borrowing capacity. If the cash flows of the merging firms are imperfectly correlated, a merger may reduce the operating risk of the combined firm relative to the weighted average risk of the target and acquirer. This should increase the optimal leverage for the merged firm, assuming a firm's debt ratio is determined by balancing its costs of financial distress and the value of interest tax shields (see Brealey and Myers, 1987). The papers reviewed in this chapter typically do not focus on the tax benefits of mergers. Instead, they examine whether there are nontax motivations for mergers.

Leveraged Buyouts

A leveraged buyout results in three fundamental changes for a firm. First, its capital structure is changed since new debt is issued and the proceeds are used to repurchase equity. The postbuyout firm therefore typically has significantly higher leverage than the prebuyout firm. Second, the postbuyout firm usually concentrates ownership in a small number of active shareholders. These may be senior management or other buyout participants. Finally, buyout firms are no longer listed on public equity exchanges. These changes create a number of potential benefits, including improvements in managerial incentives, opportunities to recontract with employees and other stakeholders, and tax benefits.

Improved Management Incentives

Leveraged buyouts are likely to have an effect on the incentives of top management. These increased incentives can arise for two reasons. First, members of top management frequently increase their stake in the firm, becoming significant equity owners in the buyout firm. Their incentives are then closely linked to the interests of other stockholders, since their wealth is directly related to the firm's performance. Second, other buyout participants, who typically own a significant stake in the new firm and are represented on the board of directors, are likely to monitor managers more effectively than are diversified owners in the prebuyout firm.

An increase in management ownership can also have perverse incentives. Since it is difficult for managers with large firm stockholdings to diversify away firm-specific risk, they may be inclined to select new projects that reduce the variance of the firm's cash flows, even if these projects have positive values. This explains why buyout firms typically have minimal investment requirements, reducing managers' ability to undertake value-reducing low-risk projects.

Recontracting Benefits

Buyouts can provide the new owners with an opportunity to renegotiate explicit and implicit contracts with employees and other stakeholders. These recontracting benefits are similar to those already discussed for merging firms.

Tax Benefits

The main tax benefits arising from leveraged buyouts are from higher interest shields on the increased debt and increased depreciation shields from step-ups in asset bases. Kaplan (1989a) estimates that for buyouts occurring between 1982 and 1985, leverage increased from 21 percent prior to the buyout to 86 percent afterwards. Because corporate interest payments are tax deductible, this increase provides the buyout firm with a substantial tax saving. Kaplan estimates that if the change in leverage is permanent, this saving can explain up to 94 percent of the premium paid by the buyout company to the existing stockholders. If the interest benefits are only available for eight years, because the new debt is repaid after eight years, the saving can explain 29 percent of the buyout premium.

While the increase in leverage is an important benefit from a leveraged buyout, it raises one puzzle. Why did the firm have to undertake a buyout to achieve this gain? A leveraged recapitalization, where the firm issues new debt and uses the proceeds to repurchase equity, would seem to be an equally plausible way to obtain the additional interest tax shields without foregoing access to public equity markets.

The second frequently cited tax benefit from leveraged buyouts is the step-up in basis of depreciable assets. As in a merger, prior to 1986 firms were permitted to write up the value of depreciable assets to their appraised market values. Kaplan estimated that the value of this benefit explains approximately 28 percent of the buyout premium for firms electing to step up asset bases.

As shown by Kaplan, the tax benefits available from leveraged buyouts can be sizable. However, the studies reviewed in this chapter examine nontax reasons for buyouts.

EVIDENCE ON EFFECTS OF CHANGES IN CORPORATE CONTROL

Several recent studies have examined accounting measures in years surrounding changes in corporate control to evaluate whether these events improve performance. While this seems like an easy task, there are some serious difficulties in constructing these measures. First, accounting information after a merger or buyout is typically not available. A merged firm reports data for the combined firms but not for the target and acquirer separately; a buyout firm is privately owned and typically does not issue public financial statements. Second, target or buyout book assets and depreciation frequently increase after a merger or buyout because of asset write-ups required under purchase accounting. Consequently, accounting earnings and accounting returns on assets before and after a merger or buyout are not comparable. Third, the capital structure of the new firm (the combined target and acquirer, or the buyout firm) is likely to change after the control change, depending on how the transaction is financed. Since accounting earnings measures do not reflect a cost of equity financing but do record interest expenses, comparisons of premerger and postmerger accounting performance are not comparable across mergers or buyouts. Finally, performance changes surrounding a merger or buyout can be affected by other events, including subsequent asset sales or acquisitions and changes in economy or industry performance.

In this section I discuss performance measures and research findings of recent studies that have examined postmerger and postbuyout performance.

Mergers and Acquisitions
Measuring Postmerger Performance

The performance measures used by three recent studies of postmerger performance are summarized in Table 5.1. Ravenscraft and Scherer (1987) examine the target line of business performance using operating earnings (earnings before interest, taxes, and extraordinary items, but after depreciation) as a percentage of book assets and sales, and cash flows as a percentage of sales in the years 1975 to 1977. To control for changes in economic conditions, these measures are compared to industry performance. There are a number of limitations to this research design. First, Ravenscraft and Scherer examine performance in three years, 1975 to 1977. However, the merger sample was selected from the period 1950 to 1977, implying that merger events could have occurred as many as twenty-seven years prior to measurement of postmerger performance. Because so many other events are likely to occur in this period, it is difficult to attribute any change in performance to the merger. Second, the main performance metric used in the study, operating return on assets, does not control for

Table 5.1 Summary of research design for studies examining postmerger performance

Study	Sample	Sample Merger Years	Performance Years Relative to Merger	Performance Measure	Performance Benchmark
Ravenscraft and Scherer (1987)	2,238 firm lines of business that engaged in acquisitions	1950–1977	1975–1977	*Premerger:* Earnings before interest, taxes, and extraordinary items as a percentage of end-of-year book assets for target and acquirer lines of business	Acquirer firm industry
				Postmerger: Earnings before interest, taxes, and extraordinary items as a percentage of end-of-year book assets and sales, and cash flow as a percentage of sales for target firms' lines of business	Target firm line of business comparison
Herman and Lowenstein (1988)	56 hostile acquisitions	1975–1983	−5 to +5	*Premerger:* Earnings after tax as a percentage of book equity, and earnings before tax as a percentage of book assets for the target and acquirer firms separately	No industry comparison
				Postmerger: Earnings after tax as a percentage of book equity, and earnings before tax as a percentage of book assets for the merged firm	
Healy, Palepu, and Ruback (1990)	50 largest mergers and acquisitions	1979–1983	−5 to +5	*Premerger:* Earnings before depreciation, net interest, and taxes as a percentage of market equity plus book debt for combined target and acquirer firms	Weighted target and acquirer *Value Line* industries
				Postmerger: Earnings before depreciation, net interest, and taxes as a percentage of market equity adjusted for merger announcement return plus book debt for the merged firm	

the effects of purchase accounting on earnings and assets. Third, it is not obvious why gains from mergers would be reflected only in the target firms' segments; synergies are just as likely to improve acquiring firms' performance. Finally, to measure target performance after the merger, Ravenscraft and Scherer use the Federal Trade Commission (FTC) line of business data, which has several potential problems. Definitions of business segments may change systematically after mergers if acquirers restructure their operations. Results of tests using segment data reported to the FTC are also likely to be difficult to interpret since reporting firms have incentives to use accounting discretion to reduce the likelihood of antitrust suits by the FTC (see Watts and Zimmerman, 1986).

Herman and Lowenstein (1988) estimate performance using return on book equity for the merged firm after the merger. This measure does not adjust for the effect of purchase accounting on postmerger earnings and equity. In addition, Herman and Lowenstein do not adjust their return on equity measure for differences in the method of financing the merger, and they fail to control for the effect of common industry shocks on postmerger earnings performance.

In a recent study, Krishna Palepu, Richard Ruback, and I [Healy, Palepu, and Ruback (1990)] attempt to address the limitations of the performance measures used in the foregoing studies. We examine postmerger performance for the fifty largest mergers between U.S. public industrial firms completed in the period 1979 to 1983. Performance is measured by the pretax operating cash flow return on the market value of assets for the combined target and acquirer in the premerger period and for the merged firm in the postmerger period. Pretax operating cash flows are defined as earnings before depreciation and goodwill amortization, before net financing charges, and before taxes. Our measure is also adjusted to control for the stock market's capitalization of any postmerger improvements in cash flows anticipated when the merger is announced. Finally, we control for industry- or economy-wide factors that could explain differences between premerger and postmerger performance by computing median cash flow returns for the target and acquiring firms' industries in years surrounding the merger. Weighted averages of these values are deducted from the combined target and acquirer returns before the merger and from the merged firm returns after the merger.

Postmerger Performance Results

Table 5.2 summarizes the main research findings on premerger and postmerger performance for the three studies. Ravenscraft and Scherer (1987) find no strong evidence of improvements in performance for the target lines of business after the merger. Herman and Lowenstein (1988) report that in the two years following the merger (years +1 and +2), merged firms have lower returns on equity and returns on assets than acquirers in the premerger period. In years +3 to +5 merged firms' returns revert to premerger acquirer levels. However, it is not clear whether this arises because mergers initially reduce the performance of the combined firms or because targets have lower returns than acquirers. Further, as noted, there are serious limitations to the performance metrics and research designs of these studies.

Our study shows quite different results (Healy, Palepu, and Ruback, 1990). We find that after the merger the cash flow rate of return on assets for merged firms is about three percentage points higher than the industry return. In contrast, prior to the merger

Table 5.2 Summary of research findings on premerger and postmerger performance

Study	Premerger Performance Results	Postmerger Performance Results
Ravenscraft and Scherer (1987)	Bidder and target lines of business earn similar operating returns on assets as their industries	Target lines of business do not earn higher operating returns on assets or operating margins than their industries
Herman and Lowenstein (1988)	Bidders and targets earn similar returns on equity and returns on assets	In years +1 and +2 return on equity and return on assets for the merged firm are lower than acquirer returns in the premerger period. In years +3 to +5 the merged firms returns revert to premerger acquirer levels
Healy, Palepu, and Ruback (1990)	Combined target and acquirer firms have same pretax operating cash flow returns on assets as their combined industries	Merged firms earn 3% higher pretax operating cash flow returns on assets than their combined industries

the combined target and acquirer show cash flow rates of return similar to the industry. The improvements in performance after the merger are statistically reliable.

One question raised by our findings is whether improvements in industry-adjusted postmerger cash flow returns are due to a relative decline in the market value of the sample firms' assets, rather than an increase in their cash flows. This could arise if postmerger cash flow improvements anticipated by the stock market at the merger announcement do not materialize. Stock prices for the merged firms would then decline relative to the industry, causing measured cash flow returns for the sample firms to be higher than industry values. We examine postmerger market equity returns for the sample firms and find that they are not significantly different from equity returns for their industries. This implies that the postmerger industry-adjusted cash flow returns are due to increases in sample firms' operating cash flows, rather than declines in their market values.

Finally, we find that there is a strong positive relation between our measure of performance, pretax cash flow rates of return on assets (adjusted for industry effects), and the abnormal stock return for the combined target and acquirer firms in the merger announcement period. Cash flow rates of return explain roughly 46 percent of merged firms' announcement returns.

Sources of Performance Improvements

As noted, the increase in operating cash flow returns after mergers can arise from a variety of sources. To provide further evidence on these sources the studies examined a number of characteristics of merged firms. The characteristics and research findings

Table 5.3 Summary of research findings on operating, financial, and investment characteristics for merger firms

Study	Firm Characteristics	Difference Between Postmerger and Premerger Measures
Herman and Lowenstein (1988)	*Financial characteristics of bidders before and after merger*	
	Debt to equity ratio	Increases after merger
	Fixed charge coverage	Decreases after merger
Healy, Palepu, and Ruback (1990)	*Operating characteristics for merged firm postmerger and combined firms premerger (both relative to combined industries)*	
	Operating cash flow margins	No change after merger
	Sales turnover	Increase after merger
	Employee growth	Decrease after merger
	Pension expense/employees	No change after merger
	Investment characteristics for merged firm postmerger and combined firms premerger (both relative to combined industries)	
	Capital expenditures/assets	No change after merger
	R&D/assets	No change after merger
	Asset sales/assets	No change after merger

are summarized in Table 5.3. Herman and Lowenstein (1988) report that merged firms have higher financial leverage than premerger bidders. However, it is not clear whether this arises because bidders increase debt to acquire the targets or because targets have higher leverage than acquirers.

Healy, Palepu, and Ruback (1990) examine operating and investment characteristics (all adjusted for industry effects). Operating characteristics include pretax margin on sales, asset turnover (sales per dollar of assets), employee growth rate, and pension expense per employee. Investment characteristics include capital expenditures, asset sales, and research and development (R&D) expenses, all as a percentage of the market value of assets. We find that asset turnover increases after the merger, and labor growth rates decline. However, the merged firms experience no significant change in cash flow margins, pension expense per employee, capital expenditure rates, asset sale rates, and R&D rates relative to their industries in the postmerger period.

The preceding findings indicate that improvements in asset productivity, perhaps arising from economies of scale or scope, are an important source of merger gains. While the merger firms also show an improvement in labor use, measured by the decline in labor growth rates, labor savings cannot explain the increase in operating cash flow return on assets because they do not lead to increased operating cash flow margins.[1] The absence of an increase in margins also suggests that the postmerger cash flow improvements are not due to increases in monopoly rents. Finally, the merged firms do not appear to focus on improving operating cash flow returns on assets at the expense of long-term investments, since R&D, capital expenditure, and asset sales rates do not change after the merger.

Leveraged Buyouts

Measuring Postbuyout Performance

Performance measures used by three recent studies of postbuyout performance are summarized in Table 5.4. Kaplan (1989b) examines postbuyout performance for forty-eight management buyouts. He estimates three measures of performance, all of which are adjusted for changes in industry conditions: percentage changes in operating income, operating income as a percentage of end-of-year book assets (return on assets), and operating income as a percentage of sales (operating margin). Operating income is earnings before depreciation and amortization expenses, before financing charges, and before taxes. This measure controls for the effect of any increase in depreciation or goodwill amortization arising from the use of purchase accounting to record the buyout. Kaplan notes that percentage changes in earnings in years surrounding the buyout are difficult to interpret because they do not allow for the effect of asset sell-offs or acquisitions. Return on assets and operating margins are therefore estimated to control for changes in firm size. Book assets are adjusted for asset write-ups recorded in the year of the buyout. While this adjustment is correct at the time the buyout takes place (year 0), it overstates the effect of asset write-ups in subsequent years (years 1 to 3) when the book values of the written-up fixed assets and inventory are reduced by depreciation and inventory sales. Consequently, return on asset measures after the merger are probably overstated. Operating margins, however, are unaffected by purchase accounting.

Smith (1990) examines the postbuyout performance of fifty-eight management buyout firms. The main measures of performance are operating cash flows as a percentage of average assets (return on assets) and operating cash flows as a percentage of sales (operating margin). Operating cash flows are cash flows from normal operations before financing charges. They therefore control for the change in capital structure of the buyout firm. Assets are adjusted for the asset write-ups. However, as noted, this adjustment overstates the effect of asset write-ups in years subsequent to the buyout, when the book values of the written-up fixed assets and inventory are reduced by depreciation and inventory sales. Consequently, return on asset measures after the merger are probably overstated. This bias is probably not severe for Smith's study, since she examines asset returns for only one year after the buyout.

Both Kaplan and Smith examine management buyout firms with financial reports publicly available after the buyout. These are usually firms that filed 10-K reports with the Securities and Exchange Commission (SEC) after the buyout because they had public debt or preferred stock outstanding, firms that filed an initial public offering (IPO) prospectus after the buyout, or firms that were acquired by a public company after the buyout and had 8-K reports filed with the SEC by the purchaser. Buyout firms that have a subsequent IPO or are purchased are likely to be the most successful buyouts. This selection bias makes it difficult to interpret postbuyout performance and is likely to be important for both studies. Of an initial sample of seventy-six management buyouts, Kaplan finds only forty-eight firms with postbuyout data. This frequency is even lower for Smith, who identifies an initial sample of 215 management buyouts and is left with only fifty-eight firms after deleting those that do not report postbuyout data.

The third study, by Lichtenberg and Siegel (1990), avoids the selection bias problems faced by Kaplan and Smith by examining a large sample of leveraged buyouts

Table 5.4 Summary of research design for studies examining postbuyout performance

Study	Sample	Sample Buyout Years	Performance Years Relative to Buyout	Performance Measure	Performance Benchmark
Kaplan (1989b)	48 MBOs	1980–1986	−2 to +3	Percentage changes in operating earnings (before depreciation and amortization, interest, taxes, and extraordinary items), and operating earnings as a percentage of end-of-year book assets (adjusted for asset write-ups) and sales for the buyout firm	Buyout firm industry
Smith (1990)	58 MBOs	1977–1986	−5 to +1	Cash flow from operations before financing charges and taxes as a percentage of book assets (adjusted for asset write-ups) and sales for the buyout firm	Buyout firm industry
Lichtenberg and Siegel (1990)	399 MBO plants and 733 other buyout plants	1981–1986	−8 to +5	Revenues for buyout plant controlling for labor and capital inputs	Buyout plant industry

using the Census Bureau's Longitudinal Research Database. This database contains plant-level information for both public and private companies. Lichtenberg and Siegel control for limitations in accounting-based measures of postbuyout performance by using changes in productivity as their performance metric. This measure is computed by comparing revenues for a buyout plant in a given year with revenues for plants in the same industry and year, controlling for differences in labor hours and economic estimates of capital.

Postbuyout Performance Results

Each of the preceding studies finds some evidence of operating improvements in postbuyout performance. Table 5.5 summarizes the findings. Kaplan (1989b) reports that buyout firms have significant increases in both operating margins and operating return on assets in each of the three years after the buyout. For example, median operating margins increase from 10.9 percent in year -1 to approximately 13 percent in year 3. These improvements are not caused by industry-wide performance, since changes adjusted for industry effects are also positive and statistically reliable.

Smith (1990) finds evidence of an increase in operating cash flow margins both before and after management buyouts. Median margins are 7.9 percent five years before the buyout (year -5), 12.4 percent in year -1, and 14.4 percent in the first complete year after the buyout (year 1). The margin in year 1 is significantly greater than the operating cash flow margin for the buyout firms' industries. This finding is consistent with the view that the financial burden imposed on buyout owners provides them with a powerful incentive to increase the firm's operating efficiency. However, Smith's findings also indicate that the buyout firms' performance improves before the

Table 5.5 Summary of research findings for studies examining postbuyout performance

Study	Prebuyout Performance Results	Postbuyout Performance Results
Kaplan (1989b)	Buyout firms have similar changes in operating return on assets and operating margins as their industries in year -1	Buyout firms have increases in operating return on assets and operating margins relative to their industries in each of the three postmerger years
Smith (1990)	Buyout firms show steady improvements in pretax operating cash flow returns on assets and pretax operating cash flow margins relative to their industries in years -5 to -1	Pretax operating cash flow returns on assets and pretax operating cash flow margins for the buyout firms continue to improve relative to their industries in year $+1$
Lichtenberg and Siegel (1990)	Buyout plants show steady improvements in productivity relative to their industries in years -5 to -1	Productivity for the buyout plant continues to increase relative to the industry in years $+1$ to $+3$ but may reverse in years $+4$ and $+5$

buyout, raising doubts about whether the postbuyout improvement is caused by the buyout.

Finally, Lichtenberg and Siegel (1990) find evidence of postbuyout increases in productivity for all buyouts and also for management buyouts. Industry-adjusted productivity changes for the buyout plants are positive and significant for three years before the buyout and continue for a further two to three years. However, it is difficult to interpret these results. First, it is not clear whether the postbuyout gains persist: there is some evidence of negative productivity changes in years 4 and 5. Second, the increase in productivity before the buyout raises the question of whether the improvement would have occurred even without the buyout. Finally, the statistical significance of the tests is suspect, because the plant data are probably not independent.

Sources of Performance Improvements

Improvements in performance after buyouts can arise for a number of reasons. To provide additional evidence on these, Kaplan (1989b), Smith (1990), and Lichtenberg and Siegel (1990) examine other characteristics of buyout firms. These include industry-adjusted operating characteristics (employee growth and sales per employee), investment characteristics (capital expenditures as a percentage of sales), and management forecasts of buyout firm performance made in the buyout prospectus. A summary of these variables and study results are presented in Table 5.6

Kaplan (1989b) and Lichtenberg and Siegel (1990) examine whether operating performance improvements arise from decreases in employment. Their findings provide some support for the view that buyouts provide new owners with opportunities to renegotiate implicit or explicit contracts with labor. However, the results are quite weak. Kaplan finds that buyout firms have lower employee growth rates than their industries for one year after the buyout. However, this decline appears to be primarily due to firms that have divestitures in that year. Lichtenberg and Siegel observe that there is a decline in nonproduction workers after the buyout, as well as a decline in wage rates for these workers. In contrast, there is no such decline in the production work force and weak evidence of an increase in production wage rates. However, it is not clear whether nonproduction workers leave the organization or are simply relocated from the plant level to corporate headquarters. Further, once again the statistical significance of the tests is suspect, because the plant data are probably not independent.

Both Kaplan (1989b) and Smith (1990) find evidence of a decline in capital expenditures to sales in the postbuyout period. There are at least three ways to interpret this evidence. One interpretation is that prior to the buyout management invested in unprofitable projects, and after the buyout the new owners eliminated this excess investment. A second interpretation is that the financial burden on the firm imposed by the buyout forces managers to focus on short-term performance to service the debt, at the expense of the long term. A third interpretation is that management completed a capital expenditure program prior to the buyout, anticipating that the investments have long-term benefits for the firm owners. In firms where investors are skeptical of the value of this program, managers will view the firm as being undervalued and will have an incentive to participate in a buyout to earn positive postbuyout returns.

Kaplan investigates whether incumbents take advantage of private information in negotiating buyouts. Lowenstein (1985) argues that buyouts occur when managers

Table 5.6 Summary of research findings on operating and investment characteristics for buyout firms

Study	Firm Characteristics	Difference Between Postbuyout and Prebuyout Measures
Kaplan (1989b)	*Operating characteristics for buyout firms postbuyout and prebuyout (relative to industry)*	
	Employee growth rate	Decreases after merger
	Investment characteristics for buyout firms postbuyout and prebuyout (relative to industry)	
	Capital expenditures/sales	Decrease in years −1, +1, and +2
Smith (1990)	*Operating characteristics for buyout firm postbuyout and prebuyout (relative to industry)*	
	Sales turnover	Increase after merger
	Employees/sales	No change after merger
	Sales/working capital	Increase after merger
	Investment characteristics for buyout firm postbuyout and prebuyout (relative to industry)	
	Capital expenditures/sales	Decrease after merger
Lichtenberg and Siegel (1990)	*Operating characteristics for buyout plant postbuyout and prebuyout (relative to nonbuyout plants)*	
	Annual wage rate	Decreases after merger for nonproduction workers and increases for production workers
	Employee growth rate	Decreases after merger for nonproduction workers, no change for production workers

have private information that their firm's future performance is likely to exceed market expectations. However, Kaplan finds no strong evidence to support this view. Management forecasts made in the buyout prospectus overstate, rather than understate, postbuyout performance. Further, insiders owning approximately 50 percent of all insider holdings prior to the buyout do not choose to participate in the buyout, indicating that they do not believe that the buyout is underpriced.

CONCLUSION

There is widespread agreement that mergers and acquisitions and leveraged buyouts increase stock prices for the combined target and acquiring firms and for buyout firms, respectively. However, there has been little evidence on whether these changes in corporate control are associated with subsequent improvements in firm performance or on sources of any improvements. The studies reviewed in this chapter provide a first attempt to answer these questions.

The results of studies of mergers and acquisitions are mixed. However, several of these studies do not control for accounting problems in measuring performance after mergers. After allowing for these effects, we find that merged firms experience a significant increase in asset productivity relative to their industries in the five years after the merger, leading to higher postmerger cash flow returns on assets. There is no evidence that mergers enable target and acquiring firms to increase monopoly rents, since the merged firms' operating margins relative to their industries do not change after the merger. Finally, merged firms do not appear to reduce their capital expenditures and R&D rates after the merger, indicating that the merger improvements do not come at the expense of long-term growth.

Management buyout firms also experience an increase in operating performance after the buyout. These effects persist for at least three years. However, since buyout firms also show improvements in performance before the buyout, there is some question as to whether the postbuyout improvements are caused by the buyout or would have occurred anyway. Further, it is not clear whether the improvements continue in the long term, since buyout firms typically reduce capital expenditures after the buyout. The only evidence on the performance of buyout firms beyond three years indicates that they underperform their industries.

The foregoing findings raise two interesting questions, which provide promising areas for future research on the effects of changes in corporate control. First, are the performance improvements caused by the changes in corporate control, or would they have occurred anyway? For example, if mergers arise from undervaluation of the target firms by the stock market, postmerger improvements in performance will occur whether or not there is a merger. Similarly, if buyouts occur when managers have private information that their firm's future performance is likely to exceed market expectations, postbuyout performance improvements will occur without the buyout. There is no strong evidence that incumbents take advantage of private information in negotiating buyouts.

A second question is, What are the economic factors that explain the cross-sectional variation in performance after changes in corporate control? While performance appears to improve for a majority of the firms examined in the studies reviewed, a significant proportion have negative performance after the control change. These firms may have performed poorly because of bad luck, or systematic business and managerial reasons may have led to these outcomes. By developing a structural model of how mergers and buyouts improve performance, it may be possible to determine whether a merger or buyout is the most appropriate form of organizational change.

NOTE

1. The cash flow margin is affected by both the number of employees and their wage schedule. If the decline in employee growth after the merger is offset by higher wages for the existing work force, margins may be unchanged. However, we are unable to test this proposition since wage data are unavailable for most of the sample firms.

REFERENCES

Brealey, R., and S. Myers. 1987. *Principles of Corporate Finance*. New York: McGraw-Hill.

Gilson, R., M. Scholes, and M. Wolfson. 1988. "Taxation and the Dynamics of Corporate Control: The Uncertain Case for Tax Motivated Acquisitions." In *Knights, Raiders, and Targets: The Impact of the Hostile Takeover*, edited by J. Coffee, Jr., L. Lowenstein, and S. Rose. New York: Oxford University Press.

Hayn, C. 1989. "Tax Attributes as Determinants of Shareholder Gains in Corporate Acquisitions." *Journal of Financial Economics* 23, no. 1: 121–154.

Healy, P., K. Palepu, and R. Ruback. 1990. "Does Corporate Performance Improve after Mergers?" MIT Sloan School of Management working paper 3149-90.

Herman, E., and L. Lowenstein. 1988. "The Efficiency Effects of Hostile Takeovers." In *Knights, Raiders, and Targets: The Impact of the Hostile Takeover*, edited by J. Coffee, Jr., L. Lowenstein, and S. Rose. New York: Oxford University Press.

Jensen, M. 1986. "Agency Costs of Free Cash Flow, Corporate Finance and Takeovers." *American Economic Review*, May, pp. 323–329.

Jensen, M., and R. Ruback. 1983. "The Market for Corporate Control: The Scientific Evidence." *Journal of Financial Economics* 11, no. 1: 5–50.

Kaplan, S. 1989a. "Management Buyouts: Evidence on Taxes as a Source of Value." *Journal of Finance* 44, no. 3: 611–632.

Kaplan, S. 1989b. "The Effects of Management Buyouts on Operating Performance and Value." *Journal of Financial Economics* 24, 217–254.

Lichtenberg, F., and D. Siegel. 1990. "The Effects of Leveraged Buyouts on Productivity and Related Aspects of Firm Behavior." Columbia University working paper.

Lowenstein, L. 1985. "Management Buyouts." *Columbia Law Review*, May, pp. 730–784.

Myers, S., and N. Majluf. 1984. "Corporate Financing and Investment Decisions When Firms Have Information That Investors Do Not Have." *Journal of Financial Economics* 13, no. 2: 187–221.

Palepu, K. 1986. "Predicting Takeover Targets: A Methodological and Empirical Analysis." *Journal of Accounting and Economics* 8: 3–36.

Ravenscraft, D., and F. M. Scherer. 1987. *Mergers, Selloffs, and Economic Efficiency*. Washington, D.C.: The Brookings Institution.

Shleifer, A., and L. Summers. 1988. "Breach of Trust in Hostile Takeovers." In *Corporate Takeovers: Causes and Consequences*, edited by A. Auerbach. Chicago: University of Chicago Press.

Smith, A. 1990. "Corporate Ownership Structure and Performance: The Case of Management Buyouts." Unpublished working paper, University of Chicago.

Watts and Zimmerman. 1986. *Positive Accounting Theory*. Englewood Cliffs, N.J.: Prentice-Hall.

COMMENTARY BY ANN LEIBOWITZ

As someone who grew up in a company which until recently regarded any kind of debt as anathema, I found it startling to consider unused debt capacity as "organizational slack," as suggested in Paul Healy's chapter. Once over that hurdle, however, I saw corporate performance as defined by earnings before interest and taxes as being a good measure for assessing the effects of a change in control. The method is particularly worthwhile in that it incorporates investment standards as external benchmarks. Mr. Healy has normalized out a lot of the vagaries of accounting that sometimes mask what might otherwise be seen as improvements in financial performance.

But three to five years isn't, in my judgment, quite a long enough period to consider. To be sure, the longer the interval between change in control and a particular financial result, the less certain the causative link, if any, between the two. But it is also possible in the first few years following a change in control to defer a considerable amount of expenditure, other than research and development, which dramatically enhances short-term performance as measured by Mr. Healy's model, but at the expense of long-term profitability. Thus the model is an excellent one worth tracking, but not to the exclusion of other performance criteria.

I would like to talk about our experience at Polaroid and corporate performance as I've seen it, not so much as reflected by our financial results (which have been quite good so far) but from a more subjective point of view. While not having undergone an actual change in control, Polaroid had a close call in 1988 when Stanley Gold of Shamrock Holdings identified us as a takeover target. At first the approach purported to be friendly, but then the dealings became decidedly hostile, and we at Polaroid pulled up our socks. We did not go through a leveraged buyout technically but we borrowed—a company that, as I said, had essentially no debt—over $300 million, quite a chunk of change, to accomplish a financial restructuring. The money was used primarily to acquire back a significant portion of our stock, which we put in our employees' hands in the form of an Employee Stock Ownership Plan. Originally 14 percent, but now about 20 percent, of our stock is held in the ESOP trust. Our employees, we feel, have been made direct participants in Polaroid's future, through the ESOP and through an ongoing communication process built around employee ownership.

In addition, we downsized, as did most, if not all, other companies which underwent actual change in control. We thus reduced our payroll by $80 million. A number of other changes were made, many of them very good. But some of the changes that were at least seriously considered, if not made, were bad. I'd like to talk about both kinds, for they all affect long-term performance.

On the good side, the takeover threat caused management to look at itself and make some very tough decisions. Polaroid was a traditional company. Many of its people had started young and had grown up with it. We did not have, and still don't have, a great deal of turnover, so projects were hung on to—some people would say out of love— but sometimes out of concern for "turf," or out of an attraction that had become outdated by the lack of real continued financial potential. Having Stanley Gold breathing down our necks made us take a hard look at some of these. Decisions were made abruptly, and sometimes surprisingly comfortably, which should have been made much earlier. The officers' and senior managers' ranks were thinned. Projects were evaluated and screened: some were postponed, some beefed up, and some scrapped altogether. Expenses were pared, and cost justifications for new expenditures became a way of life. A number of us who stayed can now see that in many respects our encounter with Mr. Gold was the best thing that could have happened to us.

But what about the bad things, the things that can adversely affect long-term performance? One example is costs for training and education. If costs are cut by reducing or eliminating training, the results may not be seen for several years, for employee training is truly long-term investment. But it is expensive, and sometimes impossible, to recoup the resulting loss once such cutbacks have been made. Once upon a time, *Business Week* referred to us as Polaroid University. I'm not sure we'd get the same accolade today.

Professional advisers, such as environmental and safety engineers and lawyers who work at the preventive end of catastrophe, are often dispensed with as part of cost cutting. You may not immediately see the effects of their loss. But until recently it would have been hard for me to imagine feeling sorry for Exxon. As I look at the disastrous oil spill in Alaska and the fact that Exxon admits to having laid off safety engineers as part of cost cutting, I wonder how much of that was driven by pressure from today's takeover climate, to get rid of employees who seemed not to be pulling their own weight on a continuous basis or who were otherwise seen as not being "cost-justified."

And work priorities may not always change for the better. I know one labor counsel at a large company that has been acquired, who used to spend most of his time developing cost-effective, thoughtful employment policies and practices. Now, he says, he has become an expert on how to run a layoff without getting sued, and that is essentially what he does 100 percent of the time.

I think what has really happened is that the threats of takeover, and actual take-overs, have filled the voids that should have been filled by boards of directors who were, after all, elected by the shareholders to represent shareholder interest and oversee management. Theoretically, of course, boards of directors are supposed to hold company officers accountable for performance and reward (or punish) them accordingly. But as a practical matter, that doesn't seem to happen very often in the absence of some external threat. Board members at most publicly held companies are more often than not elected on the basis of recommendations by the very management they are supposed to oversee. I submit that in many instances, these boards have largely ignored or abdicated their fundamental responsibilities to shareholders, not by conspiring to "entrench" management, but by neglecting to become sufficiently informed to make reasoned, sound judgments in their deliberations.

We had some embarrassment at Polaroid when our ESOP was challenged in court by Mr. Gold. Some of our board members who had approved the ESOP were asked to testify as to why they believed the plan as established was appropriate for the company and its shareholders, as distinguished from being a management entrenchment device as claimed by Mr. Gold. Fortunately, the Delaware judge decided that the plan was inherently sound and fair, but her conclusion was unlikely to have been based on the testimony of board members who were not seemingly cognizant of the whys and wherefores of some of our corporate strategy. It seems to me that if boards who are supposed to represent shareholder interest don't find a way to exercise informed discretion, judgment, and management oversight, they should know there are plenty of people waiting in the wings who will gladly replace them.

I think the system we need for corporate accountability is already in place. If it were really working well, then in most cases (assuming a competent board, of course) one would not expect to see any particular improvement in corporate performance on account of change in control, actual or threatened. The real question for me is whether, and how, we will be able to make the present system work to preserve the best of what corporate America is all about. Otherwise, as Sir James Goldsmith has indicated, we unwittingly foster the notions of those who think that corporations are there to be raided. Should this trend continue, we may as well all sit and shudder with fear—and wait.

6

The Role of the CEO in the Management of Change: The Case of Information Technology

EDGAR H. SCHEIN

Few people would question the assumption that CEOs have a major impact on the changes that occur in their organizations. Yet there is surprisingly little analysis of just what the nature of this impact is likely to be, whether it will vary by industry, company, or CEO attitude and style, and what empirical data can be gathered to begin to shed some light on these issues (Hambrick, 1988; Thomas, 1988).

The research to be reported in this chapter focuses on a particular area of CEO impact—information technology—but the hypotheses that flow from this research about CEO roles in the management of organization change are more general in nature. In particular, the research reveals that there is a diversity of attitudes and assumptions about the appropriate role of the CEO in the management of change, and we would expect such diversity to apply to areas other than the implementation of information technology.

Analyses of the implementation of information technology (IT) have noted a variety of factors that aid or hinder such implementation. For example, Markus (1984) notes that one can focus on (1) the limitations of the technology itself; (2) the resistance to change on the part of individuals based on personality, cognitive style, or position in the organization; or (3) the interaction between individuals and the technology. Kraemer, King, Dunkle, and Lane (1989) extend this interactionist perspective by referring to the role of "states of computing" in given companies reflecting the interaction between the interests of different organizational levels and different functional groups.

One of the limitations of these types of analyses is that they refer to management levels in a general way, referring occasionally to "top management" or "senior executives," but it remains unclear what is actually meant and whether any distinctions are drawn between chairmen of boards, chief executive officers (CEOs), chief operating officers (COOs), and division general managers. As Kotter (1982) and others have shown, different general managers do quite different things, so it is important to be precise in specifying whom one is studying.

In their report on the use of "executive support systems," Rockart and Delong (1988) do single out CEOs in many of their examples, but their cases are mostly an analysis of successful utilization of IT that illustrates what is possible, not what is normal. The fact that many CEOs have difficulty with IT is acknowledged but not analyzed by them or by other researchers who have focused on CEOs (Gibson and Jackson, 1987; Rockart and DeLong, 1988; Rockart and Treacy, 1982).

Surveys of CEOs, such as those done by Moore (1986), tend to identify CEOs who are successful implementers and analyze their characteristics, but they do little to help us understand the characteristics of the much larger population who are not enthusiastic about IT and who do not wish to use it themselves.

RESEARCH FOCUS AND METHOD

This study began in 1987 with a decision to interview a broad sample of CEOs in a variety of companies to try to determine in a more general way their assumptions about IT and their attitudes toward the problems of change and implementation. Ten MIT Sloan Fellows, one other graduate student, and I were able to interview ninety-four executives, all of whom were current or past CEOs and, in a few cases, COOs or presidents of divisions in conglomerates or multidivisional companies. Seventy-nine of them clearly fitted the CEO criterion. This sample was arrived at by each Sloan Fellow picking an industry that interested him or her and writing letters to CEOs in a sample of companies in that industry. Sixty percent of the persons contacted in this manner agreed to be interviewed. All were male. Some general characteristics of the sample are listed in Table 6.1.

The interviews, which were focused on personal attitudes and the use of IT, tried to elicit some of the underlying assumptions behind the behavior and attitudes. Common dimensions and variables were chosen for the interview protocol and subsequent analysis but, because we felt it essential to get the CEOs' spontaneous views, we asked our interviewers to allow each CEO to tell his story in his own way. We then combined the protocols in terms of common themes and found that coding reliability was sufficient to pursue our analysis and to develop constructs, but not high enough to allow us to generalize from this sample to the larger population of CEOs. This study should, therefore, be viewed as exploratory in nature.

Table 6.1 Characteristics of CEO sample[a]

Average age	56.3 (42–69)
Average years as CEO	7.1 (1–26)
Average number of employees	54,600 (200–800,000)
Industries and range of sales	
Insurance	560×10^6 to 650×10^6
Telecommunications	400×10^6 to 12×10^9
Services	2×10^9 to 3×10^9
Banking	2.5×10^9 to 27×10^9
Aerospace/high-tech	40×10^6 to 50×10^9
Utilities	260×10^6 to 1×10^9
Manufacturing	20×10^6 to 70×10^9

[a] Data based on 79 CEOs, COOs, and presidents. Sixty percent of persons contacted agreed to be interviewed.

Table 6.2 A stage model of planned change

Unfreezing: Creating motivation to change
  Disconfirmation
  Induction of anxiety/guilt
  Creation of psychological safety
Creating change through cognitive redefinition
  Stimulating imitation or identification
  Stimulating scanning
Refreezing: Stabilizing the change
  Integration into personality
  Integration into key relationships and social system

GENERIC CEO ROLES IN THE CHANGE PROCESS

Table 6.2 presents a model of the change process that was originally proposed by Kurt Lewin and elaborated by me to explain changes that had planned, nonvoluntary, and sometimes coercive elements to them (Lewin, 1952; Schein, 1961, 1972, 1987). Lewin correctly foresaw that in living systems any given stable state was a "quasi-stationary" equilibrium that could be unfrozen, moved, and refrozen, but he did not elaborate in detail how one actually unfreezes a system, moves it, and then refreezes it. Since organizations tend to develop stable routines and cultures, any organization change tends to occur in terms of the stages identified in this model (Schein, 1985). The critical elements in this model are the actual activities implied in each step of the change process, so our analysis focuses on those kinds of CEO activities.

As Table 6.2 shows, one can logically analyze and order the steps necessary in each stage of the change process, though these steps often occur out of sequence or simultaneously. Most of these steps occur through the intervention of some human, to be labeled for this purpose a "change agent." All of the activities of the change agent, including diagnostic inquiry, can be thought of as "interventions" in the sense that they have an effect on the people who are the target of the behavior. It is the pattern of such interventions on the part of CEOs that is the focus of this analysis.

Disconfirmation: The CEO as a Disconfirmer

Change will not occur unless there is some motivation to change, and such motivation is most often provided by information that previously held assumptions, attitudes, or behavioral routines are no longer working. The information that things are no longer working, called "disconfirmation," is typically brought into the organization by those members who are most closely in contact with the external environment, who are most responsible for the performance of the organization, and who have the most internal credibility as sources of information.

CEOs are uniquely suited to be disconfirmers. If things are not going right in their view, they have not only the opportunity but the obligation to start an organizational change process by disconfirming the present state. Normal routines that have become habits in an organization will not change unless someone ceases to respond in the expected manner. Such disconfirming responses will obviously have more weight if they come from the CEO than from someone lower in the hierarchy.

A clear example came from one of our respondents who decided to start the change process toward greater use of IT by announcing that he was personally going to start using a desktop terminal and would henceforth send all critical communications to his subordinates only via electronic mail. In other words, if they sent something by the old system, he would simply not respond, and anyone who did not get a terminal would miss important messages from him.

If there is no disconfirmation from any source, no motivation to change will be aroused. In a complacent organization, therefore, one of the CEO's most critical functions is to generate information or announce decisions that will have a disconfirming effect, thereby initiating the change process.

Induction of Anxiety or Guilt: The CEO as the "Bad Parent"

Disconfirming messages have an impact only if they connect to something we care about. If the CEO ceases to respond to subordinates' behavior in an area irrelevant to their concern, they may simply pay no attention. However, if continuing to behave in the old way makes the subordinates anxious because some important goals may not be met, or makes them feel guilty because some valued ideals will not be met unless a change occurs, then the message will be attended to and discomfort will motivate some activity. It is this step that leads to quips like "no pain, no gain" or the common assertion among change agents that "unless the system is hurting somehow, no change will occur."

CEOs are clearly in a good position to play a key role in anxiety or guilt induction because symbolically and psychologically they occupy a parent role. Probably the best examples from our interviews came from those CEOs who stated outright or subtly implied to their subordinates that the subordinates' failure to learn to use IT meant either that they would fail in their work (anxiety induction) or that they were technologically "backward" (guilt induction). Whether it is intended or not, a force toward change is induced when the subordinate feels obsolete, out of touch, or in some other way uncomfortable about maintaining his or her old behavior.

Creation of Psychological Safety: The CEO as the "Good Parent"

If too much anxiety or guilt is created, there is the danger that the change targets will react defensively. One of the most likely defenses in this situation is denial, which, in this case, means that the subordinates will cease to "hear" the disconfirming signals or will rationalize them away. Subordinates will say to themselves, "The boss doesn't really mean it; he won't persist if I don't go along," and so on.

In the case of the introduction of IT, subordinates may feel that they will be embarrassed by their slow learning ability, or by their inability to type, or by the fact that their poor grammar or spelling will be revealed—all of which they could hide by dictating directly to a secretary. A common error here is to assume that the resistance to change is only the lack of motivation or the unwillingness to put out the effort to learn something new. Much more likely is the defensive avoidance that results from inability to face one's own presumed inadequacies if one does not feel psychologically safe.

CEOs should and do attend to this issue in a variety of ways. One of the commonest is to be totally inflexible on the ultimate goals to be achieved but to be highly flexible and supportive on other issues. For example, the CEO may mandate that desktop workstations will eventually be used by all senior management but allow some leeway in (1) the pace of their introduction; (2) the degree to which selected subordinates would be allowed to continue to use their secretaries to enter data or memos, and, most important; (3) the amount and type of training help that would be available no matter what the cost. Thus subordinates for whom "going to class" created tension could use individual coaches, perhaps even for long periods of time. CEOs who feel that sending their subordinates to formal classes would threaten them further may consider an individual coach the psychological safety net necessary to support innovation.

How many CEOs played each of these three unfreezing roles cannot be determined because local circumstances varied or data are not available. However, we heard many more stories about the disconfirming and anxiety- or guilt-inducing roles than about the other roles. It was least common to hear stories from CEOs about the necessity to provide psychological safety, even though they were often in the best position to provide it. We have to assume that they are either less sensitive to the need for this role or less willing to talk about it because it appears to be "soft." It should be noted, however, that unless all three aspects of the unfreezing process occur to some degree no motivation toward change will be created.

Creating Change Through Cognitive Redefinition: The CEO as Role Model

Ultimately unfreezing creates a motivation and readiness to change. The change target becomes sensitized to the need to learn something new and starts to look around for relevant information. For lasting change to occur, however, the target not only must learn new behaviors but also must cognitively redefine or reframe the issue so that new perceptions, attitudes, and feelings are created as well. Sometimes such cognitive redefinition occurs prior to behavior change, sometimes afterwards in an effort to reduce dissonance (Festinger, 1957). But if it does not occur at all, we are dealing only with temporary change of the sort one sees when people are coerced but not convinced.

The most common source for new information is someone else in the organization who seems to be "doing it right," in the sense that his or her behavior is getting positively reinforced or "confirmed." Such role models not only provide behavioral cues on what to do, but, more important, they permit the target to psychologically identify with the model and thereby absorb some of the new cognitive point of view.

Many CEOs in our interviews discussed how the use of IT made it possible to think in a fundamentally different way about "managing the business," and part of their problem was to get across these new concepts. For some of their subordinates this meant new assumptions about what a manager does and how a business can and should be managed. They had to reframe the manager's job. If the CEO felt comfortable with his own vision and level of understanding, he became a willing role model, teacher, and object of psychological identification. If he did not, he could deliberately stay away from the situation, conceal his own behavior to a greater degree, disconfirm efforts on the part of subordinates to imitate him or identify with him, or limit his involvement to that of a "process consultant" (Schein, 1987, 1988). In that role the

CEO would help the subordinate redefine his or her own job but would not give advice or solutions.

Some CEOs were outspoken about not wanting to be role models. They sent the message "Do what I say, not what I do," a situation that arose frequently with entrepreneurs, who often recognized that their own personal style was unusual and not necessarily the correct model for others. Another reason why some CEOs deliberately tried not to be role models was that they wanted to avoid cloning themselves. They believed that an effective organization needs innovative behavior, so they stimulated as much as possible people's efforts to learn in their own way and from their own sources.

If the CEO felt that he personally was the wrong model, but he believed that a correct model existed and that learning from a role model was the best way to learn, he could, of course, manage the change process by bringing into the organization consultants, trainers, or other executives who represented what he wanted to teach.

Stimulating Cognitive Redefinition Through Scanning: The CEO as Process Consultant

Imitation and identification have the virtue that learning can occur rapidly and behavior can be standardized fairly quickly. However, if the goal is for the new behavior to be innovative, then this change mechanism is a disadvantage because it prematurely funnels all changes into the same channels. If the CEO wishes to avoid such premature channeling, he must create circumstances that will "help the subordinate to learn on his own." The CEO as a change agent can achieve this result by becoming a process consultant and/or by sending subordinates "out into the world," to find out what is out there and learn from it (Schein, 1969, 1987, 1988).

The essence of process consultation in this context is for the CEO to become genuinely interested in the subordinate as a learner and to provide whatever help the subordinate appears to need to learn new beliefs, attitudes, values, and behavior, much as a coach elicits from an athlete what that athlete is most capable of. The CEO as process consultant does not advise, teach, or tell. Instead he listens, helps the subordinate identify what the problem is, and helps the subordinate figure out what he or she will do about the problem. Suggesting that the subordinate should "scan" the environment for ideas is the basic mechanism. The CEO in this role may offer options and alternatives but never recommends any particular course of action as the correct one.

In our interviews we saw many examples of this kind of forced scanning. The CEO would announce that the company had to learn to make better use of IT, would disclaim any special visions or skills in this area, but would expect regular reports on progress. Often, with the help of the IT department, key subordinates would create committees or task forces to scan the environment, inform themselves, and begin to redefine in their own heads what tools and processes they needed. They would then be in a position to educate the CEO.

If this scanning process was to work, however, the steps involved in unfreezing had to have occurred. We found good examples of where CEOs had earlier disconfirmed present practice by strongly asserting that "something" was not right, without, however, offering a vision or a solution themselves, thus forcing scanning on the part of subordinates.

Refreezing: The CEO as Reinforcer

One of the most frustrating aspects of organizational change is that new behaviors and attitudes do not stick once the initial "Hawthorne effect" has worn off. The system either reverts to its original state or moves in some brand new direction that may not be desired by the change agent. For new responses to remain stable, they must be "re-frozen," in the sense that they must fit into the personality of the change target and into his or her key relationships. Otherwise a new unfreezing process begins because of personal discomfort or disconfirmation by others in the system.

In order to avoid either of these undesirable outcomes, change agents generally favor projects that involve as much of the total system as possible, and they encourage change mechanisms that draw more on scanning than on identification or imitation. If a person learns through scanning, he or she automatically incorporates only things that fit into the personality, whereas with imitation and identification one often adopts behavior to please the role model, only to drop it later when the role model is no longer an audience.

Similarly, if a person learns something new along with others who are part of his or her work system, the members will reinforce each others' behavior, thus making it more likely that new responses will persist if the whole team or work system has learned them together. In other words, refreezing is most likely to occur when the change occurs through scanning and when the whole work system undergoes change together, and it is least likely to occur when an individual learns alone and through imitation/identification.

The implications for CEO behavior are obvious. If the CEO is the original change agent, he must view as his change target entire groups or subsystems, not isolated individuals, and he must avoid becoming the object of imitation. Furthermore, since he is a prime audience for and reinforcer of change, when change in the right direction occurs, he should strongly confirm and reinforce the new behavior and attitudes.

We infer from our interviews that many CEOs were sensitive to these kinds of issues, but only at an intuitive level. They did not talk as articulately about group norms and the subtleties of change as they did about unfreezing and setting a direction for change. And how they chose to reinforce had much to do with their vision for IT and the longer range goals they saw for it, a topic we will discuss later.

FACTORS INFLUENCING CEO
CHANGE AGENT BEHAVIOR

Having identified the generic change agent roles, we now need to know what, if anything, will determine how a given CEO will actually behave in the process of initiating and managing change. The factors identified in this section can all be thought of as "partially causal" or influential, and they act in complex combinations rather than as single forces (see Figure 6.1). In terms of change theory, each factor can be thought of as either a "driving" force leading to increased pressure for the system to move in a certain direction or as a "restraining" force leading to resistance (Schein, 1985, 1987).

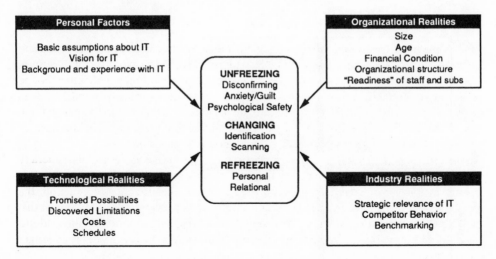

Figure 6.1 CEO change roles and their determinants.

Basic Assumptions about Information Technology

We believed that whether they were explicitly aware of it or not, all CEOs had a set of assumptions about IT and a vision of what it could or could not do for them. Table 6.3 and Figure 6.2 present a typology of such assumptions based on (1) basic faith that IT is a good thing for organizations, and (2) the conviction that those things will or will not come about.

Though the coding was not always totally reliable, we were able to agree enough on the basic types to give a rough approximation of how many of our CEOs fell into

Table 6.3 A typology of CEO assumptions about IT

Utopian idealist: This CEO sees nothing but benefits deriving from the increased use of IT in all areas of *his business and personal life.* He may not see all these benefits in actual use, but he believes firmly that in time all the benefits will be realized.

Realistic utopian: This CEO sees great potential benefits in IT but is not sure that they will all be realized because of hidden costs, resistances in others, and various other sources of difficulty that are not inherent in IT but in its implementation.

Ambivalent: This CEO sees some benefits in some areas but sees potential harm in other areas and/or perceives that the costs may in the end outweigh the benefits; therefore, he is ambivalent in the sense of wanting to push ahead but being cautious and doubtful at the same time.

Realistic skeptic: This CEO is basically doubtful about the benefits of IT, short run or long run, but realizes that the appeal of the technology will bring much of it into organizations anyway; given this reality, the CEO must control carefully what is introduced so as to minimize potential harm or excessive costs.

Utopian skeptic: This CEO believes that IT is primarily harmful in that it undermines other effective managerial processes. It is not merely excessively costly but actually harms organizational effectiveness by encouraging the use of tools, categories of information, and processes of doing work that are less effective than what is currently or potentially possible in terms of other managerial models; he therefore sees his role to be to minimize the harm that IT can do, to undermine its implementaion in any way possible, and to control its costs to the utmost degree.

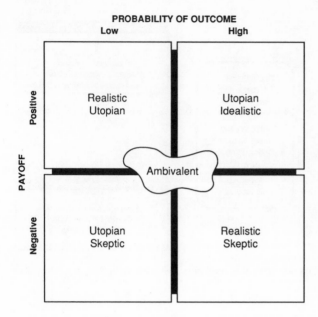

Figure 6.2 CEO assumptions about IT.

each basic category, as shown in Table 6.4 (based on the eighty-four cases analyzed).

In terms of basic assumptions, one can see a degree of realism prevailing. A few CEOs were totally utopian about the potential of IT, but the bulk of them were realistic about the difficulties of changing their organizations. Both of these groups would be expected to exert primarily driving forces in the sense that they would try to unfreeze and change their organizations. The ambivalents and those who saw IT as "merely a tool" clearly were more cautious in their approach to implementation and would thus be expected to be as much on the restraining as driving force side. There were few real skeptics, so one would not expect strong restraining forces from CEOs except in the form of caution about the potential costs of IT.

To give a flavor of the range of responses from utopianism to skepticism, we quote various comments made during the interviews in Table 6.5.

Specific Visions about Information Technology

Many CEOs had a positive vision for IT, but there was great diversity in the nature and strength of that vision. Our interviews were not specifically geared to identifying such

Table 6.4 Number of CEOs holding different assumptions

Type	Payoff	Probability of Occurrence	Number	Percent
Utopian idealist	+	+	17	20
Realistic utopian	+	−	46	55
Ambivalent	±	±	19	23
Realistic skeptic	−	+	2	2
Utopian skeptic	−	−	0	0
Total			84	100

Table 6.5 Sample comments from CEOs

Utopian responses

"IT enables you to decide where you want to be in the industry and how to get there."

"IT makes strategic decisions possible; longer range analysis."

"IT will assist in the design of new products and services."

"IT helps in generating data and performing complex analyses as input to decision making."

"IT is complex and expensive; you can't measure the benefits; it requires more people; but it is the best bargain for the money."

"IT permits real-time understanding of the business."

"IT is necessary for managing a dynamic business."

"IT lets you do things you couldn't otherwise; everything we do in the customer interface area is now done electronically; this is the key to business now and in the future."

"We will continue to use IT in the production areas of the business and in the year 2000 we will have no direct manufacturing jobs."

"New technologies attract talented people to the organiztion."

Skeptical/ambivalent responses

"Computer-generated data come to be treated as if they represent reality and are not checked for accuracy."

"Computer use can become a substitute for thinking."

"Computers are causing people to be lazy; the increasing reliance on the computer is reducing the propensity to think."

"Business becomes too numbers oriented; people look at the trees, not the forest, and miss the global aspects of the problem."

"IT provides too much information."

"I saw the last company I worked for get ruined and damn near broken by their MIS group; they are great at creating solutions to nonproblems."

"I'm not very impressed with the innovations that have come out of the computer and software industries."

"We are able to cost justify equipment, but we really don't know if it makes our people more effective."

"Computers may be used unethically; they move lies faster."

"IT leads to invasion of privacy."

visions, but they could easily be ordered in terms of a basic typology derived from other research on IT (Rockart, 1979; Zuboff, 1988). For this purpose it is useful to distinguish several levels of "impact" of IT on organizations, as outlined in Table 6.6.

The Vision to Automate

Some CEOs in our sample saw the ultimate role of IT to be a way of replacing expensive, unreliable human labor with sophisticated robots, systems, and other IT devices. The promise of IT for them was that it would ultimately save money, improve quality, and thereby make the organization more effective. They tended to look at their organizations from a manufacturing point of view and were preoccupied with cost and/or technological issues.

Such CEOs would tend to be less utopian and more ambivalent or skeptical. The

Table 6.6 CEO visions of the potential impact of IT

The vision to *automate*

The vision to *informate up*

The vision to *informate down*

The vision to *transform*

change agent role that they would be most likely to play is either to disconfirm the present cost structure by insisting on automation or to disconfirm the present use of technology by insisting on technological upgrading. In both cases they would focus more on the primary role of IT in the manufacturing process and would be relatively less sensitive either to the possible role of IT in the process of management or to the impact on the management system of the automation they were advocating.

As has also been pointed out, though this vision has long-range implications technologically and may involve major capital expenditures, it often proves to be shortsighted because the human implications are not carefully thought through and the systems in the end do not work as well as they should because they do not take advantage of operator creativity and innovation on the one hand and operator limitations in learning how to run automated systems on the other (Zuboff, 1988). In other words, the deeper assumption that human behavior can be automated in a complex technological environment may not be valid.

The Vision to "Informate" Up: "Control Utopia"

The term "informate" is taken from Zuboff (1988) and refers to the impact that IT has in making previously concealed parts of a system's processes more visible to people both higher up and lower down in the organization. For the production worker this might mean the ability to manage processes that were previously under the control of management. For managers this usually means the ability to control more precisely all aspects of the process because the information system would provide detailed performance data. For some CEOs, IT could then be the "ultimate management control tool." They assume that by installing the right kind of information system they could be completely informed about every aspect of every operation in their organization. Such information would enable them to pinpoint problems rapidly and set into motion remedial measures.

Such a vision appeals to the control-oriented executive and probably is functionally similar to the automation solution, except that what is being automated here is not the production process but the control process. The human hierarchy is being replaced with an information system. Toward this ultimate goal a number of the CEOs who insisted on installing terminals on their own and their subordinates' desks did so in order to facilitate the introduction of a complete communication network and a common information and control system. They could then determine exactly where deviances occurred and act on them immediately.

Some of the resistance encountered from subordinates was probably motivated by their recognition that once such a system was installed, it could easily be abused by a control-oriented CEO. Abuse here would be micromanagement on the part of the CEO, thereby undermining the rest of the organization, and possibly even the validity of the information fed into the system because of the tendency to falsify input data as a counterreaction to the discomfort and anxiety that the system creates. Unfortunately, the system designers often collude with this type of CEO by reassuring him that they can make the system invulnerable to any kind of falsification.

In terms of our model of change, the type of CEO who is oriented toward control via an upward informating system will be an effective disconfirmer but will have trouble unfreezing the system because he will not be sensitive to the need to provide psychological safety. He may successfully coerce change, but the change will be superficial and unstable because it will not involve any cognitive redefinition on the part of the subordinates who are the change targets.

Such CEOs may be utopian about the potential of IT, but they are expressing an extreme degree of skepticism about human behavior, typical of McGregor's "Theory X" (McGregor, 1960). As McGregor noted, the very existence of the complete information and control system signals to the rest of the organization that top management does not trust the human organization to inform and control itself adequately.

The Vision to Informate Down

"Informating down" is what Zuboff observed to be the consequences of computerizing production processes and creating automated factories. If the production process was to be automated, it first had to be understood as a total system. To teach operators how to manage the new processes, the whole system had to be made transparent to them. Zuboff observed that not everyone could make the transition from manual work and the use of all the senses to primarily mental work that required a complex diagnosis of what was going on by deciphering what a particular configuration of data on a computer screen or a control panel revealed.

For those who could make the transition, the production process was demystified. One consequence was that supervisors no longer had the power that special knowledge or understanding had previously given them. This "knowledge power" was now distributed throughout the work force. For many middle managers this loss of power was a direct threat, but for CEOs looking to create the "factory of the future" this could be an entirely positive vision if they also had a Theory Y set of assumptions about human nature (McGregor, 1960) and were willing to push operational control down in the organization.

In our interviews we could not tell whether the executive advocating this kind of IT solution was genuinely interested in "informating" his organization, or whether he was secretly hoping for lower costs and more centralized control. But at least in their words these CEOs were advocating a much more radical IT use than what was proposed in either of the previous visions.

In any case, such CEOs would be much more sensitive to the issues of creating psychological safety, both for operators who had to drastically change their concept of what their work would be in the future and for middle managers whose role might disappear altogether. They would also realize that changes of this magnitude would not occur without strong external and internal disconfirmation and induction of guilt or anxiety, and thus be forced to consider all of the stages of getting a change process started.

The Vision to Transform

A few CEOs saw IT as the basis for a complete transformation of their organization and industry. They could see how IT would change the organization's fundamental relationship to its suppliers and customers, how the introduction of networking, executive support systems, teleconferencing, and other IT innovations would fundamentally alter the nature of the products, markets, and organizational structure, and how these, in combination, would alter organizational boundaries, interorganizational relationships, and even the management process itself.

The role of hierarchy would change in that distributed information would make local problem solving and lateral information sharing much more feasible, and the role of the executive team in the strategy process would change if modeling and various kinds of decision support tools would make it possible to develop alternatives much more rapidly. In a sense IT would make it possible to be simultaneously more centralized around basic strategy and goals and more decentralized around implementation and control.

Power and authority would shift away from position and status toward knowledge and information, and leadership would become less of a role and more of a "function," that is, more widely distributed as a function of the requirements of the task to be accomplished. More emphasis would fall on groups and teamwork, and boundaries between jobs as well as roles would become more fluid. That, in turn, would require a higher level of professionalization of the work force to deal with higher anxiety levels resulting from role ambiguity (Hirschhorn, 1988).

We encountered a few executives who seemed to be pushing toward this kind of vision, but most of them acknowledged that it would take some time before IT itself would be good enough and cheap enough to make this possible. They correctly foresaw that such transformations would require major cultural change that would take some time and effort to accomplish. Perhaps most troubling to them was the implication that the present work force might not be well enough educated or trained to fulfill the necessary roles in the transformed organization, an issue that is also present in the informated organization.

Such CEOs clearly fell into our utopian idealist category and their behavior in terms of the change model seemed to be oriented toward consistent but careful unfreezing because of their concern that their organizations might not be ready to handle the level of change ultimately required. They were, in this sense, another group who would be sensitive to psychological safety as an issue in the change process.

In summary, the basic assumptions held by the CEO were obviously a critical factor both in terms of how they saw the ultimate potential of IT and how optimistic they felt about the implementation of various IT projects within their organizations. But clearly, their own assumptions were not a sufficient explanation of their behavior. We found in the interview data that a number of other factors operated as powerful driving and restraining forces.

For example, many CEOs felt the technology was not yet good enough or cheap enough to deliver on its potential. These CEOs tended to press their IT community to improve the technology while restraining the organization from "wasting money" on premature solutions. Other CEOs were greatly influenced by the behavior of their competitors, particularly in industries where IT had already proven its potential to provide strategic advantage. CEOs in larger, more diversified companies tended to let their divisions decide on the use of IT and were often reluctant to impose single systems on diverse subcultures, thereby limiting possibilities for standardization or broader systems integration. In many companies CEOs were very sensitive to the lack of readiness of the employees to utilize IT, or they had other financial priorities that made IT investments undesirable.

The factors identified by our CEOs as major influences on their decisions with regard to IT are, of course, interrelated and interactive. The most striking result, therefore, is the diversity of situations we encountered at the level of the CEO. We were seeking the common elements in how CEOs would structure their own behavior as change agents and found, instead, that the multiplicity of technological, industrial, organizational, and personal forces operating made such generalizations tenuous.

CONCLUSION

The change agent roles that these different executives take of course differ with their basic orientation and the situation of their organizations. As noted, all of the CEOs were driven by the state of affairs in their industry. Only a small number had utopian transformation visions that went substantially beyond what other companies in their industry were doing. Those few get singled out as heroic change agents by academics and the media, but the reminder from our data is that they are as yet a distinct minority.

The "bottom line" seems to be that CEOs find themselves in very complex force fields and vary their behavior as change agents accordingly. They feel that the realities of their particular situation in terms of the size, age, structure, and financial condition of their companies, the technological possibilities and limitations, industry benchmarks, employee readiness, and the credibility and skill of their IT management all have to be taken into account in deciding how far and how fast to push the adoption of new IT tools. Many of them believe, therefore, that this complexity calls for the CEO to be an integrative force instead of an IT zealot, though they acknowledge that future generations of CEOs, who will have been educated much more thoroughly in the possibilities of the computer and IT, may be able to take a much more optimistic and proactive stance toward IT.

For the IT skeptic it will be reassuring to realize that there are a good many CEOs out there who are cautious, who have been burned, and who, therefore, are quite realistic about the limitations of today's IT solutions. On the other hand, for the IT utopian it will be very reassuring to know that many of our CEO's do involve themselves actively in IT projects, even if they personally do not use desktop workstations, and many more take IT for granted as a technology and a set of tools that will help their companies in many ways.

Though the focus in this chapter was on IT, it should also be noted in concluding that the CEO change agent roles identified apply to all kinds of organizational change, especially changes of a strategic nature that may require reorganization of work, authority relationships, and management styles. In all organization change and development projects the CEO role should be carefully diagnosed and taken into account, since that role has great power in getting the change process started.

NOTE

1. The interviews were conducted and analyzed by Buzzard (1988), Carey (1988), Donaldson (1987), Glassburn (1987), Harman (1987), Homer (1988), Kelly (1987), Kennedy, (1987), Lasswell (1987), North (1987), Pilger (1987), Shuff (1988), Stewart (1987), and Sutherland (1988).

REFERENCES

Buzzard, S. H. 1988. An Analysis of Factors That Influence Management of Information Technology in Multidivisional Companies. Unpublished masters thesis. Sloan School of Management, MIT.

Carey, D. R. 1988. Information Technology: Attitudes and Implementation. Unpublished masters thesis. Sloan School of Management, MIT.

Dearden, J. 1983. "SMR Forum: Will the Computer Change the Job of Top Management?" *Sloan Management Review* 25, no. 1.

Donaldson, H. M. 1987. Executive Assumptions About Information Technology in the Service Industries. Unpublished masters thesis. Sloan School of Management, MIT.

Festinger, L. 1957. *A Theory of Cognitive Dissonance.* New York: Harper & Row.

Gibson, C. F., and B. B. Jackson. 1987. *The Information Imperative.* Lexington, Mass.: D. C. Heath.

Glassburn, A. R. 1987. A Study of Chief Executive Officer Attitudes Toward the Use of Information Technology in Executive Offices. Unpublished masters thesis. Sloan School of Management, MIT.

Hambrick, D. C., ed. 1988. *The Executive Effect: Concepts and Methods for Studying Top Managers.* Greenwich, Conn.: JAI Press.

Harman, P. E. 1987. Executive Assumptions About Information Technology in the Banking Industry. Unpublished masters thesis. Sloan School of Management, MIT.

Hirschhorn, L. 1988. *The Workplace Within.* Cambridge, Mass.: MIT Press.

Homer, P. B. 1988. A Study of Information Technology Innovation in High Technology Firms. Unpublished masters thesis. Sloan School of Management, MIT.

Keen, P. G. W. 1983. "The On-Line CEO: How One Executive Uses MIS." Unpublished working paper, Microframe, Inc.

Kelly, M. L. 1987. Attitudes and Expectations of Senior Executives About Information Technology Within the Consumer Electronics Industry with Emphasis on Japan. Unpublished masters thesis. Sloan School of Management, MIT.

Kennedy, H. E. 1987. CEO Assumptions Concerning Information Technology in High Technology Firms. Unpublished masters thesis. Sloan School of Management. MIT.

Kotter, J. P. 1982. *The General Managers.* New York: Free Press.

Kraemer, K. L., J. L. King, D. E. Dunkle, and J. P. Lane. 1989. *Managing Information Systems.* San Francisco: Jossey-Bass.

Lasswell, S. W. 1987. Chief Executive Officer Attitudes Concerning Information Technology: A Study of High Technology and Aerospace Companies. Unpublished masters thesis. Sloan School of Management, MIT.

Lewin, K. 1952. "Group Decision and Social Change." In *Readings in Social Psychology,* rev. ed., edited by G. E. Swanson, T. N. Newcomb, and E. L. Hartley. New York: Holt.

Markus, M. L. 1984. *Systems in Organizations.* Boston: Pitman.

McGregor, D. M. 1960. *The Human Side of Enterprise.* New York: McGraw-Hill.

Meyer, N. D., and M. E. Boone. 1987. *The Information Edge.* Agincourt, Ontario: Gage Educational Publishing.

Moore, J. H. 1986. "Senior Executive Computer Use." Stanford Graduate Business School Unpublished working paper.

North, J. B. 1987. Attitudes of Telecommunications Executives About Information Technology. Unpublished masters thesis. Sloan School of Management, MIT.

Pilger, D. R. 1987. Chief Executive Officer Attitudes Toward Information Technology in the Automotive and Manufacturing Industries. Unpublished masters thesis. Sloan School of Management, MIT.

Rockart, J. F. 1979. Chief Executives Define Their Own Data Needs. *Harvard Business Review*, March–April, pp. 81–93.

Rockart, J. F., and D. W. DeLong. 1988. *Executive Support Systems*. Homewood, Ill.: Dow Jones–Irwin.

Rockart, J. F., and M. E. Treacy. 1982. "The CEO Goes On-Line." *Harvard Business Review*, January–February, 82–88.

Schein, E. H. 1961. *Coercive Persuasion*. New York: Norton.

Schein, E. H. 1969. *Process Consultation*. Reading, Mass.: Addison-Wesley.

Schein, E. H. 1972. *Professional Education: Some New Directions*. New York: McGraw-Hill.

Schein, E. H. 1985. *Organizational Culture and Leadership*. San Francisco: Jossey-Bass.

Schein, E. H. 1987. *Process Consultation*, vol. 2. Reading, Mass.: Addison-Wesley.

Schein, E. H. 1988. *Process Consultation*, vol. 1, rev. ed. Reading, Mass.: Addison-Wesley.

Shuff, R. F. 1988. A Model of the Innovation Process in Information Technology. Unpublished masters thesis. Sloan School of Management, MIT.

Stewart, N. S. 1987. Chief Executive Officers: Assumptions About Information Technology in the Insurance Industry. Unpublished masters thesis. Sloan School of Management, MIT.

Sutherland, D. J. 1988. The Attitudes and Management Behaviors of Senior Managers with Respect to Information Technology. Unpublished masters thesis. Sloan School of Management, MIT.

Thomas, A. B. 1988. "Does Leadership Make a Difference in Organizational Performance?" *Administrative Science Quarterly* 33: 388–400.

Zuboff, S. 1988. *In the Age of the Smart Machine*. New York: Basic Books,

COMMENTARY BY DONALD RUNKLE

The one issue that was not discussed in this chapter was the assumption that using information technology (IT) is a very good thing to do. There is very little discussion about whether IT is really worthwhile or not, or if it is really productive. I think that's probably still on the table.

I would say that from GM's (General Motors) standpoint, we have in progress, alive and running, a fascinating test of this paper. Over the last decade we have had a pretty visionary chairman who fundamentally had the idea of an integrated company from an IT standpoint. But he didn't unfreeze the company before he decided to do the second part of it, which was to move and change it. He bought, as you know, a whole IT company, EDS (Electronic Data Systems). He spent a few billion dollars on EDS. There was little discussion about whether the acquisition was a good idea within the organization as a whole. Subsequent to the purchase he asked the company to begin the move toward an integrated company using a lot more IT, and he did that mostly through praising EDS and urging GM people to change. I would have to say that during that process the sparks flew. It has now settled down substantially, EDS has become much more flexible in the whole operation, and I think we are on our way to an integrated IT company.

I went through Professor Schein's typology, and I would have to say that our CEO is a utopian idealist. I think from the vision standpoint he would be in the category "automate," replacing expensive, unreliable people with computer technology.

In hindsight, I think that this chapter would have been a good one to read and heed before we tried to integrate EDS into GM. It would have saved us some time and energy. The CEO should have spent a lot more time unfreezing the company and getting it more interested in proceeding. Clearly you still buy a company the size of EDS in a private manner to keep the prices down, but once it was bought it could have been absorbed as a separate subsidiary and then discussed openly with the organization as a whole to let them know that we needed to move toward more IT in the workplace. I also think it would have been very helpful to articulate what is referred to here as a psychological safety net of sorts, but that was not communicated at all and resulted in a great deal of fear as to what exactly was going on. We had a lot of problems in making it all happen. Also, using what is referred to here as "scanning" would have been helpful.

Roger Smith (the chairman) was not a role model for scanning. He didn't use IT, so the scanning model could have helped us with the unfreezing process. We need to refreeze slowly, too. We are not yet fully unfrozen but are in the process of moving, and I can tell we need to refreeze slowly. My background and experience early in my career have been in this kind of area, and I am very enthusiastic about the capabilities of computers and IT. I would just say that before a company proceeds toward integration too heavily, you first need to simplify and streamline the operations. Do that first, and then document the needs and real requirements as far as what you want for IT, what you want it to do, and then automate what's left. Then book the savings in the beginning of the year, rather than implementing it and seeing what happens, and then booking it later. Put the expected gains in the budget right away.

I thought the model is worthwhile, and I just wish that the chapter had been written in 1983 so we could have read it prior to the EDS acquisition.

7

Strategic Alignment: A Model for Organizational Transformation Through Information Technology

JOHN C. HENDERSON AND N. VENKATRAMAN

As organizational transformation emerges as an important theme among both management scholars and practitioners, it is perhaps a truism that the organizations of the 1990s will be significantly different from those of the last few decades. While several factors have been postulated to influence and propel the organizational transformation process, as the chapters in this book attest, a major force lies in the recent developments and capabilities offered by information technology (IT)—namely, computers and communication technologies. This is mainly due to the acceleration of power and capabilities of these technologies with corresponding improvement in cost–performance ratio in recent years (Scott Morton, 1991). Over the last few years, several different arguments have been offered to highlight the potential of IT to influence competitive characteristics (see, for instance, Keen, 1986; McFarlan, 1984; Parsons, 1983; Porter and Millar, 1985; Rockart and Scott Morton, 1984; Wiseman, 1985) as well as facilitate and shape business transformations, but there is a glaring lack of systematic frameworks to conceptualize the logic, scope, and patterns of organizational transformation that depend on IT. To help address this deficiency, this chapter develops and presents a conceptual model with a set of propositions and management implications.

This chapter is based on a pivotal premise: recently the role of information technology in organizations has shifted beyond its traditional use as backoffice support toward an integral part of the strategy of organizations. Following King (1978), Rockart and Scott Morton (1984), and others, we differentiate among three major roles of IT—administrative, operational, and competitive. The *administrative* role signifies the scope of IT in the automation of accounting and control functions, which is reasonably well understood in the traditional literature on management information systems (see, for instance, Ein-Dor and Segev, 1978; Ives, Hamilton, and Davis, 1980). Indeed, the importance of technology for streamlining the activities of payroll, accounts payable, and accounts receivable is a given, not worth elaborating here. Suffice it to state that this role requires the deployment of an efficient IT platform (including hardware, software, and communication systems) for administration and control and is independent of the strategic management of the organization. The *operational* role is an extension of the first role and is distinguished by the creation and deployment of a technology platform that creates the capability to automate the entire set of business processes as opposed to only the administrative activities. This role requires the deployment of an IT infrastructure that responds to and supports the chosen business strategy (King, 1978; McLean and Soden, 1977).

Following Grant and King (1982), Hax and Majluf (1984), and Hofer and Schendel (1978), strategic management can be viewed in terms of a hierarchy of three levels of strategies: corporate strategy, concerned with the portfolio of and interrelationships among businesses; business strategy, focusing on developing a strategy that maximizes firm-specific comparative advantages to best compete in the marketplace; and functional strategy, reflecting efficient allocation of resources to the particular function. Within this hierarchy, IT strategy is at the functional level, with a charter of efficiently allocating its resources to best support the chosen business strategy. Thus, within these two roles, IT strategy reflects a functional, efficiency orientation (King, 1978).

In contrast, the *competitive* role represents a significant point of departure. Extending beyond the internal, efficiency focus, the capability now exists for organizations to deploy new IT applications that leverage the information and technological attributes to obtain differential sources of competitive advantages in the marketplace (Cash and Konsynski, 1985; Copeland and McKenney, 1988; McFarlan, 1984; Venkatraman and Kambil, 1991). Increased attention is being paid to the potential role of IT to influence structural characteristics of markets (e.g., see Clemons and Row, 1988) as well as shape the basis of competition (see, for instance, Malone, Yates, and Benjamin, 1987; Rotemberg and Saloner, 1991). It is becoming increasingly clear that a limited consideration of the first two roles for IT in modern corporations is suboptimal with potentially dysfunctional consequences.

More important, the emergence of this role has significant implications for organizational transformation. This is because the mere superimposition of powerful IT capabilities on the existing organizational structure and processes is unlikely to yield superior competitive benefits. This is supported by one of the central messages from a recently concluded MIT Research Project, *Management in the 1990s* (Scott Morton, 1991), that successful organizations can be distinguished by their ability to leverage IT capabilities to transform their businesses (structures, processes, and roles) to obtain new and powerful sources of competitive advantages in the marketplace.

Before discussing the competitive role in detail, we note that the existing frameworks are limited in terms of their ability to provide fundamental insights and guidance. The administrative role is supported by frameworks such as Critical Success Factors (Davis, 1979; Rockart, 1979); the operational role is supported by frameworks like Business System Planning (IBM, 1981); and Value Chain Analysis (Porter and Millar, 1985). However, insights for leveraging the competitive role, being sufficiently different from the other two, cannot be obtained from these frameworks.

Several frameworks have been proposed to address the challenge of recognizing the competitive role of IT. These include Parsons's (1983) articulation of different levels of impact of IT in the marketplace; McFarlan's (1984) adaptation of Porter's competitive strategy framework to a context characterized by the deployment of IT applications; Rockart and Scott Morton's (1984) adaptation of Leavitt's (1965) organization theory model; as well as other frameworks rooted in a set of convenient dimensions (e.g., Hammer and Mangurian, 1987; Wiseman, 1985). Based on a general assessment of these frameworks (for a systematic approach to organizing these frameworks, see Earl, 1988), we argue that they are useful for describing and highlighting the emerging interconnection between IT capabilities and organizational actions, but they fail in their lack of articulation of the fundamental logic and rationale for exploiting IT capabilities as well as the complexities of the organizational transformation required to leverage technological capabilities. More specifically, they fail to simultaneously address the business (external) and organizational (internal) requirements of transformation based on and shaped by new and powerful IT capabilities. This chapter aims to address the need by offering a model to link organizational transformation and the exploitation of IT capabilities in its competitive role.

PROPOSED STRATEGIC ALIGNMENT MODEL

The proposed model is depicted in Figure 7.1. It is based on four key domains of strategic choice: business strategy; organizational infrastructure and processes; IT strategy; and IT infrastructure and processes. We briefly describe each domain and subsequently articulate the distinctive features of the model.

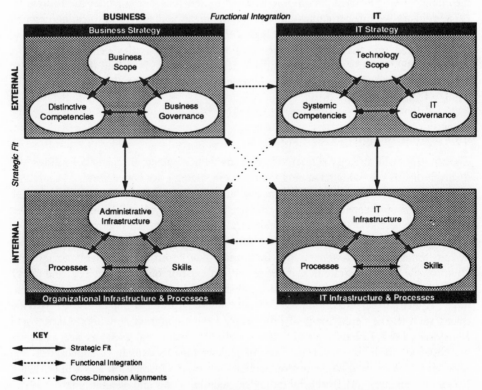

Figure 7.1 The proposed strategic alignment model.

Business Strategy

If we view organizational transformation from a "voluntaristic" as opposed to a "deterministic" perspective (Astley and Van de Ven, 1983; Miles and Snow, 1978), then business strategy is a central concept. However, the concept of strategy is overarching (Andrews, 1980; Hax and Majluf, 1984) and covers a broad terrain with multiple meanings, definitions, and conceptualizations (Venkatraman, 1989b; Venkatraman and Grant, 1986). Nevertheless, most discussions deal with three central questions: (1) business scope—choices pertaining to product-market offerings (Hofer and Schendel, 1978); (2) distinctive competencies—those attributes of strategy (e.g., pricing, quality, value-added service, superior distribution channels) that contribute to a distinctive comparative advantage over other competitors (Porter, 1980; Snow and Hrebiniak, 1980); and (3) business governance—choices of structural mechanisms to organize the business operations (e.g., strategic alliances, joint ventures, and licensing) that recognizes the continuum between markets and hierarchy (Jarillo, 1985; Williamson, 1985).

Organizational Infrastructure and Processes

The relevance of including organizational infrastructure and processes need not be extensively justified in the context of organizational transformation. However, given the challenge to specify a parsimonious set of dimensions, we consider the following: (1) administrative infrastructure—including organizational structure, roles, and reporting relationships (Galbraith, 1977); (2) processes—the articulation of work flows and the associated information flows for carrying out key activities (Thompson, 1967; Zuboff, 1988); and (3) skills—the capabilities of the individuals and the organization to execute the key tasks that support a business strategy (Fombrun, Tichy, and Devanna, 1984; Scott Morton, 1991).

Information Technology Strategy

The concept of IT strategy is relatively new and hence open to differing definitions and assumptions. By drawing an analogy to business strategy, we conceptualize IT strategy in terms of three dimensions: (1) information technology scope—the types and range of IT systems and capabilities (e.g., electronic imaging systems, local and wide-area networks, expert systems, robotics) potentially available to the organization; (2) systemic competencies—those distinctive attributes of IT competencies (e.g., higher system reliability, interconnectivity, flexibility) that contribute positively to the creation of new business strategies or better support existing business strategy; and (3) IT governance—choices of structural mechanisms (e.g., joint ventures, long-term contracts, equity partnerships, joint R&D) to obtain the required IT capabilities, involving issues such as the deployment of proprietary versus common networks (Barrett and Konsynski, 1982; Rotemberg and Saloner, 1991; Venkatraman, 1991) as well as strategic choices pertaining to development of partnerships to exploit IT capabilities and services (Henderson, 1990; Johnston and Lawrence, 1988; Johnston and Vitale, 1988; Koh and Venkatraman, 1991), including outsourcing (Loh and Venkatraman, 1991).

Information Technology Infrastructure and Processes

Analogous to organization infrastructure and processes, this domain is defined in terms of three dimensions: (1) architecture—choices pertaining to applications, data, and technology configurations (see, for instance, Parker, Benson, and Trainor, 1988; Zachman, 1986); (2) processes—the work processes central to the operations of the IT infrastructure, including processes for systems development and maintenance as well as monitoring and control systems (Bostom and Heinen, 1977; Henderson, Rockart, and Sifonis, 1987; Janson and Smith, 1985; Marcus and Robey, 1988; Martin, 1982a,b; Raghunathan and King, 1988; Rockart and Short, 1989); and (3) skills—choices pertaining to the knowledge and capabilities required to effectively manage the IT infrastructure within the organization (Martin, 1982a,b; Mumford, 1981; Strassman, 1985).

DISTINCTIVE FEATURES OF THE MODEL

Before proceeding further, it is useful to enumerate the distinctive features of the proposed strategic alignment model. Specifically, we highlight two features: (1) IT strategy as distinct from IT infrastructure and processes; and (2) the concept of strategic alignment as distinct from bivariate fit (relationships involving any two domains discussed earlier) and cross-domain alignment (relationships involving three domains). We conclude with a discussion of strategic alignment as a central element of organizational transformation.

Distinguishing IT Strategy from
IT Infrastructure and Processes

The first feature relates to the distinction between IT strategy and IT infrastructure and processes, which is critical given the general lack of consensus on what constitutes IT strategy. Thus we build from the literature on business strategy, where there is a clear distinction between *external alignment*—positioning the business in the external product-market space—and *internal arrangement*—design of organizational structure, processes, and systems (see, for instance, Snow and Miles, 1983). Within the IT arena, given the historical predisposition to view it as a functional strategy, such a distinction had been neither made nor considered necessary. However, as we consider the potential that exists to leverage emerging IT capabilities to redefine market structure characteristics as well as reorient the attributes of competitive success, the limitation of a functional view is apparent.

Indeed, the hierarchical view of the interrelationship between business and functional strategies is increasingly being questioned, given the prevalent feeling that the subordination of functional strategies to business strategy may be too restrictive to exploit potential sources of competitive advantage that lie at the functional level. Accordingly, functions are being considered as sources of competitive, firm-specific advantage. Key emerging themes include (1) strategic marketing management, recognizing the exploitation of sources of marketing advantages at the business strategy level (e.g., Wind and Robertson, 1983); (2) strategic human resource management, highlighting the explicit consideration of human resource profiles and capabilities in the formulation and implementation of strategies (e.g., Fombrun, Tichy, and Devanna, 1985); and (3) notions of manufacturing as a competitive weapon, illustrating the potential sources of advantages that lie within the production and manufacturing function (e.g., Wheelright, 1984) as well as exploring the linkage between finance and corporate strategy (Myers, 1984). A common theme is the recognition of an external marketplace, that is, a place where these function-specific advantages could be leveraged, and an internal organizational function, where the function activities should be managed efficiently. Following this tradition, we distinguish in the strategic alignment model IT strategy from IT infrastructure and processes. Four different business examples are invoked to illustrate the distinction.

The first example is American Express's decision to commit a high level of resources to its electronic imaging technology platform as a key capability to provide value-added services (by providing copies of receipts with the monthly statements) as a means of differentiating its travel-related services. This is related to its IT scope as well as systemic capabilities, which are conceptually different from its internal management of its data centers or its global telecommunications network. Both are necessary for efficient leveraging of IT capabilities, but one falls within the purview of external domain, whereas the other is concerned with internal operations.

Second, Eastman Kodak's decision to outsource its data center operations to IBM is related to critical make-versus-buy choices (IT governance) in the IT marketplace. This is logically distinguished from Kodak's decision to centralize or decentralize systems development activities across its different business units.

The third example is provided by McGraw-Hill's custom publishing strategy in its textbook business. This recently developed strategy can offer custom textbooks as an alternative to standard textbooks through a sophisticated electronic imaging technology infrastructure produced in a three-way joint venture with Eastman Kodak and RR Donnelley & Sons. This IT-based business capability, which reflects an IT strategy that shapes and supports McGraw-Hill's business strategy, is to be conceptually distinguished from its internal IT infrastructure and operational systems.

Finally, Baxter Healthcare—known for its Analytical Systems Automated Purchasing (ASAP)—recently announced the formation of a joint venture with IBM for providing software, hardware, and information-based services to hospitals, thus reflecting its IT governance posture of collaboration, which is to be distinguished from its internal management of the information systems function.

Collectively, these four business examples illustrate the importance of the three dimensions of IT strategy delineated in Figure 7.1. They also argue for the separation of IT strategy from internal management of the information systems (IS) function.

Differentiating Strategic Alignment from Bivariate Fit and Cross-Domain Alignment

The proposed strategic alignment model is more than the articulation of the underlying axes, the four domains, and their constituent dimensions. It derives its value from the different types of relationships among the four domains. Specifically, three dominant types of relationships can be delineated in the model depicted in Figure 7.1. These are termed bivariate fit, cross-domain alignment, and strategic alignment.

Bivariate Fit

The simplest type of relationship is a bivariate one, linking two domains, either horizontally or vertically. The bivariate relationship between business strategy and organization infrastructure and processes refers to the classic strategy–structure fit that has been a dominant theme in organizational strategy research (Chandler, 1962; for an overview, see Venkatraman and Camillus, 1984). Correspondingly, we specify a bivariate relationship between IT strategy and IT infrastructure and processes in this model, highlighting the need to interconnect an organization's external positioning in the IT marketplace with its approach to managing the IS function in its organizational context. These two relationships represent the classic strategy formulation and implementation perspectives for the two strategies considered here: business strategy and IT strategy.

In contrast, the other two bivariate relationships link the domains horizontally. The links between business strategy and IT strategy (i.e., articulation of the required IT scope, development of systemic competencies as well as IT governance mechanisms) reflects the capability to leverage IT strategy to both shape and support business strategy. This is particularly relevant for the competitive role of the IT function discussed earlier. Correspondingly, the link between organizational infrastructure and processes and IT infrastructure and processes reflects the need to ensure internal coherence between the organizational requirements and expectations on the one hand and the delivery capability within the IS function on the other hand—which is consistent with the notion of viewing IS as a business within a business (Cash, McFarlan, and McKenney, 1988).

Benefits and Limitations of Bivariate Fit

A major benefit of the bivariate fit perspective lies in its simplification of the relevant domain, invoking ceteris paribus conditions. If, for instance, the organizational and IS infrastructures can be reconfigured easily, then a bivariate interconnection between business and IT strategies could suffice. However, most instances of organizational transformation require adaptation across a complex set of multiple domains, thus limiting the value of bivariate perspectives. An obvious approach lies in the consideration of multiple bivariate relationships, which could lead to an error of "logical typing" or "reductionism" (Bateson, 1979; Venkatraman, 1989a).

Indeed, a major area of controversy in the literature on organizations relates to the distinction between bivariate relationships among a narrow set of variables and multivariate, holistic relationships among a set of variables representing an organizational system (McKelvey, 1975; Miller and Friesen, 1984; see also Alexander, 1968). The main controversy is that if one were to decompose the system into a set of bivariate relationships, there exists a serious possibility of internal logical inconsistencies (or mutually conflicting directions) among multiple pairwise contingencies. As Child asked: "What happens when a configuration of different contingencies is found, each having distinctive implications for organizational design?" (1975, p. 175). Extending this to the present context of strategic IT management, the limitation lies in considerations of external perspectives only (via business and IT strategies without any regard for the internal considerations) or internal perspectives only (via integrating the IS functions and activities within the overall organizational infrastructure). Alternatively, the bivariate fit could involve considerations of business and IT perspectives separately, which have been argued to be dysfunctional (see, for instance, King, 1978; McLean and Soden, 1977; Pyburn, 1983). This calls for the recognition of mutivariate relationships or, more precisely, cross-domain relationships discussed next.

Cross-Domain Alignment

The first type of mutidomain relationship involves three domains, linked sequentially. This can be conceptualized as a triangle overlaid on the model seen in Figure 7.1. Although eight combinations of cross-domain alignments are possible, we argue that four are particularly important and managerially relevant for our discussion here. As seen in Table 7.1, these are labeled strategy implementation, technology exploitation, technology leverage, and technology implementation.

Strategy implementation, as depicted in Table 7.1, is a cross-domain perspective that involves the assessment of the implications of implementing the chosen business strategy by appropriate organizational infrastructure and management processes as well as the design and development of the required internal IT infrastructure and processes. This is, perhaps, the most common and widely understood cross-domain perspective as it corresponds to the classic, hierarchical view of strategic management (see, for instance, the three-level hierarchy in Hax and Majluf, 1984). Given its widespread acceptance, it is not surprising that several different analytical methodologies are available to operationalize this perspective, where the more popular approaches include critical success factors (Rockart, 1979), business systems planning (IBM, 1981), and enterprise modeling (Martin, 1982a,b).

Technology exploitation, as seen in Table 7.1, reflects the potential of IT strategy to influence key dimensions of business strategy. Within the competitive role for IT, this perspective is concerned with the exploitation of emerging IT capabilities to affect new products and services (i.e., business scope) and to influence the key attributes of

Table 7.1 Four dominant perspectives on IT planning

Label	Cross-Domain Perspective[a]	Common Domain Anchor	IT Planning Method Example
Technology exploitation	← * ↓	Technology strategy	Opportunity identification (Sharpe, 1989) Value chain analysis (Porter and Millar, 1985)
Technology leverage	* → ↓	Business strategy	G/CUE (Gartner Group, 1989)
Strategy implementation	* ↓ →	Business strategy	CSF (Rockart, 1979) Enterprise modeling (Martin, 1982b)
Technology implementation	* ← ↓	Technology strategy	Service-level contracting (Leitheiser and Wetherbe, 1986)

[a]Asterisk (*) = domain anchor.

strategy (distinctive competencies) as well as develop new forms of relationships (i.e., business governance). Unlike the previous perspective, which considers business strategy as given (or a constraint for organizational transformation), this perspective allows the modification of business strategy by emerging IT capabilities. Beginning with the three dimensions of IT strategy, this perspective seeks to identify the best set of strategic options for business strategy and the corresponding set of decisions pertaining to organizational infrastructure and processes.

Key examples of the technology exploitation perspective include the exploitation by Baxter Healthcare (previously American Hospital Supply Corporation) through its proprietary ASAP electronic order-entry system to deliver superior value-added service to its hospital customers and the consequent implications for redesigning the internal organizational processes (see, for instance, Venkatraman and Short, 1990); the attempt by Federal Express to create a new standard for overnight delivery through its COSMOS/PULSAR system and the corresponding implications for redesigning its internal processes; and the ability of American Express's IDS division to leverage its IT infrastructure to develop capabilities for electronically filing income tax returns as well as leveraging the information for tailoring its financial products to individual needs (Venkatraman and Kambil, 1991).

Thus although much of the current excitement about IT in its competitive role lies in the technology exploitation perspective, the discussion has been at the level of the bivariate fit between IT strategy and business strategy (see, for instance, McFarlan, 1984; Wiseman, 1985). We argue that any consideration of the attractiveness of the emerging IT capabilities without corresponding attention to the redesign of internal operations is seriously limited with negative consequences for organizational transformation. This is because performance is clearly a function of both formulation and implementation of strategies, and myopic attention to any one at the expense of another could obscure the best possible mode for organizational transformation.

Technology leverage, as seen in Table 7.1, is a cross-domain perspective that involves the assessment of the implications of implementing the chosen business strategy through appropriate IT strategy and the articulation of the required IS functional infrastructure and systemic processes. The underlying rationale is that business strategy is best executed by leveraging the emerging technological capabilities rather than through the design of an efficient internal organization. For example: USAA, a leading U.S. insurance company, decided that the best strategic option involved the development of a superior document-handling system based on state-of-the-art electronic imaging technology. This was accomplished through a joint development venture with a key vendor, involving fundamental changes to the internal IT infrastructure: data, applications, and configurations.

Another example is American Express Travel Related Services, whose business strategy anchored on two technology-based competencies: quick approval of purchases and providing copies of receipts to the cardholders. The approval process on a charge card (i.e., without any preset spending limit) typically has a longer lead time than a corresponding transaction involving competitors' credit cards (with a preset spending limit). It was imperative that American Express at least match the response time of the leading competitors to avoid losing cardholders to an alternative, faster transacting card. This business strategy required a systemic competence involving expert systems (Authorizer's Assistant) as well as corresponding changes in the internal IS organization for developing, maintaining, and controlling the systems. The second component, ECCB (Enhanced Country Club Billing), refers to American Express's business competence of providing copies of all charge slips with the monthly statement. Although cardholders expressed satisfaction with this service, the cost of maintaining and distributing the slips was becoming prohibitive when the traditional mode was used. However, an optical scanning, storage, and laser printing system allowed the delivery of the same level of service more efficiently.

In terms of the proposed strategic alignment model, these examples highlight the impact of business strategy (distinctive competence) on IT strategy (IS governance and systemic competencies, respectively) and the corresponding implications for IS infrastructure and processes (IS architectures). Again, the limitations of a bivariate fit perspective are apparent. Either a formulation view (e.g., the impact of business scope on IT scope or systemic competencies) or an implementation view (i.e., the implications of systemic competencies or new IT governance for internal IS operations) is limited when viewed in terms of this model. Some emerging analytical perspectives are beginning to reflect technology leverage. As an example, Gartner's G/CUE (Gartner Group, 1989) examines an organization's business strategy and develops implications for IT strategy with respect to key trends in the IT markets via technology scanning scenarios; it also identifies the implications for migrating from the current IT infrastructure to the desired state.

Technology implementation, as depicted in Figure 7.1, is concerned with the strategic fit between the external articulation of IT strategy and the internal implementation of the IT infrastructure and processes with corresponding impact on the overall organizational infrastructure and processes. In this perspective, the role of business strategy is minimal and indirect and is best viewed as providing the necessary administrative support for the internal organization. This perspective is often viewed as necessary (but not sufficient) to ensure the effective use of IT resources and response to the growing and fast-changing demands of the end-user population. Analytical methodologies even partially reflecting this perspective require a systematic analysis of the IT markets as well as possible service contracting approaches. Examples of analytical methods include end-user need surveying (Alloway and Quillard, 1983), service-level contracting (Leitheiser and Wetherbe, 1986), and architectural planning (Zachman, 1986).

By way of summarizing the discussion on four cross-domain perspectives, we develop the following propositions:

P1: The effectiveness of strategic IT management will be significantly greater for any cross-domain perspective than any bivariate fit relationships.

P2: On average, the four cross-domain perspectives for strategic IT management will be equally effective.

The rationale for the first proposition is derived from the preceding discussion on the limitations of bivariate relationships in a complex organizational system and the need to integrate across external and internal domains as well as across business and technology domains. The rationale for the second proposition is based on the principle of equifinality, that is, multiple equally effective approaches to exploiting technology for organizational transformation, where the universal superiority of one approach over another cannot be a priori argued.

Further, from Figure 7.1 and Table 7.1, it is clear that the four perspectives discussed reflect a top-down orientation, where either business strategy or IT strategy directs the subsequent internal (organizational) considerations. As recognized earlier, it is entirely conceivable to consider corresponding bottom-up orientations. For example, the organization infrastructure could serve as a domain anchor for a process that considers the impact of organizational capabilities on business strategy and the subsequent implications for IT strategy. Such perspectives would signal the recognition of the current organizational infrastructure or IT infrastructure as the relevant starting point for deriving implications for the external strategic choices. Thus although the top-down orientations reflect the preference of strategic managers as well as the rational, analytic approach as adopted here, it is important to recognize that the proposed strategic alignment model does accommodate the possible existence of internally consistent bottom-up analysis of cross-domain relationships. In the interest of space and given the relatively limited prior attention to these perspectives, these are not discussed here.

Strategic Alignment

The final type of relationship in the proposed model is strategic alignment. It involves simultaneous or concurrent attention to all four domains and can be conceptualized in its weak and strong forms. In its weak form, it can be conceptualized in terms of a single-loop transformation process across the four domains; in its strong form, it should be viewed as a double-loop transformation process. The notion of a loop requires the specification of a starting point as well as a particular direction of transformation, and hence the distinction between a single-loop and a double-loop process (see Argyris, 1977, 1982). The former accommodates only one single direction of transformation, whereas the latter recognizes the centrality of both possible directions. The logic underlying strategic alignment is elaborated in this section by invoking two theoretical concepts, completeness and validity.

Completeness is a central concept of strategic alignment because it is clear that lack of considerations of any one of the four domains will leave unrecognized one domain and the consequent relationships. As discussed previously, each of the four dominant cross-domain perspectives does not recognize (i.e., takes as given and fixed) one of the four domains. For instance, technology exploitation (Table 7.1) does not recognize critical issues pertaining to IT infrastructure, and is therefore incomplete. Given the critical interplay among the four domains, we argue for the importance of completeness or, more formally, single-loop transformational process.

Validity refers to the degree of attention needed to explicitly overcome the possibility of bias via unrecognized or hidden frames of reference. A major concern raised by Churchman (1971), Mason and Mitroff (1981), and Weick (1979) within the context of a decision-making process relates to the potential threat to validity of decisions introduced by the existence of a domain anchor or a fixed-reference frame that remains unchallenged (for a discussion within the IS context, see Henderson and Sifonis, 1988). Following Mason and Mitroff (1981) and Argyris (1977, 1982), we call for an analytical method that explicitly challenges the assumption of a given domain anchor. More formally, the analytical method should incorporate a double-loop transformational process.

Figure 7.2 schematically represents the different types of relationships discussed here, excluding bivariate fit, which was argued to be myopic and dysfunctional.

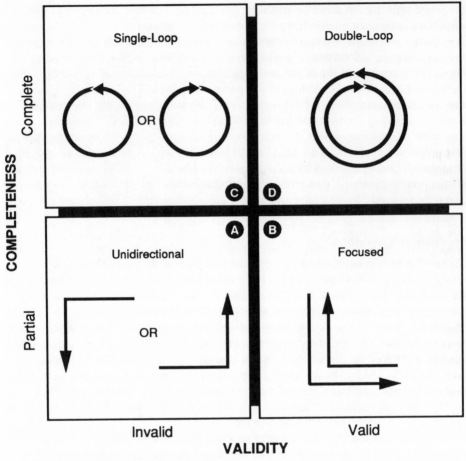

Figure 7.2   Strategic IT management effectiveness.

Specifically, two types of cross-domain perspectives exist, unidirectional and focused. The distinction is that the latter recognizes the potential sources of invalidity (or biases) and provides a correction mechanism in the pairing of the cross-domain perspectives. Extending beyond cross-domain perspectives, two forms of strategic alignment can be specified, the weak form represented as single-loop and the strong form specified in terms of the double-loop process. Thus we develop the following proposition:

P3: The effectiveness of strategic IT management is significantly greater for a complete process than for any type of cross-domain alignments, under ceteris paribus conditions.

We argue that much of the failure to translate the available opportunities to leverage IT for superior organizational performance lies in the incompleteness of the process described here. In other words, although adequate attention may be given to the four domains, the process as depicted in Figure 7.2 may not be completed. As an illustration, in our field research, we encountered a strategic IT management process that paid due attention to all the four domains represented in our strategic alignment model (Figure 7.1) but still was considered ineffective by the managers. Detailed interviews and further analysis of their process indicated that the first step reflected technology exploitation and the second strategy implementation. Both analytical steps were supported by well-known analytical methodologies. However, as shown in Table 7.1, such a process does not address the relationship between IT strategy and IT infrastructure and processes. In other words, while the relationship between business strategy and organizational infrastructure and processes was assessed twice, the process did not evaluate the feasibility of translating IT strategy into appropriate systems and processes within the IS function. Indeed, migration problems across different generations of systems emerged as a major contributor to the project's failure. More formally, we term this an incomplete process, hence weaker than a process that considers consistent cross-domain perspectives.

Other propositions derived from Figure 7.2 are as follows:

P4: On average, the unidirectional perspective is the least effective process for strategic IT management.

The rationale for this proposition is based on the fact that this perspective reflects neither completeness nor validity. In other words, it carries the risks associated with incompleteness as well as the failure to challenge the domain anchor. In the absence of both critical requirements of strategic IT management, it is straightforward to argue that this is least effective.

P5: On average, single-loop (i.e., complete but invalid) and focused (incomplete but valid) processes will be equally effective and superior to unidirectional process for strategic IT management.

Our rationale for this proposition rests on the importance of completeness and validity in addressing strategic IT issues. Although both forms of strategic IT processes are currently used (Boynton and Zmud, 1987; Rockart, 1979), there is a lack of prior theory on the relative importance of completeness versus validity. Thus we argue that the single-loop and focused processes are superior to a unidirectional process, but we refrain from any further delineation of the relative effectiveness of these two approaches.

P6: On average, double-loop (i.e., complete but valid) and focused (incomplete but valid) processes will be equally effective and superior to unidirectional process for strategic IT management.

Essentially, this proposition argues that a complete and valid process will be the most effective approach to strategic IT management. Such an approach not only addresses all the four relevant domains but also seeks to challenge the assumptions inherent in the domain anchors. However, it has a major limitation in terms of high levels of resources—both time and costs, which need to be recognized and managed depending on the specific contingencies faced by the organization.

STRATEGIC ALIGNMENT AS AN ELEMENT OF
ORGANIZATIONAL TRANSFORMATION

This chapter developed a model of organizational transformation that specifically addresses the requirements of leveraging the emerging developments in information technologies. This model is based on the need to achieve alignment across internal and external domains as well as functional integration across business and IT areas. The value of the model is argued with propositions for research and practice. Whereas this chapter provides some support for the conceptual validity of the model, the empirical validity leading to the confirmation or falsification of the propositions requires systematic field research. We are in the midst of operationalizing the key constructs and collecting multiperiod data to test the propositions offered here.

Over two decades ago, Thompson noted, "Survival rests on the co-alignment of technology and task environment with a viable domain, and of organizational design and structure appropriate to that domain" (1967, p. 147). These observations are equally valid today and apply well to the present context of exploiting IT capabilities for organization design. Our position is that strategic alignment—especially between business and IT strategies across external and internal domains—is an important element of the larger organizational transformation process. Specifically, we discuss the usefulness of the model along three lines: (1) as a descriptive model; (2) as a prescriptive model; and (3) as a dynamic model.

Strategic Alignment as a Descriptive Model

At a first level, the proposed strategic alignment model can be viewed as a descriptive model of organizational transformation. Specifically, it can be used to identify the key factors to be considered (i.e., the four domains and the twelve constituent dimensions seen in Figure 7.1) as well as the alternative directionality of transformation (i.e., the different cross-domain perspectives seen in Table 7.1). The power of the model lies in (1) the parsimonious delineation of the dimensions and (2) the conceptual separation of IT strategy from the internal IT infrastructure and processes. From a research point of view, this model can be used to describe and categorize the emerging examples of exploiting IT as a lever for business transformation. From a management decision-making point of view, this model serves the purpose of identifying the different alternatives to leverage IT for business transformations. We are aware of several organizations adopting this as the central model in their strategic management process, where IT plays a critical role in business transformation.

Strategic Alignment as a Prescriptive Model

At a second level, the proposed model can be viewed as prescribing certain alternatives and approaches. Prescriptive frameworks derive their logic and rationale from underlying theoretical arguments and/or empirical results. Although there is preliminary theoretical support for some of the cross-domain perspectives, we do not yet see it as a prescriptive model until we test these propositions with empirical data. This is because we are in agreement with Mintzberg, who noted, "There has been a tendency to prescribe prematurely in management policy—to tell how it should be done without studying how it is done and why. . . . Prescriptions become useful only when . . . grounded in sophisticated description" (1977, pp. 91–92). We believe that the topic of strategic management of IT is in a similar position—with excessive prescription based on isolated cases, which is counterproductive for both theory and practice. We are now in the midst of accumulating a set of empirical observations using this conceptual model to understand the patterns of realizing value from IT investments with the ultimate aim of developing this into a prescriptive model.

Strategic Alignment as a Dynamic Model

Implicit in the discussions throughout is that strategic alignment is a dynamic concept, best viewed as "shooting at a moving target." One of the managers interviewed in connection with the research project noted that this model is best viewed as a "journey and not as an event." This is analogous to Miles and Snow's argument that the organizational adaptive cycle—which provides a means of conceptualizing the major elements of adaptation and of visualizing the relationships among them—is a central concept of strategic management (1978, p. 27). It is also consistent with Thompson, who noted that alignment is

> not a simple combination of static components. Each of the elements involved in the [co-]alignment has its own dynamics [and] behaves at its own rate, governed by the forces external to the organization.
> . . . if the elements necessary to the co-alignment are in part influenced by powerful forces in the organization's environment, then organization survival requires *adaptive* as well as *directive* action in those areas where the organization maintains discretion. . . . As environments change, the administrative process must deal not just with which domain, but how and how fast to change the design, structure, or technology of the organization. (1967, pp. 147–148; emphasis in original)

Accordingly, we view the strategic alignment model as a dynamic model of strategic IT management requiring the organization to delineate the areas where it should maintain discretion (involving both the business and IT domains) as well as identify the approaches for transforming the internal organization structures and processes. However, we recognize that a dynamic perspective does not imply the need to manipulate and adapt all dimensions at all times, nor is it predictable in terms of specific trigger points (Child, 1975; Miles and Snow, 1978; Thompson, 1967). Indeed, the key strategic IT management challenge lies in the identification of those strategic dimensions that require modification under different contingencies for enhancing organizational performance. It is our hope that our detailed research project will offer some normative guidelines for recognizing and responding to critical contingencies.

Thus our view of business transformation explicitly recognizes the organization at the nexus of key streams of actions involving a complex set of variables—where the streams are dynamic in scope, moving in different directions at different speeds. We believe that the challenge of organizational transformation is best conceptualized as a dynamic strategic alignment process with particular considerations to those strategic components that matter at that point in time, and our argument has been that IT occupies that role at present and in the foreseeable future. We hope this chapter has provided a parsimonious model to conceptualize and manage one area of complexity inherent in managing today's organizations.

ACKNOWLEDGMENTS

The authors would like to acknowledge the contributions to this research made by Christine Bullen, Gary Getson, Charles Gold, Jim Sharpe, Cesar Toscano, and other individuals who served on our academic and industry advisory panels. This research was funded by the IBM Advanced Business Institute.

REFERENCES

Alexander, C. 1968. *Notes on the Synthesis of Form*. Cambridge, Mass: Harvard University Press.

Alloway, R. M., and J. A. Quillard. 1983. "User Managers' Systems Needs." *MIS Quarterly* 7, no. 2: 27–41.

Andrews, K. R. 1980. *The Concept of Corporate Strategy*, rev. ed. Homewood, Ill.: Richard D. Irwin.

Argyris, C. 1977. "Double Loop Learning in Organizations." *Harvard Business Review*, 55, no. 5: 115–125.

Argyris, C. 1982. "Organizational Learning and Management Information Systems." *Data Base* 13, no. 2, 3: 3–11.

Astley, W. G., and A. Van de Ven. 1983. "Central Perspectives in Organization Theory." *Administrative Science Quarterly* 28: 245–273.

Barrett, S., and B. Konsynski. 1982. "Inter-Organization Information Sharing Systems." *MIS Quarterly* (special issue, December): 93–105.

Bateson, G. 1979. *Mind and Nature*. New York: E. P. Dutton.

Benjamin, R. I., J. F. Rockart, M. S. Scott Morton, and J. Wyman. 1984. "Information Technology: A Strategic Opportunity." *Sloan Management Review* 25, no. 3: 3–10.

Bostom, R. P., and J. S. Heinen. 1977. "MIS Problems and Failures: A Socio-Technical Perspective, Parts I and II." *MIS Quarterly* 1, no. 3: 17–32; no. 4: 11–28.

Boynton, A. C., and R. W. Zmud. 1987. "Information Technology Planning in the 1990s: Directions for Research and Practice." *MIS Quarterly*, 11, no. 1: 61–69.

Cash, J. I., F. W. McFarlan, J. I. McKenney, and M. R. Vitale. 1988. *Corporate Information Systems Management: Text and Cases*. Homewood, Ill: Irwin.

Cash, J. I., and B. Konsynski. 1985. "IS Redraws Competitive Boundaries." *Harvard Business Review* 63, no. 2: 134–142.

Chandler, A. D. 1962. *Strategy and Structure: Chapters in the History of American Enterprise*. Cambridge, Mass.: MIT Press.

Child, J. 1975. "Managerial and Organization Factors Associated with Company Performance—Part II, A Contingency Analysis." *Journal of Management Studies* 12: 12–27.

Churchman, C. West. 1971. *The Design of Inquiring Systems: Basic Concepts of Systems and Organization*. New York: Basic Books.

Clemons, E. K., and M. Row. 1988. "McKesson Drug Company: Case Study of a Strategic Information System." *Journal of Management Information Systems* 5, no. 1: 37–50.

Copeland, D. G., and J. L. McKenney. 1988. "Airline Reservations Systems: Lessons from History." *MIS Quarterly* 12: 353–370.

Daft, R. L., and K. E. Weick. 1984. "Toward Model Organizations as Interpretive Systems." *Academy of Management Review* 9: 284–295.

Davis, G. B. 1979. "Comments on the Critical Success Factors Method for Obtaining Management Information Requirements in Article by John F. Rockart." *MIS Quarterly* 3, no. 3: 57–58.

Davis, G. B. 1982. "Strategies for Information Requirements Determination." *IBM Systems Journal* 21: 4–30.

Dickson, G. W., R. L. Leitheiser, J. C. Wetherbe, and M. Niechis. 1984. "Key Information Systems Issues for the 1980's." *MIS Quarterly* 8, no. 3: 135–159.

Earl, Michael, ed. 1988. *Information Management: The Strategic Dimension*. Oxford: Clarendon Press.

Ein-Dor, P., and E. Segev. 1978. "Strategic Planning for Management Information Systems." *Management Science* 24: 1631–1641.

Fombrun, C. J., N. M. Tichy, and M. A. Devanna. 1984. *Strategic Human Resource Management*. New York: Wiley.

Galbraith, J. R. 1974. "Organization Design: An Information Processing Perspective." *Interfaces*, 4, no. 5: 28–36.

Galbraith, J. 1977. *Organization Design*. Reading, Mass.: Addison-Wesley.

Gartner Group. 1989. G/Customer User Evaluation. Stamford, Conn.

Grant, J. H., and W. R. King. 1982. *The Logic of Strategic Planning*. Boston: Little, Brown.

Hammer, M., and G. E. Mangurian. 1987. "The Changing Value of Communications Technology." *Sloan Management Review* 28, no. 2: 65–71.

Hax, A. C., and N. S. Majluf. 1984. *Strategic Management: An Integrative Perspective*. Englewood Cliffs, N.J.: Prentice-Hall.

Henderson, J. C. 1990. "Plugging into Strategic Partnerships: The Critical IS Connection." *Sloan Management Review* 31: 3, 7–18.

Henderson, J. C., J. F. Rockart, and J. G. Sifonis. 1987. "Integrating Management Support Systems into Strategic Information Systems, Planning." *Journal of Management Information Systems* 4, no. 1: 5–23.

Henderson, J. C., and J. G. Sifonis. 1988. "The Value of Strategic IS Planning: Understanding Consistency, Validity, and IS Markets." *MIS Quarterly* 12: 187–200.

Hofer, C. W., and D. E. Schendel. 1978. *Strategy Formulation: Analytical Concepts*. St. Paul: West Publishing Company.

IBM. 1981. *Information Systems Planning Guide, Business Systems Planning*, 3rd ed. Report No. GE20-0527-2, White Plains, N.Y.

Ives, B., and G. P. Learmonth. 1984. "The Information System as a Competitive Weapon." *Communications of the ACM* 27: 1193–1201.

Ives, B., S. Hamilton, and G. B. Davis. 1980. "A Framework for Research in Computer Based Management Information Systems." *Management Science* 26, no. 4: 910–934.

Janson, M. A., and L. D. Smith. 1985. "Prototyping for Systems Development: A Critical Appraisal." *MIS Quarterly* 9, no. 4: 305–316.

Jarillo, J. C. 1988. "On Strategic Networks." *Strategic Management Journal*, no. 9: 31–42.

Johnston, H. R., and P. Lawrence. 1988. "Beyond Vertical Integration—The Rise of Value-Adding Partnerships." *Harvard Business Review* 66 (July–August): 94–101.

Johnston, H. R., and M. R. Vitale. 1988. "Creating Competitive Advantage with Interorganizational Information Systems." *MIS Quarterly* 12: 153–165.

Keen, P. G. W. 1986. *Competing in Time: Using Telecommunications for Competitive Advantage*. Cambridge, Mass.: Ballinger.

King, W. R. 1978. "Strategic Planning for Management Informations Systems." *MIS Quarterly* 2, no. 1: 27–37.

Kling, R. 1980. "Social Analyses of Computing: Theoretical Perspectives in Recent Empirical Research." *Computing Surveys* 12, no. 1: 61–110.

Koh, J., and N. Venkatraman. 1991. "Joint Venture Formations and Stock Market Reactions: An

Assessment in the Information Technology Sector." *Academy of Management Journal.* December.

Leavitt, H. J. 1965. "Applied Organizational Change in Industry." In *Handbook of Organizations,* edited by H. A. Simon. Chicago: Rand McNally.

Leitheiser, R. L., and J. C. Wetherbe. 1986. "Service Support Levels: An Organized Approach to End-User Computing." *MIS Quarterly* 10, no. 4: 337–349.

Malone, T. W., J. Yates, and R. I. Benjamin. 1987. "Electronic Markets and Electronic Hierarchies." *Communications of the ACM,* June, pp. 484–497.

Management in the 1990s Research Program. 1989. Final Report, Massachusetts Institute of Technology, Cambridge, Mass.

Marcus, M. L., and D. Robey. 1988. "Information Technology and Organization Change: Causal Structure in Theory and Research." *Management Science* 34, no. 5: 583–598.

Martin, J. 1982a. *Application Development Without Programmers.* Englewood Cliffs, N.J.: Prentice-Hall.

Martin, J. 1982b. *Strategic Data Planning Methodologies.* Englewood Cliffs, N.J.: Prentice-Hall.

Mason, R. O., and I. I. Mitroff. 1973. "A Program for Research on Management Information Systems." *Management Science* 19: 475–487.

Mason, R. O., and I. I. Mitroff. 1981. *Challenging Strategic Planning Assumptions: Theory, Cases, and Techniques.* New York: Wiley.

McFarlan, F. W. 1984. "Information Technology Changes the Way You Compete." *Harvard Business Review* 62, no. 3: 98–103.

McFarlan, F. W., and J. L. McKenney. 1983. *Corporate Information Systems Management: The Issues Facing Senior Executives.* Homewood, Ill.: Richard D Irwin.

McKelvey, B. 1975. "Guidelines for the Empirical Classification of Organizations." *Administrative Science Quarterly* 21: 571–597.

McKinsey & Company, Inc. 1968. "Unlocking the Computer's Profit Potential." *The McKinsey Quarterly,* Fall, pp. 17–31.

McLean, E. R., and J. V. Soden. 1977. *Strategic Planning for MIS.* New York: Wiley.

Miles, R. E., and C. C. Snow. 1978. *Organizational Strategy, Structure and Process.* New York: McGraw-Hill.

Miller, D. 1981. "Toward a New Contingency Approach: The Search for Organizational Gestalts." *Journal of Management Studies* 18: 1–26.

Miller, D., and P. H. Friesen. 1984. *Organizations: A Quantum View.* Englewood Cliffs, N.J.: Prentice-Hall.

Mintzberg, H. 1977. "Policy as a Field of Management Theory." *Academy of Management Review,* pp. 88–103.

Mumford, E. 1981. "Participative Systems Design: Structure and Method." *Systems, Objectives, Solutions* 1, no. 1: 5–19.

Myers, S. C. 1984. "Finance Theory and Financial Strategy." *Interfaces* 14, no. 1: 126–137.

Myers, W. 1985. "MCC: Planning the Revolution in Software." *IEEE Software* 2, no. 6: 68–73.

Parker, M. M., and R. J. Benson, with H. E. Trainor. 1988. *Information Economics: Linking Business Performance to Information Technology.* Englewood Cliffs, N.J.: Prentice-Hall.

Parsons, G. L. 1983. "Information Technology: A New Competitive Weapon." *Sloan Management Review* 24: 3–14.

Porter, M. E. 1980. *Competitive Strategy: Techniques for Analyzing Industries and Competitors.* New York: Free Press.

Porter, M. E., and V. E. Millar. 1985. "How Information Technology Gives You Competitive Advantage." *Harvard Business Review* July–August: 149–160.

Pyburn, P. J. 1983. "Linking the MIS Plan with Corporate Strategy: An Exploratory Study." *MIS Quarterly* 7, no. 2: 1–14.

Raghunathan, T. S., and W. R. King. 1988. "The Impact of Information Systems Planning on the Organization." *Omega* 16: 85–93.

Rockart, J. F. 1979. "Chief Executives Define Their Own Data Needs." *Harvard Business Review* 57, no. 2: 81–93.

Rockart, J. F., and M. S. Scott Morton. 1984. "Implications of Changes in Information Technology for Corporate Strategy." *Interfaces* 14, no. 1: 84–95.

Rockart, J. F., and J. E. Short. 1989. "IT in the 1990s: Managing Organizational Interdependence." *Sloan Management Review* 30, no. 2: 7–17.

Rotemberg, J., and G. Saloner. 1991. "Information Technology and Strategic Advantage." In *The Corporation of the 1990s,* edited by M. S. Scott Morton. New York: Oxford University Press.

Scott Morton, M. S., ed. 1991. *The Corporation of the 1990s.* New York: Oxford University Press.

Sharpe, J. H. 1989. "Building and Communicating the Executive Vision." IBM Australia, Ltd., working paper 89-001.

Snow, C. C., and L. Hrebiniak. 1980. "Strategy Distinctive Competence and Organizational Performance." *Administrative Science Quarterly* 25: 317–336.

Snow, C. C., and R. E. Miles. 1983. "The Role of Strategy in the Development of a General Theory of Organizations." In *Advances in Strategic Management,* vol. 2, edited by R. Lamb. Greenwich, Conn.: JAI Press.

Strassman, P. 1985. *The Information Payoff.* New York: Free Press.

Thompson, J. D. 1967. *Organizations in Action: Social Sciences Bases of Administrative Theory.* New York: McGraw-Hill.

Venkatraman, N. 1989a. "The Concept of Fit in Strategy Research: Toward Verbal and Statistical Correspondence." *Academy of Management Review* 14, no. 3: 423–444.

Venkatraman, N. 1989b. "Strategic Orientation of Business Enterprises: The Construct, Dimensionality and Measurement." *Management Science* 35, no. 8: 942–962.

Venkatraman, N. 1991. "Information Technology–Induced Business Reconfiguration: The New Strategic Management Challenge." In *Corporation of the 1990s,* edited by M. S. Scott Morton. New York: Oxford University Press.

Venkatraman, N., and J. C. Camillus. 1984. "Exploring the Concept of 'Fit' in Strategic Management." *Academy of Management Review* 9: 513–525.

Venkatraman, N., and J. H. Grant. 1986. "Construct Measurement in Organizational Strategy Research: A Critique and Proposal." *Academy of Management Review* 11: 71–87.

Venkatraman, N., and A. Kambil. 1991. "The Check Is Not in the Mail: Strategies for Electronic Integration in Tax Return Filing." *Sloan Management Review* 32, no. 3: 33–43.

Venkatraman, N., and J. E. Short. 1990. "Strategies for Electronic Integration: From Order-Entry Systems to Value-Added Services at Baxter." MIT Center for Information Systems Research working paper.

Weick, K. E. 1979. *The Social Psychology of Organizing,* 2nd ed. Reading, Mass.: Addison-Wesley.

Wheelright, S. 1984. "Manufacturing Strategy: Defining the Missing Link." *Strategic Management Journal* 5, no. 1: 77–91.

Williamson, O. E. 1985. *The Economic Institutions of Capitalism: Firms, Markets and Relational Contracting.* New York: Free Press.

Wind, Y., and T. S. Robertson. 1983. "Marketing Strategy: New Directions for Theory and Research." *Journal of Marketing* 47, no. 2.

Wiseman, C. 1985. *Strategy and Computers: Information Systems as Competitive Weapons.* Homewood, Ill.: Dow Jones–Irwin.

Zachman, J. A. 1986. "A Framework for Information Systems Architecture." IBM Los Angeles
    Scientific Center Report G320-2785.
Zani, W. M. 1970. "Blueprint for MIS." *Harvard Business Review* 48, no. 6: 95–100.
Zmud, R. W., A. C. Boynton, and G. C. Jacobs. 1986. "The Information Economy: A New
    Perspective for Effective Information Systems Management." *Data Base* 16, no. 1: 17–
    23.
Zuboff, S. 1988. *In the Age of the Smart Machine.* New York: Basic Books.

COMMENTARY BY THOMAS MADISON AND NAN LOWER

These lessons are directly relevant to the issues facing our clients at United Research. Many of these companies have IT applications that are over ten, and in some cases almost twenty, years old. We too have discovered that antiquated technologies and systems are one of the greatest barriers to positioning an organization for success. And a system that cannot support today's strategy will certainly not be able to support tomorrow's.

Our work at United Research bears this out. We have found that a holistic approach is essential to successfully planning and managing IT change. This requires integrating and aligning four key areas: business strategy, business architecture, business rules, and technology. When IT planning is not incorporated effectively into the business plan, the organization risks a significantly reduced return—or no return—on its IT investment.

Another barrier to linking IT strategy with business strategy is the lack of change management skills among IT people. Trained to manage the current business and incremental changes, they often lack the skills needed to understand shifts in overall business strategy or how such shifts will affect IT strategy. Their background thus makes them ill-suited to act as advocates of significant change.

Henderson and Venkatraman have clearly indicated how a weak infrastructure inhibits the organization from leveraging technology to achieve business objectives. I would like to see them extend their research further in this area, with a greater emphasis on identifying the actions companies must take to overcome the obstacles to successful IT strategy implementation. For example, at United Research we have found that many organizations do not formulate adequate plans for implementing changes in their business architecture or their business rules. In these situations, it is sometimes necessary to slow down, or even stop, major information systems introductions and to concentrate first on changing the business. Once the new business strategy is fully understood, one can then move on to consider new IT systems. The greatest resistance to slowing down the introduction of new IT systems comes naturally from the IT professionals themselves, who want to introduce IT as quickly as possible.

A company that does not coordinate its IT strategy with its business strategy also runs the risk of making major IT investments in areas that are about to be phased out. In fact, we have encountered situations where 50 to 60 percent of a company's investment in IT had been finalized with little awareness of a significant change in strategic direction. This sort of situation often arises as a result of turf issues: one function may be reluctant to share its data with another function. Instead of regarding all relevant information as "the company's data," everyone thinks in terms of "my data" versus "your data." If a company is to flourish in today's rapidly changing environment, it must first overcome this kind of cultural barrier.

As organizations begin to view information technology as a major resource to implement business strategies, they must consider their strategic alternatives in light of IT's potential to help them realize their goals. Companies must also recognize, and overcome, the barriers to successful implementation of their critical change initiatives. The Strategic Alignment Model provides a useful framework for working with organizations to evaluate current approaches to information systems management, to investigate and test alternative methods, and to develop new approaches to proactively plan the future.

8

Technological Change and the Management of Architectural Knowledge

REBECCA M. HENDERSON

One of the most difficult and important challenges facing many modern organizations is the need to respond to seemingly ceaseless rapid technological change. Developments in computing technology, in new materials, in medicine, biotechnology, and a wide variety of other fields present firms in industries as diverse as banking, food, capital equipment, and packaged consumer goods with both major opportunities and significant threats.

Many of these developments present a particularly difficult challenge because they cannot be easily classified as either "radical" or "incremental" innovation. Both practicing managers and academic researchers have long accepted the idea that dramatic, radical technological change often creates very significant competitive problems for established firms, whereas more minor, incremental innovation often reinforces their skills and position. The research presented here focuses upon a class of innovations that are intermediate in character between the two—innovations that build upon much of the existing experience and capability of established organizations but that still have very significant competitive consequences. Consider, for example, the case of Xerox and the introduction of small copiers.

Xerox, the pioneer of plain-paper copiers, was confronted in the mid-1970s with competitors offering copiers that were much smaller and more reliable than the traditional product. The new products required little new scientific or engineering knowledge, but despite the fact that Xerox had invented the core technologies and had enormous experience in the industry, it took the company almost eight years of missteps and false starts to introduce a competitive product into the market. In that time Xerox lost half of its market share and suffered serious financial problems (Clark, 1987).

In a recent paper, Clark and I suggested that this type of innovation should be defined as "architectural" innovation (Henderson and Clark, 1990). Architectural innovation changes a product's architecture, or the relationships between its components, but leaves the components, and the core design concepts that they embody, unchanged.

Architectural innovation often creates very significant problems for established firms because architectural knowledge is embedded in the implicit knowledge of the organization, particularly its communication channels, information filters, and problem-solving strategies, so that its obsolescence is difficult to observe and to correct. This is the kind of innovation that confronted Xerox. It destroys the usefulness of a firm's architectural knowledge but preserves the usefulness of its knowledge about the product's components.

This chapter explores the usefulness of this idea for the understanding of organizational transformation. I begin by briefly summarizing the arguments and evidence presented earlier (Henderson and Clark, 1990). The concept of architectural innovation grew out of work in the semiconductor photolithographic alignment industry, an industry in which the established firms suffered sharp declines in market share following the introduction of equipment incorporating seemingly minor innovation.

I then explore the implications of the concept of architectural innovation for organizational transformation in general. I suggest that the distinction between component knowledge and architectural knowledge has general application beyond problems of product design, and that one of the recurrent themes addressed by the other chapters in this book is the need to rethink the structure of existing systems and to rebuild tacit organizational knowledge to reflect new environmental realities. I close by suggesting that many of the proposals for organizational transformation discussed in this book can be understood as proposals for the creation of organizations that explicitly manage architectural knowledge.

ARCHITECTURAL INNOVATION

To develop the concept of architectural innovation, I focus on the problem of product development, taking as my unit of analysis a manufactured product sold to an end user and designed, engineered, and manufactured by a single product-development organization. Such a product can be usefully understood as both the product as a whole—the system—and the product in its parts—the components. This distinction has a long history in the design literature (Alexander, 1964; Marples, 1961). For example, a room fan's major components include the blade, the motor that drives it, the blade guard, the control system, and the mechanical housing. The overall architecture of the product lays out how the components will work together. Taken together, a fan's architecture and its components create a system for moving air in a room.

Successful product development requires two types of knowledge. First, it requires component knowledge, or knowledge about each of the core design concepts and the way in which they are implemented in a particular component. Second, it requires architecture knowledge, or knowledge about the ways in which the components are integrated and linked together into a coherent whole. Innovations can be understood in terms of their impact on these two types of knowledge. This idea is illustrated in Figure 8.1.

The horizontal dimension captures an innovation's impact on components; the vertical captures its impact on the linkages between components. Framed in this way, radical and incremental innovation are extreme points along both dimensions. Radical innovation establishes a new dominant design and hence a new set of core design concepts embodied in components that are linked together in a new architecture. Incremental innovation refines and extends an established design. Improvement occurs in individual components, but the underlying core design concepts, and the links between them, remain the same. Modular innovation is innovation that changes a core design concept without changing the product's architecture.

The essence of an architectural innovation is the reconfiguration of an established

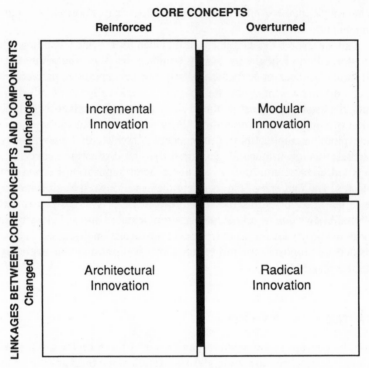

Figure 8.1   A framework for defining innovation.

system to link together existing components in a new way. This does not mean that the components themselves remain untouched. Architectural innovation is often triggered by a change in a component—perhaps size or some other subsidiary parameter of its design—that creates new interactions and new linkages with other components in the established product. The important point is that the core design concept behind each component—and the associated scientific and engineering knowledge—remain the same.

The application of this framework can be illustrated with the example of the room air fan. If the established technology is that of large, electrically powered fans, mounted in the ceiling, with the motor hidden from view and insulated to dampen the noise, improvements in blade design or in the power of the motor would be incremental innovations. A move to central air conditioning would be a radical innovation. New components associated with compressors, refrigerants, and their associated controls would add whole new technical disciplines and new interrelationships. For the maker of large, ceiling-mounted room fans, however, the introduction of a portable fan would be an architectural innovation. Although the primary components would be largely the same (e.g., blade, motor, control system), the architecture of the product would be quite different. There would be significant changes in the interactions between components. The smaller size and the co-location of the motor and the blade in the room would focus attention on new types of interactions between the motor size, the blade dimensions, and the amount of air that the fan could circulate, while shrinking the size of the apparatus would probably introduce new interactions between the performance of the blade and the weight of the housing.

These distinctions are important because they give us insight into why established firms often have a surprising degree of difficulty in adapting to architectural innovation. Incremental innovation tends to reinforce the competitive positions of established firms, since it builds on their core competencies (Abernathy and Clark, 1985), or is "competence enhancing" (Tushman and Anderson, 1986). In the terms of the framework developed here, it builds on the existing architectural and component knowledge of an organization. In contrast, radical innovation creates unmistakable challenges for established firms, since it destroys the usefulness of their existing capabilities. In our terms, it destroys the usefulness of both architectural and component knowledge (Cooper and Schendel, 1976; Daft, 1982; Tushman and Anderson, 1986).

Architectural innovation presents established firms with a more subtle and potentially equally difficult challenge, because of the way in which architectural knowledge evolves within the firm. Since architectural knowledge is usually stable during long periods of incremental innovation, it tends to become embedded in the communication channels, information filters, and problem-solving strategies of the organization. This makes its obsolescence difficult to observe and to correct.

In the first place, established organizations require significant time (and resources) to identify a particular innovation as architectural, since architectural innovation can often initially be accommodated within old frameworks. In the second place, even after the threat of architectural innovation has been recognized, the building of new architectural knowledge takes time and resources. New entrants to the industry must also build the architectural knowledge necessary to exploit an architectural innovation, but since they have no existing assets, they can optimize their organization and information-processing structures to exploit the potential of a new design. Established firms may be tempted to modify the channels, filters, and strategies that already exist rather than incur the significant fixed costs and considerable organizational friction required to build new sets from scratch (Arrow, 1974; Chandler, 1990). But it may be difficult to identify precisely which filters, channels, and problem-solving strategies need to be modified, and the attempt to build a new product with old (albeit modified) organizational tools can create significant problems.

These problems are well illustrated in the history of the semiconductor photolithographic alignment industry.

INNOVATION IN PHOTOLITHOGRAPHIC ALIGNMENT EQUIPMENT

Photolithographic aligners are sophisticated pieces of capital equipment used in the manufacture of integrated circuits. The production of semiconductors requires the transfer of small, intricate patterns to the surface of a wafer of semiconductor material such as silicon, and this process of transfer is known as lithography. The surface of the wafer is coated with a light-sensitive chemical, or "resist." The pattern that is to be transferred to the wafer surface is drawn onto a mask and the mask is used to block light as it falls onto the resist, so that only those portions of the resist defined by the mask are exposed to light. The light chemically transforms the resist so that it can be

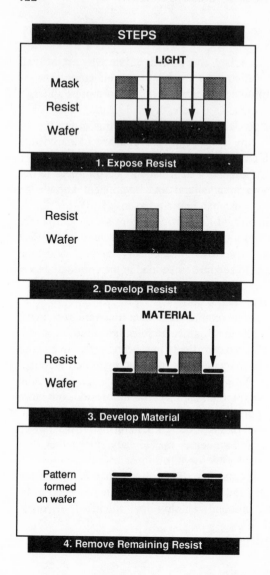

Figure 8.2 Schematic representation of the lithographic process.

stripped away. The resulting pattern is then used as the basis for either the deposition of material onto the wafer surface or the etching of the existing material on the surface of the wafer. The process may be repeated as many as twenty times during the manufacture of a semiconductor device, and each layer must be located precisely with respect to the previous layer (Watts and Einspruch, 1987). Figure 8.2 is a very simplified representation of this complex process. A photolithographic aligner is used to position the mask relative to the wafer, to hold the two in place during exposure, and to expose the resist. Figure 8.3 is a schematic diagram of a contact aligner, the first generation of alignment equipment developed. Improvement in alignment technology has meant improvement in minimum feature size, the size of the smallest pattern that can be produced on the wafer surface; yield, the percentage of wafers successfully processed; and throughput, the number of wafers the aligner can handle in a given time.

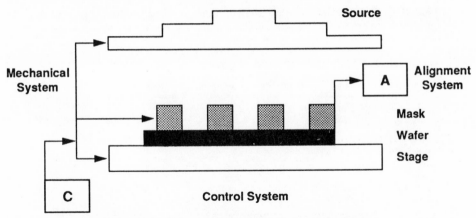

Figure 8.3 Schematic diagram of a contact aligner.

A constant stream of incremental innovation has been critical to optical photolithography's continuing success. The technology has also seen four waves of architectural innovation: the move from contact to proximity alignment, from proximity to scanning projection alignment, and from scanners to first- and then second-generation "steppers." (Photolithographic technology is described in much greater detail in Henderson, 1988.) Table 8.1 summarizes the changes in the technology introduced by each generation. In each case the core technologies of optical lithography remained largely untouched, and much of the technical knowledge gained in building a previous

Table 8.1 A summary of architectural innovation in photolithographic alignment technology

	MAJOR CHANGES	
Equipment	Technology	Critical Relationships Between Components
Proximity	Mask and wafer separated during exposure.	Accuracy and stability of gap is a function of links between gap-setting mechanism and other components.
Scanning projection	Image of mask projected onto wafer by scanning reflective optics.	Interactions between lens and other components are critical to successful performance.
First-generation stepper	Image of mask projected through refractive lens.	Relationship between lens field size and source energy becomes significant determinant of throughput.
	Image "stepped" across wafer	Depth of focus characteristics—driven by relationship between source wavelength and lens numerical aperture—becomes critical. Interactions between stage and alignment system are critical.
Second-generation stepper	Introduction of "site-by-site" alignment, larger 5× lenses.	Throughput now driven by calibration and stepper stability. Relationships between lens and mechanical system become crucial means of controlling distortion.

Source: Field interviews, internal firm records (Henderson, 1988).

Table 8.2 Share of deflated cumulative sales (%), 1962–1986, by generation, for the leading optical photolithographic alignment equipment manufacturers[a]

Firm	Contact	Proximity	Scanners	Step and Repeat (1)	Step and Repeat (2)
			ALIGNMENT EQUIPMENT		
Cobilt	44		<1		
Kasper	17	8		7	
Canon		67	21	9	
Perkin-Elmer			78	10	<1
GCA				55	12
Nikon					70
Total	61	75	99+	81	82+

Source: Internal firm records, Dataquest, VLSI Research Inc.

[a]This measure is distorted by the fact that all of these products are still being sold. For second-generation step and repeat aligners this problem is particularly severe, since in 1986 this equipment was still in the early stages of its life cycle.

generation could be transferred to the next. Yet in each case the industry leader was unable to make the transition.

Table 8.2 shows share of deflated cumulative sales from 1962 to 1986 by generation of equipment for the leading firms. Figure 8.4 shows share of sales over time for three of the leading established firms and new entrants in proximity printers, scanners, and the first generation of steppers. The first commercially successful aligner was introduced by Kulicke and Soffa in 1965. They were extremely successful and held nearly 100 percent of the (very small) market for the next nine years, but by 1974 Cobilt and Kasper had replaced them. In 1974 Perkin-Elmer entered the market with the scanning projection aligner and rapidly became the largest firm in the industry. GCA, in turn, replaced Perkin-Elmer through its introduction of the stepper, only to be supplanted by Nikon, which introduced the second-generation stepper.

In nearly every case, the established firm invested heavily in the next generation of equipment, only to meet with very little success. A reliance on architectural knowledge derived from experience with the previous generation blinded the incumbent firms to critical aspects of the new technology. They thus underestimated its potential or built equipment that was markedly inferior to the equipment introduced by entrants.

The case of Kasper Instruments and its response to Canon's introduction of the proximity printer illustrates some of the problems encountered by established firms. Kasper Instruments was founded in 1968 and by 1973 was a small but profitable firm supplying approximately half of the market for contact aligners. In 1973 Kasper introduced the first contact aligner to be equipped with proximity capability. Although nearly half of all the aligners that the firm sold from 1974 on had this capability, Kasper aligners were only rarely used in proximity mode, and sales declined steadily until the company left the industry in 1981. The widespread use of proximity aligners occurred only with the introduction and general adoption of Canon's proximity aligner in the late 1970s.

Canon's aligner was superficially very similar to Kasper's. It incorporated the same components and performed the same functions, but it performed them much more effectively because it incorporated a much more sophisticated understanding of the technical interrelationships that are fundamental to successful proximity alignment.

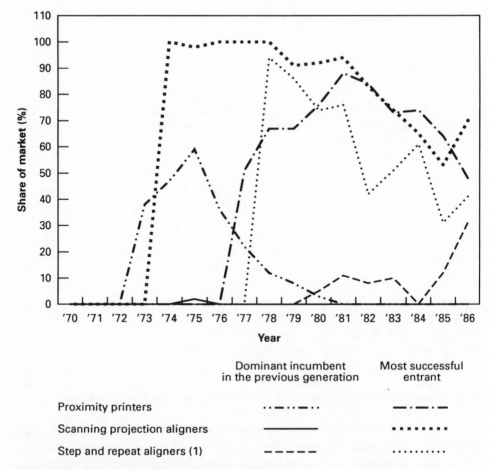

Figure 8.4 Estimated share of sales by the most successful entrant and by the most successful established firm of the previous generation.

Kasper failed to develop the particular component knowledge that would have enabled it to match Canon's design. More important, the architectural knowledge that Kasper had developed through its experience with the contact aligner had the effect of diverting Kasper's attention from the new problems whose solution was critical to the design of a successful proximity aligner.

Kasper conceived of the proximity aligner as a modified contact aligner. Like the incremental improvements to the contact aligner before it, design of the proximity aligner was managed as a routine extension to the product line. In particular, the gap-setting mechanism that was used in the contact aligner to align the mask with the wafer was slightly modified, and the new aligner was offered on the market. As a result, Kasper's proximity aligner did not perform well. The gap-setting mechanism was not sufficiently accurate or stable to ensure adequate performance, and the aligner was rarely used in its proximity mode. Kasper's failure to understand the obsolescence of its architectural knowledge is demonstrated graphically by two incidents.

The first is the firm's interpretation of early complaints about the accuracy of its gap-setting mechanism. In proximity alignment, misalignment of the mask and the wafer can be caused by inaccuracies or instability in the gap-setting mechanism and by distortions introduced during processing. Kasper attributed many of the problems that users of its proximity equipment were experiencing to processing error, since it believed that processing error had been the primary source of problems with its contact aligner. The firm "knew" that its gap-setting mechanism was entirely adequate and, as a result, devoted very little time to improving its performance. In retrospect this may seem like a wanton misuse of information, but it represented no more than a continued reliance on an information filter that had historically served the firm well.

The second illustration is provided by Kasper's response to Canon's initial introduction of a proximity aligner. The Canon aligner was evaluated by a team at Kasper and pronounced to be a copy of a Kasper machine. Kasper evaluated it against the criteria that it used for evaluating its own aligners—criteria that had been developed during its experience with contact aligners. The technical features that made Canon's aligner a significant advance, particularly the redesigned gap mechanism, were not observed because they were not considered important. The Canon aligner was pronounced to be "merely a copy" of the Kasper aligner.

Similar problems that show up in all four episodes of architectural innovation in the industry's history are typified by the case of Perkin-Elmer and stepper technology. By the late 1970s Perkin-Elmer had achieved market leadership with its scanning projection aligners, but the company failed to maintain that leadership when stepper technology came to dominate the industry in the early 1980s. When evaluating the two technologies, Perkin-Elmer engineers accurately forecast the progress of individual components in the two systems but failed to see how new interactions in component development—including better resist systems and improvements in lens design—would give stepper technology a decisive advantage.

GCA, the company that took leadership from Perkin-Elmer, was itself supplanted by Nikon, which introduced a second-generation stepper. Part of the problem for GCA was recognition, but much of its failure to master the new stepper technology lay in problems in implementation. Echoing Kasper, GCA first pronounced the Nikon stepper a "copy" of the GCA design. Even after GCA had fully recognized the threat posed by the second-generation stepper, its historical experience handicapped the company in its attempts to develop a competitive machine. GCA's engineers were organized by component, and cross-department communication channels were all structured around the architecture of the first-generation system. Although GCA engineers were able to push the limits of the component technology, they had great difficulty understanding what Nikon had done to achieve its superior performance.

Nikon had changed aspects of the design—particularly the ways in which the optical system was integrated with the rest of the aligner—of which GCA's engineers had only limited understanding. Moreover, because these changes dealt with component interactions, there were few engineers responsible for developing this understanding. As a result, GCA's second-generation machines did not deliver the kind of performance that the market demanded. Like Kasper and Perkin-Elmer before them, GCA's sales languished and it lost market leadership. In all three cases, other factors also played a role in the firm's dramatic loss of market share, but a failure to respond effectively to architectural innovation was critical.

ARCHITECTURAL INNOVATION AS A PERVASIVE ISSUE IN ORGANIZATIONAL TRANSFORMATION

Although the concept of architectural innovation was derived from a study of technological change, the idea is a source of rich insight into some of the most fundamental barriers to organizational transformation.

This is immediately apparent if we think of component and architectural knowledge in more general terms. In general, component knowledge is local, active, focused knowledge about elements of a larger problem, whereas architectural knowledge is knowledge about how these elements fit together. Architectural knowledge is more likely to be diffused within the organization and to be embedded in organizational routines rather than in the minds of individuals because during long periods of incremental innovation it is much more stable than component knowledge.

During periods of incremental innovation, there will be rich, unstructured information flows and problem-solving activities within the boundaries of a component, but the information flow and problem solving that occur across component boundaries will be much more highly structured and more diffuse. "Components" emerge as organizations learn enough about a particular organizational task to be able to fragment it into elements that can be addressed in relative isolation without the need to transport the full range of knowledge about the internal workings of other components across component boundaries. Thus component boundaries are defined simultaneously by an organization's knowledge and problem-solving capabilities and by the internal structure of any particular organizational task.

As an illustration, again consider the room fan company. If information about the design of every element of the fan could be costlessly and instantaneously transferred to all designers, the distinction between component and architectural knowledge would not be a useful one. The designers of a new blade could take full advantage of all available knowledge about motors: all knowledge would be component knowledge in the sense that it would be actively involved in problem solving and locally accessible. Architectural knowledge develops because information transfer is expensive, or, in Von Hippel's terms, because component knowledge is "sticky" (Von Hippel, 1990). In the case of the room fan, it summarizes the component knowledge of the motor designers into a reduced set that summarizes what the blade designers need to know about motors in order to design adequate blades. Architectural knowledge can thus emerge only after an organization has developed sufficient experience with a problem to be able to fragment it into elements without losing critical information.

In the case of technologies that develop hierarchically in the manner outlined by Henderson and Clark (1990), components will correspond to logically and physically distinct elements of the design, since knowledge about the technology will evolve simultaneously with the design. Thus in our analysis of the nature of architectural innovation in photolithographic design and of the problems that it created for established firms, we were able to interpret each firm's knowledge of the relationship between the physical components of the design as embedded architectural knowledge. In such a case, the component and the architectural knowledge of the organization will be a logical reflection of the internal structure of the technology, and the organization and the products that it builds will mirror each other in very specific ways.

In the case of more general organizational tasks, the development of architectural knowledge is less likely to be guided by a particular technological structure, but we can hypothesize that the information-processing constraints of the organization will nevertheless result in the formulation of architectural knowledge as soon as any particular organizational task is sufficiently stable that it can be fragmented into elements without the overall problem-solving effort suffering too greatly. Architectural innovation will in this sense be more than a technical event—it will be any innovation that requires the firm to rethink the way in which it integrates together any coherent set of organizational tasks.

For example, much of the recent stress on design for manufacturing techniques (see, for example, Hauser and Clausing, 1988; Nevins and Whitney, 1988) can be interpreted as a move to manage architectural innovation within the design process. Many manufacturing firms have historically separated their design and manufacturing efforts into "components"—that is, into centers of local problem solving which are integrated together by a reduced set of stable architectural knowledge. In some firms this knowledge took the form of beliefs such as "those guys can build anything smaller than a breadbox" or "anything made out of aluminum held together with rivets." Design-for-manufacturing methodologies represent an explicit realization that this type of architectural knowledge may be outdated or insufficient, and that the organization has to explicitly recognize the existence of a much richer set of potential interactions between design and manufacturing. In this sense richer "rules of manufacturability" (rules such as "all else equal reduce part count") are attempts to build more appropriate architectural knowledge. Extensive simultaneous engineering efforts are attempts to transfer the "component knowledge" of product and process engineers to each other.

This much broader definition of component and hence of architectural knowledge suggests that this research may have immediate relevance to more general problems of organizational transformation and to many of the other chapters in this book. For if component knowledge is local, intense knowledge about particular elements of larger problems, and architectural knowledge is embedded knowledge about the ways in which these elements interact, then many of the major challenges of organizational transformation may involve the reconfiguration of architectural knowledge, and our attempts to create "learning" organizations are attempts not only to create organizations that actively engage in the construction of component knowledge—that is, the building of richer knowledge about particular aspects of a problem—but also to create organizational forms and processes that can actively reevaluate and reconstruct new forms of architectural knowledge. The other chapters suggest that this may be quite as difficult a challenge in other fields of organizational endeavor as it is in the management of technological innovation.

Consider, for example, Bailyn's discussion of the need to consider family issues in discussions about work and human resources (Chapter 12, this volume). Bailyn suggests that one of the major challenges facing the modern U.S. corporation is the need to adapt to a significantly different kind of work force—one with much more diverse needs and expectations. She suggests that this may require a fundamental rethinking of the basic assumptions that most organizations make about personnel policies such as training, job tenure, and promotion. This can be understood as a need to rethink some of the fundamental architectural knowledge of the organization, where local problem solving about the ways in which particular employees should be treated is currently embedded in an overarching and largely implicit structure. The problems of work force diversity require a reconfiguration of the organization's thinking since the relationships among employees, their families, and the company, and the needs and demands that govern these relationships, are likely to be quite different.

The same concern with organizational change that may completely reconfigure the elements inside the corporation is evident in the discussion of corporate governance issues in chapters by Dore, Useem, and Healy. Dore suggests that many Japanese corporations are governed by quite different conceptions of the relationships between the multiple stakeholders of the firm (Chapter 2, this volume). In consequence, the set of implicit assumptions about how the stakeholders of a firm—the employees, owners, customers, and suppliers—work with each other is quite different. He implies that the set of relationships found inside such Japanese corporations may ultimately result in more successful performance, and thus that U.S. corporations may have to rethink the way in which competing interests are mediated inside the firm. The same theme is evident in Useem's work (Chapter 4, this volume). He suggests that the recent wave of leveraged buyouts and mergers is bringing about a qualitatively different relationship between owners and managers inside some American corporations. Healy's work suggests that these changes also significantly change performance (Chapter 5, this volume).

All three chapters strikingly reinforce the idea that architectural innovation can have very significant consequences and be very difficult to implement despite the fact that from some perspectives it appears to be relatively "minor." After all, changes in governance could in principle merely be changes in contractual relationships within the firm. These three chapters imply that there are major organizational barriers to these types of changes that flow from deeply held assumptions—architectural knowledge—about the ways in which the parts of the firm work together to promote the interests of the whole.

Beyond the identification of the problems that organizations face in responding to these types of architectural innovation, the central concerns of several of the other chapters can be interpreted as the development of a richer understanding of alternative organizational mechanisms that may make organizations much more capable of explicitly managing architectural knowledge.

For example, Kochan and McKersie suggest that the most successful manufacturing organizations are those that are able to take full advantage of the knowledge and capabilities of their work force (Chapter 11, this volume). This point is also made forcefully by MacDuffie and Krafcik, who suggest that historically many U.S. manufacturing corporations have maintained assumptions about the need to control and limit the involvement of the blue-collar work force in the introduction of new technologies—architectural assumptions in that they shaped the ways in which problems were solved inside the organization—that are now actively inhibiting effective performance, but that are difficult to change because they are embedded deeply in the structure of the corporation (Chapter 13, this volume). For example, Kochan and McKersie stress that minor innovations such as the introduction of quality circles are unlikely to be successful unless they are backed by fundamental changes in the firm's structure and governance.

Senge and Sterman also address this issue (Chapter 21, this volume). They suggest that one of the major problems facing organizations today is the fact that managers use inadequate or overly simplistic "mental maps" of the organization and its environment, which are rarely subject to challenge or assessment, and that these may lead them to grossly inappropriate decisions that fail to take account of the interactive, dynamic nature of their environment. They describe the development of computer-based tools that assist managers to develop much more accurate and communally understood mental maps of their environment reflecting the nature of the system with which they are confronted. These tools can be thought of as a way to make the architectural knowledge of senior managers about the interrelationships between elements of the firm and its environment explicit.

RESEARCH ISSUES AND QUESTIONS OUTSTANDING

A number of critical issues remain for further research. The most immediate is the need to build a richer understanding of the nature of architectural knowledge and the ways in which it is managed and changed within an organization. My research in the photolithographic alignment equipment industry led me to some specific hypotheses about the structure and development of technically derived component and architectural knowledge. Although I believe that these concepts may have relevance to more general problems of organizational change, much more remains to be done to make the concepts concrete and operationally useful in other settings.

For example, it will be important to build a better understanding between the concept of architectural knowledge and the internal mental maps of Senge and Sterman, the concepts of theory in use and unfreezing developed by Schein (Chapter 6, this volume), and the descriptions of organizational routines of Nelson and Winter (1982). Further field-based studies of these problems should also shed light on this issue.

Another important area for future research is the relationship between the internal structure of the tasks facing organizations and the development of architectural and component knowledge. Clark and I found the concept of the hierarchy of design extremely useful as a way to understand the development of architectural knowledge in the photolithographic industry. An interesting research question is the degree to which analogous concepts can be of use in the analysis of the development of other types of knowledge.

Answers to these questions will be fundamental to the development of a richer understanding of organizational transformation.

ACKNOWLEDGMENT

Selected passages of this chapter have been reprinted from "Architectural Innovation: The Reconfiguration of Existing Product Technologies and the Failure of Established Firms" by Rebecca M. Henderson and Kim B. Clark, published in *Administrative Science Quarterly*, Volume 35, Number 1, March 1990, pp. 9–30 © 1990 by Cornell University.

REFERENCES

Abernathy, W. J., and K. Clark. 1985. "Innovation: Mapping the Winds of Creative Destruction." *Research Policy* 14: 3–22.

Alexander, C. 1964. *Notes on the Synthesis of Form.* Cambridge, Mass.: Harvard University Press.

Arrow, K. J. 1974. *The Limits of Organization.* New York: Norton.

Clark, K. B. 1987. "Managing Technology in International Competition: The Case of Product Development in Response to Foreign Entry." In *International Competitiveness,* edited by M. Spence and H. Hazard. Cambridge, Mass.: Ballinger.

Chandler, A. D. 1990. *Scale and Scope.* Cambridge, Mass.: Harvard University Press.

Cooper, A. C., and D. Schendel. 1976. "Strategic Response to Technological Threats." *Business Horizons* 19: 61–69.

Daft, R. L. 1982. "Bureaucratic Versus Nonbureaucratic Structure and the Process of Innovation and Change." In *Research in the Sociology of Organizations,* edited by S. B. Bacharach. Greenwich, Conn.: JAI Press.

Hauser, J., and D. Clausing. 1988. "The House of Quality." *Harvard Business Review,* May–June, pp. 63–73.

Henderson, R. M. 1988. The Failure of Established Firms in the Face of Technical Change: A Study of Photolithographic Alignment Equipment. Unpublished Ph.D. dissertation. Harvard University.

Henderson, R. M. and K. B. Clark. 1990. "Architectural Innovation: The Reconfiguration of Existing Product Technologies and the Failure of Established Firms." *Administrative Science Quarterly* 35: 9–30.

Marples, D. L. 1961. "The Decisions of Engineering Design." *IEEE Transactions on Engineering Management* 8 (June): 55–71.

Nelson, R., and S. Winter. 1982. *An Evolutionary Theory of Economic Change.* Cambridge, Mass.: Harvard University Press.

Nevins, J. L., and D. E. Whitney. 1988. *Concurrent Design of Products and Processes.* New York: McGraw-Hill.

Tushman, M. L., and P. Anderson. 1986. "Technological Discontinuities and Organizational Environments." *Administrative Science Quarterly* 31: 439–465.

Von Hippel, E. 1990. "The Impact of 'Sticky' Information on Innovation and Problem-Solving." Management of Technology Department, MIT working paper 3147-90-BPS.

Watts, R. K., and N. G. Einspruch, eds. 1987. *Lithography for VLSI, VLSI Electronics—Microstructure Science.* New York: Academic Press.

COMMENTARY BY JOHN M. MATSON

After reading Rebecca Henderson's chapter I have to ask if the issue is the management of technology or the technology of management. To demonstrate what I mean, I need your help. Would everyone please stand up. In the next fifteen seconds I would like each of you to shake as many hands as you can . . . beginning now. OK, time's up. How many people shook five hands? How many shook ten? Sara Beckman shook thirteen. What did she do differently from the rest of us? She used both hands. Sara demonstrated one of the three tenets which I believe will guide our future success. The first is working with all of our intellectual faculties: right (creative) and left (rational) sides of our minds. We probably only used our right hand because that is what is comfortable. But the business climate today is demanding new solutions, which require new ways of thinking. Technology broadens everyone's job, allowing a holistic approach to management and work . . . left and right sides. The second tenet is knowing one another and working together as never before. As we evolve employees to knowledge workers, education about how to express what they think and feel along with accepting others' input will be essential. The third tenet drives the first two and that is the acceptance of continuous change along with a willingness to champion change for excellence.

At Johnson & Johnson we are trying to work through this process, so I don't have specific examples to share with you which demonstrate these tenets in action. But what we have determined is the idea of "enablers" and "realizers." Enablers are technology. Technology which is critical for empowering our employees to grow, adapt, and become fully involved. So our understanding of how to use technology is essential. But people are the realizers. They are the ones who make it happen. As a value-driven organization, we are trying to figure out how to support the change process which will evolve us into a company full of realizers. We believe that protocols assist in that process. Within this chapter is the notion of protocols—not a permanent document but a guide through the process that can help us recognize the difference between radical change and the subtleties of architectural systems change. In that process, protocols are the first step of sorting down a massive amount of knowledge into easy-to-follow steps. Often they precede the development of diagnostics for further clarification and definition of a problem. Ultimately a set of principles will evolve which will open up the ability for change in any organization at any pace and level, continuously. These are elements which I believe begin the transformation of an organization.

Dialogue on Strategic Restructuring

The chapters on strategic restructuring led to a debate over why Japanese firms manage their organizations and work forces differently from most American firms. As the following dialogue illustrates, the debate started with a discussion of differences in the incentives and controls exerted on Japanese executives by their financial institutions, moved to differences in philosophies of management, and ended with a spirited debate over how far U.S. firms are willing to go in empowering or involving their employees—from the workplace to the boardroom.

MANAGERS VERSUS SHAREHOLDERS?

Paul Osterman

Professor Dore's theory seems to be that Japanese managers act in the interests of stakeholders other than themselves personally. That is, they internalize and act on the interests of employees, the community, customers, and shareholders. They seem to somehow do a good job of balancing those interests without seeming to operate only in their narrow self-interests such as by trying to expand their own turf or empire or salary and so on. My question is, Why is this the case? Are the incentives, reward systems, or controls on top executives or the firm different in Japan than in the United States? If so, are these mechanisms transferable to the United States?

Ronald Dore

The reward system in Japan is relatively transparent; fixed according to rank and level; and not dependent upon stock options or ownership. The stock is granted in a make-order fashion and is really a very small portion of an executive's income. Stock is granted according to a set of unwritten but generally known set of rules handed down from the top. The discretion of the people at the top who are able to bargain for their own rewards is limited and the number of people with this discretion is also extremely limited. A type of bargaining over how to exercise this discretion goes on within this group. This bargaining enforces their feeling of being the elders in the community and leaders in the corporate community.

Paul Healy

I think there are differences between the corporate control environments in Japan and the United States. In Japan, the owners of most large corporations are the banks, and they have closer links with the stockholders. In Japan, the stock market and takeovers for corporate control are less important because the major players are already sitting down and talking much more readily than in the United States.

Maurice Segall

Let me just add to that. JAL (Japan Airlines) is essentially owned by its suppliers and its banks. American Airlines, roughly the equivalent of JAL, is basically owned by institutions and not by its suppliers and certainly not by its banks. Now visualize a threat to either one of these two companies—the Trump threat to American and the Trump equivalent to JAL. Visualize the reaction of both, and you'll realize you have two totally different worlds. Since I'm a director of American Airlines I can say that.

Ronald Dore

Insofar as JAL is in hock to the banks, the bankers they deal with are people they went to school with and they know.

Donald Ephlin

American managers always stress that their first responsibility is to be responsive to their shareholders. But as I see it they are not being as responsive to the shareholders as they are to Wall Street analysts. This is unfortunate because these Wall Street people, not the real shareholders, are the ones who influence managerial decision making and they are the short-term speculators. This takes American firms in the wrong direction.

But I want to emphasize another difference between Japanese and American managers that goes beyond the financial incentives and that is harder to transfer but gives the Japanese a significant competitive advantage. I've observed a real philosophical difference.

Many of you have heard about the General Motors–Toyota joint venture plant, NUMMI. We sent hundreds of GM managers to NUMMI to look at it, and they come away totally unimpressed because they don't see any new technology or any other kind of managerial razzle dazzle there. Instead, what they often overlook but would see if they looked carefully is a different philosophical approach to managing that is very effective and that gives them great competitive advantage. This, however, is one of the hardest things to transfer to American corporations, even when you understand it. Even if you send employees to Japan for a few years to learn about and understand the way the Japanese corporations do business, when they come back to America to share what they've learned, they feel completely frustrated trying to bring this philosophy into practice. So we need to keep probing at what the source of these philosophical differences is or how we can transfer this different management approach.

EMPOWERING EMPLOYEES
AS A TRANSFER STRATEGY?

Maurice Segall

Maybe we need a different approach to transferring managerial sensitivity to multiple stakeholders. What do the rest of you think about having a stakeholder—an employee—sitting on the board and really influencing fundamental decisions?

Raymond Stata

I think it's a misplaced notion. There are other mechanisms by which the employee should participate, and I think it is not necessarily crucial that they affect vital decisions directly. Representatives of employee interests are supposed to focus just on these interests and it would be unrealistic to expect them to be given the respect of the board when the board is dealing with a different set of issues. Employee issues are not to be resolved at the board level. In fact, the principal responsibility of the board is to figure out whether or not to remove the CEO. Beyond that the board must help set the firm's overall strategy and policies, so I think that employee interests are not properly moved up to that level. Are not the stockholders the owners of the corporation? If so, they are the ones who need to be represented on the board.

Donald Ephlin

I obviously disagree. I feel that employees need to be and should be represented on the board of directors in order to bring information that only employees hold to the attention of the board. On a typical board you have a number of inside management people representing one side of the equation, defending their own actions. But nobody is there to challenge them or to provide the perspective of the rest of the employees.

I had the occasion to address the Ford and General Motors boards of directors several times, and each time the outside directors of these companies complimented me afterward because they got information they had never before received. I think there is a very valuable contribution to be made by employee representatives. Second, many decisions get made that the workers react very adversely to only because they did not have all the information they could have had. So I think we would have much more well-run organizations if our boards were balanced in this way.

Laura Divine

I'd like to extend that from the boardroom down into the actual management of day-to-day operations. I support a lot of what Ray Stata is saying because it is in the actual management of the firm on a day-to-day basis that is the best place for employee involvement.

But I continue to wonder what it is that prevents management from running the business in a way that really empowers people, in a way that supports the development of capabilities, that supports the investment in employees. And when we ask for feedback from employees, why don't we listen to them? I don't think it's a matter of them not speaking up; I think it's a matter of us not listening. So I'm still questioning, What is it that holds us back?

Derek Harvey

Superior managers in Mobil are those who believe in participatory management, who empower their employees, and who seek feedback from them. They trust and have a belief in their employees. These managers are most frequently talked about, and they make a difference. This information came out in two- or three-hour interviews, where people were asked to talk about those managers they've had in Mobil they felt were superior. The data were then compared with our own "high-potential" lists, and we saw a strong correlation.

Raymond Stata

I'm a little troubled by this discussion, which seems to be saying that the stakeholder model is sort of a zero-sum game, and that it's some sort of balancing act to manage all these interests as opposed to a model that says there is no limit on the capacity of human beings to create value and wealth, and no limit to learning, and the extent to which they do these things, there will be plenty in it for everybody.

II

USING HUMAN RESOURCES FOR STRATEGIC ADVANTAGE

9

Using Human Resources
in Skill Formation:
The Role of Training

LISA M. LYNCH

As U.S. firms continue to face increasing international competition, deregulation, technological innovation, and changes in the demographic composition of the work force, they are being challenged to examine the skill formation process of their work force in order to increase productivity and remain competitive. Productivity growth in the United States in the 1970s and 1980s lagged behind productivity growth in countries such as Japan, West Germany, Sweden, Italy, and the United Kingdom. There are many reasons cited for this (see Bailey and Chakrabarti, 1988, for a comprehensive survey), but given that labor accounts for at least 70 percent of total costs, if "we could figure out a way to make labor 10 percent more efficient . . . output per hour of work would rise by about 7 percent even with no increase in capital. Such an increase in labor productivity would soon pull investment along . . . and the transitory increase in productivity growth would be impressive" (Blinder, 1990, p. 2).

There are various options and changes in organizational practice discussed in other chapters in this book that, if implemented, would improve productivity. But a necessary condition for firms to gain competitive advantage through innovative human resource utilization is that the work force is well educated, highly skilled, and broadly trained. Unfortunately, one of the major differences between the United States and its competitors is in the skill level and general training of the labor force. This chapter summarizes recent research that has begun to examine the reasons behind our apparent corporate disadvantage in skill formation and presents some examples of best practices in skill formation, which illustrate possible methods for addressing this issue.

THE LEGACY OF SPECIALIZATION

We are in a productivity crisis partly because of our past successes. By defining jobs narrowly and making each job easy to learn, many U.S. firms obtained increased productivity through specialization and through the interchangeability of workers with limited skills and experience rather than training workers to become multiskilled. As technologies change and, as noted in other chapters, the need for cross-functional competencies and problem solving increases, so too does the demand for multiskilled workers. Therefore, it is not surprising that the countries that are experiencing rapid growth in productivity today have typically followed an alternative model in which firms provide both general and firm-specific skills to their workers. This creates a new type of flexibility in the workplace which is more compatible with rapid technological change, new production techniques such as "just-in-time," and otherwise altered organizational structures. Broader skills training for all workers reduces the need for supervisors and allows the day-to-day management of the firm to be performed by workers rather than supervisors. This reduces the hierarchical structure of a typical firm dramatically. The provision of general skills training, however, is not an easy policy for U.S. firms to implement because unlike Japanese firms, where "lifetime employment" leads to low labor turnover, U.S. firms run the risk of investing heavily in workers and losing them to competitors.

As the service sector continues to grow, there is increasing need 'or "knowledge workers" in professional and technical occupations. Traditional educational institutions have not always been able to deliver programs for these kinds of workers, especially in those industries characterized by rapid technological change. Highly skilled technical jobs in professional occupations such as computer, mathematical, and operations research analysts are forecasted to grow by 52 percent and jobs for technicians and related support occupations are expected to increase by 32 percent by the year 2000 in the United States (U.S. Department of Labor, 1989). At the same time the majority of new workers will be minorities with the highest high school dropout rates or women, who, as a group, have historically been underrepresented in those occupations with the largest amounts of on-the-job training. Therefore, companies will find themselves required to develop costly internal training programs in order to remain competitive and to cope with the skill needs of their new workers in the next decade.

The skill acquisition and formation issues discussed in this chapter are closely linked to the human resource innovations presented by Kochan and McKersie (Chapter 11, this volume). A well-structured skill acquisitions or human resource development policy is a necessary precondition for a human resource strategy that seeks to more fully utilize labor. Thus the investment in workers' training must be seen as an essential part of an overall human resource management strategy that links selection, training, career planning, compensation, performance appraisal, and employment security.

This chapter summarizes the findings of a more detailed survey (Lynch, 1991b) on the role of the private sector in the skill development of workers in the United States and expands on another article (Lynch, 1989). It begins with a brief summary of the trends in the demographic composition of the work force and the implications of these trends on the training policies of firms. It then discusses who needs training, who provides training, who pays for it, some innovative "trainers" in the private sector in the United States, and, finally, the structure of training programs provided by the private sector in other countries. It concludes with a brief discussion of policy issues for private sector training in the United States.

WHO ARE THE WORKERS OF THE FUTURE?

Seventy percent of those projected to be working in the year 2000 in the United States are already in the labor force. By the year 2000, as forecasted by the Department of

Labor (1989), there will be several changes in the composition of the work force. For example, the age distribution of the work force will change substantially. Specifically, the "baby bust" will continue with young workers aged 16 to 24 representing only 16 percent of the labor force in the year 2000 versus 19 percent in 1988 and 24 percent in 1976. At the same time the "baby boomers" will be aging, resulting in the share of those 35 to 54 in the work force rising from 40 percent in 1988 to 49 percent by 2000. However, the relative share of workers over the age of 55 will remain constant over this period of time.

Participation of women in the labor force will continue to rise, with women representing 47 percent of all workers in the year 2000 as compared with 45 percent in 1988 and 41 percent in 1976. The share of the labor force composed of minorities will also increase by 2000. Blacks will represent 12 percent of the work force in 2000, up from 11 percent in 1988. Hispanics will go from 7 percent of the labor force in 1988 to 10 percent in 2000. Asians and other remaining minorities will increase from 3 to 4 percent from 1988 to 2000.

All of these compositional changes are the result of two factors, the characteristics of new entrants into the work force and the characteristics of those who leave the work force. A higher percentage of white males will be exiting the labor force from now to the year 2000 while the number of new entrants who are women, African-American, Hispanic, or Asian will be almost 70 percent. This represents a dramatic increase in the diversity of workers in the labor force and it poses many challenges with regard to training.

WHO NEEDS TRAINING?

Given these demographic changes and changes in product demand and technology, who needs training? There are four primary types of workers who need training. These include new entrants into the labor force, permanently displaced workers, employed workers, and long-term unemployed workers. New entrants into the labor force are made up of three subgroups, each with varying stocks of skill and new skills needs. These groups are composed of young people entering the work force for the first time, reentrants (e.g., women) into the labor force who may have worked in the past and are well educated but have been out of the labor force for a period of time, and immigrant workers who come with a variety of skill levels, work experience, and proficiency in English.

The second type, permanently displaced workers, may have been displaced as a result of technological change in their industry or occupation or changes in demand due to increased technological competition or deregulation. The third type of workers includes those who are employed but who need training for promotions, maintenance of already acquired skills, or new jobs following redeployment within the firm. The final category of workers with training needs is the long-term unemployed. Obviously, the range of company and government training programs that need to be provided to these four types of workers varies substantially. For example, as mentioned earlier, the occupations that are expected to grow the most over this period of time are in high-tech areas which require postsecondary education and/or training. However, minorities, who will represent an increasing percentage of new entrants, are not well represented in

Table 9.1 Training needs

Who Needs Training	General Skills[a]	Firm-Specific Skills[a]
Entrants		
Youths	**	*
Women (reentrants)	*	**
Immigrants	**	*
Displaced workers	*	**
Employed workers		
Promotion		**
Redeployment	*	**
Long-term unemployed	***	

[a]Asterisk (*) indicates the degree to which each group needs general or specific skills. Number of asterisks indicates relative need.

these occupations at the moment and they also have much lower high school and college completion rates than their white counterparts. Firms will need to develop more general training programs to enable these workers to get on track within their organizations.

Companies in the United States train their workers extensively, but their training policies have focused primarily on developing formal training programs both within the firm and off-site for young workers, reentrants, those who are being promoted, those needing skills maintenance, and those who are being redeployed. Firms also provide extensive informal training to new workers, but typically with little knowledge of how much is being done, who is receiving it, who is providing it and when, how much time it takes, and how much it costs. Seldom do firms assess the economic returns to either their formal or informal training programs. Most of the firm-provided training is specific to the particular needs of the firm or work site. More general training is left to what workers acquire on their own in the education system before they enter the workplace, or to training they receive from schools (community colleges or night schools) or proprietary institutions, such as vocational and technical institutions, after they have left school and begun to work.

In summary, there are four groups of workers who have very different training needs. New entrants typically need more general skills training (such as quantitative skills) that are relevant for a broad group of employers, while those already employed need more firm-specific skills development. Table 9.1 summarizes the differences in the need for general and firm-specific skills for these workers.

WHY IS THERE UNDERINVESTMENT IN TRAINING?

Human capital theory would predict that firms would be willing to provide general training to their employees if the employees were willing to work for lower wages to pay for this training. This theory thus assumes that general training is typically paid for by the individual employee rather than the firm. If, however, minimum wages (legislated or social norms) make this impossible, firms traditionally are reluctant to pay all the costs for general training since they cannot "capture" the return on their training investment. Another employer could induce a recently trained employee to leave ("cherry picking"), thus burdening the first employer with the training cost but no worker. Recent changes in the structure of minimum wage laws have attempted to address this issue by allowing a lower "training wage" for the first six months of employment to encourage more general training.

On the other hand, employees are not willing to pay for firm-specific training because there is often little portability of these skills to other employers. In this case firms are expected to pay for such training. If workers are constrained in their ability to acquire general training (due to limited resources or access to training providers) and firms are reluctant to pay for most general training, then we run the risk of a market failure in the provision of general skills development. In short, in the absence of other economic incentives that encourage firms collectively to invest more in training, America runs the risk of underinvesting in broad-based skill development.

THE EVIDENCE ON PRIVATE INVESTMENT
IN TRAINING

There have been few studies of training that draw on representative samples of U.S. firms, but Bartel (1989), Barron, Black, and Loewenstein (1987), and Bishop (1989), using company-based data, found that (1) large firms are more likely to provide training than are small firms; (2) formal training programs are just one part of a well-developed internal labor market; and (3) large employers appear to be paying for a portion of general training costs. But an important conclusion that flows from these studies is that firms with higher turnover rates invest less in training, which in turn has the effect of reducing the overall amount of training provided by firms in the United States. Thus if the responsibility for training is left exclusively to firms, and firms have difficulty in capturing general training investments, those workers who need general skills training may be undertrained. Therefore, it is critical to develop a national policy that increases the amount of general training provided in the private sector without further penalizing those firms that already invest more than their fair share.

WHO RECEIVES AND WHO BENEFITS
FROM TRAINING?

There has been relatively little empirical work on the impact of private sector training on the careers of workers compared with the numerous studies on the impact of government training programs. The few studies that have been done have used data from surveys of individual workers and company-based surveys (Lillard and Tan, 1986; Lynch, 1991a). The findings of these studies can be succinctly summarized as follows: (1) although the difference in the probability of males and females receiving any type of training is not significant, males are more likely to receive on-the-job training and females off-the-job training; (2) nonwhites are less likely to receive on-the-job training than whites, holding all other characteristics constant; (3) the likelihood of receiving company-provided training drops when there is high unemployment; (4) not completing high school significantly lowers the probability of receiving training; (5) company-provided training is not very portable from employer to employer for young workers;

(6) union membership significantly raises the probability of receiving on-the-job training; (7) managers and professional and technical employees are more likely to receive company-provided training than are blue-collar or clerical workers; and (8) rapid technological change in the industry of employment increases the probability of receiving in-house company training programs.

There is strong evidence that training pays off for workers. The rates of return to training on wages are quite substantial. For example, Lynch (1991a) finds that the wages of young workers with training rose 11 percent per year, whereas an additional year of tenure on the job without any training raised wages only 4 percent. Mincer (1989) finds similar rates for young workers who receive training but finds that older workers who receive training receive only a 3.6 percent increase in their wages. In summary, although more information is needed on the provision and returns to private sector training, we can say that while the individual returns to this type of training appear to be substantial, this training is unevenly distributed across individuals, occupational groups, and firms. This variance in the amount and type of training firms provide, together with the relatively high turnover rates of American workers, has led to the concern that there is underinvestment in training in the United States.

INNOVATIONS IN TRAINING

This section briefly highlights some specific examples of innovations in training programs in the United States, including the successes and difficulties that these programs have encountered. The firms described here are not the only innovative organizations in the United States, but the experiences of these organizations captures some of the key organizational issues surrounding private sector training.

In the previous section four types of workers were identified who need training. The long-term unemployed are traditionally trained through government programs in the United States, so this section focuses on private sector training programs directed toward the other three groups of workers. Special attention is given to the obstacles that need to be overcome in order to increase the diffusion of these types of firm training policies.

New Entrant Training

Designing training programs for new entrants, especially minority youths who have not completed high school or gone on to postsecondary school, is particularly challenging. The Federal Reserve Board of Boston, however, has offered training in basic business skills to ten to fifteen new inner-city employees every year since 1973 in their Skills Development Center (see Hargroves, 1989, for a complete description). The participants in this program were primarily minority, female, and young and the program trains these individuals for entry-level clerical positions within the bank. The participants are first involved in an academic program to learn basic skills and new clerical skills. At the same time they are given temporary work assignments so that they can begin to acquire valuable work experience. Once basic skills are acquired the trainees try a specific job and if the job match is successful, they are transferred to this job; if not, they return to the Skills Center. The average cost of training per worker is $7,000.

The Federal Reserve Board concluded that although the savings of such a program are not large, the program does ensure a sufficient supply of clerical workers in a very tight labor market. One of the difficulties the bank had, however, in quantifying the costs and benefits of such a program was to identify all of its "savings." Quantifying the returns to training is as difficult as attempting to quantify the long-term benefits of research and development. The long-term gains are often elusive to quantify in the short run, whereas the calculation of the immediate costs is relatively straightforward. This problem of evaluation serves to limit greater diffusion of programs such as this.

Training for the Currently Employed

IBM has developed over the years a very sophisticated approach to skills development within its organization. This Systems Approach to Education tries to divide the training process into a series of manageable steps and to facilitate careful decision making and budget planning at each stage to maintain cost control of training. IBM has developed detailed curricula for every major job category and the company uses classrooms, interactive videodiscs, self-study, supervised self-study, computer-based training, tutored video, and satellite classrooms (see Casner-Lotto, 1988, for additional information) for its training programs. One of the key features of this program is its flexibility in adapting to the different needs of the employees and the company.

Displaced and Redeployed Worker Training

The IBM Systems Approach is a useful model for skills development associated with natural promotion within an organization; firms that find themselves redeploying workers due to changes in product demand or technology have introduced other innovations in training. Three examples of such training initiatives include the experience of the computer, telephone, and auto industries. For example, Digital Equipment Corporation in 1985 introduced its Transition Process to deal with overstaffing in the company (see Kochan, Osterman, and MacDuffie, 1987, for a complete discussion of this). The process is divided into three stages: (1) selection of "available" employees; (2) counseling and training; and (3) exit from the program to another job at DEC or outside the company. DEC found that many employees were unwilling to take the risk of training for a new occupation since they were convinced that the downturn would be short and that they would be recalled to their old jobs. Thus only about 15 percent of those offered training chose this option. An important lesson from this case, therefore, is that most employees do not respond well to training opportunities that are presented to them in a crisis situation. It takes an ongoing commitment to upgrading skills to create a successful training and development program. However, the company found that the Transition Process had preserved its reputation as a firm committed to employment security, and this resulted in higher morale and loyalty during a difficult period.

Both the auto and telephone industries have reached innovative joint company–union agreements with regard to the role of training in the organizational changes both of these industries are undergoing. For example, BellSouth and the Communication Workers of America agreed to a Career Continuation Program, which takes workers who are about to be laid off and enrolls them into this program with pay and benefits. In addition, the program reimburses up to $2,500 for items such as tuition and books for courses both within and outside BellSouth. The program is an attempt to maintain a commitment to the employees to preserve jobs but at the same time implement a massive reorganization of the company necessitated by deregulation and changes in technology (see Lynch and Osterman, 1989, for additional information). One of the advantages of this program is the cap it places on the number of weeks employees can participate. If at the end of a predetermined period they are not transferred into a new job, their final severance is reduced by the number of days in the program. The hope is that the employees will feel that they are making a financial investment in the program as well as the company and that this will increase the effectiveness of the program.

The auto industry since 1982 has also had training programs jointly designed and administered by the union and the company for the skills development of active and displaced workers. These joint programs were negotiated through collective bargaining. The UAW–Ford agreement established an employee development and training program that differs from the well-established internal training programs in the company such as apprenticeships. Instead, this program provides tuition assistance for new job training outside Ford, assists active employees with advice and programs for their future both within and outside Ford, and offers training and counseling in high school completion. One unique feature of this program is that the company agreed to finance general skills training for employees who might eventually leave the firm. The auto industry has been a path breaker in the United States for the provision of general skills training, but it is not clear that this is a practice that should or will be emulated in other industries or in smaller firms.

INTERNATIONAL COMPARISONS

There are some distinct differences in the training policies and training institutions in countries such as Germany, Sweden, Great Britain, and Japan from those in the United States. For example, the system of vocational training schemes, called the dual system, is often cited as one of the primary forces behind West Germany's high productivity growth (see Disney, 1989; and Prais and Wagner, 1983; for reviews of the West German system). This system trains individuals in specific skills, but, perhaps more important, it teaches young workers that they will have to learn many new skills over their career. Training in Germany, however, is not restricted to the apprenticeship scheme for school leavers. The government created many other types of training programs to assist adult workers in retraining. These include a voucher system for training and wage subsidies to firms providing on-the-job training. Adults may enter a certified training course where the training institute is reimbursed by the government for all of the costs of training. The individual may also receive an earnings-related subsistence allowance in the form of a grant or a loan. In addition, the government supports individual firms providing training through a wage subsidy which is paid to the firm.

In Sweden, training is just one component of a very broad economic policy to promote full employment. Since the early 1980s there has been an expansion of resources devoted to providing in-house training programs to prevent job losses (see Standing, 1988, for a review of the Swedish model of training). In addition, subsidies have been given to firms that provide training for men or women in occupations that are overrepresented by one sex or the other (Sweden has greater occupational segregation than the United States even though the female–male wage differential is around 90 percent). Perhaps the most innovative and controversial policy was the passage in 1984 of legislation creating "renewal funds" whereby large establishments must put 10 percent of their net profits into a fund for research and training. Rather than raising taxes and using the revenue to provide government training programs, the government has instead required firms to set aside a minimum designated explicitly for training. The approach in Sweden thus is to encourage firms to regard investments in training the same way that they regard investments in research and development.

The current government in Great Britain recently proposed dramatic reforms to promote employment growth into the 1990s (U.K. Department of Employment, 1988) that focus on the importance of private sector training. Noting that seven out of ten of the employed workers in the year 2000 in Great Britain are already employed and that most of these workers have left school at the minimum age of sixteen and have not acquired any qualifications since then, the government has established Training and Enterprise Councils (TECs). These councils will plan and deliver training programs at the local level. Specifically, they will assess the skill needs of their local labor market and identify prospects of expanded job growth and the availability of appropriate training programs in the local area. They will then manage training programs for young people, the unemployed, and employed adults requiring new knowledge and technical retraining. There will also be additional support for small firms. At least two-thirds of the TEC members will be top management employers and the remaining members will be senior figures from local education, training and economic development agencies, and trade unions who support the aims of the council. There is, however, no mandatory role for any group other than the employers. This differs then from the German system, where there is a mandatory role for groups other than employers, especially the trade unions. In fact, the British government states, "that it hopes to 'place ownership' of the training and enterprise system where it belongs—with the employer" (U.K. Department of Employment, 1988, p. 40).

The basic educational system in Japan focuses on providing a high level of very general skills to its graduates (Sako and Dore, 1988). Therefore, more firm-specific skills must be taught at the firm level. Most of that instruction is done by the supervisor, who has the responsibility of teaching and motivating subordinates. Some firms even measure a group's performance by the percentage of the workers who can do a number of tasks. Interestingly, most off-the-job training in Japan takes place through correspondence courses. As in Germany, skills testing is an important component of training. There are testing centers in every prefect in Japan. Under Japan's Vocational Training Law, prefect governors can authorize training programs developed by employers, unions, and employer associations. Local and national governments are also required under this law to provide financial assistance to employers and employees participating in in-house training. These take the form of traineeship loans, financial assistance to firms with fewer than 300 employees, incentive grants for paid educational leave, and professional advisory and institutional services (Inoue, 1985). As in the United States, most training is done by large firms, but smaller Japanese firms are more likely than smaller U.S. firms, to try to pool their resources.

POLICY ISSUES FOR PRIVATE SECTOR TRAINING

American firms face a variety of issues and challenges as they reexamine the way in which they train and retrain their workers. The old model of mass production, which generated narrow job definitions, low skill levels, and a reliance on informal training of firm-specific skills, is not an effective structure for new production techniques that require multiskilled workers such as those described by MacDuffie and Krafcik (Chapter 13, this volume). In addition, as the service sector continues to grow there is increasing need for "knowledge workers" in professional and technical occupations. If new entrants into the labor force or older workers with limited general skills do not have the qualifications for these new technical jobs, firms will have to decide whether to train these workers or to hire qualified workers outside the firm (if they are available). This is a difficult decision because unlike Japanese firms, where lifetime employment leads to low labor turnover, U.S. firms run the risk of investing heavily in workers and then losing them to competitors. Another option would be to move production to those countries that can supply the necessary skills (although even in Europe one of the major policy issues is "skills mismatching"). Whatever decision is made, if the "skills gap" is not addressed, U.S. firms will continue to have low productivity growth.

Given the variety of workers who have training needs and the range of types of training that they need (from firm-specific to general training), it is not possible to identify one training strategy that will be effective in improving competitiveness. Rather, there exists a "menu" of options for employees, employers, and the government to choose from. For example, until now, U.S. firms, especially those in manufacturing, have relied on an informal system of training workers with workers learning on the job. However, workers who want to enter into the growing technical and professional occupations are not going to be successfully trained in this informal system. There are few training centers prepared to train these new technical and professional workers. Therefore, many firms, especially larger firms, have chosen to invest in the training of workers in-house. But often these companies have difficulty in justifying or evaluating the various training programs they offer. A large part of this is due to the difficulty in measuring the costs and benefits of various training programs. For example, do the costs of training include just the direct costs of providing teachers, materials, and tuition to run a course, or do they also include indirect costs such as lower productivity and wages paid during training? How does a company measure the costs of informal training?

For those who choose to train in-house many develop their programs with the assistance of outside training vendors. Typically, the vendors are asked to evaluate the effectiveness of their training course. Apart from the moral hazard problem associated with having the vendor evaluate the course, the evaluation criteria often focus on how "happy" the participants were with the course rather than on actual measures of posttraining performance. Although it is important to evaluate the effectiveness of training programs, many firms are reluctant to do this because they are concerned that a formal cost/benefit analysis will not measure the longer term benefits of training. However, firms make these sorts of evaluations for investments in research and development all the time, so perhaps it would be appropriate for firms to evaluate training investments the same way they consider evaluating investment decisions in the R&D.

While in-house training programs may be effective for currently employed workers, the training issues associated with new entrants are closely linked to the quantity and quality of the educational system that these young workers come from. Therefore, the establishment of links between the business community and local schools may result in upgraded schools and consequently firms would be more able to invest in incremental skills training because the ability to learn would be higher. One example of such a program is the Boston Compact, an agreement signed in 1982 committing business leaders, public educators, and local government officials to improving the quality of education in order to enhance the skill levels of Boston high school graduates entering the workplace. This program has been so successful that the National Alliance of Business has replicated the compact in ten metropolitan areas across the country.

In-house training programs and business–school links will not be sufficient to address all training needs. The encouragement of regional and industry consortia to clearly identify training and work force needs and to communicate them to local community colleges and vocational educational schools or proprietary institutions could greatly assist the skills development of displaced workers and those currently employed. In particular, smaller companies have limited resources to provide training, but at the same time often have the greatest training needs for multiskilled workers. Most of the employment growth in the United States in the 1980s and 1990s has been and will continue to be in small businesses. By pooling their resources to set up programs that provide the training for common skills needs, these smaller firms can greatly improve their productivity at a modest cost. Employers in Europe have had much more experience than U.S. employers in working in confederations to develop these kinds of programs.

Another option that has been proposed in the United States to assist firms that wish to train their workers but do not have the resources to do this is to give various tax breaks or subsidies to firms that train. This may be one way to encourage firms to provide more general training when labor mobility is high, but there are some limitations with this type of policy. For example, should firms that receive subsidies be monitored to make sure that they are using the money for training or for training they would not have otherwise provided? Should employees, and their representatives, be given a voice in the design and oversight of training programs and thereby perform part of this monitoring and quality control function? Are subsidies alone sufficient to help smaller firms? Would expansionary macroeconomic policies be more effective in raising the skill levels of workers?

Much of the recent policy discussion has focused on "privatizing" training—that is, shifting the burden of training and development to private sector employers. Although there are advantages of this strategy, such as increased relevance of training programs, there are possible dangers to a training policy that relies exclusively on the private sector. As discussed earlier, firms have an incentive to provide firm-specific training but are more reluctant to make massive investments in general skills development. One option to encourage more of this is for public policy to encourage joint participation—the consultation of workers in the design and administration of any training subsidies granted to firms. This would help ensure that subsidized training is a supplement to and not a replacement for the firm's specific training expenditures. Perhaps some demonstration projects should be encouraged along these lines.

Employers, schools, and government are not the only players that could participate in the provision of training. Labor unions should also consider becoming more vocal advocates in collective bargaining for expanded joint training programs. This could be an important component of the activities labor uses to represent current members and to recruit new members.

Finally, it is important to note that it would be a mistake to simply implement what appears to be best practice in training without understanding how training fits within a broader human resource management strategy. In other words, no firm is likely to have a successful investment program in training unless it has a corresponding commitment to human resource and competitive strategies that require multiskilled, committed, and motivated workers. Moreover, no firm will achieve the full returns to an aggressive human resource development policy unless it has a concurrent strategy to (1) establish employment security provisions and (2) fully utilize the skills by providing opportunities for workers to solve problems, influence their work environment, and share in the benefits of improved productivity and corporate performance.

Regardless of the specific training policies selected, there appears to be a need at the state and/or national level for greater coordination of training efforts by firms; local, state, and federal governments; unions; schools; and other training institutions in the United States. Thus the need for more training and skills development is just another issue among those discussed in this book that requires not only changes *within* organizations but also *across* organizational boundaries and institutions.

Our major economic competitors have implemented comprehensive plans to train and develop their workers so that they will be able to respond to the demands associated with new technologies and increasing international competition. As Europe moves toward greater coordination in 1992 it has been proposed in various European Communities Commission documents that a major part of the social dimension of 1992 will be to expand training programs. The reason behind this is that "the process of introducing new technologies would be economically more viable and socially more acceptable if accompanied by effective training and greater motivation for both workers and managerial staff" (Venturini, 1989, p. 95). The United States will be challenged to do the same in the area of skill formation if it hopes to remain competitive.

REFERENCES

Bailey, M., and A. Chakrabarti. 1988. *Innovations and the Productivity Crisis*. Washington, D.C.: The Brookings Institution.
Barron, J., D. Black, and M. Loewenstein. 1987. "Employer Size: The Implications for Search, Training Capital Investment, Starting Wages, and Wage Growth." *Journal of Labor Economics* 5, no. 1: 76–89.
Bartel, A. 1989. "Formal Employee Training Programs and Their Impact on Labor Productivity: Evidence from a Human Resource Survey." NBER working paper 3026.
Bishop, J. 1988. "Do Employers Share the Costs and Benefits of General Training?" Cornell University Center for Advanced Human Resource Studies working paper 88-08.
Blinder, A. 1990. *Paying for Productivity*. Washington, D.C.: The Brookings Institution.
Casner-Lotto, J. 1988. "Achieving Cost Savings and Quality Through Education: IBM's

Systems Approach." In *Successful Training Strategies,* edited by J. Casner-Lotto and Associates, San Francisco: Jossey-Bass.

Disney, R. 1989. "Labour Market Policies Towards the Adult Unemployed in Germany: An Overview." Draft mimeo, University of Kent.

Hargroves, J. 1989. "Basic Skills and Clerical Training for New Employees: One Bank Looks at Its Investment." *New England Economic Review.* September/October, 58–68.

Inoue, K. 1985. "The Education and Training of Industrial Manpower in Japan." World Bank working paper 729, Washington, D.C.

Kochan, T., P. Osterman, and J. P. MacDuffie. 1987. "Staffing in a Changing Environment: A Case Study at Digital Equipment Corporation," mimeo, MIT Industrial Relations Section.

Lillard, L., and H. Tan. 1986. "Private Sector Training: Who Gets It and What Are Its Effects?" Rand monograph R-3331-DOL/RC.

Lynch, L. M. 1989. "The Role of the Private Sector in Training." *Forty-Third Annual IRRA Proceedings.* pp. 387–395.

Lynch, L. M. 1991a. "Private Sector Training and Its Impact on the Earnings of Young Workers." *American Economic Review.* Forthcoming.

Lynch, L. M. 1991b. "The Private Sector and Skill Formation in the United States: A Survey," mimeo. Reprinted in *Advances in the Study of Entrepreneurship, Innovation, and Economic Growth: The Education and Quality of the American Labor Force,* edited by Gary Libecap. Greenwich, Conn.: JAI Press. Forthcoming.

Lynch, L., and P. Osterman. 1989. "Technological Innovation and Employment in Telecommunications." *Industrial Relations,* Spring, vol. 28, no. 2: 188–205.

Mincer, J. 1989. "Human Capital and the Labor Market: A Review of Current Research." *Educational Researcher,* May, pp. 27–34.

Prais, S. J., and K. Wagner. 1983. "Some Practical Aspects of Human Capital Investment: Training Standards in Five Occupations in Britain and Germany." *National Institute Economic Review,* August, no. 105: 46–65.

Sako, M., and R. Dore. 1988. "Teaching or Testing: The Role of the State in Japan." *Oxford Review of Economic Policy,* Autumn, vol. 4, no. 3: 72–81.

Standing, G. 1988. "Training, Flexibility and Swedish Full Employment." *Oxford Review of Economic Policy,* Autumn, vol. 4, no. 3: 94–107.

U.K. Department of Employment. 1988. *Employment for the 1990s.* London: HMSO.

U.S. Department of Labor. 1989. "Outlook 2000." *Monthly Labor Review,* November, vol. 112, no. 11.

Venturini, P. 1989. *1992: The European Social Dimension.* Luxembourg: Office for Official Publications of the European Communities.

COMMENTARY BY PATRICK FINCKLER

Traditionally, we have concentrated on developing employees with specialized skills rather than on developing multiskilled workers. I had previously been a proponent of specialization: it's easier to teach, and easier for employees to learn. However, I have been consistently encountering human resource stumbling blocks. In insurance, a company is divided into many small units, each of which can be brought to a screeching halt if a specialized person leaves. I believe that job specialization decreases job satisfaction, increases turnover, and lessens the dedication of the employees.

We need to develop multiskilled workers via cross-training. It will be more difficult to teach and learn but an abundance of cross-trained employees reduces turnover and its negative consequences. When you cross-train, jobs become more interesting and workers become more skilled and productive, thus allowing you to pay higher wages.

An emphasis on and commitment to cross-training also encourages the development of a cadre of workers from the top down that enjoy learning. It decreases organizational rigidities to change and eventually creates a long-term competitive advantage for your firm.

I agree that there is a relationship between turnover and training. But I wonder which is the cause and which the effect? Does the turnover result in the company's underinvestment in training (the firm feels like it's not going to keep them anyway, so why bother?) or does the lack of training result in the turnover, since workers are dissatisfied with their jobs and lack of challenge?

In my opinion, the development of a training competency within the organization is vitally important and extremely valuable in that it maximizes the productivity of short-term employees while mitigating the negative impact of turnover.

COMMENTARY BY FRAN RODGERS

I think Lisa Lynch identified the skills gap problem we have in this country very well. If anything, though, she underestimated that skill gap and America's quality worker shortage. At the present time without major efforts to reverse them, these problems are only going to get worse. We have fewer young workers, our schools are not giving our kids the skills we in industry need them to have, and children are being born disproportionately to parents without the financial resources to invest in them. At the rate we are going, the chronically unemployed of tomorrow will be today's crack babies, and today's "chronically underemployed"—those who can't read and write—will be the standard entry-level workers of tomorrow.

When we are trying to understand the cause of these problems, we can identify difficulties at the level of colleges, the high schools, and go all the way down to the elementary schools and to preschool and day care. Most efforts to "fix" labor force problems through education have started too late in children's lives; fail to address parenting, family, and workplace issues; and therefore cannot and will not succeed.

At the same time we have not faced up to education issues, we have also not ensured that we are taking advantage of the labor force that exists and can contribute. I'm a little concerned about Lisa Lynch's grouping women as though they are an "underclass." Women are now the majority of college graduates. A critical reason why we cannot capitalize on the talents and higher education of women is that we have not yet adapted to the feminization of the work force. A fundamental resistance to change has caused us to force women and men with new family structures into outmoded career molds, and this has led to massive frustration and the underutilization of talent and ambition. Barriers include a confusion of time at work with contribution, hierarchical career paths, and pervasive gender bias.

A lot of our managers don't really know how to manage at all. Training is necessary to teach managers to manage, motivate, and deal with diverse people. However, training alone can't "teach" how to manage work and families and diversity issues in the workplace. We can no longer separate the needs in the work force from business strategy. They are one and the same. Addressing issues of education and women's participation goes to the heart of our value system. But we must grapple with them if America is to be competitive.

10

Cross-Functional Teams: Blessing or Curse for New Product Development?

DEBORAH GLADSTEIN ANCONA AND DAVID E. CALDWELL

The popular literature is often prone to lambasting U.S. management practices as the culprit responsible for the trade deficit, the loss of technological leadership, and the lag in U.S. competitiveness. The cry has gone out to revamp our organizations; to move away from specialized jobs to broader work responsibilities; away from narrow functional perspectives to an enterprise-wide view; and away from rigid hierarchies to more fluid, flexible structures that can be more reactive to technological, market, and competitive change (Drucker, 1988; Kanter, 1989; Mintzberg, 1988).

In partial response to these demands organizations have set up cross-functional teams in areas such as new product and new process development (Ancona and Caldwell, 1990; Tyre and Hauptman, 1989). These teams are designed to react quickly and nimbly, from a broad perspective, and to do in parallel the tasks that used to be done sequentially. The payoff is presumed to be improved time to market, lower costs due to rework, and improved innovation and quality. In short, cross-functional teams are viewed as an important strategy for addressing productivity disadvantages U.S. firms are believed to have in moving quickly from concept to marketplace.

Yet, despite the prescriptions and increase in team activity, there is little empirical research that directly tests whether, in fact, the creation of functionally diverse teams improves new product development. The evidence that does exist comes from anecdotal case studies (Kidder, 1981) from settings outside the United States or from process rather than product teams (see Clark and Fujimoto, 1987; Kazanjian and Drazen, 1986; Tyre and Hauptman, 1989). In contrast to this optimistic scenario, theory exists suggesting that diversity may actually impede new product development.

Indeed, there are theoretical reasons to believe that simply changing the structure of teams (i.e., combining representatives from different functions) will not improve performance. It is predicted that functional diversity will improve a team's ability to communicate and coordinate with *external* parts of the organization on which it is dependent (Ancona and Caldwell, 1989; Pfeffer, 1986), but this same diversity can adversely affect *internal* group processes. Diversity has been shown to increase conflict, reduce cohesion, complicate internal communications, and hamper coordination within the team (Dougherty, 1987; Kiesler, 1978; O'Reilly and Flatt, 1989; Shaw, 1971; Wagner, Pfeffer, and O'Reilly, 1984). The conflict literature predicts intensified intragroup conflict when interdependence exists among parties with different goals, such as members from manufacturing, marketing, and engineering (Schmidt and

Kochan, 1972). The small groups literature points to the difficulty of merging different cognitive styles, attitudes, and values (Bettenhausen and Murnighan, 1985; Shaw, 1971), such as those found on teams with diverse members. If not managed effectively, these internal processes may slow decision making or result in compromise solutions rather than truly creative problem solving. Thus the question is whether diversity actually impedes or facilitates team performance.

This chapter summarizes the results of a study of team diversity, process, and performance in forty-five new product teams in five high-technology companies. This study is part of a broader ongoing research effort aimed at understanding team performance within new organization structures. The results show that the emerging consensus around the desirability of cross-functional teams may be too simplistic. Diversity appears to have contradictory, complex effects that sometimes facilitate, and sometimes hinder, innovation and success. To turn this diversity into an asset, mechanisms need to be put in place to accentuate the positive and overcome the negative effects of diversity. The final section of this chapter, therefore, outlines a series of strategies for managing functionally diverse teams.

A MODEL LINKING DIVERSITY TO PERFORMANCE

This study investigates the impact of a new product team's diversity on its performance. Diversity is predicted to affect the internal process of a group and the ways its members communicate with outsiders. In addition, both internal and external processes can influence the performance of new product groups. Finally, group researchers have long noted that team diversity can have direct, as well as indirect (through group process) effects on group performance. Figure 10.1 illustrates the various links from diversity to performance. The remainder of this section provides evidence to justify each link.

Diversity

In examining the relationship between team diversity and group process and performance, many researchers have used the research tradition of demography. This

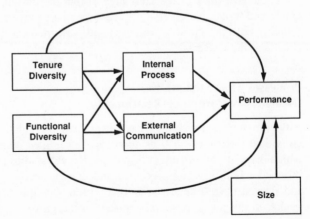

Figure 10.1 A model of new product team performance.

tradition suggests that the demographic characteristics of cohorts within a population can significantly influence a wide range of variables. When applied to organizational phenomena, for example, the demographic composition of groups has been related to turnover among university faculty (McCain, O'Reilly, and Pfeffer, 1983), top managers (Wagner et al., 1984), and nurses (Pfeffer and O'Reilly, 1987); to performance ratings of subordinates (Tsui and O'Reilly, 1989); to executive succession (Pfeffer and Moore, 1980); and to innovation in organizations (O'Reilly and Flatt, 1989). All of these studies suggest that it is the distribution of people within a group across variables such as age or tenure that influences behavior, rather than simpler descriptions of the same variables, such as the mean age of the group or the proportion of the group with a particular tenure.

Many studies of group demography have used both age and tenure measures; time of entry into the firm is thought to shape communication patterns and values while age shapes the pattern of cohorts that develop (Ryder, 1965; Wagner et al., 1984). Because we are most interested in communication patterns and values, we look at tenure diversity in new product teams.

Although not part of the demography research tradition, the most important diversity variable for development teams may be functional mix. Teams may differ in terms of the proportion of individuals from each functional area. At one extreme, a team might be made up entirely of individuals from research and development. At the other extreme, one-third of a team's members might be from research and development, one-third from marketing, and one-third from manufacturing. An entropy-based diversity index (Teachman, 1980) that captures this continuum from single function to equal proportions of members is used in this study (see Ancona & Caldwell, 1989, for more detail on measurement).

The use of cross-functional teams has been proposed as a method of speeding the product development process (see Calantone and Cooper, 1981; Cooper, 1979; Voss, 1985). These teams offer two potential advantages. First, the team has direct access to expertise and information that would not be available if all team members were from the same area. Second, since the team includes representatives from the manufacturing and marketing areas, product design and transfer will be facilitated. Despite these advantages, teams made up of individuals from different "thought worlds" may find it difficult to develop a shared purpose and an effective group process (Dougherty, 1987).

These two lines of research suggest that the design of the team as defined by the tenure and functional diversity of team members may be important variables for understanding both the group's processes and performance. This study examines both variables and their effects.

Processes That Mediate the Diversity–Performance Relationship

Although numerous studies have examined the relationship between diversity and individual outcomes such as turnover, fewer have examined the processes through which diversity has its effect in groups. Recent studies provide evidence that diversity influences both internal processes and external communication. O'Reilly, Caldwell, and Barnett (1989) demonstrate that within a sample of work teams, homogeneity of tenure on the job is positively related to the group's social integration. They further show that the aggregate social integration of the group is related to individual turnover. This suggests that at least one process by which diversity has an impact is through the development of cohesive groups. Although not part of the model they tested, O'Reilly et al. speculate that tenure similarity facilitates social integration by increasing both the opportunities for interaction and the attractiveness of members to one another. They propose that people with similar entrance dates may undergo similar experiences and develop a common perspective.

Although the demography literature most often specifies group cohesiveness or social integration as the mediating group process, for work teams the argument has been made that processes related to task accomplishment may be more important to performance than those reflecting affect within the team (Goodman, Ravlin, and Schminke, 1987). In this study rather than looking at the cohesiveness of the team, we examine the team's effectiveness in defining goals, developing workable plans, and prioritizing work. Diversity is predicted to influence performance through these intervening internal processes.

Zenger and Lawrence (1989) offer further evidence of the process by which diversity affects outcomes. Theirs is the only study that has investigated the effects of demographic composition on research and development teams. In that study, Zenger and Lawrence observed that age similarity was positively related to the frequency of communication among members of the teams. They observed a different pattern for communications with engineers outside the team. Here, similarity of tenure was more highly related to frequency of communication than was similarity of age. Thus, in addition to influencing internal processes, tenure diversity also influences communications between the team and outsiders.

Functional diversity brings together different "thought worlds" reflecting different orientations toward the product, the market, and work itself (Dougherty, 1987). Having representatives from different functions as team members is predicted to facilitate communication with nonteam members from those functions, but this structure may also create internal conflicts. Members of similar functions share a common language and orientation, which makes communication easier (Kiesler, 1978). Yet the conflicts that inevitably exist between functions get brought into a cross-functional team and may interfere with defining goals and priorities. In sum, we predict that both tenure and functional diversity will have an impact on new product team performance through internal task processes and external communication.

Predicting New Product Team Performance

Thus far we have been rather vague in defining exactly what is meant by performance. In this study we include ratings of performance made by both team members and top division managers, since many previous studies have shown little relationship between the two sets of ratings (Ancona, 1990; Gladstein, 1984). Team member scores are an average of ratings made on eight dimensions of performance: efficiency, quality, technical innovation, adherence to budgets, adherence to schedule, coordination, work excellence, and ability to resolve conflicts. For top managers analysis showed an underlying pattern of two factors or dimensions by which performance was judged. One dimension is efficiency and quality of technical innovation; the other is adherence to budgets and schedules. Based on this analysis (see Ancona and Caldwell, 1989, for more detailed statistics) we are left with three measures of performance: team-rated performance and two dimensions of managerial-rated performance.

Again, we predict that diversity influences internal process and external communication, and they, in turn, influence all aspects of performance. New product development teams are particularly dependent on communication patterns and processes both within the group and with outsiders (Allen, 1984; Katz, 1982; Tushman, 1977, 1979). These teams must obtain information and resources from other parts of the organization, interact internally to create a viable product, and transfer their work to other groups who will build and market the product (Ancona and Caldwell, 1987; Burgelman, 1983; Quinn and Mueller, 1963). Thus, in order to successfully complete a product, team members must be able to communicate with outsiders and to be able to work with one another.

Yet diversity may not act solely through internal process and external communication. Group researchers have long noted that group composition, for example, diversity, can have direct as well as indirect (mediated by group process) effects on group performance (Gladstein, 1984; Shaw, 1971). Just having the appropriate mix of skills, experience, and knowledge may influence performance. Similarly, diversity may have its effect through some process that has not yet been identified but manifests itself through a direct influence of diversity on performance.

This study thus investigates two things: the direct effects of group diversity on new product team performance and the indirect effects of diversity attributable to group process and to external communication. Diversity consists of the variability of tenure among team members and the degree of representation of multiple functions such as marketing, manufacturing, and engineering. Group process refers to the team's ability to define goals, develop working plans, and prioritize work. External communication is the average amount of communication team members had with marketing, manufacturing, engineering, and product or division management over a two-week period. Performance consists of team member overall ratings and division management ratings of innovation and achieving budget and schedule.

Complex Relationships

The link between diversity and performance may not be straightforward, since we have complicated its examination by considering two aspects of diversity—tenure homogeneity and functional diversity—and two mediating process variables—internal processes and external communications—across multiple performance indicators. For example, a high level of homogeneity within a group is likely to increase the cohesiveness and communication within the group (Festinger, 1954; Hoffman, 1985; Newcomb, 1961; Ward, La Gory, and Sherman, 1985), but this same homogeneity may act to retard external communication (Ancona, 1987; Katz, 1982). If both internal and external communications are positively related to performance, then homogeneity may be simultaneously improving and dampening performance. Similarly, functional diversity may positively influence performance through its impact on external communication, but it may simultaneously have a negative direct impact. Finally, variables that have a large impact on one aspect of performance, such as achieving budget and schedule, may have no impact on other performance measures, such as innovation. We examine these relationships while controlling for group size. The results provide greater insight into the complex impact of diversity.

New Product Team Characteristics

Before reporting on the study results we describe the new product teams that made up our sample. The study involved the leaders and members of forty-five new product teams in five high-technology companies in the computer, analytic instrumentation, and photographic industries. All of the teams were actively working on the development of new products as opposed to basic research. Each was responsible for developing a prototype product and transferring it to the groups responsible for manufacturing and marketing. For example, one team was developing a product to automate the sampling process used in liquid chromatography, and another was developing a new printing device that combined photographic and computer imaging processes. Thus each team was actively engaged in technological innovation yet responsible for ensuring the manufacturability and marketability of the new product.

Each organization was asked to provide access to a set of teams that had the following characteristics:

1. All the teams had to be working on new product development (defined as a major extension to an existing product line or the start of a new product line).
2. To ensure some broad consistency in the complexity of the products, all teams had a development cycle of one and one-half to three years.
3. All the teams had to be located within a single division to assure comparable performance evaluations.
4. Performance of the teams had to range from high to low, but company executives did not reveal how teams were initially classified until all other data had been collected.

Once the sample of teams was identified, a list of teams members was obtained from company records and verified with team leaders. The average was approximately ten.

Of the 450 questionnaires distributed to team members and leaders, 409 were returned, yielding a response rate of approximately 89 percent. Response rates were approximately equal across companies. In the final sample the average age was 38.6; 88 percent were male; 75 percent possessed at least a four-year college degree. Approximately 77 percent of the sample were engineering or research and development; the remaining 23 percent were primarily from manufacturing or marketing.

DISCUSSION OF STUDY RESULTS

The increasing reliance on teams to develop new products raises a variety of questions. One important set of questions relates to how teams should be formed. For example, should they be formed completely of engineers, or should they include a range of specialists from other functional areas? Similarly, do teams perform best when they are made up of people who have long tenure in the organization, or when they are made up of people who represent a wide range of experience? The results of path analysis

Table 10.1 Linkages between variables in the model—
directionality and significance

Variables	Direction	Significance
Tenure diversity—internal process	+	*
Tenure diversity—external communication	+	N.S.
Functional diversity—internal process	+	N.S.
Functional diversity—external communication	+	**
Tenure diversity—innovation	−	N.S.
Functional diversity—innovation	−	**
Internal process—innovation	+	N.S.
External communication—innovation	+	*
Tenure diversity—team-rated performance	−	N.S.
Functional diversity—team-rated performance	−	*
Internal process—team-rated performance	+	**
External communication—team-rated performance	+	N.S.

$*p \leq .05$; $**p \leq .01$; N.S., not significant.

applied to forty-five new product teams show that diversity influences performance both directly and through its effects on internal process and external communication. The results of the path analysis are summarized in Table 10.1 and the detailed statistical analysis from which the results are drawn are available in Ancona and Caldwell (1989).

Diversity–Process–Performance Relationships

Before discussing the relationships between group diversity and the other variables, the links between process and performance are worth noting. As in other studies of work groups, internal process is related to team ratings of performance (Gladstein, 1984). That is, teams that rate themselves as having clear goals and priorities also rate themselves as innovative, efficient, good at adhering to budget and schedule, and good overall performers. A number of explanations for this connection are possible. Members may be labeling their team as high performing if it exhibits the processes thought to be linked to performance (Calder, 1977; Gladstein, 1984). Alternatively, members who view their team as effective may attribute effective processes to it. This relationship between internal process and performance holds only for team-rated performance.

In contrast, top management ratings of achieving budget and schedule and innovation are related to the frequency of team members' external communications, although the overall model predicting budget and schedule was not significant. External communications may be of a technical nature, allowing the team to improve the quality of its product (Allen, 1984). Alternatively, they may be geared toward profile management, whereby team members try to influence key outsiders to promote and support their product (Ancona and Caldwell, 1988). Finally, it may be that teams that know they have the support of top management are more willing to communicate with outsiders than those without such support.

Although this study provides evidence that diversity influences performance through group processes, interestingly, each demographic variable seems to operate in a distinct way. The more heterogeneous the group in terms of tenure, the greater the clarity of the group's goals and priorities. In turn, this clarity is associated with high team ratings of overall performance. Thus although homogeneity of tenure is associated with greater cohesiveness in the group (Festinger, 1954; Hoffman, 1985) when it comes time to define goals and assess priorities, a group may do better with multiple experiences and perspectives that help it to define goals more in line with complex demands placed upon it. This is particularly likely with groups such as product development teams, which must operate in complex environments and respond to conflicting demands.

In contrast to tenure diversity, greater functional diversity is associated with more external communication. The more external communication team members have with other groups, the higher the managerial ratings of team innovation. When one brings representatives of different functions into the team, one gets more contacts and greater ease of communication with members of those functional groups given their shared language, socialization, and worldview (Dougherty, 1987; Lawrence and Lorsch, 1969). In turn, this greater communication across internal organizational boundaries is associated with greater innovation.

Taken together, these findings show the complexity with which diversity can influence outcomes. Further, they suggest that in order to use the results of studies of diversity each situation must be diagnosed with respect to type of diversity—tenure or functional—the nature of a group's task—simple or complex—and the type of group process—cohesiveness, task work, or external communication.

Direct Links Between Diversity and Performance

Although there is evidence of diversity's indirect effect on performance through group process, this study provides even stronger evidence of diversity's direct effect on performance. High levels of functional diversity were directly associated with lower levels of performance, particularly for management ratings of innovation and for team's ratings of their own performance. Diversity of tenure shows a similar, albeit less strong negative relationship with performance. These results are consistent with those of O'Reilly and Flatt (1989), showing a direct relationship between homogeneity and an organizational measure of innovation.

What can account for this contradictory effect of diversity? On the one hand, it produces processes that facilitate performance; on the other, it directly impedes performance. One possibility is that diverse teams are able to develop goals and priorities but not implement them because of the conflict different perspectives create. A second possibility is that diversity allows for high levels of external communication but also reduces the social integration to such a level that the group cannot effectively use the information and resources obtained from others. Third, the data from this study were all collected before the product reached manufacturing. It may be that when diversity is introduced to a team activities that were once carried out later in the development cycle are now moved to an earlier point. Teams that are struggling with diverse inputs and greater activity may seem to management to be less innovative and behind on budget and schedule early in the development cycle, yet these teams may breeze through later stages more quickly. In addition, these teams' products may better meet customer needs and have greater ease of manufacturability. Finally, diverse teams may have better processes and come up with better designs, yet because they have high visibility across much of the organization, they may be more prone to the political and goal conflict that often exists among functions. As such, diversity impedes performance by providing a forum for the rest of the organization to play out its conflicts. These conflicts impede innovation and cause numerous delays.

TURNING DIVERSITY INTO AN ADVANTAGE

The results of this study lead to two possible courses of action. Given that diversity has a larger negative, direct effect on performance than a positive, indirect effect through group process, we can go back to using single-function, tenure-homogeneous product development teams. Or we can try to implement in organizations those policies, procedures, and processes that will help to garner the positive effects of diversity rather than its detrimental ones. Here we advocate the second solution for several reasons.

First, given greater competition, consumers have come to demand the latest advances in new products coupled with high quality. These demands call for higher levels of coordination among marketing, engineering, and manufacturing than ever before. Theoretically a diverse new product team is the most efficient way to achieve such coordination. Second, organizations must find a way to do in parallel work that used to be done sequentially across functions and levels within the firm. Product development cycles must be cut dramatically in order to be first to market and to benefit from the profits and market share gain of such a position (Sasser and Wasserman, 1984). Finally, competitors from other nations—Japan and Germany, for instance—appear to have already harnessed the positive effects of cross-functional, tenure-heterogeneous teams, so the United States lags in this important area of human resources (Clark, 1988; Tyre and Hauptman, 1989; Westney and Sakakibara, 1986). Training and facilitation, changes in managerial and evaluation practices, and changes in organizational norms are needed to exploit the potential of diverse new product teams.

Training and Facilitation

The results of this study suggest that clarifying goals and priorities and communicating with external groups facilitate new product team performance, whereas an inability to implement goals, high levels of conflict, and very low cohesion inhibit performance. Therefore, if diversity is to be well managed, the team may require training in group dynamics. Specifically, conflict management and negotiation are key skills that could be used both within the team and with outsiders. These skills allow for divergent views to be combined into joint decisions without ripping the team apart.

In addition to skill acquisition, employees who are rotated across functions throughout their careers may acquire greater understanding and empathy for diverse perspectives. Exposure to those perspectives prior to a conflict situation permits a person to learn the language, time frame, and goals of other "thought worlds" so that there is more tolerance when conflict does appear.

Not only do team members need to learn new skills and perspectives, they also need to understand the complexity of team functioning. Training needs to include the teaching of models that let members analyze and understand team behavior. For example, members need to understand that both internal and external processes are needed for high performance. Yet high levels of external communication increase conflict and may slow progress in the short term. If members can predict such phenomena, they may be less frustrated with team progress.

Often, however, the team cannot manage without some help. Team members are selected primarily for technical, not interpersonal skills. Therefore, teams may need access to team facilitators, who can translate among marketing, engineering, and manufacturing representatives, arbitrate particularly difficult conflicts, provide observations of team problems, and teach team members the skills needed for current problems.

Thus, diverse teams need training in skills, perspectives, and models. To complement training facilitation helps the team through current problems. Yet the whole burden for improving product development should not fall on the team. Division and functional management and evaluation systems also contribute to team success or failure.

Management and Evaluation

The results of this study suggest that there are many different evaluations of team success. Team member ratings and managerial ratings do not correlate highly. Diverse teams that have difficulties and seem to be failing in the short term may speed through later stages and perform well in the long term. Finally, cross-functional team success may mean compromise and suboptimal outcomes for specific functions. Management and evaluation practices are needed to reconcile these divergent views.

Whereas team members see high performance resulting from smooth internal processes, management concentrates more on external communications and their impact on team output. Clearly both are necessary. Smooth internal team functioning without meeting organizational objectives is costly, but so is the loss of key members of a team that meets objectives. Just as team members must try to map and meet managerial expectations, so management must recognize and reward teams that are able to set priorities and manage conflict. These rewards need to be in the form of monetary outlay and promotions. Similarly, rewards based on group, rather than individual, output need to be put in place to create a congruence between management's message and the reward structure.

Since diverse product teams may be tackling downstream design problems earlier in the process than was previously the case, the first stages of team development may appear to be slower and more disorganized. First, more research must be done to determine whether these teams catch up and overtake the old team form later in the process. If this is the case, management must police itself not to unfairly punish those teams whose early struggles have long-term payoffs. Other studies of team performance indicate that management often makes judgments early in a team's existence that label it a success or failure (Ancona, 1990; Hackman, 1990). These judgments are then related to funding decisions, spread throughout the organization, and create self-fulfilling prophecies that ensure the label is correct. Therefore, management needs to hold off on such judgments and to change some of the time frames used in formal evaluation procedures to conform to this new model of team development.

Finally, a solution that optimizes the team's performance may be suboptimal for a particular function. If diverse new product teams are to work, then team performance must take precedence over functional interests. Unfortunately, salaries, performance evaluations, bonuses, and promotions are often determined by functional management rather than the product team leader. This situation promotes conflict within the team and often results in suboptimal decisions and products as team members strive to please functional management. Clearly we cannot set up a new structure of cross-functional teams and leave the old functional reward system in place.

Organizational Norms

The context in which the new product team operates is also key to its success. Although not specifically reported in this chapter, qualitative research from this study indicates that sometimes the whole organization must change in order for diverse teams to be a viable mechanism for product development. If a team operates in an organization where there is high conflict across functions at all levels, and where bureaucratic procedures specify transactions across functions, then it is hard for the team to be different. This is one reason why some of the most successful new product stories come from teams that have been isolated from the rest of the organization away from interference and from the old ways of doing things. If new product teams are to be successful within the corporate context, then there must be a change in mindset. The iron curtain that often exists among functions needs to be lifted, and the adherence to existing procedures needs to change to allow for more creative, flexible means to create innovative products quickly. In short, teams are very hard to create, manage, and maintain. There are many reasons they might fail, so unless an organization is going to make a serious investment in supporting these teams, they should not be set up.

The promise of diversity exists, but our empirical evidence suggests that diverse teams are not now addressing productivity disadvantages U.S. firms are believed to have in moving quickly from concept to marketplace. Diversity does help teams to set goals and priorities, and it does help them to develop and maintain external communications. However, its liabilities overcome these assets. Only with changes in training, managerial and evaluation practices, and organization norms can these liabilities be overcome to improve the product team process.

REFERENCES

Allen, T. 1984. *Managing the Flow of Technology: Technology Transfer and the Dissemination of Technological Information Within the R&D Organization*. Cambridge: MIT Press.

Ancona, D. G. 1987. "Groups in Organizations: Extending Laboratory Models." In *Annual Review of Personality and Social Psychology: Group and Intergroup Processes*, edited by C. Hendrick. Beverly Hills, Calif.: Sage.

Ancona, D. G. 1990. "Outward Bound: Strategies for Team Survival in the Organization." *Academy of Management Journal* 33: 334–365.

Ancona, D. G., and D. F. Caldwell. 1987. "Management Issues Facing New-Product Teams in High Technology Companies." *Advances in Industrial and Labor Relations* 4.

Ancona, D. G., and D. F. Caldwell. 1988. "Beyond Task and Maintenance: Defining External Functions in Groups." *Group and Organization Studies* 13: 468–494.

Ancona, D. G., and D. F. Caldwell. 1989. "Demography and Design: Predictors of New

Product Team Performance." Department of Behavioral and Policy Sciences, MIT working paper 3078-89.

Ancona, D. G., and D. F. Caldwell. 1990. "Improving the Performance of New Product Teams." *Research Technology Management*, March–April, pp. 25–29.

Bettenhausen, K., and J. K. Murnighan. 1985. "The Emergence of Norms in Competitive Decision-Making Groups." *Administrative Science Quarterly* 30: 350–372.

Burgelman, R. 1983. "A Process Model of Internal Corporate Venturing in the Diversified Major Firm." *Administrative Science Quarterly* 28: 223–244.

Calantone, R., and G. Cooper. 1981. "New Product Scenarios: Prospects for Success." *Journal of Marketing* 45: 48–80.

Calder, R. J. 1977. "An Attribution Theory of Leadership." In *New Directions in Organizational Behavior*, edited by B. M. Staw and G. R. Salancik. Chicago: St. Clair.

Clark, K. B. 1988. "Managing Technology in Technology Competition: The Case of Product Development in Response to Foreign Entry." In *International Competitiveness*, edited by A. M. Spence and H. A. Hazard. Cambridge, Mass.: Ballinger.

Clark, K. B., and T. Fujimoto. 1987. "Overlapping Problem Solving in Product Development." Harvard Business School working paper 87-048.

Cooper, R. G. 1979. "The Dimensions of Industrial New Product Success and Failure." *Journal of Marketing* 43: 93–103.

Dougherty, D. 1987. New Products in Old Organizations: The Myth of the Better Mousetrap in Search of the Beaten Path. Ph.D. Dissertation. Sloan School of Management, MIT.

Drucker, P. F. 1988. "The Coming of the New Organization." *Harvard Business Review* 88, no. 1: 45–53.

Festinger, L. 1954. "A Theory of Social Comparison Processes." *Human Relations* 1: 117–140.

Gladstein, D. L. 1984. "Groups in Context: A Model of Task Group Effectiveness." *Administrative Science Quarterly* 29: 499–517.

Goodman, P. S., E. Ravlin, and M. Schminke. 1987. "Understanding Groups in Organizations." In *Research in Organizational Behavior*, edited by L. L. Cummings and B. M. Staw. Greenwich, Conn.: JAI Press.

Hackman, J. R., ed. 1990. *Groups That Work (and Those that Don't)*. San Francisco: Jossey-Bass.

Hoffman, E. 1985. "The Effect of Race–Ratio Composition of the Frequency of Organizational Communication." *Social Psychological Quarterly* 48: 17–26.

Kanter, R. M. 1989. "New Managerial Work." *Harvard Business Review*, November–December, p. 90.

Katz, R. 1982. "The Effects of Group Longevity on Project Communication and Performance." *Administrative Science Quarterly* 27: 81–104.

Kazanjian, R. K., and R. Drazin. 1986. "Implementing Manufacturing Innovations: Critical Choices of Structure and Staffing Roles." *Human Resource Management* 25, no. 3: 385–403.

Kidder, T. 1981. *Soul of a New Machine*. New York: Avon.

Kiesler, S. B. 1978. *Interpersonal Processes in Groups and Organizations*. Arlington Heights, Ill.: AHM Publishing.

Lawrence, Q., and J. Lorsch. 1969. "Differentiation and Integration in Complex Organizations." *Administrative Science Quarterly* 12: 153–167.

McCain, B. E., C. A. O'Reilly, and J. Pfeffer. 1983. "The Effects of Departmental Demography on Turnover: The Case of a University." *Administrative Science Quarterly* 26: 626–641.

Mintzberg, H. 1988. "Adhocracy." In *The Strategy Process: Concepts, Contexts, and Cases*, edited by J. B. Quinn, H. Mintzberg, and R. M. James. Englewood Cliffs, N.J.: Prentice-Hall.

Newcomb, T. M. 1961. *The Acquaintance Process*. New York: Holt, Rinehart & Winston.

O'Reilly, C. A., D. F. Caldwell, and W. P. Barnett. 1989. "Work Group Demography, Social Integration, and Turnover." *Administrative Science Quarterly* 34: 21–37.

O'Reilly, C. A., and S. Flatt. 1989. "Executive Team Demography, Organizational Innovation, and Firm Performance." School of Management working paper. University of California, Berkeley.

Pfeffer, J. 1986. "A Resource Dependence Perspective on Intercorporate Relations." In *Structural Analysis of Business,* edited by M. S. Mizruchi and M. Schwartz. New York: Academic Press.

Pfeffer, J., and W. L. Moore. 1980. "Average Tenure of Academic Department Heads: The Effects of Paradigm, Size, and Departmental Demography." *Administrative Science Quarterly* 25 (September): 387–406.

Pfeffer, J., and C. O'Reilly. 1987. "Hospital Demography and Turnover Among Nurses." *Industrial Relations* 26: 158–173.

Quinn, J. B., and J. A. Mueller. 1963. "Transferring Research Results to Operations." *Harvard Business Review* 41 (January–February): 44–87.

Ryder, N. B. 1965. "The Cohort as a Concept in the Study of Social Change." *American Sociological Review* 30: 843–861.

Sasser, W. E., and N. H. Wasserman. 1984. "From Design to Market: The New Competitive Pressure." Harvard Business School working paper.

Schmidt, S. M., and T. Kochan. 1972. "The Concept of Conflict: Toward Conceptual Clarity." *Administrative Science Quarterly* 17: 359–370.

Shaw, M. 1971. *Group Dynamics: The Psychology of Small Group Behavior.* New York: McGraw-Hill.

Teachman, J. D. 1980. "Analysis of Population Diversity." *Sociological Methods and Research* 8: 341–362.

Tsui, A. S., and C. A. O'Reilly. 1989. "Beyond Simple Demographic Effects: The Importance of Relational Demography in Superior–Subordinate Dyads." *Academy of Management Journal* 32: 402–423.

Tushman, M. L. 1977. "Special Boundary Roles in the Innovation Process." *Administrative Science Quarterly* 22: 587–605.

Tushman, M. L. 1979. "Work Characteristics and Solo Unit Communication Structure: A Contingency Analysis." *Administrative Science Quarterly* 24: 82–98.

Tyre, M., and O. Hauptman. 1989. "Technological Change in the Production Process: Organizational Implications and Responses." MIT Sloan School of Management working paper 3050-89.

Voss, C. A. 1985. "Determinants of Success in the Development of Application Software." *Journal of Product Innovation Management* 2: 122–129.

Wagner, W. G., J. Pfeffer, and C. A. O'Reilly. 1984. "Organizational Demography and Turnover in Top-Management Groups." *Administrative Science Quarterly* 29: 74–92.

Ward, R. A., S. La Gory, and S. R. Sherman. 1985. "Neighborhood and Network Age Concentration: Does Age Homogeneity Matter?" *Social Psychological Quarterly* 48: 138–149.

Westney, E., and K. Sakakibara. 1986. "Designing the Designers: Computer R&D in the U.S. and Japan." *Technology Review,* April, pp. 25–31, 68–69.

Zenger, T. R., and B. S. Lawrence. 1989. "Organizational Demography: The Differential Effects of Age and Tenure Distributions on Technical Communication." *Academy of Management Journal* 32: 353–376.

COMMENTARY BY SARA L. BECKMAN

This chapter takes a concept many of us have struggled with and discusses some tangible aspects of it. What I would like to do is to relate the findings back to some of the themes that have come out of this conference. Although Ancona and Caldwell focus on cross-functional teams in product development efforts, their work reflects this whole issue of "permeability" that we have been talking about. I think it has some important messages in a broad sense.

All of our companies are trying to encourage cross-functional interactions in some form, whether we call them teams or something else. There is some very specific work we're doing at Hewlett-Packard along with people from other companies and organizations. Hal Edmondson (HP), Kent Bowen (MIT), Bill Hanson (DEC), and I are all involved in the "Manufacturing Vision Group," where we have been looking at case studies of new product development efforts. We almost inevitably find that these cases involve cross-functional interactions.

Internally in HP, we have been looking at the product definition process, which is the step before product development, a step which we think needs to be managed even better than the product development stage. (If the product isn't defined correctly, the entire development effort is at risk.) Here, we also find the cross-functional interactions to be critical. We also have been involved in a study with the University of Southern California's Center for Effective Organizations, actually looking at the formation of cross-functional teams in product development. We've been looking at these kinds of issues at HP, so this chapter is particularly germane to all of us at our company.

Let me go through this chapter and discuss some of the themes and concepts that strike me. First is this whole area of managing diversity. Ancona and Caldwell looked at tenure and functional allegiance as diversity measures. Lotte Bailyn's chapter and discussions here suggest that there are hundreds of dimensions of diversity that need to be taken into account when we are trying to pull together cross-functional teams. If all of this were modeled, it would present a very complex picture of the interactions between the different types of diversity and performance of the teams along a number of dimensions. I suspect we all need to pay a lot more attention to the implications of such a model in the future.

This chapter also relates to Rebecca Henderson's work and the whole concept of knowledge. The reason we create these teams in the first place is because we are trying to get knowledgeable people together from multiple functional areas. An interesting question to me is whether or not the use of cross-functional teams will help break down or make more explicit some of the tacit knowledge that Rebecca talked about.

I feel we haven't paid enough attention in our discussions to the whole area of performance measures, as well as reward and evaluation systems. We really don't know how to measure cross-functional teams, but we continue to measure them on a very functional (e.g., R&D, manufacturing) basis rather than measure the overall process the team is preforming (e.g., generating products). One interesting finding of this study is that managers evaluate teams differently than the teams evaluate themselves. Managers may not think the team is successful, when the team views itself as successful. This suggests a major disconnect in our ability to understand how to look at performance. If we can't measure performance of this disconnect in thinking about how to evaluate investment in cross-functional teams, then I think we are unlikely to evaluate the team's performance properly. This is a critical issue, and we really haven't talked much about pay and reward systems related to teams.

Finally, I'd like to discuss training and leadership. Training people to lead teams, to facilitate them, and to help them work together is critical to successful cross-functional teams.

What are the practical challenges that come out of this chapter? First of all, there is a need to create tool sets for team facilitation and communication, information systems that support cross-functional communication (rather than inventing design information systems and then inventing manufacturing information systems).

Second, there is a challenge that stems from a need to have teams actually change composition dynamically over time. From concept and customer, for example, the role of manufacturing increases and the role of R&D decreases. Marketing has a critical role in product definition, then the role of marketing falls off until the product is actually delivered to the marketplace when it increases again. So the team has to be changing continuously, to be comprised of different players at different times as their skills are required. We have looked at cross-functional teams in the task of design. How do we manage them over time so that the team changes constantly through the product life cycle, to say nothing of changing for multiple products? I challenge this group to extrapolate this work in terms of organizational need and look at the greater challenges facing our organizations.

11

Human Resources, Organizational Governance, and Public Policy: Lessons from a Decade of Experimentation

THOMAS A. KOCHAN AND ROBERT B. MCKERSIE

The past decade witnessed a tremendous amount of experimentation and innovation in human resource practices and labor–management relations. We use the term "experimentation" rather generously here since most of the changes were not planned in some predetermined or careful fashion but instead were induced by the economic pressures and structural changes felt by firms and their employees in the early 1980s. Moreover, not all of the changes prompted by these pressures proved to be effective long-run responses to the altered environment. But enough experience has now accumulated to sort out the key lessons that, if accepted and acted upon, can translate the experimental results into sustained transformations in organizational practices.

Over this past decade, faculty and graduate students affiliated with the Industrial Relations Section at MIT have devoted a great deal of effort to analyzing these developments and assessing their implications for theory, organizational practice, and public policy. This chapter draws on the results of those studies to explore their implications for the broader domains of technology and competitive strategy, organizational governance, and national policy. These extensions are appropriate since we see a close interrelationship between human resource policies and innovations, organizational governance, and national labor and human resource policies.

In the following sections we summarize the key lessons derived from the innovations in human resource and labor–management practices introduced in the 1980s. We then pose a series of challenges to traditional organizational governance arrangements and national policies affecting the employment relationship that need to be addressed if these innovations are to spread to the point that they produce significant and enduring benefits to the national economy. But first we need to outline the theoretical reasons *why* fundamental changes in human resource management and industrial relations policies and practices have been necessary.

HUMAN RESOURCES AND NATIONAL COMPETITIVENESS

There is growing recognition that for enterprises in advanced industrial societies to compete effectively in a world economy while maintaining and improving the standard of living, firms must develop and fully utilize their human resources (cf. Cyert and Mowery, 1986; Dertouzos, Lester, and Solow, 1989; Marshall, 1987; Walton, 1987). To do so in a world of shortening product life cycles, intensified price competition, greater specialization in product markets, and rapid advances in technology requires human resource practices that support (1) development of a well-educated, highly motivated, and multiskilled work force; (2) high levels of participation in problem solving and continuous improvement in productivity and quality; and (3) sustained labor–management cooperation.

Yet these are not characteristics that traditional industrial relations policies and personnel practices were designed to produce. The needs of workers, employers, and the society were quite different in the 1930s when the industrial relations system as we know it today first took shape and eventually became institutionalized following the passage of New Deal labor legislation. The major goals and achievements of the traditional industrial relations system included the steady improvement in wages and working conditions, diffusion of professional personnel management practices, achievement of industrial peace (though not necessarily sustained cooperation) through collective bargaining, a high degree of skill specialization and extensive division of labor, standardization of wage rates and labor costs in the major manufacturing sectors, and protection of management's right to make the strategic or entrepreneurial decisions and to direct the enterprise.

CHANGES IN THE 1980S: INNOVATION AND CONFRONTATION

The most forceful pressures for change in the 1980s originated from changing technologies and product markets (imports, deregulation, and shortened product life cycles) (Piore and Sabel, 1984). Thus it is not surprising that employers were the dominant actors and initiators of changes in industrial relations and human resource practices in the 1980s (Doyle, 1989; Kochan and McKersie, 1983). Employer initiatives in the 1980s took on the character of a double-edged sword. On one side, employers introduced fundamental changes in human resource practices designed to upgrade the status and influence of personnel practices in corporate decision making and to foster greater employee participation and labor–management cooperation. In both union and nonunion organizations line managers and top executives asserted greater responsibility for initiating and directing changes in human resource practices (Freedman, 1984; Kochan, Katz, and McKersie, 1986). The professional literature was replete with arguments urging management to upgrade the status of human resources by integrating human resource planning with strategic planning and decision making (Craft, 1988). "Strategic human resource management" replaced the study and practice of "personnel management" (Dyer, 1988; Fombrun, Tichy, and Devanna, 1984; Schuler, 1989). These works, and the various case studies on which they were based, suggested that at least some American firms were indeed evolving, as Walton and Lawrence (1987) characterized the transition, from a traditional human resource strategy that emphasized "control" to one that emphasized "commitment."

At the same time, however, spurred by threats from low-wage competitors and hostile takeovers and the opportunities offered by a weakened and declining labor movement, significant numbers of both union and nonunion employers implemented wage concessions, major work force reductions, and more aggressive, sophisticated, and open union-avoidance policies (Kochan et al., 1986). The maturing of product markets and the drive for leaner staffs led a number of major firms to abandon their longstanding commitments to employment security for blue- and white-collar workers (Foulkes and Whitman, 1985).

Moreover, as noted by Useem (Chapter 4, this volume), general downsizing and restructuring produced significant numbers of layoffs and severance programs to reduce white-collar and managerial workers. The net result of these changes in managerial labor markets and organizational staffing patterns, however, is rather puzzling. On the one hand, as might be expected given the pace of organizational restructuring, the ratio of white-collar to overall unemployment increased from 52 percent in 1980 to 64 percent in 1989. At the same time, the 1980s also witnessed a significant expansion in income differentials between high-level managers and middle managers. And for non-supervisory workers not only did income differentials expand, but real wages declined approximately 9 percent. Yet, despite all of the restructuring and downsizing of management, white-collar productivity decreased in the 1980s (Thurow, 1987). The net result of all of this could be called a "lose–lose" decade: managers and workers were asked to accept increased risks and at the same time economic performance did not improve as would be expected.

The escalation of employer initiatives produced corresponding efforts by unions to find ways to organize and represent their members in ways that went beyond their traditional roles and strategies in the New Deal system. Like those of employers, union strategies have been double edged. Some unions supported new initiatives to foster greater cooperation and participation at the workplace. Other union strategies served to escalate and expand the domains of labor–management conflict by bringing political and financial pressures to bear on top corporate executives whose companies were involved in major strikes, union organizing drives, corporate restructuring, and ownership battles.

Regardless of whether union leaders sought to find common ground with management or to strengthen their adversarial stance, it is clear that the decade of the 1980s witnessed a dramatic increase by union leaders in their access to key business decisions and to the line managers responsible for these decisions. The agenda of labor–management relations expanded into many new areas (technology, training, and teamwork, to mention three subjects) beyond the mandatory subjects of wages, hours, and working conditions. Thus the 1980s was a decade of intensified innovation as well as confrontation between managers, employees, and organized labor. We believe these tumultuous experiences produced a number of important lessons that should now influence policy and practice in the 1990s. These lessons emerged incrementally as experience and analysis accumulated throughout the decade. We next review them in roughly the sequence in which they arose. Some are derived from empirical research that we and others conducted over the course of the 1980s; others represent the informed consensus of management, labor, and government officials who participated in or followed these developments most closely (U.S. Department of Labor, 1989; Walton and Lawrence, 1987).

LESSONS FROM THE 1980S

Lesson 1: *The traditional New Deal industrial relations system is no longer well matched to the needs of individual workers or firms.*

One of the earliest conclusions reached by management in many firms was that the traditional industrial relations system that evolved out of the New Deal legislation of the 1930s no longer worked well for either individual firms or their employees. An early version of this view was expressed in a 1981 cover story of *Business Week,* "The New Industrial Relations." *Business Week* defined the problem as an overreliance on "adversarial" relationships at the workplace:

> Quietly, almost without notice, a new industrial relations system with a fundamentally different way of managing people is taking shape in the U.S. Its goal is to end the adversarial relationship that has grown between management and labor and that now threatens the competitiveness of many industries.

Few researchers or practitioners accepted *Business Week*'s rather simplistic argument that "adversarialism" was the sole or central cause of America's productivity crisis or that differences in economic interests could be totally eliminated from employment relationships. Yet considerable empirical evidence supported the view that adversarial relationships do impose significant costs on economic performance. For example, our own research on the effects of labor relations in the auto industry during the 1970s demonstrated that plants characterized by a pattern of high conflict and low trust—that is, plants with high levels of grievances, prolonged negotiations and disputes over work rules, and a hostile climate between workers and first-line supervisors—experienced significantly lower levels of productivity and product quality compared to plants with less adversarial patterns of interaction (Katz, Kochan, and Gobeille, 1983; Katz, Kochan, and Weber, 1985). Similar results were documented in other industries and organizations as well (Ichniowski, 1986).

But most companies did not wait for empirical verification of this hypothesis. Indeed, as early as the late 1960s, many firms sought to escape this adversarial pattern by opening new "greenfield" facilities which would operate on a nonunion basis and emphasize employee participation, flexibility in the organization of work, and decentralization of authority from traditional supervisors to work groups (Kochan et al., 1986; Walton, 1980). But abandoning existing plants in favor of new sites and work forces was neither a practical nor a desirable alternative for the majority of employers. So in the early 1980s a flurry of experimentation in existing union and nonunion facilities took place with what turned out to be a rather narrow and ultimately insufficient strategy for change, namely, quality circles (QC) or quality of working life (QWL) programs, which we consider next.

Lesson 2: *Narrow forms of employee involvement, such as QCs or QWL programs, are not powerful enough on their own to survive or transform organizations. Sustained support for innovation*

*requires giving voice to employees at all levels of
organizational decision making—including strategic
management decisions.*

By 1988 national surveys reported that over one-third of the work force was employed
in organizations with some type of employee participation experiment under way.
Larger establishments were especially likely to introduce these innovations; in fact,
over 50 percent of establishments with 1,000 or more employees experimented with
employee participation (Alper, Pfau, and Sirota, 1985). Experiments were equally
frequent in union and nonunion establishments (Ichniowski, Lewin, and Delaney,
1989).

Although many of these efforts opened the door to significant change, many also
proved to be a fad and were abandoned as soon as they experienced organizational
resistance or ran into countervailing organizational pressures. Lawler and Mohrman
(1985) estimate, for example, that the majority of QCs have been disbanded. Drago
(1988) found that the attrition rate for QCs was about 70 percent during the first two
years and that the failure rate was higher in nonunion than union establishments.
Several participants at a recent symposium on the state of the art in labor–management
cooperation suggest why this might be the case:

> If new work systems are so great, why aren't more companies getting on the band-
> wagon? . . . Many (at the conference) agreed that commitment to change must start with
> top management and be institutionalized throughout the company. . . . Within any com-
> pany, it takes years for trust to develop between labor and management . . . offi-
> cials . . . stress that building a successful program takes a great deal of hard work, self
> examination, training, retraining, and especially communication. Any company that tries to
> change must deal with individual managers and union people who have their own agen-
> das, whether it is keeping their jobs or getting re-elected. (U.S. Department of Labor,
> 1989, p. 5)

The high attrition rate for narrow employee involvement programs is not surprising, since our research showed that in most instances, as a stand-alone or isolated
strategy, narrow QCs or similarly narrow forms of employee participation did not
produce sufficient returns to productivity or product quality to sustain the commitment
of management. From the union side of the ledger as well, QWL programs often were
seen as problematical since they seldom generated major economic gains for the
members. In addition, these programs could be risky if they created the impression that
the labor leaders who were involved had compromised their independence. Moreover,
over time it became impossible to isolate these programs from other developments in
the firm. Case studies showed that the typical pattern for these experiments was a flurry
of initial enthusiasm and support followed by a plateauing of interest and a questioning
of commitment as conflicts arose with competing priorities such as downsizing, management turnover, labor–management conflicts, wage concessions, contracting out,
and organizational restructuring. The joining of these competing priorities proved to be
pivotal events in the history of these participation efforts—either the parties deepened
their commitment by applying the participation principles to these broader issues or the
process was discredited and abandoned (Cutcher-Gershenfeld, 1988). This leads to
another major lesson drawn.

Lesson 3: *QC and QWL processes can provide a good*
starting point for building trust and opening the door
to broader changes—and if they are allowed to
expand beyond the shop floor to higher levels of
policy and strategic decision making in the firm, then
they represent an effective starting point and catalyst
for the broader transformation process.

One of the themes that characterizes those situations that move beyond the initial phase is the provision of increased employment security for the employees and increased institutional security for the union. Efforts aimed at increasing the involvement of workers will not move very far beyond the experimental stage unless maximum feasible emphasis is given to long-run enhancement of employment opportunities and the institutional security of the union (Collective Bargaining Forum, 1987). A variety of imaginative arrangements have taken shape that balance employers' needs for flexibility, workers' needs for career enhancement, and unions' needs for organizational security.

It is clear that for a transformation to occur there needs to be an integration at three levels of the system: programs at the grassroots level to involve workers, policies that emphasize jointness (such as employment security), and arrangements to provide access by unions at the strategic level. The experience of Xerox over the course of the 1980s both is a prototype for successful expansion and continuity of participation and illustrates why so few firms or labor–management relationships were able to progress. In this case the parties successfully negotiated their way through a series of pivotal events in the following manner:

1. Threats to contract out work were overcome by agreeing to a task force strategy that allowed employees and managers in the units at risk to search for ways to reorganize and streamline their operations to be competitive with outside alternatives.
2. Concerns over layoffs led union and management representatives to negotiate an employment security package that provided for no layoffs in return for continued support for participation and work rule flexibility.
3. When a new plant was needed, the union participated in its design and choice of location and the company continued its longstanding practice of not opposing unionization of new jobs and work sites.
4. When confronted with management resistance to participative leadership styles the company engaged in a wholesale effort to change the culture of the management from the top executives to the first-line supervisor.

Not surprisingly, few companies or unions would be willing or able to make these types of tradeoffs of other policies to sustain human resource innovations.

But this inertia may change in the face of the impressive results achieved by companies like Xerox. Consider the comments of one senior executive from Xerox:

> As a result of our cooperative program, we've been able to reduce our unit manufacturing costs, and we've been able to get our product out to market faster. Without those changes, there's no doubt that Japan, Inc., would be able to increase its market share to our

detriment. Our top management has taken the position that it's absolutely essential to our future to continue down this path. (U.S. Department of Labor, 1989, p. 4)

Thus the summary lesson from a decade of experience with employee participation is that standing alone, it is not likely to be sustained, but if allowed to grow, exposed to broader issues and higher levels of decision making, and reinforced and supported by top management and employee leaders, then employee participation can be a powerful and effective force in helping to transform organizations. When nurtured and allowed to expand in this way, participation can have significant economic and social value for all the parties involved.

Lesson 4: *Stand-alone technology strategies neither transform organizations nor achieve world-class levels of performance. By contrast, strategies that integrate innovations in human resource management with new technologies outperform both traditional industrial relations and stand-alone technology strategies.*

One of the clearest and yet most difficult to implement lessons of the past decade is that investing in advanced technology alone is not an effective strategy for transforming organizations or enhancing organizational performance. Failure to integrate new technology with organizational changes and human resource innovations leads to an underutilization of technology and fails to capture its fullest potential. MacDuffie and Krafcik (Chapter 13, this volume) present the most dramatic evidence on this point. Other evidence suggests that the failure of technology-alone strategies generalizes to the information technology environment as well (Chalykoff and Kochan, 1989; Loveman, 1988; McKersie and Walton, 1990; Roach, 1987; Zuboff, 1988; Tyre, Chapter 14, this volume).

If the integration argument is correct, Thomas (Chapter 17, this volume) presents some sobering conclusions, namely, that the lessons of MacDuffie and Krafcik as well as Zuboff and others are very difficult to implement in organizations that continue to separate the parties and processes that design and select technology strategies from the parties and processes that manage the implementation and execution of these strategies. Thus to achieve the full benefits of technology and to integrate fully technology and human resource strategies requires a fundamental reordering of organizational roles, structures, and distribution of power. It is not surprising, for example, that the most radical reformulations of work organization and utilization of advanced technologies are found in new "greenfield" sites where human resource planners or consultants and, in a small but growing number of cases, union representatives are brought in on the ground floor, that is, at the outset of the planning and organizational design process. It is at this early stage of the planning and decision-making cycle that the most flexibility exists in the conceptions of both technical and human resource planners and representatives. Early involvement also allows for sufficient lead time to forecast the skills and to provide the training and retraining in technical and social skills required to make an integrated technical–human resource strategy work effectively. Although no hard data exist on the frequency of this type of integrated planning and design process, it appears that this is fast becoming the accepted state of the art for new facilities in most large manufacturing firms. What varies among firms in this sector is whether or not *union* representatives are included in the planning process. We suspect that in many instances, human resource planning and organizational design work proceeds without unions in order to avoid the need to recognize them when the new facility is opened.

Again, while we have only case study data to go on at this point, it appears that few organizations have made the integration of human resource and technical planning and decision making a standard practice when contemplating the introduction of new technologies or processes for existing work sites (Goodman, 1987). Most large firms can point to specific examples of "factories within factories" in which experiments with an integrated approach have been tried and implemented when major investments in new technology have been allocated, but few organizations have made this a standard practice or diffused this new model to a majority of their locations. In existing organizations traditional structures and patterns of resource allocation described by Thomas seem to endure with great resiliency. Since existing sites are where the vast majority of dollars for new technology are spent, introducing the organizational changes needed to effectively integrate technical and human resource issues in these environments remains a major challenge to management today and in the future. Until practices in these environments change, there is little reason to believe that the lessons from the micro experiments with a more integrated technical and human resource model will be diffused widely enough to produce significant and sustained improvements in aggregate productivity growth and the competitive standing of key industries.

Lesson 5: *Competitive strategies that stress low costs and low wages produce high levels of labor–management conflict, reinforce low trust, and inhibit innovation and improvement of quality.*

The corollary to this lesson is:

> *Competitive strategies that stress value added (e.g., enhanced quality) and/or product innovation require high levels of motivation, commitment, and trust in employment relations.*

One of the major developments in industrial relations and the human resource profession in the 1980s was the realization that much of the variation in human resource outcomes and labor–management relations at the workplace was determined by the competitive strategies top management chooses to follow. Recognition of this lies at the heart of the argument for integrating human resource planning with business or strategic planning (Craft, 1988). But more is involved here than simply involvement of human resource professionals or worker representatives in the *process* of strategic decision making. Of equal importance is the *substantive* choices firms make, that is, the basis on which competitive advantage is sought.

In hindsight this may seem obvious, yet the fact is that growing out of our New Deal traditions, neither personnel professionals nor union representatives had much access to or influence over these basic competitive strategy choices. Instead, like the choice of technology strategies, these decisions were left to other top executives. It was the job of the personnel professionals and labor representatives to design or negotiate employment policies and practices after these critical choices were made.

Two key lessons regarding the role of competitive strategies have emerged out of the 1980s. The first is that the separation of human resource policy and competitive strategy decision making no longer works well in environments where significant strategic restructuring is contemplated, since such changes in corporate direction inevitably require equally significant changes in compensation policies, staffing levels and patterns, and related human resource practices, all of which are part of an existing organizational culture. Second, the choice of a competitive strategy will either reinforce or weaken employee trust and support needed for other human resource innovations and pursuit of the competitive strategy itself. For example, sustaining high levels of commitment, participation, flexibility, and cooperation at the workplace requires a competitive strategy that reinforces these attributes. A strategy that emphasizes high product quality, customer service, and adaptability to change is compatible with these objectives and can sustain and reinforce these human resource innovations. A strategy that relies solely or primarily on being the low-cost competitor in either a domestic or international market is bound to conflict with and/or undermine these human resource innovations.

This lesson was most clearly brought home in the experiences of the airlines following deregulation. Consider the differences between three domestic airline firms following deregulation—Delta, Texas Air, and American. Delta historically followed the path of emphasizing quality of service, conservative financial policies, and comprehensive (some might say paternalistic) human resource policies (*Business Week,* 1981). For example, it maintained a commitment to employment security—even through a particularly difficult period in 1971 when it chose to avoid layoffs during a prolonged downturn. (In the early 1980s employees symbolically returned the favor by purchasing a Boeing 757 for Delta to show their appreciation.) Throughout the first decade following deregulation Delta stuck to this competitive strategy and its human resource policies remained largely intact. As a result it now finds itself positioned as follows in relation to other major carriers: (1) its market share has grown modestly; (2) it has the highest labor costs and staffing ratios; (3) it consistently ranks at or near the top among major carriers in low rates of passenger complaints and other indicators of service quality; and (4) it is consistently at or near the top in profitability. Thus Delta is a case in point of an organization driven by a commitment to a set of values and business strategies that support development and utilization of its human resources even in the face of intense competition. The result is a relatively high wage but also a highly profitable enterprise.

Compare this experience to the values, strategies, human resource policies, and economic results of the two largest subsidiaries of Texas Air Corporation—Continental and Eastern. Prior to deregulation Texas Air was a small regional carrier. But in the decade following deregulation it purchased a series of carriers in financial trouble—Continental, N.Y. Air, People Express, Frontier, and then in 1986, Eastern. In doing so, it became the most highly leveraged firm in the industry. By 1988 Texas Air's market share surpassed Delta and equaled its two biggest domestic competitors, American and United. At both Continental and Eastern, Texas Air adopted a low-fare–low-wage competitive strategy, even though it inherited cost structures comparable to those at Delta, United, and American. To achieve these lower costs both firms demanded deep wage cuts from employees, went through bitter and prolonged strikes and bankruptcy proceedings, and emerged as a nonunion carrier (Continental) and a significantly downsized carrier with weakened unions (Eastern). But by 1991 Eastern had gone bankrupt and was liquidated. Continental had also once again fallen into bankruptcy but continued to operate. Thus after a decade of deregulation, Eastern was out of business and Continental was positioned with: (1) a market share considerably above its share prior to deregulation but below the share it held at its peak in 1986, (2) high debt burdens, (3) labor costs approximately 40 percent below those of Delta, (4) relatively high levels of passenger complaints, and (5) persistent financial losses. Thus, in attempting to implement its competitive strategy Texas Air imposed severe economic hardships on its employees and left a trail of labor wars in its wake.

American Airlines represents yet a third approach to the business strategy–human resource policy link in the domestic airline industry. American embarked on a strategy of internal growth early in the period of deregulation. To support this growth strategy American negotiated hard with its unions to achieve a lower labor cost structure for new hires and to gain flexibility in its operations. In 1983, in return for a two-tiered wage schedule it offered the roster of employees lifetime employment security. By the end of 1989 American was positioned as follows relative to the other major carriers: (1) it experienced the greatest increase in market share of any of the major domestic carriers, (2) its labor costs approximate the average in the industry (lower than Delta's and higher than Continental's), (3) its service quality record is above average, (4) its labor–management relations are stable, and (5) it continues to be among the most profitable airlines in the industry. American continues to search for growth opportunities, most recently by purchasing landing rights and routes in Europe and South America.

Several lessons can be drawn from the experience of the airline industry. In instances where management sees labor primarily as a cost of production and presses for a reduction in labor costs so intently that the labor–management relationship is destroyed (Continental and Eastern), the long-run goal of becoming a profitable carrier is not likely to be realized. On the other hand, where labor cost concerns are matched with respect for the value employees add to an operation (Delta and American), labor–management relations can be used to help achieve the organizational changes needed for economic success. Like autos, the airline industry served as a laboratory of experimentation in the 1980s. Both labor and management learned through difficult experiences how competitive strategies, ownership changes, financial leverage, and managerial values affect human resource policies, employee– and union–management relations, and economic performance. Workers and their union representatives had been content to leave these strategic decisions to management. Given the lessons of the 1980s it is unlikely that this will be the case in the future, as illustrated by the repeated takeover attempts of United Airlines by its unions and various investors.

FROM HUMAN RESOURCE INNOVATION TO ORGANIZATIONAL TRANSFORMATION

The benefits of the lessons just reviewed will be lost unless the process of transforming human resource and industrial relations practices is both sustained in those organizations that experimented with new approaches and diffused to a broader circle of firms and employees. But if the lessons summarized here are correct, diffusion will require fundamental changes in organizational governance, management and labor values and practices, public policy, and the broad environment in which business and labor interact. We therefore now turn to changes in the broader organizational and external environment that will be needed to support and expand the transformational processes. Our key arguments are presented as propositions, since they serve as the central points requiring further research, analysis, and debate.

Proposition 1: *Management commitment alone is not strong enough to sustain and diffuse human resource innovation.*

We noted that management was the driving force for both innovation and the escalation of labor–management tensions in the 1980s. Two questions therefore arise: Have the majority of American executives internalized the values and beliefs necessary to sustain the innovative process? And can those executives who have internalized these values withstand the countervailing pressures on them to act differently? There is little evidence to answer yes to either of these questions.

Consider, for example, the following description of the dominant perspective held by American managerial leadership in the 1980s, offered by Frank Doyle, the senior vice president–corporate relations staff at General Electric:

> Economic power in the Eighties—the power to launch and sustain the dynamic processes of restructuring and globalization—has been concentrated especially in the hands of the larger companies, along with the financiers and raiders who alternatively support or attack them. If the Eighties was a new Age of the Entrepreneur—and small business did in fact account for most of the new job creation in the United States—it was Corporate America that accounted for most of the economic disruption and competitive improvement; it took out people, layers and costs while rearranging portfolios and switching industries. . . . Across the decade in the U.S. alone, there was over a trillion dollars of merger and acquisition and LBO activity. Ten million manufacturing jobs were eliminated or shifted to the growing service sector. Deals were cut and alliances forged around America and around the world.
>
> From where the shots were called was well known. Restructuring and globalization did not emerge from employee suggestion boxes; they erupted from executive suites. . . .
>
> So competitive rigor—imposed by companies in their employer roles and demonstrated by their restructuring and globalizing moves—was widely accepted because its rationale was widely understood. Given this climate—along with a political environment of relative deregulation—companies in the Eighties could focus more on portfolios than on people; fire more than hire; invest more in machines than in skills.
>
> The obvious reality of tough competitive facts inspired fear in employees and gave employers the power to act. Shuttered factories and fired neighbors is restructuring without subtlety: people could see the damage and feel the pain. (Doyle, 1989, pp. 3–4)

Thus American management suffers from a schizophrenic personality. On the one hand management has been conditioned to respond to economic pressures aggressively by cutting costs, downsizing quickly, treating technology as hardware separate from its human and organizational dimensions, and relegating concern for human resources to a second-level priority. Yet, as Doyle goes on to note, the lessons of the 1980s are that management must change in ways that recognize the lessons outlined earlier in this chapter. That is, if human resources are to become a source of competitive advantage, then human and organizational dimensions of technology must be integrated with investments in new hardware or processes, human resources must be viewed as long-term investments rather than as costs to be controlled or minimized for short-run savings, and workers and their representatives must become partners in the adjustment and management process.

Management commitment is generally accepted as a necessary condition for sustaining any significant organizational change. Yet if Doyle's characterization of American management behavior and the lessons we reviewed earlier are correct, the management values and commitment to the policies necessary to sustain innovations will be severely tested in the upcoming decade as they compete with other, more dominant pressures and styles of management behavior that destroy employee trust. Thus although management leadership and commitment are necessary for diffusing human resource innovations, they will not be sufficient. Managerial initiative will need to be supplemented and reinforced with other, more powerful and independent forces.

In light of what we know about how and why organizations change, the turbulent economic environment of the 1980s provided a rationale for management to take the lead in a wide range of restructuring programs. But while management has the credibility to drive the unfreezing and reformulating stages, it is not clear that most organizations have developed a culture to sustain and deepen the innovations during the continuing stages of the transformation process. Our most serious competitors, Germany and Japan, to name two countries, are characterized by institutions that promote continuous improvements and joint labor and management efforts that have led to a long-run performance that is difficult for our employers to match with their unilateral and crisis approach to efficiency and restructuring programs.

Proposition 2: *Continued union decline is an obstacle to diffusion of human resource innovations. Union leaders must become visible champions of these innovations for them to diffuse widely and become an ongoing part of organizational practice.*

Democratic societies normally assume that the labor movement serves as an important voice for articulating worker interests at the level of the firm and in national affairs. Labor serves to both encourage and reinforce management's positive human resource practices and to counteract or constrain management actions that are injurious to worker interests. An important task for national labor policy and for labor–management practice therefore is to ensure that workers are afforded effective means for having their voices heard.

The ability of American labor to serve this function effectively is presently at risk in the United States given the continuing long-term decline in union membership and the absence of an alternative set of institutional structures and processes for employee voice and representation. An important task for national policy and private practice in the 1990s is to reconstruct effective institutions for employee participation, broadly defined.

Throughout the 1980s the pace of union membership decline accelerated. In 1980, some 24 percent of the labor force was represented by unions. By the end of the decade the number had shrunk to less than 17 percent of all wage and salaried workers and to 12 percent for just private sector wage and salary workers. New union organizing replaces only a small fraction of the numbers lost each year through attrition in union jobs. There are many reasons for the continued decline: structural changes in the economy have eroded occupations, industries, and regions with traditionally high rates of union membership; management has become more aggressive in its union avoidance efforts; unions have not adopted new organizing themes or strategies, and some employers have adopted progressive human resource management practices that substitute for the traditional union role. We need not debate the relative importance of these factors here. Instead we want to underscore the long-term consequences of continued decline on the capacity of labor leaders to foster and sustain innovations in labor and human resource practices.

Union leaders constantly note that management resistance to union organizing and correcting weaknesses in labor law are serious barriers to union support for labor–management innovation and cooperation. It is politically difficult and risky for union leaders to champion cooperation and innovation in organized facilities of an employer when they face resistance from the same employer to the unionization of workers in new sites and other unorganized facilities. Cooperation in such a case is perceived by workers and union representatives as helping to generate resources through improved performance in the unionized facilities that are then siphoned off to expand nonunion operations.

A managerial strategy of encouraging worker and union input and cooperation in currently unionized facilities while simultaneously seeking to avoid unions in new operations also has adverse consequences for the macroeconomy and society. If played out to an extreme, in a dynamic and changing economy, such a policy will lead to further union decline and to a labor movement that sees its institutional security at risk. Support for innovation and cooperation is hardly likely to be forthcoming from an institution that is fighting for survival and is denied legitimacy by the party seeking its cooperation. Human resource innovation is not likely to be sustained if the adversarial tensions between labor and management continue to build toward a crisis point. Thus concern for diffusion of workplace innovations cannot be separated from the broader question concerning the future of worker representation and industrial relations policy.

While the decline of union membership poses a barrier to further diffusion, a resurgence of traditional unionism and traditional union–management relations is equally unlikely to support sustained innovation. Instead, the 1980s demonstrated that innovations were most likely to succeed and be sustained over time where union leaders became active partners in the management and design of innovations and became visible champions of employee participation and related practices. As yet, however, most American labor leaders have held back from making a strong endorsement of these new approaches. Indeed, an active debate is alive within the American labor movement over whether or not these innovations serve the long-term interests of workers and their unions.

Our view is that a transformed industrial relations system can be beneficial for the interests of the unions as institutions, as well as for the interests of employees and stockholders. To the extent that the new concepts of work organization and participation make the enterprise more viable, then the employment and membership interests of the union are enhanced. The ultimate proof of this proposition will come when the benefits to workers accruing from union–management cooperation are sufficiently visible to increase the interest of unorganized workers and decrease the opposition of employers to the prospect of unionization of their employment relationship. The outcome of this debate will be heavily influenced by the extent to which labor representatives are treated as legitimate partners to the change process at the level of the individual enterprise and in national policy-making. Thus we come to our final two propositions, which address the need for fundamental changes in our conception of the corporation and in the role of labor and human resource policy in national economic and social affairs.

Proposition 3: *Sustaining human resource innovations requires a multiple-stakeholder view of organizations and governance systems, which gives all employee groups a voice in the strategic directions of the enterprise.*

Recall that a bedrock principle of the traditional New Deal system—one embedded not only in law but in the ideology of American management and labor—is that management is the sole agent of shareholders and is also solely responsible for determining the strategic direction of the enterprise. This principle in turn reflects, as Dore points out (Chapter 2, this volume), the uniquely American conception that the corporation exists solely to maximize shareholders' wealth. In this view, the corporation is simply a bundle of tradable financial assets to be managed in the interests of the shareholders. This view leaves little room for employees as legitimate or valued stakeholders.

The inherent conflict between this principle and human resource innovations came into sharper focus in the 1980s as a result of developments in financial markets that created a more active "market for corporate control" (Jensen, 1989) and the increased number of hostile takeovers, leveraged buyouts, and other ownership changes described by Useem (Chapter 4, this volume). One consequence of these developments was to make labor more conscious of the need to participate in the financial marketplace and deal-making. In addition to efforts by individual unions to participate in or influence takeover efforts, the AFL–CIO announced in 1990 the establishment of an employee investment fund designed to help employee groups finance participation in firms that can be shown to have viable financial futures. Moreover, at least twenty-three states have now passed legislation allowing or requiring corporate officers and directors to take other stakeholder interests into account when making long-range strategic decisions. Thus the debate over the market for corporate control in the 1980s has opened the way for a debate over the governance of corporations in the 1990s. The 1990s, therefore, could very likely be a decade of further experimentation with new institutional forums for joining and accommodating the interests of shareholders and employees (Salter and Dunlop, 1989).

Some experience has been gained with various forums that provide employees with a limited role in organizational governance. These include representation on boards of directors, employee stock ownership plans (ESOPs), joint participation in strategic planning or design of new enterprises such as GM's Saturn Corporation subsidiary, and a variety of more informal and ad hoc strategic-level interactions that occur between worker representatives and enterprise executives. Unfortunately, this experience is both too limited and too biased toward settings where the firm was already in financial crisis prior to the involvement of employees in strategic affairs to support any broad generalizations. Moreover, the vast majority of ESOPs were enacted by managers as defensive financial maneuvers designed to ward off hostile takeovers (Blasi, 1988; Scholes and Wolfson, 1990). Very few of these provided employees any meaningful voice or influence in organizational governance. Until the definition and role of the corporation is modified to lend legitimacy to employees as stakeholders with a right to participate in strategic decisions, new institutional forums that provide an effective voice for employee interests are unlikely to emerge outside of crisis situations where designated representatives have the power to exert influence. Therefore, we believe broader acceptance of a multiple-stakeholder view of the corporation and an institutionalized role for employees in corporate governance are essential for the transformational process to continue.

Proposition 4: *Diffusion of human resource innovations requires fundamental changes in national labor and human resource policies and in the climate in which business, labor, and government leaders interact.*

The federal government was the silent partner in industrial relations and human resource developments in the 1980s. Both the innovations in human resource practices and the intensified confrontations between business and labor were largely private affairs. Although it may have been appropriate to leave experimentation with new approaches to the private parties in the initial stages of change, we are now beyond the development and demonstration phase of this transformation process. National leaders in business, labor, and government now need to make critical strategic choices over which set of forces discussed in this chapter is to dominate human resource practice and the governance of corporations in the 1990s.

Leadership choices are especially critical at this juncture since, as we have shown, individual firms have considerable discretion over how they compete, how they respond to changes in markets and technologies, and the importance they attach to human resource issues and innovation. Thus there is no guarantee that individual firms or individual labor leaders will choose these competitive strategies or champion this new model. But society has an important stake in these choices since the evidence shows that when supported by appropriate competitive strategies and managed properly, human resource innovations can enhance both competitive and human goals while the alternative approach sharpens the tradeoffs between these two sets of objectives. Thus one necessary condition has been met for these innovations to command greater support, namely, the new model that these innovations embody can contribute to both firm performance and worker welfare. It is far, however, from a sufficient condition to assure continued diffusion of the new model.

The analysis presented here suggests that for the transformation process to continue, labor and human resource policies must be changed to (1) encourage employee participation and representation at all levels of corporate governance and (2) encourage and support human resource policies as long-term investments in the future of the firm and the economy. Various specific proposals have been offered to achieve these policy objectives, including such ideas as tax incentives for investments in training and development, modification of labor law to either encourage or require employee participation councils similar to European-style works councils, modification of corporate law to encourage or require employee representation on corporate boards, and reforms of labor law to curb employer misconduct in organizing drives (cf. Dertouzos et al., 1989; Heckscher, 1987; Kochan and McKersie, 1989; Osterman, 1988; Weiler, 1990).

It is not our purpose here to argue for any specific policy initiative. Indeed, history suggests that new labor or social policies work best when they are derived both from the experience and lessons learned from private experimentation and from a prolonged process of debate, negotiations, and informed consensus among the stakeholders involved. Therefore, perhaps the best policy prescription at this point is to urge that the private experiments that began at the workplace level in the 1980s now be extended to the strategic level in the 1990s and joined by the national dialogue over the public policies and national leadership best suited for translating the lessons from these experiments into lasting benefits to the economy and work force. In the absence of some new consensus the schizophrenic pattern of corporate and labor practices of the past will continue into the future. We previously predicted (Kochan et al., 1986) that continuation of this pattern will produce a scenario of declining innovation, escalating labor–management tensions and conflicts, deteriorating economic performance, and increased risk of a major social and economic crisis. We now appear to be in the early stages of this scenario. If the lessons and propositions presented in this chapter are correct, an alternative scenario is possible; however, it will require building on and moving beyond the human resource innovations of the 1980s to achieve organizational transformations in the 1990s.

REFERENCES

Alper, W. S., B. Pfau, and D. Sirota. 1985. "The 1985 National Survey of Employee Attitudes Executive Report." Sponsored by *Business Week* and Sirota and Alper Associates.

Blasi, J. R. 1988. *Employee Ownership: Revolution or Ripoff?* Cambridge, Mass.: Ballinger.

Business Week. 1981. "The New Industrial Relations," May 11, pp. 20–33.

Chalykoff, J., and T. A. Kochan. 1989. "Computer-Aided Monitoring: Its Influence on Employee Job Satisfaction and Turnover." *Personnel Psychology* 42: 807–834.

Collective Bargaining Forum. 1987. *New Directions for Labor and Management.* Washington, D.C.: U.S. Department of Labor.

Craft, J. 1988. "Human Resource Planning and Strategy." In *Human Resource Management: Evolving Roles and Responsibilities,* edited by L. Dyer. Washington, D.C.: BNA Books.

Cutcher-Gershenfeld, J. 1988. "Tracing a Transformation in Industrial Relations: The Case of Xerox Corporation and the Amalgamated Clothing and Textile Workers Union." Washington, D.C.: U.S. Department of Labor.

Cyert, R. M., and D. C. Mowery, eds. 1986. *Technology and Employment.* Washington, D.C.: National Academy Press.

Dertouzos, M., R. Lester, and R. Solow. 1989. *Made in America: Regaining the Productive Edge.* Cambridge: MIT Press.

Doyle, F. P. 1989. "The Global Human Resource Challenge for the Nineties." Paper presented at the World Management Congress, New York, N.Y., September 23, 1989.

Drago, R. 1988. "Quality Circle Survival: An Explanatory Analysis." *Industrial Relations* 27: 336–351.

Dyer, L. 1988. "A Strategic Perspective of Human Resource Management." In *Human Resource*

Management: Evolving Roles and Responsibilities, edited by L. Dyer. Washington, D.C.: BNA Books.

Fombrun, C., N. M. Tichy, and M. A. Devanna. 1984. *Strategic Human Resource Management*. New York: Wiley.

Foulkes, F., and A. Whitman. 1985. "Marketing Strategies to Maintain Full Employment." *Harvard Business Review*, July–August, pp. 4–7.

Freedman, A. 1984. *New Issues in Wage Bargaining*. New York: The Conference Board.

Goodman, P. 1987. "New Technology and New Research Opportunities." In *Proceedings of the Thirty Ninth Annual Meeting of the Industrial Relations Research Association*, edited by B. D. Dennis. Madison, Wisc.: Industrial Relations Research Association.

Heckscher, C. 1987. *The New Unionism*. New York: Basic Books.

Ichniowski, C. 1986. "The Effects of Grievance Activity on Productivity." *Industrial and Labor Relations Review* 40: 75–89.

Ichniowski, C., D. Lewin, and J. Delaney. 1989. "The New Human Resource Management at the Workplace." *Relations Industrielles* 44: 97–123.

Jenson, M. C. 1989. "Eclipse of the Public Corporation." *Harvard Business Review*, September–October, pp. 61–74.

Katz, H. C., T. A. Kochan, and K. Gobeille. 1983. "Industrial Relations Performance, Economic Performance, and Quality of Working Life Efforts." *Industrial and Labor Relations Review* 37: 3–17.

Katz, H. C., T. A. Kochan, and M. Weber. 1985. "Assessing the Effects of Industrial Relations and Quality of Working Life on Organizational Performance." *Academy of Management Journal* 28: 509–527.

Kochan, T. A., H. C. Katz, and R. McKersie. 1986. *The Transformation of American Industrial Relations*. New York: Basic Books.

Kochan, T. A., and R. B. McKersie. 1983. "Collective Bargaining: Pressures for Change." *Sloan Management Review* 24: 59–65.

Kochan, T. A., and R. B. McKersie. 1989. "Future Directions for Labor and Human Resource Policy." *Relations Industrielles* 44: 224–243.

Krafcik, J. F. 1988. "World Class Manufacturing: An International Comparison of Automobile Assembly Plant Performance." *Sloan Management Review* 30: 41–52.

Lawler, E. E., and S. A. Mohrman. 1985. "Quality Circles After the Fad." *Harvard Business Review* 63: 65–71.

Loveman, G. W. 1988. "An Assessment of the Productivity Impact of Information Technology." MIT Sloan School of Management working paper 1988-054, Management in the 1990s Project.

MacDuffie, J. P., and J. F. Krafcik. 1989. "Flexible Production Systems and Manufacturing Performance: The Role of Human Resources and Technology." Paper presented at Annual Meeting of the Academy of Management, Washington, D.C., August 16, 1989.

Marshall, R. 1987. *Unheard Voices*. New York: Basic Books.

McKersie, R. B., and R. E. Walton. 1990. "Organizational Change and Implementation." In *Management in the 1990s Research Program Final Report*, edited by M. S. Scott Morton. Cambridge: MIT Sloan School of Management.

Osterman, P. 1988. *Employment Futures*. New York: Oxford University Press.

Piore, M., and C. Sabel. 1984. *The Second Industrial Divide*. New York: Basic Books.

President's Commission on Industrial Competitiveness. 1985. *Global Competition: The New Reality*. Washington, D.C.: Government Printing Office.

Roach, S. S. 1987. *America's Technology Dilemma: A Profile of the Information Economy*. Morgan Stanley Special Economy Study, New York.

Salter, M. S., and J. T. Dunlop. 1989. *Industrial Governance and Corporate Performance*. Boston: Harvard Business School Press.

Scholes, M. S., and M. A. Wolfson. 1989. "Employee Stock Ownership Plans and Corporate Restructuring: Myths and Realities." Paper presented at the Conference on Corporate Governance, Restructuring and the Market for Corporate Control, New York University, May 22–23, 1989. (Revised, January 1990.)

Schuler, R. S. 1989. "Strategic Human Resource Management and Industrial Relations." *Human Relations* 42: 157–184.

Shimada, H., and J. P. MacDuffie. 1986. "Industrial Relations and 'Humanware': Japanese Investments in Automobile Manufacturing in the United States." MIT Sloan School of Management working paper.

Thurow, L. 1987. "Economic Paradigms and Slow American Productivity Growth." MIT Sloan School of Management working paper.

U.S. Department of Labor. 1989. *Labor Management Cooperation: 1989 State-of-the-Art Symposium*. Washington, D.C.: Bureau of Labor–Management Relations and Cooperative Programs, Bulletin 124.

Walton, R. E. 1980. "Establishing and Maintaining High Commitment Work Systems." In *The Organizational Life Cycle*, edited by J. Kimberly and R. Miles. San Francisco: Jossey-Bass.

Walton, R. E. 1987. *Innovating to Compete*. San Francisco: Jossey-Bass.

Walton, R. E., and P. Lawrence, eds. 1987. *Human Resource Management: Trends and Challenges*. Boston: Harvard Business School Press.

Weiler, P. 1990. *The Law at Work: Past and Future of Labor and Employment Law*. Cambridge, Mass.: Harvard University Press.

Zuboff, S. 1988. *In the Age of the Smart Machine*. New York: Basic Books.

COMMENTARY BY TAPAS SEN

This is the first comprehensive essay I've seen that summarizes the lessons we can learn from human resource innovations of the 1980s. There has been an intensive growth in global competition and high technology, which has led to the need for a different set of skills in the work force, more involved workers, and a more cooperative labor–management relationship. Unfortunately, we were not smart enough to maintain this type of relationship when we went through our competitive crisis at AT&T.

The New Deal industrial relation system is no longer applicable to modern industry, but we don't know what will replace it. There isn't really a consensus, but the authors of this chapter seem to think that the participatory style will replace it. I tend to agree but I'm not sure American industry is ready for it yet. Let me illustrate by describing how hard it was to get our management—especially middle management—to commit to participation and stay committed through the crisis of divestiture.

We made a big mistake with our Quality of Work Life (QWL) process at AT&T prior to divestiture. We built a QWL superstructure but we failed to create an infrastructure that was bought into by the middle managers. When the company broke up, the middle managers had not been included in QWL, did not buy in, and were a stumbling block for us. It took a major effort and considerable lost time to overcome this problem.

What we have concluded from our experience is that if we want to facilitate a deep commitment to change we need to (1) include middle management, (2) change our managerial reward systems, and (3) invest heavily in joint union–management educational efforts. This is where, I believe, our company is headed and how we plan to compete.

Since I agree with most of the authors' points, let me turn to a few points where I might disagree or push a point even farther than the authors.

On Lesson 4, regarding the role of human resources and new technology, you need to involve all your key stakeholders up front when you are implementing new technology—your users, customers, and unions.

I'm not comfortable with the dichotomy introduced in Lesson 5, namely, the tradeoff between a low-cost and high-value-added strategy. If people are involved in the beginning, there doesn't need to be a contest between low-cost–low-wage and the value-added strategy. For example, when we were introducing fiber optics we needed to lower the cost and increase quality at the same time, so we involved all our employees in this effort. We needed to fully involve labor and management in the process to increase efficiency, save money, and become more competitive.

I also have some concern about the role of public policy in diffusing innovations. I agree that a more activist role might help, but the role of public policy should be catalytic, not coercive. For example, the Malcolm Baldrige Award (for high achievements in quality) has changed our quality perspective and done more to improve quality in companies than any regulation or new law could have achieved. Some of our customers have said that if we don't apply for this award, which will prove that we have good quality, then they will stop doing business with us. That's a powerful public policy tool for diffusing innovations. We need more policy tools like this.

Finally, I agree with the authors' emphasis on the stakeholder model. But there are at least six stakeholders that need to be taken into account when making decisions: industry, employees and unions, government, academia, the financial community, and the media. Each of these groups has important skills to offer in helping to make better choices within individual firms and in public policy. We must find better ways to bring them all into the change process and help develop a common understanding of successful competitive strategies.

12

Changing the Conditions of Work: Responding to Increasing Work Force Diversity and New Family Patterns

LOTTE BAILYN

That the work force is changing, and that the distribution of family types in the United States is dramatically different from what it has been—these are by now familiar facts. More than half of all mothers with children under one are now in the paid labor force (Hayes, Palmer, and Zaslow, 1990); 45 percent of all paid workers are women (Johnston and Packer, 1987). And 28 percent of all households are female-headed households (U.S. Department of Commerce, 1989). Further, at present, 60 percent of men in the labor force are married to wives who also hold jobs (U.S. Department of Labor, 1988b). It is not surprising, therefore, that a study by the Bank Street Work and Family Life staff has found that between two and three of every five employees are having problems managing the often conflicting demands of jobs and family life (Galinsky, 1988). Yet the structure of the workplace is still geared to the assumption that workers can commit all their energy and time to their employment.

Today, less than 10 percent of families follow the pattern of a husband at work and a wife at home caring for the children (U.S. Department of Labor, 1988a). Nor is this likely to be a transient phenomenon, as happened with the influx of women into the work force during World War II. On the contrary, these changes will be even more dramatic by the end of the century (Fullerton, 1989). These trends—combined with an increasingly aging population, an expected shortage of labor (particularly of well-educated, skilled men and women), and an increasing disparity between rich and poor, between employment in "good" companies (usually large, with many benefits) and smaller companies without benefits—these new patterns of work and family suggest a potential national crisis.

Its proportions are most evident in the decreasing welfare of the nation's children (Hayes et al., 1990), who are, after all, the future's workers, consumers, and citizens. But it affects, also, the care of other dependents (e.g., the elderly) and the fueling of the "thousand points of light," which, according to the present administration, are to substitute for government involvement. Almost alone among industrialized countries, the United States has no national family policy that can respond to the massive movement of women into the labor force.

Perhaps the best way to highlight the underlying presuppositions that govern the U.S. approach to work–family issues is to consider the situation in Sweden, which represents an entirely different picture. Swedish policy in this area is based on the following critical set of beliefs (Galinsky, 1989):

1. A basic commitment to gender equality: "Women and men are to have the same rights, obligations, and opportunities in all of the main fields of life" (Ministry of Labor Report on Equality Between Men and Women in Sweden, 1988). This premise was already stated in a report of the Swedish government to the United Nations on The Status of Women in Sweden (1971), though its implementation has only recently begun.
2. A basic commitment to economic self-sufficiency: "Every individual should have a job paid sufficiently to enable her or him to earn a living" (Ministry of Labor Report on Equality Between Men and Women in Sweden, 1988). This premise was also stated in the 1971 report, though, again, its actual implementation is a more recent phenomenon.

Together, these two commitments imply a strong belief that women should have jobs and that fathers should be involved in the care of their children.

3. The care of families, particularly children, lies within the responsibilities of the state, and is very much in its interest. Children are seen as a public good, and their proper care is necessary for the continuing success of the society.

And so the government has mandated a comprehensive set of family policies to enable these goals to be met. They are anchored in the economic reality of a longstanding labor shortage, and they are enhanced by a recent push by government to change social attitudes in the direction of valuing balance between work and family for both women and men (Galinsky, 1989).

Contrast these assumptions with those of the United States (Auerbach, 1988):

1. Families/children are in the private domain. The choice to have children is entirely personal and should neither be encouraged or discouraged. Hence any kind of government help in this area is seen as a stigma, a sign of personal failure.
2. Nurturance (children/elder care) is rightfully the province of women, either because they do it better or because it is somehow their specific job.
3. In an individualistic, achieving society, balance in life between work and personal life is not seen as a high-priority goal. Career and work success are more important.

It is important to recognize that these contrasting sets of assumptions represent different visions of the world (Dowd, 1989a) and do not necessarily reflect entirely different realities. In neither country has there yet been much change in the structure of the workplace. Nonetheless, these assumptions have differentially influenced developments in the two countries. Progress in the United States has come from allowing women to meet male work demands. But there has been little attempt to redefine gender roles. In contrast, Sweden has made a serious effort to change gender roles, primarily by urging men to be more involved in the family (Rapoport and Moss, 1990). As a result, Swedish women have a much easier time combining the conflicting demands of work and family, and have few of the feelings of conflict and guilt that are so prevalent in the United States (Galinsky, 1989). But they are even more likely than American women to have unequal work roles (Dowd, 1989a).

It is the mixture of considering family a private, individual concern and yet having to respond to the new demography of the workplace that has shaped the U.S. response to these issues. The response, as of now, has mainly come in the form of new employer-based benefits: parental leave; employee assistance programs (EAPs), originally geared to substance abuse and now more often involved in work–family issues; help of various kinds with dependent care, including flexible spending accounts; alternative work schedules; flexible benefits or cafeteria plans (Bureau of National Affairs, 1986; Employee Benefit Research Institute, 1987).

IBM, for example, recently added to its already generous family services (e.g., child and elder care referral services, EAPs, adoption assistance) two new initiatives: a personal leave program of three years during which time employees receive company-paid benefits and are assured of a job on returning; and expanded flextime, where employees have the option of starting work up to an hour before or after the normal starting time. The first initiative—personal leave—is accompanied by the option of part-time work during the first year, with the requirement that employees be available for part-time work during the second and third years if their services are needed. IBM is also starting a pilot program that will allow employees on personal leave to work at home, as long as the tasks they are assigned are amenable to this arrangement and they agree to come to their workplace location at least four consecutive hours during the week. And a new labor contract at AT&T includes a family care package consisting of a fund for the development of community child care centers and services for the elderly, grants for adoption, and parental and family illness leaves up to one year with continuation of basic benefits and a guaranteed job at the end.

Neither IBM nor AT&T, however, is representative of all U.S. employers—certainly not of small firms, or of those with fewer skill requirements or less benevolent attitudes, though similar arrangements on an *individual* basis are often possible for valued[1] employees in those cases. But since these more enlightened benefits are generally seen as a model for the U.S. response to work–family issues, it is important to subject them to analysis.

CORPORATE RESPONSE

The responses of these leading American corporations fall into two general categories, which have different consequences for other organizational concerns. First are benefits provided by employers—in the form of services or financial and information aid in obtaining these services—that allow employees with family responsibilities more easily to meet the requirements of work as currently defined. Such responses are meant, as much as possible, to help employees in different family situations and with different needs to fit the procedures originally designed for a more homogeneous work force, one where 100 percent commitment to work and organization could be presumed because an employee either was single or had family support at home. Hospitals, for example, badly in need of primarily female nursing help, often at irregular hours, frequently provide on-site child care arrangements. And at least two law firms, one in

Washington and one in Boston, recently made provision for employees' children when they are sick or when normal arrangements break down. Second are policies that create flexibility in location and time as well as varying arrangements for personal leave. The aim here is to provide employees with sufficient control and discretion over the conditions of work to respond themselves to the needs of their families.

Both sets of responses have begun to meet the needs of the current work force. But without attention to how they fit into existing organizational procedures, both may have unintended negative consequences: the first by actually exacerbating the very conditions the benefits were designed to alleviate; the second by creating—or reinforcing—a two-tier structure of employment. It is the thesis of this chapter that the introduction of family benefits must take these negative consequences into consideration, and that an effective resolution of such competing concerns will not be possible without a restructuring of the conditions of work (cf. Dowd, 1989b).

Exacerbating Family/Work Pressures

During much of this century the pressures on the conditions of employment have served to *reduce* the amount of time people spent in the workplace, but recently that trend has been reversed. Over the last fifteen years or so, work time in the United States has increased 15 percent (Gordon, 1989); among managers the increase is estimated as almost 20 percent over the last decade (Fowler, 1989). And though most European countries provide longer periods of paid time away from work than does the United States, the example of competitors in the Far East has led a number of analysts to conclude that longer working hours are necessary to bring the United States back to its previous competitive position (e.g., Subotnik, 1989; Weigand, 1986).

In particular, it is the example of Japan that is held up to support this conclusion.[2] And it is Japan, also, that serves as a model for the more participative and committed form of organization that is now recommended to increase U.S. productivity (Dertouzos, Lester, and Solow, 1989; Kanter, 1989; Lawler, 1986). Such recommendations seem to ignore the Japanese institutional norms that underlie that system, such as the role of women as family support and the economic/financial framework that exchanges employment security for total commitment in the core work force (Dore, Chapter 2, this volume). But neither of these conditions exists in the United States, and it is unlikely that either could be made congruent with contemporary American values. Yet productivity pressures, combined with globalization and increased international competition, have resulted in longer work hours just when increased family demands are also putting greater pressure on employee time. Family benefits of the first kind, which either provide or allow workers to buy family services, do not make U.S. employees less time poor. And because the availability and quality of the services thus provided are still not adequate, such responses may actually increase the work–family concerns now facing American workers.

Much of what we read about the need for organizational change in U.S. companies reflects a concern about productivity. More participation, flatter organizations, more responsibility and authority at lower levels—all of these demand increased commitment from employees, a commitment that tends, according to current rules, to translate into more time and involvement with work. But if the demographic changes over the past few decades have left the family, children in particular, as vulnerable as many now fear, then the answer is not to ensure that employees can give more time to work, but rather to find ways to make possible more time devoted to family needs. And that is the goal of the second set of benefits which the most enlightened employers are now introducing.

Creating (Reinforcing) a Two-Tier Structure of Employment

In essence, these benefits—flextime and flexplace, part-time and job-sharing opportunities, personal leaves of various kinds—are geared to freeing time for employees to attend to family needs. As such, they make legitimate a different, more accommodating set of workplace requirements. But trouble arises if other organizational procedures remain unchanged. As long as organizations continue to reward the full commitment of their employees, gauged by the amount of time spent at work, flexibility, even when available, will not be popular with core employees. Yet dependents will continue to need care. And even though the solution that evolved at the Industrial Revolution—a specialization of labor between bread winning and care taking—is no longer seen as optimal, either economically or psychologically, women still seem to be primarily responsible for care. Thus, at the present time, flexible options are more likely to be used by women than by men. And as long as such a differential pattern of use exists, it can only *increase* the disadvantages that women already face in the workplace through the feminization of poverty, the wage gap, the glass ceiling. By itself, flexibility superimposed on existing assumptions about the conditions of employment is not likely to change these basic facts. It needs to be accompanied by a reevaluation of the meaning of employment in contemporary American society—one that can provide equity and fairness along with the productive use of the nation's talents and skills. Even IBM's response, important as it is, fails to meet this challenge. And the same is true of most other examples of organizational responses to employees' family needs (see, e.g., Bureau of National Affairs, 1986; Rodgers and Rodgers, 1989).

By law, U.S. policy in these matters has been "gender-neutral." Pregnancy leave is generally subsumed under disability provisions; custody decisions in divorce cases now go as often to fathers as to mothers. But is such mandated equality equitable? Can it overcome the effect of a wage-labor system premised on an ideal worker with no family responsibilities (Williams, 1989)? Can it be equitable in the face of a deeply held cultural assumption that caring is the province of women? Does it not force everyone (both women and men) to choose between economic success without family responsibilities and economic marginalization combined with family care? And does it not, therefore, contribute to the economic vulnerability of women—as has been shown recently by the differential consequences of divorce for men and women in a "gender-neutral" world (Arendell, 1987; Weitzman, 1985)?

These are the issues involved in this second set of benefits, which provide needed leeway, under current conditions, to employees with families. But as long as women are the primary beneficiaries, these benefits may also entail a cost. As already stated for the previous category, what is needed is a reexamination of the assumptions underlying the structure of work.

CONDITIONS OF EMPLOYMENT

If it is true that American industry will require the full utilization of all talent—male and female—in order to stay globally competitive, and if we want to achieve this goal within the constraints of our notions of equity and of the needs of future generations, then a critical analysis of the premises underlying current employment practices is in order. And, just possibly, the rapidly changing demography in this country may provide the catalyst for this endeavor (cf. Briggs, 1987). But for reasons already discussed, organizations will have to do more than provide family benefits to be used primarily by women. Schwartz (1989), in her famous or infamous article in the *Harvard Business Review,* has made companies aware that family concerns must be taken into account in the conditions of employment for women. What she did not make clear is that these considerations may soon generalize to male employees, since they also, more and more frequently, do not fit the model of an employee totally committed to work with no other significant responsibilities. In this there is another compelling reason to reevaluate the basic assumptions underlying employment.

One critical issue centers on location and time (Bailyn, 1988). Too often the amount of time spent at work is seen as a prime indicator of commitment and, indirectly, of productivity; visibility is seen as a prerequisite for advancement. But long hours and a heavy workload, particularly when rigidly prescribed, are key elements in the inability to meet conflicting responsibilities. Witness the comments of a young male assistant professor: "[The university's] expectations about one's commitment to individual career—to the exclusion of spouses' career and family—make it virtually impossible to live a life in which personal goals can be considered (much less accomplished) apart from work." At that same university, two out of five young faculty parents report that they have seriously considered leaving because of conflict between family and work.

Nor is it clear that time at work is always positively related to productivity. On the contrary, some research indicates that part-time work and job sharing increase productivity per hour worked (Cohen and Gadon, 1978; Ronen, 1984). It seems important to ask, therefore, whether it is really necessary to work long hours in order to perform effectively, or whether this requirement is simply part of the traditional way to manage careers. Might long hours not be a sign of *inefficiency,* rather than of commitment and motivation? Similarly, is continuous presence at an office really required in an age of knowledge-intensive work with the aid of technology for information and communication? In a California pilot project, for example, state employees who work at home were "3 to 5 percent more productive than they would be if they spent full time in the office" (*Work in America,* August 1989, p. 8). Perhaps visibility is another proxy signal used by organizations to control employees' careers, a control that is anchored in outdated ways of managing (cf. Drucker, 1989; Dumaine, 1989; Houghton, 1989).

A second key issue, therefore, centers on new ways of managing people, a transformation that is difficult because it goes against the received wisdom about how to manage. Management by walking around, by overseeing the way subordinates work, would no longer be possible. A basic trust (in both competence and effort) would have to take its place (Perin, 1991), and managers would have to shift their emphasis away from input and concentrate on output instead. It would bring us back, perhaps, to McGregor's Theory Y—a set of assumptions that people not only enjoy their work but are willing to take responsibility for it. It has been said, for example, that the reason Sweden does not worry about employees misusing the sixty days each year they are allowed to take off for illness of children (the actual average is between six and seven) is their sense of fairness and commitment.[3] So why do U.S. (and British) managers assume that if they don't see their subordinates working, they probably aren't?

In interviews exploring the possibility of using computers to work at home during the regular work week on tasks that require cognitive concentration, Perin (1991) heard again and again managers asking, "How do I know he's working if I don't see him?" And yet they had no answer to the responding question: "How do you know he's working when you *do* see him?" Their assumptions about control stem from a scientific management model of work—McGregor's Theory X. And whether such a view makes any sense in today's world is a real question. Thus a change in management practice may be a key to effecting the kind of organizational transformation that is required—not only for individuals trying to mesh work and family concerns, but more generally for easier organizational adaptation to a rapidly changing environment.

Technology can play a role in this process. It both enables and supports, under the right conditions, changes in the organization of work that could help alleviate workplace constraints on accommodations between work and family. The ability to loosen constraints on location is a prime example of technology's potential for effecting change. So, for example, a comparison of systems developers working from home instead of being office-based shows that the former arrangement, though no substitute for child care, is associated with greater satisfaction with health and other personal concerns than is the traditional office-based pattern (Bailyn, 1989). But, as already indicated, it is difficult to convince supervisors that the arrangement is tenable (Cooperson, 1990), for it conflicts with basic cultural beliefs about time and the meaning of "office" and "home" in industrial society (Perin, 1991). Consider, however, the following example.

The task of writing a technical manual for a large consumer product manufacturer usually took about six months and required the efforts of people separated both geographically and functionally. Once an experimental network was introduced that connected these people electronically, the time to complete the task was cut to less than two months, with no change in quality. What was particularly interesting about this experiment was that one of the people involved quietly took his computer home. Other members of the group were not aware that he had changed his location, and it is interesting to speculate whether knowledge of this change would have affected the outcome.

Another example, from the same organization, relates to the introduction of computer-aided design (CAD) machines in an engineering design department. Engineering managers had been used in monitoring the work of their subordinates, seated around a large drafting table, by overseeing the process by which they arrived at their designs. But once these design engineers were huddled over individual computer screens, this control over process was no longer possible. The screen was too small for two people, and it contained more detail than could be seen as a whole. Thus supervision had to shift to the output—which appeared as a printout two floors below the design floor—and away from the input, the process by which the design was created.

The designer gained autonomy, and the supervisor had to be more trusting of the competence of his subordinates and also had to be clearer about the specifications of the final product.

What all of this indicates is that a basic change in the conditions of employment is needed for family–work issues to be usefully resolved in the context of other pressures on organizations to change. Without such systemic change, responses to family–work conflicts may lead to unintended negative consequences. To illustrate the process I would like to examine the career development system currently in use in most U.S. organizations, and to highlight the aspects of that system that would need to change.

CAREER DEVELOPMENT

Current career development procedures in organizations are based on the assumption that long-term planning for positions is not only possible but desirable. So effort is put into early identification of future potential with little concern for the long-range consequences of these decisions. Such a career system has linear continuity built into it. It assumes that the appropriate career direction is up and that what happens at the beginning is a strong determiner of the future. In one R&D lab, for example, there still is a significant positive correlation between current and starting salary twenty years into the career. And, as Rosenbaum (1984) has shown in his depiction of the tournament model, the probability of getting a promotion drops dramatically after a certain fairly clearly defined period of about seven to ten years. This procedure of early selection of high-potential employees (the fast track) ignores the possibility that the selection itself may determine the outcome—the self-fulfilling prophecy. And, most critically for the present concerns, it puts a premium on time and effort spent on work during years where family concerns are likely to make an employee particularly vulnerable.

The system is geared to matching an individual to a job that has been carefully specified independently of the person filling it. It is based on a desire to make career procedures as homogeneous as possible and to have them apply equally to all parts of the firm and to all people, whatever their individual situations. Such a system, by definition, cannot be responsive to individual needs. On the contrary, it is designed to minimize the probability of special treatment for certain groups and is supported by the legal system for just that purpose. But for a diverse work force, with employees in widely differing family situations, equality in procedures does not necessarily produce equal employment opportunity; it may produce the opposite.

Continuity, linearity, and homogeneity are already under pressure from concerns about efficiency and productivity. In particular, since the restructuring we have seen during the last decade in the United States has often been accompanied by massive displacement of workers, the assumption of continuity is really obsolete. Hence a new approach, one that would also help employees deal with family needs, may be in order. I think of such a system as "zero-based budgeting" in careers. It would involve planning for a particular career segment, perhaps of five to seven years, and then renegotiating the level of commitment, the tasks, the compensation and evaluation procedures de novo for the next segment. I have elsewhere discussed a similar idea in calling for negotiation of career procedures based on a personally defined extent of

Table 12.1 Need to change assumptions

Old Assumptions (constraining)	New Assumptions (facilitating)
Commitment/loyalty = time	Discontinuity
Manage via input; before-the-fact approval	Accountability; after-the-fact review
Homogeneity in outlook and values	Building on diversity (self-design)

occupational commitment (Bailyn, 1984). Let employees decide, at different points in their lives, the extent to which they can commit themselves to their work, and then negotiate tasks, rewards, and appraisal procedures in line with this level of commitment. Such a system would not only fit better with the current organizational reality in this country, but it would also allow employees to better mesh the needs of their families with the requirements of work. As presently constituted the career development system is geared neither to a changing organizational environment nor to the work–family issues of employees.

But changes in deeply entrenched procedures are not easily accomplished. They are anchored in largely taken-for-granted assumptions (Schein, 1985), which may have been functional at an earlier time but now serve as constraints on change. These constraining assumptions are listed in Table 12.1, which also juxtaposes new assumptions, more relevant to current needs.

The difficulties of measuring commitment and loyalty by time, particularly visible time, have already been discussed, as has the equally constraining tendency for managers to feel that they must monitor in detail the way their subordinates meet their work objectives. Together, these presumptions lead managers to walk around and to insist on the need for before-the-fact approval. Such a definition of managerial control resides in the principles of hierarchy, still firmly embedded in business organizations, and on the difficulties of specifying clearly the output goals of work. But it also represents a basic mistrust of the motivation of one's employees and of their willingness to be responsible for their work (cf. Perin, 1991). Consider, for example, the thorny question of whether employees are allowed to take time off to stay home with a sick child. In many cases no such provision is available and employees with a sick child either call in sick themselves—which some find very disagreeable—or have supervisors who are willing to accept family illness as a legitimate reason for absence. And even when organizations provide a certain number of personal days for family illness, the procedures for "applying" are sometimes so cumbersome that they are not used. Similarly, the rules for taking sick leave in some cases include a note from the doctor. (A regression to childhood where a note was necessary to excuse an absence?) If we can provide a certain number of paid work days to cover absences for personal reasons, why not leave the monitoring of their use to the employee? Why do we feel that employees will exploit this privilege? Why cannot we assume that they are mature adults, with a sense of responsibility about their work (cf. Gambetta, 1988)? In the case of the home-based systems developers, for example, there was sufficient trust that time records were completely accepted by managers, and there was no evidence whatsoever of any misuse of this trust. And a study by the National Council of Jewish Women (1987) has shown that when employers are accommodating and flexible in their policies, pregnant women take *fewer* sick days, work *later* in their pregnancies, and are *more* likely to spend time doing things related to their jobs outside regular work hours without compensation. They are also more likely to return to their jobs after childbirth (NCJW Report, 1988).

Finally, there is the presumption, despite evidence to the contrary (cf. Schein, 1987), that all people in a given organizational position should be homogeneous in outlook and values. Firms try to select for this in their hiring practices, or they count on socialization to produce it. But this attempt, besides running the risk of not being successful with the current demographic reality, also may miss a valuable source of new ideas and change. In a diverse work force employees will differ in their needs, their values, their assumptions about the role of work and career in their lives, and their approaches to work and to the people around them. And though such differences cannot guarantee adaptive change, they may provide the necessary variety from which change emerges, and may result in a rethinking of organizational routines and the establishment of new and possibly more effective procedures (cf. Weick, 1979; Weick and Berlinger, 1989).

Career procedures based on this new set of assumptions would be quite different, I think, from those now prevalent in organizations. The essence of the current procedures is an independently defined job system into which people are selected or socialized to fit. "Misfits" are weeded out in the process, and with them the potential for new ideas and approaches. In contrast, a system based on this different set of assumptions would rest on individual negotiation based on discontinuity, which would force both the system and the people in it to construct their relationship in new and different ways. More innovation would be possible; more authority could be given to those with the necessary expertise and information. Care would have to be taken that individual negotiation would be truly individual and would not turn into assignments according to stereotyped expectations about people's abilities or circumstances. None of this would be easy, but it seems to be an approach that would make it possible to combine the productivity needs of organizations with the work–family issues now confronting the U.S. work force. The alternative, of dealing with demographic and family change in isolation by superimposing family policies on the current system, might not actually improve workers' work–family conflicts and might, in the absence of other changes, reinforce the already existing gender inequity in the workplace.

POTENTIAL FOR CHANGE

These are some of the key issues that need to be confronted if there is to be an easier accommodation between organizational needs and the work–family concerns of employees. And the question now remains, where can the leverage for change be found? For there are deeply held assumptions that constrain such change. So how does one get from here to there?

There are some who say that the change in demographics itself will provide the necessary impetus. But demographic trends, and national need, tend to go in cycles, and the question of how such changes can be institutionalized remains (Rapoport and Moss, 1990). Moreover, such institutionalization will have to occur in the procedures that govern all people, not only women or mothers. Felice Schwartz, in defense of her article in the *Harvard Business Review* (1989), claims that practicality mandates a change only for women, and that the generalization to all employees, regardless of sex, will follow. Auerbach (1988), in her analysis of employer practices regarding child care, is also cautiously optimistic. She feels that these efforts already point to the acceptance by American business that the workplace and the family have changed forever—that both men and women play roles in both arenas. There is no real evidence for Schwartz's optimism or for Auerbach's. In the end, it may be that only if men's roles and men's workplace behavior change (cf. Pleck, 1989) will there be the requisite leverage to alter the underlying assumptions.

One way to guide such change is to amass information on what is currently happening. In particular, one would want to establish the family demographics of the work force, since most organizations have no notion of the families in which their employees live. The IBM data, for example, on marital status and presence of young children and elder dependents by sex, were an eye opener to management and a powerful impetus for introducing new policies. And a number of leading universities are currently engaged in similar exercises as they review their policies. The prime motivation here is the recruitment and retention of top talent. But more information than simply family demographics should be collected. Data on the problems people face in meeting current organizational requirements, indicated perhaps by absenteeism and turnover, are also required. Identification of the demographic groups that find these requirements most difficult, and the extent to which they are changing, would be a key indicator of where change is needed in order to help employees mesh their concerns with work and family.

But even more important is an assessment of the utilization and effects of new, as well as existing procedures. Policy and practice do not always go together and it is important to know who actually takes advantage of existing policies, with what consequence for their future roles in the organization. A leading university, for example, which for fifteen years has had on its books the provision of personal leave for child care for its faculty (which would stop the tenure clock), has discovered that no woman who took such a leave has ever subsequently been awarded tenure (Rowe, personal communication). Here, however, a word of caution is in order. Such information can be used to effect change; it can also be used to justify the status quo. It is just this fear that has led to so much concern over Felice Schwartz's statement that women cost the corporation more than men do. To prevent such a "misuse" of data it is critical to surface the assumptions underlying current practices (cf. Martin, 1990). Otherwise, new procedures, no matter how well meant, may have unexpected and undesirable consequences (see, e.g., Bento and Ferreira, 1990).

The most important need is for the acceptance of work–family issues as an integral part of organizational life, as an important business concern (cf. Rodgers and Rodgers, 1990), and a realization that they cannot be dealt with in a piecemeal fashion but must be central to any consideration of systemic change. Though not an easy assignment, it is possible that a confluence of forces—demographic change, expected labor shortages, an emerging national concern, models from other parts of the world, and the new technologies—may make this a propitious time to proceed in this direction.

ACKNOWLEDGMENTS

I am grateful to the Ford Foundation (grant 890-3012) for support during the writing of this chapter. I also want to acknowledge the very helpful comments given by the following people on previous drafts: Regina Bento, Rae Goodell, Deborah Kolb, Nancy Lonstein, Rhona Rapoport, Amelie Ratliff, and John Thompson.

NOTES

1. That the perceived value of employees may itself be a function of an employee's gender and family position is analyzed by Martin (1990).

2. It is ironic that Japan is currently trying to induce its workers to take more vacation time and is putting in place a whole set of interrelated procedures in order to move to a five-day week ("Coming: The 5-Day Week for All," Editorial, *The Japan Times,* August 28, 1988, p. 18).

3. Overall, however, Sweden has a very high absentee rate, something in the order of 25 percent. One company, however, found that by increasing the control of their employees over the conditions of work they reduced their absentee rate from 30 percent to 5 percent (personal communication), evidence again that one cannot superimpose family benefits on existing conditions but must accompany them by structural change in these conditions.

REFERENCES

Arendell, T. J. 1987. "Women and the Economics of Divorce in the Contemporary United States." *Signs* 13: 121–135.

Auerbach, J. D. 1988. *In the Business of Child Care: Employer Initiatives and Working Women.* New York: Praeger.

Bailyn, L. 1984. "Issues of Work and Family in Organizations: Responding to Social Diversity." In *Working with Careers,* edited by M. B. Arthur, L. Bailyn, D. J. Levinson, and H. A. Shepard. New York: Center for Research in Career Development, Columbia University.

Bailyn, L. 1988. "Freeing Work from the Constraints of Location and Time." *New Technology, Work and Employment* 3: 143–152.

Bailyn, L. 1989. "Toward the Perfect Workplace? The Experience of Home-Based Systems Developers." *Communications of the ACM* 32: 460–471.

Bento, R. F., and L. D. Ferreira. 1990. "Incentive Pay and Organizational Culture." Paper presented at the Colloquium on Performance Measurement and Incentive Compensation, Harvard Business School, June 25–26, 1990.

Briggs, V. M., Jr. 1987. "The Growth and Composition of the U.S. Labor Force." *Science,* October 9, pp. 176–180.

Bureau of National Affairs. 1986. *Work and Family: A Changing Dynamic.* (BNA special report) Washington, D.C.

Cohen, A. R., and H. Gadon. 1978. *Alternative Work Schedules: Integrating Individual and Organizational Needs.* Reading, Mass.: Addison-Wesley.

Cooperson, D. A. 1990. Telecommuting: A Way to Ease Work/Family Conflicts Through Increased Employee Time Flexibility? MIT Sloan School of Management, unpublished term paper.

Dertouzos, M. L., R. K. Lester, and R. M. Solow. 1989. *Made in America: Regaining the Productive Edge.* Cambridge: MIT Press.

Dowd, N. E. 1989a. "Envisioning Work and Family: A Critical Perspective on International Models." *Harvard Journal on Legislation* 26: 311–348.

Dowd, N. E. 1989b. "Work and Family: The Gender Paradox and the Limitations of Discrimination Analysis in Restructuring the Workplace." *Harvard Civil Rights–Civil Liberties Law Review* 24: 79–172.

Drucker, P. 1989. "The Futures That Have Already Happened." *The Economist*, October 21, pp. 19ff.

Dumaine, B. 1989. "What the Leaders of Tomorrow See." *Fortune*, July 3, pp. 48ff.

Employee Benefit Research Institute. 1987. *Fundamentals of Employee Benefit Programs*, 3rd ed. Washington, D.C.

Fowler, E. M. 1989. "More Stress in the Workplace." *New York Times,* September 20, p. D22.

Fullerton, H. N., Jr. 1989. "New Labor Force Projections, Spanning 1988 to 2000." *Monthly Labor Review*, November, pp. 3–12.

Galinsky, E. 1988. "Child Care and Productivity." Paper prepared for the Child Care Action Campaign Conference, Child Care: The Bottom Line, New York. Quoted in E. Galinsky and P. Stein, "Balancing Careers and Families: Research Findings and Institutional Responses." In *Marriage, Family, and Scientific Careers: Institutional Policy Versus Research Findings,* edited by M. L. Matyas, L. Baker, and R. Goodell. Proceedings, Symposium of American Association for the Advancement of Science, Annual Meeting, San Francisco, January 16, 1989.

Galinsky, E. 1989. "The Implementation of Flexible Time and Leave Policies: Observations from European Employers." Paper prepared for the Panel on Employer Policies and Working Families, Committee on Women's Employment and Related Social Issues, Commission on Behavioral and Social Sciences and Education, National Research Council, Washington, D.C.

Gambetta, D. 1988. "Can We Trust Trust?" In *Trust: Making and Breaking Cooperative Relations,* edited by D. Gambetta. New York: Basil Blackwell.

Gordon, S. 1989. "Work, Work, Work." *Boston Globe,* August 20, pp. 16ff.

Hayes, C. D., J. Palmer, and M. Zaslow. 1990. "Who Cares for America's Children: Child Care Policy for the 1990's." Report of the Panel on Child Care Policy, Committee on Child Development Research and Public Policy. Commission on Behavioral and Social Sciences and Education, National Research Council, Washington D.C.

Houghton, J. R. 1989. "The Age of the Hierarchy Is Over." *New York Times,* September 24, Business Section, p. 3.

Johnston, W. B., and A. E. Packer. 1987. *Workforce 2000: Work and Workers for the Twenty-First Century.* Indianapolis: Hudson Institute.

Kanter, R. M. 1989. *When Giants Learn to Dance: Mastering the Challenges of Strategy, Management, and Careers in the 1990s.* New York: Simon and Schuster.

Lawler, E. E. 1986. *High Involvement Management: Participative Strategies for Improving Organizational Performance.* San Francisco: Jossey-Bass.

Martin, J. 1990. "Deconstructing Organizational Taboos: The Suppression of Gender Conflict in Organizations." *Organizational Science* 1: 339–359.

National Council of Jewish Women. 1987. "Accommodating Pregnancy in the Workplace." *NCJW Center for the Child Report.* New York: National Council of Jewish Women.

National Council of Jewish Women. 1988. "Employer Supports for Child Care." *NCJW Center for the Child Report.* New York: National Council of Jewish Women.

Perin, C. 1991. "The Moral Fabric of the Office: Panopticon Discourse and Schedule Flexibilities." In *Research in the Sociology of Organizations,* edited by S. Bacharach, S. R. Barley, and P. S. Tolbert. Greenwich, Conn.: JAI Press. (Volume on Organizations and Professions).

Pleck, J. H. 1989. "Family-Supportive Employer Policies and Men's Participation." Paper prepared for the Panel on Employer Policies and Working Families, Committee on Women's Employment and Related Social Issues, Commission on Behavioral and Social Sciences and Education, National Research Council, Washington, D.C.

Rapoport, R., and P. Moss. 1990. *Men and Women as Equals at Work: An Exploratory Study of Parental Leave in Sweden and Career Breaks in the UK*. London: Thomas Coram Research Unit.

Rodgers, F. S., and C. Rodgers. 1989. "Business and the Facts of Family Life." *Harvard Business Review,* November–December, pp. 121–129.

Ronen, S. 1984. *Alternative Work Schedules: Selecting . . . Implementing . . . and Evaluating*. Homewood, Ill.: Dow Jones–Irwin.

Rosenbaum, J. E. 1984. *Career Mobility in a Corporate Hierarchy*. New York: Academic Press.

Schein, E. H. 1985. *Organizational Culture and Leadership*. San Francisco: Jossey-Bass.

Schein, E. H. 1987. "Individuals and Careers." In *Handbook of Organizational Behavior,* edited by J. W. Lorsch. Englewood Cliffs, N.J.: Prentice-Hall.

Schwartz, F. N. 1989. "Management Women and the New Facts of Life." *Harvard Business Review,* January–February, pp. 65–76.

Subotnik, D. 1989. "Productivity's Little Secret: Hard Work." *New York Times,* May 14, Business Section, p. 2.

U.S. Department of Commerce. 1989. *Current Population Reports* (Special Studies Series P-23, No. 159). Washington, D.C.: Bureau of the Census.

U.S. Department of Labor. 1988a. *Child Care: A Workforce Issue*. Report of the Secretary's Task Force. Washington, D.C.

U.S. Department of Labor. 1988b. *Employment and Earnings*. Washington, D.C.: Bureau of Labor Statistics.

Weick, K. E. 1979. *The Social Psychology of Organizing,* 2nd ed. Reading, Mass.: Addison-Wesley.

Weick, K. E., and L. R. Berlinger. 1989. "Career Improvisation in Self-Designing Organizations." In *Handbook of Career Theory,* edited by M. B. Arthur, D. T. Hall, and B. S. Lawrence. Cambridge: Cambridge University Press.

Weigand, R. E. 1986. "What's A Fair Day's Work?" *New York Times,* April 19, p. 27.

Weitzman, L. J. 1985. *The Divorce Revolution: The Unexpected Social and Economic Consequences for Women and Children in América*. New York: Free Press.

Williams, J. C. 1989. "Deconstructing Gender." *Michigan Law Review* 87: 797–845.

COMMENTARY BY DEREK HARVEY

Work and family issues are to the 1990s what comprehensive family medical coverage was to the 1950s. They are a necessary business expense, which includes the provision of services and policies that offer time flexibility. Time flexibility will initially include dependent care leave, flextime, and other similar tools that managers can offer their people.

In the long term, these policies will not be sufficient for dual-career employees and other heads of households. As the demand for family "care" grows so will the demand for much more substantial time flexibility. One key to achieving these changes is through management practices. Companies that appoint (or train) managers who have a value system that includes empowering employees, managing diversity, and practicing flexibility will build a climate that allows subordinates to manage their work and family lives. The manager of the nineties will be much more concerned with contribution and outcomes than the number of hours spent at the workplace.

This trend when seen alongside other trends toward flatter organizations, larger spans of managerial control, and the greater use of computer technology suggest that the workplace of the year 2000 will be radically different from today's.

Alongside these trends companies need to rethink their linear career paths and live with the reality that at different times in a career employees will give different levels of commitment.

Dialogue on Using Human Resources for Strategic Advantage

The chapters on training, work and family, and labor and human resource policies all generated vigorous debates. Included here are samples of the dialogue that ensued over the role of the government in providing training; the concerns expressed over the quality of public education and school governance; and the frustrations over our seeming inability or unwillingness to integrate family, schooling, and work issues and/or to generate the political support needed to motivate changes in public policies of transforming organizations.

EDUCATION AND TRAINING: PUBLIC, CORPORATE, OR INDIVIDUAL RESPONSIBILITY?

James Mahoney

If the government mandates certain levels of training that must be provided by companies, it will hurt those companies that already take training as a serious responsibility. Training offers an opportunity for growth and a source of competitive advantage. Private (corporate) interests and social interests diverge in this case. These training policies would be in the interests of the general public, because it would improve the caliber of our work force, but companies may not accept this as public policy because it takes away competitive advantage.

Donald Runkle

If you look at human resource development narrowly, as a strategic move, then you won't want to work together and cooperate with other companies. But training is already being shared when employees we train leave to go to work for another company. So maybe we have to look at this in the larger context of the labor markets we all draw our talent from.

Edgar H. Schein

There are deeper assumptions here. We are discussing human performance as a strategic resource. These human beings are seen as property of the organization, the organization is seen as owning the employees. It brings up questions about "Who owns a career?" Many employees are deciding that they own their careers and merely lease their talents to the companies they work for. Ideally, you would unstructure contracts and hire talents as and when you need it. That industry owns these human resources or the training problem is a big assumption.

Harold E. Edmondson

If we look at schools as a supplier, their product becomes our problem, especially if schools are providing only 30 percent of the skills we need today. And specialized, or what Lisa Lynch calls specific, training is our responsibility, but this is not a problem in a company that has continuous learning going on. Specialized training will then be the natural result.

Paul Osterman

There are many good solutions to this problem of the relationship between the role of the schools and companies in providing education and training. International comparisons are helpful. Let's look at how Germany and Japan do training. In Japan, the public schools are not vocational in the least. People are recruited into the firms with little prior skills training, but once they get into the company there is a very low turnover. Employees are then educated by the firms to meet their long-term needs.

In Germany, 80 percent of the population goes to high schools that emphasize vocational training and provide apprenticeships in cooperation with firms. Two-thirds of these individuals finish their apprenticeships and change jobs, and often even their field of employment.

In both countries, there is an educational package that is part of a larger political system. They are getting what they need in Germany and Japan. In the United States, we have no training or educational package, no constructed training path.

Nan Lower

Comparisons with countries whose policies are based on a work force, such as in Sweden, Switzerland, Germany, and Japan, are realistic and we can learn from them. But can they be adapted to the United States? How dramatic will the conflicts be, and how will we compensate for these drastic differences between organizations? We need more organizational experiments to test these questions.

SHOULD THE MANAGEMENT AND ORGANIZATION OF SCHOOLS BE TRANSFORMED?

Raymond Stata

Al Shanker, president of the American Federation of Teachers, has argued persuasively that the problem with schools is in their management. There is poor governance in our schools. We need to make changes. We need to find out how to manage people, how people learn, what a teacher does and does not do. School governance has to be radically reformed.

Robert McKersie

The state of New York has embarked on an experiment to have shared decision making in the schools by 1992. Individual districts have to empower teachers and parents, and evaluate how well they are meeting customer needs.

Laura Divine

How do we view the school system? We need to view the school system from the point of view of the students. Who is really the customer? We need to close the feedback loop, and send them feedback to see how well they are meeting the needs of the schools' customers, the students. In much the same way, the good companies view their employees as customers, and ask themselves who will provide training—government, schools, or firms.

Richard M. Locke

The high school system we have in the United States is the one that industry fought for around the turn of the century, because it was a match for the production system we had at that time. Now the market has changed. There are very few entry-level people, and organizations are downsizing. There always used to be a class of people who were the nation's unskilled labor. But today, there is such an enormous gap between the haves and the have nots that the have nots are unemployable. We need a radically different school system, which is not so much a question of resources as it is a question of managerial systems, just like the strongest companies.

SCHOOLING, FAMILIES, AND THE WORKPLACE

Derek Harvey

Is it the schools or parents that are the problem? Is there a commonality among Japan and Germany in terms of parenting? We need to think about what our companies are doing to allow us to be parents.

Fran Rodgers

No other society has tried to give women full equity in the workplace and not offered support for families and parents. Our approach in the United States is not working. Either you send the women home, which would be a disaster, or you invest in the children. If you look at the schools without looking at the breakdown of the families, it's useless. We cannot marginalize family life one bit more. Working parents can't even be involved with our schools. Companies say we need to revamp our school systems if industry is going to get the kinds of workers it needs, but then won't give their employees the time and flexibility to be involved in their children's schools. There is also no societal infrastructure in support of the schools. There is way too much being heaped on the backs of the schools, and it is weighing them down—they are expected to be day care providers, police, drug rehab counselors, and bus drivers.

Edgar H. Schein

If Fran Rodgers is right, we cannot look for merely incremental changes in either schools or company policy to solve this problem. The issue is what are the basic cultural assumptions that keep us from doing radical overhauling. Is there any evidence that flextime, family leave, and so on, would lead to a decrease in productivity? These cultural assumptions need to be examined.

Lotte Bailyn

In Sweden, they are just now beginning to do the type of thinking Ed Schein suggests. They are beginning to think about a six-hour day. Up from 2 percent, now 20 percent of men take parental leave. How, in America, do we get around the cultural assumptions that say eight, if not ten, hours of work in the office each day is best? The answer is in restructuring the conditions at work. Public policy is necessary but not sufficient to do this. But the lack of public policy in the United States is causing a social disaster.

Donald Ephlin

The concept of "transforming organizations" is exemplified by the Saturn program. It is our own best experiment and is being praised by everyone from former president Ronald Reagan on down as being what we must do to be competitive. Under our laws, though, it is probably illegal. It was illegal because we were negotiating a labor contract but had no employees at the time. GM was not willing to start up the enterprise until we had reached an agreement, so it was a Catch-22. Although we want to transform our organizations and be more competitive, even the President Commission on Industrial Competitiveness referred to antitrust laws as inhibiting us from becoming competitive. There are many public policy issues that need to be addressed. Since we have serious problems, and are now willing to work together to solve them, we want the "big three" in the auto industry to work together to solve these problems.

In the big industries, cooperation—the joint approach to problem solving—between labor and management is the best it has ever been. In the rest of America, the smaller firms, the relationship between labor and management is worse than it ever has been.

(Further discussion of Deborah Gladstein Ancona's chapter on teams is found on pages 302-304 with the Dialogue on Using Technology for Strategic Advantage).

III
USING TECHNOLOGY FOR STRATEGIC ADVANTAGE

13

Integrating Technology and Human Resources for High-Performance Manufacturing: Evidence from the International Auto Industry

JOHN PAUL MacDUFFIE AND JOHN F. KRAFCIK

For much of the last decade, technology has held the spotlight as a powerful force that has both promoted dramatic economic restructuring and offered individual firms new strategic opportunities for responding to changing competitive conditions.[1] But the enthusiastic predictions of the early 1980s about the cost-saving and quality-enhancing capabilities of advanced microprocessor-based technologies were matched late in the decade by a chorus of concern about the failure of many technology investments to yield expected performance results (Dertouzos, Lester, and Solow, 1989; Loveman, 1988; Roach, 1987).

These unrealized expectations have brought increasing attention to the organizational context into which new technologies are introduced. According to this perspective, new technological capabilities contribute effectively to improved economic performance only when the organizational skills and flexibility needed for rapid absorption and mastery of these capabilities are present and evolving simultaneously (Adler, 1988; Kochan, Cutcher-Gershenfeld, and MacDuffie, 1990; Walton, 1990).

This chapter carries this line of argument one step further, by summarizing the results of our study in the manufacturing sector of seventy automotive assembly plants representing twenty-four companies and seventeen countries worldwide. The detailed data and statistical analyses that produced these results are presented in several earlier papers (Krafcik, 1989; Krafcik and MacDuffie, 1989; MacDuffie, 1989). Our summary here emphasizes the implications of our findings for the study and practice of organizational change.

Out of our work (and that of our colleagues in the International Motor Vehicle Program) has emerged the concept of a "lean production system," that is, a production system embedded in an organizational context that takes as a premise the existence of a skilled, motivated, and flexible work force, following a logic quite distinct from traditional mass production (Kenney and Florida, 1988; Piore, 1989; Womack, Jones, and Roos, 1990). We find that plants with lean production systems have dramatically better productivity (fewer hours per car) and quality (fewer defects per car) than mass production plants.

We also find that technology is utilized differently in lean and mass production systems. Under the "organizational logic" of lean production, human resource strategy is integrated with technology strategy (Shimada and MacDuffie, 1987). Policies that develop work force skill, motivation, and flexibility and that promote ongoing problem-solving (or "continuous improvement") activity are seen as critical to the effective use of technology. This contrasts with traditional mass production, in which technological advances are expected to enhance managerial control, reduce labor costs, and minimize reliance on work force capabilities.

Accordingly, we contend that new technological capabilities will contribute more effectively to economic performance in the context of a lean production system than in a traditional mass production context. The chapter describes the "organizational logic" of lean production, explains how technology is utilized in this context, and reviews the analyses supporting this "integration" argument.

THE ORGANIZATIONAL LOGIC OF LEAN PRODUCTION

The model of lean production upon which the assembly plant study is based is drawn from Shimada and MacDuffie's analysis (1987) of the production system in Japanese-owned assembly plants located in the United States, the so-called transplants. The transplants offer a valuable opportunity to consider the structure of the Japanese approach to organizing the production system apart from the cultural context from which it emerged. Shimada and MacDuffie find that the key organizational innovations of "lean production," as developed in Japan, have been transferred nearly completely to the U.S. context, and they conclude that this approach is potentially applicable in any cultural setting.

The key organizational innovations of lean production are those linking the use of buffers and the development and deployment of human resources. We consider these in turn, contrasting the "organizational logic" of lean production and mass production.

Use of Buffers

Mass production uses highly specialized resources (both equipment and people) applied to the high-volume production of standardized products to achieve economies of scale. To ensure that these economies can be achieved, the production process must be protected as much as possible from disruptions (such as sales fluctuations, supply interruptions, equipment breakdowns) by large buffers—of inventory, repair space, extra equipment, and utility workers. These buffers moderate the tight coupling among steps in the production process, creating some slack, which minimizes the impact of contingencies.

In lean production, these buffers are seen as costly, for several reasons. The buffers themselves represent a commitment to resources not directly devoted to production. Inventories must be purchased, stored, and handled. A repair area, which provides a postprocess remedy for problems that would otherwise disrupt the primary production process, must be staffed. Inventory buffers also hinder the move from one product design to another, requiring elaborate planning to ensure that parts from the old design are used up and replaced by parts from the new design at the same rate that sales of the former product are declining and sales of the new product are increasing.

More important, buffers can also hide production problems or reduce the pressure to deal with them. A key innovation of lean production, pioneered by Taiichi Ono at Toyota, was to see disruptions to the production process as opportunities for learning (Ono, 1988). In this view, organizational slack, in the form of buffers, allows production problems to be ignored or deferred. The minimization of buffers, as exemplified by just-in-time inventory policies, therefore serves a cybernetic or feedback function, providing valuable information that can be used for continuous incremental improvement of the production system (Cusamano, 1985; Monden, 1983; Schonberger, 1982). The term "lean production" is a metaphor for this philosophy about the use of buffers.

Development and Deployment of Human Resources

This approach to buffers is inextricably linked to policies that govern human resources. For if the minimization of buffers creates the incentive to identify problems and engage in incremental problem-solving activity, it is the development and deployment of human resources that create the capability to do so effectively.

Workers must be able to identify quality problems as they appear on the line, since there is almost no stock of surplus parts and very little space to put vehicles needing repair. To be able to solve the problems they find (either alone or in a problem-solving group), they must have both a conceptual grasp of the production process and the analytical skills to identify the root cause of problems. This in turn requires a decentralization of production responsibilities from specialized inspectors to production workers and a variety of multiskilling practices, including extensive off- and on-the-job training, work teams, and job rotation within a few broad job classifications.

Furthermore, these skills and abilities are of little use unless workers are motivated to contribute mental as well as physical effort. The attentiveness, analytical perspective, and creativity needed for incremental problem solving cannot be attained through close supervision or the elaborate control systems used to ensure compliance in a mass production system.

Workers will bring those qualities to their jobs only if they believe there is a real alignment between their individual interests and those of the company, and they will commit themselves to advancing company goals only if they believe there is a reciprocal commitment from the company to invest in their future well-being. As a result, lean production is characterized by such "high-commitment" human resource policies as employment security; compensation that is partially contingent on corporate, plant, and/or individual performance; and a reduction of status barriers between managers and workers. The company investment in building worker skills also contributes to this "psychological contract" of reciprocal commitment.

To summarize, in a lean production system the stimulus to achieving cost and quality improvements is the reduction of buffers, which has both a direct effect (e.g., reducing the carrying cost of inventories) and a more significant indirect effect— providing valuable information about production problems and an ongoing incentive to utilize that information in incremental problem-solving activity. While the reduction of buffers can promote this problem-solving approach, it will be effective only when human resource policies are in place that generate the necessary skills in the work force and create a sense of reciprocal commitment between company and worker.

A "Fragile" System

Shimada and MacDuffie (1987) call attention to an important aspect of lean production's interdependence between the use of buffers and human resource policies. They characterize lean production as a "fragile" system. This is true for both components of lean production. When buffers are minimized, any minor disruption, such as the failure of a supply delivery to arrive on time, can force the entire plant to shut down. Paradoxically, the awareness of this vulnerability can strengthen the production system by providing an ongoing incentive to maintain effective communication and problem-solving skills, both within the plant and in relationships with suppliers (Nishiguchi, 1989).

Lean production is also fragile with respect to its dependence on human resources. As lean production diffuses beyond its source in Japan, it is highly vulnerable to the mass production assumptions and mindsets that have dominated managerial and engineering practice in this century. Unless managers keep the skill levels of the work force high, unless they create a culture of reciprocal commitment in which workers will be willing to contribute to process improvement, unless they accept the premise that technology must be used in a way that complements rather than minimizes the role of human resources, lean production will quickly deteriorate and revert to mass production.

Thus in practice lean production is not weaker or more prone to breakdown than mass production. Indeed, the characteristics of lean production just described often yield a greater resilience and organizational flexibility in the face of changing conditions than do those of mass production. Yet this paradox remains—that maintaining a constant awareness of lean production's "fragility" is in many ways critical to preserving this resilience and flexibility.

TECHNOLOGY IN A LEAN PRODUCTION SYSTEM

The organizational context of lean or mass production systems affects the utilization of hardware technology in several ways. One is the degree to which each production system uses resources—whether hardware or people—in a specialized way. Another, closely related to the first, is the degree to which production processes and tasks remain standardized and fixed over time. A third is the role of the work force with respect to modifying both equipment and task specifications.

A core premise of mass production is that the efficiency of production increases as the division of labor becomes more extensive and the specialization of both machines and jobs increases. This specialization is limited by the market for whatever is being produced. A sufficient volume of a product must be made to keep specialized resources fully utilized, or the inefficiencies of underutilized resources will outweigh the efficiencies of specialization.

Standardized product designs allow for the most extensive specialization of machines and jobs. The greatest efficiencies then result from producing a very large volume of such a product in very large batches, both because of economies of scale and to minimize setup costs, which are high when hardware is so thoroughly specialized around the requirements of a standard design.

The imperatives for technology under mass production, therefore, are that it be dedicated to a specific product, very efficient in its execution of a highly specialized task, and capable of operating for extremely long production runs. Once a new technology is installed, it should be modified as little as possible if it is to meet these conditions successfully. While this ideal of minimal modification is rarely achieved, it remains the primary orientation and goal of a mass production organization.

Under lean production, there is less concern with the efficiencies of specialization and more concern with the costs of rigidity in the use of technology. General purpose multifunctional or programmable equipment is favored for its ability to switch among product designs at a lower cost in time and money than specialized equipment. Production runs are short, both to provide more opportunities to switch among products and, more important, to speed the feedback that can be provided to upstream processes for problem resolution.

Most significantly for this discussion, the incremental problem-solving orientation in lean production is also applied to hardware technology. Each type of production equipment has its own idiosyncrasies that keep it from being used at full capacity; the more complex the equipment, the greater the idiosyncrasies. In both mass and lean production settings, operators, maintenance personnel, and engineers all learn over time how to minimize the impact of these idiosyncrasies.

Under mass production, the acquisition and application of this "working knowledge" about equipment glitches is constrained by the broader imperatives of specialization, standardization, and high-volume production (Hirschhorn, 1984; Kusterer, 1984). But under lean production, workers and engineers apply their problem-solving abilities to the task of improving equipment performance over time. This process of incremental improvements is commonly referred to in Japanese plants as "giving wisdom to the machine." It means that production technology need not be automatically subject to decay and depreciation but can actually appreciate in value over time.

For example, under mass production, the installation and "debugging" of a new technology are handled by staff specialists or vendors, whereas these responsibilities are often given to workers under lean production. This means that the important learning from this initial period is retained among those who will operate (and seek further improvement in) the equipment over time rather than being taken along to the next plant or customer.

Another crucial aspect of giving wisdom to the machine is the continual modification of job specifications by the work force. In some cases, these are jobs that relate directly to the use of technology, such as equipment setup times. Minimizing setup time is crucial to achieving small-lot production and the rapid feedback it provides. Therefore, workers and engineers work to improve the layout, fixtures, and procedures involved in, for example, changing a stamping press die. This type of die change once commonly took several hours (and still does in some mass production plants). But most Japanese plants and an increasing number of U.S. plants have managed to reduce this die change time to under ten minutes, often without any major capital investment.

The same principle of continual process improvement applies to all job specifications under lean production, whether directly related to technology or not. Here, too, mass production seeks to specialize and standardize as much as possible, for greater efficiency. The specification process is assigned to industrial engineers, who follow the rationalization prescriptions of Frederick Taylor to assign an appropriate work time to each process step. Workers can ease the demands of their job if they successfully fool the industrial engineer into setting a task cycle time that is greater than what they actually need to do the job.

Under lean production, workers have a major role in determining specific work procedures and methods. While production levels and the basic framework for the production process are determined by engineering requirements, teams of production workers have responsibility for developing, recording, and modifying job specifications. These specifications are extremely detailed, as much as any industrial engineering time study, but with the crucial difference that workers, rather than managers or engineers, take charge of their revision (Cole, 1990; Krafcik, 1988b; Monden, 1983).

We previously noted a tendency for mass production plants to rely on more specialized equipment and for lean production to use more general purpose equipment. It is perhaps more significant that the differences in the approach to technology in these two systems often persist regardless of the type of hardware being used. In other words, under mass production, general purpose equipment tends to be used as if it was specialized equipment intended for long, unvarying production runs. Conversely, under lean production, specialized or dedicated equipment tends to be subject to the same processes of incremental modification as general purpose equipment.

Thus there are two reasons to believe that technological capabilities will be utilized more effectively under lean production than mass production. First, the organizational context of mass production, with its prerogatives of high volume, specialization, and standardization, leads to a relatively static or rigid use of technology (Abernathy, 1978). This can be true even when the technology is inherently flexible, as with robotics and other microprocessor-based programmable equipment (Jaikumar, 1986). Second, the problem-solving orientation and skills of the work force under lean production facilitate the process of introducing *any* new technology and also yield valuable modifications over time.

RESEARCH QUESTIONS

The foregoing discussion lays out the difference in organizational logic between lean production and mass production and develops the hypothesis that the link between the minimization of buffers and the extensive development of human resource capabilities under lean production contributes significantly to such manufacturing outcomes as high productivity and high quality. It also advances the "integration" hypothesis that advanced technologies will contribute more effectively to manufacturing performance under lean production than under mass production. We next review the empirical evidence on these two hypotheses.

THE INTERNATIONAL AUTOMOTIVE ASSEMBLY PLANT STUDY

The International Automotive Assembly Plant Study was initiated in 1986. By May 1990, we had visited ninety assembly plants, representing twenty-four assemblers in sixteen countries, and seventy of those plants had responded to our survey. Almost all of the auto-producing regions of the world and all the major assemblers, with the exception of those in the Soviet bloc and China, participated in our study.

Although this chapter reports primarily on the relationship of technology and production organization to manufacturing performance, the assembly plant study was designed to address the role of other explanatory variables as well, such as model mix complexity, parts complexity, scale, and product design age. A summary of the complete multivariate analysis of these factors can be found in Krafcik and MacDuffie (1989) and MacDuffie (1991). Some of these control variables are significant, but none of them change the basic results described here. Of these, product design age was most influential. We believe that this variable is a proxy for "design for manufacturability," that is, newer products are more likely to have been designed with ease of manufacture in mind. This supports our belief that design for manufacturability has an important effect on assembly plant productivity and quality. Indeed, this is an issue we intend to study intensively in our future work.[2]

Our sample consists of sixty-two plants, all in the volume (as opposed to luxury/specialty) product category. The regional distribution of these plants (and, for U.S. plants, the region of the parent company) is presented in Table 13.1.

METHODOLOGY AND OPERATIONALIZATION[3]

Productivity

We define productivity as the hours of actual working effort required to complete a group of designated assembly plant "standard activities" on a product standardized by size, option content, and product manufacturability in the welding and painting areas. These adjustments *do* take into account differing levels of vertical integration, worker relief periods, and absenteeism. No adjustments are made for differing levels of automation, plant scale, or assembly area manufacturability. The bulk of the plants in this survey assemble products ranging in size from Ford Escort to Ford Taurus.

Quality

We used the U.S. market 1989 J. D. Power Initial Quality Survey to develop an index which reflects only those defects that an assembly plant can affect, ignoring such areas as engine performance and reliability. The emphasis therefore is on fit and finish of

Table 13.1 Composition of volume assembly plant data

Regional Category	n
Japan (J/J)	8
Japanese-parent plants in North America (J/NA)	4
U.S.-parent plants in North America (US/NA)	14
Europe (All/E)	19
New Entrants, including East Asia, Mexico, and Brazil	11
(All/NE)	6
Australia	

body panels and trim pieces, paint quality, and integrity of electrical connections. In those cases where plants in the survey do not sell products in the United States, we used internal company quality data correlated to J. D. Power figures to increase the size of the quality data base.

Production Organization Index

This index is the average of two component measures of production organization: Use of Buffers and Human Resource Management (HRM) Policies. When combined into the Production Organization Index, a high score indicates a lean production system and a low score indicates a mass production system.

The *Use of Buffers Index* measures a set of production practices that are indicative of overall production philosophy. It includes the percentage of assembly floor space allocated to final repair, the capacity of the in-process buffer between the paint and assembly areas, and a measure of inventory policy that reflects the level of inventory stocks and the frequency of parts delivery to the line. A high score for this variable indicates a minimal use of buffers and a low score indicates an extensive use of buffers.

The *HRM Policies Index* captures a wide variety of work structures and personnel practices that affect the development and deployment of human resources. Six variables reflect shop floor work organization: how direct assembly tasks are organized (the extent to which work teams and job rotation are used); how indirect tasks traditionally handled by functional specialists are allocated (the extent to which quality inspection and statistical process control are assigned to production workers); and the level of worker participation in problem-solving activity (the percentage of the work force involved in employee involvement groups and the number of production-related suggestions received and implemented).

Four other variables measure policies that affect the "psychological contract" between employees and the organization: the recruiting methods and hiring criteria used in selecting the work force, the extent to which the compensation system is contingent upon performance, the extent to which status barriers between managers and workers are present or absent, and the level of ongoing training offered to experienced production workers, supervisors, and engineers. A high score for this variable indicates a high-commitment, multiskilling bundle of HRM policies; and a low score indicates low-commitment, specializing policies.

Technology Measures

We use two complementary technology measures, the Robotic Index and Total Automation. The *Robotic Index* is the number of robots in the welding, painting, and assembly areas adjusted for the scale of the plant. Since robots are often a new investment and are by definition flexible, the Robotic Index captures these aspects of a plant's technological intent or strategy. It does, however, miss the often substantial investments plants make in fixed automation.

Our other technology variable, the *Total Automation Index,* captures the level of both flexible and fixed automation. Total Automation measures the percentage of direct production steps in the welding, painting, and assembly areas that are automated. As such, it is essentially an indicator of the total automation stock in the plant. Unlike the

Robotic Index, it does not indicate the characteristics of the automation, i.e., old or new, flexible or fixed. Also, since it measures the percentage of total direct production steps that are automated, we can expect it to be somewhat correlated with our productivity measure, which reflects the labor hours required for nonautomated direct production steps (along with all indirect and salaried/administrative labor hours). However, this allows for a conservative test of our hypothesis that a high technology level will not produce high performance in a plant lacking a lean production system.

THE SIMULTANEOUS ACHIEVEMENT OF HIGH QUALITY AND HIGH PRODUCTIVITY

Although traditional manufacturing doctrine propounds that high levels of quality and high levels of productivity are incompatible, our study results show otherwise. We divide the sample into four performance zones (Figure 13.1) and find a surprising number of plants that achieve better than average productivity and quality performance, with an overall correlation between these outcomes of .36 ($p = .007$). Further, we have identified a small group of "world-class" plants that simultaneously achieve very high levels of productivity and quality.[4]

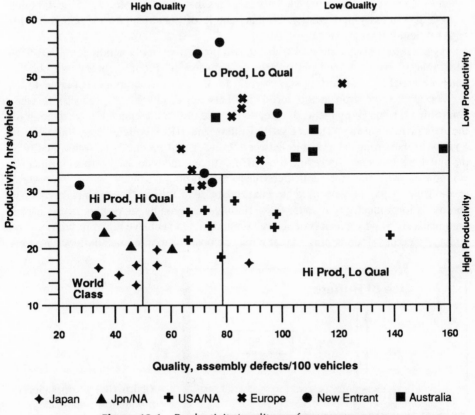

Figure 13.1 Productivity/quality performance zones.

Note that the simultaneous achievement of better than average quality and productivity is not limited to plants in Japan; six American, one European, and three New Entrant plants join five Japanese-parent plants in this zone. On the other hand, the world-class performance zone contains only Japanese plants—four in Japan and two in North America. One striking manifestation of the relationship between these outcomes is the small number of plants with above-average quality and below-average productivity, or below-average quality and above-average productivity. For the majority of the plants in our sample, quality levels and productivity levels are closely linked.

PRODUCTION ORGANIZATION, TECHNOLOGY, AND MANUFACTURING PERFORMANCE

As indicated previously, we derive the Production Organization (ProdOrg) Index as the average of two component measures, Use of Buffers and Human Resource Management (HRM) Policies. We argued that these two measures were conceptually interrelated. As Figure 13.2 shows, they are highly interrelated statistically as well.

The ProdOrg Index is strongly correlated with performance results for this sample of plants, with a simple correlation of $r = -.59$ ($n = 57, p = .000$) with productivity (hours per vehicle) and a simple correlation of $r = -.63$ ($n = 45, p = .000$) with quality (defects per 100 vehicles). This indicates that about 36 percent of the variation in both productivity and quality for this sample of plants can be explained by this organizational measure alone.

As a test of the separate effects of the two production organization components on performance, we examined the correlation between the ProdOrg Index and our key outcome variables, controlling successively for each of the components (Table 13.2).

The greater the drop in the correlation between ProdOrg and productivity when controlling for one component, the greater the role of that component in accounting for the overall relationship. Thus, Use of Buffers and HRM Policies contribute almost equally to the strong relationship between ProdOrg and productivity. With quality as the outcome measure, however, the HRM Policies measure is the most influential component, with the Use of Buffers measure contributing much less to the overall relationship. Although we would have expected Use of Buffers to contribute as much to quality as to productivity results, these findings are broadly supportive of the earlier arguments about why a lean production system is able to achieve high productivity and quality outcomes. It does suggest that it may be possible to minimize buffers for purely

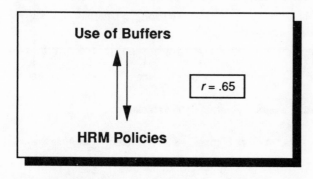

Figure 13.2 Correlation of production organization components.

Table 13.2 Correlations between production organization and key outcomes

	Correlation of Production Organization with:	
	Productivity (hours/vehicle)	Quality (defects/100 vehicles)
No controls	−.59	−.63
Controlling for Use of Buffers	−.25	−.37
Controlling for HRM Policies	−.24	−.23

cost reduction purposes, thus improving productivity, without changing the organizational processes that lead to high quality. The use of buffers must therefore be matched with HRM policies that improve a plant's capability for ongoing problem solving, as argued earlier.

The two technology measures also have statistically significant correlations with both outcomes. The simple correlation of Total Automation with productivity is $r = -.67$ ($n = 62$, $p = .000$) and with quality is $r = -.41$ ($n = 46$, $p = .002$). For the Robotic Index, the simple correlation with productivity is $r = -.55$ ($n = 62, p = .000$) and with quality is $r = -.41$ ($n = 46$, $p = .002$). Despite the differences in these measures, they result in similar characterizations of the technology levels of a given plant, as shown by the high simple correlation between them of $r = .81$ ($n = 62$, $p = .000$).

TESTING THE INTEGRATION HYPOTHESIS FOR PRODUCTIVITY AND QUALITY

Having considered the separate relationships of production organization and technology to performance, we now analyze their combined effect to assess the integration hypothesis.[5] We first examine the relationship between technology and both outcomes for subgroups of mass production and lean production plants, formed by using the sample average for the ProdOrg Index (44.6). Table 13.3 shows that the correlation between Total Automation and both productivity and quality is much stronger for the lean than for the mass production subgroup.

We then further subdivide our sample by using the sample average score for Total Automation (24.4 percent), generating four quadrants that reflect all possible combinations of technology and organizational context. In Figure 13.3, we show the average productivity and quality outcomes for each quadrant.

Table 13.3 Correlation between total automation and performance outcomes

	Productivity (hours/vehicle)	Quality (defects/100 vehicles)
LeanProd plants ($n = 21$)		
Total Automation	−.79 ($p = .000$)	−.39 ($p = .053$)
MassProd plants ($n = 36$)		
Total Automation	−.56 ($p = .000$)	−.25 ($p = .101$)

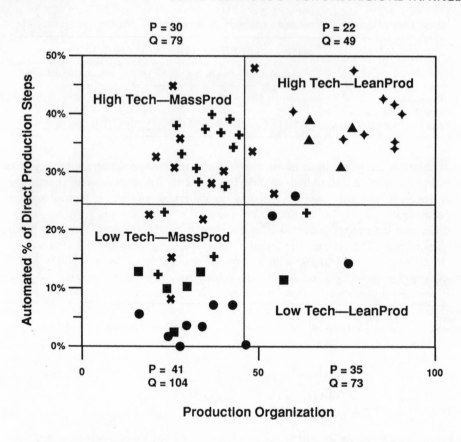

Figure 13.3 Level of automation versus production organization.

As Figure 13.3 shows, Low-Tech–MassProd plants take, on average, 41 hours to build a vehicle with a poor quality level—over 100 defects per 100 vehicles—whereas plants in the High-Tech–LeanProd quadrant have the best performance, taking only 22 hours—just over half as many hours—to build a vehicle with superior quality performance, with an average of about 50 defects per 100 vehicles. Plants in the High-Tech–MassProd group perform at the intermediate level of 30 hours per vehicle and 80 defects per 100 vehicles; the very few plants in the Low-Tech–LeanProd group have similarly intermediate results.

We now examine the integration hypothesis for overall manufacturing performance—the simultaneous achievement of high productivity and quality. Table 13.4 shows the average values of key explanatory variables, using the four performance zones found in Figure 13.1.

Total Automation is very low (15 percent) for the low-productivity–low-quality group, jumps up to 30 percent for the high-prod–low-qual and high-prod–high-qual groups, and increases modestly to 36 percent for the world-class group. The amount of technology does not, therefore, significantly differentiate among the top three performance groups. The Production Organization Index and its two component measures, in

Table 13.4 Averages for key variables by overall performance zone

Zone	n	Total Automation (% auto steps)	Production Organization (100 = Lean)	Use of Buffers (100 = Minimal)	HRM Policies (100 = HiComm)
Low-prod–low-qual	19	15.6	32.2	43.3	26.2
High-prod–low-qual	6	31.6	35.1	44.4	30.4
High-prod–high-qual	15	29.3	53.8	60.7	50.4
World class prod and qual	6	36.4	81.7	87.0	79.1

contrast, *do* differ significantly across the top three groups, with the best performing group having the most lean production system, the most minimal buffers, and the most high-commitment HRM policies. These findings confirm that the best overall manufacturing performance results when relatively high levels of automation are combined with a lean production system.

CONCLUSIONS

Support for the Integration Hypothesis

We find that both production organization and technology are important factors in explaining manufacturing performance when considered separately but contribute most significantly to high productivity and high quality when they occur together. This provides broad support for the "integration" hypothesis, which posits that a lean production system is a necessary condition for effectively utilizing high levels of automation.

To summarize our findings, the correlation between technology and performance is much stronger for LeanProd plants than for MassProd plants. High-Tech–LeanProd plants dramatically outperform Low-Tech–MassProd plants, with the latter group requiring 86 percent more hours per vehicle and yielding 112 percent more defects per 100 vehicles. But High-Tech–LeanProd plants also substantially outperform traditional plants with comparably high levels of technology—the High-Tech–MassProd plants require 36 percent more hours per vehicle and yield 61 percent more defects per 100 vehicles than this top-performing group. Furthermore, the technology measures are correlated much less with quality than with productivity, in contrast with the Production Organization measure, which is equally strongly correlated with both outcomes.

Finally, when considering overall performance (productivity and quality together), we find that technology has an important role in boosting performance as plants move from very low levels of automation to moderate levels, even in the context of a mass production system. But the performance gain in moving from moderate to high levels of automation appears to occur only when combined with the organizational, human resources, and manufacturing practices of a lean production system.

Implications for Organizational Change

While our analysis is cross-sectional, our observations of the industry suggest that the assemblers with the best manufacturing performance have approached the integration of technology and production organization by establishing a lean production system *first,* to provide a solid foundation, and then have moved to higher levels of automation. These assemblers have then been able to capitalize more quickly on new technological capabilities because their production systems facilitate learning and continuous improvement.

The value of these organizational capabilities extends to other aspects of lean production not addressed in this chapter, such as design for manufacturability. The high level of employee suggestions and of group problem-solving activity under lean production is a valuable source of ideas for design improvements and is a crucial part of the two-way flow of communication between design and manufacturing that is so critical to achieving easy-to-assemble products. Moreover, the multiskilling practices of lean production at the plant level, such as job rotation and high levels of ongoing training, are also applied at the corporate level, yielding design engineers and project managers who bring extensive manufacturing experience to their task.

As noted earlier, our study finds that lean production, despite its source in Japan, is fully transferrable to other cultural and national settings. Both the Japanese transplants in North America and a growing number of U.S.-owned and New Entrant plants (though almost no European plants) have established that the principles of lean production have universal value.

Yet the switch from mass production to lean production is far from simple. Because the bundle of practices and policies that make up lean production are so closely interrelated, transitional states between mass and lean production, in which some aspects of both systems are in place, are treacherous. When some production crisis challenges a plant in transition, the overwhelming pull is to revert to tried and true mass production principles by, for example, restoring buffers, reinstituting quality inspection, or recentralizing control over job specifications. Yet everything we know about organizational change also suggests that an abrupt shift to lean production, in response to what employees may perceive as a short-lived management fad, is also likely to be doomed to failure.

The most important first step for plants contemplating a move to lean production is education—managers, supervisors, engineers, and workers alike must understand the crucial (and not always obvious) differences in philosophy from mass production, in such areas as quality control, the use of buffers, process standardization, task specialization, and the role of the work force. Also important is the idea that work structures such as teams and quality circles are valuable only to the degree that they bring about changes in daily activities—especially the degree to which they promote ongoing problem-solving efforts from employees. Finally, those leading this change effort must understand the risks involved: lean production is a "fragile" system whose strength is realized only through prolonged efforts to minimize its vulnerabilities.

We have found that this education is best accomplished through access by managers and union officials to a learning example—a lean production plant—through either joint ventures and other forms of strategic alliance or just geographical proximity. The transplants have provided this example for U.S. companies, whereas European companies have remained mostly insulated. But for production workers, direct training in such lean production "basics" as statistical process control, the job specification process (and other tasks traditionally assigned to industrial engineers), and "hands-on" mastery of new technologies (setup, programming, preventive maintenance) are even more effective.

Once an understanding of the principles of lean production is achieved and training is under way, the change process can best be implemented through incremental steps that make clear to all the linkages between the policy of buffer minimization and the increased decentralization of responsibilities to shop floor workers (and the associated need for continued skill development). We have known some plants that have steadily closed down portions of their repair areas by roping them off or painting the floor a different color, creating more "off-limits" space by the week. Still other plants have tried to simulate the conditions of a just-in-time inventory system, even before achieving such arrangements with their suppliers, by delivering from parts storage to the line on a small-lot, high-frequency basis.

Production crises may challenge the transition to a "lean" use of buffers, but there are many other developments that can threaten the culture of "reciprocal commitment" so necessary to lean production. Demonstrating a commitment to employment security (if not an absolute "no-layoff" policy), although tough to do in the cyclical U.S. auto industry, is probably essential for lean production to take hold. We believe that the Japanese transplants have gained considerable loyalty from their U.S. workers each time they have not resorted to layoffs during a period of volume decline. Other pitfalls include the retention of visible status barriers differentiating managers and workers; compensation policies that award management bonuses in years when worker bonuses are not given; abuses of management discretion over job assignments within broad job classifications; and reliance on formal grievance mechanisms rather than informal, close-to-the-source dispute resolution.

Finally, the common separation (and even opposition) of technology strategy and human resource strategy under mass production must give way to an "integrated" perspective. As our data show, it is only through such integration that the high productivity and quality necessary for competitive success can be achieved. Many observers have noted the potential of new technologies to either enhance or constrain individual and organizational capabilities. Lean production provides the context in which the former scenario can be realized. Recognition of this fact may be the first step for any company (or country) concerned with both economic achievement and human development.

ACKNOWLEDGMENTS

The authors gratefully acknowledge the support of the International Motor Vehicle Program at the Center for Technology, Policy, and Industrial Development and of the Leaders of Manufacturing Program, both at MIT.

NOTES

1. This chapter summarizes some of the key results from the broader research project on manufacturing performance conducted by John F. Krafcik and John Paul MacDuffie under the

auspices of the M.I.T. International Motor Vehicle Program. The project grew out of Krafcik's case study of the NUMMI plant, where he developed the initial methodology for measuring assembly plant productivity and quality and from Shimada and MacDuffie's comparative case studies of Japanese manufacturing techniques found in Japanese assembly plants in North America. After Krafcik's M.S. thesis tested several hypotheses about assembly plant performance for a small sample of plants, Krafcik and MacDuffie combined forces to expand the sample and to develop and test a more complete model of the technological, human, and organizational determinants of manufacturing performance.

2. See Womack et al. (1990) for a discussion of product development processes under lean production and the link to assembly plant performance.

3. For more details on the methodology for calculating productivity and quality, see Krafcik (1988a); for the production organization index, see MacDuffie (1989); for the technology variables, see Krafcik (1989).

4. The lines separating the high and low productivity and quality zones are drawn at the sample average values for the 46 plants for which we have both kinds of data—33 hours per vehicle and 78 defects per 100 vehicles. The plants in the low-productivity–low-quality zone whose quality level is slightly better than the sample average were both few in number and virtually indistinguishable on most variables from those with worse-than-average quality. The "world-class" zone includes plants with productivity levels better than 25 hours/vehicle and quality levels better than 50 defects/100 vehicles.

5. From this point on, we present results that use the Total Automation measure of technology. This measure is more comprehensive and tends to show a stronger link between technology and performance outcomes than the Robotic Index, thus providing a more conservative test of the hypothesis that a "mass production" organizational context limits the performance contributions of technology.

REFERENCES

Abernathy, W. J. 1978. *The Productivity Dilemma: Roadblock to Innovation in the Automobile Industry*. Baltimore: Johns Hopkins University Press.

Adler, P. 1988. "Managing Flexible Automation." *California Management Review* XXX, no. 3: 34–56.

Cole, R. 1990. "Issues in Skill Formation and Training in Japanese Manufacturers' Approaches to Automation." Paper presented at conference on Technology and the Future of Work, Stanford University.

Cusamano, M. 1985. *The Japanese Auto Industry: Technology and Management at Toyota and Nissan*. Cambridge, Mass.: Harvard University Press.

Dertouzos, M. L., R. K. Lester, and R. M. Solow. 1989. *Made in America: Regaining the Productive Edge*. Cambridge, Mass.: MIT Press.

Hirschhorn, L. 1984. *Beyond Mechanization*. Cambridge, Mass.: MIT Press.

Jaikumar, R. 1986. "Post-Industrial Manufacturing." *Harvard Business Review*, November–December, pp. 69–76.

Kenney, M., and R. Florida. 1988. "Beyond Mass Production: Production and the Labor Process in Japan." *Politics and Society* 16, no. 1: 121–158.

Kochan, T., J. Cutcher-Gershenfeld, and J. P. MacDuffie. 1991. "Employee Participation, Work Redesign, and New Technologies: Implications for Manufacturing and Engineering Practice." In *Handbook of Industrial Engineering*, edited by G. Salvendy. New York: Wiley.

Krafcik, J. F. 1988a. "Comparative Analysis of Performance Indicators at World Auto Assembly Plants." Unpublished masters thesis. Sloan School of Management, MIT.

Krafcik, J. F. 1988b. "Triumph of the Lean Production System." *Sloan Management Review* 30, no. 1: 41–52.

Krafcik, J. F. 1989. "A Comparative Analysis of Assembly Plant Automation." Paper presented at the International Motor Vehicle Program Policy Forum, Acapulco, Mexico, May 1989.

Krafcik, J. F., and J. P. MacDuffie. 1989. "Explaining High Performance Manufacturing: The International Automotive Assembly Plant Study." Paper presented at the International Motor Vehicle Program Policy Forum, Acapulco, Mexico, May 1989.

Kusterer, K. 1984. *Knowhow on the Job: The Important Working Knowledge of "Unskilled Workers."* Boulder, Colo.: Westview Press.

Loveman, G. W. 1988. "An Assessment of the Productivity Impact of Information Technology." MIT Sloan School of Management working paper 1988-054, Management in the 1990s Project.

MacDuffie, J. P. 1991. "Beyond Mass Production: Flexible Production and Manufacturing Performance in the World Auto Industry," unpublished Ph.D. dissertation. Cambridge, Mass.: MIT.

MacDuffie, J. P. 1989. "Worldwide Trends in Production System Management: Work Systems, Factory Practice, and Human Resource Management." Paper presented at the International Motor Vehicle Program Policy Forum, Acapulco, Mexico, May 1989.

Monden, Y. 1983. *Toyota Production System*. Norcross, Ga.: Institute of Industrial Engineering.

Nishiguchi, T. 1989. "Strategic Dualism: An Alternative in Industrial Societies." Unpublished Ph.D. dissertation. Oxford University.

Ono, T. 1988. *Workplace Management*. Cambridge, Mass.: Productivity Press.

Piore, M. 1989. "Corporate Reform in American Manufacturing and the Challenge to Economic Theory." MIT Department of Economics working paper.

Roach, S. S. 1987. *America's Technology Dilemma: A Profile of the Information Economy*. Morgan Stanley Special Economy Study, New York.

Schonberger, R. 1982. *Japanese Manufacturing Techniques*. New York: Free Press.

Shimada, H., and J. P. MacDuffie. 1987. "Industrial Relations and 'Humanware': Japanese Investments in Automobile Manufacturing in the United States." MIT Sloan School of Management working paper.

Walton, R. 1990. *Up and Running: Integrating Information Technology and Organizations*. Cambridge, Mass.: Harvard Business School Press.

Womack, J., D. Jones, and D. Roos. 1990. *The Machine That Changed the World*. New York: Rawson-Macmillan.

COMMENTARY BY RANGANATH NAYAK

I'd like to start by encouraging continuation of this research by delving deeper into the question of what makes a high-tech–lean production system possible. This fascinating piece of analysis explains the principles of productivity and quality, yet I wonder what it is that makes a high-tech–lean production system possible in some organizations and not possible in others.

In the tradition of consulting, I decided to look at some analogies. I examined a world-class basketball team, a world-class dinner, and a world-class automobile. What makes them world class? One thing I found in all three of these is that apart from the ingredients, which must be good, there is also a master chef, a talented coach, or a very good designer who provide some sort of conceptual integrity to the thing that is being created. One of my questions to you is, Is there someone in that role in manufacturing? Is manufacturing a purely autonomous system that keeps on improving itself, or is there an external vision that creates something magnificent, which you should then keep on improving?

I looked into that question in greater detail by examining the classical planning and checking cycle. When you really start applying this cycle to a complex organization, it becomes clear that there must be a nested series of improvement and planning activities. There must be a cycle that goes on in the factory itself, on the shop floor, from which presumably there is feedback from the checking to the next level up, where people are doing product and process development; where they are doing planning for the factory. But, similarly, these planning activities also have to be subjected to some kind of plan–do–check process, taking place at some level where organization development and planning occurs.

So really my question is, Who plans what, and who checks what? Is it really an autonomous system in the factory that does it all by itself, or is there a higher level review that provides a tremendous amount of feedback and guidance?

I want to present a hypothesis that says it might take a couple of different levels of integrated planning to make high-tech–lean production processes and plants work. This planning must integrate multiple levels as well as multiple functions involving product development and design with manufacturing know-how and human resource know-how. So I might suggest that there is a correlation between planning capability and self-improvement ability at these multiple levels (guided by a common vision) and success in making a high-tech–lean production process work. I am glad to see that this is a direction the authors plan to take on their future work—to build on what they have learned in the production process and examine the role of design and product development. This should help us answer the key question: What makes high-tech–lean production possible?

14

Managing the Introduction of New Process Technology: An International Comparison

MARCIE J. TYRE

THE CHALLENGE OF TECHNOLOGICAL CHANGE

There is mounting evidence that, despite rapid advances in the technology of manufacturing equipment and systems, U.S. firms are failing to exploit these technologies for competitive benefit. Jaikumar, for instance, argues that U.S. managers "are buying the hardware of flexible automation—but they are using it very poorly. Rather than narrowing the competitive trade gap with Japan, the technology of automation is widening it further" (1986, p. 69). Thurow blames "America's poor productivity, quality, and trade performance" squarely on inferior capabilities in introducing and using process technology (1987, p. 1660). According to the Manufacturing Studies Board, U.S. companies need to "reemphasize process improvements—selecting, using, and *implementing* available manufacturing technologies—as a critical competitive weapon" (1986, p. 17).

Too often, when companies introduce new manufacturing processes they not only fail to capture competitive benefits but also experience a persistent drain on human and capital resources. One major U.S. study found that the difficulties of introducing new manufacturing equipment frequently result in productivity losses equal to or exceeding the original cost of the equipment, and that the disruptive effects can persist for two years or more (Chew, 1985; Hayes and Clark, 1985).

Yet much of the existing research on process innovation and diffusion has focused on the decision to adopt new technology, rather than on the process of learning to use a new technology once it has been brought into the organization (Kimberly, 1981; Rogers, 1982). Research on the "implementation" stage of the diffusion–innovation process has focused on developing organizational receptivity to change (e.g., Majchrzak, 1988; Zaltman, Duncan, and Holbeck, 1973). This is a useful first step, but it fails to illuminate the behaviors needed to identify and address the problems and uncertainties involved in technological process change.

The premise of this chapter is that successful process change requires not just organizational receptivity, but also active organizational efforts to adapt the new technology, the existing manufacturing system, and the organization itself to a new set of demands (Abernathy and Clark, 1985; Leonard-Barton, 1988; Van de Ven, 1986). Consequently, new process introductions often require considerable problem solving and even innovation at the plant level (Kazanjian and Drazin, 1986; Rice and Rogers, 1980).

This chapter explores regional differences in project performance and project approach within a multiplant network and seeks to identify the causes of observed differences. The chapter suggests that managerial choices that shape organizational assumptions, technical capabilities, and external linkages amount to long-term strategic decisions. These choices influence technological options and performance well into the future. Therefore, I argue that success in the manufacturing arena requires recognizing and managing the systemic linkages among technology strategy, organizational process, human resource development, and technological competence at the plant level.

ORGANIZATIONAL RESPONSES TO TECHNOLOGICAL CHANGE

Based on the literature on change in organizations and on initial fieldwork, I identified three "response mechanisms" that enable organizations to adapt, either in advance of technological change or following its introduction. These are (1) preparatory, or early, search undertaken before the new technology is put into use; (2) joint search during the start-up process with technical experts outside the factory; and (3) functional overlap between engineering and manufacturing groups at the plant level.

Preparatory search involves the investigation, modification, or "reinvention" of the new technology and relevant aspects of the receiving organization before the technology is installed in the factory (Rice and Rogers, 1980; Rogers, 1982; Van de Ven, 1986). This may involve adapting existing manufacturing systems, routines, and procedures (Bright, 1958; Chew, 1985). Coordination with (internal or external) developers of process equipment is an important aspect of preparatory search, allowing the mutual adaptation of source and user during the early phase of the project (Leonard-Barton, 1988).

The second and third response categories both involve real-time mechanisms for adapting to problems and opportunities which develop as the organization gains experience with the new technology. *Joint search* involves coordination with knowledgeable individuals from facilities or organizations external to the manufacturing plant. The notion of joint organizational search stems from the concept of an "organization set" (Evan, 1966; Thompson, 1967) or, more specifically, a unit's "technological organization set." The latter can be defined as a coalition of suppliers of technology, equipment, components, or information. Research suggests that joint problem solving among members of the relevant technological organization set can account for "a major part of the company's problem solving capability with respect to the new technology" (Lynn, 1982, p. 8; see also Ettlie and Rubenstein, 1980; Imai, Nonaka, and Takeuchi, 1985).

Functional overlap involves linking relevant functions within the organization to create "overlapping" subsystems or multifunctional teams for dealing with change

(Galbraith, 1973; Gerwin, 1981; Landau, 1969). In the manufacturing environment, key functions include the plant technical or engineering activities and direct management of production output. Tighter linkage between these areas moves the locus of decision making closer to the source of relevant information, and therefore increases the organization's ability to respond to uncertainty (Perrow, 1967).

RESEARCH METHODOLOGY

In order to understand the multiple, often subtle factors involved in introducing new process technology I collected three kinds of data: descriptive information about projects, their history, and their contexts through open-ended and semistructured interviews; specific data on project characteristics and outcomes through a written questionnaire; and documentary evidence about plant operations and projects undertaken from company archives.

Site Selection

Research was undertaken at a single leading manufacturer of precision metal components. The company is organized geographically, with operations in different countries run as separate divisions with local management. This study was carried out in three major divisions: Germany, Italy, and the United States. Two to three plants in each division were included, for a total of eight factories.

Limiting the research to one global, single-product corporation had several benefits, including controlling for most industry, product, and market variations. The design also facilitated access to detailed and confidential information about projects and their historical, technological, and competitive contexts. At the same time the design made it possible to investigate the degree to which managers in different countries took different approaches, and achieved different results, in introducing new process technology (Clark, 1989; Jaikumar, 1986; Lynn, 1982). It should be noted, however, that this study focuses on managerial processes and mechanisms within a given firm. It was not intended to highlight generalizable national or regional differences in the management of technology or to identify the influence of larger institutional or cultural factors in the countries studied here.

Sample Selection

The sample of projects studied includes all of the new process introductions identified where the technology was "new" in some way to a particular factory and which (1) were undertaken during the last four years and completed or nearing completion at the time of the study, (2) represented a total capital investment of greater than $50,000 (in constant 1986 U.S. dollars), and (3) involved participants who were available for interviews.

The sample includes a spectrum of technological process change, from improved versions of existing equipment to introductions of novel technologies and production systems. Production technologies include metal turning and precision machining equipment, assembly and inspection systems, thermal treatment and metal forming equipment, and handling systems; the range of technologies introduced in each of the three divisions is comparable. Four to eight projects were studied in each plant. A total of forty-eight introduction projects comprise the sample.

Variable Definitions[1]

Because these projects varied widely in the amount and nature of the change involved, it was necessary to measure and control for these project attributes. Measurement of *project scale* was based on total investment in new equipment, tooling, and other capitalized items (stated in constant 1986 U.S. dollars). The technological challenge involved is captured by two separate variables. *Technical complexity* measures the number, novelty, and technological sophistication of new features and improved concepts introduced (such as tooling, measurement, and control systems). *Systemic shift,* on the other hand, measures the degree to which the new equipment or system introduced fundamentally changed manufacturing tasks or operating principles in the plant. Projects rated high on systemic shift represent departures from accepted manufacturing approaches, such as moving from traditional metal removal processes to near-net-shape forming technology, or moving from reliance on buffer stocks between operations to an integrated just-in-time flow of materials. When both technical complexity and systemic shift are high, the introduction represents a "radical" shift in the technology of the factory.

The three response mechanisms described in the previous section were measured through a combination of questionnaire and interview items. *Preparatory search* measures the involvement of factory personnel in proposing and developing the technical features of the new equipment or system, including development and testing activities carried out by factory personnel before installation of the new equipment. *Joint search* measures the contribution of personnel from outside of the factory during the start-up process—that is, once the equipment is physically installed in the plant. *Functional overlap* measures the degree of integration between plant engineering and production personnel during the start-up process.

Two indicators of project success were used. *Start-up time* is based on the elapsed time between installation and productive use of new process technology. The measure used reflects the fact that the initial start-up period is typically much more disruptive for the plant than are the later phases of debugging and optimization. Start-up time is

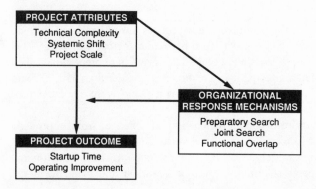

Figure 14.1 Model of process change.

defined as the sum of (1) the initial start-up period (the elapsed time in months from delivery of the equipment until parts are being made in production mode) plus (2) the introduction period (the elapsed time in months from delivery until the project is considered complete). *Operating improvement* is a composite measure reflecting the usefulness of the technical solutions implemented, the degree to which the technical objectives of the project were met, and the level of operating reliability achieved.

Variables can be organized into an operational model of process change, depicted in Figure 14.1.

RESULTS

Regional Differences in Performance: United States Versus Europe

Multiple regression analysis was used to investigate performance differences in countries or regions. Since initial analysis revealed no significant differences between the German and Italian subsamples on the dimensions examined, projects undertaken in those locations were treated as a single European sample. Performance in all regions was expected to be affected by the size and difficulty of the project. Therefore, the first analysis examines the regional effect after controlling for the three measured project attributes (Table 14.1, rows 1 and 2). In each case the effect of regional differences was significant. The results indicate that projects undertaken in the United States took an average of 8.8 months longer to complete than did projects in European plants, or an increment of almost 45 percent. The "U.S. effect" on operating improvement is comparable; at the mean, operating improvements achieved with new equipment and systems introduced in the United States were rated 48 percent below those achieved in Europe.

Next, analysis was performed to determine the source of these "regional effects." Specifically, we tested whether these differences could be explained by differential use of the three response mechanisms identified, or whether they must be attributed to other, unmeasured characteristics of the two regions. Results, shown in rows 3 and 4 in Table 14.1, demonstrate that regional differences are in fact explained largely by patterns of response to technological change. Once organizational responses are taken into account, the association between regional locus and project success becomes statistically insignificant. Specifically, the addition of preparatory search, joint search, and functional overlap reduces the effect of the region variable on start-up time by approximately two-thirds (row 3) and decreases its effect on operating improvement by approximately one-half (row 4). On the other hand, the coefficients of preparatory search, joint search, and functional overlap are consistently significant[2] and in the expected directions (at $p = .05$). That is, greater use of these mechanisms is associated with shorter start-up times and improved operating capabilities.

Organizational Responses to Change in Europe and the United States

These results suggest that preparatory search, joint search, and functional overlap are powerful mechanisms for coping with technological process change. Even more

Table 14.1 Regional difference in start-up time and operating improvement[a]

Dependent Variable	INDEPENDENT VARIABLES										
	Technical Complexity	Systemic Shift	Project Scale	Preparatory Search	Joint Search	Functional Overlap	Region = U.S.	R^2	DF	F	P
1. Start-up time	.50** (.11)	.30** (.11)	.16 (.12)				.30** (.12)	.40	44	8.7	.001
2. Operating improvement	−.23 (.14)	.13 (.14)	−.10 (.15)				−.33** (.15)	.10	44	2.0	N.S.
3. Start-up time	.54** (.09)	.69** (.14)	.33** (.07)	−.39** (.09)	−.33** (.10)	−.28* (.14)	.11 (.10)	.64	41	13.2	.001
4. Operating improvement	−.25* (.13)	−.20 (.19)	−.25 (.15)	.45** (.13)	.27** (.14)	.20 (.20)	−.16 (.10)	.31	41	4.0	.005

[a]Regression coefficients are standardized to facilitate comparison of effect sizes; standard errors are shown in parentheses.

**$p < .05$; *$p < .10$; N.S., not significant.

Table 14.2   Organizational responses to technological change

| | Organizational Response | | |
Project Attributes	Preparatory Search	Joint Search	Functional Overlap
PROJECTS UNDERTAKEN IN EUROPEAN PLANTS ($n = 31$)			
Technical complexity	$-.08$	$.51**$	$.01$
Systemic shift	$.27*$	$.29*$	$.39**$
Project scale	$.05$	$.03$	$.26*$
PROJECTS UNDERTAKEN IN U.S. PLANTS ($n = 17$)			
Technical complexity	$-.25$	$-.11$	$.31$
Systemic shift	$-.15$	$.27$	$.62**$
Project scale	$-.56**$	$.04$	$.04$

Spearman correlations; $*p < .10$; $** p < .05$.

important, they demonstrate that while the U.S. plants studied did tend to perform poorly on process introduction relative to their European counterparts, a large part of the gap can be explained by the tendency of project teams in the United States to use these mechanisms less vigorously in responding to technological change.

This argument is further supported by comparing the relationship between project attributes and organizational response variables across the two regions (Table 14.2). Project teams based in the United States were less likely than their European counterparts to respond to particularly challenging projects with intensified preparatory search during development and testing, or with greater joint search with outside experts. In fact, there is a marked tendency in the U.S. sample to undertake *less* preparatory search in advance of delivery of large-scale new equipment or systems than in smaller projects. Further, while the use of functional overlap in U.S.-based projects is strongly associated with the degree of systemic shift undertaken, absolute levels of functional overlap in the United States are still relatively low. In Europe, six projects rated either 5 or 6 on functional overlap (out of a possible high score of 8), whereas no U.S. project rated higher than 4. Conversely, five projects in the United States had an overlap rating of 0 (the lowest possible score), as opposed to one such project in Europe.

ANALYSIS OF REGIONAL DIFFERENCES

Regional differences in project performance cannot easily be attributed to underlying differences in the products produced (which are closely comparable across regions) or the difficulty of the projects undertaken: as shown in Table 14.1, significant unexplained performance differences remain even after controlling for the size and nature of the change. Rather, these results suggest that there exist managerial differences across regions which influence teams' use of the response mechanisms examined here. This finding raises important questions about the source of regional differences in search activities and technological problem-solving capabilities at the plant level.

The following section seeks to answer these questions by analyzing the evolution of the manufacturing organization and its process technology in each division. Different policy choices by managers in each region meant that regional operations evolved along different lines, acquiring divergent capabilities and operating assumptions. Further, these attitudes and capabilities, once created, proved to be long-lived and resistant to change. Starting in 1985 (the year before initiation of this study), management at the corporate and division levels began taking vigorous action to address what they viewed as historical weaknesses in U.S. operations. However, the evidence suggests that embedded organizational practices and constraints continued to affect efforts to introduce new process technology well after this date.

Organization Structure and Technology Strategy

European Operations

Local managers in the company's European divisions have a high degree of autonomy over operating decisions. However, strategic decisions relating to manufacturing operations and technology are made by centralized management committees composed of senior managers from division and central staffs. Product line rationalization, as well as process and product development, have been aggressively pursued and centrally coordinated through this vehicle in all European operations since the mid-1960s.

As a result, there has been a coherent strategy for process development in the European divisions for almost twenty years. In the early 1970s, the company's central Process Development Laboratory[3] introduced the first generation of proprietary ABC machine tools, which incorporated new concepts for precision metal finishing. German and Italian plants soon adopted the technology, completing hundreds of introduction projects. Describing the process, one senior manufacturing manager observed, "It took a *long* time to debug those early machines and we had many problems. But we learned a huge amount about the equipment, and about how to bring new technology into the plants."

In the late 1970s, the Development Lab introduced the second generation of ABC machine tools. The new line was based on existing machining concepts but incorporated a proprietary microprocessor control system. This development enabled European plants to introduce one standardized control technology from the start. As a plant manager explained, "We made sure that not one machine was introduced that did not have the possibility to communicate with other machines on the floor."

In the early 1980s, the company's development thrust turned to linking separate machines on the shop floor. The result was the introduction in German and Italian plants of a centrally controlled, fully integrated machining and assembly system capable of twenty-four-hour low-manned operation. Finally, in the late 1980s the objective was to develop more flexible integrated systems, where appropriate, for greater market responsiveness in low-volume product types.

United States Operations

Recent history in the company's U.S. division differs sharply from the European situation. Until the mid-1980s the U.S. division enjoyed full autonomy over local policies and operations, maintaining an arm's-length relationship with the parent company and its centralized management committees. Over time, these local policies created very different environments for technological change.

Until 1985, the U.S. division treated its plants as decentralized, independent profit centers. There was very little product line rationalization or coordination of process development. According to the engineering manager at one U.S. plant, "Until recently, there was no real long-term planning on the subject of manufacturing processes and equipment. Every capital request was reviewed in isolation. The U.S. division had been making money, but in a short-term mode. They were not investing systematically in technology or productivity."

Numerous early examples of internally developed ABC machine tools were introduced in the early 1970s, but process investment slowed in later years. When factories did buy new capital equipment there was no explicit effort to build on existing capabilities and concepts. Instead, U.S. plants tended to rely on external equipment vendors and traditional manual technology. There were some localized efforts to integrate separate machining operations, but plants ended up with multiple, incompatible machine control systems. Further, while the German and Italian divisions maintained active equipment development efforts to complement work at the central development lab, the U.S. equipment development center had been closed in 1972. With that move, many of the functions of the division-level technology group had been discontinued. Manufacturing engineering depth in the U.S. division was seriously eroded.

Technical Capabilities and Organizational Assumptions

Partly as a result of the pattern of decisions just described, both the German and Italian divisions boasted strong installed bases of process technology, strong manufacturing capabilities, and technically capable personnel that were largely lacking in the company's U.S. division. Productivity growth in Europe had averaged 7 percent per year between 1970 and 1985, whereas the comparable figure in the United States was 1.5 percent. Similarly, U.S. plants were judged by company management to be considerably behind their European counterparts in terms of defect and quality levels and in measures of operating efficiency such as cycle time and machine setup time.

Following the introduction of coordinated company management of U.S. operations in 1985, differences between regions in specific manufacturing performance indicators began to narrow. However, organizational assumptions and embedded capabilities developed during the earlier period continued strongly to influence the way new process technology was introduced into plants. For example, the factory environment for continuous process improvement appeared to have an important impact on the way project teams approached process innovation. In the United States, process improvement activities and their results were not tracked consistently before 1986. As one senior manager in the region explained, "There were other ways to show a profit besides worrying about operating efficiencies." According to a manufacturing engineer who had worked in both European and North American plants,

> In America, it's easy to get plant engineers to start working on large projects, with formal project management structures, but it's extremely difficult to keep attention focused on the details over time. People tend to drift away to other problems when the work is only half done, leaving all the little tasks that actually mean the difference between success and failure in a new system.

In both Italy and Germany, plant-level engineers spent a great deal of time developing and achieving annual improvement plans. These were formally specified in terms of productivity, quality, and other measures of operating effectiveness and monitored at the division (and even corporate) level. Although improvement activities were managed differently in the two European divisions, plant-level personnel in both countries generally had several process improvement projects ongoing at any time. These "mini-projects" frequently involved iterative development and testing of new tooling or devices in conjunction with the division's local technical center or (especially in Italy) with outside suppliers. According to one senior technical manager, "European plants are responsible for both product and process development. Underlying this is a strong requirement—and will—to improve on what now exists."

A related difference between the two regions concerns the plants' linkages with external sources of expertise, both inside and outside the company. While counter-examples exist, U.S. project teams generally expected to purchase solutions from equipment vendors or component suppliers, whereas project teams in Europe were more likely to use outsiders as a resource for ongoing development of a given item. This contrast is apparent in the way project teams in the different regions viewed the development of new tooling to support new process technology. In Europe, tooling development typically was viewed as a critical task requiring the combined knowledge of both plant-level engineers and suppliers' tooling experts. For instance, as one project leader in an Italian plant explained,

> We identified very early what would be the most critical problem to solve: developing tooling of sufficient precision to allow us to take advantage of the new CNC technology. And we devoted a great deal of effort to a thorough tooling study. An important part of this process was working with the tooling experts at the equipment developer to understand how to utilize this new technology.

In contrast, many U.S. project managers expressed the view that the most efficient approach was simply to purchase a satisfactory tooling package from the equipment vendor, thereby avoiding the need to invest time in tooling development. One manager attributed the problems that plagued a particular introduction to the fact that the machine had not been purchased along with a full complement of tooling from the vendor. Another project manager explained that the external supplier had delivered a tool set that "never presented a problem, so we never had to run any more trials or ask for changes."

The notion that technology can be purchased "off the shelf" extended to new manufacturing equipment from the company's process development lab. As a senior U.S. manufacturing engineer explained,

> The new machines from Central Lab require a shift in skills and operating procedures—but that is all provided. You don't need to have all the knowledge in place because the machines come complete with hardware and software, reference manuals, and service engineers from Central to do the training and initial set-up. Once you learn how to push the buttons, these machines are quite simple to use.

This expectation, however, was not borne out in practice. In almost every instance where equipment from the central lab was introduced into a U.S. plant, project participants complained that the machine did not in fact operate according to specifications, and that the service engineers who performed initial setup did not complete the task of debugging the equipment or training local operators. Engineers from the process development lab, in turn, argued that U.S. managers and technical personnel expected lab engineers to run their equipment for them. While there were notable instances in which U.S. project participants invested heavily in joint search with equipment vendors, all but one such case involved vendors external to the company and technical features which were relatively well developed (low to medium technical complexity).

European project participants also complained about the lack of technical support from the central lab, but they simultaneously stressed that part of the development responsibility must rest with the factory. As a divisional manager explained,

> Engineers in the Labs are experts in the machine technology, but we are the ones who really understand the manufacturing process. Therefore, to take a machine which meets the basic specs and make it respond to all our requirements—that's the job of the factory.

Engineering Infrastructure

The different attitudes and capabilities displayed in Europe and the United States appeared to be rooted in different engineering "infrastructures" in the two regions— that is, in contrasting approaches to the organization and development of technical talent in the manufacturing environment. Although Germany and Italy differed in many aspects of their engineering infrastructures, both divisions shared common themes which were absent in the United States.

Italy

In Italy, respondents sometimes had trouble distinguishing engineering and production as separate functions. In several cases, an individual who was described as having direct responsibility for manufacturing also maintained a seat in the plant technical office. According to the division's director of manufacturing technology,

> The word "engineer" is hard for us to define. There are at least two possibilities this can refer to within the plant. First and foremost, the backbone of this organization is the "shop floor engineer." He is in the line: generally a foreman or assistant foreman. He is responsible for production and quality, as well as for cost and quality improvements. He also has hands-on responsibility for new projects. Second, there are factory technical offices. These are the future-oriented engineers; they support production people in ongoing operations but they also develop new kinds of solutions. But they never have direct project responsibility for new process introductions. It's important that production people have responsibility for new technology from the start.

Personnel development in the Italian division includes considerable job rotation between direct manufacturing supervision and the plant technical office. All levels of manufacturing management and technical experts go through a "spiral of rotation," which begins with machine attendance and generally includes experience in a variety of manufacturing and project situations. Promising individuals also move between the division technical center and the factories. While the Italian technical center itself is very small, its staff works closely with plants to understand their needs and with outside machine shops or component suppliers to design and realize new ideas for machines or devices for use in the plants. In addition, people move between plants over the course of their careers, creating a basis for sharing knowledge and experience among plants in the division. The Italian division was noted for its ability to utilize and build on existing knowledge through extensive in-house training, team assignments, and cross-fertilization among areas and plants.

Many observers within the company pointed to the deep capabilities developed by this system at the level of production setters, supervisors, mechanics, and maintenance people. As the company's director of manufacturing described it,

> Our Italian plants put less emphasis on the pure engineering excellence of their people than do, say, the Germans; but their strength is in the very careful, conscious management of their technology. They have created a very high level of interest and ability among all their people.

The outcome, as one U.S. engineering manager remarked, was that

> the Italians are wonderful at making all kinds of process refinements—they are very conscientious about *applying* their knowledge to their operations. You take a machine which we consider great, but they make lots of little innovations and end up running twice as much product on it.

Germany

In the German division, the plant-level engineer is conceived quite differently. Engineering is organizationally distinct from production management and generally reports directly to the plant management. Many plant-level engineers have formal engineering degrees, as distinct from the apprenticeship undertaken by operating personnel. Indeed, there are important distinctions within the engineering office based on individuals' formal technical training.

Formal responsibilities in the plant are clearly bifurcated. Engineers are directly responsible for cost and quality improvements. The chief engineer is the formal project leader for planning and administration of new process introductions, and implementation is generally the direct responsibility of a process engineer in his or her group. Production managers, meanwhile, are responsible for meeting output targets in terms of quality and quantity. They are also expected to support the engineers' improvement efforts, principally by allocating people and development time to improvement and introduction projects.

However, these clear distinctions often break down—or are actively broken down—in actual operating procedures. Two of the three plants studied in Germany presented exceptions to the standard organization structure. One plant was composed of several small shops or subfactories; within them, engineers reported to manufacturing shop managers. In fact, in at least one of these shops, the production manager was also the chief engineer. In another plant, in addition to the "real" (degreed) engineers working in the technical office, there were also engineers who "sat on the production floor" in each department and reported to manufacturing managers.

Further, there was considerable technical expertise among production personnel at all levels. Production managers typically were shown considerable respect by degreed engineers on the basis of their technical know-how. As one degreed engineer explained, "The manufacturing supervisor and the department manager are really engineers too—they are the floor engineers." While their technical capabilities varied, manufacturing managers at this level all received some formal technical training, and they were the first ones to respond to technical problems on the line. Indeed, production department managers frequently came from the plant's engineering office. In many cases, junior engineers in charge of introduction projects reported in a sort of informal matrix arrangement to the production department manager.

Relative to Italy, technical personnel in Germany were less likely to rotate among plants or between plants and the division technical office. On the other hand, considerable efforts were made to link technical development activities at various facilities. First, five of the seven plants in the division (including two of the three plants studied here) were located in a geographically centralized "complex" along with the division headquarters and technical center. Especially in plants located in the central complex, there was considerable interplay between plant engineers and engineers at the technical center. Further, factory personnel with particular areas of expertise or experience were often consulted or even borrowed for projects undertaken in other plants in the complex.

Whereas Italian plants were known within the company for their penchant for "fiddling" with production equipment once it was on the floor, German plants were famous for doing a great deal of technical preparation of both the new equipment and the existing factory before attempting a new introduction. One project leader explained,

> In this project we worked explicitly to identify all the most important unknowns, and to develop solutions, before the equipment was shipped or, in many items, even before it was ordered. If you really think about it, you can identify and address 95 percent of the hard issues beforehand.

United States

The formal organization structures of U.S. factories resembled the German pattern, with separate engineering departments reporting to the plant manager. However, with the exception of the small subcomponent plant studied, informal integration of technical priorities and production requirements was often more difficult to attain. In several instances, plant-level engineers blamed delays in introducing new equipment on the difficulty of getting the production manager to set aside time for operator and supervisor training or for on-line testing of tooling or devices. Manufacturing managers, meanwhile, frequently attributed disruption and start-up delays to the absence of engineering support during start-up and later debugging of the new equipment.

Further, many individuals in the company argued that engineering capabilities in U.S. plants were too thin. In the United States, formal and in-house technical training or personnel development through job rotation received much less attention than was true in Europe. Unlike the situation in European divisions, high turnover among engineers was a frequently cited problem. As one senior manager said with dismay, "Many of the engineers in these plants are not even from our industry. They do not *really* understand the products and processes involved."

In many cases key production personnel also lacked necessary technical skills. According to one European engineer who had worked in various U.S. operations,

> There is very often a big gap at the level of the production supervisor. In too many cases, the supervisor does not have sufficient understanding of modern production technologies, so he ends up relying on operating people for process expertise. Sometimes the operators

have long experience and special aptitudes, but sometimes that is not the case. So it can be hard to carry out big projects successfully.

Another engineer explained the danger in this arrangement:

Expertise at the operator level should not be what is critical. Productivity of both old and new machines comes from the engineering backup in the plants—the engineers, maintenance people, and supervisors. That small group has got to be the organizational intelligence between management and operators. They have to be able to teach operating people, to guide them to focus on key problems, not just rely on operators' expertise. The competence of that group and how it is cultivated is the key to the ability to bring in new machine technology.

CONCLUSIONS AND IMPLICATIONS

This analysis suggests that observed regional differences in performance on new process introductions can be traced, in the short run, to underlying differences in the way project teams respond to technological change. The response mechanisms identified—preparatory search, joint search, and functional overlap—were shown to support improved project performance in terms of start-up time and operating improvement. As demonstrated, project teams in Europe and the United States differed in their propensity to use these mechanisms in dealing with challenging introductions. These differences, in turn, help to explain the relatively poor performance of U.S. plants in new process introductions.

Moreover, I have argued that these response patterns are rooted in historical differences in the way technological competencies are viewed and how they are developed. This study identified three interrelated areas where embedded managerial policies and assumptions affected the ability of the plant to introduce new technologies. The first area was strategic. In Europe a multifaceted, high-level management body was charged with the strategic guidance of process development and introduction. This body served to coordinate projects over time and across facilities. The result was that, instead of just buying machines, European plants had over the last twenty years been building the physical and human infrastructure needed to absorb the next generation of manufacturing technologies. The second area relates to the policies, procedures, and assumptions governing factory operations. European factories demonstrated a consistent, top-to-bottom emphasis on the continuous improvement of new and existing manufacturing processes. Improvement efforts were supported by a tradition of cross-boundary problem solving between the manufacturing organization and outside suppliers of technology. These efforts resulted in high levels of productivity improvement and quality performance in European divisions, and they directly affected the attitudes and assumptions that project participants brought to new process introductions. Finally, the third area of contrast across regions relates to organizational policies and practices for building technical competence at the plant level. In particular, this study points to the importance of human resource practices that build strong engineering capabilities within the plant, focusing on plant engineers, technicians, and supervisors. In Italy continuous managerial emphasis on personnel development, cross-training, and cross-fertilization appeared to have resulted in unusual plant-level technical capabilities for both ongoing process improvement and new process introductions. While German managers organized development very differently, they achieved some of the same end results. Formal and informal functional roles and development schemes combined to create a strong engineering infrastructure throughout the plants.

These arguments suggest that the successful introduction of new process technology requires more than a receptive attitude or even extensive training programs. Rather, the results suggest that the ability to make use of advanced manufacturing technology depends on the kind of organizational and human resource practices, abilities, and assumptions that have been built up over time. An interrelated set of managerial choices related to technology strategy, manufacturing policy, and human resource development molds how the organization responds to the challenge of technological change. For the U.S. plants described here, investing heavily in new process technology is likely to have little payoff unless accompanied by changes in organizational structures and competencies, by policies that support ongoing manufacturing improvements, and by a strategic framework for guiding investments in process technology.

By focusing on the problem of introducing new process technology, this chapter has highlighted the systemic nature of manufacturing capabilities. In responding to the challenge of advanced production technology, the organization is both guided and constrained by the assumptions and capabilities it has developed over time. A strong implication is that if companies are to exploit rapid advances in manufacturing technology, managers will need to examine and perhaps modify their own assumptions about the development of technological and human competencies within the organization. For many managers, the frustration will be that the development of organizational capabilities for dealing with technological change will be slower than the rate at which technology itself is changing.

NOTES

1. Further details on variable definition and measurement are presented in Tyre and Hauptman (1992).
2. The only exception is that the coefficient of functional overlap in row 4, while in the expected direction, is not statistically significant. This unexpected result is discussed in more detail in Tyre and Hauptman (1992) and Tyre (1990).
3. The Process Development Lab is located in a different European country. It is remote in location and language from any of the divisions studied.

REFERENCES

Abernathy, W. J. 1978. *The Productivity Dilemma: Roadblock to Innovation in the Automobile Industry*. Baltimore: Johns Hopkins University Press.

Abernathy, W. J., and K. B. Clark. 1985. "Innovation: Mapping the Winds of Creative Destruction." *Research Policy* 14: 3–22.

Bright, J. R. 1958. *Automation and Management*. Boston: Harvard Business School Division of Research.

Chew, W. B. 1985. "Productivity and Change: Understanding Productivity at the Factory Level." Paper presented at the 75th Anniversary Colloquium of the Harvard Business School.

Clark, K. B. 1989. "Project Scope and Project Performance: The Effect of Parts Strategy and Supplier Involvement on Product Development." *Management Science* 35, no. 10: 1247–1263.

Ettlie, J., and A. Rubenstein. 1980. "Social Learning Theory and the Implementation of Production Innovations." *Decision Science* 11, no. 4: 648–668.

Evan, W. M. 1966. "The Organization-Set: Toward a Theory of Interorganizational Relationships." *Approaches to Organization Design,* edited by J. D. Thompson. Pittsburgh: University of Pittsburgh Press.

Galbraith, J. 1973. *Designing Complex Organizations.* Reading, Mass.: Addison-Wesley.

Gerwin, D. 1981. "Control and Evaluation in the Innovation Process: The Case of Flexible Manufacturing Systems." *IEEE Transactions on Engineering Management* EM-28, no. 3: 61–70.

Hayes, R. H., and K. B. Clark. 1985. "Exploring the Sources of Productivity Differences at the Factory Level." In *The Uneasy Alliance,* edited by K. B. Clark, R. H. Hayes, and C. Lorenz. Boston: Harvard Business School Press.

Hayes, R. H., and S. Wheelwright. 1984. *Restoring Our Competitive Edge.* New York: Wiley.

Imai, K., I. Nonaka, and H. Takeuchi. 1985. "Managing New Product Development: How Japanese Companies Learn and Unlearn." In *The Uneasy Alliance,* edited by K. B. Clark, R. H. Hayes, and C. Lorenz. Boston: Harvard Business School Press.

Jaikumar, R. 1986. "Postindustrial Manufacturing." *Harvard Business Review* 64, no. 6: 69–76.

Kazanjian, R. K., and R. Drazin. 1986. "Implementing Manufacturing Innovations: Critical Choices of Structure and Staffing Roles." *Human Resources Management* 25, no. 30: 285–403.

Kimberly, J. R. 1981. "Managerial Innovation." In *Handbook of Organizational Design,* vol. 1, edited by P. C. Nystrom and W. Starbuck. Oxford: Oxford University Press.

Landau, M. 1969. "Redundancy, Rationality, and the Problem of Duplication and Overlap." *Public Administration Review* 29: 346–358.

Leonard-Barton, D. 1988. "Implementation as Mutual Adaptation of Technology and Organization." *Research Policy* 17: 251–267.

Lynn, L. H. 1982. *How Japan Innovates—A Comparison with the U.S. in the Case of Oxygen Steelmaking.* Boulder, Colo.: Westview Press.

Maidique, M. A., and R. H. Hayes. 1984. "The Art of High-Technology Management." *Sloan Management Review* 25, no. 2: 17–31.

Majchrzak, A. 1988. *The Human Side of Factory Automation.* San Francisco: Jossey-Bass.

Manufacturing Studies Board. 1986. *Toward a New Era in U.S. Manufacturing: The Need for a National Vision.* Washington, D.C.: National Research Council.

Perrow, C. 1967. "A Framework for the Comparative Analysis of Organizations." *American Sociological Review* 32, no. 2: 194–208.

Rice, R. E., and E. Rogers. 1980. "Reinvention in the Innovation Process." *Knowledge* 1, no. 4: 499–514.

Rogers, E. M. 1982. *Diffusion of Innovations,* 3rd ed. New York: Free Press.

Thompson, J. D. 1967. *Organizations in Action.* New York: McGraw-Hill.

Thurow, L. C. 1987. "A Weakness in Process Technology." *Science* 238: 1659–1663.

Tyre, M. J., and O. Hauptman. 1992. "Technological Change in the Production Process: Organizational Implications and Responses." *Organization Science,* 3.

Tyre, M. J. 1990. "Task Characteristics and Organizational Problem Solving in Technological Process Change." MIT Sloan School of Management working paper 3109-90-BPS.

Van de Ven, A. 1986. "Central Problems in the Management of Innovation." *Management Science* 32, no. 5: 590–607.

Zaltman, G., R. B. Duncan, and J. Holbeck. 1973. *Innovation in Organizations*. New York: Wiley.

COMMENTARY BY JUDITH I. ROSEN

Yesterday, Glen Urban described the mission of Sloan as serving its constituency, the business community, by improving the management of business. It strikes me that academics can do that in three ways: academic research, in my mind, must meet three criteria:

1. It must be relevant. It must solve important problems that we in industry are grappling with.
2. It must be reliable. By that I mean that it is methodologically correct and generalizable to other business situations.
3. It must be actionable, and help us develop prescriptions for dealing with similar kinds of problems.

In reading this chapter, I believe that Marcie Tyre's research meets all three of these criteria. It is quite rich on many of the dimensions that we discussed yesterday, including the importance of vision and skills and cross-functional groups, and so I'd like to encourage her to develop this work.

What I'd actually like to do is to comment on the relevance of this research to other problems I'm familiar with. As a consultant, I am consistently trying to help clients imagine the possibilities they face in order to initiate the unfreezing process. It comes from the basic notion that unless people believe they can achieve a new level of success, they will not have the required commitment to a new vision. One of the techniques we use to help clients imagine new possibilities is a best practices methodology, what we at Bain call the "best demonstrated practices." What we do is compare performance across similar units, identify the strong performers, then systematically try to understand which practices make them superior. We document those practices in great detail as the basis for introducing the most successful practices into similar units with lower performance.

To use the best demonstrated practices techniques to change behavior requires very careful analysis to remove uncontrollable differences that drive results. It is always a contentious process, because people all believe they are different and their situation is unique. Management typically says "that doesn't apply to me." This is true to some extent. Each situation is different, but what is important is that some differences are controllable and others are uncontrollable. One of the most frequently cited uncontrollable differences is regional variations. This chapter suggests that at first glance there may be some differences in regional performance at similar plants; however, when you peel the onion, you find there are some underlying systems that are neither regionally nor culturally based which actually drive those differences. I find that a very important concept for reinforcing the value of best demonstrated comparisons across regions. Using Tyre's research we can encourage clients to try to achieve new levels of success demonstrated in other regions. It confirms the fact that the best demonstrated technique does make sense if you cease being superficial in your explanation of differences and work to identify the root causes of those differences. The chapter provides the opportunity to point to academic research where regional differences, the most common objection to using the technique, did not drive real differences in performance.

The chapter is prescriptive in two ways. First, it encourages people to think of developing action plans to change performance within the historic context of the operation. I have seen many instances where understanding a company's heritage is critical because developing action plans inconsistent with the corporate heritage includes at worst a high-risk of failure and at best a long time frame. Second, the research points out the importance of systemic (rather than incremental) change as the basis for implementing dramatic changes in performance. It reinforces the need for tenacity and patience around a broad set of imperatives to produce the results we want to achieve.

15

Organizational Change and the Internationalization of R&D

D. ELEANOR WESTNEY

In the second half of the 1980s, Japanese avowals of their growing commitment to basic research and the increasing Japanese spending on research and development threw into sharp relief one of the major transformations of the final two decades of the twentieth century: the globalization of technology. As Ray Vernon pointed out, "The propensity of technology to cross national boundaries has been growing rapidly, mainly as a result of the improvement in communication and transport" (1987, p. 173). But the globalization of technology involves more than the growing permeability of national technology systems, with technology quickly moving from the most advanced to the less advanced nations. It increasingly extends to the growing interdependence of the science and technology systems of the highly industrialized countries, a development brought home to Americans with the negotiations between the Japanese and U.S. governments on U.S. military access to Japanese electronics technologies essential to the U.S. defense system.

At the level of the firm, the globalization of technology has meant increasing pressures to participate in the technology systems of countries outside the home country. A Booz Allen study of technology management conducted in the late 1980s found this consensus among managers:

> What we have called the "global network" model of technology management is clearly the "wave of the future" when it comes to competing globally. This model consists of a network of technology core groups in each major market—the U.S., Japan, and Europe—managed in a coordinated way for maximum impact. (Perrino and Tipping, 1989, p. 13)

As the managers acknowledged, building the organization to realize the strategically ideal global technology network is a formidable task. Many U.S. firms have established or acquired technology development facilities in Europe, while large European firms have built or acquired such centers in North America (Perrino and Tipping, 1989). However, both American and European firms have been much slower to penetrate the national technology systems of Asia, particularly Japan. Many are now moving to build the base for a globally integrated technology network by setting up research and development centers in Japan.

The organizational and strategic problems they are encountering in the process exemplify certain key issues in managing organizational change. One of the themes of the Report from the MIT Commission on Industrial Productivity was the resistance of organizations to change, even when the need to change is widely recognized (Dertouzos, Lester, and Solow, 1989, p. 45). The powerful internal and external forces for organizational inertia have long been a focus of analysis in organizational sociology (Crozier, 1964; DiMaggio and Powell, 1983; Hannan and Freeman, 1984; Meyer and Zucker, 1989; Stinchcombe, 1965). Perhaps just as important for today's large business organizations is the recognition of problems that occur when organizational changes are under way but are pulling in different directions. American firms trying to build up R&D centers in Japan, for example, are facing simultaneous pressures to "globalize" their technology development capabilities *and* to improve their competitiveness by reducing development times and improving the linkages among R&D, manufacturing, and marketing, tasks that are complicated rather than eased (at least in the short term) by geographic dispersal of R&D. Their relatively new R&D facilities in Japan are simultaneously under pressures to become "insiders" in the Japanese technology system, in order to have access to local centers of science and technology, to regulatory authorities, and to lead users, *and* to become trusted "insiders" in the technology system of the multinational enterprise (MNE), sharing its values and its key organizational patterns. Managing the evolution of the Japan-based R&D facilities requires not only the recognition and management of inertial forces pulling the developing organization toward entrenched but dysfunctional patterns but also the recognition of how patterns that evolve to support one desired set of changes or organizational roles may undermine the capacity to achieve another set.

As with so many other aspects of the reconfiguration of MNEs in response to the shifting patterns of national, regional, and global integration, the problems remain clearer than the solutions. This chapter explores the constraints imposed on the penetration of the Japanese technology system by the configuration of U.S.-based MNEs and by the nature of the system itself, and it examines the organizational and strategic processes involved in developing their research mandate and organization.

THE CONFIGURATION PROBLEM:
U.S. MULTINATIONALS IN JAPAN

R&D is the last major function of the multinational enterprise to be dispersed geographically: over 90 percent of the R&D expenditures of U.S. firms remain concentrated in the United States (De Meyer and Mizushima, 1989, p. 3). Even leading multinationals whose sales and investments in manufacturing abroad rival those within their home country continue to concentrate their technology development efforts at home (Doz, 1987; Hakanson and Zander, 1986), in part because control over technology remains one of the key sources of the MNE headquarters' control over its subsidiaries (Doz and Prahalad, 1981).

The pressures on MNEs to disperse their R&D geographically are increasing, however. The lead users so crucial to innovation in certain industries (Von Hippel, 1988) and the world's leading consumer markets are increasingly dispersed (Doz, 1987, p. 105). The strong NIH (i.e., Not Invented Here) syndrome of many American product development engineers has also been a powerful inducement for MNEs to try to locate technical facilities outside their home country, both to provide products better suited to local markets and to tap the expertise in science and technology that exists offshore. To refer again to the Booz Allen study cited previously, many technology managers believe that

> New technologies and the specialized talent that produces them will continue to develop locally in "pockets of innovation" around the world. Nurturing those technologies, uprooting them, and cross-fertilizing them for commercialization and global distribution will continue to be major challenges in technology management. (Perrino and Tipping, 1989, p. 13)

Moreover, governments are growing increasingly aggressive in pushing MNEs to locate technology development within their own borders as a precondition of entry into their markets.

To date, where technology development has moved offshore, it has tended to follow manufacturing, and to have its justification in the need to adapt products and processes to local conditions (Fischer and Behrman, 1979) or in government demands for value added in R&D as a condition for market access (Branscomb, 1987, pp. 252–253). This linkage between a significant technology development capability and market and manufacturing presence in a country explains in part why so few U.S. MNEs had built a significant R&D presence in Japan before the mid-1980s. One of the exceptional few is IBM, which is presented as a model of the global network in technology to which leading MNEs should aspire (Perrino and Tipping, 1989). IBM sold its first product in Japan in 1925 and established manufacturing there in 1939. After World War II, a wholly owned subsidiary resumed operations in 1950, and its first factory was opened in 1953. Twenty years later, with four factories in Japan, IBM–Japan opened a product development laboratory in Fujisawa, near one of its newer factories. In 1982 it set up the Science Institute, one of IBM's four basic research laboratories worldwide. IBM–Japan is now an integral part of IBM's technology development system and of the Japanese technology system (Miyamoto, 1986).

No other foreign firm can match the evolution of IBM–Japan's technology development capability, supported by an extensive manufacturing capacity. Given the heavy restrictions on foreign direct investment into Japan that continued until the early 1970s, most U.S. MNEs entered the Japanese market through joint ventures with Japanese firms. Sometimes these joint ventures developed a significant independent technology development capability (Sumitomo–3M, Fuji–Xerox, Yamatake–Honeywell, and HP–Yokogawa are some of the best known). But there is enormous variation across joint ventures in how effective they have been for the U.S. parent as windows into the Japanese technology system (for competitor scanning and technology acquisition) and as sources of internally generated technology. Sometimes an expansion of their roles in the MNE technology system would create potential conflicts with the interests of the Japanese parent company, especially if that expansion involves increasing activity by the U.S. parent in the joint venture and in the Japanese market. And some U.S. parent companies fear that increasing the joint venture's technology integration with the rest of the MNE's R&D organization will result in a new loss of technology to the Japanese parent, rather than a gain to their own technology system. In consequence, for many (though not all) of the U.S. parent companies, the development of an integrated global technology network requires the addition of a wholly owned R&D facility in Japan. Often, however, the MNE has not developed a significant manufacturing presence in

Table 15.1 U.S. and European corporations with R&D facilities in Japan (recent cases)

Industry	Company	Date of Establishment
Pharmaceuticals	Merck	1981
	Pfizer	1985
	Bayer	1985
	Travenol	1985
	Upjohn	1988
	Glaxo	1989
	Sandoz	1990
Chemicals	Dow Chemical	1982
	Monsanto	1984 (agricultural chemicals)
	Monsanto	1986 (silicon wafers)
	L'Air Liquide	1986
	Du Pont	1986
	Hoechst	1986
	Henkel	1987
	Celanese	1987
	ICI	1987
	Ciba-Geigy	1990
Semiconductors	Intel	1983
	Applied Materials	1984
	LSI Logic	1986
	Texas Instruments	1989
Computers	Digital Equipment Corporation	1982
	IBM	1990 (software)
Other	Eastman Kodak	1988
	Honeywell	1987
	Pioneer Seeds	1987
	TetraPak International	1987

Japan, and since it is now one of the highest cost manufacturing sites in the world, major new investments in production there are difficult to justify in financial terms. From the outset this complicates the network-building tasks of a Japan-based R&D center: it must hand off any technology it develops either across national boundaries, to production sites offshore in other MNE subsidiaries, or across the boundaries of the firm, to Japanese firms that contract for production, or joint-venture partners.

In spite of these impediments, the number of U.S. and European firms setting up R&D centers in Japan has been growing rapidly. Table 15.1 is a list of foreign companies that have established R&D centers, showing the extent of this activity. The list does not include the growing number of firms that have decided to make such an investment but are still exploring the specifics of their establishment or the firms that are making major investments in expanding a limited technology modification center into a full-blown R&D laboratory. Firms in chemicals and pharmaceuticals—industries where U.S. and European multinationals are in a strong competitive position vis-à-vis their Japanese counterparts—have been most active in setting up R&D centers in Japan, followed by firms in the information-related industries.

THE ENTRY PROBLEM: THE PERMEABILITY OF THE JAPANESE TECHNOLOGY SYSTEM

Once a corporation decides to set up R&D facilities in Japan, it faces formidable entry problems in the Japanese market for corporate control, the technical labor markets, and the configuration of the national technology system.

In many countries, the MNE can internationalize its R&D system either through setting up new facilities outside the home country or through the acquisition of local firms with established facilities (De Meyer and Mizushima, 1989). The U.S. market for corporate control has made it relatively easy for foreign firms to penetrate the U.S. technology system by acquiring a firm with a technology development capability (a mode of entry much used by European firms; see Perrino and Tipping, 1989; De Meyer and Mizushima, 1989). But this market has virtually no counterpart in Japan. The large firms that dominate Japan's technology system are shielded from outside acquisition by stable institutional shareholders, most notably banks, insurance companies, and related industrial companies (Aoki, 1988, pp. 116–127). In the few cases where foreign multinationals have been able to acquire a significant ownership stake in a major Japanese firm (such as Merck and Banyu in pharmaceuticals or Ford in Mazda), the Japanese firm has actively sought the relationship because of financial or competitive difficulties.

Medium-sized companies, on the other hand, are increasingly willing to exchange equity, even a majority interest, for access to a foreign MNE's financing and global technology networks (Vernon, 1987). However, while such acquisitions may be useful adjuncts to an MNE's technology strategy in Japan, they have significant drawbacks as substitutes for the establishment of a new wholly owned R&D center. Medium-sized companies in Japan are not likely to be core participants in the technology system, which is heavily biased toward large firms (Okimoto, 1989, pp. 145–149). Therefore, they often lack the "insider" access to information networks that the MNE is seeking. Moreover, they are unlikely to have the reputation to attract highly qualified technical personnel in Japan's exceedingly tight technical labor markets.

The technical labor markets themselves are a further impediment to entry into Japan's technology system, and here again the contrast with the United States is pronounced. The open U.S. technical labor market for new graduates and the high level of mid-career mobility means that foreign companies can readily hire researchers as consultants or as personnel for a research subsidiary. In Japan, the market for new technical graduates of the elite universities is virtually monopolized by the large firms. These firms cultivate close relationships with key professors, who allocate master's graduates from their labs to a stable group of companies (Westney and Sakakibara, 1985). Mid-career mobility, while increasing in recent years, is still extremely low by U.S. criteria.

In consequence, U.S. MNEs trying to penetrate the Japanese technology system must expend far greater effort on recruitment than they are accustomed to doing in their home country. The foreign firms that have been most successful in recruiting new technical graduates in Japan have gone to considerable lengths to cultivate relationships with key professors at certain targeted universities through research grants, consultancies, donations of equipment, and frequent visits. These serve both to inform the professors of the technical depth of the company and to reassure them of the seriousness of its efforts in Japan, both of which are essential if the professor is to encourage his students to join its R&D center. Such corporate credibility is critical in Japan, where the professor is assuming a considerable degree of personal responsibility for the subsequent career of his students, particularly for the stability of their employment and for the opportunity for them to develop their skills in the future.

Eastman Kodak, for example, began to foster its academic networks four years before opening its R&D center in the Tokyo area. One of its more innovative approaches to developing these networks was to inaugurate an annual Kodak Symposium two years before opening its center. An eminent Japanese researcher and a leading U.S. academic were invited to present research papers, with a senior Kodak researcher as commentator. The invited audience was composed of university professors and researchers from companies with which Kodak had strategic alliances or customer relations. These meetings solidified Kodak's image as a technology-intensive company of world stature and symbolized its commitment to building a technical presence in Japan. In addition, the company established Kodak Fellowships for technical students in certain key fields, a competitive scholarship program that brought the recipients to the United States for a summer of intensive English study, an American tour, and a short stint at the corporate R&D labs in Rochester. Although the fellowships carry no obligation to join the company on graduation, several recipients have done so, largely because they have become convinced through the program of Kodak's technological capacity and its commitment to its Japanese facility.

The market for mid-career researchers is quite different from the market for new graduates. Until recently, few researchers of quality were willing to leave a leading Japanese company for another employer, either Japanese or foreign. The growing number of Japanese firms whose diversification efforts make it necessary for them to hire mid-career researchers in fields outside their traditional core and the increasing number of major foreign firms entering Japan with R&D facilities have fostered the growth of a small but increasingly respectable labor market for experienced technical personnel. The hiring process is still complex and is likely to involve company-to-company negotiations. But some first-rate Japanese technical professionals are increasingly eager to spend more of their careers in technology development than the standardized Japanese corporate technical career permits (Westney and Sakakibara, 1985). They are attracted to the foreign R&D subsidiary both by the prospect of a long-term career in R&D and by the opportunity to make a major contribution to building the technical subsystem of a major multinational corporation. For some, a further inducement is the potential for contributing to the internationalization of the Japanese industrial system.

Japanese mid-career researchers and research managers play a particularly crucial role in building a technical facility in Japan. In many countries, Western MNEs are able to use their own home country employees in managerial and supervisory positions in a technical center's early years. Very few, however, have employees who can speak Japanese and are well connected in Japanese technical networks. Therefore, the facility is heavily dependent for its middle-level research managers on the recruitment of well-qualified, experienced technical employees, and considerable time and effort devoted to recruiting mid-career researchers is an essential precondition for developing an R&D center.

The locus of mid-career training for scientific and technical personnel is a third area of contrast in the relative permeability of the U.S. and Japanese technology systems and increases the importance of the mid-career hires. In the United States, although large firms play an exceedingly important role, there is a wide array of university and technical institute courses open to anyone who is willing to pay the enrollment fees. These courses range from short, intensive courses on the "state of the art" in any given field to degree-granting programs that enable a mid-career mechanical engineer to get a degree in computer science. In Japan, virtually all university courses are full time and are open only to students who have passed the rigorous entrance examinations on which the high school curriculum is rigidly focused. Mid-career training tends to be monopolized by large firms, which conduct that training largely in-house. This means that foreign companies trying to penetrate the Japanese technology system cannot turn to an extensive external educational infrastructure to enhance the technical abilities of new graduate hires or to provide access to technical communication networks for its own nationals. It also means that the capacity of the company to provide educational and career development opportunities for its employees is a critical element of its attractiveness as an employer.

All these factors mean that the MNE must devote more resources to technical recruitment and career development in Japan than is customary in its home country—indeed more than is usual in most countries in which it operates. And the key to attracting qualified technical talent, both new graduates and mid-career professionals, is the prospect of doing interesting and challenging technical work over the long term. This in turn makes the strategic mandate of the facility a matter of critical importance in developing the Japanese node in the global technology network.

DEVELOPING THE RESEARCH MANDATE[1]

The first major academic study of the internationalization of R&D was carried out in the 1970s by Robert Ronstadt. At that time, he observed four kinds of overseas research facilities in the U.S. multinationals he studied:

1. Technology transfer units (TTUs), to facilitate the transfer of the parent's technology to the subsidiary and to provide local technical services.
2. Indigenous technology units (ITUs), to develop new products for the local market, drawing on local technology.
3. Global technology units (GTUs), to develop new products and processes for world markets.
4. Corporate technology units (CTUs), to generate basic technology for use by the corporate parent.

In the complex research environment of today's multibusiness multinational corporations, it is difficult to classify the emerging overseas R&D facilities into any one category. A single overseas facility may easily be entrusted with the following research mandates:

In one business, where the facility has focused on developing expertise on a subset of the parent's technologies in that business, work is focused on modifying some major products to make them more suitable for the local market.

In another business, where the facility covers virtually the same span of technology as the parent organization, work is focused on developing new products for the regional market.

In still another business, where the facility has cultivated expertise in an area where the local science and technology system has a distinctive strength, the task is basic research aimed at the development of a new worldwide business.

It has become clear since Ronstadt's work that the strategic mandate of a facility is potentially more complex than his four categories suggest. Instead, the research mandate involves some combination of three variables: geographic scope, vertical technology scope, and horizontal technology scope.[2]

Geographic scope refers to the target market for the research: the local market, the regional market, or the world market. *Vertical technology scope* refers to the value-adding activities within R&D. The following categories are the most commonly used: (1) facilitating the transfer of technologies from the parent; (2) modifying products to suit the local market; (3) new product development; and (4) basic research. In some industries, of course, the R&D value-adding activities are somewhat different; in pharmaceuticals, for example, the distinction between basic research and new product development is extremely difficult to apply, but testing is an important technical activity. In other industries, research on process technology is a key element of the value-adding activities.

Finally, *horizontal technology scope* refers to the range of technologies covered by the facility. This can be a subset of the technologies covered by the home country R&D organization, the entire range of those technologies, or a distinctive set of technologies whose choice is shaped by local technology strengths.

These variables provide a useful way of thinking about change over time in the strategic mandate. The categories within the first two variables form a continuum from less to more complex and demanding tasks. Studies from the 1970s (Behrman and Fischer, 1980; Ronstadt, 1977) indicated that in cases where the mandate changed from less to more complex (e.g., from local to regional or to global, and from technology transfer to product development), the main initiative for the change came from the local facility. Its managers were motivated by a desire to use more fully the facility's growing capabilities and to stretch them even further. In cases where the mandate changed from more to less complex (most commonly, from basic to product development or product modification), the initiative came from the headquarters management, largely in response to a deteriorating competitive position in the market. One of the unanswered questions for the new wave of internationalization of R&D in the 1980s is whether the parent company will take on a more active role in building up the capacity of its overseas research organization and in raising the complexity of its research mandate, or whether the older pattern of the major initiatives coming from the local facility will persist.

The R&D mandates of the facility strongly influence its human resource development. High-caliber technical professionals are most likely to be attracted (and kept) by the higher value-adding activities of new product development or basic research. And the enhancement of their technical capabilities over time will be shaped by the nature of their technical activities, given the important role of on-the-job training in Japan. If the company has invested considerable effort in attracting highly qualified technical people, it has a strong stake in ensuring that their research mandate is sufficiently challenging to keep them. On the other hand, the immediate business returns are likely to be greatest if the new facility concentrates on modifying existing products for the local or regional market, a task that is unlikely to be welcomed by technical professionals who have joined a company in the expectation of spending their careers in challenging technical activities.

The research mandates also shape the key communications networks of the facility, both within the MNE and across its boundaries. The autonomy of the R&D facility from its parent organization is likely to be greatest if its mandate focuses on new product development for the local market. Its dependence is greatest when it focuses on the modification of existing products. And the demands for integration with home country R&D are likely to be greatest when the facility is doing some basic research in a unique subset of technologies that contribute significantly to the technology portfolio of the MNE as a whole. In consequence, one response to friction with the home country organization is for the local facility to turn to new product development for local markets as a way to reduce its interactions with and dependence on the parent organization.

External communications networks also depend on the research mandate. For example, a mandate in basic research will require close linkages with local basic research centers, usually universities and major research institutions such as government laboratories. A mandate in local product enhancement will require closer linkages to the customer base. Table 15.2 portrays, in highly simplified form, the key communications linkages entailed by research mandates on the two dimensions of vertical technology scope and geographic scope (linkages with production are entailed by all of the mandates except basic research). These linkages develop and become routinized over time, with repeated interactions, and switching costs are not inconsiderable.

Table 15.2   Research mandates and strategic linkages

Vertical Technology Scope	Geographic Scope		
	Local	Regional	Global
Technology transfer	Production	Production	Production
Product modification	HQ product development	HQ product development	N.A[a]
	Local marketing	Regional marketing	
New product development	Local sources of science and technology	Local sources of science and technology	Local sources of science and technology
	Local marketing	Regional marketing	Worldwide marketing
Basic research	Local sources of science and technology	Local sources of science and technology	Local sources of science and technology

[a]Not applicable by definition.

The evolution of the strategic mandate of the Japan technology center usually involves the following steps:

1. The framing, in very general terms, of the strategic role of the facility by top corporate management and headquarters R&D management, usually as part of the process by which the decision to establish such a facility is taken. Given the growing acceptance of the desirability of the coordinated global technology network as a base for competitiveness, this initial framing is often in fairly general terms of gaining access to leading-edge Japanese technology and developing the capacity for global product development that leverages that technology.
2. The development of a more clearly defined initial research mandate by top strategic business unit (SBU) management, headquarters R&D management, and the newly appointed local R&D top management.
3. The identification of a set of specific projects embodying the initial research mandate by headquarters and local R&D management and the managers of the business entities providing the research budget.

The selection of the initial project portfolio has two dimensions. The first is the output dimension: reasonable targets that enable the facility to generate visible value added for the business or businesses of the company. The second is the developmental dimension: the projects help lay the foundation for developing the knowledge base, the internal and external networks, and the research management systems of the facility.

The early project agenda has a critical influence on the subsequent development of the facility. It defines what initial knowledge base is necessary and therefore what kinds of people will be hired. It shapes the direction in which the knowledge and skills of the facility's personnel develop and begins to institutionalize the technology transfer networks that move the technology into production. It also helps to define the kinds of external linkages needed. A significant mismatch between the long-term strategic mandate and the initial project agenda can lead to serious problems. For example, if the long-term mandate is advanced product development but the initial project agenda is exclusively focused on modification of existing products, able and ambitious researchers may well be discouraged and either leave or feel resentful and frustrated that their skills are not being used and developed. If an exclusive focus on the output dimension creates a mismatch with the general long-term strategic mandate, the facility may have difficulties attracting and keeping able people and enhancing the knowledge base and networks on which to realize its long-term strategy. However, if the focus is too strongly on the developmental aspects of the project agenda, the facility's credibility with line management may suffer.

The erosion of credibility is particularly dangerous for a new R&D facility, whose legitimacy is almost by definition precarious. Any decisions about the allocation of R&D resources that involve reallocation, or even new lines of expenditure, have significant implications for organizational subunits and individual careers. While home country research managers may agree in principle with the strategic need for developing an R&D presence overseas, they may be much less enthusiastic about seeing R&D resources go into supporting projects in the new facility rather than in their own organization. The strategic mandate and the project agenda which meet the least resistance within the multinational corporation's home country organization involve either new activities, such as basic research in a new field where the foreign country's science and technology system has a clear comparative advantage and the technologies involved are demonstrably crucial to the company's future, or activities to which the existing research organization has committed a low level of resources, such as product modification or product development for a particular local market.

The internationalization of technology development is also coinciding, in many firms, with pressures to link R&D more closely to production and to customers, and to shorten product development cycles. One tool for doing this in many corporations has been to reduce corporate-level expenditures on R&D and increase the amount of R&D funding controlled by business units. Given the pressures on time to market, however, many business unit managers are reluctant to risk their R&D funding in a relatively untried R&D center offshore, especially if they have no strong personal information or experiential linkages with the researchers there. Some MNEs have responded to the difficulties of funding their developing offshore R&D facilities by earmarking certain corporate funds for them, either directly or through the business unit, which can gain access to those funds only through projects in the overseas centers. Without such efforts, offshore technology facilities often turn in frustration to developing technology for their local market rather than providing the base for a global technology network envisioned by the original strategic intent.

THE RESEARCH MANAGEMENT SYSTEM:
THE TRANSFER OF ORGANIZATIONAL PATTERNS

The development of the research management system poses distinctive problems. Because R&D has been the last function of the multinational corporation to be geographically dispersed, we are only beginning to confront one of the key organizational and managerial issues involved in internationalizing R&D: how much of the research management systems and external and internal linkage patterns from the home country to introduce and how much of the patterns dominant in the local environment to follow. Traditional views in the field of international management tended to assume that localization—adopting the organizational patterns and managerial styles dominant in the local environment—is always the best strategy. Even more recent writers, such as Kenichi Ohmae, have asserted that effective international management depends on building a cadre of local managers who manage in accordance with local patterns, especially in Japan (Ohmae, 1989b). However, such advice is largely based on the experience of marketing, which is the function where the interactions with the local environment are most dense and sustained. It is less useful in cases where organizational structures and processes are key elements of the firm's competitive advantage (e.g., in manufacturing in the Japanese auto industry) and in cases where the interactions between the local organization and the rest of the multinational firm are dense and sustained (social science research indicates that interactions are easier between similarly structured organizations).[3] The external and internal knowledge networks of the R&D organization are therefore important not only for their role in transmitting knowledge, but also because they are channels for information about organizational models and themselves exert "pulls" on the organization toward certain institutionalized patterns.

Firms differ significantly in the extent to which they regard their research management systems or their modes of internal and external linkage as key elements of their
competitive advantage. But there are some important commonalities across multinational firms on the second factor, linkages between the local organization and the rest
of the multinational. Recent shifts in the predominant patterns of organization within
multinationals—from geographic organizations to global product divisions—have
weakened the autonomy of local country subsidiaries and increased the level of interaction across borders. This has increased the costs of maintaining organizational structures and processes in the various subsidiaries that are incompatible as well as the
pressures within the MNE for greater similarity across subsidiaries. It has also increased the pressures within the R&D organization as a whole to focus on output
considerations, sometimes at the expense of developmental considerations.

Whether the R&D facility follows local or headquarters patterns or whether it
develops "hybrid" patterns of its own are matters both of conscious management
decision and of the unanticipated consequences of environmental pressures. Institutionalization theory posits that an organization that looks to another organization (or set
of similar organizations) for resources and for legitimacy will be strongly drawn to
emulate their organizational structure (DiMaggio and Powell, 1983; Zucker, 1988). To
the extent that the Japan-based R&D subsidiary looks to the local country organization
for resources, fashions a local product development mandate, and works closely with
Japanese supplier and user firms, it will be strongly pulled toward the patterns institutionalized in that organizational field. The denser its interactions with its parent organization and the greater the control of the home country business unit over its resources,
the more it will look to the MNE system for its organizational patterns. And this
structural similarity will further facilitate the intensification of interaction and communication.

One of the most important forces pulling the facility toward local patterns is the
implicit organizational model or models held by the local mid-career research managers who are recruited to staff the facility (or in the case of acquisition, are already
employed). Their experience in other organizations has given them models of how
organizations should be structured. In some cases, these are based on the organization
in which they have had their most extended working experience; in some cases, their
past experience provides them with a negative model—a strong view of what should be
avoided.

When a multinational corporation is recruiting managers for foreign R&D facilities, the process is often focused on the individual's technical abilities and accomplish-
ments, and perhaps his or her networks into universities and professional societies. It
less often explores in detail the individual's views of what constitutes a good research
management system, how the knowledge base of an R&D facility is best fostered, and
the appropriate modes of external and internal linkages (e.g., in handing off technology
to the production organization). Yet these will have a profound impact on how the
emerging facility is organized, and major incompatibility with the patterns currently
prevailing within the MNE's research organization may cause serious problems, either
for the individual or (if the person is in a top-level management position) for the facility
itself. One of the key challenges in the initial research agenda of the R&D facility is to
foster the building of the networks of communication between these upper and middle
level R&D managers and the home country R&D organization.

The major strategy for countering the inevitably strong local organizational pulls is the two-way exchange of researchers. Sending local researchers on assignment to the headquarters research organization enhances their technical abilities and provides them with a grounding in the research systems of the parent organization. Sending home country researchers to the local facility increases the number of people in the home country organization who are aware of and sympathetic to the developmental as well as the output considerations in building the R&D agenda, and it provides greater incentives to bring local research management systems into alignment with those of the parent organization.

Yet the two-way exchange of researchers between Japan and the United States is extremely costly for a U.S.-based multinational. One MNE has calculated that whereas bringing a Japanese researcher to the United States costs approximately $150,000 a year, sending an American researcher of comparable seniority to Japan costs $450,000 in the first year and increasing amounts in subsequent years. Not surprisingly, financial considerations alone dispose managers to rely on a one-way rather than a two-way flow of technical professionals.

But in addition, few U.S. MNEs have built human resource development systems for their technical people that reward international experience. Building career ladders that create and reinforce the networks among the R&D facilities worldwide may well demand a kind of personnel development structure (including the provision of language training) that the headquarters R&D organization has never previously had to generate. Long-term career planning is an essential condition for generating a cadre of home country researchers with experience abroad at critical stages of their careers (not just as senior-level administrators) and a cadre of local R&D managers with extensive experience in the headquarters R&D organization. Both are crucial for the success of the internationalization of R&D on the model of the coordinated global network articulated as an ideal by the top managers in the Booz Allen study cited earlier. However, especially for many U.S. firms, the kind of long-term, individual-specific planning required may entail major rethinking of their human resource development strategies.

CONCLUSION

Because the level of accumulated wisdom about managing the internationalization of R&D in general and in Japan in particular is still relatively low, most U.S. MNEs are adopting an emergent strategy: establishing facilities and watching to see what patterns seem to work and what structures and processes cause serious problems. This process of "mimetic isomorphism," as DiMaggio and Powell dubbed the emulation of apparently successful organizational patterns, will itself powerfully influence the development trajectory of the Japan-based R&D subsidiaries of U.S. MNEs.

The growing technological competition from Japanese MNEs will exert similar influence. Japanese firms are becoming increasingly eager to follow their growing internationalization of production with the internationalization of technology (Herbert, 1989). A survey of 177 leading Japanese firms in 1988 (*Nihon Keizai Shimbun,* September 13, 1988) found that over 80 percent of the respondents were either actively working to establish R&D bases abroad or interested in doing so.

These mimetic and competitive pressures may well provide a counterbalance to the powerful forces pulling toward a localization of the research mandate and the organization of the Japan-based R&D subsidiary. The complexity of the internal and external change processes and the iterative interaction between strategic goals and organizational change make the processes difficult to manage and the outcome in individual organizations extremely hard to predict. But where the processes are complicated by the frustrations of the participants, it is often useful to recognize that much of what they see as the pathologies of their own organization are in fact more broadly shared complexities and contradictions of the organizational changes involved in internationalizing the R&D function.

NOTES

1. The following discussion is based on interviews with technology managers in nine U.S. firms with technology development activities in Japan (five of the nine also have R&D activities in Europe).

2. This typology owes much to the three-variable typology of MNE subsidiaries developed by White and Poynter (1984), which includes geographic scope, value-added scope, and product scope, categories that are analogous to the geographic scope, vertical technology scope, and horizontal technology scope used in this chapter.

3. This is one of the pillars of the recent developments in institutionalization theory in organizational sociology. See, for example, DiMaggio and Powell (1983) and Zucker (1988).

REFERENCES

Aoki, M. 1988. *Information, Incentives, and Bargaining in the Japanese Economy*. Cambridge: Cambridge University Press.

Behrman, J. N., and W. A. Fischer. 1980. *Overseas Activities of Transnational Companies*. Boston: Oelgeschlager, Gunn, and Hain.

Branscomb, L. 1987. "National and Corporate Technology Strategies in an Interdependent World Economy." In *Technology and Global Industry: Companies and Nations in the World Economy*, edited by B. R. Guile and H. Brooks. Washington, D.C.: National Academy Press.

Contractor, F., and P. Lorange, eds. 1988. *Cooperative Strategies in International Business*. Lexington, Mass.: Lexington Books.

Crozier, M. 1964. *The Bureaucratic Phenomenon*. Chicago: University of Chicago Press.

De Meyer, A., and A. Mizushima. 1989. "Global R&D Management." *R&D Management* 19, no. 2: 135–146.

Dertouzos, M., R. K. Lester, and R. M. Solow. 1989. *Made in America: Regaining the Productive Edge*. Cambridge, Mass.: MIT Press.

DiMaggio, P., and W. W. Powell. 1983. "The Iron Cage Revisited: Institutional Isomorphism and Collective Rationality in Organizational Fields." *American Sociological Review* 48: 147–60.

Doz, Y. 1987. "International Industries: Fragmentation versus Globalization." In *Technology and Global Industry: Companies and Nations in the World Economy*, edited by B. R. Guile and H. Brooks. Washington, D.C.: National Academy Press.

Doz, Y., and C. K. Prahalad. 1981. "Headquarters Influence and Strategic Control in MNCs." *Sloan Management Review* 23, no. 1: 15–29.

Fischer, W. A., and J. N. Behrman. 1979. "The Coordination of Foreign R&D Activities by Transnational Corporations." *Journal of International Business Studies* 10, no. 2: 25–35.

Guile, B. R., and H. Brooks, eds. 1987. *Technology and Global Industry: Companies and Nations in the World Economy.* Washington, D.C.: National Academy Press.

Hakanson, L., and U. Zander. 1986. *Managing International Research and Development.* Stockholm: Sveriges Mekanforbund.

Hamel, G., Y. Doz, and C. K. Prahalad. 1989. "Collaborate with your Competitors—and Win." *Harvard Business Review* 67, no. 1: 133–139.

Hannan, M. T., and J. Freeman. 1989. *Organizational Ecology.* Cambridge, Mass.: Harvard University Press.

Herbert, E. 1989. "Japanese R&D in the United States." *Research Technology Management* 32: 11–20.

Meyer, M. W., and L. G. Zucker. 1989. *Permanently Failing Organizations.* Newbury Park, Calif.: Sage Publications.

Miyamoto, 1986. *Nihon IBM Kigyo Bunka Senryaku* (IBM Japan's Corporate Culture Strategy). Tokyo: TBS Britannica.

Ohmae, K. 1989a. "The Global Logic of Strategic Alliances." *Harvard Business Review* 67, no. 2: 143–154.

Ohmae, K. 1989b. "Managing in a Borderless World." *Harvard Business Review* 67, no. 3: 152–161.

Okimoto, D. 1989. *Between MITI and the Market.* Stanford: Stanford University Press.

Perrino, A. C., and J. W. Tipping. 1989. "Global Management of Technology." *Research Technology Management* 32: 12–19.

Porter, M. 1984. *Competitive Advantage: Creating and Sustaining Superior Performance.* New York: Free Press.

Porter, M., ed. 1986. *Competition in Global Industries.* Boston: Harvard Business School Press.

Pucik, V. 1988. "Strategic Alliances with the Japanese: Implications for Human Resource Management." In *Cooperative Strategies in International Business,* edited by F. J. Contractor and P. Lorange. Lexington, Mass.: Lexington Books.

Pucik, V., M. Hanada, and G. Fifield. 1990. *Management Culture and the Effectiveness of Local Executives in Japanese-Owned U.S. Corporations.* Tokyo: Egon Zehnder International.

Ronstadt, R. 1977. *Research and Development Abroad by U.S. Multinationals.* New York: Praeger.

Stalk, G., Jr., and T. M. Hout. 1990. *Competing against Time: How Time-Based Competition is Reshaping Global Markets.* New York: Free Press.

Stinchcombe, A. L. 1965. "Social Structure and Organizations." In *Handbook of Organizations,* edited by J. March. Chicago: Rand McNally.

Vernon, R. 1987. "Coping with Technological Change: U.S. Problems and Prospects." In *Technology and Global Industry: Companies and Nations in the World Economy,* edited by B. Guile and H. Brooks. Washington, D.C.: National Academy Press.

Von Hippel, E. 1988. *The Sources of Innovation.* New York: Oxford University Press.

Westney, D. E. 1989. "Internal and external linkages in the MNC: the case of R&D subsidiaries in Japan." In *Managing the Multinational,* edited by C. Bartlett, Y. Doz, and G. Hedlund. London: Routledge.

Westney, D. E. and K. Sakakibara. 1985. "The Role of Japan-based R&D in global technology strategy." In *Technology in the Modern Corporation,* edited by M. Horwitch. New York: Pergamon Press.

White, R. E., and T. A. Poynter. 1983. "Strategies for Foreign-Owned Subsidiaries in Canada." *Business Quarterly* 49: 59–69.

Zucker, L. G., ed. 1988. *Institutional Patterns and Organizations: Culture and Environments.*
    Cambridge, Mass.: Ballinger.

COMMENTARY BY DAVID ZNATY

When I first read this, I thought that it was not by an American. It seemed to me to be very Japanese. I will try to raise some questions that may challenge the argument advanced by the author.

If a company provides jobs in the domestic economy and has decentralized R&D, the question arises about how the firm avoids losing control of its technologies. How do you control the technology if all your R&D is decentralized, and located in many countries? These companies must respect the rules of the home economies.

In globalization of local R&D, we have the fundamental research, the applied, product-oriented research, engineering production, manufacturing, and so on. The more you make your local organization ship out its R&D, the more trouble you will have. The Japanese never decentralize R&D, and they keep it in Japan.

I want to talk about three examples. One is from my own group, the Communications Group, where we tried to organize R&D around the world. We gathered together all of our marketing managers and our fundamental researchers, and when they spoke together they realized they had not been doing research that fit in well with the firm's strategic objectives.

The second example is an American company that was producing electronic components, and it had good old machines to produce it. Then the company decided it wanted to have the local strategy group get together all of its labs and try to design a new machine. To make this electronic component, there was a very long product introduction cycle. During the project, two engineers left the company to join the competition. The American company is trying to sue these two people for copyright infringements. The company is now owned by an international holding company, and it will be a very difficult case to win.

The third example involves taking care not to create competitors in the countries in which you do your R&D. Some of the countries learn very fast. The Japanese are a perfect example of this.

In summary, I think we have to admit today that there are very few countries that should be the centers for American R&D. New technologies and innovations need to be introduced and formulated at home, especially if American companies want to use R&D as part of a strategy for transforming their organizations. The best way to fix or to change a company is education within the company. This is very difficult to do if R&D is done elsewhere.

16

The Effects of Information Technology on Management and Organizations

MICHAEL S. SCOTT MORTON

BACKGROUND

The Management in the 1990s Research Program was created in 1984 to examine the profound impact that information technology (IT) is having on organizations of all kinds. Its mission was to explore how IT will affect the way organizations will be able to survive and prosper in the competitive environment of the 1990s and beyond. This chapter summarizes the program.

The program began with two basic premises:

1. The business environment is and will remain turbulent.
2. IT will continue its rapid evolution over at least the next decade.

It is important to look more closely at these premises and at the way the program was organized to pursue its study.

Turbulent Business Environment

Turbulence in the business environment puts pressure on organizations to be sure they can effectively meet the fundamental changes that are occurring. The program identified four kinds of changes with which organizations must contend.

Social Change

The heightened expectations on the part of the population of the nations of Western Europe and North America are giving rise to pressures to improve the quality of working life and the quality of the environment, and this is resulting in a changing concept of what constitutes "value." This is particularly true of the prices people are willing to pay for products and services and the amount of damage to the environment that they will tolerate.

Political Change

The changing regulatory and governmental roles of the Western governments have resulted in a new competitive climate and a new set of rules on how to compete. This has its counterpart in other parts of the world; Gorbachev's *glasnost* is an example and is typified by the coming together of the European Community as an active force, with the symbolic 1992 "deadline."

Technical Change

There is obviously technical change in the IT area, a subject which is raised later, but in addition we have significant changes in other areas such as materials, with advances in superconductivity, ceramics, and advanced composites, to name just three. There are also major changes in the biosciences and bioengineering, both of which have had major technical breakthroughs recently and are likely to continue to evolve rapidly.

Economic Change

The twin deficits in the United States—in the budget and in trade—will continue to cause economic turbulence for some years. The fact of considerable global trade, particularly among the "Triad" (EEC, North America, and Japan), will merely exacerbate the uncertainty surrounding firms. This trade results in shifting benchmarks as to what is acceptable product quality and places new demands on corporations and nations.

The Rapid Evolution of Information Technology

The second premise behind the 1990s Research Program is that information technology now consists of a powerful collection of elements that are undergoing change and that have wide and significant applicability. These elements go well beyond what has been available during the last thirty years, in what might be termed the "data processing era." In the 1990s we expect organizations to experience the effects of the integration and evolution of a set of elements that collectively we term information technology. The research program considered these elements to consist of:

1. *Hardware,* ranging from large-scale mainframe computers to small-scale microcomputers.
2. *Software,* ranging from traditional languages such as COBOL and their fourth-generation equivalent to expert systems that have emerged from developments in artificial intelligence.
3. *Networks,* in particular telecommunications networks, ranging from public to private, broadband to narrowband.
4. *Workstations,* ranging from those designed for engineers, with large computational capabilities and the ability to display dynamic, three-dimensional color graphics, to professional workstations used by a bank lending officer or a market analyst in a consumer goods company. The latter rely on models, heuristics, and simple graphics and often have very large databases included in the system.
5. *Robotics,* ranging from robots with "vision" and "hands" used on the factory floor to a variety of devices familiar to the average person on the street, such as banks' automatic teller machines.
6. *Smart,* or *"intelligent," chips,* used in products to enhance functionality or reliability. For example, they are used in automobile braking systems to prevent

skidding and in elevators to improve response time and to detect impending failures. In simpler forms they now appear in products such as the "active card" that is used to track, via satellite, the movement of shipping containers.

The continuing evolution and integration of these six elements of IT have now reached a threshold of cost and ease of use that is enabling widespread organizational impact when the organization has the ability to harness the technology effectively.

Change

Both premises, business turbulence and technological change, imply potential organizational change. The external forces associated with environmental turbulence must be met for survival. IT offers the opportunity for organizations to react to these forces constructively. Because of the combined effect there is no reason why organizations will necessarily continue in their present form.

These challenges suggest that it will not be possible to survive as a company just by working harder within existing organizational structures and using conventional practices and tools. Given what IT now allows an alert organization to do, an organization that merely does its existing work faster and works harder will become uncompetitive in the global marketplace of the 1990s and beyond.

INFORMATION TECHNOLOGY IN PERSPECTIVE

IT has important general purpose power to manipulate symbols used in all classes of work, and therefore as an "information engine" it can do for business what the steam engine did in the days of the Industrial Revolution. It goes beyond this, however, as it is a technology that permits one to manipulate models of reality, to step back one pace from the physical reality. Such an ability lies at the heart of IT's capacity to alter work fundamentally.

Despite IT's uniqueness it does have a history. The telegraph and telephone were its forebears and were central to the rise of the modern industrial corporation. The result of the application of those technologies was the mass production, vertically integrated, hierarchical organization. But there is nothing sacred about such an organizational form. At a particular moment in time, around the turn of the century, the conditions in the marketplace of the newly industrializing Western world were conducive to the emergence of this organizational form. The pressures of global competition and the enabling coordinative capabilities of IT have led to experimentation with organizational forms. Thus it can be expected that an evolution away from the traditional hierarchical organization will take place.

Economics

Information is the lifeblood of any organization. Little can be done successfully without it. Hence the cost of handling and processing information is important. In the data processing era this was also true, but it was less critical to organizational success, as data processing principally dealt with back office clerical functions and the technology

Table 16.1 Computing cost–performance trends

	1980	1990	2000
Constant functionality[a]	4.5 MIPS	4.5 MIPS	4.5 MIPS
Cost			
Original projection (1981)	$4.5 million	$300,000	
Modified projection (1988)		$100,000	$10,000
Number of people of equivalent			
cost			
Original projection (1981)	210	6	
Modified projection (1988)		2	0.125

[a]Metaphor for constant functionality is millions of instructions per second (MIPS).

was still expensive. Technology costs have dropped and one can go beyond numerical data for algorithmic processing and move to qualitative information and heuristic manipulation. This, in turn, can be combined with the ability to work with pictures and drawings, and then one can connect all this to virtually any location in the world. Such power is new in kind; it represents a step function change from what was available before.

As important, the economics of IT have changed both absolutely and relatively. At an absolute level, we are expecting to see IT cost–performance ratios continue to change in the range of 20–30 percent a year. Such change can lead to very considerable differences over relatively short intervals of time. Table 16.1, based on results of an early MIT 1990s project (Benjamin and Scott Morton), illustrates the profound consequences of such a compounding change. In 1980 the cost of a computer with a processing power of 4.5 MIPS was $4.5 million, the cost equivalent of 210 employees of a certain skill level. The cost of a machine of this power was projected to decline to $300,000 in 1990, the cost equivalent of 6 workers of the same skill level. The actual 1990 cost is closer to $100,000. The cost of such a machine in the year 2000 is likely to be no more than $10,000, the cost equivalent of only a fraction of that same worker. Thus organizations are faced with radically different tradeoffs over time among processing power, human effort, and dollars with which to best meet the organization's objectives.

The relative costs of IT are also changing. The cost of IT relative to the cost of other forms of capital equipment is widening. Thus it is *relatively* cheaper today to invest in IT capital than it is in any other form of capital. This relationship, based on thirty years' data, is seen in Figure 16.1.

Information Technology Is Different

IT exerts such a strong influence because it can affect *both* production and coordination. Production refers to the task of producing any good or service that the organization is in business to sell. It is not limited to physical production but includes the intellectual production of things such as loans or other "soft" products. The production jobs that are most affected by IT are those in which information and/or knowledge makes a difference. We call these production workers "information workers" or "knowledge workers." The fraction of the work force that falls into this category has grown to be very large. In manufacturing industries it averages around 40 percent; in

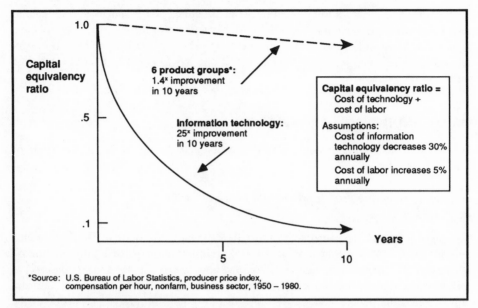

Figure 16.1 Capital equivalency ratio: information technology versus six product groups. (From U.S. Bureau of Labor Statistics.)

service industries, over 80 percent. The information worker processes information without significant modification, a task that is typically classified as clerical, such as order entry. The knowledge worker category covers those who add value to the original information. For example, this would include engineers and designers required to design new products; those who trade in the securities markets; those in financial institutions who lend money to companies or individuals; and all those who produce budgets, market research analyses, legal briefs, and so on. The use of IT to change the nature of both such categories of production work is widely recognized.

Just as important is the use of IT to change the ways in which coordination activities are carried out. Coordination tasks make up a large part of what organizations do. With IT the effects of both distance and time can be shrunk to near zero. For example, it is possible today to make financial trades in global markets anywhere in the world from any of the major cities of the world. A similar activity is that of placing orders to a supplier's plant or accepting orders directly from a customer's site to your own organization. The airline seat reservation systems are one of the most visible and oldest examples of such coordination.

Organizational memory is another feature of coordination that is affected by IT. Corporate databases now provide an enormous reservoir of information that can be used for constructive management of the organization. Personnel records indicating who has had what job, what salary, and what training form the basis for understanding the skill mix in a company and help identify possible candidates for certain jobs. Thus IT can be thought of as affecting coordination by increasing the organization's memory, thereby establishing a record that allows for the detection of patterns. Although this has been true of data for some time, the added power of heuristics and artificial intelligence provide important additional tools with which to use information.

In summary, the traditional organizational structures and practices do not have to stay the same as we move into the 1990s. All dimensions of the organization will have to be reexamined in light of the power of the new IT. The economics are so powerful and apply to so much of the organization that one has to question everything before accepting the status quo.

MAJOR FINDINGS OF THE RESEARCH

The research has six major implications. The first and most basic is that the nature of work is changing.

Finding 1: *IT is enabling fundamental changes in the way work is done.*

The degree to which a person can be affected by the rapid evolution of IT is determined by how much of that person's work is based on information—that is, information on what product to make or service to deliver and how to make it (the production task) as well as when to make it and in conjunction with whom (the coordination task). In many organizations the people in these two categories account for a large proportion of the work force.

It should be noted at this point that IT is a strong enabler, but it is not in and of itself a driver of change. The driver of change is people, normally the management, and without leadership and initiative work does not in fact really change.

We saw change in three kinds of work being enabled by IT in ways that portend the kind of patterns we expect throughout the 1990s.

Production Work

The potential impact of IT on production work is considerable. This is most apparent when the nature of production work is broken up into three consistent elements:

1. Physical production that is affected by robotics (increasingly with "vision"), process control instrumentation, and intelligent sensors.
2. Information production that is affected by data processing computers for the standard clerical tasks such as accounts receivable, billing, and payables.
3. Knowledge production that is affected by CAD/CAM tools for designers, work-stations for those building qualitative products such as loans or letters of credit, and workstations for those building "soft" products such as new legislation or new software with Computer Aided Software Engineering (CASE) tools.

These forms of change are readily understood in the case of physical products and standard information processing but do not seem to be as easily grasped and exploited when it comes to knowledge work. As a result organizations appear to be very slow in exploiting and utilizing technology in ways that increase the effectiveness of knowledge production.

Coordinative Work

IT, as it has been defined in this research program, includes six elements, one of which is communications networks. These are currently being installed at a rapid rate by nations and organizations and we expect this to continue throughout the 1990s. Such networks are being utilized within a building, within an organization, between organizations, and between countries. However, their use has been less than anticipated because existing standards do not permit easy connectivity. This situation has begun to improve and we can expect this improvement to accelerate through the 1990s as the enormous economic benefits to industries and societies become more obvious.

The new IT is permitting a change in the economics and functionality of the coordination process. As a result we can see changes in three areas:

1. Distance can be shrunk toward zero. That is, distance can become increasingly irrelevant as far as information flow is concerned. Thus the location of work can be reexamined as can potential partners. Even in 1989 leading companies have design teams in different countries linked electronically and working together on a single product.

2. Time can be shrunk toward zero or shifted to a more convenient point. Airline reservation systems are a leading example of using IT in a time-critical setting. Organizations that are required to work together although located in different time zones are utilizing store and forward and common databases as a way to shift time.

3. Organizational memory, as exemplified by a common database, can be maintained over time, contributed to from all parts of the organization, and made available to a wide variety of authorized users.

Beyond memory is the organization's ability to share skills. In a sense, such "group work," or the utilization of teams, combines the three aspects of coordination: distance, time, and memory. This combined effect has more impact than do the three elements by themselves.

This change in the economics and functionality of coordination fundamentally alters all the tasks in an organization that have to do with coordinating the organization's delivery of products and services to its customers and the actual production of such goods and services. To the extent that an organization's structure is determined by its coordinative needs, it too is subject to potential change.

Management Work

The third IT-enabled change in work is the work done by managers. The principal dimensions of management work that can be most affected by IT are those of direction and control. "Direction," as used here, is concerned with sensing changes in the external environment and also with staying in close touch with the organization and its members' ideas and reactions to their views of the environment. Relevant, timely information from these two sources can be crucial input to the organization's direction-setting process. This is as true for a sophisticated strategic planning system as for an informal executive support system or customer feedback system.

The "control" dimension of management work has two key aspects for our purposes here. The first is the measurement task, that is, measuring the organization's performance along whatever set of critical success factors has been defined as being relevant. The second aspect is to interpret such measures against the plan and determine what actions to take.

Effective control is a critical dimension of organizational learning as it feeds back to future direction setting and both of these can be fundamentally changed by the increasing availability of IT.

We have seen IT to be a strong enabler of fundamental changes in how work is done in three areas: production work, coordinative work, and management work.

IT is available to radically alter the basic cost structure of a wide variety of jobs, jobs affecting at least half the members of the organization. IT is only an enabler, however; changing jobs takes a combination of management leadership and employee participation that is, thus far, extremely rare.

Finding 2: *IT is enabling the integration of business functions at all levels within and between organizations.*

The continuing expansion of public and private telecommunications networks means that the concept of "any information, any time, anywhere, and any way I want to look at it" is increasingly economically feasible. The infrastructure to permit this is being put in place by different companies at different rates. In many cases only those organizations that have created a significant enterprise-level infrastructure will be able to compete effectively in the 1990s. Additionally, the ability to electronically connect people and tasks within and between firms will increasingly be available and affordable. In a real sense, boundaries of organizations are becoming more permeable; hence, where work gets done, when, and with whom is changing. However, this can be a difficult, often revolutionary, move whose impact is blunted by people's unwillingness to exploit the new opportunities. However, there are a few situations where components are being designed *with* suppliers in weeks, not months. Parts are ordered from suppliers in hours, not weeks, and questions are answered in seconds, not days. This enormous speed-up in the flow of work is enabled by the electronic network. The integration it permits is showing up in four forms:

1. *Within the value chain.* Kodak, among many others, connected design, engineering, and manufacturing personnel within its system of local area networks (LANs) and created a team focusing on one product. Such teams have accomplished tasks in shorter time with greater creativity and higher morale than with their previous tools and organizational structures. There is no part of an organization which, in principle, is excluded from the team concept.

2. *End-to-end links of value chains between organizations.* A supplier's shipping department can be electronically connected to the buyer's purchasing department and the sales force directly connected to its customers. This form of electronic integration is a powerful way of speeding up the flow of goods between organizations. It has been reported in the press using various terminologies such as electronic just-in-time (JIT) or electronic data interchange (EDI). This can be thought of as the boundary of the organization being permeable to IT. It can also be thought of as shifting the boundary of the organization "out" to include elements of other organizations, thus creating a "virtual" organization.

3. *Value chain substitution via subcontract or alliance.* This occurs when an organization takes one stage in its value chain and subcontracts either a specific

task or the whole stage to another organization. A common example is when a firm asks a supplier to design a component for it. Modern CAD/CAM environments permit a supplier's designers to be electronically linked to the host team to allow the data exchange needed to accomplish a joint design. Ford Motor Company's agreement with Ryder Truck to handle Ford's new car shipments is an example of a subcontracted task that could not work without electronic integration. These collaborations are enabled by IT and would not be feasible without it. They lead to the host organization being able to take advantage of the economies of scale and unique skills of the partner. To be of lasting value, of course, there must be reciprocal benefits.

4. *Electronic markets.* This is the most highly developed form of electronic integration. Here, coordination within the organization or among a few organizations gives way to an open market. Travel agents, for example, are able to electronically reserve airline seats from all the major carriers and can look around for the best price at which to complete the transaction. Electronic markets will be increasingly prevalent in the 1990s as IT costs continue to drop and thereby reduce transaction costs to the point where the "market" becomes economically effective.

These four forms of electronic integration have, to varying degrees, the net effect of removing buffers and leveraging expertise. Shrinking time and distance can have the effect of allowing the right resources to be at the right place at the right time. In effect this removes the need to have people and other assets (such as inventory or cash) tied up as unproductive buffers.

It should be noted that it appears to be required that an organization have the necessary infrastructure of communications, data, applications software, and educated and empowered users before any of these four forms of integration can be fully exploited.

We have found that each of these four forms of integration is visible in embryonic form in some organization. However, the real economic impact and rate of dissemination of the integration varies enormously and in no case has there been a clearly sustainable transformation. Some of the major reasons for this are discussed in Finding 6.

Finding 3: *The introduction of IT, resulting in changes in the degree of interrelatedness, is causing shifts in the competitive climate in many industries.*

The first two findings, which are at the level of the organization, have their equivalents at the level of the industry. This takes the form of the unique impact of IT on the competitive climate and its effect on the degree of interrelatedness of products or services with rivals. This can lead to unprecedented degrees of simultaneous competition and collaboration between firms. This effect of IT on the nature and extent of interrelatedness between organizations is spreading rapidly. For example, parts suppliers that are linked electronically with purchasers for design and manufacturing are now not uncommon.

Another illustration is the creation of an electronic linkage between the U.S. Internal Revenue Service (IRS) and tax preparation firms. The linkage was created to enable the electronic filing of individual income tax returns prepared by those firms. This has opened up opportunities for lending or borrowing what is, in aggregate, some $70 billion. This is fostering the creation of new arrangements between multiple financial services firms (Venkatraman, Chapter 5 in Scott Morton, 1991).

The second unique impact of IT on competitiveness concerns the importance of standards. It is now important to know when to support standards and when to try to preempt competitors by establishing a proprietary de facto standard. Every industry has an example. For illustration here, consider the attempt by the major insurance companies to tie agents to their system. The general agents retaliated by using the industry association to grow their own network with its open standards to protect themselves. Understanding the changed nature of one's competitive climate is important in an era of growing IT pervasiveness.

This framework adds a new dimension to the classic economic analysis of competition, a dimension here termed "interrelatedness." Such an expanded analysis has shown that as traditional economic forces (such as competitor actions) change, or as the economics and functionality of IT change, the position of an organization relative to competitive organizations will change. In both cases there is no technical or economic reason (such as ownership of patents) that can allow one organization to capture excess "economic rents" from the use of IT for any sustainable period of time. Competitive and technological forces simply do not permit any single organization to enjoy a sustainable competitive advantage merely from its use of information technology.

It is possible, however, for an organization in the decade of the 1990s to capture benefits. This appears to come from being an early (or different) mover with a business benefit enabled by IT and then investing actively in innovations that continue to increase the benefits to the user of the innovation. In other words, the benefits do not flow from the mere use of IT, but arise from the human, organizational, and system innovations that are added on to the original business benefit. IT is merely an enabler that offers an organization the opportunity to vigorously invest in added innovations if it wishes to stay ahead of its competitors.

The empirical fact that existing organizations constantly move—or are moved—to different points in the competitive matrix and that new organizations appear on the competitive horizon adds considerable importance to the functions of scanning and environmental monitoring. Effective scanning of the business environment to understand what is changing is critical if an organization is to proactively manage its way through an environment made additionally turbulent with changes in technology.

Finding 4: *IT presents new strategic opportunities for those organizations willing and able to step back and reassess their mission and operations.*

A turbulent environment, the changing nature of work, the possibilities of electronic integration, and the changing competitive climate are all compelling reasons for the third stage in the evolution of the organization of the 1990s. In short, automate and "informate" set the stage for transformation.

Research during the 1990s program suggested that the three findings just discussed—the new ways of doing work, electronic integration, and the shifting competitive climate—present an organization with an opportunity, if not a pressing need, to step back and rethink the mission of the organization and the way it is going to conduct its operations.

There appear to be three distinct stages that organizations are going through as they attempt to respond to their changing environments.

Stage 1. Automate

IT applications in this stage are designed to take the cost out of "production." Savings are usually achieved by reducing the number of workers. For information handlers such as order entry clerks this can result in effectively being eliminated from the work force. For other production workers manual operations are replaced by machine actions under computer control. For example, an operator no longer has to change valve settings by hand but instead watches a computer screen and types instructions.

This requires fewer operators with consequent direct cost savings. Beyond process control and automation of traditional paper processing (e.g., bank check clearing), IT is being used for automation with the scanner and bar code, the universal product code (UPC). This is now used not only for packaged goods but also for inventory in warehouses and a host of other "tracking" applications. These kinds of IT tools can give rise to enormous cost reductions for firms.

The new IT tools, used by the "production" workers that are left after automation, often generate information as a by-product. This is clearly seen in the case of process control, where the operators have information from multiple sensors and watch screens and type in instructions. In the automate stage, however, little or no use is made of this new information beyond direct control of the existing process.

Stage 2. Informate

"Informate" is a term (coined by Shoshana Zuboff) that describes what happens when automated processes yield information as a by-product. The informate stage as we saw it in this program has three distinguishing characteristics. The first of these is that production work involves new tools that provide information needed to get the job done; for example, the operator must read the screen to see if the process is within tolerance. This work can be fairly "simple," as in monitoring machines, or it can involve complex new skills, an example of which is using a three-dimensional dynamic color workstation for engineering design. Similarly, the foreign exchange trader working in several markets on a real-time basis has to use a set of computer-based tools that are quite different from the telephone and voice with which the job used to be done. At a more mundane level, a salesperson making a presentation to a potential customer uses financial models to demonstrate the savings on this month's "deal." All these knowledge workers are having to develop new skills to work with new information tools. These often involve new ways of thinking.

The second distinguishing characteristic of the informate stage is that the new IT tools often generate new sorts of information as a by-product of the basic task. For example, the process control operator might notice that one limit is always exceeded when the weather is hot; the foreign exchange trader may notice that certain accounts are building a position in certain currencies; or the salesperson, by analyzing twelve months of sales data, notices buying patterns in some of the customers. The process of using the new IT tools thereby develops some by-product information that in turn can require a different kind of conceptual grasp by the person concerned. Thus "invisible" work is going on in the worker's mind. This kind of work may require changes in skills and management practices if it is to be used successfully to improve the organization's performance. It requires an ability to see patterns and understand the overall process rather than just looking at controlling the information on the screen. In this situation the production worker becomes an "analyzer," a role involving a level of conceptual skill different from what was needed before as a "doer," or machine minder.

The third distinguishing characteristic of the informate stage is that the new skills and information are developed to the point where new market opportunities can be opened up. This may require a broader view of one's job and an identification with the whole organization rather than one's narrow piece of it. For example, American Hospital Supply (AHS) was able to sell the patterns of their customers' buying behavior, detected by the AHS sales force, back to the producer of the original product. The salespeople concerned had noticed that there were patterns with certain kinds of customers. They alerted their management to these patterns and in turn came up with the idea that this would be a valuable by-product that could be sold and thus form the basis for a new business.

Stage 3. Transformation

The changing nature of work does not stop with the informate stage but goes on to the transformation stage. The term "transformation" was chosen deliberately to reflect the fundamental difference in character exhibited by organizations (or parts of organizations) that have been through the first two stages and have begun on the third.

I contend that many successful organizations in the 1990s will pass through this stage, a stage characterized by leadership, vision, and a sustained process of organizational empowerment so basic as to be exceptionally hard to accomplish. In a way it can be thought of as being the necessary follow-on to "total quality." The total quality programs are a uniquely American phenomenon of the late 1980s. They served as a very useful rallying cry to energize organizations so that they could fix the woefully inadequate practices that had crept into their operations and management procedures. The concept of transformation includes the broad view of quality but goes beyond this to address the unique opportunities presented by the environment and enabled by IT. A process to help accomplish this, the strategic alignment model (SAM), emerged from the 1990s research (this is discussed in Scott Morton, 1991, Chapter 5).

Finding 5: Successful application of IT will require changes in management and organizational structure.

The 1990s Program has shown that IT is a critical enabler of the re-creation (redefinition) of the organization. This is true in part because it permits the distribution of power, function, and control to be moved to wherever they are most effective, given the mission and objectives of the organization and the culture that it enjoys.

Organizations have always managed some form of matrix structure, a matrix involving functions, products, markets, and geography in some combination. With the new IT, unit costs of coordination are declining significantly. This means that over the next decade we can afford more coordination for the same dollar cost. In addition, IT is causing changing economies of scale. For example, flexible manufacturing permits smaller organizations to also be low-cost producers. Thus IT is enabling a breakup, a dis-integration, of traditional organizational forms. For example, multiple skills can be brought together at an arbitrary point in time and location. In short, ad hoc teams are enabled by IT. Digital Equipment Corporation, among others, has all its engineers on the same network; thus an engineer anywhere in the world can share information, ask for help, or work on a project as needed. As these ad hoc teams become an effective way of working they give rise to the "networking" organization. In such organizations horizontal and vertical working patterns can be created as needed. This will not be the most appropriate organizational form for all tasks and all organizational cultures; however, it is increasingly an option. IT's ability to affect coordination by shrinking time and distance permits an organization to respond more quickly and accurately to the marketplace. This not only reduces the assets the organization has tied up but improves quality as seen by the customer.

Put another way, the 1990s research suggests that the metabolic rate of the organization, that is, the rate at which information moves and decisions are made, is speeding up and will get faster in the 1990s. This is partly because the external environment demands responsiveness and partly because IT has enabled changes to be made in how work is done. In both cases the availability of electronic tools and electronic integration permits this responsiveness. Since global competitive forces do not permit an organization to ignore its competition, as one firm picks up the new options the others must follow. Thus the management of interdependence in the 1990s will take place in a dynamic environment. This in turn requires new management systems and processes. Thus the measurement systems, rewards, incentives, and required skills all require rethinking in the new IT-impacted world. For example, the use of an electronically based JIT system obviously requires new production planning and control processes. The use of small autonomous product teams that combine design, engineering, and manufacturing raises issues of rewards, evaluation, and reassignment. The changes in work created by the use of new technology requires new skills and totally new ways of doing the job.

Management has the challenging task of changing the organizational structure and methods of operation to keep it competitive in a dynamically changing world. Research has shown that IT provides one set of tools that can enable such change. However, to think through the new systems and processes so that they can be exploited effectively is a major challenge for line management.

Finding 6: *A major challenge for management in the 1990s will be to lead organizations through the transformation necessary to prosper in the globally competitive environment.*

Before looking at the findings about organizational transformation it is useful to consider some context. An organization can be thought of as being comprised of five sets of forces in "dynamic equilibrium" among themselves even as the organization is subjected to influences from an external environment. This is represented in Figure 16.2. In this view, a central task of general management is to ensure that the organization, that is, all five forces (represented by the boxes), moves through time to accomplish the organization's objectives.

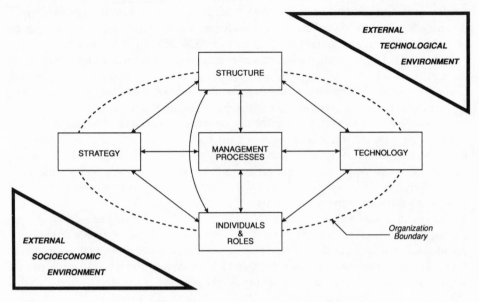

Figure 16.2   The MIT 90s framework.

Within this context it would appear that IT should affect the tasks in the organization and ultimately its strategy. However, the evidence at the aggregate level does not indicate any improvements in productivity or profitability. One illustrative early data point from the United States is growth in number of white-collar workers in 1985:

Executives and managers	+5.6%
Support staff	+3.5%
Growth in U.S. output	+3.0%

Possible reasons for this lack of visible improvement are many but they can be grouped into three broad categories. The first of these is that the benefits are there but simply are not visible. This could be true because the right data are not available or because there is a time lag between the impact of IT and the time when the benefits show up in the data. In addition, to some extent the nature of the impact may not be measurable. For example, the satisfaction derived from finding out one's bank account status on one's PC without leaving home may be a very real benefit to some people, but it does not show up in the statistics on productivity that can be collected.

A second category of explanation is that the Western psyche does not permit the West to be flexible enough to learn new ways. People are used to doing things in a certain way and do not want to change. This difficulty is compounded by having few effective enabling national institutions to encourage or foster change.

The third category is the most disturbing, namely, that there really is no bottom-line impact from IT investment in many firms. This may have happened for one or more of three reasons. The first is that many firms have applied IT to areas of low payoff. The literature is full of examples, such as elaborate refinements of financial accounting systems. The money invested in these cases has in fact produced no real economic payoff for the organization. A second reason is that too often IT is laid on top of

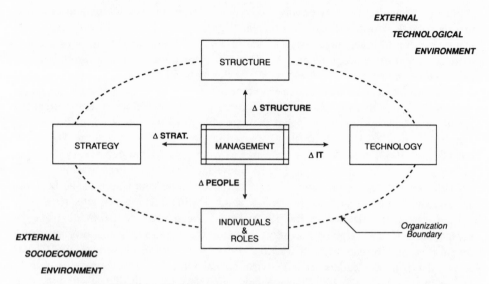

Figure 16.3 The role of management in the change process.

existing practices. Thus there was no real cost reduction, just cost displacement. People were removed as automation was implemented but were replaced by IT and other system costs. No one stepped back and rethought and improved the overall process in such cases. The third reason is that the change was managed superficially and was not absorbed by the organization. In short, the organization did not make real changes in the way it worked or was organized.

The 1990s research has pinpointed some characteristics of the organizations that will be able to successfully go through the transformation process. The first, and obvious, fact is that none of the potentially beneficial enabling aspects of IT can take place without clarity of business purpose and a vision of what the organization should become. A clear mission visible to, and understood by, the organization is a well-known prerequisite for any major organization change. However, when the issue at hand is organizational transformation, enabled by technology, it appears particularly important to invest a large amount of time and effort in getting the organization to understand where it is going and why. This effort is further complicated by the lack of knowledge and skills, not to say fear, of new technology. There appear to be two other important preconditions of successful transformation. One is that the organization has been through a process of "aligning" its corporate strategy (business and IT), information technology, and organizational dimensions. The second precondition is that the organization have a robust information technology infrastructure in place, including an electronic network, and understood standards. Given that there is a vision and an understood view of the business purpose, the challenge in the management of transformation is summed up in Figure 16.3.

Research suggests that the "gray ellipse" in Figure 16.2 and the three forces in it that represent the "people issues" are critical in the transformation process. One root cause for the lack of impact of IT on the improved economic performance of organizations is an organization's unwillingness to invest heavily and early enough in human resources. Changing the way people work can be extremely threatening and therefore takes a great deal of investment. There must be investment in new skills, in psychological ownership of the change process, and in a safety net under the employee so that there is no fear of taking prudent risks. These investments are required throughout the organization as management itself is part of the required change.

The ultimate goal of this change is to give all employees a sense of empowerment. They need to feel that they can make a difference, that their efforts directly affect the organization's performance, and that they are able to take on as much responsibility and commensurate reward as they are willing to work for. Such a Theory Y (McGregor, 1960) view of an organization is a long way from our history of large, hierarchically organized mass production command and control organizations.

However, the economic realities engendered by IT and the nature of the business environment suggest that if the foregoing factors are in effect the attributes needed by the successful organization of the 1990s, as has been suggested, moving from the present state of most large organizations to the next generation organization requires a transformation. Research (Scott Morton, 1991; Allen and Scott Morton, 1991) has shown that if all the leadership and environmental conditions are adequate, then there are three stages—unfreezing, change, and refreezing (or embedding)—if organizational transformation is to be successful.

CONCLUSIONS

This chapter has discussed the six major impacts of IT that have emerged from the research carried out by the 1990s Program. These can be focused and regrouped to correspond to the five forces in an organization shown in Figure 16.2.

Technology

IT will continue to change over the next decade at an annual rate of at least 20 to 30 percent. This will lead to greater shrinkage of time and distance effects, greater interconnectedness, and better organizational memory with greater capture of organizational "rules" (heuristics).

Individuals and Roles

People will have new tools with which to work and increasing connectivity to information and other people. Much additional training will be needed to ensure effective use of the tools and more education will be required to allow individuals to cope with the blurring of boundaries between job categories and tasks.

Structure

As the way work is performed changes, and as coordination costs drop enormously, new organizational structures become possible, as do new ways of working. Ad hoc teams will become more attractive as a way to get jobs done. IT will be a critical enabler of organizational restructuring.

Management Processes

Changes induced by IT will cause a redistribution of power and control. In addition, the shrinkage of distance and time effects can cause a speed-up in information flow. Thus new methods of planning and control will be required, as organizations design ways to cope with a different kind of "management of interdependence."

Strategy

IT changes the nature and degree of interrelatedness within an industry and organization. As a result boundaries blur and new collaborations are possible. However, IT by itself does not provide any sustainable competitive advantage. Such advantage comes from a sustained effort by line management to use IT to get closer to the customer's real needs. This constant flow of innovation and improvement requires vision and implementation skills if it is to be effective.

THE CHALLENGE OF THE 1990S

No impact from IT is yet visible in the macroeconomic data available. A very few individual firms are demonstrably better off, and there is a larger group of isolated examples of successful exploitation in particular individual functions or business units. However, on average the expected benefits are not yet visible.

One major explanation of this lack of impact lies in the enormous strength of historical precedence. The Western economies have had over half a century of doing business in certain ways. These ways are very hard to discard, and it appears to be harder yet to learn new ones.

Understanding one's organizational culture, and knowing what it means to have an innovative culture, is a key first step in a move toward an adaptive organization. This in turn seems to require innovative human resource policies that support the organization's members as they learn to cope with a changing and more competitive world. To accomplish this successfully is one of the major challenges for an organization in the decade of the 1990s.

IMPLICATIONS AND POSSIBILITIES

As organizations invest heavily in people, changes in organization structure, and new management processes, they can begin to move toward a new form of organization—the flexible organization. Its characteristics are a high level of responsiveness to external needs, increasingly effective use of all assets, employees that behave as owners and actively contribute to the goals of the organization, and management systems that provide feedback in ways that promote learning.

The results of this, already partially visible in some innovative, successful organizations, is a firm that is smaller (for the same level of output), flatter, and makes more use of ad hoc teams that are based on relevant expertise. Since IT is able to span organizational boundaries, the flexible corporation makes use of alliances and various forms of partnerships as it seeks to stay focused on its core competencies while supplementing these with other needed skills.

Such a flexible organization is a goal which is enabled by IT, a goal that is a long way from reality in many organizations. With a clearly articulated vision, a robust infrastructure, investment in human capital, and creative human resource practices it can be achieved. To achieve it is one of the challenges of the 1990s.

REFERENCES

Allen, T. J., and M. S. Scott Morton. 1991. *Information Technology and the Corporation of the 1990s: Research Studies*. New York: Oxford University Press. Forthcoming.

Benjamin, R. I., and M. S. Scott Morton. 1986. "Information Technology, Integration, and Organizational Change." Cambridge: Management in the 1990s Program working paper 86-017. (See Scott Morton, Appendix B, for a complete list of working papers.)

McGregor, D. M. 1960. *The Human Side of Enterprise*. New York: McGraw-Hill.

Scott Morton, M.S., ed. 1991. *The Corporation of the 1990s*. New York: Oxford University Press.

Zuboff, S. 1988. *In the Age of the Smart Machine: The Future of Work and Power*. New York: Basic Books.

COMMENTARY BY SARITA NARANG

I have three comments to make about why the results of new information technology are not showing up.

The first gets into American tradition and culture. If you think about some key tenets of the American value system such as freedom of choice, creativity, the value of entrepreneurs, and the "I did it my way" attitude, what you will notice is that what that has produced in terms of information technology is this: we have had a tremendous development of high-tech, high-speed information technology. Along with that, the individuals who have created these systems have been artists of a sort. As a result, there has been limited standardization.

In our company, for example, we have a billing system that was created by a set of programmers who really were artists. They created something that worked, and as additional customer requests came on, they added and patched on to the point where it is now a Winchester Mystery House, and we don't know how to effectively change the system to come up with a new one. This lack of standardization might be one of the causes why results are not showing up. We need to think of the implications of limited standardization, and what it does to the end-users. Does it turn them away from actually using the product?

The second is about the notion of time. We now have the capability to send information across the world in almost zero time. But as human beings, do we have the capability to really understand all those data, take them in, and work with them? It seems to me there are two notions of time in today's world. When I sit in front of my terminal processing my electronic mail, the few seconds that it takes to enter and get something back seem like forever. In contrast, I went back to where I grew up in Delhi a couple of years ago, and went to an ivory mart. There was an ivory carver there who was carving a magnificent piece. I asked him how long he had been carving the ivory, and he said about fifteen years. I then asked him how long it would take to complete it, and he said about seven more! People have different senses of time, and in putting together this wonderful technology, we don't consider what we can really do with it as human beings.

The last point really is, What do we need to do? We need to really look at the human element of business. We need to work on building the capability of people to manage the technology that's emerging, and also put in place some reinforcing systems such as measurements or compensation, that are in concert with the expectations we're asking of them.

What does it really take for people to change? I suggest that we look at some other systems. We may need to go into the realms of anthropology, to see what it is that causes primitive cultures to change. What are the high-leverage points that allow people to embrace change in a quicker fashion? We might look at sociology, political science, and philosophy. What comes up is the notion of dealing with technologies. If we plug in people, like changeable parts, we're using workers and technology until both are used up. Will employees really want to use the new technology that's coming up? Or might we approach employees with: "We've created this technology so that your work can be better and your quality of life improved"?

17

Organizational Change and Decision Making About New Technology

ROBERT J. THOMAS

Recent reports on the "state of manufacturing" emphasize the critical role technology can play in the achievement of strategic advantage.[1] Two of the key requirements for gaining strategic advantage through technology are speed, particularly in the movement from concept to implementation, and effectiveness or usability of the new technique or system. Unfortunately, the studies that make these claims tend to underplay the complex organizational challenges which can slow the development and introduction of new technology and, in some cases, prevent its most effective use. For example, efforts to implement new technology can be stymied by existing organizational structures, especially when technology implies changes that threaten the distribution of authority, responsibility, and status among different functions, occupations, and professional groups (Crozier, 1964; Pettigrew, 1973). However, it is important to recognize that new technology also challenges the "historical" organization, that is, the routines, vested interests, and customs that accumulate as an organization ages. Technology-induced changes in organizational structure may be difficult and even painful. But changes in the historical organization are doubly trying because they tend to encounter hidden obstacles: first, routine ways of thinking and acting, entrenched interests, and tradition permeate each moment or stage in the process of technology development and implementation (Nelson and Winter, 1982); and second, they can prevent opportunities for change from ever being recognized (Henderson and Clark, 1990; Tushman and Anderson, 1986). Such phenomena as the "not-invented-here syndrome" and technological stagnation have their roots in the historical organization. When core assumptions derived from past successes permeate present structure, they can easily constrain the range of options visible to the organization as a whole and, perhaps most important, to the parts responsible for identifying and developing new technologies.

For these reasons, any effort to understand how technology can contribute to strategic advantage must take into account the challenges posed by new technology *to the organization* and, conversely, the challenges posed by the organization *to new technology*. In this chapter, I argue that one potentially useful way to understand that reciprocal relationship is to analyze the dynamics of organizational decision making around new technology. A focus on organizational decision making forces us to examine the *entire* sequence of activities associated with technological change. Instead of attending only to the "impacts" of technology on organization, I suggest that it is essential to also investigate "where technology comes from." That is, three questions should occupy our attention:

1. How do characteristics of organizations influence the choice of problems to be solved by technology?
2. What role does the process of resource allocation play in connecting technology development to strategic business objectives?
3. How does the social organization of the production process influence the success or failure of implementation efforts?

These questions and this approach transform the problem from one that is static and outcome oriented to one that is dynamic and that creates an organic connection between process and outcome.

In the next section, I outline three models of decision making—rational actor, garbage can, and political models—and suggest what each leads us to expect to see as characteristic of choice processes around technological change. I summarize three case studies of technological change and compare them with the expectations drawn from the decision-making models. In the conclusion I discuss the implications of the case studies and the conceptual approach for organizational efforts to achieve strategic advantage through new technology.

A CONCEPTUAL FRAMEWORK

Technological change can be characterized as a set of decisions. Decisions have to be made as to how an organization's resources should be invested in equipment, training, and support for new technology and whether it is better to develop systems in-house or buy them outside (Bower, 1970; Dean, 1987). Product and product market characteristics obviously influence investment alternatives. But, equally important, organizations must also decide who or what function will be given authority and responsibility for selecting among alternatives, what criteria or goals must be satisfied to justify the allocation of resources, and how new equipment or processes are to be implemented in the technical core.

Research on decision making provides three distinctly different models that can help us analyze the process of technological change. Each offers an independent perspective on the dynamics of choice behavior which can be linked to the core research questions described earlier.

First, the *rational actor model* characterizes organizations as conscious utility maximizers. That is, organizational members begin from a set of shared objectives (e.g., profit maximization) and construct a clear preference ordering to guide their decision-making behavior (see Allison, 1971; March, 1978; Simon, 1955). In an effort to cope with the inevitable uncertainties that derive from dealing with a changing environment, organizations place a high value on acquiring information and developing analytical tools with which to construct and evaluate alternative action strategies. To the extent that they can, organizations also seek to achieve full knowledge of their internal operations, particularly those bearing upon core production technologies. In practice, the rational organization scans the environment for technological opportunities which it can incorporate in its core and evaluates those opportunities in terms of criteria that flow logically from its broad strategic objectives.

Second, the *garbage can model* argues that a theory of rational action, although not necessarily a fiction, overstates the degree to which organizations do (or even can do) the complex calculations necessary to warrant the label "rational" (Cohen, March, and Olsen, 1972). Detailed examinations of actual decision processes suggest that preferences are rarely as orderly or as well understood as the rational actor model contends (Allison, 1971); quite often, strategic objectives are vaguely worded and offer insufficient guidance in uncertain situations. By contrast, the garbage can model suggests that decision making is far more contingent, perhaps even random, because the core ingredients for choice do not necessarily all come together neatly or simultaneously. That is, decision making ought to be thought of as the convergence of four different streams: problems, solutions, participants, and choice opportunities. For example, decision making may involve a problem in search of a solution and the two may be pursued in a linear, sequential fashion; however, it is equally possible that a solution will appear without any immediate connection to a problem but may "find" a problem to which it can be attached. Likewise, the problems which attract participants' attention may not be objectively more important than problems which do not; yet the distribution of participants' interests can create the perception of greater importance. In practice, then, the garbage can model suggests that the absence of a clear preference ordering renders the decision-making process dependent on the rate and the timing of the appearance of problems, solutions, participants, and choice opportunities.

Third, the *political model* suggests that whereas broad objectives may provide a point of consensus among organizational members, other factors, including differences in perspective created by organizational structure or occupational/professional distinctions, tend to generate multiple and competing interpretations of organizational goals (Bacharach and Lawler, 1980; Bower, 1970; Pettigrew, 1973). This means that organizational decision making may not be as anarchic as the garbage can model suggests; but neither is it as ordered, predictable, and linear as the rational actor model anticipates. The key difference resides in the structure of interests and interest groups: the political model suggests that organizations will be characterized by multiple interest groups competing for influence in the determination of organizational goals and the means with which to achieve them. Under these circumstances, rational calculation of alternative actions is difficult to accomplish because evaluative tools can be undermined by agreements reached through political coalitions, negotiations, or the exercise of formal or informal power. The political model does not deny the possibility that decisions will be made in reference to objective calculations of cost and benefit; however, it does suggest that the choice of strategic direction and, by extension, the choice of evaluative criteria may themselves have more to do with power and influence than with objective information and analysis. In practice, then, this suggests that decision making around technological change may be more directly influenced by the distribution of power (e.g., who or what function has the power to choose problems and solutions) than by the "objective" circumstances facing a firm.

Comparing these models along four major dimensions of decision making in Table 17.1, we can see that the *rational actor* model suggests that firms will (1) place heavy emphasis on identifying problems that can be clearly and unambiguously linked to strategic objectives, (2) use cost/benefit criteria derived from those strategic objectives

Table 17.1 Major dimensions of decision-making models

Dimension	Model		
	Rational Actor	Garbage Can	Political
1. Link between strategy and problem identification	Strong; strategy provides clear guidance	Weak; diffuse strategy often fails to provide guidance	In between; strategy emphasized but subject to battles over interpretation
2. Link between strategy and evaluative criteria	Direct	Indirect	Direct but loose under conditions of uncertainty
3. Use of analytical tools to guide resource allocation	Heavy reliance	Used but often inadequate	Used but often manipulated
4. Structure of decision-making process	Optimized to fit nature of product and product markets	Loose and often informal	Decision-making conducted through coalitions, power brokering, bargaining

to evaluate investment alternatives, (3) rely on objective analytical tools to determine how resources ought to be allocated, and (4) structure the decision-making process to optimize the distribution of people, resources, expertise and power.

The *garbage can* model suggests that firms will (1) lack a clear set of strategic objectives and therefore will tend to identify problems and make choices based on the flow of people, problems, solutions, and choice opportunities, (2) have an unclear decision technology and therefore will rely on a number of evaluative criteria, some of which may be analytical and others of which may be intuitive, (3) allocate resources on the basis of both active decision and active indecision (e.g., allowing past budgeting rules to substitute for continuous recalculations), and (4) attempt to structure the decision-making process formally but will have great difficulty enforcing a standard set of procedures due to the uneven flow of participants, problems, solutions, and choice opportunities.

Finally, the *political* model suggests that firms will (1) emphasize agreement about broad strategic objectives but will, in practice, justify the problems identified through interest group–specific interpretations of those objectives, (2) employ cost/benefit criteria but will subject them to interpretation as well, allowing for the possibility that under conditions of uncertainty the objective criteria will play only a small role in the decision-making process, (3) apply analytical tools in support of specific interest group objectives, and (4) structure the decision-making process as a series of contests in which the content of change proposals, the choice among competing proposals, and the funding of proposals for change will be decided by coalition and bargaining.

THE RESEARCH DESIGN

To assess how closely any one (or a combination) of these models characterizes the actual process of decision making around technological change, I undertook a series of case studies in the commercial manufacturing organization of a major North American aerospace and electronics manufacturing firm over the course of three months in 1987 (see Thomas, 1991 and 1989 for a more detailed discussion). The company employs over 100,000 people worldwide and has contracts with several major North American unions.

Three recent technological changes were selected for the research. The cases were chosen to meet three general criteria: (1) to represent new and substantially different technologies being applied in three of the company's major manufacturing facilities; (2) to share certain generic similarities to technologies being developed or applied in a wide range of manufacturing industries; and (3) to vary in their overall cost and magnitude of impact (i.e., from higher cost, leading-edge systems to lower cost, incremental changes in equipment or technique). The following cases were chosen: a flexible machining system, or FMS (medium cost, leading edge); a robotized assembly cell, or RAC (higher cost, leading edge); and a new generation of computer numerical control, or CNC, machine tools (lower cost, incremental). As it turned out, each change had a distinctly different origin in the company: the FMS was a division-level effort; the RAC was a corporate initiative; and the CNC machine tools were requested by factory management.

The case studies were chosen without any intention to evaluate managerial practice or to explain the success or failure of a given instance of technological change. This is important because the research was intended to be largely exploratory in character; that is, this represents an effort to understand in detail an extraordinarily complex process. Even though it would be desirable to consider these cases typical, most readers will understand that there are no typical instances of technological change, particularly changes of the scale in which I am interested.[2]

Data collection consisted of three main activities:

1. In-depth semistructured interviews were conducted with participants in the decision-making and development processes. Initial interviews were conducted with division-level operations and research and development (R&D) managers and representatives of allied functions. Later interviews were conducted with corporate officials, line managers, union representatives, and workers. Sixty-four people were interviewed.
2. All available documentation associated with these projects was analyzed and every effort was made to corroborate dates and events from those records.
3. Field notes were kept on observations of the equipment at work and questioning the operators and others about the technology, particularly in terms of how it departed from past practices.

CASE STUDIES OF TECHNOLOGICAL CHANGE

Each case will be presented and analyzed in a format that attempts to document the chronology of events and, perhaps more important, to capture the dynamics of change, particularly as they reflect the perspectives and the influence of the different organizational actors involved. Specific attention will be paid to the three questions identified at the outset: (1) how characteristics of the organization (particularly its structure) influence the choice of problems to be solved by technological change; (2) what role resource allocation processes played in connecting technology development to strategic business objectives; and (3) how the social organization of the production process influenced implementation efforts. The cases will also be compared along these dimensions.

The Flexible Machining System

The automation of machining processes has been an area of great interest to engineers, managers, and academics for well over thirty years (Bright, 1958). However, the creation of *flexible* machining systems (or cells, referring to a series of linked machines) is a relatively new development (Jaikumar, 1986). Until recently, the complexities and high cost of sensor technology have made it uneconomic to automate a machining system unless the volume of parts being produced was high and the variability of the cuts was low. The FMS project initiated in 1980 represents a major departure from this company's prior experience and put it at or near the leading edge of such developments in industry.

The full cycle of the development effort (from concept to implementation) took a division-level manufacturing research and development team nearly four years to complete. Since the company maintained a relatively decentralized process or manufacturing R&D effort, the bulk of the FMS story involved divisional personnel and processes. However, the projected cost of the effort necessitated corporate review of the capital expenditures. Thus the process of problem identification and selection began at the divisional level but eventually involved corporate evaluation.

Problem Identification

On an annual basis, divisional executives were presented with a budget for updating, repairing, and/or replacing capital equipment and manufacturing facilities. From this budget they generated a portfolio of investments in the manufacturing process to support corporate production objectives. Interviews with divisional executives, especially the manager of operations (to whom the manufacturing R&D group reported), revealed that the corporation rarely dictated where the budgeted dollars were to be spent. This led divisional management into a process of interpreting the organizational objectives set forth by corporate management in terms of the performance criteria established for the division, the size of the budget allotted for capital equipment purchases, and the opportunities made possible (or impossible) by the amount of money available. In this instance, the operations manager said he'd offered hints to his R&D people about what he felt were some of the major production problems in the division but that interpretation and those hints were largely "echoes of the message we got from corporate"—to curb costs, increase productivity, and, in his words, "to lose heads," or reduce the amount of direct labor. In passing on the message to his staff, including but not limited to R&D, he said: "I sort of threw down the gauntlet to my people to see who would respond."

The gauntlet arrived in the form of memo sent out in June 1980, and by October a portfolio of a dozen proposals was constructed. Two proposals stood out—both in terms of their projected expense and in their focus on technologies that were unprecedented in the division. One, expressed in a terse memo from a pair of production superintendents, called for a computer-controlled system with robot carriers and fork-lifts to automate the storage and retrieval of parts in several shops. It offered little in the way of expectations for the cost of the system, the savings it might generate, or guidance as to who in the organization would take responsibility for overseeing its use. The other proposal, for a flexible machining system, came in from R&D complete with transparencies and preliminary cost justifications. The proposal carried with it a fairly dramatic statement of the problem: "Of the total time a part spends in the shop, only 5 percent is spent on a machine. For the remainder of the time, the part is either waiting for processing or is in transit from one station to the next." The proposal came close on the heels of a major machine tool show in Chicago which had featured the first fully integrated FMS, a system created by a major equipment manufacturer. Several R&D engineers had attended the exhibition and their estimate of machine usage closely resembled the phrasing that appeared in brochures extolling the virtues of the system on display.

Although divisional executives found merit in both the "big-ticket" proposals, the operations manager found the FMS more appealing on three grounds. First, the FMS promised to reorganize the system of parts handling and inventory tracking that the operations manager argued was "antiquated" and "out of control," and which served as a "screen for sloppy shop-level management." Second, the proposal claimed it would reduce the amount of direct labor in that portion of the shop by two-thirds. According to the operations manager, these two features—gaining control and "losing heads"—would help him sell the proposal to his superiors. The third appeal of the FMS coincided with a more personal objective for this manager: "I wanted to be the guy who did it first." But, in order to do it first, he argued, it had "to be done right, done cheaply, and done quietly."

Resource Allocation

However appealing the FMS proposal was in its initial form, success in the process depended heavily on the ability of R&D and divisional management to justify the FMS economically and to set the stage for its eventual implementation. With regard to economic performance (as measured in "payback," or return on investment [ROI], calculations), the critical issue was staffing. Reductions in direct labor figured promi-nently in ROI calculations and therefore in the FMS's funding chances in competition with other investment alternatives. A survey of vendors and users in other companies showed that there was no consistency in staffing practices and that the introduction of the FMS technology could generate considerable heat from workers and their unions. The R&D manager consulted staff in the industrial engineering department to come up with acceptable figures. An industrial engineer later reported, "I'm not going to tell you how we generated that ROI because it was really silly. We had a number to hit and we hit it." By making a supervisor the equivalent of the system operator and gambling that the union would not learn of the impending changes, it was possible to "finesse the ROI" and thus to anticipate the economic evaluation that would later be made by corporate financial staff.

Although the proposal had already achieved backing from operations management, in many respects the content of the proposal still remained to be determined. That is, a "problem" had been successfully identified and compellingly presented, but the future performance of the FMS would depend on both the ability and the willingness of other functional groups (e.g., quality control, scheduling, and maintenance) and production supervisors to make it work. Equally important, a fight over the proposal at this stage would undermine the effort to proceed quickly, quietly, and cheaply and sink its chances for funding later. Thus the operations manager stressed that completion of the first phase of proposal development constituted only a "set-up" for another, more critical phase: "framing" the problem and solution so as to organize the support—or placate the resistance—of those groups affected by the change. Framing proceeded in three directions, outward, downward, and upward.

Outward Framing. Several members of the project team were dispatched as emissaries to allied functions. Their prepared scripts made it clear that, despite higher level backing, the project representatives were willing to bargain with allied groups over the ultimate configuration of the FMS. As important as the bargaining, however, the presentations were designed to provide allied groups with a frame in which to pitch the projects to their own superiors. Through an iterative process of problem-finding, deal-making, and persuasive argumentation, which took the better part of a year and a half, the proposal was given final form.

Downward Framing. Since shop-level supervisors and workers had already been identified as part of the problem to be "solved" by the FMS, it is not surprising that downward framing left few openings for further refinement of the content of the proposal. Even though the operations manager instructed the project team to assemble a "user group" with a shop-level supervisor as its nominal leader, several R&D engineers complained that the exercise was futile since, as one put it bluntly, "Most of those guys have to be dragged kicking and screaming into the twentieth century." Higher level management displayed a similar kind of skeptical regard, though it was generally tempered with some compassion for the shop management's myopia: "Shop supervision had the same concern about job security that the guys operating the machines did. In other words, if you don't need as many machine operators, you don't need as many supervisors to supervise them." Neither the union nor workers in the area were included as part of the downward framing process.

Upward Framing. The operations manager's presentation to the top divisional manager and then to corporate management underscored the importance of finding a way to frame the proposal in terms of organizational objectives. When asked how he described the FMS to his bosses, he responded: "Oh, I don't try to get technical. I go on emotion as much as anything. It's got to be something that turns them on. They can visualize in their own mind that this is going to be a good idea, it's going to solve the problem—at least in the way we've set up the problem—and it'll get good savings." Since appeals to emotion are commonly not persuasive to financial staffs, the process of upward framing was not complete without supportive economic figures. As described earlier, this base has been well covered with the "finessed" ROI calculations—so well covered, in fact, that the plans to eliminate direct labor entirely meant that there would be *no* direct cost associated with the operation of the FMS. In the end, funding was approved and the FMS project was launched into its final stages.

Implementation

The FMS came "on-line" early in 1984 within budget and on schedule. However, shortly after it was formally turned over to the shop, problems began to occur. The expense of programming support and maintenance was far greater than anticipated. The union was called in by the workers whose machines had been set aside for the FMS. Without mentioning the ROI calculations that had been used to justify the machines, company representatives claimed that there were no grounds for a grievance because no one had been displaced by the new technology. The workers were reassigned and, as a result of negotiations with the union, the FMS operator would remain in the union bargaining unit. Arriving late in the game, union representatives angrily pointed to the FMS as an example of the company's policy of "keeping the union in the dark."

Within a year, the major software problems had been resolved and the FMS appeared to be an efficient system; for example, when it was operating at capacity, it cut the flow time for parts by a factor of three. The operations manager who had shepherded the project was promoted and sent to a much larger division of the company. However, despite the vigor with which economic calculations dominated the early phases of proposal formation and resource allocation and the undermining of some of the major assumptions behind those calculations in the first year of its operation, there was no postimplementation audit of the economic performance of the system.

Robotics Assembly Cell

This effort (initiated in 1982) to create a fully integrated robotics cell (robotized assembly cell, or RAC) for parts assembly offers two important points of comparison. First, and most significant, this move into robotics applications for assembly operations was initiated outside the normal divisional budgeting process. By contrast to the FMS, data collected in this case indicated that the initial development efforts were encouraged by upper levels of divisional and corporate management. Second, even though an earlier manufacturing R&D team had successfully adapted a relatively simple robot to one highly repetitive segment of the assembly process, the integrated cell concept multiplied the number and complexity of operations to be performed. Most important, it introduced a feedback dimension of much greater sophistication (and therefore of greater potential difficulty).

Problem Identification

Early intervention by high-level management strongly influenced the development process. One R&D engineer put it succinctly: "We were given a mandate from our bosses. Robotics was something that was hot and it ought to be applied in our operation." Early participants revealed two specific elements to that mandate: (1) the division was told by corporate management that money would be available to automate/robotize labor-intensive activities; and (2) the division had to figure out ways *both* to gear up for more cost competition by "getting labor out" and to dampen the fluctuation in the demand for labor. Given this stimulus, the initial R&D team began a search for portions of the assembly process that might be adaptable to robotics. They eventually settled on an especially labor-intensive subassembly whose parts volume and variety appeared to justify the use of a flexible assembly cell.

Enthusiasm for the new technology could not, however, easily bridge the gap between the competence necessary to apply the solution (once a problem had been found) and the competence available in R&D. This led the project team to be far more dependent on other departments inside the company and on external equipment vendors. As the team began to develop a proposal, it consulted two robotics manufacturers to assess the match between the problem and the solution. One vendor produced a videotape demonstrating that most of the things that R&D wanted done could be done. More important than simple confirmation, the videotape provided sufficient justification to request additional funding for the project.

However, when division-level industrial engineering was called in to provide an economic assessment of the system, questions began to arise. Industrial engineers viewed the videotape closely and discovered that at least some of the functions represented were incomplete or incorrect. Exchanges with the vendor revealed even greater uncertainties as to the effectiveness of the solution and therefore the vendor's calculations regarding its economic performance. Industrial engineering's objections opened the door to other groups, including shop management and the facilities maintenance organization; in particular, the latter group argued that other equipment was needed far more than this "exotic" solution.

Disputes about the validity of the videotape forced the manager of R&D to expand the project team to include representatives from the major functional support areas and from the shop. The expanded team worked to accommodate the conflict first by focusing on technical issues. Plans for the assembly cell were scaled down to reduce its complexity and several steps were removed from the process. After eight months of work, the R&D engineers persuaded the expanded project team that they had developed a workable plan that could achieve a reasonable return on investment.

Resource Allocation

The proposal for the revised assembly cell was submitted to a review with divisional management and then passed along to corporate staffs as part of a bundle of proposals for funding. The funding was approved without an overt discussion of the problems encountered previously. Several divisional managers made it clear in later interviews that they remained skeptical; the fact of high-level corporate support encouraged them to avoid further public dispute.

Yet once bid specifications were drawn up and distributed and three proposals came in for review, the expanded project team resuscitated the earlier debates. They failed to agree on a clearly superior alternative and split into three factions. What appeared to be the only possible compromise appeared: the contract should be let to the lowest bidder.

The system was promised for delivery in twenty-six weeks. However, the actual (and incomplete) delivery occurred sixty-six weeks later. According to R&D personnel, "Everything that could have gone wrong went wrong." The numerous problems included hardware and software failures; organizational failures (e.g., turnover in the vendor's engineering and sales ranks); economic failures (the vendor had been stretched to the limit in terms of its obligations to new and existing contracts, culminating in the firm standing at the brink of bankruptcy); and reorganization, as the vendor was acquired by another company and forced to reorder its priorities. At several points along the line, R&D engineers proposed that the vendor be bought to ensure that the work would be completed. Failing that radical a solution, R&D was forced to salvage what it could and attempt to finish the process of development.

Implementation

At the end of the case study investigation, the robotics assembly cell had been installed and R&D personnel were still struggling to make the overall system work. Problems with pieces of the system continued to foul up the whole. To make a semblance of progress, the system was scaled back to a simple set of chores. However, the chores to which it was assigned were identical to the ones that an earlier project team had devised for a very simple and (in relative terms) a very inexpensive single robot some four years earlier. To make matters worse, a year later the parts which the cell had been intended to build were redesigned as integrated units no longer requiring assembly.

Shop Programmable Machine Tools

Shop programmable machine tools (or computer numerical control, CNC) stand out as departures from the now-familiar numerical control (NC) machines, including the FMS described earlier, in that each is equipped with its own small computer which can be programmed on the shop floor by a trained operator. Operators input data on the type of work to be done, the type of material to be machined, and the tolerances required in cutting and the computer generates a program that can be stored on a floppy disk. In mid-1986, four of these new machine tools were purchased and introduced into one of the large machine shops in the company's parts fabrication division. They replaced six profile and tracing mills, which, at an average of twenty-five years old, were judged too costly to repair. The shop in which they were placed was divided into two parts: one side contained a variety of large NC machines dedicated to relatively long production runs; the other side, referred to as the "conventional side of the house," contained smaller NC and operator-controlled machine tools and was largely used to produce parts runs in smaller batches. The CNC equipment was brought into the conventional side.

Problem Identification

The CNC equipment represented a relatively modest change in scope or technological sophistication, certainly by comparison with the FMS and the RAC described earlier. However, those differences alone offer only limited clues as to why this technology was given priority by shop management or why it was deployed the way it was. Interviews with representatives of shop management and the facilities maintenance department revealed that the central attraction of the CNC machines for shop management resided in their potential to gain a measure of *control for the shop* over the work environment, especially the scheduling of jobs. A significant chunk of the work performed in the conventional side of the shop consisted in emergency orders for customers in need of out-of-stock replacement parts and new parts being produced in relatively small numbers. The unpredictable arrival of emergency orders, as well as competing demands from various sources for small production runs, led to a great deal of negotiation and juggling as well as occasional overt conflict between shop management and the internal and external customers making claims on the shop's machining capacity.

A major contributor to the tension experienced by shop management was the shop's dependence on external departments for the plans and programs necessary to meet the orders they received. In particular, the Resource Planning and the NC programming groups exercised a claim to "configuration control" that directly affected shop management's ability to accommodate the demands of its various customers. When parts were previously cut on NC equipment, the Resource Planning group supervised the documentation of revisions and directed the flow of parts and programming. If the shop acquired the machines, it would also acquire the ability to write and store its own programs and to directly influence the scheduling of its workload—short-circuiting the otherwise highly centralized system. From the viewpoint of shop management, therefore, dependence upon Resource Planning and NC programming was the problem to be solved and the CNC equipment was the solution.

Resource Allocation

Each year the shop submits to divisional management a five-year plan which prioritizes needs for equipment replacement or repair. This process routinely takes place outside the purview of R&D, and, in this division at least, it is part of an activity orchestrated by the facilities maintenance department. Prior five-year plans had included requests for replacement of several worn machine tools with newer but largely similar versions. Starting with the 1985 plan the request specified CNC equipment; however, because CNC was not well defined, it was not particularly clear that "shop programmability" was the underlying desire.

In the normal course of its duties, the facilities department helped devise the formal proposal, including calculating the payback periods for the investment. The payback figures appeared respectable, but again there was some question regarding the accuracy of the calculations. When asked how the figures were arrived at, shop managers admitted that they were "based as much on guess as on fact." To that was added the admission that there were never more than four people operating the six machines being replaced (i.e., due to the extensive downtime of the older machines). Although shop management felt they had the numbers to justify the CNC equipment, they also recognized the potential for open conflict with the Resource Planning and NC programming groups. Since premature disclosure of their plans might result in failure to achieve their objectives, shop management made a conscious effort to proceed quietly.

Downward Framing. Gaining a measure of independence from other departments may have been a major part of shop management's private goal in seeking the new machines, but the manner in which they were selected and deployed was profoundly affected by social organization at the level of the shop floor. In the words of one manager close to the process, the CNC equipment was attractive because it would "preserve and extend" the skills of machinists already in the shop. Four of the workers who ultimately came to staff the machines were consulted in advance about equipment feasibility and were later sent out for special training. The significance of this move is greater because, as other researchers have noted (see Kelley 1986; Whittaker, 1988), the machines do not presuppose a lengthy apprenticeship in the range of machining skills in order to be run adequately.

Interviews with the CNC equipment operators revealed that shop management's action was appreciated but, at the same time, it was also expected. A machinist in the area argued that shop management's closeness to the work being done in the area made them "aware of what it takes to get the most out of this equipment." That awareness, he suggested, derived in large part from the fact that several of the higher level supervisors in the shop had begun work as hourly machinists there. Whether motivated by regard for machinists' skills, commonality of experience, or desire to avoid confrontation, shop management made local conditions a significant factor in the selection and deployment of the new technology. This approach had a substantial payoff in the enthusiastic response of the area machinists: several machinists suggested that the new equipment represented a welcome challenge and reported spending lunch and break periods discussing ways to maximize the capabilities of the technology.

Upward Framing. With a "pitch" and transparencies prepared by the facilities maintenance department, shop management presented its proposal for the acquisition of four CNC machines. The presentation was concise and carefully timed to fit into an agenda of more than two dozen other presentations. According to several observers, the large number of presentations reduced the evaluation process to a review of problem statements, estimates of productivity increase, and cost projections. The CNC proposal urgently requested replacement of worn-out equipment and showed acceptable payback periods. Divisional management approved the request without discussion.

Implementation

Although the Resource Planning group was unaware of the events that led up to the acquisition of the CNC equipment, it found out soon after the equipment arrived. For many of those involved, including the R&D group, what transpired was further evidence that "the shop ought not be left to its own devices." In the words of one well-placed observer, "What you see there is a demonstration of how oriented shop management is to their own small world and to their personnel. And, obviously, they grew up in the shop. They came up through there. So, when you analyze what they tell you, you have to remember where they came from." Within six months after the equipment arrived, the aggrieved stakeholders (which by that time included Resource Planning, NC programming, and Manufacturing Engineering) began meeting to formulate a response. According to one engineer, "What we're doing now is getting the procedure changed so . . . we have a say because we're more closely associated to the prime divisions. I think in that regard we know a little bit more than the shop." In finding a means to satisfy its positional objectives, shop management attempted to sever a few of its external dependencies. What might have appeared as a straightforward process quickly generated a decidedly negative response.

DISCUSSION

These three cases of technological change defy neat encapsulation by any of the models of decision making presented at the outset. From the perspective of the rational actor model, all three cases appeared to coincide in very general ways with espoused corporate goals. That is, each certainly paid attention to the general mandate to curb costs, lose heads, and increase productivity; but none of the three cases was dominated by that link. Equally important, given the array of ways the resources could be allocated, it was not especially clear that these changes could be justified in terms of the evaluative criteria drawn directly from those goals. Information was collected in the course of each development effort but the information search was also limited. For example, the operations manager in the FMS case basically stopped looking after two big-ticket proposals came in and one seemed to fit his functional, managerial, and personal goals. Finally, uncertainties about the "true" benefits of all three solutions rendered economic evaluations questionable. Yet the knowledge that the "right" numbers were essential to a positive outcome higher up in the decision structure—coupled with the lack of a postimplementation audit—encouraged proponents to finesse the ROIs anyway.

From the perspective of the garbage can model, the three cases show that decision making is significantly influenced by the flow of problems, solutions, and participants and by the structure of the decision process. The RAC, in particular, offers a classic case of a solution in search of a problem. The iterative process of development, with multiple starts and stops and ambiguity about goals, coincides with the garbage can critique of linear, rational models. Rationality was certainly bounded (March, 1978) by the unwillingness of managers and engineers in both the FMS and the RAC cases to effectively incorporate shop-level knowledge about the context into which the equipment would be placed. Yet, as suggested earlier, the problems were chosen with goals in mind and, although these goals may not have been strongly linked to the evaluative criteria, the choices were neither haphazard nor random.

In several respects, the case histories seem to accord best with the political model. Corporate strategic objectives provided a point of consensus, yet they were sufficiently broad to allow disputes in interpretation of their meaning. Broadness in wording and decentralization of responsibility for problem finding enabled divisional managers and engineers to seek ways to achieve their own functional and personal objectives through technological change and to manipulate evaluative criteria to justify their efforts. But, even more compellingly, close examination of the way the proposals for change were formed suggests that power considerations are intimately linked to technology: the FMS offered a way to "get control" over the shop and required a coalition to be built with lateral groups quietly; the RAC set off internal border warfare, which perhaps impaired the selection of both the problem and the vendor; and, in the CNC case, shop management's effort to get control over its own affairs led it into a coalition with machine operators and, later, into a fight with those functions it sought to escape.

Yet to characterize these decision processes as merely political would overlook how the uncertainties and ambiguity associated with change, especially technological change, cause difficulties for even the most well-ordered system. As I noted at the outset, new technology challenges both the existing structure and the "historical" organization; that is, it challenges well-understood formal roles and relationships and it provokes vested interests and traditions. The latter, in particular, are commonly invisible but, as the case studies showed, when they are given the opportunity to *guide* the choice, the shaping, and the implementation of problems and solutions, they can have a powerful influence on the capacity of an organization to innovate *and* to use innovations effectively.

Thus, rather than suggest that these cases be dismissed as simple political machinations in a complex organization, I would argue that they provide a significant insight on the nature of decision making around new technology. More specifically, the case studies suggest that a distinction should be made between two spheres in decision making around new technology: the *contest over resources* and the *contest over content*. By contest over resources I mean the process of allocating resources between organizational units (e.g., operations, engineering, research and development, marketing, finance) each of which presses what it perceives to be legitimate claims to resources. By contest over content I refer to the process whereby technological change proposals are generated and selected for presentation as contenders for organizational resources. The critical contribution of this formulation resides in its expansion of the analysis of organizational decision making *beyond* the allocation of resources. Although the allocation of scarce dollars and personnel is important, an exclusive focus on resource allocation would lead us to neglect the content of the proposals themselves and, in the process, to overlook factors that may influence the choice of technological alternatives, that is, the core issues in the call for using technology to strategic advantage.

The term "contest" connotes that choices are made within a context of finite resources and that contestants are compelled to present their ideas/proposals as organizationally legitimate claims that are, despite their legitimacy, incompatible with one another. Framed this way, decision making with respect to new technology is neither the sole province of top managers nor restricted to any single moment in time (e.g., annual capital or budgetary allocation). Instead, it allows for the possibility that, for example, choices about the creation or adoption of a given technology (or, more generally, a given form of work organization) may be made at a time and in an organizational "place" (level or function) far distant from top managers and periodic resource allocation processes.

The point can be stated even more strongly: the contest over content mediates the relationship between technology and organization. There are three basic reasons behind this contention. First, the hierarchical structure of most firms—and especially large manufacturing enterprises—tends to place top decision makers at some remove from the details of the proposed technological changes or the technological alternatives discarded prior to the initiation of the contest over resources. As the case studies showed graphically, this invites change proponents to frame their proposals in the language of organizational objectives *even when they are uncertain as to whether those objectives can ever be met.* Second, when top decision makers establish performance goals or missions for subordinate units and their managers, they encourage individual managers to be especially attentive *to their own domain* and to the *implications of any change in process or technique for their ability to meet the objectives and/or fulfill the missions established for them.* Third, the division of labor below the level of top decision makers or resource allocators tends to create and reinforce bounded rationality not only with respect to organizational goals but also with respect to the relative importance of different problems to organizational functioning. In other words, discrepancies between what *is* done and what *could* or *should* be done become central to the process of problem identification and help steer the search for solutions which enable managers to satisfy the demands imposed from above. Thus the effect of hierarchy will be to render the contest over content relatively invisible to top decision makers (and therefore to observers of the contest over resources) but of great importance for individual managers in their effort to accomplish what is expected of them. And differences in pressures or missions, in fields of expertise, and therefore in models of the production process will lead to competition and conflict over the content of technology proposals.

Hierarchically imposed pressures and functional differentiation may encourage managers and engineers to eliminate obstacles to performance within work domains over which they are formally expected to exercise control, but these two factors are of limited utility in explaining which obstacles or problems are selected and how they are solved. Two insights from the case studies help clarify the situation. First, managers and engineers routinely confront a greater number of problems to be solved than they have resources or opportunities to pursue. This requires that they establish at least an implicit preference ordering to aid in the choice among problems and solutions. They are guided in this effort in part by the nature of the pressures for performance to which they are subjected and the activities in which they must engage in order to acquire resources. Second, the nature of the work context, particularly the social and political organization of work, also conditions the choice of problems, solutions, and the manner of their implementation. If, as the case studies demonstrated, a problem appears intractable or a potential solution "will not fly" in the context of the existing arrangement of management, unions, workers, or, more broadly, the social organization of work, then it is far less likely to be addressed.

How that social structure is conceived of by change proponents, how the groups that compose it are (or are not) represented in the change process, and how the social structure responds to the challenge will therefore be central factors for understanding both the process and the outcomes of the contest over content. Building from earlier arguments about the effects of hierarchy and differentiation, I would suggest that the higher the level of origin, the less likely that proposed changes will give consideration to the existing social structure of the production system. In other words, organizational, functional, and physical distance between those who are proposing the change and those who are the object of change will directly influence the perceived importance of the social structure of the production system in the contest over content. As the FMS case showed, higher level managers and technically oriented engineers will be less likely to recognize the interests of workers, unions, and lower level supervisors for several reasons: (1) their efforts to respond to hierarchically imposed pressures will orient them more to *outcomes* which alleviate those pressures than to the interests and relationships that make up the social system; (2) their ability to garner resources to undertake change (i.e., to succeed in the contest over resources) will be strongly influenced by the promise of outcomes aligned with organizational objectives (e.g., return on investment); and (3) they will be less aware of the informal agreements and customs that constitute the social structure of the production system. As the CNS case showed, lower levels of management and staff departments will, by contrast, be much more directly aware of worker, union, and supervisors' interests precisely because they are more thoroughly enmeshed in that social system. The content and scope of their proposals are thus more likely to be influenced by the complex of rules, obligations, and informal agreements that govern workplace relations (Thomas, 1991).

Failure to investigate the capacity or the willingness of a work system to change can lead to conservative outcomes where vested interests, traditions, and routines rule certain solutions out of bounds. Conversely, conscious refusals to take into account the knowledge, interests, and aspirations of those who are the object of change (much less involving them in the process of choosing technology) may be expedient for those seeking to alter existing arrangements, but they also make the process of technological change secretive and political and virtually guarantee that change will be perceived as a challenge (or threat) to the social organization of the production system.

CONCLUSION

Analysis of the case studies and their implications for how we conceptualize decision making around new technology leads to two conclusions relevant to the themes of this book:

1. Uncritical acceptance of the existing structure and the historical organization leads to a bounded contest over content and a conservative set of problems and solutions.
2. Refusal to heed the existing structure and the historical organization leads to a less restricted contest over content and a more innovative set of problems and solutions.

Whereas the former approach may make it possible to avoid overt conflict and accomplish change more smoothly, it does not prepare the organization for rapid or discontinuous shifts in technology. Thus what may be gained in effectiveness in use may be lost in speed of adaptation. And although the latter approach may make it possible to respond rapidly to external developments, it increases the probability that change will be accompanied by conflict, extensive efforts to defend the status quo, and less effective use of technology.

What is needed to achieve the optimal combination of innovativeness, speed, and effectiveness? If the case studies and the conceptual framework are any guide, three issues are important:

1. We should recognize that ambiguity, uncertainty, hierarchy, and differentiation combine to make the process of technological change political in character. However, rather than recoil in horror or clamor for evaluative measures that will "ensure" rationality, we should seek out those changes in structure, process, and management practice which enable us to better cope with uncertainty.
2. We can begin to employ analytical techniques that are better suited to political situations. Stakeholder analysis, for example, might make organizations more sensitive to the obvious and not-so-obvious participants in the process of change. One of the simplest techniques is to begin redefining the contest over content as a multiparty process which includes those immediately responsible for identifying problems *and* those who are ultimately the object of change.
3. We can recognize that there are multiple sources of information and expertise *inside* organizations that rarely are approached in the search for problems, solutions, and means to match them. The effective "coalition" between shop-level managers and workers in the CNC case offers some indication of how knowledge sources at the organization's disposal are overlooked in all but the exceptional circumstance.

NOTES

1. See, for example, Dertouzos, Solow, and Lester, *Made in America: Regaining the Productive Edge* (1989), and Hayes, Wheelwright, and Clark, *Dynamic Manufacturing* (1989).

2. However, as part of a current research effort I am engaging in comparative studies of technological change in a much larger, cross-sectional sample of manufacturing firms.

REFERENCES

Allison, G. 1971. *The Essence of Decision*. Boston: Little, Brown.

Bachrach, S., and E. J. Lawler. 1980. *Power and Politics in Organizations*. San Francisco: Jossey-Bass.

Bower, J. 1970. *Managing the Resource Allocation Process*. Boston: Harvard Business School Press.

Bright, J. R. 1958. "Does Automation Raise Skill Requirements?" *Harvard Business Review*, July–August, pp. 85–98.

Cohen, M., J. March, and J. Olsen. 1972. "A Garbage Can Model of Organizational Choice." *Administrative Science Quarterly* 17: 1–25.

Crozier, M. 1964. *The Bureaucratic Phenomenon*. Chicago: University of Chicago Press.

Davis, L., and J. C. Taylor. 1976. "Technology Effects on Job, Work and Organizational Structure." In *The Quality of Working Life*, edited by L. Davis and J. Taylor. New York: Free Press.

Dean, J., Jr. 1987. "Building the Future: The Justification Process for New Technology." In *New Technology as Organizational Innovation*, edited by J. Pennings and A. Buitendam. Cambridge, Mass.: Ballinger.

Dertouzos, M. L., R. K. Lester, and R. M. Solow. 1989. *Made in America: Regaining the Productive Edge*. Cambridge, Mass.: MIT Press.

Hayes, R., S. Wheelwright, and K. Clark. 1988. *Dynamic Manufacturing*. New York: Free Press.

Henderson, R., and K. Clark. 1990. "Architectural Innovation: The Reconfiguration of Existing Product Technologies and the Failure of Established Firms." *Administrative Science Quarterly*, 35: 9–30.

Jaikumar, R. 1986. "Postindustrial Manufacturing." *Harvard Business Review*, November–December, pp. 69–76.

Kelley, M. 1986. "Programmable Automation and the Skill Question." *Human Systems Management* 6: 223–241.

March, J. 1978. "Bounded Rationality, Ambiguity and the Engineering of Choice." *Bell Journal of Economics* 9: 587–608.

Nelson, R. R., and G. S. Winter. 1982. *An Evolutionary Theory of Economic Change*. Cambridge, Mass.: Harvard University Press.

Pettigrew, A. 1973. *The Politics of Organizational Decision-Making*. London: Tavistock.

Simon, H. 1955. "A Behavioral Model of Rational Choice." *Quarterly Journal of Economics* 69: 99–118.

Thomas, R. J. 1989. "Organizational Politics and Technological Change." MIT Sloan School of Management working paper 2035-88.

Thomas, R. J. 1991. "Technological Choice and Union-Management Cooperation." *Industrial Relations* 30, no. 2: 167–192.

Tushman, M., and P. Anderson. 1986. "Technological Discontinuities and Organizational Environments." *Administrative Science Quarterly* 31: 439–465.

Whittaker, D. H. 1988. "New Technology and Employment Relations." Unpublished Ph.D. dissertation. University of London, Imperial College.

COMMENTARY BY H. KENT BOWEN

I found this a very challenging and interesting chapter. The author makes some conclusions that I wish we could dismiss, since they are all totally against my upbringing as an engineer, and my engineering sense. There are three models—the rational model, the garbage can model, and the political model—and we see from the evidence that it is really the political model which seems to best describe how decisions were actually made. As I read the chapter, examined the evidence, and looked at my own experiences, I regret to have to admit that it is probably true. The things that get done do depend upon who asks the questions, who votes, who sets the agenda, and who sets the timetables.

Thomas argues that there is a contest for resources, and a contest for content. Those are interesting notions, particularly in light of this idea of the "zero-sum game." We would hope that there is a higher plane at play, but if we look at the realities of the past, we will see that knowledge has not been used quite appropriately, that people have not been empowered as they should have been. We see that, in fact, it just may be a zero-sum game. But one wonders whether there would not be this conflict between content and resources had there been clearer communication of the strategic intent, and if the decisions were based on real data, and whether the political model would then be the only model that works.

I yearn for a prescription—not a description of what people actually do, but a prescription for what they might do. And I wonder whether this wonderful new look at the way things get done, the nonrational model, should encourage us to do some experiments. We had one experiment on the flatter organization described which is now three or four months old, but we may need a lot more of those experiments to see if we can turn our organizations around.

Is the political model the model that works because we are in turmoil and disorganized? Is the rational model just a dream, or could it really be put into place?

Finally, I'd like to come back to the issue I keep hearing about, that managers are not as familiar with technology as they could be. My belief is that engineers are people who can frame the problem, solve the problem, and teach, and anybody that can't do all three of those things should turn in his or her engineering degree. But I would say that managers ought to be similar to engineers in that respect. If managers can be teachers, then they could teach their employees, and we could get out of the politically driven, "pretend" process, and get down to the facts and realities.

Dialogue on Using Technology
for Strategic Advantage

The discussion on the use of technology for strategic advantage paralleled a theme developed in the chapters on this topic by focusing on the organizational and human resource policies relevant to making technology work rather than on the technologies per se. A sampling of this discussion is reproduced here starting with issues related to interactions with the education and skills of the work force, followed by a discussion of the ways information technology can best be used to promote changes in organization policies, and concluding with a series of exchanges over how to make effective use of cross-functional teams in new product or process development efforts.

TECHNOLOGY AND HUMAN RESOURCE SKILLS

Derek Harvey

Marcie Tyre says the educational levels are higher in the German than the American firm and this is a key reason why the Germans seem to be better at continuously improving and making better use of technology. We have had similar experience at Mobil. Our Indonesian plant outperforms similar plants around the world because the company trains the work force from the ground up. Workers start from ground zero and actually learn basic engineering while they are employed by our company. This gives them an advantage over plants where workers lack the basic math skills needed to absorb the training required for simple engineering work.

John Paul MacDuffie

Our work suggests that education and training levels are only half the answer to gaining advantage from technology. Technological skills have to be utilized as well. For example, in our sample European workers are better educated than American workers, but, on the whole, European plants have lower productivity and quality. European plants are adhering most strongly to traditional mass production practices and don't fully utilize the skills of their educated work force. They are trying to increase the production volume by catching up and mastering the Ford model of mass production. The European plants may have an advantage over their U.S. counterparts in terms of education, but thus far the European firms have been unable to tap this resource as effectively as they might.

TECHNOLOGY AND ORGANIZATIONAL LEARNING

Glen L. Urban

The MacDuffie and Krafcik chapter concludes that new technologies or manufacturing policies alone do not automatically translate into high levels of organizational performance. Instead, the results suggest that these policies must be combined with a host of other practices. Is there some unifying theme to all these interactions? In other words, how do we take these findings and decide what to do?

John Paul MacDuffie

The various practices discussed in the chapter are important, but to be effective they must be grounded in an underlying culture that promotes problem solving and learning. There are some firms that have all the right structures and formal policies but don't have effective problem-solving processes. But where the right policies go together with effective problem solving you get the positive performance results discussed in the chapter.

Thomas A. Kochan

That leads me to a point I'd like to make about organizational learning. Given that these policies are so interrelated, how can we translate them into a learning process? We have written a teaching case based on the results of the MacDuffie and Krafcik research. The case is accompanied by a computer model derived from this research. We use this model to simulate the effects of alternative policy choices on the net present value of an investment in a new plant. The model provides an analytical device that stimulates debate among the students over *how* to implement these policies. They see the potential benefits of different policy mixes and then often ask themselves: "Well, it looks pretty clearly like if we implement the MacDuffie and Krafcik production system and invest a moderate amount in new technology, we will get the kind of economic results that we want. But can we do that in our organization? Do these approaches fit our culture? How will we get the actual problem solving that we need to make these model practices work for us?"

By combining the use of a computer model with an interactive group exercise we have been able to get our students to see how human resource issues, organizational design, technology strategies, and broader corporate strategies are interrelated. This makes for a powerful learning tool. We believe this approach could be used in actual organizations to facilitate organizational learning and change.

CAN INFORMATION TECHNOLOGY CREATE COMPETITIVE ADVANTAGE?

Robert B. McKersie

I'd like to ask what the pathways are for using information technology to achieve organizational change. Why is there so little evidence that information technology pays off? There seem to be two models. In one top management implements new information technology and then uses it to drive or force change. GM has been criticized for using its purchase of EDS in this fashion but once EDS is fully integrated it may be able to promote or drive organizational change. Another model is to let organizational changes "pull" in new information technologies. Although the authors here seem to prefer this pull model, I'm not convinced that this is the only model that will work, especially in the future as the power of information technology grows.

Michael S. Scott Morton

Sometimes we tend to use technology as a forcing function. But organizations need to be careful when they use it this way and make sure that they are using technology as an enabler, not a way of forcing some particular, narrow, or totally preconceived organizational change. Organizational change and the use of new technologies need to be motivated by a vision of what the organization is striving to become and then let the particular solutions evolve.

John M. Matson

I don't believe that information technology has been as much of a failure as it seems. It all depends on how it is used. You can either use IT for real-time information and data—actionable information, if you will—or you can use IT to collect historical data. I think we are now in the process of switching from historical to real-time data. So I believe that IT will be the driver for transforming organizations in the future and competitive advantage will come to those organizations that can handle IT effectively. I appreciate Ed Schein's analysis of the different styles CEOs have in approaching the use of IT, but I think they no longer have any choice. They may continue to have different styles, but they better recognize that IT can be and will be an enabler of significant organizational change and a source of competitive advantage.

Maurice Segall

Maybe a little historical perspective will help on this question. In the 1960s information technology was not the driver, but now it has accelerated at such a pace that there is clear, sustainable competitive advantage to that firm that gets a handle on it before its competitors. Let me give several examples.

Clearly SABRE was a driver in the airline industry. With the SABRE reservation system, American Airlines forced every other airline to use its system or to develop something comparable. If an airline doesn't now have a well-functioning reservation/yield management system, it can't survive. In this case IT drove change in the industry and forever transformed American Airlines.

In retail, having inventory on hand is absolutely necessary and stores often find themselves out of stock, particularly in fashion retailing. The Limited clothing chain has gained tremendous competitive advantage from its use of IT to solve this problem. It is by far superior at monitoring and planning how to buy, deliver, and handle merchandise. The Limited's inventory management brought it to a new level, making the company a market leader.

In banking, Bankers Trust today is the IT leader and has used its leadership position to radically change the banking industry.

There seems to be a pattern. When one or two firms become the innovators in using IT they achieve a sustainable competitive advantage. If other firms don't quickly catch up and institute their own IT system and reorganize accordingly, they are in trouble.

ORGANIZATIONAL DESIGN AND TECHNOLOGY/PRODUCT DEVELOPMENT: THE CASE OF CROSS-FUNCTIONAL TEAMS

Harold E. Edmondson

Our concept of cross-functional teams at Hewlett–Packard does not go quite as far as is perhaps described in Ancona and Caldwell's chapter. For one thing, we don't want to do in parallel all work that traditionally was done in series. The design of a product, for instance, should be clearly the job of the engineering department, but you have to have manufacturing and some marketing people there to make sure that the engineering people do a complete job, and that it gets done right the first time, rather than having to do it over again because you neglected to account for a manufacturing constraint. I think the assignment of responsibilities in parallel is a productive way to initiate this kind of change that gets around some of the problems you were considering. They are valid problems, and you need to address these changes as a new way of doing business and understand that there is a lot of education that must go on within the company, too.

The second step after establishing responsibility is to get rid of the wasted time step. The process can still happen in series, but if you strip away from each segment of the process the unnecessary wasted time, you will be much better for it. I think you can do this through cross-functional teams. For instance, if you are using a CAD system that happens to work with the CAM system you've got, you have a lot better chance of getting your prototype back in a day and a half than in the three months or three weeks that it takes today. The cross-functional teams can be responsible for carving out those wasted blocks.

The last step—and I'm not sure if we'll ever get to this, although I'd like to—is to do the work in parallel. By this I mean to get ready for the manufacturing of the product at the same time you are designing and inventing it. When I consider the way we do our R&D and engineering work, I'm really not sure if we can ever do this. Optimally, we will do away with prototypes. You don't need them, because you can simulate the product in design. We are also striving for zero ramp-up time in manufacturing. You are so confident that your engineers designed it right that you can start right up. Separately, these two things are miracles, but together they are even more.

Deborah Gladstein Ancona

A lot of time is lost in "throwing it through the transom," so even if you are not going to begin doing things in parallel immediately, you will save time when you stop doing this and change your process.

William C. Hanson

The term "cross-functional" seems to me to cause people to feel a loyalty to their own function. At Digital Equipment Corporation, we call them cross-functional teams, too. But I wonder if that does not force our employees to think too much about their functional area. Isn't there a better term for these teams?

Tapas Sen

At AT&T, we're drifting away from the term "cross-functional" and now use "business teams" since we realized that people had been overly protective of their own functions. These business teams worry not only about concept to market, but also from market to concept.

Deborah Gladstein Ancona

It is true that the term may prove to be a self-fulfilling one. But in my research I didn't see much variance as a result of the term used to describe such a group. If you have warring functions in your organization, then that's the way it is. You can't blame the teams for the way the organization views its functional areas.

So it really isn't a question of the terms you choose to use. Successful teams usually have a strong senior sponsor so they are not isolated from the rest of the organization and have political access to resources, and they have a well-developed, effective team language.

Successful teams are usually made up of people who have extensive networks and a broad range of contacts in the organization. They generally have the ability to negotiate, too, but it is the vast number of individuals across the organization that the team members know which helps them to be successful.

Derek Harvey

Core competency, no matter what the term you use to describe the team, will make the team work for your firm. You need to determine which employees in your organization have core competency, and then go about assigning these individuals to the appropriate teams.

Robert J. Tuite

Do we have the internal mechanisms within our organizations to help team members to learn and to develop core competency?

Deborah Gladstein Ancona

I think that core competency can be learned. Again, I don't think the problem is as much with the people as it is with the reward systems they operate under.

Older, more established firms can be seen as having advantages over younger, newer firms in some respects. For instance, older firms probably have a better idea of what the customer wants and expects, and probably have a more stable customer base as well. Outside that frame of reference, however, some of the companies we studied are so deeply entrenched and so inertial that they cannot change. Younger firms tend not to be as strictly defined and seem not to have as many of these problems.

Teams take on a "personality" of their own shortly after they are formed. They are defined by the answers to two questions: "What is the strategy of this team?" and "What are the tasks the organization needs the team to complete?" The nature of your team must be well suited to your expectations for what that team can accomplish.

So in the end, managers cannot force a particular style on the teams from above, they can only reward effective team performance.

Robert J. Thomas

Several people have asked what we can do to make team members behave constructively. Since this whole issue is about managing diversity, a company's teams will inevitably have conflicts about desired outcomes and perceived company goals.

Some firms create teams under the illusion that they will avoid these conflicts. But this seldom happens and if they work too hard at avoiding or ignoring the real differences in perspectives, they will defeat the purpose of bringing diverse experts together and won't be effective in solving the problems they were asked to address.

IV

REDESIGNING ORGANIZATIONAL STRUCTURES AND BOUNDARIES

18

Work, Labor, and Action:
Work Experience in a System
of Flexible Production

MICHAEL J. PIORE

Since 1987 the Institute of Labour Studies of the International Labour Organization in Geneva has been examining the changing size distribution of firms in industrial economies. At the heart of the Institute's work is a set of commissioned papers reviewing the evolution of small businesses in nine countries. The papers collect both quantitative evidence and qualitative material, drawn largely from case studies of industrial regions where small business has been particularly prominent. The papers confirm the general impression of policymakers and practitioners that in all of these countries there has been a trend, since the 1970s, toward smaller business units. This represents a reversal of the trends of earlier postwar decades, which in some countries can be traced back to the nineteenth century, toward large business units (Sengenberger and Loveman, 1987). Most surprising, however, is the finding that many small businesses—or at least the industrial districts that are constituted by them—exhibit a dynamism in the creation of new products and in the evolution of productive technology which we conventionally associated with large corporate organizations. The technical dynamism of industrial districts is especially prominent in central Italy, but it can be found in all of the countries studied.

A parallel development is occurring in the corporate sector. The belief is spreading within a number of firms that have historically been organized in a tight, vertically integrated, hierarchical structure that the decentralization of power and responsibility along lines which resemble that of the industrial district will reinvigorate them and enable them to compete more effectively in the world market. A great many of these major corporate enterprises have begun to move in this direction.

As Sabel and I argued in *The Second Industrial Divide*, conventional theories of industrial development do not provide an adequate understanding of trends of this kind (Piore and Sabel, 1984). The theory of mass production, as developed out of the work of Smith, Marx, Taylor, and Ford, fails to account for the technical dynamism of small firms in industrial districts or of the newly decentralized corporate structure. That dynamism is captured by the neoclassical competitive market model or, at least, the Austrian variant, which emphasizes the role of the innovating entrepreneur. But the importance this model places on the independence and the social isolation of the business firm and on the competitive pressures of the marketplace fails to capture the heavy emphasis upon the role of cooperation and community that one finds in every single ethnographic study of industrial districts and in the corporate enterprises which are being used by big business as models for their reforms. Sabel and I attempted to think of these developments as a turn toward the craftswork of the nineteenth century, but the kind of cooperation among individuals and firms which one observes is not really consistent with the image that craftsmanship evokes. The division of labor does not respect the old crafts jurisdictions. New jurisdictions consistent with modern technology are conceivable but not as obvious or as compelling as a meaningful analogy to a craft organization would seem to require.

This chapter is offered as a contribution toward an alternative analytical perspective which does capture the characteristics of the newly emergent forms of industrial organization. For these purposes it draws heavily upon a set of philosophical categories developed by Hannah Arendt in *The Human Condition* (1958). It tries to show not only how these categories help us to capture the salient organizational features of these districts but also the basic difference in the perspective which they suggest from that in which we conventionally view these phenomena and to indicate what that difference in perspective suggests about the problem of establishing and maintaining structures of this kind through public policy.

THE "FACTS"

The Characteristics of Industrial Districts

There is now a large and growing case study literature on industrial districts. Virtually all of these studies were conceived and executed to examine a set of expectations formed by theories of mass production and the large hierarchical corporate enterprise that has been its most characteristic institutional form. The studies are thus implicitly comparative, and they suggest a list of factors that distinguish the institutions of these districts either from the large business enterprise or from the institutions associated with the technologically stagnant small firms, which are consistent with the expectations of mass production.

At the top of the list are the two factors that we already emphasized: the technological dynamism of the districts and the combination within them of the apparently contradictory traits of competition and cooperation. Technological dynamism is the essential criterion used in picking the studies from which the list is drawn. The peculiar combination of competition and cooperation figures prominently in virtually every single study on the list, most of which were conceived independently without prior knowledge of other studies of similar areas.

A third characteristic of virtually all of the districts is that they are characterized as embedded within the "culture," the "social structure," or the "community." Many of the studies emphasize the importance of the family structure, or of the structures of political parties (particularly the Communist party in central Italy) and of the church. One French-language study of North African districts coined the term "ethnoindustrialization" to characterize the process (Bouchara, 1987). The correct English translation of ethno is anthropological, but the English term can be applied directly to many districts in the United States, which are embedded in the social structure of immigrant groups with common ethnic origins. Even the high-tech districts of silicon valley and Route 128 are described as embedded in a culture derived from the universities and the social or communal structure associated with them. Giacomo Becattini (1987) characterizes the historical emergence of industrial districts in central Italy as "a *'thickening'* of industrial and *social* interdependencies in a certain place." Another metaphor which is sometimes used is one that likens an "industrial district" to a language community: the members share a common mode of discourse about the productive process.

Fourth on a list of characteristics of industrial districts which emerges in case studies is the idea of these districts as *networks*. The term is designed to capture the contrast between relationships in an industrial district and the strict line of authority and communication in the hierarchical corporation. But it also suggests a richness of communication which escapes the directness and simplicity of the price signals in a competitive market where communication is also lateral and multidirectional.

The fifth characteristic of the industrial district studies is the spontaneous and unpredictable character of success and failure. People do not seem to be able to plan, or even to approach their problems in a fully systematic or rational (or at least controlled) way. Instead, they try a number of different things, some of which "work" and some of which do not. This is especially true of changes in the product, where the market seems to select the winners and losers. But it is also true of innovations in productive technique. The linguistic metaphor appears here again: innovation in an industrial district is like the changes in a language over time. The result of the unpredictable nature of innovation is the phenomenon that gives rise to the emphasis on the combination of competition and cooperation in the literature, where competitors are continually forced to turn around and shift to a subcontracting relationship with each other because the chances of gaining a market are simply too slim to maintain sufficient capacity to meet demand when one does. But it also gives rise to frequent bankruptcies, and the result, in a number of districts ranging from traditional garments to high-tech silicon valleys, is that bankruptcy is not considered a catastrophic event and has little impact upon an individual's reputation or capacity to engage in business in the future.

Closely connected to the spontaneity and unpredictability of the evolution of the districts is what is frequently described as the amoebalike quality of their evolution (see, especially, Imai, 1985, and Imai, Nonaka, and Takeuchi, 1985). The patterns of change in the array of products and in the techniques of production tend to evolve continuously. The set of things being done thus seems to expand and contract around the perimeter. This is often contrasted to the discontinuous leaps that occur from one generation of products to another in mass production. It is closely associated in the literature with two other traits of the process of production and innovation.

It is associated first with what Becattini calls the "bottoms-up" approach to innovation. Changes in production technology and in the product itself arise either in the shop or in collaboration with the shop. Second, the shop itself is open. Producers visit each others' firms and freely discuss their production problems with one another, comparing notes and ultimately sharing innovations. Again, we see this as an aspect of cooperation or community that seems contradictory to the competitive spirit which we also observe among these small firms. It is as if there are no trade secrets.

Public Policy

Finally, on the list of stylized facts about industrial districts, one would like to include the role of public policy in their creation and maintenance. Unfortunately, however, the material in the case studies on this question is extremely diffuse. The principal "fact" about public policy in industrial districts is that *it is too diffuse to be characterized in terms of conventional categories of analysis.* Nonetheless, one can make a series of generalizations.

The Provision of Particular Services

A first set of observations concerns the role of public authority in the provision of particular services. It is possible to draw up a list of particular services which successful industrial districts need and which are not provided by the firms themselves. This list differentiates this form of production from mass production, where the firm does provide the services, basically because it is able to capture internally an economic return for doing so. The most important of these services appears to be twofold: research and development and training and education. But in a number of areas, public or cooperative authorities also provide financial services, marketing, material purchasing services, managerial consulting services, as well as common eating facilities, medical care, and the like, which in Italy a number of small firms often share within a single industrial park. And in some areas, one or another phase of the production process in which there is a special economy of scale may be performed communally as well. A further paradox to be noted is that in the competitive market model many of these services, most particularly training but also medical services and the canteen, are paid for directly by employees, and it is not at all clear why this does not seem to happen in industrial districts.

A list of services does not, however, go very far in characterizing public policy because while services are sometimes provided by the government authority, usually at the regional or municipal level, they are all just as often provided by some other communal organization or institution: the trade union, a business association, a collective agreement between the union and an employer association, some form of cooperative venture, or, more rarely, by a religious group or a political party. Moreover, the division of labor among these different organizational forms does not have an obvious pattern. Not only does it vary from one district to another but it also varies within any given district in the sense that some of the services on the list are provided in one way and some in another.

The list of services, moreover, is in no way sufficient to guarantee the success of an area as a dynamic industrial district. The recent vogue of state and local economic development policy in the United States, for example, has succeeded in generating virtually every item on this, or any conceivable list, without anything like a comparable success in generating industrial districts. One is led to wonder whether the preoccupation with a list of functional prerequisites may not actually be a source of the problem which these policies face.

A second set of observations concerns the rules and standards of behavior governing the operation of these communities. In a sense these are laws or quasi laws. The process through which they are created and enforced and through which disputes about them are adjudicated constitutes the classic legislative, administrative, and judicial functions of government. Here again, however, the roles and the rule-making processes are not readily understood, at least insofar as we attempt to encompass them within accustomed analytical categories. Thus, for examples, virtually every study suggests that there must be a set of rules and that their chief function is to curtail the kind of exploitation among members of the community that would foreclose cooperation among them. This is generally perceived as a set of limits upon competition and phrased in terms of restraints upon wage competition, procedures for distributing demand which ensure the full employment of the communities' resources or the sharing of the burden of unemployment, and the like. Here, as in the case of community services, one can probably generate a list. Because both the services and the rules impose burdens and confer benefits upon the community as a whole, it appears that the community must have a parameter that defines membership. The definition and the maintenance of that parameter might be taken as a second functional requirement of the policy-making body.

On the other hand, the way in which these rules emerge and the level at which they are understood and enforced is not easy to delimit and understand. It is illustrated by two points that emerged in the discussion of the country reports at the ILO. First, there was a discussion of rules limiting competition and promoting cooperation. Conventional economic jargon has increasingly talked of the issues at stake here in terms of "opportunism" or "the free-rider problem." Much of academic theory is concerned with a range of institutional structures and devices which overcome the incentive of individuals to cheat the community when it is to their personal advantage to do so, even though they also have an interest in the survival of the community as a whole. A typical example is one of whether an individual will voluntarily pay union dues. The conclusion of the ILO group was that such models were not appropriate to the understanding of industrial districts because allegiance to them existed at such a profound level that problems of opportunism never arose: once the members of a community had posed the problem in those terms, it was argued, and began to look for solutions of the kind which neoclassical economic theory was increasingly seeking to offer, it was already too late; the problem had become too severe to be overcome. The extension of this point, however, seems to imply that industrial districts of this kind could be found but they could not be made, that the rules which hold them together exist at a level much more fundamental (or subconscious) than that at which public policy operates.

But here the second point made at the meeting seemed to contradict the first. Charles Sabel argued, from his study of the German textile machinery industry, that one could identify a historical process through which such communities were made and the process was more or less conscious; that it involved a chain of concrete material conflicts between the different groups and individuals which came to compose the community; and that the characteristic of each conflict was that the parties came to see in it a choice between their own immediate interest and that of the survival of the community as a whole and were led to compromise in order to preserve the community. In other words, there was in fact a series of critical rule-making episodes, where the conflict between the community and particular interests became explicit and those interests were compromised to preserve community.

The final point about the policy-making process which seems to emerge in these studies concerns the nature of the political leadership itself and its activities. Here again information is scarce but the one study that focuses on this process explicitly suggests that the major part of the leadership's time seems to be spent as mediators in disputes, a point which seems to fit with the preceding observation about conflict and compromise (Ritaine, 1987). A subsidiary observation in central Italy stresses another point: the active leadership of business organizations seems to be drawn from the ranks of small business and seems to be able to compete in terms of interest and prestige with business management as an activity, although the knowledge and skills required to perform these offices effectively would enable one to run one's own business.

HANNAH ARENDT AND THE HUMAN CONDITION: HOW MIGHT ONE ATTEMPT TO UNDERSTAND THESE STYLIZED FACTS?

Of the frameworks which have been developed for the analysis of work and production, the one that seems most useful in this regard was developed by Hannah Arendt in *The Human Condition* (1958, 1963; Young-Bruehl, 1982). Her categories of analysis are strictly speaking philosophic. They are not empirically derived, nor are they grounded in an analytical structure. On the other hand, they do have a certain empirical basis in the actual structure of the ancient Greek city-states, from which the philosophical tradition in which they are grounded derives, and they have been molded in the light of modern analytical structures, particularly those deriving from Marx, and the contemporary understanding of the evolution of work and the productive structure in modern times.

Arendt distinguishes between three modes of productive activity: labor, work, and action. Work and labor involve the relationship between man and the physical world. The distinction between them rests essentially upon the durability of the product. The product of work is permanent. It achieves a durable place in the world in the sense that it outlives the creator, the worker, and in that specific sense it achieves an independent existence. Because the product is durable, man is able to attain through work a certain kind of immortality. By contrast, labor in ancient Greece was an activity associated with the biological process and was designed to ensure basic needs or more literally human survival. By extension, therefore, it is closely associated with consumption; often it does not yield in and of itself an independently identifiable physical product. When it does, that product has only an ephemeral existence. Arendt relates this distinction to the epistemological distinction between the words *labor* and *work,* a distinction that exists, she asserts, in every language, although it has been generally lost in common usage. It continues nonetheless in certain specific usages. The original distinction, and the distinction she wants to make between the two as types of productive activity, is captured by the fact that we speak of the birth process as *labor* and of an artistic creation as a *work* of art. The words *Arbeit* and *Werk* are used in the same way in German; *travail* and *oeuvre* in French.

Arendt's third category of activity is action, which, unlike labor and work, involves a relationship among men and women. It is the activity through which individuals reveal themselves to other individuals, and through which they achieve meaning as persons. For Arendt, as for the Greeks from whom she draws her understanding, action was the most noble of the three activities. Although not synonymous with speech,

Arendt's concept of action involves a discourse among people. Speech and action depend on human plurality, "the twofold character of equality and distinction." If people were not equal, they would be completely unable to understand each other; if they were not distinct, they would need neither to speak nor to act in order to reveal themselves to each other. Thus action needs a community of equal persons to provide, as it were, the context for their actions.

Because it is through action that people define themselves as men and women, action is, for Arendt, an end in itself. But each action is also part of a process through which people come to exist in the world and give meaning to their lives. The sequence of actions of an individual over his or her life constitutes a story, and it is through that story remembered and retold in the community that individuals achieve immortality and overcome the biological processes. In this sense, action is also a means, and thus it becomes a means and an end at once.

Because actions take place within a community of differentiated persons and involve the interaction among them, because in effect one person's actions lead other persons to act in their turn, the consequences of action are unpredictable. The story of one's life which emerges in the process of action is thus not a creation but a revelation of self, a self one cannot control and which one does not even know except through action in the community.

Thus action is like work in the sense that it gives a person a kind of immortality. It is like work also in that the story of actions, which is an individual's life, has a beginning and an end. Labor, in contrast, is caught up in the biological processes and is thus a continual repetition of activity in an endless process, to produce a product that disappears in the act of creation. But action is like labor and unlike work, in that it is not a means toward an end but an end in itself, and it achieves its ultimate meaning as an element in a *process*. The notion of a strong distinction between means and ends, and of an activity which is defined clearly by an output—namely, the work that is produced—rather than in terms of a process, is peculiar to work, not to labor and not to action.

Work occurs in isolation; it is only the end product that is presented to other people. The workman works alone. Action takes place in a community of men and women. The activity of labor is often performed among other persons, but the people among whom it is performed are undifferentiated.

In ancient Greece, labor was an activity of women and slaves performed within the household; work was the activity of the craftsman and the artist; action was the political activity of the Greek citizen in the civic life of the city-state. Arendt argues that in modern times the craftsman's work has been reduced to labor through mass production. What was once politics has been reduced to technical decisions made by policymakers and carried out by bureaucrats, so that it too becomes labor. Action has disappeared as a realm of human activity. To the extent that we retain a refuge from labor in modern times, it is by divorcing contemplation from work, to which it was linked in ancient times, and making it into a separate realm of activity. We thus survive in an age of mass production by withdrawing into ourselves, cutting ourselves off from other people and losing our capacity to act.

In the notion that work has been reduced to labor through mass production, Arendt follows Marx; this assertion and its analytical implications are essentially coincident with the theory of mass production as developed by Marx and later by Taylor and Ford.

Most efforts to understand industrial districts and what Sabel and I have called flexible specialization have defined it as a return toward craft production or, in Arendt's terms, work. From this point of view, the important insight of *The Human Condition* is the third realm of action. Perhaps flexible specialization can be best understood in terms of this third realm.

INDUSTRIAL DISTRICTS AS ACTION

To accept Adam Smith's pin factory as prototypical of production in the modern age is virtually to accept the notion that economic development through mass production has been a transformation of production from work to labor.[1] Could the emergence of dynamic industrial districts imply that labor is now being transformed into action?

What might it mean to think of production as a form of action? It means that the production process becomes for the people who participate within it a public space like the political forum of ancient Greece, that they see that space as a realm in which they reveal themselves to each other as individuals. The central activity occurring in that space must, therefore, not be the creation of physical goods, or even the improvement of the instruments that are used in production, but the discourse which surrounds the production process, and the opportunity which that discourse provides for each person to reveal himself or herself as an individual to his or her interlocutors and collaborators. To say that production is basically an occasion for the discourse is not to say that people only talk to each other. The process could well—does, in fact—involve physical acts of constructing and changing instruments of production and using them to actually produce goods and services. But it is always the act of doing these in collaboration and interaction with others which is central, because that collaboration and interaction is the characteristic of action. And since production is the occasion for discourse, and it is the discourse that matters, the subject matter can move as easily toward marketing or the distribution of productive activity among firms, to compensation or to the politics of the industrial district, as toward production itself without threatening the essential quality of the process; indeed, by extending the realm of discourse, and hence action, that quality might actually be enhanced.

Certain characteristics of the districts, which otherwise appear irrelevant or even contradictory, become self-evident once production is conceived as the arena of action. The openness of the production process and of the innovations in the instruments of production becomes almost a prerequisite for their existence. If production is to serve as an arena of discourse and a stage for action, the interlocutors and the audience obviously have to be allowed to enter the theater. Similarly, the apparent ease with which people move from production to the politics of the organization of production— the fact that businessmen are so willing and able to become spokesmen for and organizers of the business community—reflects the fact that both production and politics are for them essentially the same thing.

The paradox of competition and cooperation, which is so central in every characterization of these districts, also dissolves. Both competition and cooperation lose their meaning. They are terms of reference in a model in which production is a means and the ends which it serves are the product that can be sold in the market for income. They imply a district whose members are ultimately motivated by profit. Each individual is a potential competitor because his or her sales threaten the profit which any other member can obtain. Cooperation can be understood only by the ultimate need of the individual for the help of the other members and of the district as a whole, if profit is to be earned at all. It is paradoxical because it is hard to understand how the drive for individual profit can be made consistent with the need for collaboration or, conversely, how the possibility of regular collaboration can be sustained over time in the face of the constant temptation to compete offered by the market.

But once one sees the industrial district as essentially a forum for action, it becomes clear that what is involved is not competition and cooperation at all. We have mistaken competition for the individual's attempt through action to differentiate himself or herself. What appear to be collaborators or cooperators in the market model are really interlocutors in the discourse through which the differentiation of the individual occurs and the audience for the story of a life which actions create. Or, to put it in a somewhat different way, what we have seen as cooperation is the quality of equality without which the discourse would be impossible and the differentiation achieved through it meaningless.

In much the same way, the problem of opportunism—a preoccupation that infuses the new economics of industrial organization—also dissolves. That problem too derives from the model in which activity is a means toward the end of individual income. It is generated by the conflict between one of the means (collaboration through community) and the ends, or, as Marx might have put it, between the collective nature of the means and the private nature of the ends. Thus the view that once the problem is conceived as one of opportunism it is too late to solve it takes on a new meaning. It is not that individuals in the community need to suppress opportunism at a subconscious level. It is not, in other words, an issue of internalizing social restraints. It is rather a question of how one conceives of and understands the process itself. If one conceives of production as a realm of action, the other members of the community cannot ever be dispensed with without making one's acts meaningless.

This new conception clearly forces us to rethink the idea that what is peculiar about these industrial districts is that the economic structure is embedded in the social structure. Or, rather, it suggests that we must disentangle a set of concepts which are used interchangeably in the literature: society, community, and culture. The critical concept in Arendt's view of action—and by extension the understanding of industrial districts—is the notion of a community of equals. Only within such a community can one differentiate one's self: if the other members of the community are not like one, they cannot appreciate one's differences. Arendt also believes that such a community must be relatively small, small enough so that its members can see and know each other as persons. This rules out large aggregates such as national or international communities and explains why we are looking at relatively limited and contained geographic areas. It also suggests why traditional societies, where such contained areas are relatively common, that is, relative to modern society, may be particularly hospitable to the development of such districts.

But community in this sense is not synonymous with either society or culture. The community does not necessarily coincide with the society and production does not need to be embedded within the social structure. Some social structures may be compatible with community, moreover, and others may not. The Greek social structure generated such communities and maintained them by creating a category of *citizens*, who were equal, but whom the rest of the social structure, in which individuals were very unequal, labored to sustain. But one could well imagine that in some societies, particularly some traditional societies, people were so highly differentiated that it would be impossible to create a community of equals as Arendt understands that term.

Similarly, the society or its culture (here one probably ought to speak of "culture," not "society") may or may not value *action* enough to generate a dynamic productive realm even if it is capable of sustaining a community in which action could occur.

PUBLIC POLICY

What does this ultimately suggest then about the "public policy problem" of creating and sustaining districts of this kind? It suggests that the problem may be divided into two distinct components. The first is the problem of how to generate a concern with action. The second is what would be called, in Arendt's terminology, the problem of labor.

About the first problem, very little can be said either from theory or from the case study material. But it is obvious that if one adopts the framework of analysis which we have been developing, it becomes a central problem for further study.

A good deal more can be said, analytically at least, about the second problem. Relative to the social structures of mass production, flexible specialization involves an inversion of ends and means. Whereas in mass production the production process is a means for the attainment of income, it becomes in flexible specialization an end unto itself, or rather the action which occurs in the realm of production becomes an end in itself. But since action, which gives meaning to people's lives, does not ensure survival, communities that are organized for action need some other means of ensuring survival. This is exactly the problem upon which Hannah Arendt focused in the ancient Greek city-state: in Greece, it was resolved through the *labor* of women and slaves in the private sphere. In the industrial districts of the case study literature, it is solved by selling the output of the production process in the market to obtain income, income that can in turn be converted into the means of survival. Thus these districts invert the relationship between income and production which prevails in mass production: income becomes the means and production is the end. But because it is the production that generates the income, the relationship becomes extremely complex. Production is not just an end; it is also a means to the end. The balancing of these two purposes, so to speak, of the production process becomes a central problem which the industrial district has to solve. The analytical question, thus, is, How is it possible to ensure that production serves as an effective means for the community's survival without having the members of the community become so preoccupied with income that action, which makes the community dynamic in the first place, loses its centrality in the community's value system? One can suggest some clues to how this problem might be investigated. Obviously, the conflict is lessened if the community has secure sources of income through, for example, the welfare state, a minimum of subcontracts from some large producers, or the monopoly position that the craft guilds enjoyed in the medieval world. But none of these measures would seem to completely dissolve the paradox, particularly if the community were at all conscious of the need to maintain its guarantees or became concerned with their extension.

The paradox is reinforced if one begins to think about industrial districts as a so-called policy problem because the way that policy problems present themselves, the industrial districts are of value precisely because they are technologically dynamic and generate high income. Our argument has been that they do these things by forgetting income and focusing upon production as a realm of action. And yet this implies that it is the task of the policymaker, who is interested in income, to induce the community to forsake an interest in income for action. As suggested earlier, one of the ways this seems to be solved in central Italy is that the community comes to see the process through which the institutions that ensure survival are created and maintained as a realm of action in much the same way as production is a realm of action. But whether this is a general solution to the problem—or ever could be—is doubtful. And thus, ultimately, it, like the value placed upon action in the first place, becomes a central concern of public policy and hence a focus for further research.

What does it imply for the conventional view of public policy in terms of lists of services and the intermediary institutions that provide them on the one hand or of rules that govern behavior on the other? These old issues remain, but they are transformed through this focus on action and the conflict between income and action as opposing goals for production. For example, one becomes interested in the services not only because of the functions they perform from a narrow economic viewpoint but also because of the values they instill. Do schools, for example, teach skills or do they instill in the students the value of action? And the way in which a service is provided may also become more important because of the impact it has on values than because of the service itself. If the community does not, for example, come to see the provision of these services as a realm of action, would it be better for services to be provided from outside the community by a distant state? Much the same change occurs in the issues surrounding the list of rules. Rules may still be important, but now it is not rules that manage the conflict between competition and cooperation or foreclose opportunism, for these are, as we have seen, no longer issues; instead, what is important is the value that the rules place on action and the way in which action, and not income, is rewarded and sustained.

ACKNOWLEDGMENTS

This is a condensed version of a paper originally prepared for the New Industrial Organization for the Institute of Labour Studies of the International Labour Organization. I am especially indebted to my colleagues in that endeavor, Gary Loveman and Werner Sengenberg, who have directed the project of which this is a part and discussed the results and their interpretation with me at length over the course of the last year. The chapter also benefited from the comments of my colleagues and students at the Massachusetts Institute of Technology.

NOTE

1. This leads us to see flexible specialization as a reversal of the classic development process, a movement back toward craftsmanship. But this is not surprising since the distinction which Arendt makes between them is drawn as much from classical economics as from ancient

Greece, the social structure of which, as we have just seen, hinged much more on the distinction between labor and action than on that between labor and work.

REFERENCES

Arendt, H. 1958. *The Human Condition*. Chicago: University of Chicago Press.

Arendt, H. 1963. *On Revolution*. New York: Viking Press.

Becattini, G. 1987. "Small Business Development in Italy." Paper presented at the ILO–Institute of Labour Studies project on The New Industrial Organization, Spring 1987.

Bellandi, M. 1986. "The Marshallian Industrial District." Dipartimento di Scienze Economiche, Universita degli Studi di Firenze, working paper 42.

Bouchara, M. 1987. "Industrialization Rampante en Tunisie." *Economie et Humanisme*, September.

Brusco, S. 1982. "The Emilian Model: Productive Decentralization and Social Integration." *Cambridge Journal of Economics*, no. 6, pp. 167–189.

Capecchi, V., and E. Pugliese. 1978. "Bologna Napoli: Due città a confronto." *Inchiesta*, no. 35–36, pp. 3–54.

Clark, R. 1979. *The Japanese Company*. New Haven: Yale University Press.

Foucault, M. 1979. *Discipline and Punish: The Birth of the Prison*. New York: Vintage Books.

Granne, B. 1983. *Gens du cuir . . . Gens du papier: Transformations d'Annonay depuis les années 1920*. Paris: Editors du CMRS.

Imai, K. 1985. "Network Organization and Incremental Innovation in Japan." Institute of Business Research, Hilotsubashi University, Kunitachi, Tokyo, IBR discussion paper 122.

Imai, K., I. Nonaka, and H. Takeuchi. 1985. "Managing the New Product Development Process: How Japanese Companies Learn and Unlearn." In *The Uneasy Alliance*, edited by K. B. Clark, Cambrige: Harvard Business School Press.

Lazerson, M. H. 1988. "Organizational Growth of Small Firms: An Outcome of Markets and Hierarchies." *American Sociological Review* 53 (June): 330–342.

Perulli, P. 1987. "Flexibility Strategies: Employers, Trade Unions and Local Government: The Case of Modern Industrial Districts." Paper presented at the New Technologies and Industrial Relations Conference, Boston, February 22–24, 1987.

Piore, M. J. 1989. "Corporate Reform in American Manufacturing and the Challenge to Economic Theory." MIT, Department of Economics working paper 533.

Piore, M. J., and C. Sabel. 1984. *The Second Industrial Divide*. New York: Basic Books.

Puel, H., and J. Saglio. 1979. "Concentration industrielle, mutation sociopolitique et développement urbain dans les villes moyennes: Oyonnex, formation du capital industriel et transformations urbaines." Lyons: Groupe lyonnais de sociologie industrielle.

Raveyre, M. F., and J. Saglio. 1984. "Les sytemes industriels localise: éléments pour une analyse sociologique des ensembles de P.ME industriels." *Sociologie du Travail*, no. 2, 157–176.

Ritaine, E. 1987. "Prato ou l'exaspiration de la diffusion industrielle." *Sociologie du Travail*, no. 2: 138–156.

Sengenberger, W., and G. Loveman. 1987. "Smaller Units of Employment: A Synthesis Report on Industrial Reorganisation in Industrialised Countries." International Institute for Labour Studies, New Industrial Organisation Programme, discussion paper 3.

Watanabe, S. 1970. "Entrepreneurship in Small Enterprises in Japanese Manufacturing." *International Labour Review* 102, no. 6: 531–576.

Young-Bruehl, E. 1982. *Hannah Arendt: For Love of World*. New Haven: Yale University Press.

COMMENTARY BY JAMES MAHONEY

As the chapter mentions, prior to 1970 the trend was toward larger, hierarchical organizations, especially in the industrial sector, and to some degree in the corporate sector. Since 1970, that trend has evolved into one where we see the beginning of smaller units. Piore makes reference to the technological advantages that were being achieved by the smaller industrial districts and the interdependence of the players, both from a cooperation standpoint and in terms of the feeling of community. He also notes the need for a set of rules to help distribute demand and to regulate competition and capacity.

The chapter shows that action was an opportunity for people to reveal themselves, which triggered in my mind some of the activities in our operation for talking about work in a different context. Rather than just working to gain financial rewards to help you to do other things, work can also be seen at a deeper level as a means of self-satisfaction. If we look at mass production, it was the inability to have discourse and to be able to display your efforts that resulted in a work force that withdrew into themselves and cut themselves off from other people.

I look back at the early 1970s, when we first started a movement within our own company to be vision-driven. Over the last twenty-odd years we have started to make some progress in that area, and one of the tenets we used back then was a book by E. F. Schumacker called *Small Is Beautiful*. The author said that the fundamental task was to achieve smallness within large organizations. That has been the process that we've tried to evolve, and we have begun to move from a hierarchical organization to a flatter one. Now we have local operating companies that have the authority and autonomy and responsibility to get things done. Similar to industrial districts, we have set up a system of governance made up of internal boards of directors that deal with local operations. In terms of allocating demands and capacity, we have resorted to the theory of "the commons," where we have encouraged everyone to maintain an entrepreneurial spirit yet at the same time recognize that there is a big picture to consider.

The only issue that we have that is analogous to a mass production process is in the claims part of our business. There are so many difficulties that can arise in that this is much more of a process-oriented area than other parts of the company. Interestingly, it is also the area where we had our highest turnover and level of job dissatisfaction. I find myself asking whether those people saw their jobs as simply "jobs" or if working for the company was a "profession" to them. After reading this work and getting some exposure to the information on the human condition, I was forced to ask myself whether or not there was something we could do to give employees an enhanced appreciation of what it is they are doing and to raise their commitment level. I guess one of the beauties of having a flatter organization and having the focus on learning is that we are able to tie together technology and human resources. I think we have made a pretty good beginning, but we have a lot of work left to do to expand this to the rest of the company.

19

Informal Information
Trading Between Firms

STEPHAN SCHRADER

Employees frequently exchange proprietary information informally with colleagues in other firms, including direct competitors. Such information exchange builds on reciprocity. Information is traded for other information. Employees give information in the expectation of receiving valuable information in return (Von Hippel, 1987).

This chapter[1] argues that informal information trading across firm boundaries can be in the economic interests of the involved firms, as long as employees adhere to certain guidelines with respect to what to trade and not to trade. In many situations, firms can reap an economic advantage from swapping information. In other situations, however, it might run contrary to a firm's interests to trade information with another firm. This chapter presents empirical evidence on information trading in the U.S. specialty steel and minimill industry. This evidence suggests that employees trade information so that it creates an economic benefit for the participating firms.

This finding has important consequences for the management of informal communication across organizational boundaries. It contradicts the widely shared view that firms have to implement organizational measures to prevent any outflow of valuable information that is not governed by contractual arrangements. Firms that make their boundaries impenetrable to informal information trading may prevent not only leakage of information but also its acquisition. Employees who cannot provide information will not receive information from colleagues outside the firm. Consequently, an important source of information is not available to these firms. As several studies have shown, informal interorganizational communication networks provide an effective possibility to acquire needed information (e.g., Allen, 1984; Bradbury, Jervis, Johnston, and Pearson, 1978; Czepiel, 1974).

This chapter first characterizes informal information trading. It then investigates circumstances under which information trading is economically advantageous for firms. Next, methods are described that were used to study informal information transfer in the U.S. specialty steel and minimill industry, and the results of this study are presented. The empirical evidence supports the notion that, in the industry investigated, employees trade information within the economic interests of their firms. Finally, ways in which these results might change aspects of our understanding of firm boundaries are discussed.

DESCRIPTION OF INFORMATION TRADING

Information trading refers to the informal exchange of information between employees working for different, sometimes directly competing firms. Employees provide colleagues working at other firms with technical advice in the expectation that their favors will be returned in the future. To illustrate the process, consider a medium-sized steel minimill in which a new continuous caster was installed. Unforeseen technical difficulties in the start-up process were encountered. The superintendent responsible activated his network of personal contacts by phoning a colleague who worked for a directly competing firm; the two men meet frequently at meetings of the Association of Iron and Steel Engineers. The colleague, whose firm was using the same piece of equipment, had to decide whether to provide the information requested. In this case, he provided the needed help, and the technical problem was solved swiftly. (If he had thought that providing the information would create a disadvantage for his firm, he probably would have refused the request.) The superintendent who received the help knew that he was incurring an obligation to provide similar assistance in the future. Reciprocity appears to be one of the fundamental rules governing information trading.

INFORMATION TRADING AS ECONOMIC
EXCHANGE BETWEEN FIRMS

Under what circumstances can information trading be expected to be in the economic interests of the involved firms? Von Hippel (1987) argues that, in principle, information trading could benefit firms if employees adhere to certain guidelines with respect to what they do and do not trade.

It is advantageous to trade information if the information offers "relatively little competitive advantage" (Von Hippel, 1987, p. 298). In this context, competitive advantage is defined as "the extra increment of rent which the firm can expect to garner if it does not trade the unit of proprietary know-how" (Von Hippel, 1987, p. 298; see also Carter, 1989). This extra increment of rent depends on the specific situation. The same information might offer a great competitive advantage relative to one firm, but no competitive advantage, or only a small one, relative to another. Providing this information to the first firm reduces the information provider's expected rents to a considerable extent, whereas providing the information to the second firm changes the rent expectations only slightly. Thus it is conceivable that transferring information to another firm creates little costs to the providing firm even if the information is generally of high value to the latter. In such situations, trading this information for similar information can benefit both trading partners.

Take, for example, two firms, A and B, that compete primarily on product quality. Assume firm A possesses information that could help both firms to simplify the production process but not to improve product quality. Even if A provides this information to B, A still benefits from the simplification. In other words, the rent that A expects to draw from this information is largely unaffected by whether firm B also knows the information. Transferring the information creates little costs to A.[2] Firm B, however, might benefit greatly from receiving the information, creating an obligation to reciprocate information that could benefit A in turn. Thus both firms would gain from trading this type of information. The following subsections discuss the costs and benefits of trading information in greater detail.

Cost of Transferring Information

The cost of transferring information equals the amount by which the firm's rent expectation changes if the information receiver also knows the information—everything else being equal and abstracting from the costs of the diffusion process itself. Here three factors are discussed that should influence the degree to which an information transfer affects the rent expectations of the transferring firm: (1) the degree of competition between the involved firms; (2) the availability of alternative information sources; and (3) whether the information relates to a domain in which the involved firms compete.

Degree of Competition

The rent that a firm can expect to gain from a specific unit of information is likely to remain unchanged by disclosure of the information to a noncompetitor—provided the receiving firm does not give the information to another firm that is a competitor. Cooperation between partners with diverging competitive goals allows one partner to benefit without the other partner losing (Hamel, Doz, and Prahalad, 1989).

A different situation exists if the receiving firm is a competitor. Take, for example, the disclosure of some information to a competing firm that puts the recipient in a position to improve product quality without increasing cost; assume that the two firms compete with regard to product quality. Receiving this information enables the competitor to improve its position in the marketplace. In such a situation, the rent expectations of the original owner of the information must be revised downward. This specific information no longer gives its owner a competitive advantage relative to the information receiver.

Under certain circumstances, however, providing information to a competitor means little or no cost for the information provider, especially if the inquirer could have received similar information without great difficulty from another source, or if the transferred information does not relate to a dimension on which the firms compete with each other.

Availability of Alternative Information Sources

The degree to which a transfer changes the rent expectations of the transferring firm partly depends on the time span for which the information would have given its original owner a know-how advantage relative to the inquirer (Porter, 1983). The shorter this time span, the smaller the change in value of the information caused by a transfer, all else being equal.

Often, proprietary know-how can be independently developed by any competing firm that needs it, given an appropriate expenditure of time and resources. In a survey of 650 high-level R&D managers representing 130 lines of business, most of the respondents indicated that other firms can duplicate typical unpatented process and product innovations within a reasonable time span, and at costs considerably less than those of the innovator (Levin, Klevorick, Nelson, and Winter, 1987, p. 809). In addition, similar know-how frequently can be obtained from other sources—for example, from suppliers or from other firms in the same industry. In these cases, the competitive advantage caused by an informational lead would probably be lost even if the firm had refused to transfer the information.

Consequently, if the receiving firm could easily develop the same or similar know-how internally or if similar information is available to the receiving firm from other sources, transferring information reduces a firm's rent expectations only slightly.

Impact of Information on Domains of Competitive Importance

Transferring information tends not to alter the competitive relationship between the information-providing and the information-receiving firm, assuming the information relates to a domain in which the firms do not compete with each other (Hamel et al., 1989). Thus handing over such information creates little or no costs for the information-providing firm; the firm's competitiveness is not diminished. Nevertheless, obtaining this information may benefit the receiving firm considerably. In the steel industry, transferring information that helps firms improve product quality (e.g., how to control specific parameters of the melting process so as to reduce the occurrence of lead strings in the rolled steel) tends to be more damaging for a firm's competitive position, relative to the information receiver, than is transferring information that leads to a reduction in production cost. Why should this be? Steel firms compete primarily in three dimensions: product quality, price, and service (Barnett and Crandall, 1986). Supplying a competitor with quality-related information helps that competitor improve on a dimension of competition—product quality—and is therefore disadvantageous for the transferring firm. By enabling a competitor to produce and sell a better product, the transferring firm puts its own competitive position at risk.

On the other hand, transferring cost-related information (e.g., how to improve lubrication of the fabric bearings of a rolling mill so that their pass life increases) is less likely to be disadvantageous. In the steel industry, prices are set rather independently of marginal costs. The large proportion of fixed costs and the high barriers to exit are responsible for the fact that it is often more economical for firms to sell their products below cost than to leave expensive capacity unutilized. Thus information leading to cost savings will contribute to the improvement of a firm's profit margin but will not necessarily lead to a price decrease. A notable exception is radical cost savings large enough to allow strategic price cuts that cannot be matched by competitors (Porter, 1985). Therefore, a transfer of nonradical cost-saving information is not likely to create a disadvantage for the transferring firm, provided the receiving firm does not use the additional profit to finance measures detrimental to the transferring firm that would not have been financed otherwise.

Benefit of Transferring Information

Empirical evidence by Von Hippel (1987) and Rogers (1982) suggests that transferring information is part of exchange relationships grounded in reciprocity. In exchange relationships, providing another party with a favor obliges that party to reciprocate in order to maintain the balance of benefits and contributions, even without an explicit agreement (e.g., Levine and White, 1961; Macaulay, 1963; Miller and Berg, 1984).

Several studies offer support for the strength and extent of the quid pro quo norm (see the overviews presented in Gross and McMullen, 1982, and Miller and Berg, 1984).

The literature proposes, first, that receiving a benefit is likely to increase the probability that the receiver will provide a similar benefit in the future. Second, the literature suggests that the change in the receiver's willingness to provide a benefit depends on the value of the benefit that he or she received (e.g., Adams, 1965; Blau, 1964; Clark, 1985; Emerson, 1976; Mills and Clark, 1982; Walster, Berscheid, and Walster, 1976). Thus if informal information transfers constitute exchange relationships, then the benefit of providing information depends on the degree to which giving help increases the chance of receiving help. This in turn depends on the value of the provided information to the receiver: the more important the information to the receiver, the stronger his or her obligation to reciprocate, and the greater the future benefit for the information provider.

Nonetheless, even if the information receiver is eager to reciprocate, this cooperation is without benefit to the information provider if the former cannot return information of relevance to the latter. This leads Carter (1989, p. 157) to propose that a trader might "favor partners that promise the most useful information in return for his own." Consequently, it should be more in the interest of a firm to exchange information with another firm at the forefront of technological development than to maintain an information-trading relationship with a firm barely managing to keep up with technological advances.

Table 19.1, which summarizes the preceding discussion, lists the variables expected to influence an employee's decision about whether to provide information to a colleague in another firm, assuming that the employee trades information according to the economic interest of his or her firm. The empirical analysis presented in the next two sections tests whether employees orient their information-exchange behavior along the variables discussed.

Table 19.1 Hypothesized influence of discussed variables on employees' decision whether to transfer information to colleagues from other firms

Variables	Likelihood of Transfer of Requested Information if Variable Takes on High Value
INFLUENCING THE COSTS OF TRANSFERRING INFORMATION	
Degree of competition between information-providing firm and information-receiving firm	Less likely
Availability of alternative information sources to information receiver	More likely
Information's impact on domains of high competitive importance	Less likely
INFLUENCING THE BENEFITS OF TRANSFERRING INFORMATION	
Likelihood that information receiver will reciprocate information	More likely
Value of transferred information to information receiver	More likely
Technical expertise of information receiver	More likely

Source: Schrader (1991).

METHODS

The empirical investigation concentrates on the U.S. specialty steel and minimill industry, a segment chosen because it is characterized by considerable nonradical technical advance. An example of the technological advance in the minimill industry is provided by a 70 percent reduction in the average tap-to-tap time from 1975 to 1985. (The tap-to-tap time is a parameter describing the efficiency of the melting process.) During this same period, average worker-hours per ton fell by 47 percent (Barnett and Crandall, 1986, p. 57). This progress, however, is not due to radical technical change. The basics of the underlying technologies (electric arc furnace, continuous caster, rolling mill) remained unchanged during those ten years. Rather, the continuous improvement of existing technology was the key to the industry's progress (Barnett and Crandall, 1986). Consequently, information about small improvements, which is often transferred informally, has a significant impact on firm performance in this industry.

Data Collection

A mail questionnaire was used to learn about employees' decisions to transfer information to colleagues in other firms and to test whether informal information transfers are part of information-trading relationships.

The questionnaire was sent to 477 technical managers, all of those listed under one of the 127 specialty steel or minimill companies appearing in the *1986 Directory of Iron and Steel Plants*[3] and identified by their job title as being directly responsible for technical matters and not belonging to top management. Typical job titles are plant manager, superintendent of the rolling mill, superintendent of the meltshop, and chief engineer.

In the questionnaire, half the employees surveyed were asked to think back to the last instance in the past year when someone from another steel firm had requested technical information and they had provided the desired information (version 1 of the questionnaire: transfer situation). The other half of the respondents were asked to think back to the last instance when they had been asked for information and had not provided it (version 2: no-transfer situation). Both situations were to be described in terms of the same variables, using primarily seven-point scales.

The idea behind this approach was to collect two samples, one consisting of cases in which employees are willing to transfer information; the other, of cases in which employees refuse to transfer information. Using these two samples, transfer and no-transfer situations could be compared systematically, and the variables that help discriminate between transfer and no-transfer situations could be identified.

The variables that were used for characterizing the specific information-transfer decision can be divided into two groups: variables describing the context of a transfer decision (e.g., characteristics of the information seeker and of the firm he is working for; attributes of the relationship between the information owner and the information seeker) and variables relating to the desired information itself.

The questionnaire was mailed to the 477 selected managers in August 1987. In twenty-nine cases, the employee could not be reached or had retired. Of the 448 employees reached, 297 returned the questionnaire. Three questionnaires had to be discarded, either because most questions were not answered or because the answers contained obvious inconsistencies. The remaining 294 questionnaires yielded a response rate of 65.6 percent (64.7 percent for version 1, transfer situation; 66.5 percent for version 2, no-transfer situation). Of the 127 firms included in the sample, 103 were represented by the returned questionnaires. To test whether the employees who received and returned version 1 of the questionnaire were significantly different from those who received and returned version 2, the two groups were compared in regard to demographic and firm-specific characteristics. No significant difference could be detected.

Due to the specific design of the questionnaire, not all respondents had to answer the part that refers to the employee's most recent information-transfer decision: forty-four respondents could not answer this part because they had not been asked for information during the year before the survey; forty-three of the respondents who received a questionnaire that inquired about a rejection of an information request indicated that they had not rejected any requests; three of the employees who were asked to describe a transfer situation indicated that they had rejected all information inquiries by colleagues from other firms. Altogether the survey yielded 204 characterizations of information requests, of which 119 referred to transfer situations and eighty-five to no-transfer situations.

Determining Underlying Factors

Several variables measured by the questionnaire correlate strongly, opening up the possibility of reducing the number of variables and detecting underlying dimensions by factor analysis of the data. Eight factors emerged from this analysis. In all cases, the factor loadings are distinct and can be interpreted meaningfully. Each of these factors represents a specific dimension either of the context of transfer decisions or of employees' perceptions of characteristics of requested information. Table 19.2 describes the eight factors. (The factor loadings are given in Schrader, 1991.)

None of the variables that characterize the context of the transfer decision relates directly to the degree of competition between the two firms. The degree of competition is operationalized by combining two variables. It is assumed that firms that sell similar products to the same customer group are likely to be direct competitors, whereas firms that sell different products to different customer groups are not direct competitors. Thus the corresponding variables from factor 2 and factor 4 can be used to calculate an indicator for the degree of competition (for details, see Schrader, 1990). Employees were not asked directly whether the inquirer's firm was a direct competitor since the pretest of the questionnaire had shown that this would have decreased the acceptance of the questionnaire to a considerable extent, possibly due to employees' perceptions of socially desirable behavior.

The following analysis includes one further variable. As discussed, information transfers are expected to be part of reciprocal relationships. Therefore, the surveyed employees were asked to indicate to what extent they expected their transfer decision to change the inquirer's willingness to provide information to them in the future—that is, the extent to which they expected their specific information-transfer decision to

Table 19.2 Factors derived from analysis of 204 transfer decisions

Factor	Content
CONTEXT OF TRANSFER DECISION	
Strength of relationship or friendship	Describes aspects of the relationship between the information owner and the person inquiring for information; takes on a high value if the two employees have exchanged information in the past and if a close personal relationship exists between them
Similarity of market segment	Indicates extent to which the two firms sell their products in the same regionally defined markets and to the same customer groups
Technological knowledge of inquiring party	Takes on high value if the information owner perceives the inquirer's firm as one of the technological leaders in the industry and inquirer as having large degree of technological expertise
Similarity of technology	Describes extent to which the two firms employ comparable production technologies and produce similar products
CHARACTERISTICS OF REQUESTED INFORMATION	
Importance to deciding party	Describes information owner's perception of the importance of the requested information to himself and to his firm
Importance of information to inquiring party	Describes information owner's perception of the importance of the requested information to the inquirer personally and to his firm
Degree to which information relates to domains of low competitive importance	Indicates the extent to which requested information relates to domains that might be important for a firm's overall performance, but which are not domains in which the firms compete fiercely with each other
Availability of alternative information sources	Reflects whether the information owner thinks that other alternatives are open to the inquirer to cover his informational needs; alternatives are developing a similar information internally or acquiring a comparable information from other external sources

increase their chance of receiving information (or, if they had refused to provide the requested information, the extent to which they expected the transfer to decrease their chance of receiving information).

Contrasting Transfer Versus No-Transfer Decisions

Probit analysis was used to contrast circumstances under which employees were willing to provide requested information with those under which no informal information transfer took place. The probit analysis included as independent variables all factors described earlier (except the two factors that jointly constitute the indicator for the degree of competition), as well as the indicator for the degree of competition and the measure of the expected change in the inquirer's willingness to reciprocate information (for further details, see Schrader, 1991). The probit analysis helps to determine which of these factors and variables influence the information-transfer decisions of employees. Table 19.3 summarizes the results.

Table 19.3 Observed influences on employees' decision whether to transfer information to colleagues from other firms

Independent Variable/Factor	Likelihood of Transfer of Requested Information if Variable/Factor Takes on High Value
Intensity of competition	Less likely
Availability of alternative information sources	More likely
Importance of information to deciding party	Less likely
Degree to which information relates to domains of low competitive importance	More likely[a]
Expected change of inquirer's willingness to reciprocate information	More likely
Importance of information to inquiring party	No significant impact
Technological knowledge of inquiring party	More likely
Strength of relationship or friendship	No significant impact

[a]This factor has a significant impact only if a modified data set that includes estimates of missing values is used (Schrader, 1991).

RESULTS

The hypothesis was put forward earlier that a manager's information-transfer decision is strongly influenced by the perceived costs and benefits that a transfer creates for his or her firm—costs through reducing the rent that the firm can expect to draw from the innovation, and benefits through increasing the chance of receiving valuable information in return. As shown in the following subsection, the data strongly support this proposition.

Information Trading

The decision patterns observed (Table 19.3) provide substantial evidence for the general hypothesis that technical employees trade information. The surveyed employees appear to exchange information in such a way that a transfer creates few costs but potentially high benefits for the firms involved. Information is provided in the expectation that this will significantly increase the likelihood of receiving valuable information in return. The expected change in the inquirer's willingness to provide information, as well as the technological knowledge of the inquiring party, discriminate strongly and positively between transfer and no-transfer situations. At the same time, employees also take into account the variables influencing the costs of transferring information.

Cost of Trading Information

It was argued earlier that transferring information creates high costs for the transferring firm if the information is provided to a competitor, if it relates to a dimension on which the involved firms compete, and if no other sources for the same or similar information are available to the inquirer. Under such circumstances, transferring information leads to a considerable competitive backlash. If the hypothesis that employees trade information within the economic interest of their firms is correct, then employees should be less inclined (ceteris paribus) to exchange information in situations in which transferring information is likely to generate considerable economic costs.

This hypothesis is supported by the data. The likelihood of an information transfer significantly decreases if the firms are direct competitors, if the information is not easily available from alternative information sources, and if the information is of high importance to the firm of the employee who is making the transfer decision. Also, if information relates to domains of low competitive importance, then apparently it is more likely to be transferred. The coefficient for the last factor, however, is significant only if a data set including estimates of missing values is used.

The intensity of competition between the involved firms is one of the variables that discriminate strongly between providing and not providing information. Nevertheless, in 29.4 percent of the situations in which information was transferred, the information-receiving firm and the information-providing firm are likely to be competitors.[4] Keep in mind that handing information to a competitor does not necessarily harm the information-providing firm. For example, if information does not relate to a domain in which the firms compete or if the inquirer easily can obtain similar information from another source, then transferring this information—even to a competitor—does not put the transferring firm at a disadvantage. The results show that employees decide accordingly.

To sum up, the data support the hypothesis that the decision to provide requested information is strongly influenced by the economic costs for the transferring firm. Information transfer is more likely to occur the less the transfer reduces the rent that the transferring firm is expected to derive from the information.

Benefit of Trading Information

It was proposed earlier that informal information transfer creates not only costs but also economic benefits for the transferring firm, benefits in the form of receiving valuable information in return. Information trading yields a net gain for the firm if the benefits outweigh the costs. The probit analysis (Table 19.3) strongly supports the proposition that information is provided in circumstances in which it is expected that considerable benefits for the providing firm will be generated.

Transferring information considerably increases the provider's chance to obtain information from the receiver. In 72.6 percent of the transfer cases, employees assumed that providing information would improve their chance of receiving information from the inquirer. In 32 percent of the no-transfer situations, they expected that the refusal to transfer would reduce their chance to receive information.

It has been hypothesized that, because the receiver's obligation to reciprocate is expected to increase with the value received, information is more likely to be exchanged if it is of high importance to the information-receiving party. The probit analysis, however, does not detect a direct effect of the importance of the information for the receiving party on the transfer decision. A significant relationship between the importance of the information to the receiving party and the expected change of the receiver's willingness to provide information in the future, however, can be reported. Employees who transferred information that they considered important to the inquiring party expected that this would considerably improve their chance of receiving information more often than did employees who transferred information they considered to be of low importance to the receiver (Table 19.4).

Table 19.4   Importance of the transferred information and expected change of the inquirer's willingness to reciprocate (percentage of cases per group)

Importance of Transferred Information to Inquiring Party[a]	Expected Change of Inquirer's Willingness to Provide Information (%)[b]				
	0	1	2	3	Σ
Low (n = 58)	31.0	20.7	27.6	20.7	100% (n=58)
High (n = 59)	25.4	5.1	39.0	30.5	100% (n=59)

Source: Schrader (1991).

[a]Information is classified as being of low importance to the inquiring party if the value of the relating factor is less than the median. A value equal to or above the median serves as an indicator for high importance. The data are from the 119 descriptions of transfer situations. Two of these cases had to be eliminated due to missing values.

[b]A 0 indicates no change; 3 indicates the inquirer is much more likely to provide information.

Chi-square = 8.121; $p < .05$.

Even if the inquirer is eager to reciprocate, his or her cooperativeness remains without economic value if no relevant information exists that could be returned. Therefore, as hypothesized previously, employees should be more inclined to exchange information with a colleague whose firm controls a state-of-the-art know-how pool and who is knowledgeable himself or herself than with someone who is barely keeping up with technological change. This hypothesis is strongly supported by the data. The probability of an information exchange increases significantly if the inquiring party is known to control considerable technical knowledge (Table 19.3).

In summary, the data provide strong evidence for the hypothesis that information is traded with the expectation of receiving economically valuable information in return. Information is transferred when it is expected that doing so creates an economic benefit for the transferring firm.

The Impact of Friendship

Several studies have demonstrated the importance of friendship and personal trust for the disclosure of information (Berg and Clark, 1986; Miell and Duck, 1986; Sitkin, 1986). These studies, however, do not discuss whether friendship fosters information transfer because it encourages asking for information or because it encourages providing information.

The factor analysis yielded one factor—strength of the relationship/friendship—that describes the personal relationship between inquirer and information owner and that characterizes their information transfer history. No significant impact of this factor on the probability that a specific information is transferred can be detected (Table 19.3). Apparently, in making the decision to provide requested information, whether the inquirer is a friend is of secondary importance. This finding does not necessarily contradict other studies that have found friendship to be an important characteristics of information-transfer networks. Friendship may define the network within which information is exchanged. Gross and McMullen (1982), for example, argue that asking a friend for help creates fewer psychological costs than asking a stranger. Once the network is established and once a person has created the need for a transfer decision by asking a colleague for information, however, friendship has little impact on the transfer decision.

Information Trading and Firm Performance

The data presented so far support the notion that employees trade technical information within the economic interest of their firms—as they perceive it—and that friendship plays a secondary role in the decision to transfer specific information. The question that must now be addressed is whether informal information trading creates an observable benefit for the firms.

The managers surveyed were asked to indicate the general propensity of their firms to participate in the informal exchange of technical information. In addition, they were asked to rate the economic success of their firms in comparison to the industry average by using a seven-point scale, with 1 meaning "well below average" and 7 "well above average" economic performance.[5]

The data suggest a connection between the inclination of a firm to participate in informal information trading and its economic performance. The degree to which a firm's employees participate in the informal information exchange correlates positively ($r = .19$, $p < .001$) with the firm's economic success as evaluated by the surveyed employee. Managers who worked for firms that did not participate in the informal information exchange indicated, on average, a significantly lower economic performance for their firms (mean $= 4.7$) than did managers whose firms actively participated in this kind of information transfer (mean $= 5.8$; significance of mean difference, $p < .001$).

In summary, the survey offers suggestive evidence for a positive link between the economic performance of a firm and the participation of its employees in informal information trading. It should be noted that the survey itself cannot determine cause and effect. Since employees' information-exchange behavior appears to be oriented toward their firms' benefit, however, it can be postulated that participation in informal information transfer drives economic performance of these firms.

DISCUSSION

The observed decisions reveal information-transfer patterns that strongly support the hypothesis that employees trade information and that information trading is desirable from a firm's point of view. Employees are less inclined to provide a specific piece of information if doing so is likely to considerably hurt their firm's ability to capture economic rents from the information; they are more willing to provide information if they can expect to receive valuable information in return. Factors like friendship or duration of the relationship with the inquirer appear to be of secondary importance for the decision to provide a specific unit of information. (Such factors, however, may be significant for defining the network of personal contacts within which information is exchanged.) In addition, the evidence suggests a positive link between informal information trading and a firm's economic performance.

One important limitation of this study must be pointed out. All empirical data are drawn from one industry, the U.S. specialty steel and minimill industry. It remains untested whether the close alignment of managers' and firms' interests that apparently exists in the steel industry can also be found in other industries. Different information-trading patterns may be expected in those industries characterized by high job mobility and difficulties linking employees' contributions to the performance of their firms (Rogers, 1982). A pilot study in the aerospace industry, however, suggests that, even in such an industry, information-trading patterns similar to those found in the steel industry can be observed (Gavrilis, 1989).

Several interviewees pointed out that the inclination to cooperate and to participate in informal information trading has increased considerably with the entrance of new competitors, whether foreign competitors or domestic ones coming from outside the traditional boundaries of the industry. The managers argued that foreign competition forces them to innovate constantly in order to remain competitive. Under such circumstances, they asserted, firms cannot afford not to cooperate; they must use available know-how efficiently. Informal information trading can contribute to this goal.

Many circumstances are conceivable under which an information exchange is in the economic interest of the involved firms, yet under which formal transfer mechanisms are ruled out because they are too expensive. Unlike formal information transfer, the informal transfer entails limited transaction costs. In particular, contracting costs and control and enforcement costs are insignificant in comparison to the formal transfer: no lengthy negotiations are required and no costly legal institutions are necessary to monitor the information exchange. These simplifications are made possible at the expense of legal mechanisms that could be used to force the trading party into fulfilling its obligations. Fortunately, other, less costly control mechanisms do exist. For example, news about uncooperative behavior of a player appears to travel fast within the surveyed industry. Thus by not cooperating in one relationship, a player puts several relationships in jeopardy—a strong mechanism for enforcing cooperation.

Information leading to incremental improvements is especially likely to fall into the category of information not suitable for formal transfer agreements. Firms that do not use informal information trading for acquiring this kind of information are sacrificing an important information source. Several empirical investigations have shown that incremental improvements can be very important to a firm's economic success (Enos, 1962; Gold, 1979; Hollander, 1965).

The notion of information trading challenges some aspects of our traditional beliefs regarding the desirable permeability of firm boundaries. It is a widely shared view that firms have to seal or at least control their boundaries to prevent information leakage. Measures are advocated that restrain employees from transferring information informally across organizational boundaries (e.g., Hamel et al., 1989). Firms that make their boundaries impenetrable to informal information transfer, however, may prevent not only leakage of information but also its acquisition.

Opening a firm's boundaries to allow information trading can create economic benefits, though entailing the risk that employees exchange information against the firm's interests. As shown here, information trading is not always desirable. It is advantageous if employees are aware of when to exchange and when to hide information and if they act accordingly. Conceivably, several mechanisms can be employed to induce desirable information-trading behavior. A fine-grained rule system is one possibility. Such a system, however, is likely to be inflexible, difficult to keep updated, and potentially demotivating. In the context of this study, no firm was encountered that had established such a system. Another possibility is to (1) provide employees with an incentive scheme that motivates them to act in the interests of the firm and (2) enable them to make well-informed decisions. A need to improve ongoing practices in the management of technically oriented employees appears necessary, especially with regard to the second point. Data from Germany show that middle-level managers who are responsible for technical areas, e.g., R&D managers, believe that they are not well informed about their firm's goals and strategies (Pritzl, 1987). This entails the possibility that due to insufficient managerial information, some information is traded against a firm's interests, even if the individual manager intends differently.

Information trading creates incentives to innovate. Internally generated technical knowledge not only is used within a firm, but also is bartered for further knowledge— as long as the benefits outweigh the costs. A firm that does not keep up with technical change loses its attractiveness as a trading partner. Thus reducing internal technology development at the same time inhibits the ability of a firm to acquire information externally. Internal technology development and information trading are not substitutes, but rather complements.

NOTES

1. This chapter draws on "Informal Technology Transfer Between Firms: Cooperation Through Information Trading." *Research Policy* 20 (1991), by the same author.

2. Transferring this information creates costs for firm A only if the resulting costs savings induce B to finance measures that affect A inversely and that would not have been financed otherwise.

3. The directory, considered by industry experts to be a comprehensive source, lists specialty steel companies, minimills, and integrated steel companies by type, providing the names and titles of top- and middle-level managers in each firm.

4. In these situations, the indicator of competition, ranging from 1 to 7, is equal to or larger than 5. That is, the firms sell similar products to the same customer group.

5. This performance measure was used because several of the firms surveyed do not publicize financial information. Because in 244 of the 294 cases, at least two respondents belonged to the same firm, the reliability of the performance measure can be determined through an analysis of variance with firm success as a dependent variable and firm as the independent variable. The resulting coefficient of determination $r^2 = .59$ ($p < .001$).

REFERENCES

Adams, J. 1965. "Inequity in Social Exchange." In *Advances in Experimental Social Psychology*, edited by L. Berkowitz. New York: Academic Press.

Allen, T. J. 1984. *Managing the Flow of Technology: Technology Transfer and the Dissemination of Technological Information Within the R&D Organization*. Cambridge: MIT Press.

Barnett, D. F., and R. W. Crandall. 1986. *Up from the Ashes: The Rise of the Steel Minimill in the United States*. Washington, D.C.: The Brookings Institution.

Berg, J. H., and M. S. Clark. 1986. "Differences in Social Exchange Between Intimate and Other Relationships: Gradually Evolving or Quickly Apparent?" In *Friendship and Social Interaction*, edited by V. J. Derlega and B. Winstead. New York: Springer.

Blau, P. M. 1964. *Exchange and Power in Social Life*. New York: Wiley.

Bradbury, F., P. Jervis, R. Johnston, and A. Pearson. 1978. *Transfer Processes in Technical Change*. Alphen aan den Rijn, The Netherlands: Sijthoff & Noordhoff.

Carter, A. P. 1989. "Knowhow Trading as Economic Exchange." *Research Policy* 18: 155–163.

Clark, M. S. 1985. "Implications of Relationship Type for Understanding Compatibility." In *Compatible and Incompatible Relationships*, edited by W. Ickes. New York: Springer.

Czepiel, J. A. 1974. "Word-of-Mouth Processes in the Diffusion of a Major Technological Innovation." *Journal of Marketing Research* 11: 172–180.

Emerson, R. M. 1976. "Social Exchange Theory." *Annual Review of Sociology* 2: 335–362.

Enos, J. L. 1962. *Petroleum Progress and Profits: A History of Process Innovation*. Cambridge: MIT Press.

Gavrilis, T. G. 1989. Information Trading in the Aerospace Industry. Unpublished masters thesis. Sloan School of Management, MIT.

Gold, B. 1979. *Productivity, Technology and Capital: Economic Analysis, Managerial Strategies, and Government Policies*. Lexington, Mass.: Lexington Books.

Gross, A. E., and P. A. McMullen. 1982. "The Help-Seeking Process." In *Cooperation and Helping Behavior*, edited by V. J. Derlega and J. Grezlak. New York: Academic Press.

Hamel, G., Y. L. Doz, and C. K. Prahalad. 1989. "Collaborate with Your Competitors—And Win." *Harvard Business Review* 67: 133–139.

Hollander, S. 1965. *The Sources of Increased Efficiency: A Study of Du Pont Rayon Plants*. Cambridge: MIT Press.

Levin, R. C., A. K. Klevorick, R. R. Nelson, and S. G. Winter. 1987. "Appropriating the Returns from Industrial Research and Development." *Brookings Papers on Economic Activity*, no. 3: 783–820.

Levine, S., and P. E. White. 1961. "Exchange as a Conceptual Framework for the Study of Interorganizational Relationships." *Administrative Science Quarterly* 5: 583–601.

Macaulay, S. 1963. "Non-Contractual Relations in Business: A Preliminary Study." *American Sociological Review* 14: 55–69.

Mansfield, E. 1985. "How Rapidly Does New Industrial Technology Leak Out?" *Journal of Industrial Economics* 34: 217–223.

Miell, D., and S. Duck. 1986. "Strategies in Developing Friendships." In *Friendship and Social Interaction*, edited by V. J. Derlega and B. Winstead. New York: Springer.

Miller, L. C., and J. H. Berg. 1984. "Selectivity and Urgency in Interpersonal Exchange." In *Communication, Intimacy, and Close Relationships*, edited by V. J. Derlega. Orlando, Fla.: Academic Press.

Mills, J., and M. S. Clark. 1982. "Exchange and Communal Relationships. In *Review of Personality and Social Psychology*, vol. 3, edited by L. Wheeler. Beverly Hills, Calif.: Sage.

Porter, M. E. 1983. "The Technological Dimension of Competitive Strategy." In *Research on Technological Innovation, Management and Policy*, vol. 1, edited by R. S. Rosenbloom. Greenwich, Conn.: JAI Press.

Porter, M. E. 1985. *Competitive Advantage: Creating and Sustaining Superior Performance*. New York: Free Press.

Pritzl, M. 1987. *Die Bedeutung der Zielklarheit für die Führungskräfte des Unternehmens: Eine empirische Analyse*. Munich: GBI.

Rogers, E. M. 1982. "Information Exchange and Technological Innovation." In *The Transfer and Utilization of Technical Knowledge,* edited by D. Sahal. Lexington, Mass.: Lexington Books.

Schrader, S. 1990. *Zwischenbetrieblicher Informationstransfer: Eine empirische Analyse Kooperativen Verhaltens.* Berlin: Duncker & Humblot.

Schrader, S. 1991. "Informal Technology Transfer Between Firms: Cooperation Through Information Trading." *Research Policy* 20: 153–170.

Sitkin, S. B. 1986. *Selective Exposure: Determinants of Secrecy Behavior Among Engineers in Three Silicon Valley Semiconductor Firms.* University of Texas at Austin. (photocopy)

Walster, E., E. Berscheid, and G. W. Walster. 1976. "New Directions in Equity Research." In *Advances in Experimental Social Psychology, Volume 9: Equity Theory Towards a General Theory of Social Interaction,* edited by L. Berkowitz and E. Walster. New York: Academic Press.

Von Hippel, E. 1987. "Cooperation Between Rivals: Informal Know-How Trading." *Research Policy* 16: 291–302.

COMMENTARY BY CLAUS G. SIEGLE

At Ford Motor Company in Europe we did discuss our organizational strategy with our employees; we simply cascaded our business plans down from the very top of the organization to the lowest level of the plant, the workers. At Autolatina, we had not allowed our employees to be well informed about business plans and business strategy. They were not given the broader vision of where the company was headed and their role in making this vision reality.

We are now starting to ask our workers for their opinions about our manufacturing process: "What should we change?" "Based on your experience, is there something we can do better?" Our employees are starting to make contributions to the company; we are sure that over time they will be very proud of this participatory system and its efficiency. In Europe, workers know things today that they in their position would not have been privy to earlier. Our workers also report feeling pleased with their contributions. Problems result when employees may feel the information they have is their own, and share it in inappropriate ways. The company may lose strategic advantage, certainly, but there also is a question of whether or not it is even "good" information, since it is usually the impressions and suggestions of the worker. It may paint a different picture than the reality of the situation.

We also use cross-functional teams, particularly when making prototypes, where you need to have people in product development working closely with people in manufacturing and engineers. We have a new problem as a result of these cross-functional teams, which is that our employees do not know or understand the rules regarding which issues are proprietary and which are not, or what they can safely say and what they cannot. These rules were very often not clearly spelled out by management. This is worth thinking about, because you would not want to lose competitive advantage simply because your employees did not know better. An example of this occurred a few years ago, in Spain, when a Fiat dealer in that country began telling me about the new Ford Fiesta. He told me all and everything about the car—positive and negative—including a defect that it had but that I had never realized. This was very top-secret and powerful information. In any case, it pays off to involve the total work force.

On the topic of joint ventures, I have to say that I have started to work in a joint venture—Ford and Volkswagen—in Brazil. I am sitting together with VW and with Ford employees. We are all certainly getting a lot of firsthand information from both companies—from Volkswagen in Germany and Ford in Detroit. I have information from VW, VW is competing heavily with Ford in Europe, but I cannot give the information to my cohorts at Ford where it would do them a lot of good. I think that is an ethical question!

You mention a very good point about how you tell your people about what information can be shared, what information cannot be shared, and how to possibly bring information they get from informal sources into the company, while weeding out the bad or unreliable information. I think as we continue to increase the level of employee involvement, the issue of how you tell your employees what to do and what your employees do with information they would not normally have access to will become increasingly important.

20

Strategic Alternatives for Technology-Based Product and Business Development

EDWARD B. ROBERTS

Many of the world's major corporations need effective development of new technology-based product lines and new businesses that offer significant potential for added sales and profits. This need arises from dramatic changes in several critical dimensions of global technology-based competition. Competition has intensified in expense and pace; it has become global in the "home" countries of key competitors as well as the location of the multiple R&D, manufacturing, and marketing/distribution activities that each firm needs to integrate. Now even relatively simple products depend upon the integration of multiple core technologies. Market opportunities that are growing most rapidly are coming from emerging technological fields. As a consequence, every firm has now become what I call a "minority" technology player; that is, no one corporation any longer controls a majority of the relevant sources of innovation or even has internal mastery of the relevant technologies for its own strategies. Instead, in every industry undergoing significant technological change, the world outside of any single company now contains the majority of technological innovation. This leads to the growth of new organizational forms: competition has forced cross-linkages, partnerships, alliances, and consortia to become the way of life, and it will be more true five years from now than it is today. These dramatic unidirectional changes have already occurred, forcing many firms to play "catch up."

What kind of strategic needs must a corporation satisfy through technology? First, companies need significant enhancements to their current product lines, including not just new products but also substantial cost reductions and quality improvements. Second, companies need technological contributions to the initiation and growth of major new business areas, entailing the development of new production processes as well as the new products for these businesses. Assessment of the empirical innovation literature on alternative strategic approaches to new business development, combined with a pilot research study in one major diversified corporation, suggests a framework for rationally pursuing these corporate objectives.

THE INNOVATION DILEMMA

As these objectives are sought by corporations, what problems must be overcome in achieving them? Here is where we encounter what I label the "innovation dilemma." It consists of two propositions. The farther that any company seeks to innovate, as measured by degrees of change from its base markets and technologies, the greater the likelihood that its innovation efforts will fail. Yet the less that a firm seeks to innovate, across the board, the greater the likelihood that the corporation itself will fail. I will provide support for these propositions throughout the chapter.

The Familiarity Matrix

As a framework for resolving this dilemma I use a diagram introduced a few years ago (Roberts and Berry, 1985), called the "familiarity matrix" (Figure 20.1). The familiarity matrix visualizes in terms of degrees of market and technology change from a firm's base business three different zones of potential change in developing new products or new businesses. The bottom left corner represents a company's present business position, its base technology and its base market. That area is completely familiar to the firm. The company is in possession of and has widely applied the base technology to its own products and manufacturing processes for many years. The firm knows the base customers and their competitors, their expectations, and their likely behaviors. For many firms that "base–base area" is presently under attack or is expected soon to be losing attractiveness in regard to profitability and/or growth. Erosion of the base is the prime motivator for pursuing more ambitious business innovation. In the zone that immediately surrounds its base business, a company deals with new but familiar changes in technology and/or new but familiar changes in market. This is a zone of minimal change. If a company engages in innovation efforts within this first zone, few of its projects are likely to fail. And yet the firm will not be achieving meaningful expansion of its base of opportunity, in terms of new and substantially different markets. Each individual innovation activity in this zone is by definition an incremental innovation.

If the firm moves its innovation efforts to the second zone in the familiarity matrix, the zone pictured at the diagonal in Figure 20.1, it is shifting further outward from its base but holding some key business variable fixed. Perhaps the base market is being kept the same and the firm is attempting to create and/or utilize new but unfamiliar technology. Or the company may be holding its technology more or less fixed and trying to enter a new but unfamiliar market. Or perhaps the company adopts a compromise position and seeks to apply new but familiar technology to a new but familiar market, trying to achieve what here might be called moderate change, but on both competitive dimensions of market and technology. This zone represents a middle ground in which the risks of failure of each individual innovation effort are increased substantially from incremental changes. But now the business opportunity available to the company is likely to be far more expansive.

If the corporation attempts significant change, moving to the outer zone of the diagram, the zone of least familiarity, the zone characterized simultaneously by both unfamiliar technology and unfamiliar market, its efforts are accompanied by the high-

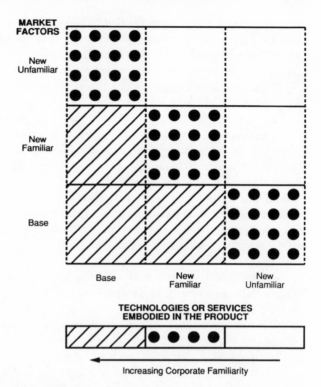

MARKET FACTORS

New Unfamiliar

New Familiar

Base

Base   New Familiar   New Unfamiliar

TECHNOLOGIES OR SERVICES EMBODIED IN THE PRODUCT

Increasing Corporate Familiarity

Figure 20.1
The familiarity matrix.

est degree of likelihood of failure. To fulfill their needs and/or aspirations, many companies concentrate their innovation efforts in the moderate to significant change zones and consequently encounter a high rate of failure of individual innovation efforts. High-percentage failure in and of itself is not necessarily bad, since the few successes achieved may provide vital advances for the firm. But companies need better understanding of how to couple alternative strategies for innovating with the degree of change they are seeking.

STRATEGIC ALTERNATIVES FOR DEVELOPMENT

A number of strategic options are available for developing major new product lines and businesses. These include internal development or major internal ventures, acquisitions, licensing, joint ventures or alliances, venture capital, and "educational alliances." Strengths and weaknesses of each are discussed next.

Internal Development or Major Internal Ventures

The principal advantages of internal development or major internal ventures are the use of existing resources of the company accompanied by total control of the activity. (Elsewhere I focus upon the substantial differences between these two approaches; Roberts, 1980.) All of the professional staff are employed by the firm, self-contained within the corporation, subject to its planning and control, its resource allocation and direction. Despite the frustration that technology managers usually express about how little they can actually control R&D people, nevertheless, of all the strategic options internal development, or major internal ventures, provides the maximum for self-directed leadership or influence, if not exactly control.

The major disadvantage of internal development as a strategy for new business development is the long time lag before a substantial new effort can achieve profitability and significant impact. 3M's executives have long said that thirteen to fifteen years, on average, elapse from initial R&D to cash flow break even in launching a major new business activity with prospects of $100 million or more in annual revenues. The second major disadvantage of relying upon internal development is that, to the extent the company is trying to move its technological resources toward new market opportunities, corporate lack of familiarity with new markets is likely to lead to significant errors in targeting, focusing, specification writing, and proper identification of customer needs and user demands. Consequently, many firms have experienced technical successes from internal development efforts but failed to accomplish business objectives.

Major internal ventures have similarly had a mixed record of success in trying to achieve bold departures from present base business lines. A few spectacular successes provide the encouragement to continue despite the high-percentage failures of the many. For example, Du Pont's record in major venturing reflects important differences between those cases where the company has been able to achieve strong integration of marketing considerations and market understandings with new and innovative technology and other situations where it hasn't been able to master this combination. Corfam, Du Pont's venture aimed at developing and commercializing synthetic shoe leather, is a case where the company had good technological skills but lacked understanding of the market. It resulted in the largest single venture development write-off in Du Pont's history: $160 million at the departmental, not the corporate, level of the company. In contrast, the Du Pont Photo Products department has produced a string of dramatic successes, generating about $2 billion a year of revenues from internal ventures that launched electronic chemicals, like photoresists, and electronic systems businesses, like color proofing systems and the clinical analyzer, with additional venture product spinoffs into Du Pont's biomedical area.

The 3M Company, well known for its excellent track record in the area of internal new business development, has for years been able to generate many new product entries to the market. Yet its numerous product entries have been less consistent in launching major businesses that have dramatically changed 3M's overall base. A few years ago 3M publicly released some performance data, describing technical audits carried out on 100 internal new product programs involving unrelated technology. These data are presented in Figure 20.2.

For these 100 situations of unrelated technology, the upper left quadrant presents 3M's record of 25 percent significant successes when it entered unrelated markets but with high degrees of product uniqueness. 3M achieved the same score in the bottom right sector, with situations of related market and unrelated technology, but where the product offerings lacked uniqueness. When 3M combined product uniqueness with its own understanding and capabilities in related markets (the bottom left corner of Figure 20.2), the company achieved its best performance with a record of 67 percent major product successes. The top right quadrant shows the contrasting dismal results of no

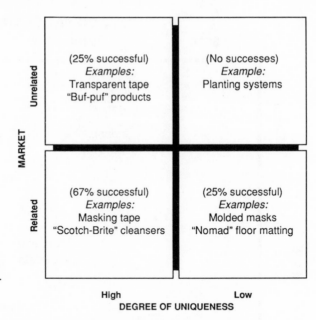

Figure 20.2 New product programs at 3M in areas of unrelated technology (n = 100 internal technical audits). (From *3M Today,* vol. 1, no. 3, March 1985.)

stellar successes whatsoever when 3M concurrently pursued both unrelated market and unrelated technology, and offered low product uniqueness as well. The 3M Company's own database shows that even a firm with a great reputation for internal venture success finds that it must hold some changes under control to be able to establish a pathway of success. Going for broke, in terms of multiple degrees of change sought simultaneously, doesn't work. These efforts at all-out innovation seem to work least when they are needed most.

Figure 20.3 illustrates that the IBM Corporation has encountered similar difficulties in launching major internal ventures. Its display of projects on its own grid of market and technology change reveals mainly products that have never reached the marketplace, especially when they entailed extreme desired change from IBM's base–base position.

Acquisitions

Mergers and acquisitions have accelerated dramatically in recent years, despite the enormity of evidence that demonstrates great problems with acquisitions as a major new business strategy. The chief advantage of acquisitions is rapid market entry. The major disadvantage occurs when a corporation uses an acquisition to move away from its base business. That new business area is by definition unfamiliar to the acquirer and very high likelihood exists that the acquiring company will encounter failure.

In his classic work Rumelt (1974) found that primarily related acquisitions had positive and significant performance results for acquiring companies. Porter's data (1987) (thirty-three U.S. firms) on acquisitions carried out from 1950 through 1980 indicates that 74 percent of unrelated acquisitions were sold off within a few years after the acquisition was made originally. Foster (1988) cites a recent McKinsey & Company analysis (200 largest U.S. firms) of major acquisition programs from 1972 through

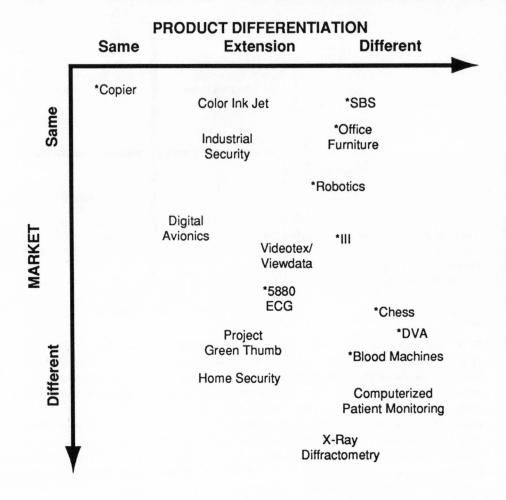

Figure 20.3   Major venture portfolio of the IBM Corporation.

1983 that shows only 23 percent of merger and acquisition programs succeeded in meeting internal return on investment requirements of the companies carrying out the programs. A 92 percent failure rate was recorded in the area of unrelated acquisitions. In their study of lines of business acquisitions, Ravenscraft and Scherer (1987) found similar results: unrelated acquisitions are more likely to fail and to be sold off. Acquisition usually works only when a corporation focuses on building the base business it is already in, adding to what it already has or in a zone of incremental change around the base. For movement away from a firm's base business toward new areas, acquisitions are a "nonstarter."

Licensing

Licensing technology from other firms is widely practiced, but usually to provide new performance features for present products or manufacturing processes or to enable extension of existing product lines. Seldom does a license permit effective diversification into new fields. Its strength as an option lies in the rapid access established to technology already proven by another firm, with the attendant reduced financial exposure that comes from being able to avoid undertaking a development program. But that is also the root of the weakness of licensing. The technology is seldom proprietary once transferred, having been developed by another firm, and it is often about to be replaced by a next generation of technology. Furthermore, the licensee frequently ends up being dependent upon the technology source. The licensee organization does not enhance its internal technical competence by the mere fact of the license; it must take more intensive investment steps to develop capabilities that would enable building upon the licensed technology. Licensing is far more suited to support current business or as part of a new business strategy based upon one of the other alternatives identified in this chapter.

Joint Ventures or Alliances

Growing dramatically as a chosen major new business development strategy is the use of joint ventures or alliances. Advantages arise from this approach primarily when technological and market unions formed between two or more companies can create and exploit synergy. This occurs especially when the coupling is between large and small companies teaming together, where the large company brings in resources, manufacturing capabilities, and distributional capacities worldwide and where the small company takes advantage of its ability to innovate rapidly to bring in new and emerging technologies. In these circumstances alliances and joint venture activities, not acquisitions, work well. Furthermore, financial and technical risk is distributed among the multiple partners to a new venture. The major disadvantage of joint ventures or of alliances is the great potential for conflict between partners. Substantial problems are often encountered when two very different organizations try to come together, to work together over an extended period of time, especially in a major new business development endeavor. At the heart of these problems too is the lack of true familiarity of each partner with the other, and of each partner with the complementary resources of knowledge and skills brought by the other firm.

A joint venture or alliance is a situation in which two or more organizations pool complementary resources in an arrangement that is less than a full merger or acquisition. But many of the issues posed by unrelated acquisitions are also valid for unrelated alliances or joint ventures. When one company begins ongoing working relationships with another firm that is significantly different, with different market capabilities and channels, different technical capabilities and know-how, the possibility of achieving novel and valuable new business development does exist. But along with this possibility come the likely problems of effectively managing the interfirm ties. Indeed, these problems exist even when the partners are two divisions of the same company, a growing form of alliance.

Joint ventures and alliances come in many shapes and forms. Many alliances are between two or more large companies, most being what I call "distributional alliances." One company focuses on the marketplace in which it already has access to a country or an area of distribution, the other company already has a product and a manufacturing process. These alliances or joint ventures are being pursued increasingly today in search of globalization. They are not difficult to conceive or even to implement, although many straightforward management problems do take place at the organizational boundaries. Lack of cross-cultural familiarity is especially troublesome.

Alliances that have high potential payoffs but are very difficult to initiate and carry to success include what I call "developmental alliances." Here both parties to the alliance bring in pieces of technology in an attempt to put together or more likely to develop a common new capability, a capability that neither partner has at the outset, that will be manifested in new product and/or process. This type of alliance or joint venture requires a jointly executed development program. One company that has mastered this kind of alliance well is Corning Glass Works, now Corning Inc. Corning over its long and innovative history has found ways of teaming together in joint ventures with other partners of comparable size in building totally new businesses—for example, Dow-Corning, Owens-Corning, and Siecor—usually tying Corning's basic technology to a more applied partner. Corning's senior management provides ongoing commitments to welding fifty-fifty trust relationships that are jointly nurtured and that succeed.

Three other structural forms of joint ventures or alliances also serve the primary purpose of joint technology-based development of new businesses. These include the many new alliances between large and small companies that I have discussed previously (Roberts, 1980). Still other developmental relationships are between industry and universities, a relatively new pattern that has grown dramatically during the 1980s, and that will grow still further during the 1990s. And Europe has already experienced what is a new possibility in the United States since passage of the 1986 Technology Transfer Act, alliances between industrial organizations and government laboratories. Of course, the United States has had a long history of industry working with the government as its R&D sponsor or as its business regulator, but with rare exceptions (e.g., the aircraft industry with the former NACA laboratories) not previously with government as a technology development partner in search of commercial outcomes. Already the National Institutes of Health have initiated large numbers of new agreements with industry as a result of this act, but potential benefits of these relationships are still largely unrealized and their likely problems yet untested.

To understand better the potential benefits from alliances I turn to what I think is the most successful new business development alliance, one that was both well structured and implemented, the IBM personal computer. It is most important to realize that the IBM PC has been pictured in the business press as an internal venture, a model of internal entrepreneurship in IBM. In reality, however, the PC was a multifirm strategic alliance, in which internal to IBM, IBM controlled and took responsibility for overall design and integration of the product concept and the final product. That internal planning and control group within IBM was organized "entrepreneurially" as what IBM labeled an IBU, an independent business unit. That venture group turned to the outside world, to vendors that were not owned by IBM, companies without even minority shareholdings by IBM, for external technology, manufacturing, and even distribution. First, the major hardware components and systems were developed and produced outside of IBM. For example, the largest stand-alone hardware system, the printer, was developed and produced by the Epson Division of Seiko. Other major companies supplied practically all the other elements of the hardware system. All of the software also came from outside of IBM. The operating system, MS-DOS, came from Microsoft, presumably with some financial help from IBM, but the product innovations were launched by the outside small company. The major applications software, initially Visicalc, which had been developed originally for the Apple Computer, and then the Lotus 1-2-3 software, the major user tools on which the IBM hardware platform was sold to industry, came from outside small firms.

Astonishingly, given IBM's outstanding strength in distribution and marketing, all initial channels of distribution for the IBM PC came from outside of the company. Apparently IBM's marketing department refused to distribute the PC, perhaps properly sensitive to the unfamiliar market being targeted. New alliance relationships with Computerland and Sears Roebuck, which was starting an internal venture called Sears Business Centers to sell office products, provided IBM the initial channels of distribution for moving the PC products to customers. How else could a corporation ramp up from zero market penetration to multi-billion dollars of sales in such a short period of time, were it not taking advantage of other companies' already existing technical and marketing resources, which IBM was instantly able to access, integrate, and manage effectively in an alliance fashion?

The early success of the PC then led IBM to take a series of appropriate next steps. IBM correctly reintegrated that successful venture into its mainstream management pattern as the Entry Systems Division, subject to the management control systems and management hierarchy that is proper for the handling of a multi-billion dollar business. And IBM then did the next important thing that a corporation ought to do after it succeeds in launching an alliance-based business. It began as quickly as its agreements and resources allowed to try to substitute itself for its outside partners in as much of the high-value–added chain as possible. So today, if you buy an IBM PC, IBM is hoping that an IBM Proprinter will be attached to it, not an Epson printer. Today, IBM has packaged software from many outside vendors under its own label, in an attempt to capture at least some of the large margins associated with the PC software. And today, IBM channels of distribution, not just external channels, are attempting to sell that PC product.

This case illustrates that one proper way to launch such an unfamiliar new venture is to use the external resources to help get started, to move the corporation along in building familiarity of technology and familiarity of market as rapidly as possible, intending gradually to reintegrate such a business if it succeeds into the parent firm. As long as a company tries to move concurrently into an unfamiliar market and an unfamiliar technology and to do that all internally, the firm will have high likelihood of failure. Only as the company masters this balancing act between the inside and the outside, between the familiar and the unfamiliar, can it resolve the innovation dilemma.

Alliances or joint ventures face many problems but space permits identification of only the most common difficulty, the "impedance mismatch" issues arising from cultural differences between the two or more partners. Especially as firms necessarily move toward global alliances, they will need to deal with the cultural differences originating from different homelands, different nationalistic tendencies, different regulatory systems in the countries in which people have been accustomed to doing business. These major problems will be accelerated, not reduced, by the expected European Community changes of 1992. A concluding note is that despite the problems of implementing alliances, the familiarity that an alliance will produce from working together may well provide the bases for later acquisitions that are more likely to be successful.

Venture Capital

Another widespread approach to business development is external venture capital investment. A major company typically buys a minority equity interest in a young technology-based firm, primarily seeking to gather information informally through a "window" on an emerging technology or market. Financial goals and objectives of both near-term and eventual acquisition of technology and/or the young company itself may also be served by corporate venture capital activities. A potential "window" is at best an opening to more intensive corporate actions to develop new products and businesses. Information is hard to access through this channel, the window seems "opaque," unless the investor devotes considerable staff support effort, in addition to its initial funding, to seeking this knowledge transfer.

Most corporate venture capital is invested through the intermediary of "pooled" funds managed by professional venture capitalists. Unless these managers understand the technology strategy of the corporate investors and are committed to assisting in achieving the linkage between the large and small firm, little will be accomplished in the domain of new business development. Monsanto mastered this approach in its search for insights and technology for the biotechnology field through careful selection of cooperative venture capital funds, establishment of noncompeting investment relationships, and strong commitment of senior Monsanto management to provide backup for the investments. Computer Services Corporation (CSK-Japan) gained entry to the artificial intelligence business via contacts established through its investment in a U.S. seed capital firm.

But increasingly corporations are attempting to carry out direct venture capital investments without the help of fund managers. These efforts frequently fail because of the corporate staff's lack of familiarity with the process of small company venture investment and nurturing as well as from the corporation's absence of heavy "deal flow" in investment opportunities with emerging technology companies. Olivetti has overcome these problems by recruiting a successful electronics entrepreneur to run its electronics-focused venture capital investments. But even successful investing only provides greater familiarity with technological and market opportunities. Follow-on commitments of licensing, alliances, acquisition, and/or internal development are needed to create new products or businesses for the investing corporation. Kubota Corporation has boldly coupled its direct venture capital investments with concurrent technology licensing and joint ventures in its aggressive efforts to enter the computer business. Time is needed to assess the effectiveness of Kubota's strategy.

Educational Acquisitions

Absent from the managerial literature is the last business development method to be described in this chapter, what I have named the "educational acquisitions." Companies can use small acquisitions of young firms as windows on new technology and/or market, and at the same time acquire a core of people on which a future business can be built. The acquisition obviously must be in an unrelated area in order to serve the purpose of horizon expansion for the acquirer, but it had better be both small, to lessen risk, and carefully executed. Many acquisitions of small technology-based companies in the United States lead to almost instant departure of key people, with possible formation of competitive firms. To avoid this the acquiring company should structure incentives for retaining the key staff members of the small firm, involving them as integral parts of the acquiring firm's plans for future business growth and development. Handled effectively, the acquired human resources transfer their knowledge base to their new parent organization, enabling a period of assessment and further investment that might generate new products and product lines. Thus Harris-Intertype turned its acquisition of Radiation Dynamics into the base for its own long-term diversification into computers and communications, eventually becoming Harris Corporation.

CHOOSING THE MOST APPROPRIATE NEW BUSINESS DEVELOPMENT APPROACH

Figure 20.4 shows results from our study of one multi-billion dollar diversified corporation, in which we looked at a series of fourteen new business development episodes. The stars indicate success, the black dots are failures. Note first the characteristic intensifying of failures as the firm moves away from its base business: the farther from the base that one attempts to innovate, the more likely are failures to occur. These data support the 3M and IBM evidence presented earlier. The stars tend to be close to company areas of existing knowledge, understanding, and capability. The diagram supports in general my innovation dilemma arguments, but it also reveals different patterns of results stemming from use of different new business approaches. Cases D, E, and F are failures from improperly positioned—that is, overly aggressive—internal developments; J, K, and L are failures from incorrectly targeted acquisitions.

A company needs to select the new business development approach that is most appropriate to the degree of technical and market change being sought. Figure 20.5 summarizes the arguments developed in this chapter. If the company is seeking to achieve only a small shift in technical or market positioning, it should use internal development or acquisitions. Licensing can be added too if the company wants to move a bit farther out in search of technical change. If the corporation is attempting to achieve a moderate degree of market or technological change, moving away from its base business by more than just a small extent, then it had better consider more active use of major internal ventures, joint ventures, and alliances with outside partners to couple some of their external skills and familiarity with the firm's own internal knowledge and capabilities.

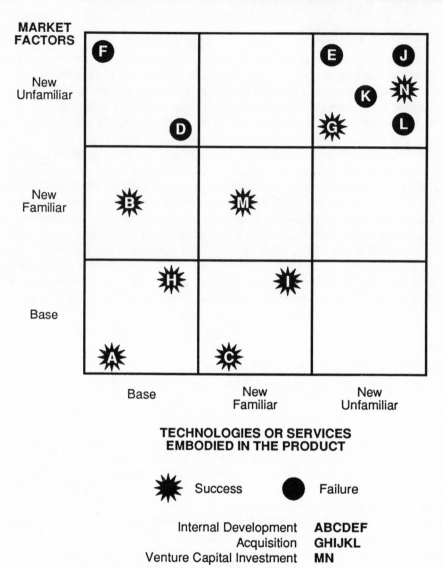

Figure 20.4   New business outcomes on the familiarity matrix.

If a corporation really needs and wants to achieve significant change, then it must eventually perform what I call generically the "two-step"; more specifically, it must adopt one of several alternative "multistep" patterns. Namely, it first makes one partial move toward its goal, followed by another appropriate-sized step, just like we all learned in the children's game of Giant Steps. This attempt to two-step the change, not trying to do everything at once, allows gradual development of market and technical familiarity in the direction of desired change. Each step along the path is thus more subject to effective internal managerial control and influence. For example, the first step might appropriately be venture capital or educational acquisitions in the unfamiliar

MARKET FACTORS

	Base	New Familiar	New Unfamiliar
New Unfamiliar	Joint venture	Venture capital or "educational" acquisition	Venture capital or "educational" acquisition
New Familiar	Internal development or acquisition or joint venture	Internal development or acquisition or license	Venture capital or "educational" acquisition
Base	Internal development or acquisition	Internal development or acquisition or license	Joint venture or strategic alliance

TECHNOLOGIES OR SERVICES EMBODIED IN THE PRODUCT

Figure 20.5 Appropriate strategies for corporate new business development.

zone, using relatively low resource commitment to gain sufficient technical/market familiarity to enable doing alliances or joint ventures next. The external venture capital investments in small firms seek to create a window on technology to gain more understanding and to begin building partnerships aimed at future payoff. The relationships acquired by this means cannot have short-term impact and can generate only long-run benefits (or losses). Monsanto's multistep movements into biotechnology reflect precisely this mode of strategic change, beginning with venture capital. Instead of or in addition to venture capital, the company might initially undertake small educational acquisitions, done solely for the sake of developing insights while building a base of core staff in a new area, not for the sake of market positioning. These are indeed actions in largely unrelated areas, but they are tempered by their small size and associated modest financial risk. A company that attempts actions more aggressive than those indicated in Figure 20.5 should proceed with great caution. "Giant steps" of product/business change, such as unrelated major internal new ventures and unrelated acquisitions, generally fail. Exxon Enterprises' expensive attempts to enter the computers and communications field reflect the lessons taught in Figure 20.5: external venture capital was appropriately and successfully employed for initial entry to unrelated business fields, but major unrelated internal ventures led to predictable disasters (Sykes, 1986).

Moving differently, the first step toward significant change might be a somewhat more aggressive commitment in the familiar zone, such as an alliance, accomplishing part of the ultimate desired move toward the unfamiliar territory. That would produce a new base of market and technical knowledge, permitting a later next step to achieve the original goal. Allen-Bradley's successful conversion from leadership of the electromechanical industrial controls business to an even stronger position in the solid-state controls field evidences proper use of the full variety of options listed, with alliances prominent in its strategy (Fusfeld, 1989). One final means for implementing the multistep approach to significant change is seen in Clark, Chew, and Fujimoto's (1987) work on innovation in the world automobile industry. They demonstrate the much greater tendency of Japanese producers to undertake several sequential incremental steps, using internal development for each step, whereas European and American firms attempt bolder, more complex innovation efforts. Putting together a large number of serial small changes appears to generate significant change much faster than trying to make single major moves.

This chapter reinforces an argument embedded in other contributions to this book: taking effective advantage of new technological or market opportunities requires careful selection of organizational forms. Moreover, the more radical the departure from prior company strengths, described here in terms of "familiarity," the more a firm needs to develop the organizational and human skills needed to manage cross-boundary linkages. Understanding how firms can meet this challenge should feature prominently in the future research agenda for those interested in managing corporate development.

REFERENCES

Clark, K., W. B. Chew, and T. Fujimoto. 1987. "Product Development in the World Auto Industry: Strategy, Organization and Performance." Paper presented at the Brookings Microeconomics Conference, December 3–4, 1987.

Foster, R. 1988. Address to Industrial Research Institute conference, Boston.

Fusfeld, A. R. 1989. "Formulating Technology Strategies to Meet the Global Challenges of the 1990s." *International Journal of Technology Management* 4, no. 6: 601–612.

Porter, M. E. 1987. "From Competitive Advantage to Corporate Strategy." *Harvard Business Review*, May–June, 43–59.

Ravenscraft, D. J., and F. M. Scherer. 1987. *Mergers, Sell-Offs, and Economic Efficiency.* Washington, D.C.: The Brookings Institution.

Roberts, E. B. 1980. "New Ventures for Corporate Growth." *Harvard Business Review* 58, no. 4: 134–142.

Roberts, E. B., and C. A. Berry. 1985. "Entering New Businesses: Selecting Strategies for Success." *Sloan Management Review* 26, no. 3: 3–17.

Rumelt, R. P. 1974. *Strategy, Structure and Economic Performance.* Boston: Harvard Business School, Division of Research.

Sykes, H. B. 1986. "Lessons from a New Ventures Program." *Harvard Business Review* 64, no. 3: 69–74.

COMMENTARY BY ROBERT J. TUITE

In the twenty years since my first management position in the Kodak Research Labs, I can see three distinct phases in the complex process of technology management for business. At that time, the prevailing view was that technology should be developed in lock step with business strategy, the "just-in-time" approach. That Utopian view has long been made obsolete by the increased pace and global dispersion of technology. We then had the "make versus buy" approach, in which companies considered technology as any other business commodity, which could be purchased from any number of vendors. Finally, we arrived at the "strategic partnership" approach in which both the supplier and the user of technology negotiate to ensure a harmony of interests and share in the risks and the rewards.

Professor Roberts's chapter introduces the "familiarity matrix" as a way to view the various approaches companies have used to manage the risks involved in technology-based business development. Market familiarity (the demand side) is plotted on one axis; technology familiarity (the supply side) on the other. Risk then increases exponentially the further out you go on either axis, leading companies to supplement internal development with a variety of other approaches, generally involving external partners.

Kodak has had some experience with each of the approaches outlined, with mixed results that are generally consistent with this chapter. Acquisition in particular has been a difficult management challenge for Kodak; the company swallowed a number of small fry before bringing itself to swallow a whale—Sterling Drug—which we are still trying to digest.

My involvement has primarily been with R&D management and with internal ventures, using a modification of the venture capital process. Business proposals were evaluated, developed, seeded, and "sold" to the existing business units or to a corporate venture board set up to fund internal start-ups. Thus the program was oriented primarily toward opportunistic, as opposed to strategic, new business development.

A few specific comments about the paper before discussing opportunities for future research. First, I would make a distinction between "technology" and "product," where product represents the embodiment of a technology for a given customer application. Both the IBM and 3M examples cited used a product axis rather than a technology axis. Second, I would distinguish between "venture capital" and "direct investment." Kodak has a venture capital development function which participates in a number of venture capital pools to provide a window on technology. Any direct investment in a specific company, however, must be made by a business unit because it views it as in its strategic interest. Finally, I prefer the word "partnership" to "alliance" in that it better conveys the concept. The partnership approach is now used throughout Kodak as part of a total quality management process, both between internal units as well as with external organizations.

In terms of opportunities for further research, accepting the proposition that the risks increase exponentially as one ventures out the familiarity axes, and yet companies continue to use these various approaches in the never-ending quest for sources of new business growth, I would target the following issues for future research:

1. What are the critical success factors that distinguish successful companies in these high-risk endeavors, that is, "best practice"? We have found that when there is a harmony of objectives, a partnership type of operating style, a reasonable level of autonomy, and a share in both the risks and the rewards, success is more likely. Acquisitions are the worst of all possible worlds because they "monetize" the risk at the time of the transaction, often against a plan which is overly optimistic, thereby removing the shared risk–reward aspect so critical to success.

2. What has been the experience with "reintegration"? It is one thing to get a new business or acquisition up and running, but at some point, it needs to be folded back into the mainstream of the company with all sorts of implications for the managers and employees of the venture. Reintegration of the IBM PC venture did not go smoothly.

3. The business community has not been kind to "intrapreneurs" whose projects have fallen short of expectations; how have companies handled the career development issues? I believe that companies need to institutionalize the new business development function and give it a stature comparable to R&D. In that way, we can recycle our most entrepreneurial people, thereby providing them with a rewarding career doing what they do best and what the country needs most.

21

Systems Thinking and Organizational Learning: Acting Locally and Thinking Globally in the Organization of the Future

PETER M. SENGE AND JOHN D. STERMAN

THE "NEW WORK" OF MANAGERS

Eroding competitiveness, declining productivity growth, and explosive technological, political, and environmental change form the familiar litany of problems that threaten traditional organizational structures and management practices. Organizations stressed by these pressures have worked to clarify their missions, visions, and values. Many seek to reorganize into leaner, more locally controlled, and market-responsive structures. Yet all too often the core operating (as opposed to espoused) policies guiding organizational behavior remain unchanged. Efforts to improve strategic management often founder because new strategies and structures threaten traditional habits, norms, and assumptions. The problem lies, in part, with failing to recognize the importance of prevailing mental models. New strategies are the outgrowth of new world views. The more profound the change in strategy, the deeper must be the change in thinking. Indeed, many argue that improving the mental models of managers is the fundamental task of strategic management:

> The choice of individual courses of action is only part of the manager's or policy-maker's need. More important is the need to achieve insight into the nature of the complexity being addressed and to formulate concepts and world views for coping with it. (Mason and Mitroff, 1981, p. 16)

> Strategies are the product of a world view . . . the basis for success or failure is the microcosm of the decision makers: their inner model of reality, their set of assumptions that structure their understanding of the unfolding business environment and the factors critical to success. . . . When the world changes, managers need to share some common view of the new world. Otherwise, decentralized strategic decisions will lead to management anarchy. (Wack, 1985, pp. 89, 150)

In response, managers and academics alike have identified organizational learning, the process whereby shared understandings change, as a key to flexibility and competitive advantage in the 1990s. In a recent study of the beleaguered manufacturing industries, Hays, Wheelwright, and Clark (1988) conclude: "There is one common denominator in high-performance plants: an ability to learn—to achieve sustained improvement in performance over a long period of time. When assessing a manufacturing organization, learning is the bottom line." Analog Devices's CEO Ray Stata (1989) argues that "the rate at which individuals and organizations learn may become the only sustainable competitive advantage" (p. 64). Arie de Geus (1988), former chief of planning at Royal Dutch/Shell, observes that an organization's ability to survive depends on "institutional learning, which is the process whereby management teams change their shared mental models of their company, their markets, and their competitors. For this reason, we think of planning as learning, and of corporate planning as institutional learning" (p. 70).

All agree that learning organizations will require profound shifts in the nature of managerial work. William O'Brien, CEO of Hanover Insurance Companies, sees the learning organization of the future abandoning "the old dogma of planning, organizing, and controlling" for "a new 'dogma' [of] vision, values, and mental models" (Senge 1990a, p. 299). Similarly, the "quality of organizational learning," in Don Schön's view (1983a), is determined by the quality of the "organizational inquiry that mediates the restructuring of organizational theory-in-use."

Organizational learning processes are most effective when they help managers develop a more systemic and dynamic perspective. Organization development professionals have long advocated a systems perspective for effective change (Beckhard and Harris, 1987; Katz and Kahn, 1978; Schein, 1985; Weick, 1979). A recent strategic management text begins by citing the views of Bruce Henderson, a "senior statesman" of the strategy field, who criticized "the essentially static nature of . . . earlier work . . . [which neglected] time, second order effects and feedback loops . . . the ingredients for the insightful analysis that was needed to move the field of strategy its next step forward" (Lorange, Scott Morton, and Ghoshal, 1986, p. xviii). The challenge is how to move from generalizations about accelerating learning and systems thinking to tools and processes that help managers reconceptualize complex issues, design better operating policies, and guide organization-wide learning.

One new approach involves "learning laboratories" or "microworlds"—microcosms of real business settings where managers play roles in a simulated organization. As an aircraft flight simulator allows pilots to try new maneuvers and experience extreme conditions without risk, so too a learning laboratory provides a flight simulator for managers. A microworld compresses time and space, allowing managers to experience the long-term, system-wide consequences of decisions (Graham, Senge, Sterman, and Morecroft, 1989; Sterman, 1988a). But an effective learning laboratory is much more than just computer simulation. It trains managers and teams in the full learning cycle, as originally conceived by John Dewey: discover—invent—produce—reflect. Learning laboratories help managers see through superficial symptoms to the underlying causes of complex phenomena, reorganize perceptions into a clearer, more coherent picture of business dynamics which can be effectively communicated, and create tools that can accelerate the learning of others.

SYSTEMS THINKING: NEW INSIGHTS, NEW PERSPECTIVES

The research draws on the system dynamics methodology developed originally at MIT (Forrester, 1961, 1969; Roberts, 1978). For systems theorists, the source of poor performance and organizational failure is often to be found in the limited cognitive skills and capabilities of individuals compared to the complexity of the systems they are called upon to manage (Forrester, 1961; Perrow, 1984; Simon, 1979, 1982). A vast body of experimental work demonstrates that individuals make significant, systematic errors in diverse problems of judgment and choice (Hogarth, 1987; Kahneman, Slovic, and Tversky, 1982).

Dynamic decision making is particularly difficult, especially when decisions have indirect, delayed, nonlinear, and multiple feedback effects (Dörner, 1989; Kleinmuntz, 1985; Kluwe, Misiak, and Haider, 1989; Sterman, 1989a, 1989b). Yet these are precisely the situations in which managers must act. Systematic dysfunctional performance due to misperceptions of feedback have been documented in a wide range of systems:

Managers in a simple production–distribution system generate costly fluctuations, even when consumer demand is constant (MacNeil–Lehrer Report, 1989; Sterman, 1989b).

Managers of simulated consumer product markets generate the boom and bust, price war, shakeout, and bankruptcy characteristic of industries from video games to chain saws (Paich and Sterman, 1990).

In a simulation of People Express Airlines, students and executives alike frequently bankrupt the company, just as the real management did (Sterman, 1988a).

In a publishing industry simulation, people often bankrupt their magazines even as circulation reaches all-time highs, as happened to a number of real publications (Hall, 1976, 1989).

In a forest fire simulation, many people allow their headquarters to burn down despite their best efforts to put out the fire (Brehmer, 1989).

In a medical setting, subjects playing the role of doctors order more tests while the (simulated) patients sicken and die (Kleinmuntz, 1985).

These studies all show that performance deteriorates markedly as the time delays grow longer and the feedbacks more powerful (Diehl, 1989). Market mechanisms and financial incentives do not eliminate the errors (Camerer, 1987; Smith, Suchanek, and Williams, 1988). Experience and training do not solve the problem: professional economists create depressions in simple economic models (Sterman, 1989a); in simulations of real estate and shipping, a majority of managers tested go bankrupt at least once before learning how to survive, despite experience in these industries (Bakken, 1990); government officials playing an economic development game often impoverish their simulated nations through foreign debt, poison their environments, and starve the population (Meadows, 1989).

These findings have significant implications for learning. In the past simulation models were often constructed by expert consultants, who then explained their operation to policymakers. The "traditional consulting" approach has produced many notable successes, and use of system dynamics in a variety of industries is growing (Cooper, 1980; Morecroft, 1988; Roberts, 1978; Weil, 1980). Nevertheless, while models developed and interpreted by outside experts may change what managers think about a particular issue, they rarely change the way managers think about future issues. In contrast, the model builder often acquires enduring insight. Why? Model development creates a laboratory microworld in which hypotheses must be tested, evaluated, and revised. Model builders learn about the substantive issues *and* develop skills in scientific method and critical thought.

LEARNING LABORATORIES

Our research attempts to develop learning processes aimed at improving managers' shared mental models and altering the character of those models so that they become more systemic and more dynamic. In our view, this can be achieved only if managers themselves become the modelers to a far greater extent than in most prior work. Researchers in system dynamics and other systems traditions have experimented with many processes to catalyze systems thinking in management teams. While effective learning processes are iterative and flexible, for purposes of exposition they can be divided into three stages:

Mapping mental models—explicating and structuring assumptions via systems models
Challenging mental models—revealing inconsistencies in assumptions
Improving mental models—continually extending and testing mental models

Mapping mental models involves the explication and sharing of the managers' assumptions. These mental models typically are very poor maps of the terrain. Axelrod's (1976) study of the cognitive maps of elites painted a "picture of the decision maker . . . [as] one who has more beliefs than he can handle, who employs a simplified image of the policy environment that is structurally easy to operate with, and who then acts rationally within the context of his simplified image." But flaws in mental models cannot be corrected until mental models become more explicit. Forrester (1971, p. 3) argues:

> The mental model is fuzzy. It is incomplete. It is imprecisely stated. Furthermore, within one individual, a mental model changes with time and even during the flow of a single conversation. The human mind assembles a few relationships to fit the context of a discussion. As the subject shifts so does the model . . . each participant in a conversation employs a different mental model to interpret the subject. Fundamental assumptions differ but are never brought into the open.

Many cognitive mapping tools have been developed to elicit and portray the mental models of individuals and groups (Checkland, 1981; Eden, Jones, and Sims, 1983; Hall, 1984, 1989; Morecroft, 1988; Richardson and Pugh, 1981). Good mapping tools help people capture the time delays, long-term effects, and multiple impacts of decisions—the characteristics which cause the most serious misjudgments in dynamic decision making. The more effective tools, increasingly computer-based, also facilitate group input and rapid revision (Morecroft 1982, 1988; Richmond, 1987). In the mapping stage there is no attempt to converge upon a single, integrative model. The most important result of the mapping stage is to uncover critical assumptions and set the stage for challenging them.

Challenging mental models is testing for internal and external validity. Once team members have gone public with their mental models they can begin to discover internal inconsistencies and contradictions with data and others' knowledge. Experienced managers frequently have accurate perceptions of causal structure and decision-making process but draw erroneous conclusions about what happens when different parts of a system interact. Challenging models thus requires an inference engine to deduce the consequences of interactions among the elements of the map. Simulation provides that engine. For simulation to be effective in challenging the managers' mental map, the team members must have a high level of ownership of the simulation models. Managers should be able to construct the models themselves in a short period of time. Managers must understand the software without computer expertise or technical training. We have used STELLA, software for graphical construction of dynamic simulation models on microcomputers (Richmond, Peterson, and Vescuso, 1987). STELLA is widely used in the natural sciences, and applications in management and economics are growing rapidly (*Health Care Forum,* 1990; Milling and Zahn, 1989; Nyhart, 1988; Nyhart and Samarasan, 1989; Solomon, 1989). STELLA is designed to be used first as a mapping technology. The simulation model is then built directly from the cognitive map. Managers frequently can learn the mechanics of STELLA in an hour.

The "reality check" models developed at this stage are designed to uncover overlooked dynamics which bear on the success of the team's strategy. A good reality check model is simple. It should be a straightforward translation of the team's strategy map, and typically it is built up from pieces that are well understood and agreed upon in the mapping stage.

Challenging mental models is delicate. Managers' beliefs are called into question. Inconsistencies are revealed. If trust and openness are not well established, individuals may be threatened and react defensively. It has often proven useful to work with the team members on developing inquiry skills and recognizing defensive routines. A number of approaches to team development have been used successfully in conjunction with mapping technology, including Ed Schein's process consulting (Schein, 1969, 1987) and the action science approach of Chris Argyris (1982, 1985) and colleagues (Argyris, Putnam, and Smith, 1986; Argyris and Schön, 1978) among others (e.g., Dyer, 1987; Schön, 1983b).

Improving mental models is the open-ended process of explicating, testing, and revising managerial assumptions. Now the team expands the simple reality check models to include potentially important feedback dynamics. Assumptions about exogenous factors are questioned. Factors excluded from the initial maps are brought inside the boundary of the model. Linkages with other functions in the organization, and with other organizations in the environment, are considered.

The key to the process is the discipline imposed by the modeling tools. Ideas for improvement must be translated into specific changes in policy and structure. There is no guarantee the models will predict what would occur if a new policy were implemented. But the assumptions behind new initiatives will be explicit and subject to continued testing and improvement. The managers become experimentalists practicing scientific method to improve the structure and functioning of their organization.

The full benefits of the learning process may accrue over a considerable period of time, in some cases several years. New conceptual perspectives are assimilated gradually, stimulated by ongoing processes of dialogue and debate (Levitt and March, 1988). Eventually, new perspectives lead to new perceptions. The formal process is best viewed as catalyzing a larger, more diverse organizational learning process, gently nudging managers toward a more systemic and dynamic view of their world.

CASE STUDY: THE INSURANCE CRISIS

A number of learning laboratories and management microworlds have been developed. One of the more interesting has been developed for a leading American property and liability insurance company to address the runaway costs that threaten the entire liability insurance industry—the tort system in the United States consumes more than 2.5 percent of GNP, the highest in the world. Premiums on auto insurance doubled from 1983 to 1988. Between 1979 and 1985, the number of product liability cases increased 150 percent. The average size of jury verdicts increased fivefold from 1973 to 1985. Public backlash against escalating insurance premiums is growing: outraged Californians recently passed ballot referenda rolling back automobile insurance premiums. In New York state, rate caps have left all five providers of medical malpractice coverage technically bankrupt (Richardson and Senge, 1989).

Commonly cited causes of the crisis include the abundance of lawyers in the United States, increasing litigiousness of society, juries that side with victims rather than uncaring big business, and the growing technological complexity of society (Huber, 1987). Notably absent from such accounts are explanations relating to the management practices of insurers themselves. Why are there so many tort lawyers and lawsuits? Why are insurers perceived to be uncaring? Some of the top managers at Hanover Insurance, of Worcester, Massachusetts, were asking the same questions. These managers intuitively felt that their own management practices had contributed significantly to the problem. They distrusted easy explanations which fix the blame on outside forces. Blaming greedy lawyers, juries, and policyholders is psychologically safe, absolving insurers from responsibility. While not denying the role of these factors, they also saw that blaming the problem on external forces prevented the company from contributing to constructive solutions.

Hanover Insurance is a medium-sized firm specializing in property and casualty. In 1989 Hanover earned $83 million on premium income of about $1.5 billion. Assets were $3 billion. Founded in 1852, Hanover went through a dramatic transition in the last twenty years. In the mid-1960s the company was at the bottom of the industry. In 1969 State Mutual purchased a 50 percent interest in Hanover, injecting much-needed reserves and installing a new president, Jack Adam. With his marketing vice president and eventual successor, Bill O'Brien, Adam began to reorient the company around a new set of guiding principles designed to address deeply rooted problems in Hanover's traditional authoritarian management style:

Purpose—an antidote to a weak sense of common direction
Merit—an antidote to rampant politics and bureaucracy

Openness—an antidote to widespread game playing through hoarding information or operating from private agendas

Localness—an antidote to institutional blocks to strong morale and decision making by front-line units

Vision—an antidote to low self-image and difficulties in communicating the scale of the firm's aspirations

The new culture did not quickly take root. Personnel and structural changes accompanied the internalization of the new philosophical foundation. Many of Hanover's original managers were unprepared for the organization Adam and O'Brien envisioned. During the early 1970s management turnover was high. A level of regional management was eliminated to encourage local autonomy and authority. Later, internal boards of directors were established to further strengthen the autonomy of local business units.

By the mid-1980s Hanover emerged as a leader in the property and liability industry. Hanover's combined ratio, the ratio of operating expenses to premium income (a measure of the profitability of the insurance side of the business), has bettered the industry average in each of the past eleven years. During the same period Hanover grew 50 percent faster than the industry as a whole. There is a widespread belief in the organization that the company's business success is linked to its guiding principles (Bergin and Prusko, 1990).

One logical starting point for Hanover to apply the systems approach was claims management. The problem is highly dynamic: Hanover's growth placed ever greater demands on the claims operation. There were more complex claims and increasing numbers of claims requiring litigation or subrogation (recovering costs from other insurers). The problem cut across all levels of management, corporate functions, and regions. Most important, Hanover's nonauthoritarian culture and emphasis on local decision making meant the systems approach could not be successful if members of top management were the only participants in the process.

The project has proceeded in three stages. First, a team of top managers worked with MIT researchers to develop shared models of the problem. Next, a simulation model developed in phase one was converted into an interactive "management flight simulator." The Hanover team designed a three-day workshop, the Claims Learning Laboratory, using the flight simulator. Over one hundred managers have now participated in the CLL. In the third stage, now under way, a second workshop is under development to help in managing change, systems thinking tools are being introduced throughout the firm, and the effectiveness of the approach is being evaluated through longitudinal studies.

The first stage involved a management team consisting of the senior vice president for claims and two of his direct reporters. The team met every two weeks for about a year with the MIT researchers. The group appeared to have a high level of openness and mutual trust, reflecting several years of working together in Hanover's culture. At the first meeting the team developed an initial statement of objectives, strategies, and problems. The team's vision statement expressed their intent to be preeminent among claims organizations in the insurance industry, to provide "fair, fast, and friendly" service. Their image of the ideal claims adjuster soon emerged: a person capable of conducting thorough professional investigations, possessing excellent communication and negotiation skills, keeping accurate and complete records, and able to educate claimants regarding the fair value of their claims while spotting those with the slightest fraudulent inclinations. They enumerated ten measures of performance and a dozen strategies to achieve them.

When asked to discuss the problems they faced, the claims VP talked about having too many "balls in the air," the challenge of simultaneously keeping many performance standards on target, like a juggler. Whenever Hanover worked to improve performance on a particular objective, such as controlling settlement costs, there was backsliding on others, such as prompt settlement of claims. Typically, the team's vision statement expressed high aspirations but was unconnected to the current situation or how to get there from here. They had created a laundry list of disjoint problems and solutions. Interconnections were expressed through operationally vague metaphors such as the juggler with too many balls in the air.

The process of mapping, challenging, and improving mental models began in the first meeting. STELLA was used to map assumptions of the current strategy. Simple reality check models quickly showed a mismatch between the anticipated growth in underwriting volume and the resources allocated for claims settlement. The team was soon developing and testing its own models (Senge, 1990b, provides a detailed description). The final model was comparatively simple, though more complex than the original map. It had been thoroughly tested. Most important, it was the team members' model. They had built it. They knew what was assumed and why. The laundry list had been transformed into a sophisticated theory of the problem dynamics.[1] Moreover, the team's model carried potentially significant implications for longstanding management practices.

The analysis suggested rising settlement costs are largely caused by systematic, long-term underinvestment in claims adjusting capacity. Hanover simply has too few adjusters, with inadequate skills, experience, motivation, and incentives, to provide the quality of investigation and personal attention to the customer required to be fair, fast, and friendly. Figure 21.1 shows the feedback structure which underlies the drift to low performance that Hanover, and the industry, has experienced. Individual adjusters in a claims organization constantly adjust the pace of work to control the backlog of pending claims. A high pending pool means more dissatisfied customers as claimants find themselves waiting longer. Claims processing centers carefully monitor the pending pool, regularly reporting various measures of work flow. An increase in incoming claims causes the pending pool to rise, intensifying the time pressure on each adjuster. Time pressure measures the adequacy of the adjuster staff and skills available to handle the current caseload. High time pressure can be relieved only by (1) devoting less time to each claim, (2) increasing work intensity, or (3) adding adjuster capacity. Each option forms a balancing feedback process that seeks to restore time pressure to normal. However, the three channels for controlling the work flow involve very different time delays, costs, and side effects.

Adding adjuster capacity means hiring additional adjusters, improving training, and reducing turnover, thus increasing time available and settlements, reducing the pending pool, and relieving time pressure (the capacity loop in Figure 21.1). But building adjuster capacity takes time. New adjusters must be found, hired, and trained. Adjusting is a highly skilled profession, and the ability to handle complex claims effectively requires years of experience. Building capacity is also expensive and requires

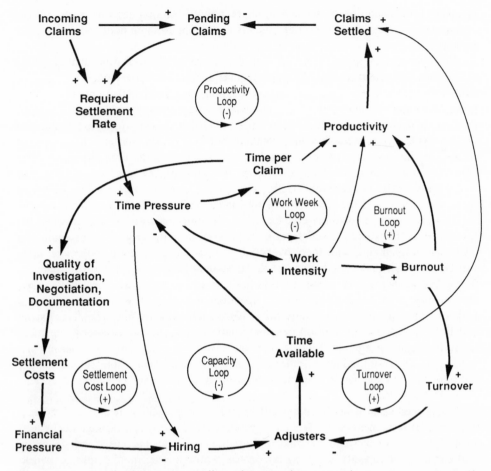

Figure 21.1 Feedback loops controlling claims settlement, with processes causing self-reinforcing erosion of quality and increasing settlement costs.

top-management authorization. Adding adjuster capacity was therefore the last resort in the organization.

Increasing work intensity means longer work weeks, fewer breaks, and less time spent in "nonproductive" activities such as talking with colleagues or training, increasing the time spent settling claims and draining the pending pool (the work week loop). Overtime is frequently used to control the pending pool. However, sustained high work intensity produces stress, low morale, and burnout, lowering productivity and increasing turnover. These delayed side effects form reinforcing feedbacks, vicious cycles, which can actually worsen time pressure (the burnout and turnover loops in Figure 21.1).

By far the easiest and quickest way to control time pressure is to settle each claim faster. Individual adjusters have a high degree of control over the time they spend on a claim. They decide how aggressively to pursue investigation, whether to visit the claimant or handle the claim by "telephone adjusting," how long to negotiate with the claimant, how much time to spend keeping records. When time pressure rises, adjusters cut back on all of these activities, quickly cutting the pending pool and easing time pressure.

However, spending less time on each claim inevitably erodes the quality of the settlements for several reasons. First, inadequate attention to documentation means the firm is less successful in litigation and subrogation, increasing settlement costs. Effort is wasted trying to locate and reconstruct evidence improperly recorded at the time of the loss, increasing the time required to settle and further intensifying time pressure in a vicious cycle. Moreover, less investigation and negotiation means settlements are likely to be inflated. Settlement costs increase as adjusters under time pressure tend to agree to a claimant's initial request, up to the amount they are authorized to pay without a supervisor's approval: "Hello, Mr. Smith? Your basement was flooded? How much was your loss? Fine. The check will be in the mail tomorrow." Finally, telephone adjusting and limited customer contact reduce customer satisfaction. Experienced adjusters report that customer satisfaction arises more from the process of listening to a customer, empathizing with them over their loss, and negotiating a settlement value that the customer understands than the dollar amount of the settlement. After hanging up the phone, Mr. Smith's first reaction is likely to be "they gave me what I asked for—it must have been worth more!" Spending less time on each claim creates a paradox: costs increase *and* quality falls. Worse, the unhappy policyholders, having had little opportunity to develop personal relationships with the company, are more likely to litigate or attempt fraud, further increasing the burden on the adjusters and legal staff. The result is higher settlements and increased financial pressure to control costs, making it even harder to increase adjuster capacity—another vicious cycle (the settlement cost loop).

These feedbacks describe a system biased toward quality erosion and gradual escalation of settlement costs. Whenever pending claims increase, management exerts strong pressure to increase the rate of settlements. Given the costs and delays in building adjuster capacity, adjusters are driven to process ever more claims per week. To the individual adjuster lowering standards is the easiest way to relieve the time pressure. In the short run spending less time on claims appears to increase productivity. But in the long run customer dissatisfaction, inadequate investigation, and poor documentation cause settlement costs to rise. The financial burden created by higher losses creates organization-wide campaigns for cost reductions and further reductions in capacity, intensifying time pressure and forcing quality standards even lower.

Counterpressures to the erosion of quality are weak. Management focuses on the tangible, measurable aspects of performance: settling claims, controlling the pending pool, and controlling expenses. Quality, in contrast, is hard to assess. It is multidimensional. Customer feedback about quality is delayed, diffuse, and often distorted by customers' desires to influence their settlements—and by management's suspicions about customer motives. The claims VP called these intangible aspects of quality "the fuzzies," saying, "In this business there are lots of ways to look good without being good." Feedback from poor quality is not only delayed; it is manifested in other areas such as increased litigation, market share erosion, and pressure for government regulation. By the time low quality is apparent, rising settlement costs, increasing turnover, low morale, and high stress may prevent the organization from increasing quality.

Periodic campaigns to increase quality fail because they increase time pressure, causing powerful compensating pressures to settle claims more rapidly.

The culture of the claims organization changes as quality erodes. Adjusters who reduce quality to handle a backlog crisis quickly learn lower standards are not only acceptable but even rewarded since they allow the adjuster to excel on the salient measures of production. Because turnover is high, new adjusters enter a culture which increasingly focuses on processing claims swiftly, and they are neither trained in nor asked to perform to the old standards. The firm's response to high turnover is to routinize the adjuster's job to reduce training costs and minimize the skill level and salary requirements of recruits. Bob Bergin, senior manager for property claims at Hanover, notes:

> In my thirty years in the business, I have seen a steady decline in the pay and status of insurance adjusting. Once it was a respected profession. Today, most adjusters are young college graduates with no aspirations to a career in adjusting. Our management practices both react to and reinforce this attitude.

The insidious aspect of these dynamics is the gradual shift in the burden of controlling the workload from capacity expansion to quality erosion. The erosion in quality standards becomes self-reinforcing: *once time pressure is relieved, so are the signals that more capacity is needed.* In the short run, slipping quality standards works. Pending claims drop. Time pressure is relieved. Management will not authorize an increase in adjuster head count since there is no apparent problem. In fact, management attention shifts to other problems, for example, what appears to be an inadequate legal staff to handle a growing volume of litigation—litigation brought on, in many cases, by insufficient adjuster capacity.

There are several implications of the feedback processes revealed by the model. First, the adequacy of capacity cannot be assessed through comparisons to competitors. The claims vice president wondered aloud if perhaps "we may have half the adjusting capacity that we actually need for our current caseload, from the standpoint of high service quality and low total costs." One of us (Senge) responded that it seemed quite possible. He said, "You don't understand what a crazy thing I am saying. We *already* have a lower caseload per adjuster than almost all of our competitors." When all firms suffer similar quality erosion none serve as role models to demonstrate the potential leverage of increased adjuster capacity. Entire industries can thus experience eroding quality standards, as exemplified by many U.S. firms in the 1960s and 1970s.

A second implication is that simply increasing the adjuster head count will not solve the problem. Low quality standards have been institutionalized. Adjuster skill levels are constantly depleted by high turnover. Ambitious and talented people avoid claims and seek careers in underwriting, finance, or marketing. Increases in resources will be effective only in concert with changes in the prevailing mental models throughout the organization.

Yet the potential impact of increased investment in adjuster capacity is substantial. The model, consistent with the judgment of the project team, suggests reductions in settlement costs of 5 to 20 percent may be realized by increasing investigation and negotiation quality (Moissis, 1989). Since settlements comprise about two-thirds of all expenses, a reduction of 10 percent would more than double net income.

THE CLAIMS LEARNING LABORATORY

After working for a year with the claims managers, the MIT team felt that the model captured the causes of important dynamics. The managers had been intimately involved in conceptualizing and analyzing the model. They could articulate the policy implications of the model with clarity and conviction. A traditional consulting project might have ended here with high confidence of implementation. In fact, the results of the model were virtually unimplementable. The model suggested a need for investment in adjuster capacity at a time when the firm, and the entire industry, is under intense pressure to cut costs. Moreover, the model implied that responsibility for the insurance crisis rests in part with established management practices, when most within the firm regard the problem as externally caused. Specifically, the model suggested that established policies had produced declining quality and increasing settlement size—precisely the opposite of the organization's lofty vision and espoused policies.

The problem now facing the team was how to develop shared understanding throughout the organization. The managers who went through the intense learning process could not expect those who had not to agree with its "counterintuitive" implications. At Hanover, and increasingly in other firms, decision-making responsibility is widely distributed. There are hundreds of individuals who implement new policies and may easily thwart new initiatives. For significantly new policies to come into practice, each person must go through his or her own personal learning process. There is no substitute.

The team decided to develop a workshop for claims managers to stimulate rethinking of established policies and practices. The workshop had to compress into a few days the process of mapping, challenging, and improving mental models the team itself went through in the previous year. The resulting Claims Learning Laboratory (CLL) is a three-day workshop attended by groups of about fifteen managers. It was impractical in a workshop format to have each group of managers build their own model from scratch. Instead of STELLA, the CLL employs a computer simulation game or management flight simulator embodying the model. The game uses easily learned software to simulate a claims processing center together with the decisions, data, pressures, and constraints characteristic of the real organization. Significantly, the Hanover team developed and delivers the CLL without substantial assistance from the MIT modelers (Bergin and Prusko, 1990; Kim, 1989; Moissis, 1989).

The CLL has now been in operation for about two years. Almost all claims managers, and a surprising number of managers from other functional areas, have attended. Bob Bergin and Gerry Prusko, two of the managers who deliver the workshop, report:

> The results of the learning laboratory have been positive. It has been credited with:
>
> 1. Shortening the learning curve for new managers
> 2. Improving communication skills
> 3. Creating an atmosphere for organizational learning
> 4. Clarifying and testing assumptions
> 5. Making mental models explicit
> 6. Integrating qualitative with quantitative measures of performance
> 7. Providing a shared experience for decision-making and problem analysis.

> When claim managers integrate the systems thinking approach into their own decision making, they accelerate the changes that need to occur in the organization. (Bergin and Prusko, 1990, p. 35)

Many managers report the CLL to be their most meaningful training experience. Although it is too early to judge the long-term effects, managers are beginning to develop a language for discussing interactions between workload, quality, and costs. Follow-up study (Kim, 1989) shows that some managers continue to use the mapping tools after the CLL. Causal diagrams are becoming commonplace inside Hanover. Experiments with new policies and strategies are starting. One recent participant reports:

> When I came back from the learning laboratory, I had a much better understanding of what the important issues were. Before the lab, I would have said that lack of quality was the only important factor. After the lab, it was obvious to me that productivity was also a key issue. So I restructured some units to enhance their ability to settle claims. After I saw dramatic increases in productivity [in the real organization], I applied pressure to improve quality—and I have seen a difference. (Bergin and Prusko, 1990, p. 35)

LESSONS: ELEMENTS OF EFFECTIVE LEARNING LABORATORY DESIGN

Experiences at Hanover and elsewhere point to three lessons for designing effective learning laboratories: (1) focus on conceptualization; (2) design opportunities for reflection; (3) beware the computer.

Conceptualization

Most of the first half of the CLL is spent in a series of conceptualizing exercises. Managers discuss basic questions such as "What determines adjuster productivity?" and "What influences investigation quality?" to help them identify interdependencies. They gradually build up a causal map of the relevant feedback processes. The mapping accomplishes several goals. First, the participants *participate*—they discuss the issues of concern to them rather than receiving wisdom transmitted from the workshop leaders.[2] Second, cognitive mapping tools are introduced as a language for systems thinking. The participants learn causal diagramming in the process of mapping their own mental models. Finally, the mapping process brings to light many of the relationships in the simulation. When the computer is introduced, it is no black box—the relationships in the model have already been discussed.

Reflection

In early tests of the simulation we found the manager-players were thoroughly engaged within fifteen minutes. They were literally on the edges of their seats. They argued with one another about the next decision. They bragged about cost reductions they achieved. But afterwards none could articulate a significant new insight about claims management. They had played to win without pausing to reflect or to formulate and test theories about the causes of the problem.

These managers had fallen victim to the "video game" syndrome. To enable managers to experience the long-term side effects of decisions, simulations compress space and time. Good simulations also enable rapid trials with different strategies. But these very capabilities allow people to play without careful experimentation and without reflecting on the causes of the outcome. The players try a strategy; if it doesn't produce the desired outcome in a few months, they improvise. Rather than a series of controlled experiments, managers tend to vary multiple factors simultaneously. Instead of sticking with a strategy to see its long-term consequences, people quit a game which is going badly and start another (Moissis, 1989). They behave the same way they do in real life. Trial and error produces little insight, whether performance is good or bad. Treated as a game, simulations can reinforce the misperceptions of feedback and cognitive errors in dynamic decision making (Brehmer, 1980; Dörner, 1989; Hogarth, 1987).

To compensate for the managers' tendency to undermine their own learning, simple learning scenarios are used to introduce the game. The learning scenarios help develop disciplined strategic analysis and scientific method. Working in teams to encourage articulation of their reasoning, players are presented with a problem such as an unanticipated increase in incoming claims. They are first directed to focus only on the work flow and rebalance the pending pool. Each method of controlling work flow (hiring adjusters, increasing work weeks, or allowing quality standards to drop) is tried separately to isolate the different feedbacks and side effects associated with each. Before playing, the managers must state their strategy and what they expect to happen. After playing, they compare the actual results to their expectations and explain any discrepancies using their map of the causal relationships, then they present their analysis to the group. The process of reflecting on discrepancies between expectations and outcomes establishes a discipline the managers then carry forward to experiments with new strategies. Without such discipline, simulation all too quickly becomes mere game playing.

The Computer

The participants in the Claims Learning Lab do not see the computer for the first day and one half. For many people, the computer is a predictive tool, a source of information, or a means of control (Orlikowski, 1988; Weizenbaum, 1976). It is not often seen as a tool for learning. In a successful learning laboratory, managers must perceive that the process is about their ways of thinking, their strategies, their problems—not about the computer. When the computer is introduced the problems of the claims organization are the focus of attention.

Learning laboratories such as the CLL represent what Donald Schön calls a "virtual world," a "constructed representation of the real world." Schön (1983b) shows how virtual worlds play a critical role in learning among professionals. Constraints on experimentation are reduced. The pace of action can be varied. Actions that are irreversible in the real world become reversible. Changes in the environment can be eliminated. Complexity can be simplified. But Schön cautions that "the representational reliability of the virtual world has its limits." Learning always involves experimentation and reflection in the virtual world *and* the real world.

Herein lies a next major challenge for firms seeking to promote organizational learning. We must learn how to design and manage the process whereby managers move continually between the virtual world of the learning laboratory and the real world of management practice. Experiments in the virtual world should lead to hypotheses which are tested through measurement and experimentation in the real world. Conversely, actions taken in the real world will continually provoke new questions and present new puzzles which can be illuminated in the virtual world.

Current research concerns the transferability of the lessons of early experiments with learning laboratories to new organizational settings. The process and modeling tools described here are now used successfully by organizations in diverse industries, including oil, chemicals, finance, health care, heavy manufacturing, consumer products, computers, and high tech. The library of microworlds embodying different general theories of business dynamics is gradually growing (Graham et al., 1989; Sterman, 1988a). Experiments with learning laboratories in firms and universities are leading to improved methods for team learning.

Managers and organization theorists often point to high-performing teams in sports or ensembles in the performing arts as role models of flexibility, learning, and consistent quality. Yet most firms, unlike a basketball team or symphony, have no practice fields where managers' skills can be developed and team competencies enhanced. Opportunities to reflect, to experiment, to challenge and revise mental models may be even more important for learning in firms than in sports or the arts. Learning laboratories are becoming an important tool of successful learning organizations to create meaningful practice fields to accelerate team learning. Simulation is increasingly important in recreating the full range of interpersonal and substantive challenges confronting managers attempting to think globally while acting locally.

NOTES

1. The model contains numerous nonlinear response functions, many of which involve "soft variables" for which there are few quantitative data. Estimation of model relationships was based on quantitative data where available, supplemented by expert judgment. The use of the model depends more on the qualitative features of these relationships than on precise numerical values. For example, it is more important for managers to understand that building adjuster capacity involves long delays than to know the exact length of these delays, or to recognize that increasing work intensity eventually causes burnout rather than knowing exactly how many extra hours adjusters in a given office are prepared to work. The role of soft variables in simulation models and criteria for validation of simulation models are discussed by Sterman (1988b).

2. Of course, the importance of participation and the perception of control over process and content have long been recognized in education, organization development, and psychology. We stress that introduction of systems thinking and computer simulation does not require taking control away from participants. Indeed, well-designed flight simulators enhance participants' control over the learning process.

REFERENCES

Argyris, C. 1982. *Reasoning, Learning, and Action*. San Francisco: Jossey-Bass.
Argyris, C. 1985. *Strategy, Change, and Defensive Routines*. Boston: Pitman.

Argyris, C., B. Putnam, and D. Smith. 1986. *Action Science.* San Francisco: Jossey-Bass.

Argyris, C., and D. Schön. 1978. *Organizational Learning: A Theory of Action Approach.* Reading, Mass.: Addison-Wesley.

Axelrod, R. 1976. *The Structure of Decision: The Cognitive Maps of Political Elites.* Princeton, N.J.: Princeton University Press.

Bakken, B. 1990. "Transfer and Learning in Simulated Dynamic Decision Environments." System Dynamics Group, Sloan School of Management, MIT, working paper D-4017.

Beckhard, R., and R. T. Harris. 1987. *Organizational Transitions, Managing Complex Change.* Reading, Mass.: Addison-Wesley.

Bergin, R., and G. Prusko, 1990. "The Learning Laboratory." *HealthCare Forum Journal* 33, no. 2: 32–36.

Brehmer, B. 1980. "In One Word: Not from Experience." *Acta Psychologica* 45: 223–241.

Brehmer, B. 1989. "Feedback Delays and Control in Complex Dynamic Systems." In *Computer Based Management of Complex Systems,* edited by P. Milling and E. Zahn. Berlin: Springer Verlag.

Camerer, C. 1987. "Do Biases in Probability Judgment Matter in Markets? Experimental Evidence." *American Economic Review* 77, no. 5: 981–997.

Checkland, P. 1981. *Systems Thinking, Systems Practice.* Chichester: Wiley.

Cooper, K. G. 1980. "Naval Ship Production: A Claim Settled and a Framework Built." *Interfaces* 10, no. 6: 20–36.

De Geus, A. P. 1988. "Planning as Learning." *Harvard Business Review,* March–April, pp. 70–74.

Diehl, E. 1989. "A Study on Human Control in Stock Adjustment Tasks." In *Computer Based Management of Complex Systems,* edited by P. Milling and E. Zahn. Berlin: Springer Verlag.

Dörner, D. 1989. "Managing a Simple Ecological System." Lehrstuhl Psychologie II, University of Bamberg, working paper.

Dyer, W. G. 1987. *Team Building: Issues and Alternatives,* 2nd ed. Reading, Mass.: Addison-Wesley.

Eden, C., S. Jones, and D. Sims. 1983. *Messing About in Problems.* Oxford: Pergamon Press.

Forrester, J. W. 1961. *Industrial Dynamics.* Cambridge: Productivity Press.

Forrester, J. W. 1969. *Urban Dynamics.* Cambridge: Productivity Press.

Forrester, J. W. 1971. "Counterintuitive Behavior of Social Systems." *Technology Review* 73, no. 3: 52–68.

Graham, A., P. Senge, J. Sterman, and J. Morecroft. 1989. "Computer-Based Case Studies in Management Education and Research." In *Computer Based Management of Complex Systems,* edited by P. Milling and E. Zahn. Berlin: Springer Verlag.

Hall, R. I. 1976. "A System Pathology of an Organization: The Rise and Fall of the Old Saturday Evening Post." *Administrative Science Quarterly* 21: 185–211.

Hall, R. I. 1984. "The Natural Logic of Management Policy Making: Its Implications for the Survival of an Organization." *Management Science* 30: 905–927.

Hall, R. I. 1989. "A Training Game and Behavioral Decision Making Research Tool: An Alternative Use of System Dynamics Simulation." In *Computer Based Management of Complex Systems,* edited by P. Milling and E. Zahn. Berlin: Springer Verlag.

Hays, R. H., S. C. Wheelwright, and K. B. Clark. 1988. *Dynamic Manufacturing: Creating the Learning Organization.* New York: Free Press.

HealthCare Forum. 1990. *HealthCare Forum Journal* 33, no. 2.

Hogarth, R. 1987. *Judgement and Choice,* 2nd ed. Chichester: Wiley.

Huber, P. 1987. "Injury Litigation and Liability Insurance Dynamics." *Science* 238 (October 2): 31–36.

Kahneman, D., P. Slovic, and A. Tversky, 1982. *Judgment Under Uncertainty: Heuristics and Biases*. Cambridge: Cambridge University Press.

Katz, D., and R. L. Kahn. 1978. *The Social Psychology of Organizations*. New York: Wiley.

Kim, D. 1989. "Learning Laboratories, Designing Reflective Learning Environments." In *Computer Based Management of Complex Systems*, edited by P. Milling and E. Zahn. Berlin: Springer Verlag.

Kleinmuntz, D. 1985. "Cognitive Heuristics and Feedback in a Dynamic Decision Environment." *Management Science* 31, no. 6: 680–702.

Kluwe, R. H., C. Misiak, and H. Haider. 1989. "Modelling the Process of Complex System Control." In *Computer Based Management of Complex Systems*, edited by P. Milling and E. Zahn. Berlin: Springer Verlag.

Levitt, B., and J. March. 1988. "Organizational Learning." *Annual Review of Sociology* 14: 319–340.

Lorange, P., M. S. Scott Morton, and S. Ghoshal. 1986. *Strategic Control Systems*. St. Paul: West Publishing Company.

MacNeil–Lehrer Report. 1989. *Risky Business—Business Cycles*. Public Broadcasting System, aired October 23, 1989. (video)

Mason, R., and I. Mitroff. 1981. *Challenging Strategic Planning Assumptions*. New York: Wiley.

Meadows, D. L. 1989. "Gaming to Implement System Dynamics Models." In *Computer Based Management of Complex Systems*, edited by P. Milling and E. Zahn. Berlin: Springer Verlag.

Milling, P., and E. Zahn, eds. 1989. *Computer Based Management of Complex Systems*. Berlin: Springer Verlag.

Moissis, A. 1989. Decision Making in the Insurance Industry: A Dynamic Simulation Model and Experimental Results. Unpublished masters thesis. Sloan School of Management, MIT.

Morecroft, J. 1982. "A Critical Review of Diagramming Tools for Conceptualizing Feedback Models." *Dynamica* 8, no. 1: 20–29.

Morecroft, J. 1988. "System Dynamics and Microworlds for Policymakers." *European Journal of Operational Research* 35: 301–320.

Nyhart, D. 1988. "Computer Modeling in Dispute Resolution—An Overview." *Dispute Resolution Forum*, April, pp. 3–15.

Nyhart, D., and D. Samarasan. 1989. "The Elements of Negotiation Management: Using Computers to Help Resolve Conflict." *Negotiation Journal* 5, no. 1: 43–62.

Orlikowski, W. 1988. "Computer Technology in Organisations: Some Critical Notes." In *New Technology and the Labour Process*, edited by D. Knights and H. Willmott. London: MacMillan.

Paich, M., and J. Sterman. 1990. "Riding the Rollercoaster: Dynamic Decision Making in Corporate Strategy." Paper presented at the conference on Behavioral Decision-Making Research in Management, The Wharton School, June 1–2, 1990.

Perrow, C. 1984. *Normal Accidents: Living with High Risk Technologies*. New York: Basic Books.

Richardson, G. P., and A. Pugh. 1981. *Introduction to System Dynamics Modeling with DYNAMO*. Cambridge: Productivity Press.

Richardson, G. P., and P. Senge. 1989. "Corporate and Statewide Perspectives on the Liability Insurance Crisis. In *Computer Based Management of Complex Systems*, edited by P. Milling and E. Zahn. Berlin: Springer Verlag.

Richmond, B. 1987. *The Strategic Forum: From Vision to Operating Policies and Back Again*. High Performance Systems, 45 Lyme Road, Hanover, NH 03755.

Richmond, B., S. Peterson, and P. Vescuso. 1987. *An Academic User's Guide to STELLA*. High Performance Systems, 45 Lyme Road, Hanover, NH 03755.

Roberts, E. B. 1978. *Managerial Applications of System Dynamics*. Cambridge: MIT Press.

Schein, E. 1969. *Process Consultation: Its Role in Organization Development*. Reading, Mass.: Addison-Wesley.

Schein, E. 1985. *Organizational Culture and Leadership*. San Francisco: Jossey-Bass.

Schein, E. 1987. *Process Consultation*, vol. 2. Reading, Mass.: Addison-Wesley.

Schön, D. 1983a. "Organizational Learning." In *Beyond Method*, edited by G. Morgan. London: Sage.

Schön, D. 1983b. *The Reflective Practitioner*. New York: Basic Books.

Senge, P. 1990a. *The Fifth Discipline: Mastering the Five Practices of the Learning Organization*. New York: Doubleday.

Senge, P. 1990b. "Catalyzing Systems Thinking in Organizations." In *Advances in Organization Development*, edited by F. Masaryk. Norwood, N.J.: Ablex.

Simon, H. A. 1979. "Rational Decision-Making in Business Organizations." *American Economic Review* 69: 493–513.

Simon, H. A. 1982. *Models of Bounded Rationality*. Cambridge: MIT Press.

Smith, V., G. Suchanek, and A. Williams. 1988. "Bubbles, Crashes, and Endogenous Expectations in Experimental Spot Asset Markets." *Econometrica* 56, no. 5: 1119–1152.

Solomon, J. 1989. "Now, Simulators for Piloting Companies." *Wall Street Journal*, July 31, p. B1.

Stata, R. 1989. "Organizational Learning—The Key to Management Innovation." *Sloan Management Review*, 30, no. 3: 63–74.

Sterman, J. D. 1988a. *People Express Management Flight Simulator*. Software and Briefing Book. Available from author, Sloan School of Management, MIT, Cambridge, MA 02139.

Sterman, J. D. 1988b. "A Skeptic's Guide to Computer Models." In *Foresight and National Decisions*, edited by L. Grant. Lanham, Md.: University Press of America.

Sterman, J. 1989a. "Misperceptions of Feedback in Dynamic Decision Making." *Organizational Behavior and Human Decision Processes* 43, no. 3: 301–335.

Sterman, J. 1989b. "Modeling Managerial Behavior: Misperceptions of Feedback in a Dynamic Decision Making Experiment." *Management Science* 35, no. 3: 321–339.

Wack, P. 1985. "Scenarios: Uncharted Waters Ahead," and "Scenarios: Shooting the Rapids." *Harvard Business Review*, September–October: 72–89; November–December: 139–150. (two-part article)

Weick, K. E. 1979. *The Social Psychology of Organizing*. Reading, Mass.: Addison-Wesley.

Weil, H. 1980. "The Evolution of an Approach for Achieving Implemented Results from System Dynamics Models." In *Elements of the System Dynamics Method*, edited by J. Randers. Cambridge: MIT Press.

Weizenbaum, J. 1976. *Computer Power and Human Reason: From Judgment to Calculation*. San Francisco: W. H. Freeman.

COMMENTARY BY WILLIAM C. HANSON

I would like to first touch on this whole notion of the practice field. In manufacturing we need to continually practice in order to continually improve. This notion of computer modeling and computer simulation which allows you to have time to practice is a very key point. There are a lot of times when we inside industry do something or make a major decision and we haven't had a chance to practice it. I think the idea of modeling and simulation will allow us to do that, so we are intrigued about the notion.

I certainly agree with Senge and Sterman when they say that models being used are built by somebody else—not by my managers or by people on the line—and that is the problem. The real learning will come from actually building those models. The notion of the learning lab is powerful because it can help the line organization take the time, discipline, and rigor needed to develop a model. But there lies a problem: Will we in industry take the time, spend the money, and have the discipline to in fact create these learning labs and then have them used by line managers to build and use the model?

For us at Digital Equipment Corporation, this is where the irony lies, because DEC is in the computer business and we cannot survive without using computer simulation and modeling for the development of our products. We use it very extensively for the development of our products. We spend a lot of time, money, and rigor to get our line organizations involved in developing a model for our products. The irony is that we do not use models for our management processes. Again, the reason for that is because we perceive that it takes too much money, time, and effort and we can't get the commitment of line management behind it to do it for management processes. We have developed simulation models for management processes and activities, but unfortunately they have been developed by "techies" and therefore line management hasn't really embraced them.

One of the things we could be doing at DEC is to reduce our day sales outstanding (DSO) which is how we measure our accounts receivable. If we could take twenty or twenty-five days out of DSO, we could probably save greater than $500 million in cash. Management of DSO is a management process that lends itself to computer modeling, but it would require a major investment to develop the model. We use computer simulations to develop a new product, and over the lifetime of the product we'll expect and in fact generate millions of dollars of cash and profit for the corporation. The irony in all this is that while we are willing to devote this sort of rigor to developing new products we have not attacked management processes with the same techniques—and the results would be the same or more impressive. I expect the initial investment costs will be as high as they were for product simulation, but I also expect that the results and savings will be equally high and beneficial. That is our dilemma.

This chapter has certainly provoked me to think about why we are willing to devote these resources and this energy on one side and not on the other.

Dialogue on Redesigning Organizational Structures and Boundaries

An interesting discussion of the dilemmas associated with sharing information across boundaries (among firms, between labor and management, between top executives and middle managers) ensued after presentation of the papers on changing organizational structures and designs. As the following dialogue illustrates, there is considerable unease within managerial ranks over the risks associated with broad information sharing. In addition, even among those who support expanded information sharing and communication, there is uncertainty over how to do it. And, as the first two comments from Ann Leibowitz from Polaroid and Bob Tuite from Eastman Kodak illustrate, sometimes what starts off as a cooperative exercise in information sharing of technical data between scientists and engineers can turn into a legal battle between armies of corporate lawyers.

Ann Leibowitz

How do companies think about cooperation, interaction, and sharing? It is very interesting. You hear a lot about how Polaroid and Kodak are locked in combat, but it wasn't always like that. Kodak made our negatives when we began, and we were heavily dependent on them. If it wasn't for Kodak, Polaroid would be a very different kind of company. This relationship had nothing to do with trust, with all due respect to my Kodak colleagues. We trusted them then; we trust them now. It isn't a matter of trust but of accountability and mutual interest. The real question was, What is Kodak's objective, and what is ours? So decisions on whether or not to cooperate and share data were made based on what was seen as being in the best interests of each firm.

Even today, I'm sure there are lots of people in our research labs who would love to ask their counterparts in some competitor, "How the hell do you make that dye, anyway?" Whenever this type of question arises the definition of proprietary information needs to be considered. Although we do exchange some information, we still have lots of questions about how and when to do it. For example, how do you transmit to people what information is proprietary and what isn't? How do you begin defining what the company's "crown jewels" are? What actions put the corporation at risk, and what, on the other hand, are techniques that can be learned and shared? Do you, Bob, want to provide the Kodak perspective?

Robert J. Tuite

I only lament the fact that the scenario (referring to a major lawsuit between Polaroid and Kodak over the technology for instant photography) wasn't different. I think when we started out we had a different view of what the response was going to be to our relationship. As everybody knows, we had more lawyers working on our instant film program than we had scientists and engineers.

Sara L. Beckman

We have similar questions to the ones raised by Ann Leibowitz. We often ask ourselves how we can train people in the organization to know what to share and what not to share. It's critical that we improve performance measures and do competitive benchmarking of processes. But that is where we seem to get into difficulties. There is a tremendous fear that comes along with alliances. In our relationship with DEC, we wanted DEC and HP people to get together and deal with environmental issues. Apparently, both sides did not get the idea that it was to be a cooperative discussion, and each brought about forty lawyers. So obviously, there are different levels of cooperation.

Donald Runkle

American firms' failure to cooperate was pointed out in *Made in America* as one of the shortcomings in the United States. I sense a major shift, though. On the way to the airport, my counterpart at Ford called me on my car phone to talk about possibly cooperating on the electric car project. Where could we cooperate, and where would we compete? Should we cooperate on batteries, converters, or something else, and then compete in sales? We agreed that I would draw up a plan that seems to make sense and then get the folks in the legal department to work out the details. We have an Advanced Automotive Components Consortium of Ford, General Motors, and Chrysler that is very successful, in addition to the Auto/Steel Partnership we've had for the past three years. An attorney sits in the room during our discussions and tells us what we can and cannot talk about.

We make light of the fact that we are still able to cooperate more easily with companies in Japan than we are with the companies fifteen miles down the road. That is fundamentally troublesome. I feel a shift here, though, and I hope the government encourages it and assists in the process. American laws are still placing U.S. firms at a disadvantage, which the government needs to do something about. When it comes right down to it, America has to decide what share of the world automotive industry and electronics market it wants to get, and then use the best technical information available to shape an overall industry policy. There is some movement on this front, but not nearly enough.

Tapas Sen

At AT&T, we are very keen about improving communication and increasing cooperation, because some of our biggest competitors are also our customers. One such example is IBM.

And this issue extends beyond sharing of certain business information to sharing professional expertise. For example, the last round of labor negotiations between AT&T and the union went very well. However, at one of the regional Bell operating companies, NYNEX, the most recent labor negotiations were extremely adversarial. So we agreed to let one of our senior labor professionals join that company to work on improving relations. Why did we do that? Because we both benefit from labor–management peace. As long as the strike went on, we could not deliver our products to them. And they are one of our biggest customers.

Sara L. Beckman

I want to give another example of how the sharing goes beyond technical data to information that is relevant to organizational learning and change. And it doesn't just involve top executives. Xerox has a terrific course on competitive benchmarking, which is given to employees at all levels of the organization. We have used their materials. In turn, we share what we are doing in this area with them and other companies.

Donald Ephlin

Trading information on labor–management relations in the automobile industry is something the companies used to do to conspire against the unions. We raised all kind of hell about it. Now that we are working more closely together with individual companies, they don't want us to be talking to or helping their competitors. Roger Smith called me a traitor for three years because I was helping Ford to stay alive.

V

LEADERSHIP AND CHANGE: THE PRACTITIONERS' PERSPECTIVE

22

A CEO's Perspective

RAYMOND STATA

Today, management innovation, more than conventional technological innovation, is the highest leverage point for improving organizational performance and competitiveness. The complexity of modern organizations, coupled with rapid changes in technology and society, escalates challenges to management at a time of rising customer expectations and competitive threats. Therefore, this book addresses a desperate need of many corporate managers.

Bob Solow pointed out that the dominant criterion for the survivability of living organisms is their efficiency of reproduction. I would suggest the criterion for the survivability of human organizations is their efficiency of learning—not just learning by the parts but, more important, learning by the system as a whole. For me organizational learning is a helpful concept in thinking about how to effect organizational change. By organizational learning I mean not only the acquisition of new knowledge but the transformation of this knowledge into new skills which are manifest in behavior and action. It also relates to an organization's ability to sense changes in its environment and to respond to these changes. In fact, I believe the rate at which an organization learns is its only sustainable, long-term competitive advantage.

The challenge, then, is to better understand the methods and conditions that promote organizational learning, how they differ from and yet depend on individual learning, and how organizational and societal learning are related and dependent.

If you wish to make revolutionary changes, that is, to materially accelerate the rate of learning, then several conditions are required. There must be a high degree of motivation, there must be a credible vision of a new reality or benchmark of performance, and there must be leaders with the skills and knowledge to manage the organizational change progress or, alternatively, there must be an external change agent to guide the change process. As I look back on my experience since the early 1980s in trying to upgrade the performance and management of Analog Devices, nearly all of these conditions were missing at least to the degree required to achieve revolutionary change. We made progress, but the rate of learning was excruciatingly slow, and as I look across the industrial landscape, I'm convinced that my experience is not unique.

I have been convinced since the early 1980s that we need to significantly upgrade the management of the company and that the ideas and methods underlying total quality management (TQM) were the best avenue for improvement. However, emotional motivation was missing. That is, although we needed to improve, we were doing well by most standards and there was no credible threat to our leadership or survival.

That changed in October 1987, when our stock plunged by a factor of three and has yet to recover. Now I have a sense of urgency. Not only is the threat of a takeover very real, but the financial community has delivered a message that does not correspond with our vision of the future. Pride as well as fear is a powerful motivating force. No group which considers itself the market leader relishes the label of has-been. It makes you look more carefully at which judgment of the future is real and why the judgments are so different. So now we have genuine motivation, but what about a vision for how to fix it?

Only recently have I fully begun to understand the vision of a new reality, and ideally what we are trying to achieve in a management transformation. Still missing are the leadership skills and knowledge to manage the change process. We are fully motivated and ready to change—now we have to learn how to do it.

I had the good fortune recently to meet Professor Shiba, a guest lecturer from Japan to the Manufacturing Leaders Program. I asked his advice on how to accelerate the rate of learning and change. Initially our discussions broadened my conceptual understanding of what TQM is all about. In essence, TQM is a methodology that promotes organizational learning by systematic discovery of high-leverage problems and by agreement to solutions by those who are empowered to act or make changes. TQM is also a management philosophy that redefines the purpose of work in terms of customer satisfaction and provides feedback to continuously improve the process by which work is performed in order to achieve this purpose. It also envisions every employee at every level in every function as a learner, with the responsibility of continuously discovering new and better ways to do their jobs. In this sense TQM is a mass movement aimed at all employees, not just managers.

But even more important, Professor Shiba convinced me that working alone on TQM in isolation was not going to work. That way we would never catch up with Japanese managers. His reasoning was as follows. Management is an empirical science. Best practice is discovered by experimentation, by trying different approaches and comparing notes on what works best. Thus the rate of learning is determined by the number of experiments being performed and by how openly and effectively the results of these experiments are being shared. Shiba says what we are lacking in America is a learning network through which best practices can be shared, not only within organizations but between organizations. In other words, we have not accepted the importance of mutual learning and have not focused on the organizational infrastructure and methods to encourage the learning process.

In Japan, the Japanese Union of Scientists and Engineers (JUSE) and Japanese Scientists' Association (JSA) provide this function and have been doing so for forty years. Japanese corporations broadly share management knowledge and promote mutual learning through these networks, even though they compete viciously in the marketplace.

As an experiment, with the encouragement and help of Professor Tom Lee and Professor Shiba, a group of seven companies here in Massachusetts founded the Center for Quality Management (CQM) to provide this function. We thought that if we were successful, perhaps this would serve as a model for other parts of the country and also a vehicle for societal learning which could bring schools, hospitals, and government agencies into the revolution of management thinking now under way. Already we have had Florida Power and Light and Xerox give seminars, and Motorola is scheduled next. Ten executives and three professors from MIT spent five weeks full time designing a plan for CQM which involved a visit to some of the best practitioners of TQM in Japan and the United States.

One of the conclusions of this five-week effort is something we already know but often tend to forget; that is, a revolutionary change of management practice and culture will not occur without very strong leadership and know-how from the top. To a large extent I have been a cheerleader and spectator of the process, but not a participant. I have not learned new skills that have materially modified my behavior and actions. Obviously that has been a foul-up in the process, which can be corrected only if I spend the same time and effort to learn as I expect from others.

Another conclusion is that organizational leaders often will not become convinced that they must change until they see and hear about personal experiences coming from other organizational leaders who have gone through the change process. One of the early goals of the Center is to arrange a trip for about ten to fifteen CEOs to Japan to go through a structured transfer of knowledge and to witness firsthand a vision of what is possible. When you look at companies like Xerox, Hewlett Packard, and Florida Power and Light you find that they had the benefit of this kind of firsthand exposure to the new reality.

Revolutionary change will generally occur only when there is some kind of external change agent. Deming and Juran were change agents in Japan, but until very recently they have had little impact here. I was aware of the work of Deming, Juran, and Crosby, but they had little impact on me compared to Shiba. The new reality exists in Japan, and you have to be in touch with that reality to effect change.

Another aspect of organizational learning which is becoming more visible to me is that the effectiveness of group or team communications within our company is just terrible if you think in terms of group learning as a goal. First, there is a lot of jockeying for position, and a lot of games are being played out. All of the cards are not on the table. Second, when we talk to each other it's like ships passing in the night. Often we don't understand one another or what the other intends to say.

One of the basic tests of TQM is a commitment to get to the facts in defining problems and finding solutions and to avoid blame in finding out what is wrong. In the early phases of TQM implementation, especially in manufacturing, most of the facts can be represented quantitatively. But as top management gets involved in TQM the facts are represented by language, concepts, and propositions. It takes a special effort and new methods to make sure that higher level abstractions and propositions are firmly anchored in reality. In Japan they have come a long way in developing tools to facilitate group communications and mutual learning—for example, the seven management tools, especially the K-J method. But few American managers even know about these tools, let alone have the skills to use them.

We are beginning to understand that organizations are very complex human systems and that the performance of these systems depends more on how well the parts interrelate than on how well each part performs separately. Reductionist methods of dividing the whole and analyzing and managing the parts separately don't produce high-performance systems. Most managers today are reductionists in their thinking. They don't have the systems skills to optimize the performance of the whole; to design processes and policies that take into account the interrelationships of the parts; to see themselves as managers of interactions as opposed to actions of subordinates; to understand their role as facilitators of learning processes. The challenge we face in industry and you face in business schools is to develop managers with these systems skills.

The starting point is a clear definition of what you want and don't want in this new breed of leader. I'm speaking here about not just CEOs but leaders at every level of the organization. At the top of everyone's list is the leader as facilitator, coach, and counsel. However, this attribute has been narrowly construed to imply facilitator of individual learning and development. The more difficult challenge is to become a facilitator of organizational or group learning and development.

We want our leader to understand organizations in system terms and to be skilled at designing processes, policies, and structures to optimize the performance of the whole.

We want our leader to be skilled at aligning individual interests and goals with group interests and goals and at resolving conflict where it arises.

We want our leader to have TQM knowledge and skills; that is, systematic methods to identify high-leverage problems and implement solutions in a complex organizational setting and to identify best industry practice as a benchmark of performance.

Finally, we want our leader as a professional manager to understand and value the contributions of professional knowledge workers such as engineers and to see them as essential, equal partners with whom he or she must share power in deciding the strategies and policies of the firm and not as hired hands to be controlled and manipulated.

Someone asked earlier, what are the fundamental constraints to progress and change? I would answer that ideas and beliefs borne out of past success are the principal constraints to change. The challenge is to envision new and better ways to achieve our purpose in a continuously changing world—ways that are often in conflict with what worked well in the past.

23

A Labor Leader's Perspective

DONALD EPHLIN

Leadership in today's environment is a very important topic for discussion. Years ago when I served on an air force bomber, I was introduced to the team concept in the truest sense. The pilot had power not because he was the highest ranking person on the plane, but because of his knowledge. But even if the lowest ranking person on the plane had looked out his window, seen one of the engines was on fire, and yelled "Hey, the engines on fire, bail out," no one would have questioned his rank and waited for someone of higher rank to verify what he had seen. Everyone would simply have bailed out. That is teamwork.

Today, many of our leaders are inexperienced in how to deal with the people they are supervising. All the training and expertise are of no value to the company if you are unable to effectively deal with the troops.

People tend to want facts that support their point of view rather than finding answers to the problems confronting the company. Many are very willing to blame the unions, for example, rather than taking responsibility for their own part of the problems. Some don't mind going down with the ship as long as they can convince themselves and others in the company that it was the unions and others who were to blame, not themselves. But if you merely blame the workers, you miss the solution to the problem. If you work with the unions and use them as allies, you can solve the problems together and possibly not have to go down with the ship at all.

The 400,000 workers at GM were a huge resource for CEO Roger Smith, who looked at the union leadership as an ally. Worker involvement was much more successful as a result. Bob Stempel, soon to be the CEO at General Motors, said that quality is not a bargainable issue at General Motors not because he was hiding from it but rather, as he said, because we all agree on the need to improve quality. Few of the people in management in many of the companies I have worked with over the years were strong enough to accept what the union had to say. Some were leaders in the company only because of their position and rank. They were not leaders in the truest sense of the word.

Many of the management leaders in Japan attained a much broader background and experience as they moved through their career paths toward the top. Leadership requires a great deal of training, knowledge, risk taking, and the willingness to take responsibility for decisions and actions. This is also true on the union side. Today's union leaders need to take more responsibility and must have a much greater understanding of the intricacies of the business with which they are dealing. Even if being a leader is a new role for you, you must realize that your ability or lack of ability to lead your cohorts directly affects the quality of their working environment and that your performance is crucial to the well-being of all those you represent.

At Ford, CEO Phil Caldwell agreed to have an outside analyst make a comparison of Mazda and Ford so that we would have a common database about the so-called landed cost differential. This outside analyst was accountable only to the union and management and the results were never publicized, but his study contained a great deal of analysis that was news to the Ford management. Chairman Caldwell still acknowledges that he learned a great deal from the study because it pointed to areas that were high cost but not contributing to the productivity of the operation. This was very helpful as Ford went through the process of reducing its break-even point and eliminating unnecessary overhead.

Also, at Ford the union and management were trying to launch the employee involvement process. Once Chairman Caldwell became convinced that this process was highly beneficial to Ford in its efforts to improve quality and the effectiveness of the operations, he not only supported it quietly, but in fact gave real, visible leadership to the effort. He appeared in plants and sat in on problem-solving teams; company newspapers publicized these efforts so that everyone in the union and management understood fully that Ford management was committed to making this happen. Thus there was no longer an adversarial union–management relationship and the workers were able to become the asset that they could have been all along. These efforts proved highly successful in turning Ford around in its darkest hours.

The hourly workers can be very helpful in training other people and in improving operations. Smart management leaders use unions as an ally in introducing technology and new ideas into the company. At one point, Roger Smith wanted people to have a better understanding of what was happening in General Motors with regard to new products and new processes, so he had the company stage a very large show called Teamwork and Technology. This show was presented all over the country to audiences that consisted of shareholders, employees, suppliers, dealers, and others interested in the company. Speakers at these programs on teamwork and technology included the chairman and president of General Motors as well as the director of the union's GM Department—me. This was a visible demonstration to one and all that improving quality, turning General Motors around to make it more effective, was not an adversarial posture but rather one in which we shared a desire and a willingness to make improvements.

A very effective motivational speaker named Graham has remarked that every time he gives one of his motivational talks to senior management people, they become very enthusiastic about what he has said, frequently saying to him, "I wish my employees could have heard you, they really need it." It's amazing—"they" always need to be motivated; the leader does not think he needs it.

Let's compare three Japanese plants located in the United States to see the role of leadership and motivation. There was no consistent pattern to the way the Japanese manage in America. The NUMMI plant, which is the joint venture between General Motors and Toyota in California, was an old plant that had very strong union leadership and a militant work force, but there was very good communication and cooperation between labor and management in putting together the joint venture and in getting it started. This extended from the regional director of the union and the director of the

General Motors Department to the local union leadership and the employees on the shop floor. That experiment has been a huge success.

When Mazda started up operation in the suburbs of Detroit, it had a brand new plant. Employees mostly were inexperienced in the auto business and as a result inexperienced in union leadership. They were not really successful at the beginning because the union leadership was not able to help put together the program that would make it run effectively.

The third company, Nissan, came to the United States and would hire only workers with absolutely no past union relationship. As a result of this anti-union stance Nissan has already alienated over one-third of its employees, who have already voted in favor of having a union. So as you see, there is no consistent pattern to Japanese management in America. But one thing is clear: if you have good union–management relations, strong leadership on both sides, you are more likely to succeed. It all depends on the level of cooperation and teamwork demonstrated by the leadership on both sides.

Sometimes the old leadership styles seem safer. If it is confrontational and you are a manager or union official, you can devote your energies to managing conflict rather than solving the problems and getting the job done. You definitely don't need to understand the total problem or be able to manage people as well because you always have those on the other side of the table to blame and can make them the scapegoat. Risk taking is essential to change that.

Without leaders to spread the news of the good things we've learned, without really shifting, we don't have a chance to become competitive. We must realize that leadership must come from the highest ranking person in the company and also from those within the unions if we are to have a chance to save what is left of America's heavy industry and to once again assume the leadership role that we so long had in the industrial world.

Dialogue on Leadership and Change

Ray Stata and Don Ephlin's comments sparked a discussion around two controversial points. First, do CEOs learn only from each other and not from others in their organizations? If so, does this CEO, top-down leadership and change process produce or retard organizational learning? Second, can we transfer "best practices" from Japan or elsewhere into our organizations or is each organization a cultural island unto itself?

THE CEO, MIDDLE MANAGERS, AND ORGANIZATIONAL LEARNING

Robert McKersie

I have a question to start us off. Do CEOs feel really comfortable learning only from others at the top, other CEOs?

Raymond Stata

A revolutionary change in paradigm from within the organization is very rare. It's usually from an external source.

James Mahoney

The idea that a CEO can learn only from other CEOs and not from others in his organization is an ego problem on the part of the CEO. A CEO who learns only from others at his own level in other organizations will delay growth and learning within the company.

Ann Leibowitz

Ray Stata said that top management was not communicating with middle management, and middle managers have been cut out of the loop. An excited CEO comes to the troops and gets them fired up with his ideas. When he goes right to the bottom levels of the organization to communicate his message, he is leaving out the middle managers.

We must remember that it is the middle managers who implement, and when you don't include them from the beginning, they are all suddenly jockeying for position with upper management and not even really meeting with employees. If I don't feel valued as a middle manager, maybe I'm too afraid to lead the change.

Raymond Stata

The bottleneck is occurring at the top of the organization, not in the middle. The CEO is far too busy to be trying to promote and manage change alone but is holding down the specialized managers like dead weight. Top management is not leading the change. How does top management learn, how does top management lead?

Fran Rodgers

Leadership from the top is necessary but not sufficient. There must be commitment from the top, the middle, and all the way down to the bottom of the organization. But you do need to start at the top, and work your way down.

I also want to refer to Ray Stata's comment that "group communication is a circus." Is that because group members are not listening to one another, because of ego problems, or because they do not speak a common language? If so, how do you break through that?

Raymond Stata

We now know how to move this communication along, and how to get our own language and definitions straight. We have to learn how to neutralize the competitiveness of managers all jockeying for position and resolve the differences among us about what exactly "reality" is. It's destructive and wasteful for people in organizations to play games.

Sara L. Beckman

Our problem is that we imbue the importance of performance in our children, and rate on performance rather than learning. We don't share information in business because other people knowing and learning about what you know diminishes and dilutes your success. So we are naturally uncooperative. If we could promise employees that the more they learn, the more they will advance rather than having it based on the way they perform, things would change and we would be a lot more cooperative.

Derek Harvey

When we look at our people in Mobil, when we see them posed with a problem, we have determined that a superior performer—a leader—is someone who can ask "Who can I get to help me on this?" An average performer thinks "I need to do this myself, be rated on it alone, and receive credit for my work alone."

Maurice Segall

We're turning over managers in our companies the way I used to sell shirts. American industry is churning out people so fast that I wonder who is going to be around to be on the learning curve. In retailing, there is hardly a company that doesn't have frequent switches in leadership and management. Does this type of rapid turnover handicap an organization's ability to learn, and slow that process?

Derek Harvey

When you have high turnover, your trust within the company and your teamwork are hurt. In my company, we relocate 2,000 of our 14,000 managers to points within Mobil every year. Our population seems to think it's in a rut if each person doesn't change jobs every eighteen months. But when you relocate this frequently, the depth of contribution that can be made is questionable.

Tapas Sen

Our business schools need to examine the type of leaders they are producing. If we are sticking with the "fast track" system even though we are unhappy with it because of inertia, then we clearly have a problem.

Robert B. McKersie

Most of our students do expect to be on a career fast track. Society reinforces the feeling that to be on the fast track in a lot of these companies, you need to switch jobs every eighteen months in order to continue to advance. When people do switch jobs that frequently, the trust is never built between them and the work force that is needed to achieve change.

Fran Rodgers

Who can expect these students to give loyalty when there is none given them in return?

William C. Hanson

It seems that when we ask questions about loyalty and express our concern about it, we are possibly putting ideas into the heads of the students. They will mirror what they think is the "fast track" thing to do. The Leaders for Manufacturing students, on the other hand, are saying they will be committed.

Thomas A. Kochan

The Leaders program involves a good faith commitment on the part of the students, and it's a bona fide attempt to build the trust you have been talking about. The students want to make a commitment, but they want employers to do likewise. They wonder, "Will the organization invest in me?" We don't know yet if mutual investment will work, but that is an important part of the experiment the Leaders' program has embarked on.

CAN BEST PRACTICES BE TRANSFERRED?

Raymond Stata

There is a lot of fundamental knowledge about what works out there in organizations; in fact, we have thirty years of trial and error experimentation. The skill is in translating this great body of knowledge into practice. Learning can take place concurrently throughout the organization via learning networks. Figuring out best practices is a good model for moving forward and learning from one another. There is already a group of universal principles and best practices in organizational management. We are behind the state of the art in these principles, the majority of which are generated in and incorporated into practice in Japan.

Edgar H. Schein

We seem to be falling into that best practices trap again. We need to discuss the nature of core technology, environmental issues, and the type of industry it is before we can determine the best practice. What the organization needs to learn is dependent on these factors. Learning needs are different for each company.

Lotte Bailyn

I'm a bit skeptical about the notion of universal principles, especially when you use the Japanese as the model. As Ronald Dore pointed out, the Japanese have a lot of homogeneity in their values. A comparison between the United States and Japan with its homogeneous values will not be a successful one.

Raymond Stata

There are two fundamental principles that I'm talking about, and they are not "Japanese." The first is that the purpose of work is to satisfy the customer. You should measure the customer's satisfaction via feedback, and make any changes necessary to increase that satisfaction. The second is the dual function concept of those who work in your firm—they are both operators and innovators. They must change, improve, and approve of the operations.

Lotte Bailyn

Your assumption is that people are there only for their work, which is a Japanese concept. They have the infrastructure in Japan to support the assumption that people are there only to work, but that infrastructure just does not exist in the United States, as evidenced by the lack of training and programs like day care.

Robert J. Thomas

A lot of people work in order to live, and certainly don't live to work. We are now asking our employees to give more than they are justifiably willing to give, and more than American industry is willing to support them in giving.

CONCLUSION

24

Creating the Learning Organization

MICHAEL USEEM AND THOMAS A. KOCHAN

The process that resulted in this book was conceived as an inductive search for a new and more satisfactory model or theory of organizational change than the models inherited from prior generations of behavioral scientists. We were not disappointed. As the dialogue between researchers and managers included with each chapter demonstrates, the participants were impatient with most of the existing frameworks. Rational decision making, traditional design principles, power- and leadership-based models, shareholder- or financial market-driven change, organizational development, and the stakeholder view of the corporation all came in for criticism. None of these served as a comfortable metaphor for describing the challenges facing contemporary organizations for either the academics or the practitioners who participated.

Instead, what emerged were two overriding themes. The first was an emphasis on change that challenges and reconfigures the tacit knowledge or deep assumptions about how organizational boundaries, technologies, strategies, and human resources should be arranged. The chapters and the dialogues implicitly call for systemic changes that alter the relationships among organizational components or practices, not just changes within each activity area. The importance of systemic change introduced in Chapter 1 was affirmed.

Second, most participants found a consensus on the concept of the "learning organization." This metaphor captured the vision of individuals, groups, and organizational networks committed to and capable of continuous learning through information exchange, experimentation, dialogue, negotiation, and consensus building. The studies and cases reported in this book suggest that such a learning organization must both build on the major forces for change and institutionalize the process of change so that it becomes a continuous and routinized part of organizational life.

In this chapter we continue the inductive process by developing what we interpreted as the key lessons that can be drawn from the research and practical dialogue. We believe these lessons combine to produce a challenging model of a learning organization. In presenting this model here we do not pretend to have done anything other than open debate on its validity and merits. The model's elements should be viewed as working propositions induced from available evidence and experience—but also as propositions yet to be proven or fully confirmed. We seek to foster a concerted agenda for the future study and practice of organizational change and transformation.

This chapter focuses first on the costs of resistance to organizational change and the resulting problems faced by managers. Second, it turns to the major forces that drive (or resist) organizational transformation. Third, though these forces may push organizational change, they do not determine its course, and we focus on the influence that politics and power, organizational history, and managerial discretion exert on the course. Fourth, the chapter specifies characteristics that the previous chapters suggest should be built into an organization that can optimally learn and thus generate continuous systemic change. Fifth, the process by which managements can effectively import innovations from other organizations and national settings is examined. Finally, organizational change cannot occur in isolation, and the importance of creating corresponding societal changes is stressed.

THE COSTS OF ORGANIZATIONAL INERTIA

Continued and systemic forms of change may be essential for organizational competitiveness or even survival. Yet change is not a natural state for many organizations, and it does not occur automatically in response to cues from some invisible hand. Organizations typically display enormous inertia in some areas, as well they should. Without continuity in reporting relations and stability in manufacturing methods, completing even the most mundane task becomes prohibitively costly. Indeed, over time an organizational culture, or set of shared assumptions and norms of behavior, tend to develop that protects organizations from the lure of passing fads, false market signals, or overly self-interested "outsiders." The latter are unable to penetrate well-embedded norms and behavioral patterns. Yet the costs of failing to overcome the inertia can also be the decline or end of the organization.

The risks of failing to engage in continuous systemic change are evident in many of the studies in this book, especially when, as in the current environment, the forces driving or calling for change are mainly external to the organization. During the 1980s the driving forces for change came from evolving technologies, work forces, financial markets, and organizational innovations that promised to be superior to traditional patterns. Ignoring these cues—both opportunities and pressures—proved to be costly for many organizations, managers, and employees.

Perhaps nowhere is this more starkly depicted than in Rebecca Henderson's analysis of innovations in photolithographic technologies for silicon chip production. Five distinctive technologies dominated the process in succession. In each case, one company that had adopted the lead technology came to dominate the market. But in all cases, the leading producer then failed to incorporate the next generation of technology, and its market dominance was swiftly—and in most instances completely—displaced by a new producer. The analysis reveals that the organizations that did innovate were those that had first managed to reconfigure the components of the production process, to build a new architectural knowledge.

The failure to initiate and sustain systemic organizational change can also result in a loss of far more than market share, especially in a period of active contest for corporate control. The 1980s witnessed the emergence of innovations in financial markets that gave rise to leveraged buyouts and other devices to strengthen the hand of owners and dominant shareholders in decisions that had since the advent of the modern corporation been largely delegated to managers. Many managements unwilling or unable to implement organizational changes found that outside groups sought in the name of "unlocking shareholder value" to do it for them. Takeover groups often moved in to institute changes, for better or for worse, that incumbent groups could or would not take.

Since the intensifying market for corporate control struck at the heart of top management power and prerogative, it is not surprising that most top managers mounted a strong counteroffensive to protect the organization—and themselves—from this threat. Poison pills, employee stock option plans, and downsizings represented short-term organizational changes made in response to the external threats. But did these responses add value for other organizational constituents? And did they stimulate the process of continuous learning that will be needed in organizations in the future? Or did they create a new form of organizational cocoon that insulates the firm from outside pressures and constructs stronger internal walls between owners, managers, and employees? Although the evidence from empirical research is not yet adequate to answer these questions, experience and intuition led our participants to take a negative view of restructuring strategies that generated short-term gains for some shareholders and managers at the expense of other constituencies. Restructuring strategies that integrate the long-term interests of stakeholders were judged, by contrast, to provide a more suitable foundation for cooperation, learning, and innovation.

These issues are in need of further research and public debate since they underlie a critical question (and one that we return to at the end of this chapter): What vision does society have of the corporation and its functions and responsibilities? Or, in the generic terminology of contemporary organizational development: Who should be the corporation's customers, and to whom should it be responsible?

The studies reported here also confirm that organizational change limited to single components may have limited impact at best. Organizational change, drawing on one standard usage, has been defined to include changes in policy, products, goals, market, technology, and relations among units (Zald, 1970, p. 242). The present studies, however, imply that these components are too interrelated to permit effective tinkering with single strands alone (a conclusion reached by others from other information sources; see, for instance, Nadler, 1977, and Nadler and Tushman, 1988). The studies of Edgar Schein and Michael Scott Morton suggest that the introduction of new information technologies without a concomitant opening of the organization and empowering of work force users can leave the new systems' potential largely unrealized. The introduction of employee stock ownership plans may significantly increase a firm's productivity, report other studies, but only when they are also accompanied by the introduction of employee involvement in company decision making (Conte and Svejnar, 1990). Similarly, John Paul MacDuffie and John Krafcik's analysis of new technologies in auto manufacturing reveal that the technologies realized their potential only when integrated with innovative human resource policies stressing work force skill, motivation, and flexibility. And Lisa Lynch's study shows that training is likely to be effective only if employees are also empowered to shape their work environment. The book's studies thus affirm the importance of integrated and consistent change among an organization's major components.

THE FORCES FOR ORGANIZATIONAL TRANSFORMATION

Instigating systemic change depends on the presence of underlying forces that ready the organization for transformation. Economists and organizational theorists have long recognized the power of changing product markets in signaling the need for organizational change. While the importance of product markets was recognized by the participants, three additional forces behind contemporary organizational change attracted considerable attention: technological innovations, shifting financial markets, and work force developments.

Technological Innovations

The potential power of new technologies as a force for change is acknowledged in all the research investigations included in this book. Yet it is also clear that new technologies do not automatically signal which strategic response, organizational form, or human resource practice will achieve the full benefits of technological changes. For example, Edward Roberts' investigation of the development of technology-based new product lines reveals a landscape littered with failed initiatives, even though the lines had seemed to represent logical directions at their launchings. Technology therefore can be a powerful enabler or catalyst, but it is not a singular determinant of systemic organizational change.

Shifting Financial Markets

The chapters by Paul Healy and Michael Useem imply an increasing influence of financial markets on organizational change. Institutional stockholders and hostile raiders pressed for increased returns, and many companies as a result came to be shaped more by financial considerations and less by strategic and constituency considerations. Ann Leibowitz's chronicle of Polaroid Corporation's response to a hostile takeover effort is illustrative. After successfully rebuffing the acquisition, management made numerous organizational changes in response to the financial threat. Among these were a restructuring of the senior ranks, paring of the work force (the company payroll dropped by some $80 million), and a scaling back of training and professional advisers. "Nothing focuses the mind more quickly," Leibowitz observed, "than a takeover threat." But the comparative perspective introduced by Ronald Dore shows that financial market developments are mediated by the institutions in which society embeds their ties to corporate clients. This perspective shows that, like product markets, financial markets do not operate as invisible or unilateral forces.

Work Force Developments

The research of Lisa Lynch, Lotte Bailyn, and others, indicates that a third driving force for change is one often least apparent to managers—the work force itself. The 1980s were times of great experimentation with employee participation and changes in the organization of work and relationships at the workplace. Much of this was pushed not so much by management as by the employees themselves and their changing demography. This pressure for change was sometimes viewed as forcing decisions that involved zero-sum tradeoffs between shareholder and employee interests. Increasing dividends must come at the cost, it was presumed, of lower wages, reduced employment rolls, and lessened participation. Perhaps, but as argued by Robert McKersie and Thomas Kochan, the low-cost, disempowered work force concept employed by some companies has often meant less, not more, for the shareholders. Ignoring or resisting changes in the work force may prove convenient, but it may also prove costly as a foregone opportunity for building upon a powerful force for organizational change.

THE PATHS OF ORGANIZATIONAL TRANSFORMATION

Although technology, financial markets, and work force developments are often the driving factors of organizational change, they determine neither that change will occur nor the course it will take. For these issues one must turn to other organizational factors. Three key attributes emerged from our research and dialogue: power and politics, organizational history, and, perhaps most important, managerial discretion.

Power and Politics

The actual path of organizational change is highly dependent upon the relative mobilization and balance of power among groups promoting or opposing change. As a case in point, Robert Thomas's studies of the adoption of new manufacturing technologies revealed that a "rational" model of technological choice and resource allocation is a less accurate description of how new technologies are introduced than what is termed a "political model." The advocates tended to possess surprisingly little knowledge of the new technology's expected financial, organizational, or human impact. Yet, motivated by other concerns, they persevered and finally prevailed through persuasion if not always a strictly rational argument. The commitment and relative power of a championing group, one that reflects the diversity of those affected by the change, and not the intrinsic merits of the new technology, were key to the outcome. In light of these findings, ignoring or attempting to eliminate the political aspects of technical change is thus unrealistic and may actually slow the process of implementation and encourage underutilization. The task should instead be to acknowledge and then harness the political power.

Organizational History

Also important to the course of change is the organizational history that the competing groups bring to the process. Marcie Tyre's comparative assessment of U.S. and European plants of a leading manufacturer testifies to the continuing legacy of the past. The differences in start-up times and operating improvements following the introduction of new process technologies could be traced to different problem-solving capabilities. The superior problem-solving approaches in the German and Italian plants, however, were not simply a matter of better management decisions. Rather, they reflected deeply embedded decision-making styles. Despite a common parent, local plant histories in the United States discouraged what might have otherwise been seen as logical actions.

Richard Locke's account of the contrary courses of industrial restructuring at Fiat Auto and the Italian textile district of Biella illustrate how different the approaches can be within the same national context. In one case, management reorganized its production by confronting labor; in the other, it successfully negotiated the changes with its unions. Local historical and organizational traditions, not industrial or technological differences, explained the alternative strategies. If the past sometimes constrains the present, these studies also offer a cautionary reminder: whatever the organizational change undertaken today, it may unwittingly impose significant constraints on change in the future.

Managerial Discretion

Within these contending pressures, management possesses considerable discretionary power to shape the final course of action. As good as a new product may be in principle, without a product champion the concept is sure to be stillborn. New technologies can be viewed as enablers of change, observes John Matson from his Johnson and Johnson experience, but without "champions of change" as their realizers, the technologies are likely to remain in the laboratories.

Senior management must often define a course of change among conflicting pressures from stockholders, customers, employees, and other constituencies of the firm. Such conflicts and the managerial choices they imply are partly a unique product of American business culture. Japanese managers, according to the analysis of Ronald Dore, tend to view the organization's interests as superseding all internal differences. They downplay the opposed stakes of the organization's substrata, placing greater emphasis on general employee welfare. By contrast, American managers attribute little transcendence to the organization or its general welfare, choosing instead to see the task as adjudicating conflicts among the contending groups.

In a highly politicized environment, with stockholders, employees, and other groups pressuring management for favor, management may feel compelled to seek courses that involve constituency tradeoffs. This has often meant favoring powerful interests at the expense of the weak, and short-term interests at the sacrifice of the long-term. But the results of such political expediencies are likely to be an underutilization of organizational resources. Aggregate gain is sacrificed for parochial advance. If so structured, organizational change would hardly be systemic, could not be transformative, and certainly would not produce a culture conducive to organizational learning.

Overcoming parochial organizational politics and setting a transformative course, chapters of this book suggest, is within the power of managerial discretion. Senior management typically has the power to reconcile and align the agendas of the organization's forces for change and its contending groups. That discretion can even extend to redefining the groups' interests away from a conflict model altogether. The introduction of new information technologies, according to the studies of Michael Scott Morton, Edgar Schein, and others (e.g., Zuboff, 1988), has sometimes been seen as a powerful instrument for better monitoring and controlling the work force, thereby enhancing productivity. In other companies, by contrast, the information system is conceived as an instrument for unleashing creativity and empowering the work force. Despite a relaxing of worker oversight, productivity is still enhanced, often to a greater extent than if management had chosen to deploy the system as a traditional means of controlling, rather than working with, its employees. Information technologies were used to reconcile rather than exacerbate constituency conflicts, and to align them around organizational goals.

The book's studies and dialogue point to a number of areas where opportunities for managerial intervention abound. One managerial action, the strategic use of performance and reward criteria, was identified as particularly pivotal. If financial criteria serve as the sole performance criterion to which managers are held accountable, then little wonder that customers, employees, and other groups receive short shrift. But we know from counterexample that performance measures can be expanded and diversified without damage to company earnings. Hewlett–Packard is among those companies that view a purely financial emphasis as an anachronism. The company has built an attractive work environment by expanding its evaluation measures, observed Harold Edmondson and Sara Beckman, with an extension to team as well as individual performance. The work environment in turn has served as an important ingredient in the firm's continuing growth. Management's choice of performance measures can thus serve to drive organizational change by signaling and rewarding alternative courses of action.

The divergent approaches to organizational change, then, are not technologically, financially, or work-force determined, though they may be so driven. The studies reported here repeatedly reveal that alternative paths are available, and that management retains considerable discretion in selecting a path or even whether to follow a path at all.

THE LEARNING ORGANIZATION

Making organizational change continuous through the building of a "learning organization" emerged as a central theme in the discussion of the papers presented at the conference and included as chapters in this book. Perhaps it attracted such interest because it envisions a broader, more sustained approach to organizational change and transformation than most previous change models. It points to a restlessness among both academics and practitioners with the partial change models of the past. Perhaps it also portends a decade of more radical departures among the actors who will drive and participate in organizational change, the substantive topics or issues open to negotiations in the change process, and the multiple organizational levels and boundaries that will be permeated by future changes. It is the ferment that comes prior to a significant shift in conceptual paradigms and the emergence of new ways of thinking about and guiding practice. In diagnosing the past, the book's studies and dialogue offer a model for the continuous organizational change. In this section we build upon the participants' collective research insights and practical experience to formulate this model. In doing so, we are implicitly offering both hypotheses for future research and prescriptions for future practice.

The chapters and dialogue suggest that learning is the essential capacity if an organization is to engage in systemic change on a continuing basis, and if it is to go beyond the isolated changes and periodic lurching steps observed in so many organizations. Although the wrenching consequences of market defeats, ownership turnover, and labor strife can induce long-needed changes, the central hypothesis or argument embedded in this new model is that the organization that has learned how to learn can preemptively and thus more effectively master those challenges.

Many of the features necessary to create a learning organization challenge prevailing management norms. One of the most basic principles under challenge is the culture of radical individualism prevalent in some managerial circles. Drawing on the American traditions of open opportunity and individual achievement, business values place great premium on the independence of the firm and its management. The company should be unfettered in its pursuit of profits; senior managers should be free to select whatever means they deem necessary to achieve that end. Such assumptions are historically rooted, Reinhard Bendix (1963) has shown, in the emergence of managerial ideologies accompanying the early rise of American capitalism. Subsequent studies confirm the antipathy of American management toward working with government, labor, and other groups (e.g., Lodge, 1990; Silk and Vogel, 1976). Other studies reveal widespread acceptance of this radical individualism among the public as well (e.g., Bellah, Madison, Sullivan, Swidler, and Tipton, 1985).

Radical individualism may have well served business growth in early periods of expansion, and it remains an important source of entrepreneurship and innovation today. Yet one aspect has left both managers and their organizations isolated from the information needed for transformative change. The sense of self-direction, a virtue for some purposes, has encouraged many managers to eschew inputs from other constituencies. Some would seemingly prefer to dwell in a state of corporate autarky. The lingering belief in self-sufficiency and nonreliance on external input and negotiation furnishes an inertial anchoring but discourages forward learning. Its persistence is increasingly at odds with daily organizational reality. This is evident at the individual level, for instance, within Mobil Oil Corporation. Derek Harvey reports Mobil research showing that people who know how and when to ask for help receive superior performance ratings. Those who want to complete a task themselves may provide an admirable display of self-confident independence, but they receive lower performance reviews. It is also evident at the organizational level: the performance of Japanese firms can be traced in part to development of enduring ties and cooperative contracts with one another, their employees, and government agencies, all done far more freely than has been the practice among U.S. firms. The U.S. syndrome of "not invented here" and other forms of parochialism remain a significant barrier, a kind of learning disability.

Overcoming the isolation by moving from independence to interdependence requires a range of organizational inventions to ensure a two-way flow of information and action. The studies in this book point toward three mutually reinforcing learning features that would help organizations to better read and act upon their internal worlds and external environments: transcended boundaries, a learning culture, and a diverse and flexible work force.

Permeable Boundaries

To achieve faster innovation and flexibility, traditional organizational forms that stress hierarchic authority, centralized control, and fixed boundaries must give way to organizational designs that rely upon work teams, decentralized decision making, and informal networks crosscutting formal boundaries.

The creative energy of such initiatives is evident in Michael Piore's study of the technologically dynamic populations of small firms concentrated in industrial districts. Much of their motivation can be traced to the informal communities which their managers have spontaneously created by virtue of geographic proximity. The findings of Deborah Ancona and David Caldwell's work on cross-functional teams and Stephan Schrader's study of information trading across company boundaries offer corroborating evidence on other aspects of boundary crossing. So too does Raymond Stata's commentary on the significance he attaches to information sharing among chief executive officers, one of his most important channels of learning. Eleanor Westney's chapter confirms the importance of crossing national boundaries as well if companies are to take maximum advantage of research and development opportunities abroad.

The concept of crossing boundaries should even be extended to the traditional divide between work setting and family context. Organizations have generally chosen to ignore family constraints in designing jobs and careers. Yet Lotte Bailyn's chapter makes it clear that the changing gender composition of the work force, the new divisions of responsibility within the family, and the intrusion of family issues into the workplace are making the boundary more permeable, at least in principle. It has remained in practice a particularly formidable boundary, however, despite the evident costs. As Fran Rodgers notes, "a fundamental resistance to change has caused us to force women and men with new family responsibilities into outmoded career molds," and among the results have been a "massive frustration and underutilization of talent and ambition." A learning organization, therefore, will need to transcend the traditional work–family divide.

These studies provide empirical underpinning for the general thesis on the value of boundary spanning, an old proposition but one recently embraced by a range of observers (e.g., Kanter, 1989; Meyer and Gustafson, 1988). Yet this book also offers a warning. Merely transcending organizational boundaries will not assure success. For these channels to be effective and thus create value, they must foster reciprocal information sharing and be built around shared commitment to sustained cooperation and a common set of values. They must also be anchored in organizations that know how to make use of the exchanged information. In short, they must be accompanied by parallel nurturing of a learning culture.

A Learning Culture

With organizations less compartmentalized, data and ideas can begin to flow more freely across boundaries. Yet new ideas and implementing actions are only as good as their receivers' processing. Knowing how to encourage and make use of information trading is an acquired capacity. As Stephan Schrader's study notes, too often top executives tend to believe that information exchange is useful and appropriate for them but is to be avoided or controlled in their subordinates. Learning cultures require multiple antennas to receive and transmit information across external and internal boundaries. A multichanneled flow helps ensure that innovation information is effectively diffused and captured.

What is often lacking is an explicit tool that promotes a learning culture and makes clear its value to the organization. The "microworlds" simulation developed by Peter Senge and John Sterman illustrates the kind of experiences that can be created to build a culture of systemic and organization-wide learning. A similar simulation model has been built on the basis of John Paul MacDuffie and John Krafcik's auto industry research. These models offer vehicles for both overcoming the legacy of historical assumptions and learning about the integral relationships among technologies, human resources, and organizational designs in contributing to organizational performance and development.

A learning culture would stress learning not only about the organization's components but also about the relations among them. Borrowing from Rebecca Henderson's analysis, new architectures are needed not only in the technologies of production, but also in the organization of production. Just as in the case of photolithographic alignment procedures for semiconductor manufacturing, the absence of architectural learning in the organizational sphere may prove fatal. Certainly this is the warning from Derek Harvey in reflecting on recent changes at Mobil Oil Corporation: "If we don't look at the core architecture issue, we will fail in all other attempts to transform organizations." Relational learning can thus prove just as important as component learning.

A Diverse and Flexible Work Force

Realizing the full potential of boundary crossing and a learning culture also depends on whether the organization capitalizes upon and further expands the diversity of its work force. Lotte Bailyn's work demonstrates that the concept of diversity should be enlarged to reflect not only social groups traditionally excluded but also work patterns conventionally ignored. The concept should be further expanded, suggests the study of Deborah Ancona and David Caldwell, to include organizational diversity in addition to demographic variety. This would include cross-functional groups, joint ventures, business–educational alliances, labor–management partnerships, and other means by which those with diverse perspectives are brought together.

While "managing diversity" or "valuing diversity" is often viewed as a reactive necessity given the changing demographic composition of the work force, diverse composition should be recast as an opportunity for a learning advantage. Homogeneity may be important for efficient teamwork. But by drawing on the complementary strengths of varied backgrounds, experiences, and contacts, heterogeneity can be used to net advantage. If viewed as a managerial opportunity rather than a problem to be managed, diversity should generate a broader range and more nuanced set of ideas and perspectives. Managing or valuing diversity should therefore give way to *learning from diversity* as an organizational norm.

To make this feasible organizational participants need to be empowered and accepted as legitimate and valued partners in decision-making and problem-solving processes. Participation should be broadly defined to include individuals and representatives of differing functions, organizational levels, and demographic groups within the organization along with representatives of a spectrum of organizations and institutions outside.

Again, this is a controversial proposition because it challenges norms and prerogatives that management has built for itself over the years. Some of the most spirited discussion at the conference occurred as senior and middle managers, business and labor representatives, academic researchers, and managerial practitioners discussed such issues as labor participation in strategic decision making, accommodating family constraints in the workplace, and the responsibility of business toward schooling. These discussions were microcosms of the challenge of moving from managing diversity (often achieved by managers attempting to balance off narrow and defensive interest group pressures) to learning from diversity. The first step of such a transition requires careful listening to the unique information and perspectives of people of diverse backgrounds and experiences. The subsequent step is to treat that information as valued input, whatever the source, in a process intended to build a consensus or reach a decision which people are committed to support and carry forward. The third and most far-reaching step is to empower the groups to make the decision and take responsibility for its implementation and evaluation.

Even greater work force and interorganizational diversity can be expected in the future. Yet fostering and sustaining change from below is a task most senior managers are ill-prepared to perform. Human resource specialists seldom have sufficient power to drive or even sustain these workplace innovations. Union representatives can add a powerful and independent voice to the change process, but too often they either bring or are treated by management in an arms-length or adversarial manner. Thus diversity and pressures for change from lower level employees or their representatives often become translated into a battle over contending forces rather than as a channel for learning, listening, and innovating. The organizations that are most successful in the future will be those that learn to capture the innovative potential of all participants. A breaking down of traditional ideological or psychological barriers to vertical learning and change efforts is required, and that will depend upon a tenor of openness that only senior management can set.

Flexibility of the work force is also important for rapidly applying the lessons of new experiments and past mistakes. It should be viewed as a precondition for virtually any organizational change. "An abundance of cross-trained employees," observes Patrick Finckler from his experience with Hanover Insurance Company, ensures that his organization can avoid being "brought to a screeching halt" by inevitable turnover and change. Yet while the development of human resources is a vital objective of building a learning organization, doubts remain about the ability of firms to implement the principle. Left to their own devices, companies tend to undertrain employees in general skills, according to Lisa Lynch's analysis, and public agencies will tend to undertrain in firm-specific skills. Thus, particularly in the human resource domain, creating a learning organization requires building a capacity to work effectively with multiple organizations and public agencies.

Participants became restless with the traditional criticism often voiced by senior managers that there is a shortage of talented people in the middle ranks of the work force. Instead, the challenge was raised to create the talent by empowering the middle and lower ranks, to give them the authority to "manage." Listening to their diverse viewpoints was viewed as essential, moving beyond a tendency for CEOs and other top managers to listen only to themselves and the more homogeneous viewpoints they represent. If the spirited discussion that occurred in the two days of the conference is any indication, the era of management as a separate class or the decade of CEO adulation in the business press and popular management writing may be coming to an end. To be sure, the CEO is a key change agent in the firm, but as Edgar Schein demonstrated, not all CEOs are up to the task—some bring mindsets that are too skeptical and serve as restraining forces on the innovation process. In short, we may be entering an era in which change is too important to be left to the control of the CEO and his or her senior management. Valuing the varied knowledge of a diverse work force and building upon leadership initiatives throughout the ranks will be essential.

Going a step further, we might argue that if the learning organization is to be qualitatively different from and better than traditional organizations, discovery and action cannot be limited to a privileged few at the top of the hierarchy. If everyone in the organization must be prepared to change, then everyone must be capable of learning and empowered to act on their new knowledge. Information must no longer be a source of power to be guarded and used for tactical advantage. It must be disseminated widely to add to the organization's collective knowledge base. Neither top management nor functional specialists can claim special status and power due to the information they possess. This in turn implies that the status barriers that traditionally separate top managers and functional experts from others in the organization must be eliminated.

ADAPTIVE LEARNING: IMPORTING INNOVATIONS
FROM OUTSIDE THE ORGANIZATION

Although many innovations can be transferred across organizational or national boundaries, they cannot be simply or automatically transplanted. Instead, organizations must become skilled at what we might call *adaptive learning,* the process of customizing innovations from outside the organization to fit the local context.

The difficulties of importing innovative technologies or organizational practices cannot be a pretext for ignoring them. Hiding behind the walls of an embedded organizational culture in a world of global competition and rapid transmission of information is a sure ticket to organizational obsolescence. Yet outright copying of the innovation without appreciation of the context from which it is drawn and into which it is inserted can be a ticket to an equally adverse fate.

Robert Cole (1989) and Eleanor Westney (1987) developed evidence elsewhere showing that effective learning organizations are those that adapt applicable innovations from other cultures in ways that take into account their own cultures. They envisioned ways to translate information on "best practices" elsewhere into innovations that worked within their own organizational contexts. Learning from best practice requires organizational adaptation, not imitation.

The concept of adaptive learning therefore resides between the opposed positions of a longstanding debate about the value of importing best practices. On the one side have been the economic determinists who argue that if there exists some objectively superior practice, the forces of global competition will mandate its adoption or lead to a loss of competitiveness. On the other side have been those who view each organizational setting as unique, bound by its specific culture and historical experience. The book's chapters and an animated conference discussion, however, indicate that neither position is a useful guide to organizational change. Some organizations can and under certain circumstances do learn from the successes of others, even those in diverse national settings. Yet the most lasting applications have come when the innovations have been crafted to fit local conditions. This is one reason why the concept of "competitive benchmarking" has gained such widespread acceptance since it reflects the advantage of adaptive over imitative learning.

The importance of adaptive learning is illustrated by John Paul MacDuffie and John Krafcik's study of auto manufacturing performance. Information on variability in productivity and quality is well known in the auto industry and the best practices are equally well known. Yet the leading edge competitors in this industry are, they find, those which understand the leverage points in their own organizations and have the commitment needed to learn from demonstrated best practices elsewhere, but also know which elements to apply within their own organizations.

SYSTEMIC SOCIETAL CHANGE

As suggested previously, organizational transformation requires permeability of organizational boundaries and an increased capacity for cross-organizational collaboration and learning. This in turn challenges us to create theories and strategies that move beyond the boundaries of the firm to encompass social as well as organizational change. What is being called for then is a change process that is powerful enough to question and, where appropriate, alter the boundaries of individual firms.

The need for broader theories was illustrated by conference commentary of Robert Solow on why no single company had been able to market a keyboard based on superior principles of key placement. Studies had amply confirmed the greater typing efficiency of the alternative key arrangement. Yet firms found they could not take it to market unless a host of other firms, including many competitors, would make the change as well. Innovating organizations tend to be pulled back to their prior states by powerfully conservative forces if they are unable to bring their competitors and other economic and social institutions along with them. Aspects of organizational change without a corresponding societal or institutional change can thus be highly constrained.

Achieving this type of institutional change requires broadening the constituencies or frames of reference incorporated in our change models and processes. Richard Walton's book *Innovating to Compete* (1987) shows that societies that have been most successful in diffusing organizational innovations are those that have strong industry–labor–government institutions for promoting and reinforcing the change process. Robert Cole's *Strategies for Learning* (1989) suggests the need for national infrastructures that support diffusion of social and organizational innovations. A range of other research studies confirm the importance of "organizational fields" for the transfer and adoption of new ideas and practices (e.g., DiMaggio and Powell, 1983; Fligstein and Dauber, 1989). An adequate theory of organizational change, therefore, must move beyond the boundaries of the firm to incorporate an understanding of how collective learning and change occur in our society.

Changing individual firms will thus not be sufficient to affect the competitiveness of a national economy or the standard of living of a significant part or all of the population. Building systemic societal change requires a vision that is clear on what functions and responsibilities society wants the modern organization to perform and accept.

CONCLUSION

Much of the debate over the future of the corporation can be expected to revolve around the two competing organizational models that we introduced in Chapter 1: the traditional shareholder-maximizing, hierarchical, management-driven model versus the transformed stakeholder model. The traditional model of the organization is increasingly archaic, that much is clear. Far less certain are the emergent properties of the transformed model. The research studies and case experiences reported in this book have pointed toward at least five emergent properties, each requiring further analysis. We set these forward as a tentative image of the future, remembering that a transformed model can never be fully prescribed and must always be experimentally evolved.

1. Organizational change should be systemic. The technological, organizational, and human resources must be altered together, since the potential of one can be fully realized only when developed with all. Moreover, systemic change involves more than changes within each of these components. It challenges the underlying assumptions, tacit knowledge, and standard relationships that link these different organizational components—a capacity for what we in this book have labeled architectural change.

2. Creating change requires transcending the legacies of past rivalries and traditional status distinctions in order to mobilize an organization's many constituencies. This requires confronting rather than suppressing organizational politics by acknowledging different constituencies' competing concerns. Yet at the same time it requires a closer alignment of these concerns with the long-term needs of the organization, best achieved by directly engaging the several constituencies in organizational learning, problem solving, and decision making.

3. While management cannot create the systemic change on its own, it plays a critical role in defining the organization's vision. Management can choose to empower all organizational participants in a way that creates a collective learning culture. Or it can choose to see itself as the receptor and sole guardian of privileged information and new ideas. The alternative paths are many, and management has power to set its course.

4. Other organizational stakeholders—whether shareholders, employees, consumers, or public-policy makers—face the same critical choices. They may opt to join in fostering an organization's transformation by helping to shape and therefore identify with the organization's long-run objectives. By doing so they can help create a learning network or community. Alternatively, individual stakeholders can choose to stand in the way by focusing on their specific interests or remain on the sidelines and watch their knowledge, skills, and value to the organization atrophy.

5. Continuing systemic change depends on the building of a permanent learning capacity across as well as within organizations. A learning society, one capable of fostering institutional change, is essential to sustaining a learning organization. Central components of a learning society include a capacity for negotiation and problem solving across organizational boundaries; an interactive mode stressing data, experimentation, and feedback rather than rhetoric and ideology;

and the ability to learn from diverse representatives of multiple organizations and institutions. Just as achieving systemic change within organizations requires architectural change, systemic institutional change requires transforming many traditional arms-length or adversarial relationships.

A key management challenge of the future is to develop the skills and perspectives needed to build and integrate these components. In so doing, it will be important to unfreeze the organization to start the process, but it will be equally important to avoid refreezing in a way that stops the process and waits for external pressures to build up to the point that reactive change is once again forced on the organization. The pressures of global competition and changing technologies will ensure that managements will face ample pretext—and at times the necessity—for initiating strategic restructuring of their organization. It is in these periods that the potential for unfreezing is greatest, but so too is the danger of refreezing. Thus Kurt Lewin's traditional three-stage change model of unfreezing, transformation, and refreezing must be replaced by a model that stresses continuous learning, experimentation, and a commitment to improvement, while retaining a constancy in certain core elements.

While firms in all advanced societies are recasting their strategies and organizations to respond to the changes, a variety of different approaches have been observed in the studies of this book. The approaches reflect variant management philosophies and organizational histories as much as market or technological necessities. With an organization's actual approach is thus often a matter of management choice, the high road will consist of overcoming the legacies of radical individualism on the one hand and avoiding conflicting stakeholder politics on the other. Strategies that treat the organization and its employees as a community built around relationships of trust are more likely to produce and sustain the learning configuration.

Organizational change cannot be an isolated affair, left for each management to confront and solve. Public policies ranging from education and training to labor, antitrust, and securities regulations shape the capacities and willingness of managements to effect change. The debate over organizational transformation therefore becomes in part a society-wide debate as well. The outcome of the broader debate will determine whether organizational transformation and corresponding societal changes become the norm or just another minor deviation in a seemingly steadier and conventional path of business history.

Finally, transforming organizations depends on how well the process is understood. Here there is no substitute for careful analytic research. Management prescriptions too often sound right but prove wrong. Raymond Stata avows that a sine qua non for any organizational change is "fact-based management." Translating this into action, Judith Rosen of Bain and Company urged more research that is relevant, reliable, and actionable. Many of the chapters in this book sought to meet these criteria, but much remains to be examined if organizational transformation is to be factually guided during the years ahead.

ACKNOWLEDGMENTS

The authors gratefully acknowledge the helpful suggestions of Deborah Ancona, Lotte Bailyn, Robert McKersie, Paul Osterman, and Robert Thomas on an earlier version of this chapter.

REFERENCES

Bellah, R. N., R. Madison, W. M. Sullivan, A. Swidler, and S. M. Tipton. 1985. *Habits of the Heart: Individualism and Commitment in American Life*. Berkeley: University of California Press.

Bendix, R. 1963. *Work and Authority in Industry: Ideologies of Management in the Course of Industrialization*. New York: Harper & Row.

Cole, R. E. 1989. *Strategies for Learning: Small-Group Activities in American, Japanese, and Swedish Industry*. Berkeley: University of California Press.

Conte, M. A., and J. Svejnar. 1990. "The Performance Effects of Employee Ownership Plans." In *Paying for Productivity: A Look at the Evidence*, edited by A. S. Blinder. Washington, D.C.: The Brookings Institution.

DiMaggio, P., and W. Powell. 1983. "The Iron Case Revisited: Institutional Isomorphism and Collective Rationality in Organizational Fields." *American Sociological Review* 48: 147–160.

Fligstein, N., and K. Dauber. 1989. "Structural Change in Corporate Organization." *Annual Review of Sociology* 15: 73–96.

Kanter, R. M. 1989. *When Giants Learn to Dance: Mastering the Challenge of Strategy, Management, and Careers in the 1990s*. New York: Simon and Schuster.

Lodge, G. C. 1990. *Perestroika for America*. Boston: Harvard Business School Press.

Meyer, J. R., and J. M. Gustafson, ed. 1988. *The U.S. Business Corporation: An Institution in Transition*. Cambridge, Mass.: Ballinger.

Nadler, D. A. 1977. "Concepts for the Management of Organizational Change." In *Perspectives on Behavior in Organizations*, edited by R. Hackman, E. Lawler, and L. Porter. New York: McGraw-Hill.

Nadler, D. A., and M. L. Tushman. 1988. *Strategic Organization Design*. Glenview, Ill.: Scott, Foresman.

Silk, L., and D. Vogel. 1976. *Ethics and Profits: The Crisis of Confidence in American Business*. New York: Simon and Schuster.

Walton, R. E. 1987. *Innovating to Compete: Lessons for Diffusing and Managing Change in the Workplace*. San Francisco: Jossey-Bass.

Westney, D. E. 1987. *Imitation and Innovation: The Transfer of Western Organizational Patterns to Meiji Japan*. Cambridge, Mass.: Harvard University Press.

Zald, M. N. 1970. "Political Economy: A Framework for Analysis." In *Power and Organizations*, edited by M. Zald. Nashville: Vanderbilt University Press.

Zuboff, S. 1988. *In the Age of the Smart Machine: The Future of Work and Power*. New York: Basic Books.

Contributors and Participants

The following individuals contributed to the book and/or participated in the working conference that facilitated preparation of the book. The institutional affiliations are identified as at the time of the conference (May 1990).

Deborah Gladstein Ancona, Associate Professor of Organizational Studies, Sloan School of Management, M.I.T., Cambridge, Mass.

Lotte Bailyn, Professor of Organizational Psychology and Management, Sloan School of Management, M.I.T., Cambridge, Mass.

Sara L. Beckman, Product Generation, Change Management Team, Hewlett–Packard Company, Palo Alto, Calif.

H. Kent Bowen, Professor of Materials Science and Engineering, M.I.T., Cambridge, Mass.

David E. Caldwell, Associate Professor of Management, Leavey School of Business, Santa Clara University, Santa Clara, Calif.

Gary L. Cowger, Director of Manufacturing, Cadillac Motor Car Division, General Motors Corporation, Detroit, Mich.

Laura Divine, Director/Quality, Pacific Bell, San Ramon, Calif.

Ronald Dore, Professor of Political Science, Department of Political Science, M.I.T., Cambridge, Mass.

Harold E. Edmondson, Vice President, Corporate Manufacturing, Hewlett–Packard Company, Palo Alto, Calif.

Donald Ephlin, Senior Lecturer, Sloan School of Management, M.I.T., Cambridge, Mass.

Patrick Finckler, Vice President, Hanover Insurance Company, Worcester, Mass.

William C. Hanson, Vice President of Manufacturing, Digital Equipment Corporation, Maynard, Mass.

Derek Harvey, Manager, Planning & Analysis, Mobil Corporation, New York, N.Y.

Arnoldo Hax, Deputy Dean and Alfred P. Sloan Professor of Management, Sloan School of Management, M.I.T., Cambridge, Mass.

Paul M. Healy, Associate Professor of Management, Sloan School of Management, M.I.T., Cambridge, Mass.

John C. Henderson, Associate Professor of Management Science, Sloan School of Management, M.I.T., Cambridge, Mass.

Rebecca M. Henderson, Assistant Professor of Management, Sloan School of Management, M.I.T., Cambridge, Mass.

Thomas A. Kochan, Leaders for Manufacturing Professor and George Maverick Bunker Professor of Management, Sloan School of Management, M.I.T., Cambridge, Mass.

John F. Krafcik, Product Program Analyst, Business and Strategy Group, Alpha Project, Ford Motor Company, Dearborn, Mich.

Ann Leibowitz, Senior Corporate Attorney, Polaroid Corporation, Cambridge, Mass.

Richard M. Locke, I.R.I. Career Development Assistant Professor of Management and Political Science, Sloan School of Management, M.I.T., Cambridge, Mass.

Nan Lower, Consultant, United Research Co., Morristown, N.J.

Lisa M. Lynch, I.R.I. Career Development Associate Professor of Industrial Relations, Sloan School of Management, M.I.T., Cambridge, Mass.

John Paul MacDuffie, Doctoral Candidate, Sloan School of Management, M.I.T., Cambridge, Mass.

Thomas Madison, Vice President, United Research Company, Morristown, N.J.

James Mahoney, Vice President, Hanover Insurance Company, Worcester, Mass.

John M. Matson, Corporate Director, Operations and Technology Development, Johnson & Johnson, New Brunswick, N.J.

Robert B. McKersie, Professor of Industrial Relations, Sloan School of Management, M.I.T., Cambridge, Mass.

Sarita Narang, Manager, Pacific Bell, San Ramon, Calif.

Ranganath Nayak, Senior Vice President, Arthur D. Little, Cambridge, Mass.

Paul Osterman, Associate Professor of Human Resource Management, Sloan School of Management, M.I.T., Cambridge, Mass.

Michael J. Piore, Professor Economics and Management, Sloan School of Management and Department of Economics, M.I.T., Cambridge, Mass.

James Rebitzer, Assistant Professor of Management, Sloan School of Management, M.I.T., Cambridge, Mass.

Edward B. Roberts, David Sarnoff Professor of Management of Technology, Sloan School of Management, M.I.T., Cambridge, Mass.

Fran Rodgers, President and Founder, Work/Family Directions, Watertown, Mass.

Judith I. Rosen, Vice President, Bain and Company, Boston, Mass.

Donald Runkle, Vice President, Advanced Engineering Staff, General Motors Corporation, Warren, Mich.

Roger Samuel, Executive Director, International Center for Research on the Management of Technology, and Director, Management of Technology Program, Sloan School of Management, M.I.T., Cambridge, Mass.

Edgar H. Schein, Sloan Fellows Professor of Management, Sloan School of Management, M.I.T., Cambridge, Mass.

Stephan Schrader, Assistant Professor of Management, Sloan School of Management, M.I.T., Cambridge, Mass.

Michael S. Scott Morton, Jay W. Forrester Professor of Management, Sloan School of Management, M.I.T., Cambridge, Mass.

Maurice Segall, Senior Lecturer, Sloan School of Management, M.I.T., Cambridge, Mass.

Tapas Sen, Division Manager, Human Resources, American Telephone and Telegraph, Morristown, N.J.

Peter M. Senge, Director, Systems Thinking and Organizational Learning, M.I.T., Cambridge, Mass.

Claus G. Siegle, Director, Manufacturing, Autolatina Comercio Negocios e Participacoes Ltda., São Paulo, Brazil.

Robert M. Solow, Institute Professor, Department of Economics, M.I.T., Cambridge, Mass.

Raymond Stata, President and Chief Executive Officer, Analog Devices, Inc., Norwood, Mass.

John D. Sterman, Associate Professor of Management, Sloan School of Management, M.I.T., Cambridge, Mass.

Robert J. Thomas, Leaders for Manufacturing Associate Professor, Sloan School of Management, M.I.T., Cambridge, Mass.

Lester C. Thurow, Dean and Professor of Management and Economics, Sloan School of Management, M.I.T., Cambridge, Mass.

Robert J. Tuite, Director of New Opportunity Development, Eastman Kodak (executive loan to High Technology of Rochester), Rochester, N.Y.

Marcie J. Tyre, Assistant Professor of Management, Sloan School of Management, M.I.T., Cambridge, Mass.

Glen L. Urban, Deputy Dean and Dai-Ichi Kangyo Bank Professor of Management, Sloan School of Management, M.I.T., Cambridge, Mass.

Michael Useem, Visiting Professor of Management, Sloan School of Management, M.I.T., Cambridge, Mass.

N. Venkatraman, Assistant Professor of Management, Sloan School of Management, M.I.T., Cambridge, Mass.

Veikko O. Vuorikari, Managing Director, Eficap Oy Venture Capital Company, Lappeenranta, Finland

D. Eleanor Westney, Associate Professor of International Management, Sloan School of Management, M.I.T., Cambridge, Mass.

David Znaty, Société de Gestion et D'Informatique Publicis, Paris, France.

Index